THE SOUTHWEST

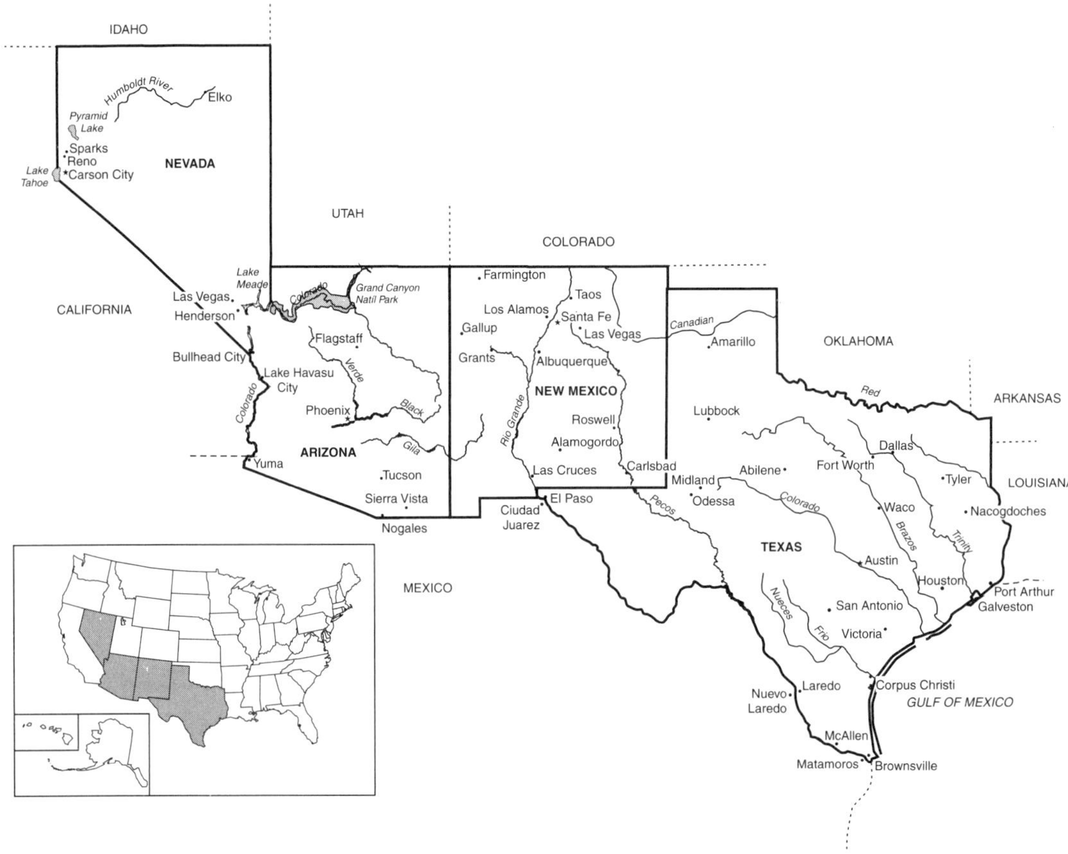

IDAHO
NEVADA
Humboldt River
Elko
Pyramid Lake
Sparks
Reno
Carson City
Lake Tahoe
UTAH
COLORADO
CALIFORNIA
Lake Meade
Colorado
Grand Canyon Natl Park
Las Vegas
Henderson
Bullhead City
Flagstaff
Verde
Lake Havasu City
Colorado
Phoenix
Black
Gila
ARIZONA
Yuma
Tucson
Sierra Vista
Nogales
Farmington
Taos
Los Alamos
Santa Fe
Gallup
Las Vegas
Grants
Albuquerque
Rio Grande
NEW MEXICO
Roswell
Alamogordo
Las Cruces
Carlsbad
El Paso
Ciudad Juarez
MEXICO
Canadian
Amarillo
OKLAHOMA
Red
ARKANSAS
Lubbock
Dallas
Fort Worth
Abilene
Midland
Odessa
Tyler
LOUISIANA
Pecos
Colorado
Waco
Nacogdoches
Brazos
Trinity
TEXAS
Austin
Houston
Port Arthur
Galveston
San Antonio
Nueces
Frio
Victoria
Laredo
Nuevo Laredo
Corpus Christi
GULF OF MEXICO
McAllen
Matamoros
Brownsville

[redacted]

THE SOUTHWEST

The Greenwood Encyclopedia of
American Regional Cultures

Edited by
Mark Busby

Foreword by William Ferris, Consulting Editor

Paul S. Piper, Librarian Advisor

GREENWOOD PRESS
Westport, Connecticut • London

Library of Congress Cataloging-in-Publication Data

The Southwest : the Greenwood encyclopedia of American regional cultures / edited by Mark Busby ; foreword by William Ferris, consulting editor.
p. cm.
Includes bibliographical references and index.
ISBN 0–313–33266–5 (set : alk. paper)—0–313–32805–6 (alk. paper)
1. Southwest, New—Civilization—Encyclopedias. 2. Southwest, New—History—Encyclopedias. 3. Southwest, New—Social life and customs—Encyclopedias. 4. Popular culture—Southwest, New—Encyclopedias. 5. Regionalism—Southwest, New—Encyclopedias. I. Busby, Mark. II. Series.
F786.S747 2004
979'.003—dc22 2004056067

British Library Cataloguing in Publication Data is available.

Library of Congress Catalog Card Number: 2004056067
ISBN: 0–313–33266–5 (set)
0–313–32733–5 (The Great Plains Region)
0–313–32954–0 (The Mid-Atlantic Region)
0–313–32493–X (The Midwest)
0–313–32753–X (New England)
0–313–33043–3 (The Pacific Region)
0–313–32817–X (The Rocky Mountain Region)
0–313–32734–3 (The South)
0–313–32805–6 (The Southwest)

First published in 2004

Greenwood Press, 88 Post Road West, Westport, CT 06881
An imprint of Greenwood Publishing Group, Inc.
www.greenwood.com

Printed in the United States of America

The paper used in this book complies with the Permanent Paper Standard issued by the National Information Standards Organization (Z39.48–1984).

10 9 8 7 6 5 4 3 2 1

First, I wish to thank all the contributors to this volume for their hard work and commitment to the project. I would also like to thank Rob Kirkpatrick and Anne Thompson of Greenwood Press for their vision and persistence; my assistant at the Southwest Regional Humanities Center, Sharon Pogue, for her steady help; the other Center faculty and staff, Dickie Heaberlin, Twister Marquiss, Terry Vaughn, and Beverly Waddill, for their continuing enthusiasm for the Southwest; and my wife, Linda, again, for her fine editing and for her support.

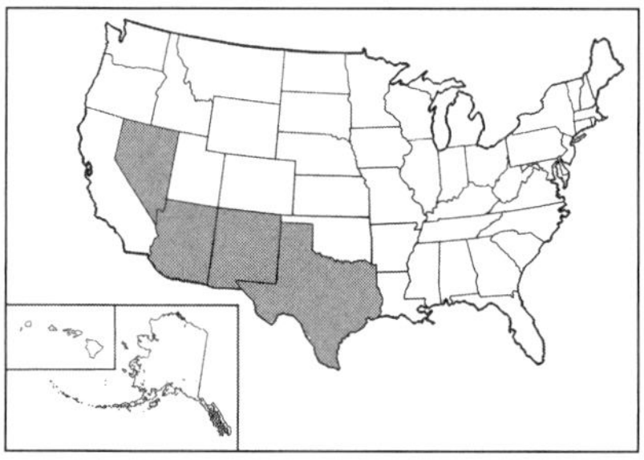

CONTENTS

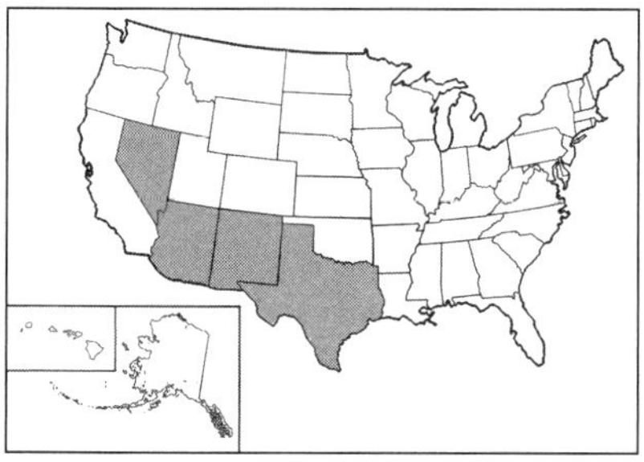

FOREWORD

Region inspires and grounds the American experience. Whether we are drawn to them or flee from them, the places in which we live etch themselves into our memory in powerful, enduring ways. For over three centuries Americans have crafted a collective memory of places that constitute our nation's distinctive regions. These regions are embedded in every aspect of American history and culture.

American places have inspired poets and writers from Walt Whitman and Henry David Thoreau to Mark Twain and William Faulkner. These writers grounded their work in the places where they lived. When asked why he never traveled, Thoreau replied, "I have traveled widely in Concord."

William Faulkner remarked that early in his career as a writer he realized that he could devote a lifetime to writing and never fully exhaust his "little postage stamp of native soil."

In each region American writers have framed their work with what Eudora Welty calls "sense of place." Through their writing we encounter the diverse, richly detailed regions of our nation.

In his ballads Woody Guthrie chronicles American places that stretch from "the great Atlantic Ocean to the wide Pacific shore," while Muddy Waters anchors his blues in the Mississippi Delta and his home on Stovall's Plantation.

American corporate worlds like the Bell system neatly organize their divisions by region. And government commissions like the Appalachian Regional Commission, the Mississippi River Commission, and the Delta Development Commission define their mission in terms of geographic places.

When we consider that artists and writers are inspired by place and that government and corporate worlds are similarly grounded in place, it is hardly surprising that we also identify political leaders in terms of their regional culture. We think of John Kennedy as a New Englander, of Ann Richards as a Texan, and of Jimmy Carter as a Georgian.

Because Americans are so deeply immersed in their sense of place, we use region like a compass to provide direction as we negotiate our lives. Through sense of place we find our bearings, our true north. When we meet people for the first time, we ask that familiar American question, "Where are you from?" By identifying others through a region, a city, a community, we frame them with a place and find the bearings with which we can engage them.

Sense of place operates at all levels of our society—from personal to corporate and government worlds. While the power of place has long been understood and integrated in meaningful ways with our institutions, Americans have been slow to seriously study their regions in a focused, thoughtful way. As a young nation, we have been reluctant to confront the places we are "from." As we mature as a nation, Americans are more engaged with the places in which they live and increasingly seek to understand the history and culture of their regions.

The growing importance of regional studies within the academy is an understandable and appropriate response to the need Americans feel to understand the places in which they live. Such study empowers the individual, their community, and their region through a deeper engagement with the American experience. Americans resent that their regions are considered "overfly zones" in America, and through regional studies they ground themselves in their community's history and culture.

The Greenwood Encyclopedia of American Regional Cultures provides an exciting, comprehensive view of our nation's regions. The set devotes volumes to New England, the Mid-Atlantic, the South, the Midwest, the Southwest, the Great Plains, the Rocky Mountains, and the Pacific. Together these volumes offer a refreshing new view of America's regions as they stretch from the Atlantic to the Pacific.

The sheer size of our nation makes it difficult to imagine its diverse worlds as a single country with a shared culture. Our landscapes, our speech patterns, and our foodways all change sharply from region to region. The synergy of different regional worlds bound together within a single nation is what defines the American character. These diverse worlds coexist with the knowledge that America will always be defined by its distinctly different places.

American Regional Cultures explores in exciting ways the history and culture of each American region. Its volumes allow us to savor individual regional traditions and to compare these traditions with those of other regions. Each volume features chapters on architecture, art, ecology and environment, ethnicity, fashion, film and theater, folklore, food, language, literature, music, religion, and sports and recreation. Together these chapters offer a rich portrait of each region. The series is an important teaching resource that will significantly enrich learning at secondary, college, and university levels.

Over the past forty years a growing number of colleges and universities have launched regional studies programs that today offer exciting courses and degrees for both American and international students. During this time the National Endowment for the Humanities (NEH) has funded regional studies initiatives that range from new curricula to the creation of museum exhibits, films, and encyclopedias that focus on American regions. Throughout the nation, universities with regional studies programs recently received NEH support to assist with the programs that they are building.

The National Endowment for the Arts (NEA) has similarly encouraged regional initiatives within the art world. NEA's state arts councils work together within regional organizations to fund arts projects that impact their region.

The growing study of region helps Americans see themselves and the places they come from in insightful ways. As we understand the places that nurture us, we build a stronger foundation for our life. When speaking of how she raised her children, my mother often uses the phrase "Give them their roots, and they will find their wings." Thanks to *American Regional Cultures*, these roots are now far more accessible for all Americans. This impressive set significantly advances our understanding of American regions and the mythic power these places hold for our nation.

William Ferris
University of North Carolina
at Chapel Hill

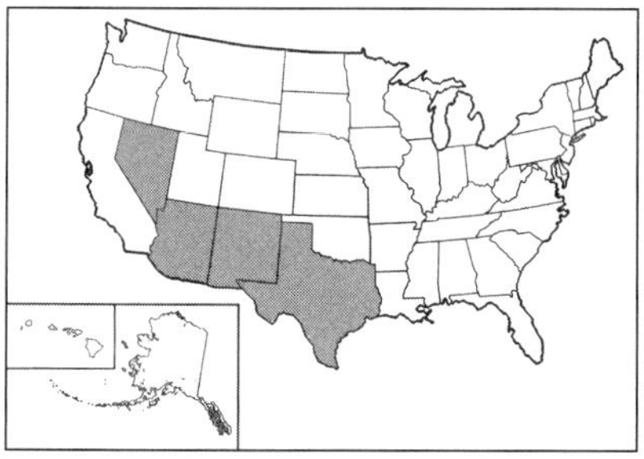

PREFACE

We are pleased to present *The Greenwood Encyclopedia of American Regional Cultures*, the first book project of any kind, reference or otherwise, to examine cultural regionalism throughout the United States.

The sense of place has an intrinsic role in American consciousness. Across its vast expanses, the United States varies dramatically in its geography and its people. Americans seem especially cognizant of the regions from which they hail. Whether one considers the indigenous American Indian tribes and their relationships to the land, the many waves of immigrants who settled in particular regions of the nation, or the subsequent generations who came to identify themselves as New Englanders or Southerners or Midwesterners, and so forth, the connection of American culture to the sense of regionalism has been a consistent pattern throughout the nation's history.

It can be said that behind every travelogue on television, behind every road novel, behind every cross-country journey, is the desire to grasp the identity of other regions. This project was conceived to fill a surprising gap in publishing on American regionalism and on the many vernacular expressions of culture that one finds throughout the country.

This reference set is designed so that it will be useful to high school and college researchers alike, as well as to the general reader and scholar. Toward this goal, we consulted several members of Greenwood's Library Advisory Board as we determined both the content and the format of this encyclopedia project. Furthermore, we used the *National Standards: United States History* and also the *Curriculum Standards for Social Studies* as guides in choosing a wealth of content that would help researchers gain historical comprehension of how people in, and from, all regions have helped shape American cultures.

American Regional Cultures is divided geographically into eight volumes: *The Great Plains Region*, *The Mid-Atlantic Region*, *The Midwest*, *New England*, *The Pacific Region*, *The Rocky Mountain Region*, *The South*, and *The Southwest*. To ensure that cultural elements from each state would be discussed, we assigned each state to a particular region as follows:

The Great Plains Region: Kansas, Nebraska, North Dakota, Oklahoma, South Dakota
The Mid-Atlantic Region: Delaware, District of Columbia, Maryland, New Jersey, New York, Pennsylvania, West Virginia
The Midwest: Illinois, Indiana, Iowa, Michigan, Minnesota, Missouri, Ohio, Wisconsin
New England: Connecticut, Maine, Massachusetts, New Hampshire, Rhode Island, Vermont
The Pacific Region: Alaska, California, Hawai'i, Oregon, Washington
The Rocky Mountain Region: Colorado, Idaho, Montana, Utah, Wyoming
The South: Alabama, Arkansas, Florida, Georgia, Kentucky, Louisiana, Mississippi, North Carolina, South Carolina, Tennessee, Virginia
The Southwest: Arizona, Nevada, New Mexico, Texas

Each regional volume consists of rigorous, detailed overviews on all elements of culture, with chapters on the following topics: architecture, art, ecology and environment, ethnicity, fashion, film and theater, folklore, food, language, literature, music, religion, and sports and recreation. These chapters examine the many significant elements of those particular aspects of regional culture as they have evolved over time, through the beginning of the twenty-first century. Each chapter seeks not to impose a homogenized identity upon each region but, rather, to develop a synthesis or thematically arranged discussion of the diverse elements of each region. For example, in turning to the chapter on music in *The Pacific Region*, a reader will discover information on Pacific regional music as it has manifested itself in such wide-ranging genres as American Indian tribal performances, Hawaiian stylings, Hispanic and Asian traditions, West Coast jazz, surf rock, folk scenes, San Francisco psychedelia, country rock, the L.A. hard-rock scene, Northwest "grunge" rock, West Coast hip-hop, and Northern California ska-punk. Multiply this by thirteen chapters and again by eight volumes, and you get a sense of the enormous wealth of information covered in this landmark set.

In addition, each chapter concludes with helpful references to further resources, including, in most cases, printed resources, Web sites, films or videos, recordings, festivals or events, organizations, and special collections. Photos, drawings, and maps illustrate each volume. A timeline of major events for the region provides context for understanding the cultural development of the region. A bibliography, primarily of general sources about the region, precedes the index.

We would not have been able to publish such an enormous reference set without the work of our volume editors and the more than one hundred contributors that they recruited for this project. It is their efforts that have made *American Regional Cultures* come to life. We also would like to single out two people for their help: William Ferris, former chairman of the National Endowment for the Humanities and currently Distinguished Professor of History and senior associate director for the Center for the Study of the American South, University of North Carolina at Chapel Hill, who served as consulting editor for and was instrumental in the planning of this set and in the recruitment of its volume editors; and Paul S. Piper, Reference Librarian at Western Washington University, who in his role as librarian advisor, helped shape both content and format, with a particular focus on helping improve reader interface.

With their help, we present *The Greenwood Encyclopedia of American Regional Cultures.*

Rob Kirkpatrick, Senior Acquisitions Editor
Anne Thompson, Senior Development Editor
Greenwood Publishing Group

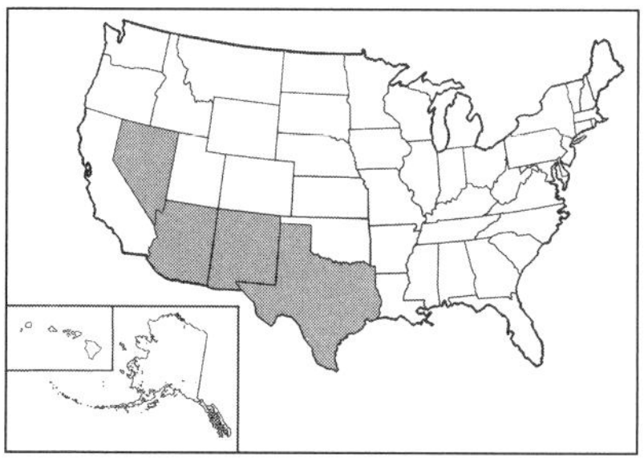

INTRODUCTION

The purpose of this volume is to discuss the environmental and cultural variety of the American Southwest, which like other regions of the United States exists clearly in the imagination but is more difficult to define. To understand any region requires knowing its geology, geography, ecology, biology, anthropology, prehistory, history, and sociology; the cultural contributions of art, architecture, literature, music, dance, drama, and film; and the region's political and social conditions. We must know the plants and animals, landforms and topology, languages, myths and legends, sweep of time, stories, painting, sculpture, and movies that have defined the place—all of these create the place itself or demonstrate the various cultural values that a place inspires. Still, very few places have a pure regional identity. Cultural geographers speak of regional areas as having a core and periphery. The core New England space is somewhere near Boston, the core of the Southwest is the plaza in Santa Fe, New Mexico, and for the South it is the fictional Tara of *Gone with the Wind*. Places on the periphery often have mixed identities, and such is the case with much of the Southwest.[1]

So the questions are: What is the region we call the Southwest? What defining traits mark the Southwest?

To illustrate the difficulties of constructing such a definition, consider the following: Several years ago Steve Goodman and David Allan Coe created the perfect country and western song, "You Never Even Called Me by My Name," which had to include getting drunk, getting out of jail, mothers, trains, and pickup trucks. The resulting line tells a story about the speaker being drunk the day his mama got out of prison, and as he drove his pickup truck to pick her up in the rain, he got run over by a train. Others have tried to define regions with a similar construction. Pat Conroy once defined Southern literature this way: "All Southern literature is about this: 'Mama died the night the hogs ate Willy when she heard what Papa did to Sister.'"[2]

I've been trying to come up with something as succinct for defining the Southwest. Let's try this: "The Indian boy sat on his horse looking out over the buttes, mesas, and arroyos dotted with Saguaro and sage, Joshua trees, prickly pear, and lechuguilla. He was listening to the mournful wailing of the lobos and coyotes, when suddenly a rattlesnake's chilling warning was drowned out by the jet's low approach to the airport, bringing the weekend's load of gamblers, miners, computer programmers, and big-business felons."

So it is appropriate to begin by examining the various ways the Southwest is defined, as well as its characteristics and qualities. In *The Southwest: Old and New* (1961) W. Eugene Hollon writes, "the term 'Southwest' as hereinafter used refers only to the four large states of Texas, Oklahoma, New Mexico, and Arizona."[3] Kenneth Kurtz's definition is clear and easy: his Southwest is Arizona and California.[4] In *Our Southwest* (1940) Erna Fergusson draws a triangle from San Antonio to Los Angeles and then back to Fort Worth: inside is the Southwest; outside is not.[5] Bookman Lawrence Clark Powell's Southwest is "the semi-arid land from the Pecos of New Mexico-Texas to the Salinas of California, including deserts, mountains, and river valleys, cities and seacoast."[6] Charles DiPeso specifies a large region bounded by the 38th parallel on the north (from Wichita, Kansas, to San Francisco), the Tropic of Cancer (23° 27' north latitude) on the south, the 97th meridian on the east, and the Pacific Ocean on the west.[7]

For historian Bertha Dutton the "Southwest is an area with no specific limits or definite boundary, but for the purpose of culture studies, ancient and modern, it includes all of New Mexico and Arizona, the southwest corner of Colorado, southern Utah, southwestern Nevada, and the California border of the Colorado River. The Greater Southwest adds the southern California Indians to the Pacific coast, western Texas, and then dips down into northern Mexico on occasion."[8] In *Sky Determines* (1934) Ross Calvin focuses on climatic factors, particularly aridity and its related topics: precipitation, native flora and fauna, crops, and underground water storage and recharge.[9] Rupert N. Richardson and Carl Coke Rister, in *The Greater Southwest* (1935), say that Kansas, Oklahoma, Texas, Utah, Colorado, Nevada, New Mexico, Arizona, and California constitute the "Greater Southwest."[10] Historian Herbert Eugene Bolton's *The Spanish Borderlands* (1921) delineates the Southwest as being made up of regions that had been conquered by, occupied by, and culturally influenced by Spain and Mexico.[11] Historian Howard Lamar uses the term "the far Southwest" in 1970 to refer to Utah, Colorado, Arizona, New Mexico, and most of Nevada.[12] And Dan Flores, in *Horizontal Yellow: Nature and History in the Near Southwest* (1999) states that his book is about

> Kansas, New Mexico, Texas, Oklahoma, with slices of Colorado, Kansas, Louisiana, and Arkansas—divided politically and culturally, but linked by water: All these seemingly disparate places constitute a distinctive bioregional watershed, an ecology fashioned by geology and gravity and defined by how the rain and snow draining eastward off the Southern Rockies gets to the ocean. . . . The second is history. . . . The last is sensory impression. While landscapes that are vertical or green may make up some of its most dramatic spots, the Near Southwest's characteristic topography is one of the grandest, most windswept landscapes of plains, tablelands, and deserts on the planet. . . . Horizontal Yellow, a land stretched taut like a drumhead as if from the sheer weight of the overarching blue, and for almost the entire year round

> yellowed (the way anything exposed yellows) by the suck of the sun on an ocean of grass.[13]

Stanley Vestal (Walter S. Campbell's pseudonym), in *The Book Lover's Southwest* (1955), gives the somewhat tautological description: "By the Southwest I mean West Texas, the western half of Oklahoma, New Mexico, and those parts of Kansas and Colorado which are definitely Southwestern in background and outlook." Vestal excludes Arizona and California because they "seem a long way off and no part of the [Southwesterners'] world."[14] Tom Pilkington, in *My Blood's Country* (1961), is more precise: "Texas, New Mexico, and Arizona, plus parts of Oklahoma, Colorado, Utah, Nevada, and Southern California (excluding Los Angeles)."[15] Keith L. Bryant, in *Culture in the American Southwest: The Earth, the Sky, the People* (2001), identifies the Southwest as "a vast region located to the west and south of a line drawn from Houston up to Tulsa to Colorado Springs and westward to Los Angeles. The Southwestern boundary blurs along the political border with Mexico where Mexican, Hispanic, and Anglo cultures mingle, largely without distinction." Bryant, then, defines the Southwest by urban sites.[16]

No doubt, the most flexible definition comes from J. Frank Dobie, in his *Guide to Life and Literature of the Southwest* (1942): "The principal areas of the Southwest are . . . Arizona, New Mexico, most of Texas, some of Oklahoma, and anything else north, south, east, or west that anybody wants to bring in."[17]

As all these definitions indicate, although the greater Southwest is a physical region that runs from the piney woods of East Texas to the Gulf Coast, across the rolling Texas Hill Country to the dry deserts and arroyos of Trans-Pecos West Texas, New Mexico, Arizona, Nevada, Utah, southern Colorado, and southern California, and includes the several states of Northern Mexico, this volume will primarily follow the National Endowment for the Humanities' designation of the Southwestern region as Texas, New Mexico, Arizona, and Nevada.

Critical to the Southwest is a comprehensive knowledge of how the various cultures in the Southwest—Native American, Mexican American, African American, and Euro American, and so forth—have been affected by and have altered the natural environment. Understanding the region requires knowledge of a mix of cultures that have been determined by geographical, geological, and biological forces, shaped through historical development and literature, and altered by various languages. Moreover, it requires recognizing the relationship between the region and the broader national identity. The harsh Southwestern landscape has historically led Southwesterners to glorify an American individualism long celebrated in our national documents; frontier attitudes have often characterized Southwestern culture. Many of our historical and literary texts demonstrate how Anglo-American settlers entered an unknown world and saw nature as a resource for their singular use, whereas many minority cultures have questioned the emphasis placed on individuality instead of community. Their response to the hot, arid land of scorpions and rattlesnakes, Saguaro and sage, has been to band together in communal, supportive societies.

The region's history reflects the lives and interaction of diverse peoples. Alvar Núñez Cabeza de Vaca was the first European to travel through part of the region and document his observations after he was shipwrecked on the shores of present-day Galveston in 1528. He wandered through Texas, New Mexico, and Mexico before returning to Spain in 1537, and his stories of golden cities to the west led

Coronado to search for the seven cities of gold in 1540. When Juan de Oñate settled New Mexico in 1598, he brought cattle and horses, animals that would eventually transform the natural environment through overgrazing and alter the human landscape when the Plains Indians, particularly the Comanche and Apache, discovered that on horseback they were even more powerful hunters and warriors. For the next two centuries, having found an inimical landscape and no great wealth, the Spanish slowly settled in the Southwest, which served as a buffer for Spanish developments in Mexico. After Mexico achieved its independence from Spain in 1821, the Mexican government offered land grants in Texas to Anglo settlers such as Moses Austin and his son Stephen, and the Anglo migration into the Southwest began.

That resettlement set in motion the major events that shaped the region in the nineteenth century: Texas' independence, the U.S. war with Mexico, the Gadsden Purchase, fur trapping, the discovery of gold in California and silver in Nevada, the coming of railroads, the American Civil War and Indian wars, and the growth of the cattle and mining industries. The twentieth-century Southwest witnessed the Mexican Revolution and its effects on the border, World War I, the Great Depression and the Dust Bowl, World War II and the internment camps and so-called relocation centers for Japanese Americans, nuclear testing, increasing immigration, a growing drug trade, and NAFTA. As the Southwest saw a radical change in the way it was perceived, its image transformed from a vast desert wasteland hostile to humans to a beckoning sunbelt. Cattle and ranching gave way to oil, aircraft, and space industries, then to high finance, high technology, and legalized prostitution and gambling in Nevada and to casinos on Indian reservations.

The Southwest has figured prominently in national mythology and political reality, producing such major political figures as Arizona's Barry Goldwater, Morris K. (Mo) and Stuart Udall, Sandra Day O'Connor, and John McCain; New Mexico's Pete Domenici and Bill Richardson; Nevada's Paul Laxalt and Harry Reid; and Texas' Lyndon Johnson, Barbara Jordan, Ann Richards, George H. W. Bush, and George W. Bush.

PREHISTORY TO CONTACT

The long prehistory of the native peoples of the Southwest—Mogollon, Hohokam, Anasazi, and the relatively unknown Patayan—continues to enter the American imagination, primarily through the cliff dwellings preserved across the region and especially at Mesa Verde National Park in the Four Corners region where Colorado, New Mexico, Arizona, and Utah meet. The Southwest fell into history at first contact with Europeans, and in the Southwest, the first person was Cabeza de Vaca. In 1527 he was appointed treasurer of a royal expedition of about 300 men, led by the Spanish explorer, Pánfilo de Narváez, to Florida. In April 1528 the expedition sailed into Tampa Bay, began an overland march to Apalachee Bay, and then attempted to reach Mexico in makeshift boats. Separated from Narváez, Cabeza de Vaca led a small band of shipwreck survivors to an island, probably Galveston (which he called Malhado or Misfortune Island, the Island of Doom), where native people captured them. Early in 1535 Cabeza de Vaca and the three other survivors of the ill-fated expedition—Dorantes, Castillo, and Esteban the Moor—escaped and began a journey across what are now the southwestern United States and northern Mexico. In 1536 they reached a Spanish settlement on the

Sinalo River in Mexico. In 1537 Cabeza de Vaca returned to Spain and was rewarded by being appointed governor of Río de la Plata (now largely Paraguay).

His account of the Narváez expedition, *La Relación*, and his tales of the Zuni and their villages, the legendary Seven Cities of Cíbola, encouraged other expeditions to America. Also, *La Relación* is the first book recounting a confrontation and reconciliation between the European explorers and the native peoples, and it has all the elements of good literature—structure (escape and return, journey, mythic parallels, frontier myth, regeneration through violence) and the elemental theme of a man's survival after having been stripped of all resources but his own mind and imagination.

For historians Cabeza de Vaca's importance comes from his having been the first European to travel the Southwest and to write reports that spurred increased exploration of the region, in particular the expeditions of Hernando de Soto and Francisco Vásquez de Coronado. For anthropologists Cabeza de Vaca's reports on his journey across the Southwest include information about numerous tribal bands—the Karankawas, Caddoes, Atakapans, Jumanos and Conchos, Pimas, Opatas, and the loose bands of hunter-gatherers now called Coahuiltecans. Unlike the organized, and sometimes quite complex, tribes of many other indigenous peoples through much of North America, Cabeza de Vaca encountered small wandering bands of people constituting small family groups that congregated seasonally for celebrations called Mitotes. For the most part they were egalitarian, with no chiefs and usually no more than twenty-five people. Cabeza de Vaca's discussion of these archaic groups is the only anthropological record about many of them.

For literary scholars Cabeza de Vaca's book serves as the prototype for much American literature that followed. As Tom Pilkington notes, the book's theme of the "physical, emotional struggle for an accommodation between races" is "a conflict that has never been very far removed from the American consciousness and one that has always been a factor in the works of our best and most vital writers."[18] And Frederick Turner, in *Beyond Geography: The Western Spirit against the Wilderness*, suggests that Cabeza de Vaca's story serves as the first captivity narrative, which became the most significant early American story and was and continues to be the basis for the fiction and movie genre, the Western.[19]

THE FRONTIER SOUTHWEST, THE COWBOY, AND THE MODERN SOUTHWEST, 1821–1960

Cabeza de Vaca's narrative led later Spaniards and their horses and cattle to the Southwest, although the explorers never found the golden cities they sought. After Mexico achieved independence from Spain in 1821 and began offering land grants to Anglo settlers, the next major era began. Nineteenth-century Southwestern literature is mostly about the various travelers to the region and the folktales and songs that grew up with them. The Southwestern story thus reflects the larger Western one about the influence of the frontier and often reflects the much explored, powerful theme of being drawn to a dream of paradise.

The cowboy is one of the dominant icons of the frontier myth. As Henry Nash Smith demonstrated in *Virgin Land*, the story of the cowboy emerged in dime novels toward the end of the nineteenth century and notably in former Pinkerton agent Charlie Siringo's popular memoir *A Texas Cowboy* (1886). The dime novels gave way to serious literary treatments such as Owen Wister's *The Virginian* (1902) and Andy Adams' trail drive novel, *The Log of a Cowboy* (1903), as well as to the first narrative film, *The Great Train Robbery* (1903). These works led to the recognizable attributes of the Western genre: nineteenth-century setting, cattle, cowboys, horses, Indians, and outlaws.

The cowboy is chiefly a figure of Texas and the Southwest. After the Civil War, when Texas veterans discovered their homes and livelihoods in disarray and herds of wild cattle roaming the land, some enterprising veterans began to round up the cattle, which began the trail drives that are at the heart of cowboy legend. That life lasted for about twenty-five years, from 1870 to 1895, when barbed wire, the opening of train service, and economic downturns ended the golden days of trail driving. But the cowboy is still an internationally recognizable American symbol representing the freedom of the frontier and independence.

In the last quarter of the nineteenth century the Southwest was dominated by Indian wars. Eventually the Comanche were defeated at Palo Duro Canyon in Texas when General Ranald MacKenzie slaughtered 1,400 of their horses, the Navajo were forced to make the long walk to Bosque Redondo in New Mexico, the Utes were relocated to Colorado, and the Apache held out until Geronimo was captured in 1886. The beginning of the twentieth century saw an increased interest in the cowboy as the embodiment of frontier values at the same time that Americans, influenced by Frederick Jackson Turner's famous 1893 address, feared that the end of the frontier signaled the end of those same traits that had defined the country. The old order, based on the ranching system with clear goals and methods of behavior and societal expectations, was crumbling because of overgrazing, drought, the closing of cattle trails, and quarantine laws. The new order, which began with large-scale farming that utilized irrigation systems and continued with the introduction of refrigerated railroad cars, began to take its place.

THE TWENTIETH AND TWENTY-FIRST CENTURIES

The large farms and then the large oil companies introduced a corporate economy with a value system based on business, capitalism, and exchange of labor. The discovery of oil had a marked effect on much of the Southwest, especially Texas and New Mexico. The growth of nuclear energy for warfare and industry continued to alter the Southwest, almost as much as the introduction of hooved animals had. Uranium mining and nuclear testing have become central to Southwestern history and to much Southwestern literature, figuring prominently in Edward Abbey's *Desert Solitaire*, Leslie Silko's *Ceremony*, Cormac McCarthy's *The Crossing*, and much of the literature written about Nevada. The "Atomic City" of Los Alamos, New Mexico, and the Trinity test site south of there represent for many the ultimate separation between nature and humankind that the environmental movement of the late twentieth century, which has continued into the twenty-first, seeks to heal.

SOUTHWESTERN QUALITIES AND MYTHOLOGY

Historically, travelers journeying across the Southwest—from explorers such as Cabeza de Vaca to twentieth-century nature writers such as John Graves of Texas and Abbey of Arizona—have attempted to capture their responses to the natural and cultural phenomena they experienced. Many emphasize encountering and coming to terms with a rich variety of human cultures, but just as often they explore the challenges posed by the natural conditions of the Southwest, where lush pine forests give way to empty plains that sometimes stretch so far that "the eye yearns for even the slightest hill to lean itself against" (as Roy Bedichek commented in his 1947 *Adventures with a Texas Naturalist*), where most of the indigenous vegetation is thorny and fruitless, and where often there is insufficient water to sustain either cities or livestock.[20] The harsh natural environment of the Southwest, with its variety of landscapes as beautiful and appealing as they are dangerous and frightening—arid Chihuahuan, Sonoran, Mojave, and Great Basin deserts; jutting Rocky Mountains; eroding Caprock canyonlands; rolling Llano Estacado plains; roiling Gulf Coast; and lush East Texas forests—inspires deep ambivalence among its inhabitants.

The variety of landscapes, called metaphorically *Mountain Islands and Desert Seas* in a natural history book by Fred Gehlbach, is one of the region's defining features. Although its aridity, quality of light, or melding of cultures often defines the Southwest, arguably no other region in the United States is visualized so fully by its landscape. C. Hart Merriam (1855–1942), chief of the U.S. Bureau of Biological Survey beginning in 1886, identified six life zones in the Southwest, separated by the altitudes in which they occur: the *Lower Sonoran* (below 3,500 feet) includes the hot deserts of the Southwest (the Mojave, Sonora, and Chihuahua) and is distinguished by creosote bush and other desert shrubs and succulents; the *Upper Sonoran* (3,500–6,000 feet) is characterized by its ecosystem of desert grasslands that is dominated by live oaks and piñon pines; the *Transition Zone*'s (6,000–7,500 feet) principal ecosystem is coniferous forest dominated by ponderosa pine; the *Canadian* (7,500–9,000 feet) is also dominated by coniferous forest but composed of different species such as Douglas fir and white pine; the *Hudsonian* (9,000–11,000 feet) consists of coniferous forest that includes Englemann spruce, bristlecone pine, and blue spruce: and finally the *Arctic-Alpine* (11,000 feet) with its dominant ecosystem of alpine tundra.[21]

In 1853 and 1854 Frederick Law Olmsted, later to become known for designing New York City's Central Park, traveled by horseback across Texas and then published his experiences as *A Journey through Texas*. Traveling is a natural act in a region with long distances. Texas, for example, covers 266,807 square miles. It is 801 miles from the Panhandle in the north to Brownsville in the south and 773 miles from the easternmost bend in the Sabine River to the westernmost point of the Rio Grande near El Paso. With all this territory, journeying continues to be a necessary reality for the region. And many titles by Southwestern writers reflect the fundamental importance of journeying: *Waltz across Texas*; *North to Yesterday*; *Moving On*; *Horseman, Pass By*; *Leaving Cheyenne*; *The Trail to Ogallala*; *We Pointed Them North*; *Goodbye to a River*; *Pale Horse, Pale Rider*; *Down the River*; and others.

Journeying has continuing importance in the Southwest both literally and metaphorically. Many Southwestern narratives are structured by journeys, with searching used as a metaphor for the existential reality of life. From Saul on the road to Damascus, Oedipus on the way to Thebes, Odysseus headed home, Huck on the river, and Gus and Call going up the trail, the journey's power as archetype gains added heft in an area where expanse beckons and hinders.

The mythology of the Southwest is clearly grounded in frontier mythology central to the larger American experience.[22] Frontier mythology refers to a cluster of images, values, and archetypes that grew out of the confrontation between the uncivilized and civilized world, what Frederick Jackson Turner called the "meeting point between savagery and civilization." Civilization is associated with the past and with Europe, with society—its institutions, laws, demands for compromise and restriction, cultural refinement and emphasis on manners, industrial development, and class distinctions. The wilderness that civilization confronts offers the possibility of individual freedom, where single individuals can test themselves against nature without the demands for social responsibility and compromises inherent in being part of a community.

Southwestern mythology draws from frontier mythology, particularly the emphasis on the Southwest as a land of freedom and opportunity, where individuals can demonstrate those values that the Anglo myth reveres—courage, determination, ingenuity, loyalty, and others. The major indigenous American hero—the cowboy—is a product of Texas' frontier legacy. But the Southwest's frontier history and geography produce deep feelings of ambivalence. The very term *Southwest* is ambivalent since it leads in two directions at once, to the south and to the west. On the one hand, the vastness of its area seems to negate borders; on the other, the region's location on the edge of Southern and Western culture and along the long Rio Grande border with Mexico reinforces an awareness of borders. As Tom Pilkington pointed out in *My Blood's Country*, Texas is a land of borders: "Men have always been fascinated by rims and borders, ends and beginnings, areas of transition where the known and the unknown merge. In the Southwest one feels something of this fascination, because one of the central, never-changing facts about the region, I believe, is that it is a borderland."[23]

Both borders and the frontier suggest a line where differing cultures, attitudes, and factions meet. In fact, one of the major features of Southwest is ambivalence—the act of being torn in several directions at once. Early settlers who both conquered nature and felt simultaneously at one with it began the feelings of ambivalence that Larry McMurtry admitted still cut him "as deep as the bone" in his luminous essay "Take My Saddle From the Wall: A Valediction" in *In a Narrow Grave*.[24] Ambivalence is also at the center of McMurtry's epigraph for *Lonesome Dove*, which is a quote from T. K. Whipple's *Study Out the Land*: "All America lies at the end of the wilderness road, and our past is not a dead past, but still lives in us. Our forefathers had civilization inside themselves, the wild outside. We live in the civilization they created, but within us the wilderness still lingers. What they dreamed, we live, and what they lived, we dream."[25]

The ambivalence of being drawn at the same time toward such opposing forces as civilization/wilderness, rural/urban, individuality/community, past/present, aggression/passivity, and numerous others is central to the Southwestern legend, and it grows in intensity in the contemporary Southwest as the schism between old and new tears more strongly at the human heart. Often Southwestern writers examine the sharp division between the frontier myth that lives inside and the diminished outside natural world fraught with complexity, suffering, and violence but leavened with humor, compassion, and love.

Historian Larry Goodwyn identified three other important elements of the Southwestern frontier myth in a 1971 essay entitled "The Frontier Myth and

Southwestern Literature." Goodwyn first concluded that the "frontier legend is pastoral" with a strong emphasis on the primitivistic belief that being outdoors leads to living moral lives. Second, "the legend is inherently masculine: women are not so much without 'courage' as missing altogether; cowgirls did not ride up the Chisholm Trail." And third, Goodwyn found that the frontier myth "is primitively racialist: it provided no mystique of triumph for Mexicans, Negroes, or Indians."[26]

Much of the ambivalence that later writers exhibit finds their history here, in these fundamental conflicts and primitive legends. Bookish people spend much of their time inside libraries or sitting in front of word-processing machines while they contemplate the expanse of space that defines the region. And these writers know that the majority of Southwesterners—over 82 percent—live in urban areas. They also realize that many of the region's remaining natural areas along rivers and coastlines are threatened by some of the foulest polluters, who are free to exercise the liberty that a "guvment"-hating area allows.

Early works often demonstrate the sexism and racism of the old legends and have called forth important answers from Southwestern women and ethnic writers, thinkers, filmmakers, and artists who articulated their own views of the world and from others who are sensitive to these ugly legacies. Outstanding contributions have been made by Mary Austin, Sarah Bird, Willa Cather, Sandra Cisneros, Naomi Nye, Carolyn Osborn, Katherine Anne Porter, Carmen Tafolla, Leslie Silko, Georgia O'Keeffe and other Indian, Mexican American, and African American Southwesterners such as N. Scott Momaday, Simon Ortiz, Rudolfo Anaya, Dagoberto Gilb, Rolando Hinojosa, Robert Rodriguez, Ralph Ellison, J. California Cooper, and Reginald McKnight.

To these elements of Southwestern mythology—journeying, ambivalence, primitivism, racism, and sexism—another ambiguous element continues from the frontier past: violence. In an *Atlantic* essay in 1975, McMurtry excoriated Texas, noting that the frontier emphasis on violence was one of the few vestiges of the old world still hanging on: "If frontier life has left any cultural residue at all, it is a residue of a most unfortunate sort—i.e. that tendency to romanticize violence which is evident on the front page of almost every Texas newspaper almost every day."[27] Richard Slotkin examined the implications of the myth of violence in three books, beginning with *Regeneration through Violence: The Mythology of the American Frontier, 1600–1860*, in which he identified the archetypal pattern—the American hunter who journeys out into the wilderness, confronts the Indian in a violent confrontation, and regenerates himself and his people.[28]

ARRANGEMENT

Like the other books in this series on regional culture, this book includes chapters on architecture, art, ecology and environment, ethnicity, fashion, film and theater, folklore, food, language, literature, music, religion, and sports and recreation. Each chapter identifies and examines many significant elements of its topic as it relates to the American Southwest, and together they form the whole that is the region's identity.

Maggie Valentine of the University of Texas–San Antonio evaluates the architecture of the Southwest and considers a wide variety of structures, from the pit houses and cliff dwellings of pre-Columbian peoples to the European structures imported after contact and the cityscapes of the twentieth and twenty-first centuries. Valentine notes that the architectural structures reflect the responses to the climate and varied cultures of the Southwest, resulting in hybrid styles.

Holle Humphries of Austin and Lubbock surveys Southwestern art by defining art broadly, from fine art to folk art, and including painting, sculpture, woodwork, weaving, pottery, jewelry, basketry, metalwork, and photography in her discussion. She notes the powerful effects of Native American and Mexican American art forms on national visions of the Southwest and examines the notable movements, or schools, that appear in the Southwest, including the Taos Society of Artists and the Lone Star Regionalists.

Benjamin Johnson of Southern Methodist University in Dallas examines the ecology and environment of the area ranging from Palo Duro to the Grand Canyon, from the eastern to the western Colorado River, providing a historical narrative on how humans and nature have interacted or collided within the region over time. He notes how the land shapes our understanding of the American Southwest, influencing how geophysical factors, such as landforms, weather, and climate, and especially water sources from rivers to aquifers, play a major role in a region popularly recognized for its aridity.

Ruben G. Mendoza, director of the Institute for Archaeological Science, Technology, and Visualization at California State University, Monterey Bay, and David L. Shaul of Venito García Library and Archive, Tohono O'odham Nation, discuss Southwestern ethnicity, providing an overview of the ethnodemographics of the Southwest, a region often defined by the clash and cooperation of varied cultures. Arguably no other region in the United States has historically been identified as fully as the Southwest has been through its ethnic mixture of Native American, Mexican American, African American and Anglo cultures. Mendoza and Shaul examine the region's ethnic groups, discussing the prehistoric Anasazi, Hohokam, and Mogollon cultures, the famed historic Indians tribes—Comanche, Apache, Pueblo, Navaho, Hopi, Ute, Caddo, Paiute, Shoshone, Tohono O'odham (Papago), Akimel O'odham (Pima), Havasupai, Kiowa, Cherokee, Kickapoo, Tigua, Tonkawas, Wichitas, Creek, and Coahuilteca, Mexican American melding, and then the incorporation of the Southwest by the varied Anglo cultures, and the variety of ethnic groups in the twentieth and twenty-first centuries.

Brenda Brandt, education and community outreach manager at the Arizona Capitol Museum in Phoenix, contributes the chapter on fashion. She looks at fashion trends in the Southwest dating back to Native American and frontier cultures. Brandt notes prehistoric peoples' use of native fibers such as cotton and yucca and seashell adornments and then traces the changes introduced first by the Spanish, and later Mexican, cultures, immigrant Anglo cultures, and especially the power of vaquero/cowboy attire on the real and then the mythic Southwest of film and literature. She points to the significance of such recognizable Southwestern clothing as Levi jeans and bolo ties, as well as the growth of the Dallas fashion industry typified by Neiman-Marcus.

Mark Busby, the director of the Southwest Regional Humanities Center at Texas State University–San Marcos and editor of this volume, traces Southwestern film and theater, detailing the importance of the Southwest historically in providing the powerful archetypes that define the broader American experience. Busby notes the historical connection between film and theater and Wild West shows and rodeo. He points out the growth of Southwestern regional theaters like the Dallas Theater Center and Houston's Alley Theater, and he examines the national importance of such Southwestern playwrights as Sam Shepard, Preston Jones, and Denise Chavez. He argues that perhaps the film genre called the Western more rightly ought to be called the Southwestern and traces Southwestern film from silent film to such classics as *Stagecoach* and *Red River* to *Bonnie and Clyde*, *The Wild Bunch*, and *Lone Star*.

J. Rhett Rushing of the Institute of Texan Culture in San Antonio considers Southwestern folklore, in particular the popular legends, tales, myths, songs, and superstitions that originated in the region, such as Native American creation myths—Emergence and Earth Diver, Mexican American tales of *la llorona*, *corridos* about Gregorio Cortez, folk medicine such as *curanderismo*, and the urban legends that connect Southwestern folklore with that of the rest of the nation. Rushing notes that Southwestern folklore often is about borders and identity, insiders and outsiders.

Jay Cox Hayward of Tucson examines the many different ways in which Southwestern cuisines define the region and how Southwestern foodways enact a series of performances by the various folk groups—indigenous and immigrant—and have, over time, created a hybrid cuisine that reflects the same mixture of influences that we find in other aspects of Southwestern culture.

Carol Lea Clark of the University of Texas–El Paso traces the various native languages in the region, focusing on the three distinct Pueblo language families (Keresan, Tanoan, and Zunian), the Athabascan speakers (Navajo and Apache), and the introduction of Spanish, French, English, German, Basque, and Czech. She notes that Spanglish, the mixture of Spanish and English, also called code switching, is now commonplace in the Southwest and points out the growing bilingualism in the region.

Cory Lock of St. Edwards University in Austin concludes that much of the literature of the Southwest reflects the overwhelming vastness of the landscape—of territory, sky, possibilities, and diversity. Lock documents Native American oral tradition; the work of Spanish explorers such as Alvar Núñez Cabeza de Vaca; nineteenth century Southwestern writers such as Josiah Gregg, Lewis Garrard, Frederick Law Olmstead, and Mary Austin Holley; twentieth-century writers who define the power of the Western myth in the Southwest such as Gene Rhodes, O'Henry, Zane Gray, J. Frank Dobie, Larry McMurtry, and Elmer Kelton, some of whom, like McMurtry, have also revised the Western myth. Lock points to the variety of Southwestern literature at the end of the twentieth century and the beginning of the twenty-first by evaluating environmental writers like Edward Abbey, African Americans like J. Mason Brewer and Anita Bunkley, Native Americans like N. Scott Momaday and Leslie Silko, and Mexican Americans such as Américo Paredes and Rudolfo Anaya, as well as Southwestern poetry and journalism.

Richard Holland, founding curator of the Southwestern Writers Collection at Texas State University–San Marcos, who now teaches in the honors program at the University of Texas–Austin, notes that Southwestern music offers a rich combination of styles and types—blues, country, jazz, western swing, honky tonk, conjunto, Tejano, rock n' roll, singer-songwriters, and Las Vegas performers. Holland focuses on the importance of musicians such as Blind Lemon Jefferson, Woody Guthrie, Bob Wills, Huddie Ledbetter, Ernest Tubb, and many others across the region.

Jeremy Bonner of Baltimore demonstrates the importance of religion in the Southwest, tracing the significance and variety of Native American religious beliefs, especially the connection between religious practices and the land. Bonner points out that there are three distinct sections: the Bible Belt's westward edge in East Texas; the Catholic core in West Texas, New Mexico, and southeastern Arizona; and the region made up of northern and western Arizona and Nevada, historically Catholic but increasingly Mormon or completely uninterested in religion.

Margaret Dwyer of the University of Texas–Arlington discusses sports and recreation in the region, beginning with the prehistoric Hohokam's use of rubber balls for games. She also demonstrates the importance of sports across the Southwest—rodeo, baseball from Little League to professional, football at all levels, basketball, fishing, boating, hunting, wrestling, soccer, camping, hiking, horse racing, auto racing, and skiing. Dwyer notes that football dominates Texas, basketball is the major sport in New Mexico, golf is popular in Arizona, and besides the casinos in Nevada, skiing and mountain sports are prevalent.

Taken together, these essays demonstrate the power of Southwestern culture. The Southwest has a vibrant, diverse landscape; rich history; varied languages and ethnicity; and distinctive art, architecture, folklore, music, film, theater, literature, religious experiences, and sports and recreation. Despite the national fear that corporate forces are tending toward a "McWorld" that destroys regional differences and leaves only a kind of strip mall sameness, this collection of essays emphasizes the continuing power of Southwestern regional uniqueness where mesas, buttes, cacti, cowboys, vaqueros, Indians, and casinos continue to capture the imagination.

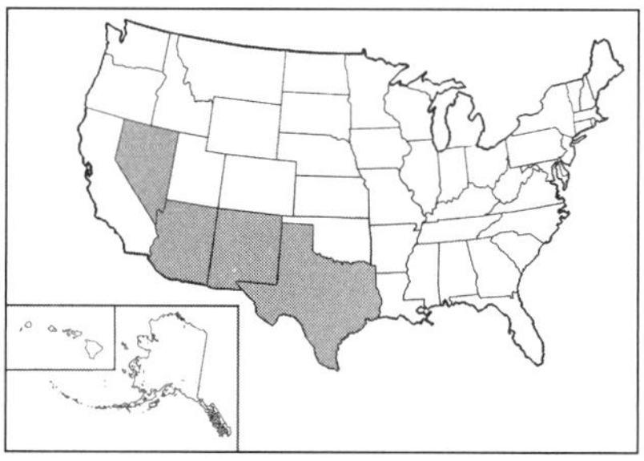

ARCHITECTURE

Maggie Valentine

The quintessential Southwestern architecture is that found in Santa Fe and Taos, New Mexico—hand-crafted adobe structures in shades of warm oranges and sunset reds, with flat roofs and projecting *vigas*. This style suggests centuries of cultural and environmental adaptation, evoking a simpler time and a very specific place. However, this stereotypical icon, like the Indian trading post, while true, is only part of the story. On closer examination the forms disclose much more about the histories of the place and the attitudes of power than that which is at first revealed. This shorthand symbol, in fact, codified into aesthetic guidelines by the City of Santa Fe, New Mexico, nevertheless, is, an oversimplified depiction of time and place that blurs the actual morphology of Southwestern architectural forms and their meanings into a coyote cliché.

The states of Arizona, Nevada, New Mexico, and Texas are located in a geographical region containing mountains, deserts, and canyons. Northern Nevada is vastly different than eastern Texas, which shares as much with Louisiana as the former does with Idaho and Utah. West Texas is arid and largely treeless, whereas East Texas is semitropical and heavily forested. Most of Nevada is part of the Great Basin, whereas Texas is at the southern end of the Great Plains. Elevations range from 9,000 ft. to sea level. Much of this part of the United States is very inhospitable during a large portion of the year. It is seasonally hot and mostly arid or semiarid. In some places, temperatures range from below freezing to triple digits over the course of a few days. The geography, climate, and topography have always limited the possibilities of the built environment in terms of materials and form, and each successive immigrant group faced the same frontier conditions. Some tried to accommodate these conditions, building in sympathy with the environment, and some to defy them, planting front yards of green grass in the desert, where there was no water.

Geographically the American Southwest is a desert, split by a national boundary. The borderland quality reflects the dual heritage of the land, and the entire area projects a feeling of isolation attributable to the vast spaces and the cultural independence it encompasses. Anyone who has driven across this area in any direction has experienced the separateness of this place and the time it takes to get from one place to another. Even when one has finally arrived in Virginia City, Phoenix, Tucson, Albuquerque, San Antonio, Abilene, Amarillo, or Brownsville, one still feels largely isolated from the rest of the United States. These cities in the center of the Southwest pride themselves on those differences that distinguish them from other places, even within the same region. Cities on the rim of the geographical Southwest but located within the political boundaries of these four states, such as Fort Worth, Dallas, and Houston, are, in fact, transitional cities that reveal the boundaries at the edge of the Southwest. They are less connected to the Indian and Spanish traditions and express more of the frontier Anglo identity. (The Southwestern term *Anglo* refers to non-Indian and non-Hispanic culture.) Likewise, Las Vegas, Nevada, on the western edge of the region, is more of a link to get-rich-quick Yankees and a West Coast oasis. The Rio Grande as the southern political border marks a boundary that is obvious in both the landscape and in history.

Another defining element of the Southwest is the quality of light, which exaggerates both the distance between places and the beauty of the natural landscape in this thirsty land. When one is traveling, the sun is direct and almost unbearable. When one stops to look at the land, the sun highlights a range of colors and forms found nowhere else. Georgia O'Keeffe and countless others were drawn to this place and tried to capture on canvas and film the light and shadows created on the land. The sun both reveals and hides natural forms and articulates the essence of the primitive built environment—the massing of hand-shaped, load-bearing adobe walls built of the earth itself—as well as the modern, high-rise cities.

The area contains the oldest and some of the newest parts of the United States. New Mexico houses the longest continually inhabited cities but was the forty-seventh state to enter the union. Thousands of years ago the region was home to scores of Native American tribes, ranging from Plains to Pueblos, who built private homes and public spaces of earth, stone, and wood, which to this day are the primary building vocabulary, even when assisted by a twenty-first-century steel frame.

Architecture is herein defined as the built environment—the exteriors and interiors of buildings' open spaces and resultant communities, shaped by the people living there. It includes the official and often monumental edifices of a culture as well as the commercial and residential buildings. It encompasses urban and rural structures, those designed by architects and those built by developers to serve perceived individual needs or on speculation, and the anonymous vernacular types designed to satisfy practical rather than aesthetic needs. Architecture is both an art and a science—an aesthetic form shaped by functional necessities. It is the one unavoidable, but often ignored, art form, yet it is primarily formed by practical considerations and limitations. It is experienced in four dimensions but is most often portrayed in two-dimensional pictures that ignore the essential third dimension of space, which, in turn, is changed in both function and memory by the fourth dimension of time. All architecture is a response to and a reflection of several characteristics of place and people. These elements include the environment (climate, topography, and natural resources); the economy (available materials and technology); the social-political organizations of the inhabitants or their conquerors; and

This abandoned structure near Abiquiu, New Mexico, reveals the structural composition of adobe bricks, external adobe plaster, vigas to support the roof, and wooden window frames inset into the adobe brick wall. Courtesy of Maggie Valentine.

the religious-cultural beliefs of the people(s) inhabiting and using the space. In any place, it describes the changing context of people and groups in terms of power, knowledge, and tradition.

In the Southwest this context was influenced primarily by three distinct groups who used common materials as dictated by shared physical conditions but shaped by diverse cultural values: Native Americans; Hispanic settlers from Mexico and Spain; and Anglos from the eastern United States and western Europe, who arrived in that order. Each group encountered the same geographic conditions and needed to contend with the other cultures, but their first responses were determined by cultural values and their own connection to the land and environment. Later arrivals freely borrowed and mixed elements they found with the skills and knowledge of architectural forms they brought with them. The physical appearance as well as the romantic imagery of the twenty-first century built environment is a result of the distinctions and sharing among these three groups, as well as of the shifting balance of power among the form-givers.

The regional architecture of the Southwest is the product of a uniquely Indian-Latino-Anglo culture; the architecture exhibits an identifiable hybrid style and reflects two traditions. The first tradition was the unique, place-defining forms such as the pueblo, plaza, and courtyard, which resulted from the beliefs, materials, and conditions of the place. As cultures merged, forms were confiscated, usually without a full understanding of their significance. It was ever a question of who owned and who controlled the use of those forms and assigned new meanings.

The second tradition was that of the dominant American catalogue of styles and approaches, transported from Eastern and Southern cities or European building traditions, either translated into a Southwestern language or simply overlaid on it. This included the grid, period revival styles, skyscrapers, and military and retirement communities. The Anglo tradition was also forged from an economic basis unknown to previous settlers, including large-scale resource extraction—for example, of gold, silver, and oil, leaving in its wake the two extremes of ghost towns and metropolitan centers. Consistent over time were differences in perspective and cultural assumptions about the basic meaning of the land itself and the role of humankind *in* versus *on* it.

The result of these competing interests and the common opponent of a harsh land, was a series of alternating hybrid cultures and statements of independence and confusion. The built environment was produced by the interaction of the three main populations, by importing and exporting different patterns from one part of the Southwest to another, but all the architecture is stamped by regional characteristics—the material, climate, and light that desert conditions and landscape dictate.

ARCHITECTURE OF INDIGENOUS PEOPLES

According to anthropologists, the first human inhabitants of this area arrived from Asia across the Bering Strait more than 10,000 years ago. According to most native traditions, people originated from the underworld, located in the belly of the earth. Native peoples shared a reverence for the land as a sacred source of power and saw the life cycle as cyclical, not linear; living things started within the earth and returned to it. The earth was thus the source of life that contained the before and the after—both ancestors and descendants. Therefore, the relationship with the land was of utmost importance for keeping harmony as one lived, literally, between the past and the future. To native peoples, time, life, and the land in which they were bound together were truths, not commodities.

The predominant native groups in the Southwest were the Mogollon, Hohokam, Anasazi, and the relatively unknown Patayan, which constituted the four major cultural traditions in the heart of the Southwest, Arizona and New Mexico; the Shoshone and Paiute in Nevada; and the Apache and Wichitas in Texas. For each of these culture groups, which encompassed dozens of tribes, the residential and community structures reflected their economic basis, as well as their sociopolitical hierarchies. The specific building forms each tribe constructed mirrored their beliefs about origins and natural law. This is especially seen in the concept of the living house and in the replication of the mythic First House, both of which are common themes among many tribes.

Typical are the Pueblo and Navajo myths. First Man and First Woman emerged from the underworld in Beginning Time when the earth was young. They climbed through a series of unlivable underworlds, until they found this one, where they were greeted by the creator god who made the first hogan and kiva. The Corn Mothers brought food with them from the earth to sustain life on the surface of the earth, gifts which are given annually.

Thus the kiva and the hogan reflect these sacred origins and describe the individual's place in the cosmic realm. The kiva, where the sky meets the earth, is surrounded by family houses. Round or rectangular, the kiva, usually partially submerged, is the place the Pueblos go to revisit the gods of the earth. It is made of adobe and entered through the top by climbing down a ladder, where the space surrounds the occupants like the sky. The interior walls are covered with murals, and the *sipapu* (small, symbolic hole) in front of the altar marks the symbolic place of emergence from the earth. The only opening is the hole in the roof, through which smoke escapes, people enter and exit, and the sun illuminates the inner space. The hogan (Navajo for "home place") is a winter dwelling made of logs stacked horizontally and covered with mud, based on the First Hogan, or Planning Hogan, which was modeled on the cosmos. Each log belonged to one of the gods of the four directions. The completed structure was a sacred and beautiful home for the First People, or Holy People, where creation and order of the outer world began and where their descendants regrouped. The shape and structure evolved, but its meaning reflects its sacred origins; the sky itself is a hogan, sheltering the earth.

The house is a living thing, a member of the family, and, like all family members, contains elements of ancestors, brothers, sisters, and heirs. It is the center of the world, the product of the union of Earth and Sky. The Blessingway (Navajo religious ritual) of the Diné (Navajo term for themselves meaning "the people") prays that you may walk in beauty—beauty in front, behind, on both sides, above, and below—to live in harmony with the earth. These six directions are sacred because they describe the cosmos and time itself. The houses take advantage of the gifts from the six sacred directions, materials supplied by the earth, and the breezes and insulation the earth provides.

While relationships between mythic beliefs and living patterns can be inferred, specific knowledge about and meanings of the native traditions and cultures often remain unknown. Native peoples depended on oral history and secrecy to keep their culture alive. Like an egg, the life and power contained within would be broken if they were revealed. While the Ancient Ones did not write down their history, they did build it. But interpretations, for the most part, are the result of ethnocentric observers who use a different base of assumptions about time, significance, and the nature of the universe. Even the names assigned to these people are not those chosen by the members of the group but are assigned by outsiders to describe what are perceived to be common attributes, whether it is language groups or pottery patterns.

Prehistoric architectural traditions included rectangular structures with multiple rooms arranged in villages in Arizona and New Mexico; earthlodges, grass houses, and tipis in Texas at the southern end of the Great Plains; and wickiups and tipis in Nevada at the edge of the Great Basin. Absent were the huge cities and monumental structures of the Aztecs in Mexico and the Mayan temples of Central America. North American Indians lived in smaller groups and built closer to the ground.

The Mogollon, Hohokam, and Anasazi are the names assigned to the pre-Columbian culture groups in the Southwest and used to categorize the ancestors of tribes currently living in the heart of the Southwest. They shared a common architectural beginning, well adapted to the hot, dry mesas. The Mogollon (early basketmakers named for an eighteenth-century Spanish colonial governor of New Mexico), the earliest of the Indian groups, lived in south-central Arizona and southwest New Mexico and flourished from the second century B.C.E. to the thirteenth century C.E. The Hohokam (a Pima term meaning "all used up") lived in southwestern Arizona, and the Anasazi (Navajo for "ancient ones" or "enemy ancestors"), often referred to today as the Ancestral Puebloans, were scattered throughout north-central Arizona and northwest New Mexico.

The First Houses of Indigenous People

The first houses of each group were pit houses, partially submerged in the earth, and covered with organic materials—similar to early shelters found across the northern stretches of Asia, Europe, and Canada—arranged in villages and towns. Pit houses were circular or square spaces, excavated into the earth, and arranged on defensible sites, such as mesa crests. The sides of the 3 ft. excavations were the side walls of the house. The space above ground was built up with branches and the roof supported by heavy logs on the interior. The rafters were made up of smaller branches and covered by a mat of mud, brush, and earth. A Mogollon settlement consisted of between five and fifty houses, surrounded by a simple masonry wall, with a special pit house for ceremonial purposes. Later they moved into the valleys, began joining their houses together around a central plaza, and built them up to two stories in height. By the fifteenth century, these sites had been abandoned and the people had disappeared.

The Hohokam, living along the rivers in southwestern Arizona, had more organized settlements, with a sophisticated irrigation system and pyramidal earth mounds to support ceremonial temples and spaces. They lived in shallow pit houses and above-ground dwellings. When agricultural cultivation replaced hunting and gathering, villages evolved, and with them, town planning. The ruins of Snaketown, twenty-three miles southeast of Phoenix in southern Arizona, which show some similarities to Meso-American civilizations, was settled circa 300 B.C.E. and occupied for seven hundred years. Early Hohokam settlements, called *rancherias*, consisted of small groups of detached houses built for extended families. In the thirteenth and fourteenth centuries these evolved into the *casas grandes*, multistory houses built in the flood plains, whose remnants can be seen in Casa Grande near Coolidge, Arizona, or in Pueblo Grande, today incorporated into a Phoenix park.

The Anasazi who had developed an agricultural lifestyle by circa 450 C.E., also first lived in villages of pit houses up to six feet deep. The pit house contained a small hole dug into the earth, which represented the mythic *sipapu*. Like their ancestors, the Anasazi gradually emerged from the earth, moving from subterranean pit houses to unit pueblos arranged linearly on top of the mesas. Beginning around 700 C.E., they began to live in these above-ground houses during the warmer part of the year, farming the land around them. These unit structures were roofed like the pit houses but made of adobe, sandstone, and masonry. The doorless, windowless units were joined together, so neighbors shared walls with units arranged in a community around a plaza. The communities had separate ceremonial structures, a sophisticated system of food production and storage, and a trading network with neighboring villages. By about 950 C.E., these above-ground square shelters were used year-round, and the pit-house form was adopted for the sacred space, or kiva, into which they could symbolically return to the earth and reemerge during sacred ceremonies.

Ancient Cities and Towns of Indigenous People

Sophisticated and highly organized cities developed in Chaco Canyon, New Mexico. Pueblo Bonito, the largest but not the earliest city, had a population of 15,000 at its peak. The city was founded in the early tenth century and lasted as a trading center for 150 years. It was organized around a D-shaped plaza, with four- to five-story contiguous masonry buildings with terraced apartments surrounding the central plaza. The construction methods were much advanced from those of the pit house villages. A veneer of dressed stone, carefully laid and fitted, covered the rubble core of thick walls laid on wide foundations, with doorways precisely aligned to create elegant walls. Small clan kivas served the residents, in addition to two huge kivas for the community. Careful planning went into the creation of these communities, which were connected by a system of roads. The four corners of the Great Kiva at Casa Rinconada, in Chaco Canyon, for example, aligned with the cardinal points, and there is evidence to suggest that other key buildings and whole towns were laid out in alignment with celestial patterns of solar and lunar orientations, marking the solstices and equinoxes.

About the time Chaco Canyon was abandoned, other Anasazi began nesting inside the cliffs below the mesa, but high off the canyon floors near the Four Corners area. Building to align themselves with the angles of winter sun for warmth and the summer sun for shade, the Cliff Dwellers translated their stick-and-adobe pit house and pueblo structures into stone, carving them out of the hillside and stacking them atop one another, sometimes up to four levels high. These terraced apartments were similar to the buildings in Chaco Canyon but shaped more by the topography. Cliff walls, not geometry or cardinal directions, molded the shapes and edges of the communities. Wood had to be carried down from atop the mesas for use in ceilings that supported the floors of the structure above it. These log beams, or vigas, were supported by joists and placed atop the walls and extended beyond them, the ends of the beams remaining visible. Smaller logs were laid across the stout logs at sharp angles and then covered with branches and adobe. Small windows admitted light and air. Many of the doors and windows were in a distinctive T formation, perhaps to allow space for bundles to be carried inside but also providing ledges at the entrances. Several houses were arranged around a kiva that was several feet in diameter, covered with mud, and had a small opening in the roof for access and a ventilation shaft that provided fresh air. The cliff dwellings varied in overall size and acted as a natural defense system from invaders while providing natural warmth and shade. More natural than man-made, these forms are a powerful example of the vernacular tradition—building with the natural environment.

There are at least two thousand known Anasazi sites left in the sandstone cliffs, many of them protected today by the federal government. The ruins were preserved from all but the elements—hidden in plain sight until the end of the nineteenth century. The Anasazi flourished in this area for nearly three thousand years. When they abandoned the cliffs circa 1300, they moved south and east into the flatter lands of Arizona, New Mexico, and southern Nevada, where many of their descendants still live.

At the base of the mountains they copied the same forms they had built into the mountains: stacked housing arranged around family and clan kivas, asymmetrically arranged to echo the mountainscape and in accordance with the angle of the sun. Here they built with mud and coarse rubble, not dressed stone. The adobe structures were covered with tree trunks, branches, and mud. Both the structures and the communities were labeled *pueblos* (villages) by the Spanish when they discovered them in the sixteenth century. As early as circa 900, there was a village at the site that became Taos, New Mexico, in north-central New Mexico. It evolved into a plaza-type pueblo settled between about 1275 and 1598 by the descendants of the Ancestral Puebloans and the ancestors of the present residents. Adobe buildings were stacked up to five stories, in stepped terraces of 50–500 rooms each. The most interior spaces were used for storage and the outermost for living, accessed by ladders that led to openings in the roof and to the terraces. The house forms have changed very little since the eighth century, except for the addition of ground-level doors and windows in the nineteenth century. The present buildings have been inhabited and altered since circa 1300.

Acoma (People of the White Rock), about 70 miles southwest of Albuquerque, which also dates from circa 900, was built on a soiless, sandstone mesa 365 ft. high. It is all but invisible until one is upon it, offering protection from unwanted visitors. This native Acropolis is probably the oldest continually inhabited community in the United States and is an example of a parallel street pueblo, in which parallel rows of contiguous adobe houses line the streets and the plaza is off to the side. All the materials—the adobe and the wood—had to be carried up by hand to build this 70-acre city in the sky. In both Acoma and Taos, the adobe houses are still built and annually repaired by the women of the tribe, following the tradition of the Ancient Ones.

Seasonal Shelters

As the Apache moved into the Southwest from the Great Plains, they split into nine tribes, with two major types of houses. Those settling in the west continued to use brush-covered shelters, known as wickiups, whereas the eastern tribes in Texas adapted the tipi. The wickiup was a bent-frame structure that could be erected quickly. A skeleton of bent branches that had been lashed and twisted together was covered with twigs and thatch made from whatever grasses were available. The house sat in a circular trench, and outer rings of branches over the thatch—attached with animal skin or string—held the structure in compression. A hole in the domed or pointed roof allowed smoke to escape.

Both the Apache wickiup and Navajo hogan were seasonal shelters. Even though the Navajo shared many belief systems with the Puebloans, their house forms differed greatly, demonstrating the differences between social and environmental determinants of built form. Hogan was a gift from Talking God, and the term was used to describe the single-room house in which they lived in the winter. The hogan could take the form of a conical-shaped building, a rectangular leaning-log structure, and a corbelled log building. The door always faced the rising sun in the east, and there was a hole in the roof to release smoke from either the central floor fireplace or wood-burning stove that provided heat. The *ki* and the *ramada* were also seasonal shelters, designed for the warmer months. The ki was a single-family shelter up to 10 ft. in diameter, made of brush and covered with mud. The ramada was an arbor, usually extended from the ki, used as summer shelter. It was supported by tree trunks and covered with logs and branches.

Most tribes in the Southwest were nomadic and did not require permanent shelter. The Paiute lived at the edge of the Great Basin, where the land alternated between high mountains and flat desert. Summer is hot and arid, with occasional thunderstorms and floods, and cold in the winter. The Kiowa, Comanche, eastern Apache, and Wichita lived on the southern edge of the Great Plains, where the land is mostly level and semiarid, with few trees. It is usually a temperate climate, but temperatures can be extreme with very little rainfall. In the north there are also cold, bitter winds and snow storms. All of these nomadic tribes first lived in natural shelters such as caves and rock overhangs. Over time they built temporary and portable structures in the form of wickiups and tipis, using organic materials. In some oral traditions, the original grass house wickiup of the Wichita was designed by Red Bean Man, a messenger of the Great Spirit; other versions credit an eagle. Both myths emphasized following very specific instructions in the building process that would result in strong houses and keep the village in harmony with nature. The house was framed with poles bent over an interior ring of posts and beams, covered with thatch, and bound together into a spire at the top. Rows of stringers kept the thatch covering tied in bunches around the exterior, which was up to 60 feet in diameter at the base.

The Kiowa built three-pole tipis, while the Comanche constructed four-pole tipis. Both were covered with buffalo or, later, canvas hides and had adjustable flaps for emitting smoke and hot air and admitting or excluding cold air at the base. An inner liner covering the lower section also helped regulate temperatures. Comanche tipis were not true cones but had a steeper side facing the bracing winds. Neither were they perfect circles, but ovoid, and their doorways faced the rising sun. The interior seating, sleeping arrangements, and placement of objects were according to social custom.

Native American architectural forms evolved slowly, adapting to changes in location, seasons, the hunt, and ideas about social organization, but the builders' belief in harmony with the natural environment and the cosmos always underlay these forms. This balance between continuity and change held true for a millennium before the tribes were discovered and conquered by Europeans, who had advanced technologies and a very different view of the world order.

HISPANIC ARCHITECTURE

One year after Christopher Columbus claimed America for Spain in 1492, Pope Alexander VI divided the New World between Spain and Portugal. Spain received North America with the blessing of the Church but not the permission of the North Americans. The presence of other European powers in North America was perceived as a threat to Catholic Spanish rule, so Spain began a systematic program, to be carried out by conquistadors and friars, of securing the land for crown and church.

Actual Spanish conquest of the Western Hemisphere began in 1519, when Hernán Cortés defeated the Aztecs in Mexico. The Spanish then turned their sights northward for additional conversion of land and souls. Taos was discovered in 1540 and Acoma a year later. The Spanish introduced new livestock, new agricultural and building techniques, new fatal diseases, and Christianity. In 1583 Spain issued a royal decree to organize the settlement of "New Mexico," an area that would become parts of Arizona, New Mexico, and Texas. In 1598, accompanied by friars and soldiers, Spanish-appointed Governor Don Juan de Oñate set out from Mexico to establish a permanent presence in the extension of Northern New Spain. In villages the Spanish conquered, like Taos and Acoma, they established churches and confirmed their authority, imposing taxes to support the building program of Catholic churches.

The Spanish missions introduced to the native peoples a new understanding of sacred space. Franciscans built churches not to commemorate the sacred space they found but to enclose the space they created. European Catholic traditions had shaped the space over time, and it became sacred only after the ritual was given form at the altar. The mission church included a longitudinal nave approaching the altar to separate the priests from the parishioners. Although it was not essential, the Latin cross shape was preferred because of its obvious symbolism and because the side aisles and transept provided extra space. In fact, it frequently turned out to be impossible, given the available building materials. A *convento*, a courtyard that included living quarters for the resident priests, was, however, required.

Upon his arrival in 1598 Oñate named the Indian village straddling the river Taos (Our Village) and ordered a mission church built, which he named San Jerónimo de Taos. The original church, begun in 1617, was built of adobe brick, a technique introduced by the Spanish, who had learned it from the Moors. By 1628 there were 2,500 Christian converts living in Taos, not all of them willing converts. The people of Taos found Spanish rule intolerable and threw them out. The church, damaged in the Pueblo Revolt of 1680, was destroyed and rebuilt several times, the last time in 1706. It was finally destroyed beyond repair by American troops in 1847 during the U.S.-Mexican War. The adobe brick ruins still stand at the edge of the pueblo and are surrounded by an Indian-Christian cemetery.

The Acoma Pueblo met a similar fate. Oñate's taxation was met with resistance, resulting in the arrest and severe punishment of the Acoma people. By 1603 Acoma Pueblo had been rebuilt, emerging as a Hispanic-Indian pueblo. The church of San Estéban was built from 1629 to 1642 on the south edge of the plaza. The Franciscan priests were trying to copy the cathedral in Mexico City (built 1563), but without sophisticated tools, with materials limited to what could be brought up to the mesa top by hand, and using native labor, who had never seen a Catholic cathedral. The wood for the altar and the vigas had to be brought from miles away, and since it was consecrated could not touch the ground on its journey to the mesa top. The battered walls, 8–10 ft. thick at the bottom, were a rubble core faced with adobe brick and a smooth overcoat of adobe. The nave was 150 ft. long and 33 ft. wide, had no transept, and was lit by clerestory windows. A convento for resident friars adjoined the church, creating a cloistered courtyard between the buildings.

Early Spanish-Influenced Churches and Dwellings

During the first Pueblo Revolt, 1680–1692, churches and other symbols of Spanish rule were destroyed. But mostly it was the wooden members and the icons that were destroyed; the adobe and stone shells survived. When the Spanish reconquered the area in 1692, they began rebuilding the churches, including those at Acoma and Taos. It is those rebuilt and restored churches one sees today, their patched skins and hybrid retablos that show both Christian and native symbols.

San Francisco de Asís at Rancho de Taos is one of the most beautiful and one of the most primitive churches in form, although it was built comparatively late, 1805–1815. Its powerful massing, the result of traditional materials and methods, has been beautifully respected and preserved. The mud surface is still replastered by hand. Best known for its back side, which one sees first, this view of the church has become a Southwestern icon. The Indian influence—the windowless, hand-formed, battered wall protected by clumsy buttresses—is apparent, but the front reflects the Hispanic religious tradition—symmetrical towers, a carved wooden door and white crosses. San José de la Laguna (1699–1706) in the Laguna Pueblo is another intimately scaled Hispanic-Indian church that shows the importance of siting. The white-washed church appears to float above the darker adobe houses of this small town. The church ceiling is spanned with crude vigas supported on corbels and covered with painted branches laid in a herringbone pattern. The Catholic reredos contrasts with the pagan images painted in bright colors on the side walls, but they work together to proclaim the faith in a new harvest.

The adobe walls of San Francisco de Asís in Rancho de Taos, New Mexico (1805–1815) are still replastered by hand. Courtesy of Maggie Valentine.

These churches mix Spanish Catholic religious concepts with New World materials and Native American technologies to produce a unique kind of structure that still shapes architecture and construction in this region. Native laborers built the buildings, but the Spanish introduced refinements in the techniques; for example, the use of wooden forms to shape adobe bricks instead of piling and puddling mud by hand. Adobe is an ideal material for the climate; it has good thermal qualities and the construction process is simple. The use of standardized bricks improved the process by making the wall faster and easier to erect and enhancing structural integrity. The Spanish also improved roofing techniques so the flat roofs drained better, and they used lime plaster to protect the buildings from wind and rain, to prevent them from melting back into the earth. Roman elements, such as arches, domes, vaulted ceilings, and plank construction, used in Spanish Renaissance cathedrals began appearing in the American desert.

Spanish building techniques were also used in house construction. For example, the *fogón* (bell-shaped fireplace) replaced the central hearth in traditional pueblos, adding flues and chimney pots to release the smoke. The *horno* (beehive-shaped exterior oven) was added to the pueblo terraces and used for baking traditional frybreads. *Canales* (water spouts carved into the ends of the extended vigas) helped the water drain from the flat roofs. Eventually wood-frame windows and doors brought in visitors, light, and air at ground level. Although the outside appearance of these traditional Indian houses was altered, the Indians did not add such Spanish features as the wrap-around portico or carved lintels and corbels. These features distinguished Spanish adobe structures, which also, in the traditional Mediterranean house form, were built around courtyards as a means of taking advantage of natural cooling breezes and maintaining privacy.

When the Spanish retook New Mexico in 1692, ending the Pueblo Revolt, which had begun in 1680, they realized the importance of establishing a presence in Texas and Arizona as well. In addition to colonizing existing Indian pueblos, they also established three kinds of new settlements in northern New Spain: religious missions; military presidios to protect the missions; and towns for the civilian population, which included the soldiers' families and nonmilitary settlers. Each settlement type had its own set of rules, and some sites, such as San Antonio, Texas, contained all three.

Spanish Missions

The mission was a religious complex with the power of church and state, and the church facade was its symbol. The role of the Spanish mission, introduced as an entity outside existing towns in 1682 as a direct response to the Pueblo Revolt, was to "civilize the heathens," making them colonials, loyal to the Spanish monarch and to the Catholic Church. To achieve this goal required an enclosed fortress-compound including both sacred and secular structures. Texas missions even operated as self-sustaining ranches or small towns. Although the layout varied with the location, the plan was based on the medieval monastery and on the missions already established in New Mexico. The church, usually forming one long side of the complex, was used by both the religious and the lay population, with the space around the altar carefully segregated.

The chapel was built first, using local materials, with a permanent stone structure to follow later. The architectural styles were imported from Spain, where the Churrigueresque Baroque was in fashion, but tempered by the realities of place. The church was still the most ornate building in the compound; sometimes Mexican tiles covered the exterior and opulent window frames and carved saints were installed at the entry. This ornamentation was in contrast with the very plain facades of the Spanish tradition and made even more exaggerated given the simple adobe and stone construction of the building. In Arizona and Texas, the churches more closely resembled those found in Baroque Mexico, whereas the New Mexican churches look more like the vernacular pueblos. Those early friars were not trained as architects, and Indians were not members of the European guilds. The result was a simpler building, as striking as the European churches, but the source of its power was its heavy massing, hand prints embedded in the walls, primitive interior paintings, and bold forms highlighted by the beautiful desert light.

While the New Mexican edifices retained more native influences, in the Spanish churches in Arizona and Texas the conquerors showed a heavier hand. The first

Texas missions were built in the east, near the Louisiana border, as a buffer against the French, and along the Rio Grande near El Paso. Because of increased Apache raids, the eastern missions were abandoned in 1721 and reestablished in San Antonio a decade later. They were rebuilt as ornate, permanent stone structures in Catholic Spanish settlements. These were new structures in new Spanish communities, located near sedentary tribes, not built as symbols of conquest in existing native cities, as in Acoma or Taos.

The mission complex served many purposes and constituted a town within walls. For the padres, there was a dormitory, kitchen, dining room, cemetery, and hospital, as well as farm buildings, corrals, and storehouses. There were shops and facilities for the nonreligious personnel—segregated quarters for the unmarried Indian men and women who lived at the mission and for the domestic servants, as well as an adjoining village for the Indian families who worked within the mission. There was also a military guardroom for the soldiers assigned to protect the mission. These various buildings were arranged around a courtyard serving as a plaza, not as formal as a cloister, but frequently arcaded. Young men and women lived at the mission and courted through the barred windows of the convento dormitory. After marriage, the family moved to the village.

The Texas missions were officially secularized in 1794, although it took thirty years to accomplish this. Lands owned by the church were distributed among the members of the congregation, and, in fact, most missions are still active parish churches. The missions in San Antonio are among the most beautiful and best preserved of the mission compounds. Four of the five still serve as active parish churches, while the grounds are protected and maintained by the National Park Service. Some of the *acéquias* (irrigation systems) are still in operation for nearby fields. Missions Concepción, Espada, San Juan Capistrano, and San José, as they are known locally, were built of local tufa and limestone in the Mexican Baroque tradition and survive in varying degrees of neglect and restoration. Collectively, they display remnants of the diversity of Spanish Southwestern churches: twin bell towers, vaults and domes, ornate wooden and stone carvings. Espada's fortification tower is intact, and all have some original outbuildings. Traces of the colorful geometric paintings that once decorated the outside can still be discerned in patches. The interior paintings include a mixture of Spanish and Indian images and motifs. The most famous surviving element is probably the Rose Window at San José; according to legend it was carved by Pedro Huizar and typical of the exquisite craftsmanship that went into the buildings. The Rose Window has come to symbolize the city, and it appears frequently as a motif, in uses as diverse as tourist brochures, new church designs, and department-store window surrounds.

The fifth, Mission San Antonio de Valero, more commonly known as the Alamo, is better known for the battle that took place outside its walls in 1836. The structure, begun in 1755, was never finished according to the Baroque blueprints. Following the battle, the ruined building was used as a warehouse. In 1850 the U.S. Army chose not to preserve the battle scar and ignored the original drawings. Instead, they added the now-familiar parapet atop the facade, which has been erroneously copied throughout the state as a historic symbol of Texan independence, initiating an inauthentic regional style that might be called Alamo Revival.

The most European of the mission compounds in the Southwest was Churrigueresque San Xavier del Bac, near Tucson, Arizona. It was begun in 1776 and

San Xavier del Bac near Tucson, Arizona (1776–1797), is the most Churrigueresque baroque of the missions built in the American Southwest. Courtesy of Maggie Valentine.

completed in 1797, under the direction of the Gaona brothers. It stands like an oasis in the sunlit desert, which exaggerates and highlights its picturesque Baroque forms and details. The cruciform church is surrounded by a low wall that frames the elaborately carved facade. The tripartite exterior's richly carved brown entrance is flanked by plain white bell towers. Curved brackets support twin belfries, and the elaborate dome over the crossing is visible from the exterior. The interior reveals complex domes and vaults instead of the flat ceilings found in New Mexican churches.

In addition to missions, which were religious administrative offices, the Spanish built parish churches for worship in towns, cities, and pueblos. Grand churches, such as San Fernando Cathedral in San Antonio, Texas (congregation founded 1731; original building begun 1738; new facade circa 1873), marked the center of the city; highway mileage is still measured from the center of the old dome. Formal and informal community chapels, *oratorios* (prayer chapels), private shrines, and *Penitente morada* (houses of worship) were also built over the centuries to serve the faithful. These mostly vernacular structures, with their adobe bricks, colorful tiles, and images of Our Lady of Guadalupe and other miracles, still stand as evidence of the Catholic heritage of the area.

Spanish Presidios

The first presidios—military compounds designed to guard the missions and the Spanish land claims—were constructed simultaneously with the first mission settlements. They worked in tandem, but not always in harmony, with the missions.

Originally called *casas fuertes* (fortified houses), the presidios were based on defensive plans the Spanish had learned from the Moors. Transferred to the New World, they were built of local materials, which might be adobe, log, or stone. The complex was square or rectangular and had high walls, a parapet roof (ideal for shooting), and at opposite corners round or octagonal *torreones* (bastions) fitted with loopholes for firing. The presidio was surrounded by a stockade, which also enclosed the storage facilities, quarters for the officers, and a chapel. Occasionally the presidio had no walls, towers, or barracks, but these tended to be in urban settings, such as San Antonio and Santa Fe, where the soldiers lived with their families. Some soldiers brought families, others married native women, but most stayed to become permanent residents in the new Spanish towns.

The best extant example of a presidio is Nuestra Señora de Loreto de la Bahía, established near Goliad, Texas, in 1749 (its third site) to protect the nearby Mission Nuestra Señora del Espíritu Santo de Zúñiga. The mission, which once owned over 40,000 head of cattle, fell into ruin after 1830. The Civilian Conservation Corps completed some reconstruction of the mission between 1933 and 1941. The presidio, which saw action as a fort during the skirmishes between Texas, Mexico, and the United States during the early nineteenth century, was from 1963 to 1967, restored to its 1836 appearance, including the barracks, officers' quarters, guardhouse, and bastions, and a working canon in front.

Spanish Towns

The third type of new settlement was secular, motivated by politics (pueblos or villas) or by economics (ranchos), and it included both official cities and vernacular towns. Each served a different kind of population and contained different housing types, assigned according to social class. Almost all housing types and forms, no matter what size or status, were laid out in an introverted fashion, having a formal front on the street and a private courtyard for the family either in the back or center of the house. This form was a microcosm of the city itself, which commonly featured a shared courtyard in the center.

The Laws of the Indies were developed by Spain over centuries, and they governed the political, social, and religious layout of new towns. Inspired by Vitruvian principles and Roman outposts, the periodically revised and codified royal decrees dictated that all new Spanish colonial settlements were to follow the same physical pattern, reinforcing the power of the crown and the church. Statutes regulated the site selection and layout of civil settlements of a specific size, including Santa Fe, the new Spanish capital of North America. The nature and climate suggested the use of insulated materials and cross-breezes, and houses were whitewashed to reflect the sun's rays.

After the site and the siting of a new town were determined, the plaza was laid out first, its size and proportions determined by the size of the city. It was square or rectangular, located in the center of the city, ideally fed by four principal streets perpendicular to the middle of the sides of the plaza, and by four secondary streets that surrounded the plaza and crossed at each corner. The width of the streets depended on the climate and the local need for defense. Additional streets emanated from the plaza so as to keep it in the center and to allow for growth.

On its surface, this approach to community planning resembled native traditions, but its motivations were different. While the Indian plaza (so-named by the Spanish because it resembled their own) reinforced commonality and shared sacred space, the Spanish plaza was dictated by law as a reminder of conquest, and the placement of buildings and land ownership around the plaza reflected the social hierarchy.

The principal secular buildings were built on the plaza. This included the *cabildo* (municipal building), city arsenal, and royal residences. Buildings faced the four sides of the plaza, where *portales* (covered walkways) protected the pedestrians and the sidewalks. Ideally the church was not on the main square but separated from it on a raised area so its visibility was increased. The cathedral or the church often found itself facing the plaza, as happened in Tucson. Housing and farming lots were located in the next ring around the plaza, and the hospital, cemetery, and slaughterhouse were removed from the civic and business center.

The initial buildings often resembled native pueblo design—adobe walls, flat roofs, and protruding vigas in both public and commercial buildings. Two of the best examples of early secular Hispanic buildings are the Palace of the Governors in Santa Fe (1610–12) and the mislabeled Spanish Governor's House in San Antonio (1749). Even though the latter was built later, it is probably a more accurate representation of the early Spanish buildings than was the Santa Fe version, whose best-known feature is the Anglo-Hispanic corbelled portal across the front, which was added to the building in 1913. The Palace in San Antonio was the home of the *comandancia* of the presidio and faced Military Plaza. It's laid out in a traditional Mexican domestic pattern of adjoining rooms facing an inner courtyard with a formal garden.

The Palace of the Governor in Santa Fe, one of the oldest surviving non-Indian buildings in the United States, began as part of the presidio, the *Casas Reales*, which contained barracks, a chapel, and offices, in addition to the palace. It was a singular row of adjoining rooms and offices. Both buildings faced a plaza at the front and a courtyard at the rear and took advantage of cross-ventilation. The Santa Fe building was damaged in the Pueblo Revolt of 1680, repaired in 1693, altered in the eighteenth century, shortened when the road was widened in the 1860s, restored in 1912, and periodically corrected since.

Spanish New World Residences

Towns also grew up around the ranch and the New World interpretation of the Mexican hacienda. The enclosed Spanish hacienda, or *casa-corral*, was a fortified compound, an introverted L- or U-shaped or completely enclosed ranch house, built around one or more courtyards. These windowless, fortified houses for wealthy landowners were made of adobe or caliche (soil and lime). A massive front gate, wide enough for a wagon to enter, opened into a covered passage, or *zaguán*. The gate incorporated a small wooden door for pedestrian entry into the courtyard, onto which all rooms opened.

The Hacienda de los Martinez in the city of Taos, New Mexico, begun in 1804 and subsequently enlarged, was the home of the Severino Martinez family. The ruins were purchased in 1964 and the structure restored to the 1820s period. The *casa mayor* at the front is a series of rooms linked by a walkway that surrounds the *placita*, or courtyard. Another courtyard in the back, connected to the front of the house by an arched entry, is also surrounded by workrooms and features a separate covered passage to admit livestock for protection in case of attack.

Jacales (huts), the most primitive of the Hispanic structures, were indigenous to Mexico. Four corner poles that were forked at the top to hold the ends of vigas supported the frame in the rectangular, one-room palisade house made of sticks and mud. Other upright posts were crossed with horizontal sticks, creating a web that could be filled with grasses, stones, mud, or rubble. The vertical wood planks that made up the frame of the walls were set into a trench at the foundation and held in place at the base by stones. Often, split mesquite was laid across horizontally, creating a *jacal de leña* (hut of firewood). The walls were chinked with rubble or daubed with mud and sod, then painted white or left their natural color. The pitched roof was covered with thatch and later tin.

The walls were 6–10 in. thick and plastered on both sides with adobe, mud, or lime mortar. The well-insulated houses were generally 10–12 ft. wide by 18–24 ft. long, depending on the length of both the branches used as ridgepoles and the vigas. The roof was steeply pitched to enable the house to stand up to the weather. It was thatched with local grasses tied in bunches and had to be rethatched every 3–4 years. Eventually, if the jacal was still standing, the thatched roofs were replaced with wood shingles or galvanized metal. The house may have had one window, and the floor was made of packed and hardened dirt or sometimes *chipichil* (a mixture of lime, sand, and gravel). The picket-and-sotol house was an adaptation

Adobe jacal demonstrates building methods typical of south Texas. Both the vertical cedar post walls and the horizontal laths are chinked and then plastered with adobe. Courtesy of Maggie Valentine.

of the jacal built by sheep and goat herders in southwestern Texas but built with less wood. Jacales were found throughout the southwest on ranches, especially in West Texas, and in barrios and the poor sections of cities, wherever first-generation immigrants lived, into the twentieth century.

Hispanic houses were sited directly on the sidewalk, turning their backs to the street. The front was a mostly blank wall, and the house opened onto or often surrounded a courtyard in the rear, which was a protected outdoor living space for the family. In homes of the wealthy, the courtyard was surrounded on all sides by the family house. Other houses were L- or U-shaped, and the wall often extended to adjoining houses, creating a shared courtyard or *plazuela* (courtyard finished by a wall). This pattern can still be seen in El Presidio in Tucson; along Canyon Road in Santa Fe; and in Mesilla, New Mexico. Mesilla, founded in 1848, was preserved by accident and neglect when the railroad bypassed it, in favor of Las Cruces. The town retains early Hispanic patterns, and its church is on the plaza. The plaza currently has an Anglo feel because of the gazebo and the parking lots, but one can still perceive the pattern in the surrounding adobe and wooden commercial buildings and in the concentric rings of adobe houses whose backs are to the street.

ANGLO SETTLEMENTS

Although parts of the Southwest remained under Spanish and Mexican control until the middle of the nineteenth century, 1821 marked a turning point. That was the year the first Missouri trading expedition arrived in Santa Fe and Mexico won its independence from Spain. Anglos were invited into Texas the same year to establish permanent communities and lured into Nevada and California a few years later with promises of gold and silver. Americans next filled in the land in between, rationalizing it through Manifest Destiny, claiming a God-given nation that spanned "from sea to shining sea." Miners used the land and left; ranchers, settlers, and cowboys stayed and fought over how to use the land. They fought with each other, and they fought with those who were there first. The federal government encouraged American citizens to settle the land as a buffer against both old enemies and the changing political balance along the borders. Texas declared its independence and fought a civil war with Mexico, then joined the United States and, together, they goaded Mexico into a war over land ownership, the demands of which required the United States to establish more military posts in the region. The resulting Treaty of Guadalupe Hidalgo, which ended that war in 1848, and the subsequent Gadsden Purchase of 1854, encouraged more American immigration.

Early Houses

The earliest Anglo pioneers brought their homes with them to the frontier, both literally and figuratively. In North Texas, they first lived in their wagons, then in dugouts and sod houses, until they could build a respectable Yankee frame house. Dugouts were dug into the ground or hillside and covered with brush or earth for insulation. Logs chinked with mud or local fieldstone often helped define and protect the exposed walls. The typical house was approximately 13 ft. square, had a

El Santuario de Chimayó, New Mexico (1814–1816), combines the formal and vernacular characteristics of Hispanic and Anglo buildings. Courtesy of Maggie Valentine.

central beam supported by a post in the center of the single room, was warmed by the earth behind and the landscape overhead, and had little light. Dust was controlled by plastering the walls, draping a piece of canvas over the ceiling, and tamping the floor. Residents were nicknamed "prairie dogs."

Sod-block houses, also made from the earth, required slightly more work. The sod was cut into blocks, using a spade, and the blocks were laid in courses, grass side down, and held together with intertwined roots, creating walls 8 ft. thick. A typical house was 16 ft. by 20 ft. and had a door frame and usually two window frames set into the walls. The frames were made in the east, and they arrived by wagon. The roof was also finished with blocks of sod, although they were thinner than the blocks used in the walls. Although the dugout and the sod-block houses were well insulated, they were dark and small, vulnerable to the wind and rain, and in continual danger of collapse.

As the family's situation improved, they moved into a frame house, and the old sod house, gradually being reclaimed by nature, was ceded to livestock. The frame house was a simple frontier structure consisting of a living room, dining room, and loft for sleeping, with a lean-to used as a kitchen, very similar to the East Coast hall-and-parlor house.

One type of house that was adapted to look Eastern but act Western was the dogtrot, the roots of which were found on both sides of the Atlantic. This basically was an East Coast hall-and-parlor house, which is divided front to back by

Adobe zaguan at the historic Hacienda de los Martinez in Taos, New Mexico (begun 1804). The entry is wide enough to allow passage of animals and carts into the courtyard where they are protected behind the fortress-like walls of the enclosed hacienda. Courtesy of Maggie Valentine.

an open hallway where the dog (or the family on hot Texas nights) could sleep. They might be wood-frame houses or log cabins, well suited to humid eastern Texas but not to the cold winters of northern Texas.

Log houses, an American folk tradition, were the first frontier houses for many different groups. Locally grown timbers were piled horizontally to create walls and notched together at the corners according to whatever ethnic custom had been handed down from generation to generation. An inch or more of space was usually left between the logs and chinked with wood chips, rocks, grass, or mortar to counteract the natural warping and tapering of the logs. The gabled, rectangular house could be a single or double pen, open or partitioned into small rooms, usually one story, often with a loft for sleeping. As the family grew, rooms could be added, and, whenever possible, there was a porch at least the width of the front of the house. A close examination of the corner joints, as well as the shape of the logs and the chinking technique, identifies which part of the United States or Europe the family left behind.

By mid-century Texas had attracted a large number of German immigrants who established towns and built houses according to their traditions. New Braunfels (1845) and Fredericksburg (1846) were founded by German aristocrats who formed an association called the Aldersverein for the purpose of encouraging German immigration and attracting farmers, intellectuals, and freethinkers. The immigrants settled in those towns and in Comfort (1854). The towns were laid out on a grid, the streets were named for the Old World, and the house forms were adapted to New World conditions. This meant log houses and dogtrots, as well as

The tin-roofed, limestone Sunday House was used by German settlers who lived on ranches and farms in the Texas Hill Country for weekend visits to the city to attend church. Courtesy of Maggie Valentine.

the German folk-tradition known as *fachwerk*, half-timbered frames with infill of mud, brick, or, in Texas, limestone. The interior and exterior surfaces were then covered with stucco, hiding the pattern created by the timber members. Once they realized that the local stone was strong enough not to need a wood frame, the settlers began to build houses out of stacked limestone blocks. Limestone cuts easily when freshly quarried, then hardens with exposure to air. These buildings would typically be roofed with galvanized metal sheeting that had been crimped into standing seams. The Breustadt House (1858), now a museum in New Braunfels, Texas, is an excellent example of a middle-class German-American house, and it demonstrates the construction techniques of the period. Many houses were started in one period and added onto later, which can create a record of the evolution of construction techniques. A Texas tradition known as the Sunday House was developed by German-American farmers who lived in the rural Hill Country and attended church in the city. The family would build a small townhouse for weekend visits. The miniature houses were accessed by an exterior stairway and consisted of one room and a sleeping loft.

Nevada was slower to develop cities. The state had attracted temporary campers—explorers and trappers—in the late eighteenth century, but it was the Gold Rush in California that spurred development, because the forty-niners needed supply stops. Unlike New Mexico and Arizona, native architecture had little impact on nineteenth-century Anglo developments in Nevada; new settlers chose instead to import types familiar to them. Mormon settlers built the oldest structures extant in the Las Vegas area, an adobe fort and log cabin (1855); they also established one of the first Anglo cities in Nevada, Genoa (1851). Mormon town patterns followed the biblical blueprint found in the New Testament's description of the Heavenly City, a New Jerusalem with a rational gridiron of wide streets and spacious blocks. The cities were absorbed when the Mormons were recalled to Salt Lake City in 1857, although many returned to live in southern Nevada and northern Arizona. Another group attracted to the foothills in Nevada were the Basque sheepherders, who saw the open ranges as a familiar environment, although they ran into conflicts with the ranchers. The Basques did leave a distinctive building type in Nevada: the Basque hotel. These simple wooden or brick structures provided room, board, and social centers for new immigrants and a home base while the sheepherders spent months on the range. A few examples of these structures have survived in northern towns, including Gardnerville, Winnemucca, and Elko.

Townships

New American townships also copied East Coast patterns. They continued the layout advocated by Thomas Jefferson and established the first federal lands by the Land Ordinance of 1785. The plan was an orthogonal grid based on the mile-square grid, laid down with no allowance for changes in topography. A six-mile by six-mile township was the basis for the new settlement, with certain squares in the checkerboard reserved for common use, schools in particular. The remaining squares were set aside for houses, divided into lots 25 ft. on the street side and 50–100 ft. deep. Although the Indian plaza, the Hispanic plaza, and the American grid appear similar, their meanings were very different.

Mexico encouraged settlement in Texas by giving impressarios land grants in return for bringing in a minimum number of recruits. Virginian Steven F. Austin was one of the most successful of these developers, founding San Felipe and Columbus in 1823, as his headquarters in Texas. The former didn't survive, but the latter, laid out by Austin according to a square-block grid, is the oldest Anglo town in the West. The new arrivals built all sizes and shapes of American frame houses in fashionable Greek Revival and modified styles. Other towns soon followed, and more Yankees moved in. By the time the Mexican government decided this was not a good policy, the Anglo population was well established in Texas and pondering independence. The new Republic of Texas welcomed Americans, and urban centers began appearing, including Houston and Galveston (1836), which became port cities; Beaumont (1837), which became a market center; Austin (1839), the new capital; and Dallas (1842), which emerged as a trading center. Perpendicular streets, named alphabetically in one direction and numerically in the other, made it easy to find one's way in these new American cities. Other cities, such as San Antonio and El Paso, were Anglicized, their primary Hispanic grids converted to the American standard. The same pattern of new American cities and Anglicized old cities was repeated in Arizona and New Mexico. Well-to-do families built impressive Greek Revival, Italianate, Stick-style, and Second Empire houses. Common folk built smaller-scaled houses and log cabins. In general, they did not copy either the Indian or Hispanic forms that suited the climate but imitated East Coast traditions in both sophisticated and frontier examples.

Mining Towns

The discovery of the Comstock Lode in 1859 led to the first immigration in large numbers of Anglo-American men who set up temporary camps and built what they needed out of what they had. Instant cities, such as Virginia City, "Queen of the Comstock," demonstrated the three phases of mining-town development. The rapid *settlement phase* consisted of tents and log cabins, laid out in no particular plan. The *camp phase* witnessed a more permanent population living in communities that utilized a traditional American grid plan. False-front vernacular versions of Eastern commercial-style buildings appeared, complete with decorative details in the fashionable (and loosely interpreted) Italianate, Second Empire, or Queen Anne styles, or some combination thereof. Wood was brought in for Victorian houses as well as for commercial buildings; sometimes whole buildings arrived from the East, especially as the development entered the *town phase*. Stone and brick were used for public buildings in the center of the town, and grand opera houses announced a sophistication previously unknown in these parts. They were usually pretentious vaudeville houses and early movie venues. Company towns—built by mining enterprises—examples include McGill, Nevada, and Ajo, Arizona—consisted of corporate headquarters, stores, and housing for the managers and workers, who were mostly single men. In Nevada boomtowns, tin cans were sometimes flattened and recycled for use as shingles and siding.

All too often, Nevada and Arizona experienced a fourth phase: abandonment, as occurred in cities such as Virginia City, Nevada; Jerome, Arizona; and the appropriately named Tombstone, also in Arizona. Towns were left to decompose, and buildings were abandoned or moved to more promising sites. Building booms and busts followed the mining economy. This economic cycle also meant that county seats moved frequently.

Homesteaders in the Southwest

By 1876 the buffalo were gone from the High Plains and the Indians with them, clearing the way for European settlers and displaced Americans—mostly Confederate soldiers and freedmen from the vanquished South—to migrate west. The U.S. government encouraged this migration through the Homestead Act of 1862, when they offered 160 acres of federally-owned land to anyone who would live on and farm the land for the requisite number of years. In repetition of an earlier pattern, settlers' first homes were what they brought with them (covered wagons and tents) or what they found they could quickly rearrange into housing (dugouts and sod). Later they built or imported frame houses, copying the forms they had lived in in the states.

Homesteaders were farmers or ranchers who battled cowboys for land. Farmers needed enclosed spaces for their livestock and to protect their crops from the cowboys, whose cattle grazed on long cattle drives until 1891. Ranchers raised livestock in one place. They needed large acreage with a source of water and a large workforce. Barbed-wire fences eventually helped settle the argument and encouraged the development of the large, self-sufficient ranch. The complex included a ranch house for the owner, a bunkhouse for the workers, and various outbuildings to service people as well as livestock. The Texas ranch house was a one- or two-

Three generations of a homesteading family in front of their sod house in Arizona, 1913. Courtesy of Maggie Valentine.

story frame building, depending on the size of the rancher's family, and it had a porch along the south side that served as a breezeway and provided shade. The house had no locks. Since the nearest neighboring house might be miles away, the ranch house provided a shelter for anyone who needed it in inclement weather, which included frequent dust storms and occasional blizzards. The bunkhouse was a separate structure, built of logs or fieldstone. A typical Texas bunkhouse consisted of a single room approximately 16 ft. by 33 ft.; there were windows at either end, a front and back door, and a shingled roof. The hired hands often slept in shifts on cots, bedrolls, or makeshift bunks, warmed by a woodstove and strong coffee.

BECOMING A U.S. TERRITORY BRINGS CHANGES

By the mid-nineteenth century, the Hispanic Southwest had become United States territory. The arrival of the railroad meant the arrival of tourists and more settlers in the next quarter century, and as a result Hispanic towns and cities became increasingly Anglicized. The grid was superimposed on or surrounded the old Hispanic hub, and adobe houses were replaced with wood-frame structures. The plaza was converted into a genteel Main Street park, or it disappeared altogether. For example, Tucson, Arizona, which began as a Spanish military post in 1776, was drastically altered a century later to accommodate a new and rapidly growing population. The presidio wall was removed and old buildings replaced. All that is left now are a few houses and the remnants of irregular street patterns in the heart of the city. The most historic part of contemporary Tucson dates from the Territorial period between 1850 and 1880, and most of that fabric was lost in the Urban Renewal of the 1960s, as were any vestiges of the original plaza. Likewise, there is little traditional architecture left in the Spanish-era settlement of Albuquerque (1706) in New Mexico, except for Old Town, and even there the buildings surrounding the plaza and even the parish church were given Victorian facades in the 1870s.

Capital City Architecture

Capital cities, including Austin, Texas (1839), Prescott (1864), the first capital of Arizona, and Phoenix (1876), the current capital, were new cities, laid out in the traditional American grid. Greek Revival houses and Classical domed government buildings identified the centers of the new cities as being American. Plazas were redefined as courthouse squares. Santa Fe, founded in 1609 as the Spanish provincial capital, became the American territorial, and then state capital, and got a new classically inspired capitol to prove it, whereas in many new southern Texas towns founded after statehood, Hispanic plazas were included in the town layout to reinforce their borderland identity.

Housing Styles in the Nineteenth and Early Twentieth Centuries

During the second half of the century, between annexation and statehood, Hispanic buildings began to change and reflect an Anglo influence. As houses were altered or enlarged, Anglo elements appeared, eventually resulting in a hybrid house type, a mixture of the flat-roofed adobe front, with pitched-roof additions that featured windows. The houses began to face the street and have articulated front entries. The Territorial Style, as it came to be called, was a regional Greek Revival. It developed in New Mexico and was created with small-scale changes to existing buildings, giving the Hispanic cities an Anglo icing. Arriving wagon trains and then railroads brought new building supplies, including frames and moldings for doors and windows, wood pediments, new tools, and lumber. They also brought the latest Anglo ideas in architecture. Adobe houses began to acquire new vertical windows, trim, and hints of Greek temple details. Classical pediments and architraves appeared, along with wooden balconies and brick coping atop the walls. Porch columns now had carved bracket capitals, highlighted with new paint. The introduction of new materials and details changed the proportional system and the feeling of the wall as an architectural element. The relationship of the members (doors, windows, and cornice details) to the whole (wall and building) changed, corrupting the visual integrity of the adobe structure. The massing of the wall and of the building changed the vocabulary from mostly wall with small openings to one of windows done in a small-scale pattern framed by a wall. The houses looked less like pueblo shelters that grew out of the earth and more like pitched-roof Eastern houses that sat on the land.

These architectural changes were accompanied by modernized lifestyles. Native Americans were bribed or forced into giving up their religion, hairstyles, and language. Their children were sent away to Indian schools where they were taught American ways of dress and speech. Reservation buildings were until recently designed by white employees of the Bureau of Indian Affairs. Manufactured lumber, railroad ties, and milled lath replaced the traditional materials of the *ramada*, resulting in the "sandwich house," in which the walls consisted of horizontal 1 ft. by

4 ft. frames filled with adobe between corner posts, then plastered inside and out. The *ki*, however, was often preserved as sacred space.

Railroad Towns

When the railroads arrived in the Southwest, railroad towns came with them. These towns developed as temporary stops on the trip to California or Oregon and were a form of company town. A Stick-style or Mission Revival depot often served as the company office as well as City Hall. Harvey House restaurants, hotels, and railroad housing were the common thread, and one town was not that different from the next. The railroad delivered finished lumber and manufactured trim to build and decorate the multistory Victorian houses. The towns were usually laid out very neatly with streets of small cottages paralleling the tracks and emanating from the railroad depot, which was located on Main Street or Central Avenue.

Unlike in the Hispanic tradition, Anglo houses were set back from the street by a front yard and set off from each other by side yards. Porches along the front of the house, sometimes extending around the corner, provided a semiprivate outdoor living space where one could watch the neighborhood and converse with neighbors if desired. A large, clearly visible front door and large windows and a front walk that led to front steps and a front porch marked the front of the house. The facades represented fashionable styles: Greek Revival, Carpenter Gothic, and Italianate. Later, Prairie and Craftsman bungalow styles were imported from Chicago and California, respectively. They also built in Period Revival styles made popular at the world's fairs, including American Colonial, Tudor, and French. Public buildings, especially county courthouses, were dressed in Richardsonian Romanesque, Second Empire, and other popular Victorian styles. They were designed mostly by local architects, such as Alfred Giles, James Riely Gordon, and James Wahrenberger, who adapted popular American monumental buildings into smaller-scaled versions made from local stone. One of the most beautiful, although not a typical example, is the Ellis County Courthouse (J. R. Gordon, 1895) in Waxahachie, Texas, a Victorian streetcar suburb of Dallas.

Downtowns

Burgeoning downtowns reflected the new Commercial-style office buildings in Chicago and other established cities. The most well-known architectural firm in the area at the turn of the century was Trost and Trost. Henry C. Trost (1860–1933), in practice with his brothers, shaped architecture in the Anglo Southwest from 1903–1940. He introduced mainstream American styles, including Prairie-style houses; Commercial (Chicago) style, Neoclassical, and Spanish Colonial Revival commercial buildings; and Art Deco skyscrapers. The firm was especially prolific in El Paso but was active in West Texas, Arizona, New Mexico, and Colorado. Trost introduced the ideas of Louis Sullivan and Frank Lloyd Wright to the region but adapted the "styles" to his own vision; he was also fluent in Pueblo Revival. The firm's most well-known buildings include the Turner House (El Paso Museum of Art, 1906); his own home (1908); the Mills Building (allegedly the second reinforced-concrete skyscraper in the country, 1911); El Paso

This view of Alamo Plaza in San Antonio, Texas, shows how the Spanish plaza was Anglicized into a Victorian park by the 1890s, complete with gazebo. Courtesy of Maggie Valentine.

del Norte Hotel (1912); the Orndorff (Cortez) Hotel (1926); Bassett Tower (1930); and more than two hundred other houses, commercial buildings, and schools in El Paso.

TWENTIETH-CENTURY ARCHITECTURE IN THE SOUTHWEST

One of the tenets of modern architecture was that, in general, place didn't matter, although siting did. Architectural solutions could be applied anywhere and were not limited by the traps of historical references and context. These were consciously new designs that utilized new materials (steel) to serve new building types (high rises) dependent on new technologies (air conditioning) to overcome any obstacles. The Corbusian and Miesian solutions were labeled *International* because they were building systems, applicable anywhere in the world. They reflected the time—the twentieth century—not the place. There were stylish interpretations along the way, such as Art Deco, Streamlined Moderne, the stripped classicism of WPA Moderne, and glass-skin facades, but the cities were considered interchangeable.

Twentieth-century architecture in the Southwest was for the most part in the mainstream of American design, from International Style to Postmodern to Deconstructivist. Even Indian reservations and casinos, built in response to the economic disenfranchisement created by land ownership and political domination, utilized American, not Southwestern, conventions. By the middle of the century, the Southwest began to look more like the rest of America. This was especially true in Houston, an American city with a Southern accent, full of glass-skinned skyscrapers, built without benefit of zoning laws. The skyscrapers were mostly developer-driven copies of those in New York, Chicago, and L.A. At the same time, the museum districts of these Texas cities contained some of the best modern architecture in the country, designed by world-class architects. The high-tech Menil Collection (Renzo Piano and Partners, 1987) is blocks away from the abstract Rothko Chapel (Howard Barnstone and Eugene Aubry, 1971), and the Byzantine Fresco Chapel Museum (Francois de Menil, 1997) creates a stark contrast in art and architecture. The Museum of Fine Arts is a lesson in architectural history, beginning with the 1920s Neoclassical facade by Ralph Adams Cram and expanded over the years with buildings and additions designed by Mies van der Rohe (1958–1969) and Raphael Moneo (1999). The playful Children's Museum was designed by Robert Venturi and Denise Scott-Brown (1992), and the University of St. Thomas is Philip Johnson's Miesian interpretation of Jefferson's university. One of the best expressions of pure sculptural quality of space can be found in the University Chapel of St. Basil (1997) at the end of the mall.

Louis Kahn's Kimbell Museum (1972) in Fort Worth is a superb essay in the interplay of spatial form and light. Across the street is the new Modern (2002), Tadao Ando's first American building, where glass-enclosed steel-frame buildings sit in quiet pools of water that together communicate the attitude of the art that the museum contains. In the same city, Bass Performance Hall (David M. Schwarz, 1998) demonstrates what might have happened if there had never been a modern movement. Reminiscent of European opera houses, it utilizes modern technologies but ignores the less-is-more ban on ornament in favor of two 48 ft. angels carved in limestone, their heralding trumpets projecting into the street.

The Modernist philosophy promised an increased standard of living through mass production and technological solutions. Beginning in the 1920s, new suburban developments began to move away from the grid, resulting in intricate aerial labyrinths of interlocking geometries and cul-de-sacs. The single-story houses were cookie-cutter versions of white stucco and red tiles that repeated in endless imitations. Houses were fronted by a small green lawn next to one- and, later, two-car garages and had swimming pools in the back yard. The houses looked alike, the streets repeated variations of the same names, and the interchangeable names of the developments all promised sunshine and escape. The subdivisions were connected to the cities by wide, hot, treeless miles of asphalt in boulevards and freeways. This kind of development became standard in the postwar era, promising a homogenized lifestyle that could not be supported in the desert. The result is increased pollution and travel time, energy crises and power outages, and a loss of identity.

Eventually, Modernism even caught up with Nevada. There were only eleven self-identified architects in the state of Nevada in the early twentieth century (.001 percent of national total), and it wasn't until 1949 that both the State Board of Architects and the American Institute of Architects established a presence in the state. Architects were imported from out-of-state for large or important buildings. Most of what was built in the state was vernacular—pragmatic buildings of the people, by the people, and for the people. There were few large permanent cities in the state; it was still largely a transitory environment built by and for the temporal mining industry.

The federal government, which continues to own most of the property in the state, built much of Nevada's architecture, using traditional government planning methods, materials, and styles. Forts followed an established military pattern, and marble and masonry Neoclassical government buildings and boxy post offices adorned with eagles were built in the cities. New Deal programs built and renovated schools, post offices, and courthouses in an abstracted Deco-Classical-Modern style that came to be known as WPA Moderne. The Works Progress Administration (WPA) and the Civilian Conservation Corps (CCC) also built large-scale projects throughout the state, including bridges and dams, most notably the Hoover Dam. Postwar developments were often centered on defense, because the wide-open spaces provided testing opportunities. The towns and cities that supported these endeavors echoed the transitory nature of the state's history, as evidenced by mobile homes and "temporary" bungalows for school buildings.

In addition to government industries, Nevada's twentieth-century economy was built on quick divorces, gambling, and tourism. The architecture of these industries merged building types into fantasy images, marked by over-scaled, well-lit signage and buildings that didn't follow the academic canons but instead encouraged commercial imagination. Robert Venturi (1925–) and Denise Scott-Brown (1931–) embraced this tacky and blunt character as being an honest approach to the state's industries as well as a more accurate tool of communicating with people in the consumer age. They encouraged their design students to "learn from Las Vegas" how to communicate in architecture using contemporary signs instead of literary symbols. Since their postmodern architectural dispensation, Las Vegas and Reno have become unapologetic and respectable. They are now family destinations, capitalizing on their symbolism. Form doesn't follow function: the neon medium is the message.

AMALGAMATION: CONTINUITY AND TRANSFORMATION

The First Half of the Twentieth Century

In 1916 Bertram Goodhue, known for his Spanish Colonial Revival innovations, was commissioned by the mining company Phelps Dodge to plan a million-dollar model mining town for the workers at their open-pit copper mine. Tyrone, New Mexico, was planned around a plaza near a railroad station. The Anglo amenities of the company town (movie theatre, office buildings, stores, hotel, and library) were lined with Spanish arcades. The mine closed in 1921, however, and the unfinished town became a Spanish Colonial Revival ghost town; it was destroyed in the 1960s in favor of a new pit. The drawings showed a community resembling early Santa Barbara—without the retrofitting. Laid out in a grid were streets filled with modest off-white houses that had flat roofs and were shaded by low trees and framed by the mountains. An example of American Progressive reform experiments applied to architecture and city planning, it demonstrated a Beaux Arts, World's Fair–inspired city plan built for the working class in a romantic style that recalled the area's roots.

Santa Fe Style

Other twentieth-century architects attempted to connect their work to its regional roots. The so-called Santa Fe style that is synonymous with Southwestern style to most tourists and merchants, began shortly after the turn of the century, capitalizing on the new status and old heritage of the area. The style was an amalgamation of custom and ordinance that recalled the area's architectural history—its ancient past, the Territorial style of its Anglo beginnings, and the Pueblo Revival style, which was becoming a national trend in the early twentieth century. It was developed, refined, and promulgated by architects, the Museum of New Mexico, and the AT&SF, which was celebrating statehood and encouraging tourism as part of the "see America first" campaign. The adoption of the Santa Fe style was motivated by a search for an accurate historical identity that would distinguish the regional architecture from the California Mission Revival, a desire to draw tourists, and to develop a building style appropriate to the climate and that reflected the progression of local traditions. Pueblo Revival featured flat, stepped roofs, adobe-looking walls in warm earth tones, blunt angles, vigas, canales, and wooden columns with Santa Fe bracket capitals. The Hopi House, a tourist hotel built in 1905 at the Grand Canyon, was designed by an architect from St. Paul, Minnesota, Mary Colter (1869–1958), in the Native American style of Chaco Canyon. Pueblo Revival was declared the official style of the University of New Mexico the following year, and in 1908 the oldest building on the campus, the Richardsonian Romanesque Hodgin Hall, was remodeled in the new old style.

Shortly after New Mexico joined the union in 1912, designers and anthropologists Sylvanus G. Morley (1883–1948), Jesse L. Nusbaum (1887–1975), and Edgar Lee Hewitt (1865–1946), who was working on his dissertation in anthropology at the time, were commissioned to remodel the 1610 Palace of the Governors. But instead of taking it back to its original form, it was restored to its 1770s appearance. In the process of uncovering the history of the place, Morley, Hewitt, and especially Nusbaum were increasingly convinced that the flat-roofed, pueblo-shaped courtyard building with its adobe walls and Anglo-Hispanic corbelled colonnade, was the appropriate architectural image for the region. They devoted much of their time trying to convince the city council and business interests of Santa Fe to amend the Plan of 1912 to declare this the official style of their City Beautiful. Their success is measured in the fact that, as Hewett observed, between 1912 and 1917, 90 percent of all remodelings and 50 percent of all new houses were in the Pueblo style.

History was altered when necessary to present this image. Victorian facades facing the pueblo had to be replaced, as did Isaac Hamilton Rapp's state capitol and governor's mansion. Through his plans for the New Mexico Building at the 1915 Panama-California Exposition in San Diego, California, Rapp (1854–1933) helped popularize Pueblo Revival. The pavilion was a synthesis of several New Mexican missions. That same year, the firm began work on the Museum of Fine Arts in Santa Fe, which is adjacent to the plaza. It was modeled on the church at Laguna Pueblo and other, similar buildings and designed around an interior courtyard. Rapp also designed the original La Fonda Hotel (1920) in Santa Fe.

John Gaw Meem (1894–1983), a civil engineer who had worked on the New York subway system, was suffering from tuberculosis and came to Santa Fe for the cure, staying at the Rapp-designed Sunmount Sanitarium. He stayed to become

San José de la Laguna in Laguna Pueblo, New Mexico (1699–1706), was the inspiration for the Museum of Fine Arts in Santa Fe, inaugurating the Santa Fe style. Courtesy of Maggie Valentine.

an architect, studying under Rapp, and worked on preserving the old mission churches. He also remodeled old buildings and designed new houses and public buildings in the old style. He enlarged Rapp's La Fonda Hotel to be even more pueblo-like, opening the lobby to the inner courtyard and emphasizing its puebloesque features. As campus architect at the University of New Mexico for thirty-five years, he was instrumental in reestablishing Pueblo Revival as the official style of new campus buildings, remodeling older buildings as necessary.

Harvey House Buildings

Mary Colter was commissioned by the Fred Harvey Company to design or remodel the Harvey House chain of restaurants, hotels, and gift shops, which were located along the path of the AT&SF Railway from Chicago to California. The railroad had originally bypassed its namesake of Santa Fe because of topographic difficulties, but city fathers arranged for an eight-mile spur from Galisteo to downtown Santa Fe. The AT&SF was already promoting its excursions through the exotic Southwest using Thomas Moran's romantic paintings when they teamed up with the Harvey Company. The imagery created by Colter distinguished most of the depots throughout the Southwest and helped popularize this multicultural and souvenir-ready style. The company institutionalized the image in its promotions and advertising, and in the 1920s they introduced Harveycars, chauffeured Packards that carried "de-tourists" on one- to three-day tours through the Indian country. The La Fonda in Santa Fe, promoted as "the Inn at the End of the Trail," was leased by the Harvey Company to serve as its center of operations and remodeled again by Colter using Indian and Hispanic themes.

Other Styles

Boosters were not the only ones who capitalized on romantic imagery to promote place. The University of Texas at El Paso (founded in 1913 as the Texas State School of Mines and Metallurgy) distinguished itself through its use of Bhutanese Revival, building a Himalayan monastery on campus, to be used as a place to study. The dean's wife had seen pictures of a lamasery in *National Geographic*, and the setting reminded her of El Paso. The architects complied. Even New Deal public buildings, which were built with federal funds and local talent, bought into it. In addition to the cookie-cutter schools, courthouses, and post offices, distinguishable only by the lobby murals painted by local artists and depicting themes of local history in the Southwest, architects utilized Pueblo Revival motifs. This can be seen in the courthouse at Las Cruces, New Mexico, and in new buildings at the University of Arizona in Tucson.

Southwestern Organic Tradition

Frank Lloyd Wright (1867–1959) tried to decipher what was unique about this region in terms of climate and material to produce regional, organic architecture when he created Taliesin West outside Scottsdale, Arizona, in the 1930s, the winter version of his Taliesin Fellowship in Wisconsin. Wright described the results as "desert rubblestone" or "desert masonry." Large stones were randomly set into concrete mortar as a means of highlighting their color and texture; surplus mortar was chipped away after it hardened, revealing the stone surface. The design for the Taliesin complex—a residence, studio, and school—was based on interlocking triangles in plan and elevation, which echoed the lines of tents and the angle of the setting sun. Linen canvas in redwood frames sheltered the studio while allowing the air to penetrate.

Wright's hands-on approach to architectural education required that each new apprentice spend several nights camping in the desert around Taliesin in order to understand the essence of shelter in this environment. They built small desert shelters for themselves only after they understood the nature of the environment, the critters, and the effects of wind, rain, the daytime sun, and the night air.

The two dozen other Wright designs executed in Arizona, New Mexico, and Texas between 1927 and 1959 continued the use of textiles (Biltmore Hotel, Phoenix, 1927), Usonian Houses (the "Usonian automatic" do-it-yourself Pieper and Adelman Houses, Phoenix, 1951), and concentric geometry (Friedman Lodge, Pecos, New Mexico, 1945; David Wright House, Phoenix, 1950; Gillin House, Dallas, 1950; Boomer House, Phoenix, 1953; and Grady Gammage Auditorium, Tempe, Arizona, 1959), adapting these designs to the desert.

Wright's organic philosophy taught that buildings must relate to nature in terms of materials, siting, form, and ecology. His Southwestern heirs pursued the evolution of these ideals and forms in their own vocabularies and interpretations of the desert-organic approach. After studying at Taliesin, Paolo Soleri (1919–) began building Arcosanti near Cordes Junction, Arizona, in 1970, an ongoing experiment in "arcology" (architecture + ecology) with his own apprentices. Man-made caves and complex concrete forms rise from the desert to create an energy- and space-efficient urban Utopia that will eventually house 7,000 people and run on solar power. Most of the land is reserved for agriculture in this alternative to urban sprawl and dependence on automobiles.

Bart Prince (1947–), architectural heir to regional architect Bruce Goff (1904–1982) and third-generation Wright disciple, is based in Albuquerque, New Mexico, where he creates fantastic futurist visions of houses in Pueblo Revival neighborhoods that erupt from first-floor adobes into swirling shapes of wood, metal, and glass, taking Southwestern organic visions to the next level. Cantilevered geometries are crossed with biomorphic shapes that defy scale and definition. His is a regional tradition that rejects representational style in favor of representing the nature of place and time.

The Santa Fe style was finally canonized in 1957 by the City of Santa Fe, in a comprehensive historic preservation ordinance that required all new buildings within the historic district to resemble handmade adobe cottages or chapels with vigas or to reflect the Anglo Territorial style, which is characterized by brick cornices, white window frames, and distinctive posts and capitals. Downtown Santa Fe lost many Victorian and early-twentieth-century buildings to replacement with Anglicized pueblos. Steel-framed structures were coated with terra-cotta-colored stucco; parking garages, fast-food franchises, and ATMs gained aluminum vigas.

Some architects focused on the desert condition and traditions without being told to. Texas architect O'Neil Ford (1905–1982) utilized the tradition of Mexican-American craftsmanship by creating homes that reflected both Modernism and Regionalism. Enormous handcrafted doors opened into white-walled spaces arranged around landscaped patios that became outdoor rooms. In a Modernist interpretation of Baroque, open spaces and plain walls contrasted with colorful and intricate details, including handcrafted *bóvedas* (traditional brick vaults built without scaffolding by Mexican craftsmen). Ford always strived to find a Minimalist interpretation of the rich Texas traditions he loved and helped preserve.

The Environment and Southwest Architecture

Architects, developers, and legislative bodies are increasingly aware that respect for the natural and historical qualities of a place is more than a matter of stylistic appearance. Federal and local governmental restrictions are working to protect the environment through building restrictions. Builders living near Tucson must prove they have a one hundred-year water supply before breaking ground and are responsible for protecting endangered flora and fauna of the Sonoran Desert that will be affected by development. Civano, a master-planned suburban development southeast of Tucson, is attempting to merge Southwestern design elements with contemporary ideas of New Urbanism, Smart Growth, and sustainability. The developers, in conjunction with the City of Tucson, are creating a model community with narrow, tree-lined streets curving through a pedestrian-scaled neighborhood that is also a sustainable community. Individual houses, community centers, and shops draw on the vocabulary of abstract Pueblo Revival, integrating flat roofs, pergolas, porches, warm colors, and the look of adobe brick walls to connect to the past and establish a sense of place. The multiuse development utilizes straw-bale construction and reclaimed water. Buildings employ solar heating and are designed to reduce energy and water consumption generally to avoid putting the additional financial burden of the development on the city and to protect the future of the desert environment.

The massing of Antoine Predock's (1936–) Nelson Fine Arts Center at Arizona State University in Tempe (1989) makes the building look like a red and purple pueblo on the campus. Like a pueblo, it is introverted and its activities are protected from the sun. An exterior plaza attached to the building provides a stage for dance performances. Despite these bold forms and broad spaces, there is a subtlety in the transition between them that helps the visitor respond to sun and shade. Predock explains it as "naked architecture": the massive walls stand up to the sun, which doesn't allow for detail on the exterior, but creates a prelude to the surprise of color on the interior.[1] His Las Vegas Library/Discovery Museum in Nevada (1990) achieves the same effect in a similar physical setting but a very different social context. In a city where artificial light, swirling lines, and brash colors are used to capture the attention of adults, this building uses natural light, simple shapes, and warm natural colors to draw in children. Inside the building, the forms and spaces encourage discovery rather than entertainment. To deal with the environment, Predock used grills to temper the sun, placed fabric roofs over the courtyards to block the harsh light, and bathed an exterior wall with water, which flows into the lobby and adjacent courtyard.

Other contemporary architects throughout the region are dealing with issues of place and form to address the ecology of place in the Southwest. Mexican architect Ricardo Legoretta (1931–) uses color to express the physical reality of the climate and the region's Mexican heritage, as seen in his design of the Zócalo condominiums in Santa Fe (2002) and the San Antonio Public Library (1995). The library is a massing of bold geometric forms in bright colors, which residents have nicknamed "enchilada red." Will Bruder (1946–) explored the effects of light and illusion in his design for the Phoenix Public Library (1995), which he describes as "a curving copper mesa split by a stainless steel canyon." The building reflects the colors of the Arizona desert and captures the sun's rays at summer solstice in the reading room on the top floor. In both cities, library use has increased dramatically since the new buildings were completed. Lake/Flato, winner of the 2004 AIA Architecture Firm Award, is also exploring regionalism without period-revival quotations. The firm utilizes indigenous materials and works with the site to capture the sense of place in the houses, ranches, churches, and museums it designs.

Modern Mexican-American folk dwellings celebrate the hybrid traditions through vernacular adaptation. Immigrants who moved into Anglo neighborhoods and houses adapted bungalows, folk Victorian dwellings, World War II houses, and postwar suburban ranchettes. Houses are separated from their neighbors by wooden, masonry, wrought iron, or even chain link fences that mark the property lines, beginning at the sidewalk. The house itself is painted vibrant colors, regardless of the style or materials. Bright and pastel blues, greens, and hot pinks contrast with each other and with the trim. Yard shrines can be found in the back or front yards, reflecting the Roman Catholic traditions of the house's occupants. A patron saint, surrounded by other religious icons, is enclosed in a partially enclosed and covered *nicho* (niche) or *capilla* (little chapel) that faces the street. On July 4th, the piñatas and *papel picados* (cut paper art) share space with the red, white, and blue bunting, streamers, and flags.

What these traditions have in common is a response to climate and culture.

Themes and images find their expression by means of the unique climate, materials, and quality of light found here, as well as from the separateness and isolation of the desert condition. The region contains some of the great monuments of American architecture, such as the Kimbell Museum, Louis Kahn's spiritual study of light, space, and mass; the bleached Baroque oasis of San Xavier del Bac; Philip Johnson's Water Garden, an unknown urban treasure of peaceful escape in downtown Fort Worth; the timelessness of Taos Pueblo's sculptural assembly; and the powerful massing of the nearby San Francisco de Asís church in Rancho de Taos. Other expressions are idealized visions of the Southwest, such as the intimate, gingerbread-colored houses on Canyon Road in Santa Fe; the string of regional railroad depots and the neon outlines of Route 66 motels and coffee shops along the "Mother Road"; adobe ranches and haciendas amid Saguaro cacti; the dude ranch; the ruins of Virginia City; and drive-in wedding chapels. They are at once mythic images of America and the Southwest.

RESOURCE GUIDE

Printed Sources

Beasley, Ellen, and Stephen Fox. *Galveston Architecture Book.* Houston: Rice University Press, 1996.

Bunting, Bainbridge. *Early Architecture in New Mexico.* Albuquerque: University of New Mexico, 1976.

Carter, Thomas, ed. *Images of an American Land: Vernacular Architecture in the Western United States.* Albuquerque: University of New Mexico Press, 1997.

Chipman, Donald E. *Spanish Texas, 1519–1821.* Austin: University of Texas Press, 1992.

Fox, Stephen. *Houston Architectural Guide.* Houston: AIA, 1990.

Jackson, J. B. *Discovering the Vernacular* Landscape. New Haven, CT: Yale University Press, 1984.

———. *Landscape in Sight: Looking at America.* New Haven: Yale University Press, 1997.

Markovich, Nicholas C., Wolfgang F. E. Preiser, and Fred G. Sturm, eds. *Pueblo Style and Regional Architecture.* New York: Van Nostrand Reinhold, 1990.

McAlester, Virginia, and Lee McAlester. *A Field Guide to America's Historic Neighborhoods and Museum Houses: The Western States.* New York: Alfred A. Knopf, 1998.

Meinig, D. W. *Southwest: Three Peoples in Geographical Change, 1600–1970.* New York: Oxford University Press, 1971.

Morgan, William N. *Ancient Architecture of the Southwest.* Austin: University of Texas Press, 1994.

Nabokov, Peter, and Robert Easton. *Native American Architecture.* New York: Oxford University Press, 1989.

Newcomb, Rexford. *Spanish-Colonial Architecture in the United States.* New York: J. J. Augustine, 1937.

Nicoletta, Julie. *Buildings of Nevada.* New York: Oxford University Press, 2000.

Oliver, Paul, ed. *Encyclopedia of Vernacular Architecture of the World.* Cambridge: Cambridge University Press, 1997.

Scully, Vincent. *Pueblo: Mountain, Village, Dance.* New York: Viking, 1975.

Simons, Helen, and Cathryn A. Hoyt. *Hispanic Texas: A Historical Guide.* Austin: Texas Historical Commission, 1992.

Stanislawski, Stan. "Early Spanish Town Planning in the New World." *Geographical Review* 37 (1947): 95–105.

Wilson, Chris. *The Myth of Santa Fe: Creating a Modern Regional Tradition.* Albuquerque: University of New Mexico Press, 1997.

Web Sites

"Architecture and Urbanism of the Southwest," University of Arizona.
http://www.elearn.arizona.edu/adobe/intro.html

The Handbook of Texas Online
http://www.tsha.utexas.edu/handbook/online/index.html

Journal of the Southwest
http://digital.library.arizona.edu/jsw

"Native American Virtual Reality Archaeology: An Architect's Perspective."
http://www.dennisrhollowayarchitect.com/html/VRChapter.html

New Mexico CultureNet
http://nmculturenet.org/heritage/architecture

Society of Architectural Historians
http://www.sah.org

"Southwestern Wonderland"
http://www.library.arizona.edu/branches/spc/pams/architec.html

"Teaching Resources," Museum of New Mexico
http://www.museumeducation.org/curricula.html

University of Nevada Las Vegas Architecture Library
http://library.nevada.edu/arch/rsrce/resguide/vegas.html

Organizations, Museums, Special Collections, Libraries

Institute of Texan Cultures
The University of Texas at San Antonio
801 S. Bowie St.
San Antonio, TX 78205-3296
http://www.texancultures.utsa.edu/public/

Museum of Fine Arts, Santa Fe,
107 W. Palace Ave.
Santa Fe, NM 87501
http://www.nmculture.org/cgi-bin/instview.cgi?_recordnum=MFA

Southwest Center
University of Arizona
1052 N. Highland Ave.
Tucson, AZ 85721
http://info-center.ccit.arizona.edu/~swctr/

The University of Arizona Library, Special Collections
University of Arizona
P.O. Box 210055
Tucson, AZ 85721-0055
http://www.library.arizona.edu/branches/spc/homepage/

"Walk Through Texas"
San Antonio Botanical Garden
555 Funston at North New Braunfels Ave.
San Antonio, TX 78209
http://www.sabot.org/

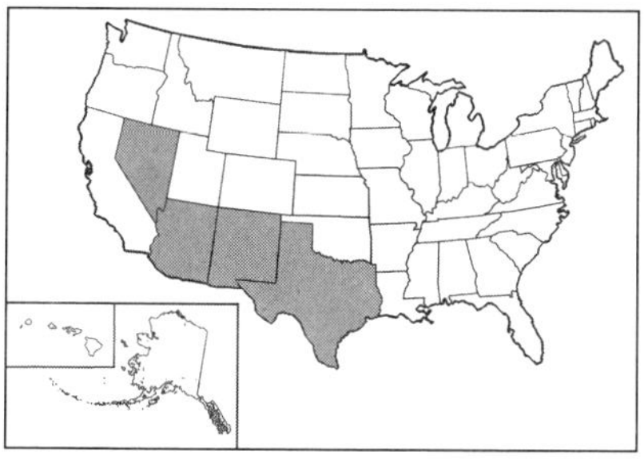

ART

Holle Humphries

Imagine that you are standing on the apex of the Continental Divide, located high in the Rocky Mountain ranges of northern New Mexico. Here, the air you inhale, although dry and thin of oxygen at such altitude, is cool and crystal clear. Because of your proximity to the equator, the sun beats down at a nearly vertical angle, etching all things on the human retina in sharp, clear focus. In a semiarid atmosphere, light is not refracted or diffused by droplets of moisture in the air, and so it is direct and brilliant in impact: nearly blinding. Shadows and contours crisply define the edges of all objects, both far and near.

Turning to all four compass points to survey the surrounding landscape, you are struck at once by the wide expanse of limitless horizons and amazing complexity in terrain—mountains, canyons, flat mesas, deserts, grasslands—its contrasting cool and warm colors, the variegated and roughly hewn textures, the apparent scarcity of water. It is a feast for artists' eyes: barren red rock plateaus and crooked, sheer sandstone canyon lands surrounded by stands of evergreen trees that cling to the rocky slopes of jagged mountains, which seem violet when viewed from a distance; inland prairie and plains grasslands of palomino gold and silvery sagebrush green; dunes of snow-white gypsum sand; gray and dun brown stretches of desert soil bristling with spiky growth that bursts forth in spring with the first rains in a riot of lavender, magenta, apricot, vermilion, and scarlet flowers; and the precious water from the infrequent thunderstorms and high-elevation snows in the mountains running sometimes blue, sometimes brown like the soil it carries, snaking along in rivers and elusive streams, or pooling in playa ponds and lakes, all of which during periods of drought sometimes disappear into their own beds, water unseen.

During the season of snowmelt in the spring and sudden cloudbursts of summer rain, the tumultuously full streams and rivers flow away from you in one of two directions. Waters that fall to the east of you drain the plateaus and plains of New Mexico and Texas and eventually empty into the Gulf of Mexico and the Atlantic

Ocean. Waters that fall to the west of you flow off the Colorado Plateau and travel all the way to Arizona to empty into the Gulf of California and the Pacific Ocean.

You are standing not only at the geographical apex of the continent east to west but on the borderlands of cultures that have clashed and blended throughout hundreds of years, crossing each other's territories north and south: Paleoindian, Mesoamerican, Native American, Hispanic, and Anglo-American. All contributed influences to the distinctive art traditions of the Southwest.

As in any region, the characteristics of Southwestern art result from the degree to which people (1) found and used, when they first arrived, what is unique to the physical environment, (2) brought their own intact culture with them, and (3) synthesized all this to create new, adaptive skills and practices—or regional culture.

PHYSICAL GEOGRAPHY: THE UNIQUE ENVIRONMENT

Aesthetic Qualities of the Region: Terrain, Space, and Light

The visual arts of the Southwest reflect human aesthetic responses to the physical environment of Texas, New Mexico, Arizona, and Nevada. And everywhere in this region, the land is bathed in light. The distinctive experience of inhabiting a spectacular space of wide-open, panoramic terrain bathed in undiluted golden light that illuminates a warm, earthy palette of hues typical of the rocks and plant life of the region, all glowing against the contrasting color of a turquoise sky, characterize life in the Southwest region. The visual art that emerged from the minds and hands of people who passed through or remained to dwell in its lands are unified by two aesthetic qualities seemingly infinite and dimensionless in the environment that surrounds them: space and light. Artists have, for centuries, been inspired by this, regardless of era or their ethnicity, culture, or country of origin.

The sense of space is visible in Native American crafts that depict their cosmological beliefs and myths of how the world was arranged, echoed in the symbols of the Southwest they used in their jewelry, baskets, pottery, sculpted talismans, hammered silver, and woven rugs.

In fine art, the paintings and photography are the windows opening to the expansive grassland, plains, mountain ranges, desert, and canyon lands of the Southwest. Those who stood proudly and carved a life within that space are regularly featured as subjects of sculpture.

The sense of light is present in the colors derived from natural pigments that Native Americans and early settlers extracted from indigenous minerals and vegetation and used as paints, slip glazes, and dyes for pottery and textiles. It is also reflected in the replication of the colors of the landscape when paint is applied to canvas.

Natural Resources Provide Materials and Symbolic Content for Art

The raw materials available in the physical environment provide people with the resources they need for food, clothing, and shelter that will enable their survival in a new situation. The raw materials the Southwestern environment offers thus exerted a major impact on lending distinctive characteristics to the local practices, cultures, and objects that were developed by its inhabitants to adapt to its special challenges.

Trees and Plants

Trees are not plentiful in the Southwest and are usually found in great numbers only in the eastern piney and oak woods of northeastern Texas, at mountain elevations, and along river valleys. Therefore, wood does not figure prominently in Southwestern art, except as small, carved figures. Plants such as yucca, sotol, river willow, devil's claw, arrowweed, squawberry, sumac, greasewood bush, rabbitbrush, and beargrass yielded fiber that nomadic Indians used as long ago as 5,000 B.C.E. to weave baskets. Tightly woven baskets served a necessary function for gathering nuts and berries and storing food. When lined with piñon pine resin, the baskets could be used for transporting water, and when coated with clay, for cooking food over fires.

Many plants of the Southwest region supplied pigments for producing paints and textile dyes. For example, the prickly pear cactus harbors the cochineal scale insect, which can be used to produce a red pigment for textile dye and paint common in Navajo rug weaving. The leaves of the Rocky Mountain wild bee plant produce a black pigment that Pueblo potters boiled to produce a thick paste, called *guaco*, which after drying and hardening, was mixed with water and applied to clay pots with a brush. Some Indian artists who dye woven wool rugs and paint their pottery today continue to use such natural sources for textile dyes and paint pigments.

In an indirect way the plentiful grass of the Southwest region also provided a resource for art. The abundant grass and brush suitable for grazing allowed raising horses, cattle, sheep, and goats to become an industry for Spanish mission settlements, Native Americans, and Anglo-Americans. The introduction of the horse in the sixteenth century sparked a transformation of culture for nomadic hunter-gatherer Indians of the Southwest, notably for the Comanche, Kiowa, Wichita, and the Apache, and their warrior deeds on horseback became the content for art centuries later. Sheep raised on mission lands in the seventeenth century provided wool for weaving and rug making, arts for which the Navajo later became famous. The cattle industry that emerged in the nineteenth century gave rise to cowboy culture and the cowboy art that followed.

Wildlife

Wildlife of the Southwest region provided meat for food and leather hide for shelter and clothing. However, the hide from bison or buffalo and deer hunted by nomadic Native Americans of the prairies and plains also served as a natural canvas for art.

Animals distinctive to the Southwest region embodied qualities either much admired or feared by its human inhabitants, and so they function as important symbols in the region's art. When seen in art bison, pronghorn antelope, coyotes, jackrabbits, javelinas, and armadillos all convey that the art has Southwestern origins. Cougars, bears, and wolves, although not specific to the Southwest, and scarce if not absent from its landscape today, remain as iconic figures represented in the art of Native Americans who still live in the region. The Zuni regard animals as being closer than humans to the powers of nature. Because they view these animals as embodiments of the protective forces of nature, the Zuni therefore carve them from semiprecious stones to function as protective fetishes.

Unique mountain, desert, and borderland creatures continue to be depicted frequently in Southwest Native American and Hispanic art. The jaguar, famously known as El Tigre in Mesoamerican mythology, was viewed as a god of the underworld, and when depicted in art, symbolizes power. Serpents in general figured hugely in ancient Mesoamerican mythology and hence in derivative Southwest Native American and Hispanic imagery. Hundreds of species of birds pilot the Southwest's skies and waters, as a portion of this territory falls within the great migratory flyway. The majestic bald eagle is among them and therefore frequently appears in Southwestern art. Its symbolic associations also are Mesoamerican in origin; in that culture the eagle was viewed as the messenger of forces of the sky and universe. The roadrunner, which can be glimpsed scurrying across bare patches of ground in grasslands and desert basins, is uniquely associated with the Southwest region and figures prominently in popular animation art of the twentieth century. Bird feathers were much valued as symbols of flight that transported messages to the spirit world beyond the sky and with rain. Pueblan pottery therefore features an extensive array of bird and feather motifs, such as the "rainbird" motif of unknown origin. Insects were regarded as important harbingers of rain, climate, and condition of the land, so they, too, are present in Southwestern art, particularly in silver pendants on squash-blossom necklaces and on *ketohs*, or silver amulets, and painted as decorations on Pueblan pottery.

Soil and Minerals

The Southwest region abounds in natural surface clays. Descendents of the Paleoindians who lived more settled lives in village pueblos created pottery vessels out of clay that were used for storing food and carrying water. The clays they used contained naturally forming mineral content; this and the firing methods collectively produce the distinctive colors associated with pottery created by regional Native American artists.

The earth in the Southwest has provided the colors of clays and slips used by Pueblo potters for two thousand years. Artists used common surface clays of the land they lived on, which fired to gray, buff, red, or brown colors. For example, the warm yellows, tans, oranges, and reds so characteristic of Hopi pottery are a direct result of the amount of iron, manganese, and titanium oxide in the clays near their homeland. Uniquely, the Acoma Pueblo artists of New Mexico, like their Anasazi and Mogollon ancestors, found a secret source of grayish, kaolin-type clay that fires nearly white.

The artists who have produced pottery for generations have long maintained an aesthetic preference for decorating the surfaces of the vessels with colors natural to the environment. They chose to decorate pottery generally in one of two different ways. Artists might burnish the clay vessel by rubbing it all over with a polishing stone to create a luster on its surface before firing, or they could suspend different-colored clays in water to create a thick solution like paint, called slip, and use it to paint on decorations before the vessel was fired.

The Southwest harbors as part of its geological base deposits of copper, calcium, iron, and silica, as well as rich veins of turquoise. Native Americans have mined turquoise for over two thousand years in the Southwest region. This turquoise was traded avidly throughout North and Central America to procure the treasures of other regions. Today, turquoise continues to be mined in New Mexico, Arizona, and Nevada. Other semiprecious and common stones of the region have been carefully selected and carved by the Zuni for fetishes. These include jet (New Mexico), serpentine (New Mexico and Arizona), travertine and azurite (Arizona), malachite (Arizona), pipestone (Arizona), and alabaster (Nevada).

Metal ores plentiful in the Southwest area include copper and silver, and in Arizona and Nevada, gold as well. Silver was mined extensively in the New World following the arrival of the Spanish in the sixteenth century. Silver, a mineral famously discovered in 1859 at the Comstock Lode near Virginia City, Nevada, is associated with the Southwest, primarily due to the fact that the Spanish introduced uses of metal to the region. Their taste for silver decoration on horses and saddles and as personal adornment became widely noted and admired. Although silver was mined in the region, it was converted into currency and was not readily available for jewelry. Therefore, at first, jewelry and other forms of embellishment for clothing and horses were made from copper, brass, and "German silver," an alloy of copper, nickel, and zinc. The only way silver could be obtained by artisans not working directly under commission to the Spanish was to melt down silver coins. After the 1880s, this began to change when trading post merchants devised ways to make legitimate sources of silver available to artisans, particularly the Navajo.

CULTURAL GEOGRAPHY AND INDIGENOUS ART

The Southwest harbors verified evidence of the oldest known continuous human habitation by Paleoindians in North America. At the twelve-thousand-year-old prehistoric Lubbock Lake site on the High Plains of Texas there is an exhibit of a first form of art in the shape of beads made from shell, stone, and bone strung on plant-fiber string. The Southwest also is home to the oldest continuously occupied towns in all of the United States: Acoma Pueblo, built on a mesa in northwest New Mexico, and Old Oraibi, perched on the Third Mesa of Hopi lands of Arizona, have both been occupied since before the twelfth century. Their descendents continue a two-thousand-year-old tradition in creating pottery.

Over the centuries, the regional artists of the Southwest have combined in their art the influences of several dominant cultures; in particular, the ancient agrarian (Hohokam, Mogollon, and Anasazi), Mesoamerican, Native American, Spanish, and Anglo-American. Such cultural influences are sometimes subtle and diffuse but reflect the impact of religious beliefs, economic systems, new art forms, and symbols brought into the region by contact through trade, conquest, and marriage between families.

Ancient Agrarian Cultures

Three distinctive ancient agrarian groups include the Hohokam, Mogollon, and Anasazi. The Hohokam lived in the south central and western Arizona regions of the Sonoran Desert. The Mogollon occupied the forested mountain ranges and high Chihuahuan Desert basins of southeastern Arizona, New Mexico, and western Texas. The Anasazi dwelled in the arid canyons and mesa lands of the Colorado Plateau region.

Art Forms

The first art forms devised by these early inhabitants of the Southwest evolved as practical objects used to ensure survival. They were decorated or made beautiful to connote a special function in the lives of those who created them. All were created within an overarching religious belief system. Some were used as intermediary devices to appeal to supernatural deities. The significant art forms developed by these early agrarian peoples include baskets, jewelry, *kachina* effigy figures, pottery, and rock art. Recognizable symbols are incorporated into these art forms.

Baskets

Baskets and, later, pottery were vital for collecting and preparing food and transporting water. Baskets were light and easily transportable. Artists wove baskets from native plants harvested from their surroundings, finding necessary materials throughout the Southwest in the plains, mountains, and desert lands.

Jewelry

Jewelry provided a tag of identity to ensure social cohesion and communicate the status and role of the wearer in order to mitigate tension or confusion about who played what role in the culture. The earliest inhabitants of the Southwest left behind jewelry made from beads of bone and semiprecious stone such as turquoise strung on sinew or woven grass fiber.

Kachina *Effigy Figures*

The general scarcity of water in the region due to the low amounts of rainfall did not provide optimal conditions for subsistence agriculture. Finding water resources in a land that receives as little as ten inches of rain a year became a focus of concern. The ancient agrarians developed a complex religion that revolved around the agricultural cycle of a year. Artists created ritual and sacred objects to secure divine intervention from supernatural deities, the spirits of departed ancestors, and the forces of all living things in order to bring rains and aid in ensuring the success of their crops and thus the well being of the people. These deities, ancestors, and forces, called *kachinas* (also *katsinas*), were painted as symbols on pottery or carved in cottonwood as small wooden representations, or effigy figures, that today are called kachina dolls.

Pottery

Inhabitants of settled agrarian communities no longer had as great a need for lightweight, portable containers for transporting personal belongings from one campsite to another. By then, people had learned to line their baskets with clay on the inside and outside to make them watertight and pest-free and fireproof so they could be used as cooking vessels. It is believed that when the clay covering the baskets became hardened from exposure to heat over fires, the means of creating pottery was discovered. Artists learned to gather the native surface clays of their local region, use the coil method of hand building to construct vessels, and fire them in bonfire pits to bake the clay and make the vessels durable. Gathering clay from the surrounding environment and using it to create vessels became an activity enmeshed with spiritual practices. The ancient agrarians left behind some of the most beautiful handmade ceramic pottery produced in the first millennium in the United States. The Hohokam were noted for their red-on-buff pottery, the Mogollon for black-on-white, and the Anasazi for using design motifs that echoed their basketry. The pottery tradition begun in the first millennium by these people has continued unabated in the Southwest for two thousand years.

Rock Art

Pictographs, or paintings on rock walls in chambers of worship or at outdoor sacred sites, and petroglyphs, or images incised onto outdoor rocks and canyon walls, all served to mark territory and perpetuate religious beliefs. Many rock sites exist in the Southwest (see Table 1).

The Southwest is home to more intact rock art than any other place in North America. Rock art made its first appearance sometime during the Desert Archaic period of 6500 B.C.E. to 1200 B.C.E. The earliest rock images appear as painted or pecked-out simple dots or lines, repeated in sequences to form rows, patterns, or simple geometric shapes, as though someone were leaving a mark to imply a simple concept or to keep count of quantities. Later rock art images are more complex and depict anthropomorphic and zoomorphic shapes. The artists produced representational images of hunters, game, predators, weapons, shamans, horned masks, mythological figures, handprints, footprints, reptiles, and insects. Some of the images are portrayed in isolation, others randomly overlap one another, but many are arranged in pictorial space to convey relationships of some sort or to record an event.

Rock art may have been executed for different reasons from era to era. Specific sites repeatedly attracted the talents of rock artists from many cultures over time. Early images may represent expressions of the great effort required to take large game with only the most primitive weapons, necessitating invocations to deities and magic in the process.

Rock art painted in some parts of the Southwest uniquely reflects the particular area's distinctive cultural geography. In the lower Pecos River region of West Texas, there are pictographs that exhibit striking similarities in style painted by Paleoindian and Desert Archaic artists from 6000 B.C.E. to 600 C.E. Images of elongated figures, men with horns, and deer with antlers are overpainted one on top of the other. Historian W. W. Newcomb believes that these places served as sites for regular convocations and initiation ceremonies for shamanistic, medicine-man, or hunting societies. Caches of Texas mountain laurel mescal beans were found nearby, and aware of the Native American medicine men's use of hallucinogenic agents such as mescal and peyote to aid mediation between the material and spirit world, Newcomb conjectures that the beans and drawings were part of an initiation rite. He further conjectures that initiates were required to ingest the beans (ground up as a fine powder), and after waking up from the twenty-four-hour hallucinogenic trance induced, paint the visions they had seen in their dreams. Newcomb notes that the stylistic similarities in these pictographs can be seen within

Table 1. Major rock art sites of the Southwest region

Texas	Amistad National Recreation Area	http://rockart.esmartweb.com/ texas.html
	Big Bend Ranch State Park	
	Franklin Mountains State Park	
	Guadalupe Mountains National Park	
	Hueco Tanks State Historical Park	
	Lower Pecos River area	
	Paint Rock	
	Purtis Creek State Park	
	San Angelo State Park	
	Seminole Canyon State Park	
New Mexico	Bandelier National Monument	http://rockart.esmartweb.com/ newmex.html
	Carlsbad Caverns National Park	
	Chaco Canyon	
	Conchas Lake	
	Crow Canyon	
	El Malpais National Monument	
	El Morro National Monument	
	Gila Cliff Dwellings National Monument	
	Navajo Reservoir District	
	Petroglyph National Monument	
	Three Rivers Petroglyph Site	
Arizona	Canyon de Chelly	http://rockart.esmartweb.com/ arizona.html
	Casa Malpais	
	Council Rocks	
	Deer Valley	
	Fort Apache	
	Grand Canyon National Park	
	Homol'voi State Park	
	Lake Mead National Recreation Area	
	Little Black Mountain	
	Long Canyon Trail	
	Lyman Lake State Park	
	Moab Regional Park	
	Monument Valley	
	Navajo National Monument	
	Painted Rocks	
	Palatki Indian Ruins	
	Petrified Forest National Park	
	Raven Site Ruins	
	Rock Art Canyon Ranch	
	Saguaro National Park	
	South Mountain Park	
	White Tank Mountains Regional Park	
Nevada	Grapevine Canyon	http://rockart.esmartweb.com/ nevada.html
	Grimes Point Petroglyphs	
	Hickison Petroglyph Recreation Area	
	Las Vegas area	
	Red Rock Canyon National Conservation Area	
	Valley of Fire State Park	

the same geographic area as the range of the mescal bean—ranging clear to the Gulf Coast and into Mexico.

Another unique rock-art tradition is exhibited in the Southwest Chihuahuan Desert of West Texas and southern New Mexico, where the ancient Mogollon culture flourished between 700 and 900 C.E. Rocks and caves hold images—such as the bear paw, deer, mountain sheep, and horned masks—of an earlier Desert Archaic hunter-gatherer culture. Alongside these appear Mesoamerican mythic and religious motifs such as the jaguar; the goggle-eyed god Tlaloc, an avatar of Quetzacoatl; the horned serpent; and the stair-step design for the rain god's altar. This suggests that a fusion occurred between these two cultures, forming the Mogollon culture. The hunters of the north assimilated influences from the Mesoamerican agricultural civilization to the south. The symbols suggest that this evolution occurred to elicit all supernatural forces possible in order to maximize opportunities for fertility and regeneration in an area that received little rain and, consequently, growing crops was a risky prospect. A syncretic art tradition possibly resulted, culminating in the development of a masked spirit religion that eventually developed into the Pueblo kachina cult still evident today in the art of the Zuni and Hopi.

Symbols in Indigenous Art

One of the most ubiquitous symbols of this time period that first appeared on rock art 3,000 years ago and that continues to be seen everywhere in Southwest art today is that of the hunchbacked flute player. Images of him have been reported from Peru all the way to Texas; one was reported even as far north as Canada. But nowhere is he as visible as in the Southwest, where vestiges of him can be found painted on kiva walls and pottery and carved into rocks and boulders. Due to this omnipresence, apparently he was held in high regard by ancient agrarian cultures. Today, he is still the emblem of the Hopi Flute Society, one of many secret societies concerned with rain, war, and healing powers.

Although the flute player is a prehistoric Southwestern "personage," his image became blurred in the twentieth century with a character currently called Kokopelli, the iconic figure saturating tourist kitsch. However, the attributes assigned to Kokopelli today—those of a Dionysian-type fertility Trickster, rife with music, goodwill, and sexual mischief—have been superimposed on a more ancient and messianic-type figure who has prehistoric origins in Hopi creation myths.

In his original incarnation, as portrayed on early petroglyphs, he may have been a symbol of the *maahus*, or cicada (locustlike), people who, according to myth, accompanied the Hopi people in their emergence out of the Underworld into the Fourth World of the present. The maahus were greeted by an eagle, a messenger for the Creator with dominion over the sky. The eagle demanded that they pass a test of courage before proceeding farther. The eagle shot each one in the legs with an arrow. The maahus bravely withstood the pain by playing music on their flutes (much as locusts do their legs), and the soothing sound as well as the heat they could generate from within the earth, healed their wounds. The eagle thereafter allowed the maahus to proceed. Four maahus led the Hopis to disperse by migration across the four compass points of the barren earth in order to settle and replenish it. To aid in this mission, the maahus preceded them, scattering a gift of seeds from burden baskets or bundles on their backs. They then played their flutes over the seeds, entreating the warm energy of the earth with music to make the seeds grow.

The maahu of myth may be the origin of the flute player who appears in rock art with a humped back, sporting antenna. In its insect form, the cicada also has what appears to be a hump on its back; its loud trilling sound can resemble the sound from a flute; and its music accompanies hot weather, portending good crops for the future. Linguist Ekkehart Malotki notes that the Hopis call the rock-art flute-player images Maahu, not Kokopelli. Malotki conjectures that over time, the messianic version of Maahu as a healer and harbinger of fertility who helped transform barren land became overlaid with the Hopi kachina figure named Kookopölö, who is a Trickster character associated with Dionysian-like human and vegetal fecundity, promiscuity, and sexual mischief. He is regularly portrayed as having a hump, bulbous antennae, and a prominent phallus, but he is not associated with being a flute player. Instead, he has attributes of the humpbacked robber fly, called Kookopölö or Kokopelli, an insect known for its aggressive promiscuous behavior. The kachina by this name is accorded similar attributes.

Mesoamerican Culture

The extent of Mesoamerican influence on the early people of the Southwest area is unknown. By 2000 B.C.E., the Mesoamerican culture flourished as a highly advanced civilization, and in the first millennium, well-established trade routes connected it to the Southwest area. Mesoamerican trade objects such as copper bells, pyrite mirrors, and seashells have been unearthed in archaeological sites in the Southwest. Montezuma II, the last Aztec ruler, wore, as protective amulets, necklaces and pendants made from Cerillos turquoise mined in New Mexico. Echoes of Mesoamerican economic systems, religious beliefs, symbols, and art forms can be seen in the evolution of regional art.

Religious Iconography

Mesoamerican culture revolved around a religion based on a cyclical calendar that was governed by what was the world's most accurate reading of the movement of stars and planets to establish the passage of time. The Mesoamerican culture's affinity for seeing the forces of life, death, and nature in the rain, wind, thunder, lightning, and personifying these forces as deities, can still be perceived to influence the symbols woven into Southwestern baskets and painted on pottery. Some of these concepts and symbols were assimilated into Pueblo culture under different guises and given different names, but the imagery remained startlingly similar.

Symbols in Mesoamerican Art

Several Mesoamerican mythological symbols can be found in rock art and on the pottery of the ancient Pueblos. Among them are Tlatoc, Quetzacoatl, and the Hero Twins. The Toltec Tlaloc (He Who Makes Things Sprout) is symbolized as a large-eyed, large-headed anthropomorphic figure who brings rain to crops. This symbol can be found in petroglyphs and pictographs throughout the Southwest.

The Aztec Quetzacoatl is a cosmic symbol of the universe represented as a feathered serpent and given the power for creation of heaven, earth, and human beings. His plumes associate him with birds of the sky above, and his form as a snake, with the earth below.

Tlaloc and Quetzacoatl share a close relationship with one another and with weather; they are forces that collectively make rain fall to the earth and hence give life to plants. The undulating motion of the serpent, like that of Quetzacoatl, is thought to represent energy that pulls rain to earth.

The Mayan Hero Twins, Hunahpú and Xbalanqué, are twin brothers always pictured together. They symbolize the contrasting forces in creation necessary to maintain balance in cosmic energy, such as light and dark and good and bad. Mayan twin mythology correlates to legends about twins retold among the Navajo, Zuni, and Hopi, with images of twin figures often seen in art. The Twin stories echo themes of injury or death to one of the twins, which results in a loss of life essence and power until the other assists in his resurrection or rebirth. This reflects universal notions that human beings face duality in life and that all efforts to achieve balance require sacrifices before a rebirth of harmony can occur. Art forms such as Pueblo pottery exhibit symmetrically balanced designs that reflect this concern for achieving harmony in life.

Native American Culture

The Spaniards' arrival in the New World in the 1500s marked the end of the prehistoric period in the Americas. European accounts defined distinctions among the Native American cultural groups they discovered, which they defined as "tribes" with different names. Some of these cultural groups and their arts and crafts survived intact for the next five hundred years of European conquest. Others developed art forms through European influences, such as making silver jewelry and weaving wool rugs. Today, these Native American arts and crafts are considered important components of Southwest regional art.

Religion

The spiritual beliefs of Native Americans gave shape to their arts and crafts. For most Native Americans, the metaphysical order of the world was linked to a cosmology or creation myth. Such myths explained the existence of the universe as the work of a Great Spirit. The Great Spirit consisted of a three-layer holistic structure: the middle realm, the Earth; suspended between the vault of the Sky World above; and the realm of the Underworld below. All living creatures, including human beings and material things, dwelled in the middle region. Human beings as dwellers of the Earth were responsible for maintaining a sense of balance in the state of ongoing flux in the three realms of the world and among all its inhabitants.

Many Native Americans saw the physical geography of the land where they lived as being animated with a life force that suffused everything. Therefore, any object made from natural materials of the earth was imbued with spiritual qualities. The process of creating such an object was viewed as part of religious ritual, like saying a prayer. In an arid land where many relied on hunting animals, gathering wild plants, and subsistence agriculture for food, religion provided a means for appealing to higher deities for rain and fertile yields of plants, crops, and game. Art objects thus were fashioned not only to satisfy practical needs, such as gathering food or water, but to function as spiritual instruments that expedited such prayers, as vehicles to seek spiritual intervention, or as expressions of religious belief. Therefore, art forms of the Southwest Native Americans served dual spiritual and pragmatic functions.

Tribal Art

The physical geography of the land in the Southwest and the various skills that people developed to adapt to it over time, gave rise to distinctive tribal groups. By the time the Spaniards arrived in 1540, the Southwest included many distinctive Native American cultural groups. Not all indigenous people in the Southwest region survived European contact and Anglo-American settlement. Those who did were removed from their native territorial lands in the nineteenth century and placed on reservations elsewhere. This includes people of the Great Plains cultures who hunted buffalo and once frequented Texas and New Mexico, such as the Comanche, Wichita, and the Kiowa. Many other Southwestern Native American groups survived and even today remain within the region. Among those who managed to keep some of their art heritage alive, the Apache of Arizona, Akimel O'odham (Pima) and Tohono O'odham (Papago) of Arizona, and the Shoshone, Paiutes, and Washoe of Nevada, continue their traditions of basket weaving. But in the twentieth century among the most significant contributions to the evolution of Southwest regional art have been those made by the Pueblo and Zuni of New Mexico; the Hopi of Arizona; and the Navajo of New Mexico and Arizona for their creation of pottery, kachinas, silver jewelry, and woven woolen rugs.

Pueblos and Zuni of New Mexico and Hopi of Arizona

The Pueblos and Zuni of New Mexico and the Hopi of Arizona all descended from ancient agrarian cultures. When the Spaniards arrived in the 1500s, their economic and spiritual life revolved around the cultivation of corn.

But more particularly, all their art forms were directly related to water. For example, the pottery created by the Pueblo people served as a vessel to carry water. The *ollas*, or pottery water jars, that women made by hand, fired, and used to carry water from the river were decorated with symbols connoting water, such as clouds, rain altars, rainbirds, and the *avanyu*, or water serpent. Because the creation of pottery was bound up in religious belief, and the Pueblos practiced their religion secretly in underground kivas, their tradition of making pottery was shielded from extinction, despite the pressure applied by conquerors to assimilate practices of their societies. Today, members of intact Pueblo communities throughout New Mexico and Arizona continue to create pottery works of lasting beauty. Each family of artists in a Pueblo community is noted for distinctive clay forms, clay colors, and methods of decoration that are derived from clay resources in their local surroundings and represent traditions passed down among family members for generations.

Navajo of New Mexico and Arizona

The Navajo, a nomadic people, came from Canada and migrated southward into the Southwest region between the twelfth and sixteenth centuries. They remained nomadic hunter-gatherers until the mid-sixteenth century. The Navajo acquired sheep from the Spaniards, marking their transition from cultivating cotton for their textiles to using wool. They sheared the wool from their flocks, washed, carded, and spun it, and then dyed it using native plants such as wild walnut, lichen, and rabbitbrush. They traded chief's blankets to other Native Americans throughout the Southwest and Great Plains regions. But by the twentieth century, on the advice of their reservation trading post merchants, many Navajo switched to weaving rugs to sell to tourists. Although the Navajo adopted some agricultural practices learned from their neighbors, their economy primarily revolved around sheep.

The Navajo were slow to relinquish their warrior ways. The warriors ranged far and wide to resist Spanish, Mexican, and then Anglo-American domination. When the Anglo-Americans acquired Southwest lands from Mexico, violence broke out between the Navajo and the U.S. Army that had been sent into the frontier to protect settlers. Finally, in 1864, the Navajo were defeated and forcibly imprisoned at Fort Sumner (Bosque Redondo) in New Mexico. This left the Navajo decimated by disease and starvation, and in 1868 the U.S. government relented and returned them to their territorial lands on a reservation that straddles northwestern New Mexico and northeastern Arizona, created for the Navajo. They reestablished their flocks of sheep and regenerated their economy by weaving wool blankets and learning to create silver jewelry from a former artisan of the Spanish mission system. Thus, art provided a means for the Navajo's economic survival.

Spanish and Anglo-American Cultures

The Europeans who came to the New World beginning in the sixteenth century were unprepared for what they encountered. It is difficult to imagine the contrast in the two worlds in terms of civilization versus wilderness. Europe was a continent that for centuries had been settled by human societies and overrun by wars. It was a land of known, if disputed, boundaries, established roads, ancient cities, and domesticated landscapes, where every plot of land had been spoken for until reconquered in times of war. By contrast, America was an untamed wilderness and one which the Europeans assumed to be populated with savages. In the quest for riches, new souls to convert to Christianity, or religious freedom they proceeded to subdue all that was wild—in both land and people.

Although the Europeans initially arrived in the New World with the mind-set of conquerors bent on securing land and riches, the challenges they faced and the solutions they arrived at over time shaped their perceptions and hence the culture that evolved as they adapted to their new environment. This transformation over time also contributed to the evolution of regional art in the Southwest.

Spanish Culture

Recently reconquering their own country after seven centuries of Moorish domination (711–1492 C.E.), the Spanish *conquistadores*' exploration of the New World was funded by newly enthroned monarchs Isabella and Ferdinand. They were charged by the Catholic Church with seeking souls to convert to Christianity and by so doing attaining a secure place in Heaven for themselves in the afterlife. By setting up missions with adjacent presidios and nearby colony settlements, the Spaniards Christianized and assimilated the native populations, and infused the region's art forms with the legacy of their own three cultures: Spanish, Christian, and Islamic.

Religion

The first Roman Catholic missionaries arrived in Mexico in 1523, two years after Hernando Cortés defeated the Aztec Emperor Montezuma at Tenochtitlán. Their conversion efforts achieved success after an alleged miracle. Legend has it that in 1531 a beautiful, dark-skinned woman appeared as a vision to the Indian peasant Juan Diego on Tepeyac Hill in Mexico, said she was the Virgin Mary, and told him to tell Bishop Juan de Zumarraga to establish a church in her name on the site. As proof of her visitation and plea, her image miraculously appeared on his cape. Ironically, the Virgin Mary had appeared on the site of an Aztec temple, which Bishop Zumarraga previously had ordered destroyed, dedicated to Tonatzin, earth goddess to the Aztecs, mother to their pantheon of gods, and guardian of humanity. The friars encountered less resistance to conversion among the indigenous Indians of Mexico and, later, the Native Americans after hearing this tale of the dark Virgin who had appeared to one of their own. Consequently, the Virgin of Guadalupe became, in time, one of the most popular images in Southwest regional art.

The tenets and practice of the Catholic faith echoed much that was already familiar to Pueblos: mysticism, elaborate ritual, a cyclic calendar of feast days and celebrations, a creation myth, a supreme god, a sanctified mother, a son regarded by his people as a hero for his sacrifice; and a pantheon of lesser, intercessional deities, which the Catholics deemed to be *santos* (saints).

By adopting what was most appealing about the new faith—its images and rituals—and by attending its worship services, gestures which satisfied the Spaniards, many Pueblos succeeded in simply overlaying Christian motifs on already intact belief systems. Transferring worship from an all-embracing earth mother goddess to a benevolent Virgin Mary did not require a great leap of faith nor strain credulity. Because many Spaniards were unaware that much of Native American religion was embedded in the Pueblo artists' work, the artists were able to continue to create their art and pass its traditions—and thus their identity—down from generation to generation by means of oral tradition and physical demonstration.

The Spaniards devoted considerable resources to establishing missions, presidios, and colonized estates nearby and to importing Catholic clergy, soldiers, and colonists to oversee operations in their frontier territories. In this manner, Spanish arts and crafts taught as trades to the local inhabitants subsequently gave rise to the introduction of new arts industries that became mainstays of Native American economies and initiated the spread of Spanish Colonial arts. (The artistic production of Spain's colonies in the New World followed the historical development of styles established previously in Spain, with original features in different regions that produced a unique mix of Spanish and indigenous elements.)

Art Forms Resulting from Indirect Influence

The Spaniards' most significant, if indirect, contribution to art of the American West and Southwest was the horse, which they reintroduced to the Americas in the sixteenth century. The horse transformed the culture of the Plains Native Americans, providing a means of transportation and freedom of mobility for following and hunting bison hitherto unknown to them. With the Spaniards' horses came the beginnings of the American cowboy, through their cattle-raising enterprises tended by *vaqueros*, or "cowmen" mounted on horses. An extensive culture grew up around the cattle-raising industry that the Spanish first imported into New Mexico then into the rest of the Southwest and California.

Thus, to the first permanent Spanish colony in New Mexico, established in 1598 by Juan de Oñate, can be attributed the genus for the cattle and ranching industry in the United States, the arts and crafts that grew up around vaquero traditions, and later, the fine-arts genre known as "cowboy art" that celebrated them. The culture of the *rancho*, or farm (or in this case, Spanish gentleman's estate in New Mexico), and the associated vaquero lifestyle of the mounted cowboys who worked the cattle on Spanish mission lands and ranches, eventually became an economic foundation of basin and range regions throughout the American Southwest. Many folk arts and crafts traditions evolved from cattle-ranching culture. These include blacksmithing, saddle making, saddle-blanket weaving, boot making, and a number of the vaqueros' own traditions, such as braiding rawhide and horsehair into *reatas* (lariats), halters, bridles, and reins. To this day, the cowboy is an icon of the independent spirit of the American West and is still celebrated in the enduring cowboy-art genre. Nineteenth-century artists Frederic Remington (1861–1909) and Charles M. Russell (1865–1926) generally are credited as the most significant progenitors of this genre, although neither hailed from the Southwest.

The Spaniards also imported the churro sheep, a hardy animal suited to the arid climate, sparse vegetation, and environment of the Southwest. These sheep were acquired by the Navajo for use in textiles, beginning in the nineteenth century.

Art Forms Resulting from Direct Influence

Trained Spanish artisans instructed Indians of the mission communities in their arts and crafts traditions. Some of these forms of art were secular and others parochial in nature and function. Collectively, they became known as Spanish Colonial arts because they were produced during the Spanish Colonial period (circa 1540–1821 C.E.). These include the art forms listed by the Museum of Spanish Colonial Art in Santa Fe, New Mexico, seen in Table 2.

Secular Art Forms

Through the Spanish colonial settlement and mission system, Spanish blacksmiths who came to the New World introduced the techniques of metalworking to the Southwest. They knew how to create decorative objects, such as bowls and chalices and ornaments for gates, windows, and doorways. These skills were transferred to making jewelry. The Spanish taste for silver ornamentation on saddles and bridles, buttons and buckles, gave rise to a demand among those around them for similar items. Around 1850 a Mexican blacksmith named Nakai Tsosi, who also had learned the more subtle skills of jewelry making, taught his skills to a Navajo man named Atsidi Sani (Old Smith). Sani in turn taught his sons, and this is how the Navajo tradition of working silver began.

Table 2. Spanish Colonial arts

Santos	Depictions of religious figures in the form of *retablos* that are painted on wooden panels, and *bultos* that are painted and unpainted carvings in the round.
Bultos en nichos	*Bultos* or carved wooden saints placed in *nichos*, or niches, placed in the home. When sited outdoors these are called *grutas*, or grottoes. Both function as folk shrines.
Altar screens	Altar screens intricately carved for placement in the church.
Furniture	Usually made from pine using mortise and tenon joints.
Relief carving	Gesso relief retablos and relief carved wooden panels similar to ones incorporated into furniture and doors.
Ironwork	Hand-forged into tools, fastenings, and a variety of household objects.
Tin work	Cut, punched, and worked into a variety of utilitarian or decorative objects.
Precious metals work	Silver filigree and silver objects for daily or sacred use.
Bonework	Decorative items, *anillos* (rings), and tool handles carved from bone.
Leatherwork and rawhide work	Items such as boots, saddles, and belts decorated with hand-tooled leather designs.
Pottery	Hand-built, unglazed utilitarian vessels made from micacenous clay, primarily used for food storage and preparation, as well as decorative items.
Weaving	Loom weavings, traditionally made from hand-spun vegetable-dyed yarns.
Colcha	Unique regional embroideries using the colcha stitch.
Straw appliqué	Crosses, chests, and boxes decorated in intricate designs of straw cut and applied in intricate designs.
Ramilletes	Decorative cut paper garlands.

Note: The Spanish Colonial period officially lasted from 1540 to 1821. Artisans brought by the Spanish to New Spain and the Southwest during that time period succeeded in disseminating knowledge about their arts and crafts to the local population. These art forms continue in many manifestations today and are sometimes also referred to as Mexican Folk Art. (From the Museum of Spanish Colonial Art, "Traditional Arts," http://www.spanishcolonial.org/arts.html)

Parochial Art Forms

The Spanish friars and priests who came in the sixteenth and early seventeenth centuries to establish missions in the New World wanted them adorned with art. Initially, missions were decorated with paintings created on animal hides or plastered walls. By the second half of the eighteenth century, however, established mission communities had successfully trained local Indians to become *santeros*, or those who made religious images of saints and holy figures. These artists created *retablos*, or portraits of saints on wood, *bultos*, or figures of saints carved from wood, and altar screens.

The santeros were schooled in methods of artistic expression originating in Baroque traditions imported from Europe. However, the santeros of the Southwest developed a style of artistic expression all their own. They needed to meet a pragmatic need: the religious edification of their audience. Many santeros were less concerned with achieving naturalism in recreating a biblical person or event than they were with communicating a symbolic idea or making an emotional impact. Because their audience was illiterate, the santeros used graphic means to get their message across. Each holy figure painted or carved had to be instantly recognizable and its function as a moral lightening rod for certain causes immediately identifiable. The santeros created each of the saints with crisp lines and form and attired them in clothing with costumes, props, and colors that never deviated from a formula based on the standard story line ascribed to them. The santeros created a pantheon of saints who could each be clearly identified and whose symbolic significance could be readily understood by the audience.

Symbols in Spanish Southwestern Art

Due to Spanish influence, Southwest culture and art eventually began to feature visual symbols of the Christian religion. Images of the cross, the crucifixion, the crown of thorns, portraits of members of the holy family, and representations of the apostles and saints all began to make their appearance in art. Such symbols began to appear outside parochial settings and merged with folk practice. For example, the dark-skinned Virgin of Guadalupe, surrounded by a full-body *mandorla* (halo) and wearing a blue cape of stars, is one of the most popular and prevalent Christian figures to appear in Southwest parochial and secular art today. The patriarchal cross imported by the Spaniards, which features two horizontal bars instead of one, made its way into silver jewelry created by Native Americans because it resembled the symbol they used for dragonflies, harbingers of water, in their art.

Over time, the cross as a symbol of the Christian faith became assimilated into folk-art practices unique to the Southwest. The *Descansos* (roadside memorials) signifies the site where someone has died and, it is believed, the soul departed from the body upon death. Such a site is regarded as more significant, perhaps, than the place in the cemetery where the body is buried later. This practice reflects ancient Indian belief that the world is alive with supernatural forces and that those of life and death animate the landscape. Thus, the practice of using descansos to mark a site where the spirit has departed from the body explains why along roadsides in Texas and New Mexico today, one can see little crosses decorated with flowers and wreaths.

Another legacy of Spanish influence originates in the Islamic symbols that long had been integrated with their own cultural arts because of the Moorish occupation of Spain. For example, the Navajo squash-blossom necklace incorporates two Moorish-inspired decorations: the pomegranate blossom and the *naja*, or Islamic crescent-shaped pendant. Additionally, the Western saddle with its leatherwork embellishment has origins in the Moorish cavalry. The tradition of carving intricate floral designs into the leather used for belts, boots, and saddles stems from Moorish leatherworking traditions that respected Islamic strictures against representing animals or people in art.

Anglo-American Culture

When it secured its independence from Spain in 1821, Mexico acquired as a spoil of war all Spain's colonial empire in North America. Anglo-Americans, lit with the zeal of expansionism, described in 1845 as being its Manifest Destiny, turned their eyes toward lands that seemed tempting for takeover in light of Mexico's tentative hold on them. In 1821 Mexico permitted commerce via the Santa Fe Trail, which joined with the Old Spanish Trail that traversed southern Nevada into California. When the way West became accessible and known to Anglo-Americans, an inexorable trickle and, eventually, a tide of humanity began to surge across the lands of the Southwest.

The Anglo-Americans brought fine-arts traditions with them, which artists used to tell the story of a particular place as it was unfolding in space and time. In visually narrating the story of the Southwest, artists of the nineteenth and early twentieth century tended to adopt one of two aesthetic paradigms in their approaches: empiricism or romanticism. Empiricism was characterized by the objective documentation of observable physical characteristics, people, and events. Romanticism placed more emphasis on subjectively expressing their emotional responses to such places, people, and events, sometimes using their art as a voice of conscience in the process. These artists provide us with much evidence about the relationship between physical geography and culture that evolved in the Southwest region.

The Subjects of Anglo-American Art

Anglo-Americans looked out on the land with a perspective shaped by their European cultural origins: they viewed it as a commodity to be conquered, bought, and sold to individual landowners, with its natural resources transformed into products to yield profit in an economic system based on capitalism. In the Southwest, Anglo-Americans rapidly appropriated the land to put it to such uses, and artists documented these practices in their art.

Trailblazers

Wilderness trappers and traders were the first to come and seek safe routes through the Southwest. Throughout the nineteenth century, explorers, military leaders, and surveyors followed in their tracks and continued to extend knowledge of pathways through the Southwest territory that most Anglo-Americans thought of as dangerous and forbidding.

Miners and Oilmen

The routes that trailblazers established by the mid-nineteenth century provided a thoroughfare for a traffic jam of hopeful, get-rich-quick prospectors stampeding West at the announcements of the discovery of gold in California (at Sutter's Mill, 1848) and silver in Nevada (the Comstock Lode,

Artists of Military Expeditions, the Railroad, and Geological Surveys

Many military expeditions and railroad and geological surveys brought artists along to document the region visually. Between 1840 and 1890 these artists created the first views of what would one day become iconic scenes of the Southwest. These views and artists include the Texas Guadalupe Mountains by John Russell Bartlett (1805–1886); Spanish churches and presidios by Seth Eastman (1808–1875) and Edward Everett (1818–1903); the adobe town of Santa Fe on the plateau of northern New Mexico by Worthington Whittredge (1820–1910); the Taos valley of New Mexico and the Anasazi ruins tucked up in the cliffs of the Canyon de Chelley in Arizona by Richard H. Kern (1821–1853); the Casa Grande ruins of Arizona by John Mix Stanley (1814–1872); the Grand Canyon carved by the Colorado River in Arizona by Heinrich B. Möllhausen (1825–1905) and William H. Holmes (1846–1933); and Pyramid Lake in Nevada by Charles Preuss (1803–1854).

1859). The stream of prospectors continued unabated with revelations of additional gold and silver veins found in Nevada, Arizona, and New Mexico in the 1880s and oil in the twentieth century, starting with Spindletop (the most famous early oil discovery in Texas), which was drilled in Beaumont, Texas, 1901.

Mineral Wealth and Artistic Representation

The discovery of mineral wealth in the Southwest, the oftentimes unsavory get-rich-quick types of people it attracted, and the degradation of the environment that resulted subsequently became subject matter for art by Anglo-American artists. Photographer Timothy H. O'Sullivan (1840–1882), who in 1867 accompanied Clarence King and his U.S. Geological Survey of the 40th parallel along the route subsequently taken by the Union Pacific transcontinental railroad, photographed the mining camps of Nevada along the way.

Nearly one hundred years later, Arizona photographer Mark Klett (1952–) participated in a project to rephotograph sites in the Southwest that had been documented by nineteenth-century survey photographers such as O'Sullivan. Klett used the ostensibly empirical eye of photography to assess how the cultural geography of human beings had transformed the physical geography of the Southwest in the past and present.

Social commentary on the consequences that discoveries of mineral resources exerted on both the physical and the cultural environment of the Southwest can be discerned in the 1940 painting *Oil Field Girls*, by Jerry Bywaters (1906–1989). In this work Bywaters, a Texas regionalist, comments on the parasitic nature of the individuals who were attracted almost overnight to oil strikes throughout the Southwest.

Ranchers

When Spain ceded its lands to Mexico in 1821, many of the Spanish *criollo* cattle that had been marked for ownership by branding had been allowed to roam mission lands freely, with the intent that they would be rounded up later by vaqueros. After Texas passed into Anglo hands in 1836, the cattle on mission lands eventually mingled with European cattle brought by Anglo-Americans. Left to graze at will on large tracts of unoccupied land, they evolved into the tough longhorn cattle breed. At the end of the Civil War, Texans found their grazing lands abundant with these free-ranging cattle. For twenty years of open range that followed, 1866 to 1886, cowboys escorted cattle north to railheads once a year for slaughter and shipment to markets in the east and west hungry for beef. The time period when cowboys, who had learned their trade from Mexican vaqueros, rode the open range and herded cattle on the long trail drives up north was, in actuality, brief, but those times have endured in Southwestern legend and art.

Farmers

Settlers eager for land traveled in the footsteps of their pioneer predecessors to the Southwest, such as the first Anglo-American colonists who followed developer Stephen F. Austin to Texas in 1821. Others went soon thereafter, filled with hope by the Homestead Act of 1862, which promised that 160 acres of free land could be theirs if only they could successfully cultivate it, as proof of improvement, after five years. Most homesteaders failed, ignorant of dryland farming and irrigation techniques necessary to survive in the land of little rain. As a result, Dust Bowl conditions of the 1930s to 1950s prevailed in Texas, New Mexico, and Arizona.

Railroads

The increase in human traffic and the commerce this engendered created a demand for mail and goods shipped as freight by rail. Railroad magnates set their gaze on connecting the country by transcontinental railway. This goal was achieved near Promontory Point, Utah, in 1869, with a golden spike joining the Union Pacific with the Central Pacific. Within thirteen years, railroad trunk lines, such as the Texas and Pacific (1881), the Southern Pacific (1883), and the Atchison, Topeka, and Santa Fe (AT&SF) (1883), interconnected all the Southwestern states in interstate commerce.

Removal of Native Americans

The only way that Anglo-Americans were able to accomplish the objectives of their Manifest Destiny was to remove the major obstacle in their way: Native Americans. U.S. policy toward its Native American population throughout the nineteenth century was characterized by attempts to remove, relocate, and sequester onto reservations Indians who got in the way of prospectors greedy for natural resources, ranchers and farmers hungry for land, and business magnates eager to secure right-of-way across Indian lands to construct a profitable ocean-to-ocean transcontinental railroad system.

Cowboy Art

The twilight era of the cattle drives proved to be the inspiration for a Texas regional artist of the nineteenth and twentieth centuries, Charles Franklin "Frank" Reaugh (1860–1945). Reaugh, born in Illinois, moved with his family in 1876 to Terrell, Texas, where he spent his time drawing the longhorns that grazed near the family property. In the 1880s he documented the roundups of the longhorn on ranches near Wichita Falls, Texas, and rode north across the Red River on the cattle drives from Texas to Kansas. A contemporary of the cowboy artists, Reaugh focused on depicting the raison d'etre of the artists' existence—the longhorn—placed like ships in oceans of grass on the plains with limitless horizons. Reaugh was among the first artists in Texas to celebrate the distinctive physical geography of the Southwest through landscape painting. His works convey a sense of romance tinged with regret for the passing of the open range.

The urge to immortalize cattle-ranching traditions subsequently gave rise to an entire American genre known as cowboy art, best exemplified by early masters of it such as Charles M. Russell (1864–1926) of Montana and Frederic Remington (1861–1909) of New York. Cowboy artists themselves conceived of forming the Cowboy Artists Association (CAA) in a meeting conducted in 1965 in Sedona, Arizona. Today its headquarters are in Kerrville, Texas. The artists of the CAA strive to document the authentic as well as romantic experience of cowboys of the past and present, as did Russell and Remington.

Anglo-American Innovations That Shaped Regional Arts

Ultimately, Anglo-Americans introduced an economic system to the Southwest based on capitalism, which demanded unrestrained access to and exploitation of natural resources, the enthusiastic embrace of materialism, and the mass disenfranchisement of indigenous peoples. Like Native Americans, the precarious environmental matrix that makes the Southwest special—its crystalline air, wide-open spaces, diverse wildlife, and breathtaking terrain—came under threat as well. These were the negative aspects incurred by the influx of the Anglo-Americans. Many of these issues became political subject matter in Southwest regional art produced in the twentieth century. But as with all change, positive benefits accrued as well and produced much that came to be celebrated in art thereafter.

The positive benefits conferred by changes brought by Anglo-Americans included new trade and transportation routes, which in turn introduced new materials and technology, new markets, and new forms of art.

New Materials and Technology

By the beginning of the nineteenth century, the materials of European and Anglo-American culture already had found their way into Native American arts.

Beads, for example, had replaced porcupine quills for decoration on clothing. By the mid-nineteenth century, traders were instrumental in supplying additional materials that were incorporated into the arts, such as calico cloth, aniline dyes, commercially spun yarn, and silver coins. However, the availability of convenient, ready-made cooking utensils nearly brought to a halt the creation of traditional handmade clay pottery vessels previously used for cooking by Native Americans. Similarly, brightly hued and colorfast aniline textile dyes supplanted more delicate, subtle, and unstable dyes that had been derived from native plants and minerals.

Increased commerce and trade brought other benefits to regional artists. By 1878 the traders who had established themselves outside of Indian reservations and near railheads played important roles in preserving and advancing Native American arts. In exchange for what the traders supplied in the way of tools, raw materials, household goods, and food, the Indians traded sheep, wool, and the products of their handiwork, including baskets, pottery, woven blankets, and jewelry they fashioned from the metal and semiprecious stones provided by the traders. Anxious to draw in tourists and make sales to generate a profit, the traders became advocates for Native American artists and catalysts for promoting and preserving an art heritage that otherwise might have died out. By conveying suggestions from their customers to the artists, they frequently were responsible for promoting the evolution of new regional art forms for the Southwest.

Agricultural Art

Although the Southwest is an important agricultural region, the enterprise of farming the land as a subject for its regional art has generally not received the same degree of attention from artists as has ranching. The ceaseless toil of farming the land holds less attraction for artists than the romantic allure of depicting cowboys as knights on horseback monitoring intractable beasts who roamed far and wide over the land.

But several artists who painted in the Southwest trained their artistic eye on agriculture when the Texas Wildflower Competitive Exhibitions, sponsored from 1927 through 1929 by San Antonio philanthropist Edgar B. Davis and the San Antonio Art League, created a separate category for cotton farming to highlight the regional attributes of Texas. Prize money was an added incentive. For his competition entry, *Picking Cotton* (1929), José Arpa (1858–1952), known for his ability to depict brilliant sunshine, conveyed the stark nature of work conducted under the hot sun when cultivating the crop of "white gold" that provided the Southwest region and Texas with economic clout.

By the 1930s, much of the Southwest was gripped in the chokehold of the Dust Bowl, which owed its severity to cyclical drought and farming methods ill-suited to the semiarid region. Unsurprisingly, during this time artists saw little to celebrate in agricultural enterprise, as conveyed in Alexandre Hogue's (1898–1994) painting, *Drouth Stricken Area,* created in 1934. Hogue, a member of a twentieth-century group of regional painters known as the Dallas Nine, perceived that failure to respect the balance of nature wreaked devastating repercussions on the environment in the Southwest. He saw that the once-great American wilderness had become a barren wasteland due to human greed and ignorance.

New Markets

The railroad's arrival in the Southwest opened up new markets for regional art. By 1883 rail lines linked most of the region. During this time period, an entrepreneur named Fred Harvey approached the AT&SF railroad officials and proposed a plan to build hotels and restaurants along the railroad stops all across the Southwest. Harvey Houses not only facilitated tourist travel, they provided a venue where Native American artwork could be displayed and marketed. Sales of their art to tourists provided economic income for many Native Americans who otherwise had little means to acquire revenue when restricted to reservations. This also provided them with incentive to preserve and continue to develop their traditional art forms.

The AT&SF railroad company also became a patron of the fine arts. In 1892 it began to offer direct commissions to famous national artists to travel the railway into the Southwest and produce paintings of its panoramic vistas. For nine decades (1903–1993) the AT&SF paid artists of the region and of the Taos and Santa Fe art colonies to paint views of the Southwest territory made accessible by railway.

New Forms of Art

Anglo-Americans contributed three forms to the region's art: the quilt and the fine arts of painting and photography. These are not distinctive regional art forms unto themselves, but once transplanted into the region, they became vehicles for artists to express uniquely regional content.

Quilts

As with the Native American art forms of basketry and pottery, the quilt's primary purpose was a practical one. Quilts were necessary for keeping warm when the frigid winds blew in the winter, particularly so in the Southwest plains, where little fuel was available to stoke fires.

Quilts have been made in Texas since 1731, according to San Antonio archival records. An entire quilting culture flourished in Texas, because of the cheap tracts of land there that attracted families anxious to establish homes for themselves and because of the availability of cotton from Texas fields. In families of scarce financial means, women (and sometimes men) pieced together fabric scraps they had on hand into blocks to form a top cover, added a cloth backing and cotton batting between them for warmth, and then stitched, or quilted, the layers together.

Those who quilted brought traditional quilting patterns with them from back East. Once settled in the Southwest, they developed designs and patterns specific to their environment, as seen in a survey of quilts created in Texas from 1836 to 1986, conducted by scholars Karoline Bresenhan and Nancy Puentes. Some designs are pictorial, featuring appliquéd patterns of local birds, trees,

Railroad Art

The railroad altered the Southwest terrain in significant ways, and one artist created a visual record of its impact on one area of the Southwest. Alfred A. Hart (1816–1908), hired after 1864 as the official artist for the Central Pacific Railroad (CPRR), used his camera to record the progress of its construction as men laid the miles of track through the West. Other artists, such as Carlton E. Watkins (1829–1916) and Andrew J. Russell (1830–1902), also used their cameras as tools to objectively document the greatest technological engineering achievement of the day, as it advanced, railroad tie by railroad tie, across each mile of alkaline desert and through the forbidding Sierra Nevada. Lawrence Hersh (n.d.), a twentieth-century photographer, retraced Hart's odyssey through Nevada one hundred years later to assess again the degree to which these changes altered the landscape, either temporarily or forever.

Buffalo Soldiers

The clash between cultural groups wrestling for dominance over the Southwestern frontier was documented by New York artist Frederic Remington (1861–1909). In 1888 he rode with the 10th Cavalry of Buffalo Soldiers stationed at Fort Grant, Arizona. Based on this experience, he portrayed in his art a phenomenon of the cultural geography in the Southwest that otherwise went unrecognized until the late twentieth century: a part of the African American cultural legacy subsumed by dominant Anglo-American traditions but mirrored in the lives of the Buffalo Soldiers encamped on the Southwestern frontier.

flowers, or even entire landscapes of bluebonnets, live oaks, prickly pear cacti, and the Yellow Rose of Texas, and picture-postcard scenes from around the state. Other quilts are more abstract. In these, the artist distilled the essence of something observed in the environment into the simplest artistic elements of color, line, and shape to form a motif. For example, for her *Indian Teepee* quilt created in 1885, Mary Jane Reese Findley (n.d.) of East Texas based her quilt-block designs on a traditional Sugar Loaf quilt pattern. Findley converted the triangles normally used into Indian teepees and arrowheads to commemorate the locale. Her home was near Caddo Indian burial mounds and Cherokee Lake, which was named for the Indians who once inhabited the area under a Mexican treaty but who were chased out of Texas in the Cherokee War of 1839. Similarly, on the High Plains artists developed geometric quilt-block designs to suggest windmill blades or echo the rhythm of plowed furrows in the soil that stretched on for miles to a flat horizon.

Fine Arts

Until the late nineteenth century, there was very little drawing, painting, or sculpture initiated by Anglo-American inhabitants of the Southwest. People were too busy trying to fulfill their basic needs for food, clothing, and shelter.

For the most part, until the 1890s production in the fine arts originated in the activity of a few professional artists who either were traveling through the area, had emigrated from other parts of the country, or were hired by government survey expedition leaders to document the terrain, flora, and fauna of the region visually. Wealthy Anglo-Americans also brought traditions and examples of fine art with them. Engaging in the fine arts was considered by almost everyone else to be a luxury, and few had training to create it. The fine arts are usually differentiated from craft only in that a fine art object does not first satisfy a basic necessity for survival, such as to transport water, as a clay pot does, or provide warmth, as a blanket does.

Empiricism and Romanticism in the Fine Arts of the Southwest

As with all art of the American West, the dual aesthetic sensibilities of empiricism (visual accuracy) and romanticism (emotional expression) have dominated the regional fine arts of the Southwest since the arrival and settlement of the Anglo-Americans in the nineteenth century. Anglos who came to the American West and Southwest perceived that they were part of an unfolding, unique story. As a result, conscious of their contribution to the settlement of a continent, they came to view the role of the artist as that of documentarian and storyteller, with the mission of art being a visual narrative to convey the saga of their epic experience.

Over the years, Southwestern regional fine art began to attain distinction. Artists, whether itinerants, foreign immigrants, or natives of the territory, could not help but respond to the dynamic heritage of the region and palpable sense of place. Characteristically, their paintings and photographs portray the seeming endlessness of the land and sky and capture the sparkling light. The distinctive animals and plants of the land, such as the bison, Texas bluebonnet, Southwest prickly pear, and Arizona Saguaro cactus, sometimes received particular attention.

The portraits of people and the events significant to their lives are played out against this backdrop of spectacular scenery. The people portrayed dominantly tend to be those of Native American, Hispanic, and Anglo descent who have been the most visible in making contributions to its cultural heritage. Artists painted, printed, and photographed genre scenes that portrayed ordinary lives. And many artists were commissioned to create historical paintings and sculptural monuments to commemorate individuals who were viewed as frontier legends, both victors and vanquished, and the events that stamped them as unforgettable. These can be found in places of honor in state buildings and history museums in Texas, New Mexico, Arizona, and Nevada.

Empiricism in the Southwest

One of the first explorers of the Southwest to bring artists with him was Major Stephen H. Long of the Corps of Topographical Engineers. In 1820 he was dispatched to discover the source of the Platte River and return by way of the Arkansas and the Red rivers to the Mississippi. Artists Samuel Seymour (1775–1823) and Titian Ramsay Peale (1799–1881), a topographer and a naturalist, respectively, accompanied him. They created the first known drawings and paintings by Anglo-Americans of the land along the Red River.

From 1820 through 1874 nearly a dozen artists followed, joining in exploratory military expeditions, railroad surveys, and geological surveys to document the lands of Texas, New Mexico, Arizona, and Nevada. Their role was seen as a dual one of artist and scientist. Although none could be called regional artists in the strict sense, their work signifies the importance that Anglo-American culture ascribed to visual documentation, and they were among the first to establish the iconography of the Southwest, by drawing and painting the region's terrain, landmarks, flora, fauna, indigenous people, and ancient ruins. These artists—including John Mix Stanley (1814–1872), George Catlin (1796–1872), Richard H. Kern (1821–1853), Friedrich Wilhelm von Egloffstein (1824–1898), and Heinrich B. Möllhausen (1825–1905)—provided the viewer with a sense of scale for comparing the size of the human being to the immensity of the terrain. They also were among the first to draw likenesses of the inhabitants in a straightforward and realistic way.

In the late nineteenth century, photographers began to be able to provide more accurate depictions of terrain than could be attained in paintings or drawings. A few—notably William Henry Jackson (1843–1942), John K. Hillers (1843–1925), Timothy H. O'Sullivan (1840–1882), William W. Bell (1830–1910), and Carleton E. Watkins (1829–1916)—created some of the most memorable images ever made of the Southwest.

Romanticism in the Southwest

Photography

Once photographers could be called in to do the job of accurately documenting the terrain and its features to meet practical needs, artists were released from the obligation to work strictly from the paradigm of scientific empiricism. Artists who journeyed to the Southwest began to work from a romantic paradigm.

Thomas Moran (1837–1926) was one of the first artists who rose magnificently to the challenge of doing nothing less than conveying the power of the land to inspire awe in all who looked upon it. Between 1871 and 1892, Moran served as an artist on three government expeditions and made five other trips to the West. In 1873 John Wesley Powell (1834–1902), heading one of the U.S. Geological Survey teams, brought Moran with him on an expedition down the Colorado River of the Grand Canyon. In response to its beauty, Moran produced the large-scale panoramic landscape work *The Chasm of the Colorado*, painted between 1873 and 1874. Working from a romantic sensibility, he did not place emphasis on scientific accuracy. Instead, he combined composite sketched views to create a scene, and he exaggerated color in his use of expressive aesthetic qualities in response to viewing such scenery. Moran went on to create many paintings that conveyed the sublime majesty of the land he saw in Arizona and New Mexico.

Thomas Moran. *The Mountain of the Holy Cross* (1876). Courtesy of the Library of Congress.

Ansel Adams (1902–1984), like Moran, came to the Southwest as a visitor and was swept away by its grandeur. Adams did as much as Moran to establish the Southwestern landscape in the minds of many Americans. In the early years, he inadvertently over-exposed his pictures until he adjusted his technique to the remarkable high-altitude light of the Southwest. But Adams' masterful knowledge of camera mechanics, photographic technique, and darkroom methods allowed him to convert his early "mistakes" into a powerful medium for artistic expression. Exemplified in his famous photograph "Moonrise over Hernandez, New Mexico" (1941), his landscapes read as places suffused with atmosphere: brooding, haunting, majestic, and mysterious.

A similar sense of romanticism permeates the works of two photographers who recorded two worlds that they thought were mysterious and vanishing: those of the Native American and the working cowboy. Edward Lee Curtis (1868–1952) documented all the Indian peoples of North America, a task that occupied him from 1907 to 1930. His series of moving portraits of Southwestern Indians feature people who look out at the viewer with their personality, strength, dignity, humanity, and sometimes ferocity starkly apparent. Erwin E. Smith (1886–1947), a native son of Texas, lived and worked on ranches as a cowhand throughout his life. Sensing extinction about to occur in the traditions of the working cowboy's culture, in the years spanning 1905 to 1912, he began to use his artistic training and

Ansel Adams. *Moonrise over Hernandez*, New Mexico (1941). © Ansel Adams Publishing Rights Trust/Corbis.

camera to document cowboy life on ranches in Texas, New Mexico, and Arizona. Smith's love for the romance of cowboy life is revealed in skillful compositions and lighting that dramatically highlight daily activities.

Sculpture

Sculpture's origins as a regional art form can be traced to the carved wooden kachinas of the Hopi and the bultos made by santeros in the Spanish Colonial arts tradition. However, sculpture as a fine art form did not become a common part of the region's art until late in the nineteenth century, because sculpture executed in carved stone or poured bronze requires extensive training on the part of artists, expensive studio and foundry facilities, and funding for materials. Additionally, New Mexico and Arizona already harbored a wealth of striking forms out-of-doors in nature and fabulous ruins of ancient cultures. Perhaps little need was felt for additional aesthetic adornment; one needed only to look outside the window to find beauty in three-dimensional form. Nevada's most striking forms of sculpture came late in the twentieth century, as its population grew. The earliest and most plentiful forms of fine-art sculpture in the Southwest are found in Texas, possibly explained by a perceived need or desire to embellish the landscape in lieu of spectacular scenery.

Sculpture in Texas predominantly celebrates the romanticism of regional heroes and cultural heritage. Until the twentieth century, the state of Texas routinely commissioned artists to create sculpture that honored its pioneer founders and Confederate heroes. The Texas centennial celebrated in 1936 brought about a renewed flurry of this type of activity. Most of the sculpture produced in the state up to that time, and all through the remainder of the twentieth century, reflects a preference for a dual empirical and romantic approach in that sculpture had to look like the person portrayed, and the likeness was expected to convey a heroic theme.

In the mid-twentieth century, sculptors began to honor other aspects of Texas culture. Sculptor Alexander Phimister Proctor (1862–1950) created a moving monument to the wild mustang at the behest of Texas historian J. Frank Dobie, who is quoted on the sculpture's base as saying that they "carried the men who made Texas." The larger-than-life bronze work, created in 1941, features one stallion and four mares in full gallop, accompanied by a foal. Dobie's words are a fitting description for the many equestrian sculptures around the state that feature those who "made Texas great" on horseback. These sculptures honor Texas leaders from the beginning of the state's history through the modern era. Some of the honored include Captain Blas María de la Garza Falcón, the Spaniard who secured the first Spanish land grant in Texas and introduced the principles of cattle raising into

Edward S. Curtis. *Canyon de Chelly, Navajos* (1904). Courtesy of the Library of Congress.

Erwin E. Smith. *The Horse Wrangler* (1910). Courtesy of the Library of Congress.

South Texas; General Sam Houston, hero of the Texas Revolution of 1835; and Terry's Texas Ranger's Memorial honoring the 8th Texas cavalry of volunteers who fought in the cause of the Civil War.

Equestrian sculpture erected in the twentieth century also pays homage to the working men and animals of Texas—the cattlemen, ranch owners, trail drivers, cowboys, cow ponies, and longhorn cattle that formed the backbone of the most romanticized industry of the Southwest. Any one of these sculptures memorializing the cattle industry would be equally appropriate in New Mexico, Arizona, or Nevada.

"The Mustangs of Las Colinas"

A fitting bookend to a discussion of sculpture that pays tribute to the horse and its influence on the cultural heritage of Texas is a mention of a sculpture that mirrors Proctor's mustangs theme. The 1984 sculpture, titled *The Mustangs of Las Colinas* and created by Robert Glen (1940–), was mounted in Williams Square, an urban space in the Las Colinas complex in Irving, Texas. A landscape site sculpture, it features nine larger-than-life horses cast in bronze, with each placed as though galloping across the plaza and a stream. The flat stone environment functions as a metaphor for the prairie, as Irving is sited in the Blackland Prairies region of Texas. This artwork celebrates features of the land, its space, and those uniquely shaped by it, who in turn affected it with their presence, whether they were a mustang or human being.

Museums in the Southwest

After the Civil War, Anglo-Americans began to import into the Southwest a variety of institutions and practices that promoted cultural heritage and fine-arts-related activities. These led to the eventual establishment of museums that collected ethnographic artifacts and arts and crafts.

Cultural Museums

An early example of a regional cultural museum is the Museum of New Mexico, founded in 1909. Dr. Edgar Lee Hewett, director of the Museum of New Mexico and the newly created School of American Archaeology, was interested in preserving the artistic traditions of the Southwestern Indians, and he hired artist Kenneth M. Chapman to curate a collection of Native American arts for the museum. They conducted an archaeological dig of twelfth- and fourteenth-century Pueblo ruins on the Pajarito Plateau west of Santa Fe, New Mexico. In the summer of 1907 and 1908, Hewett hired several San Ildefonso Pueblo men to assist on the dig, among them Julian Martinez (1879–1943). When the workers unearthed several shards of pottery at the site, Hewett and Chapman wanted to know if anyone in the Pueblo could make pottery like their findings. Julian and his wife, María Martinez (circa 1889–1980), who had been taught how to create traditional Pueblo pottery by her aunt, accepted the challenge. After a year of experimentation with clay bodies and slips, María and Julian finally arrived at what was nearly a replica of the archaeological find. Hewett and Chapman purchased all of the pots they made. Afterward, María and Julian rediscovered how to recreate the black-on-black pottery known to their Pueblo ancestors, for which the couple subsequently became famous. They taught other San Ildefonso Pueblos these skills, and once again traditional art derived from the land of the Southwest provided the means to attain economic viability.

Fine-Art Museums

By the late nineteenth century, as small towns and cities became established across the Southwest, civic-minded citizens began to look for opportunities to sponsor community art organizations, exhibitions, museums, and schools that featured and trained local artists. Philanthropists, seeking ways to establish monuments to their memory as a legacy, either provided funding for exhibitions, buildings, or institutions, or they endowed institutions with their private art collections that they had used their fortunes to amass over the years. These institutions and the exhibitions they sponsored were critically important in establishing, celebrating, and promoting regional artists, the art they produced, and the land and people they portrayed.

For example, in Texas the San Antonio Art League (SAAL) Museum started out as several art organizations that agreed to join forces in 1912 in order to achieve common goals. The SAAL wanted to provide artists with a place to exhibit their works, acquire paintings for the public's enjoyment, and start an art school. In 1927, 1928, and 1929, the SAAL conducted the Texas Wildflower Competitive Exhibitions, funded by philanthropist Edgar B. Davis. These exhibitions brought national attention to the region's art.

SOUTHWEST REGIONAL ART OF THE TWENTIETH CENTURY

In the twentieth century, the influences of physical geography and cultural geography, all of which shaped a constellation of aesthetic paradigms, coalesced to produce the distinctive forms of art associated with the Southwest. Three aesthetic paradigms prevailed. What was valued as art either had to be pragmatic (serve a useful purpose); reflect empiricism (visual accuracy in detailing the specific cultural and physical geography of a specific "place" in terms of its people and the terrain, space, light, and color unique to the region); or reflect romanticism (function as a narrative of person or place—of a specific locale).

The collision and subsequent commingling of the three cultures that were dominant in influence—Native American, Hispanic, and Anglo-American—have resulted in many and diverse art forms that today are recognized as those associated with the Southwest region.

Southwestern regional art of the twentieth century represented a continuation of traditions adapted to changing times, new circumstances, and, in some cases, new materials. Anglo-American artists trained in the European fine-arts traditions of studio-style painting showcased themes specific to the Southwest, such as highlighting the beauty of its vistas or the mystique of the ancient Native American cultures. Crafts and fine art were transformed in the hands of innovative artists who acquired experience in manipulating new materials such as fiberglass and neon lighting. Some artists of the Southwest adapted traditional art forms to reflect multiethnic themes, multicultural attitudes, or political and social issues, which sometimes gave rise to an interesting syncretism in artistic intentions, art forms, and art works. But the work invariably reflects the influences of the unique place that is the Southwest.

New Art Derived from Old: The Pueblo Indian Painting Style

After the Civil War and up through 1934, the U.S. government took steps to assimilate Native Americans into the dominant Anglo-American society. Indians were not permitted to practice their religious rites, and their children were required to attend boarding schools away from home and the influences of their parents and culture. Regardless of government policy, a few enlightened administrators and teachers sought enterprising ways to provide young Native Americans with opportunities to practice their arts.

In 1908 Edgar Hewett hired Crescencio Martinez (1877–1918), and Alfredo Montoya (1892–1913) of the San Ildefonso Pueblo to document the ritual dances and processions of the Pueblo culture by painting watercolor pictures of them on paper. The two artists developed a style similar to what they had seen in rock art, on kiva walls, and in designs on Pueblo pottery. Developing what was later called the Pueblo Indian Painting Style, they drew figures with strong contour outlines, applying color in flat planes. They did not use illusionistic techniques such as tonal shading, linear perspective, or cast shadows to suggest three-dimensional space.

Ten years later, Elizabeth DeHuff (1887–1983), wife of the superintendent at the Santa Fe Indian School, hired seven young, homesick Pueblo boys to paint pictures of Pueblo ritual dances in her home. The boys adopted a style similar to that of Martinez. Dr. Hewett mounted their work for an exhibition in the museum in 1919. In 1920 the works went on exhibition in New York. Thereafter, Hewett hired some of the boys to paint full-time for him and create a visual ethnographic record of Pueblo and Hopi traditions before all memory of them vanished. With this patronage one of the schoolboys, Fred Kabotie (1900–1986), who was originally from Second Mesa, Arizona, emerged as one of the most famous of the Pueblo Indian painters, who throughout his artistic career, documented Hopi rituals, ceremonial dances, and daily activities. He then became an art teacher and guided future Native American students.

In 1932 Dorothy Dunn (1912?–1992), a teacher at the Santa Fe Indian School, initiated the Studio for art instruction. Against government policy, she impressed on the students the need to focus on Indian subjects and to develop a style uniquely suited to their own cultural heritage. The painting style the students learned under Dunn's guidance at the Studio echoed the work done by Martinez and Kabotie.

Collectively, the efforts and collaborations of these people launched the beginning of a new Pueblo art form and the careers of a whole new generation of Native American artists. The evolution of the Pueblo Indian Painting Style resulted in iconography immediately identifiable with Southwest regional art traditions. It influenced future generations of contemporary Native Americans who later achieved fame as artists, one of whom, Allan Houser (1914–1994), was a Chiricahua Apache whose father had been imprisoned for twenty years for fighting in the last stand of the Apache band in Arizona in the 1880s. Houser used sculpture to express subjects and themes drawn from his Native American heritage, and in 1992 President George H. W. Bush bestowed on him the highest art award offered in the United States, the National Medal of Arts, for his work as an artist and teacher.

Old Art Traditions Embrace New Themes: Romanticism and Regionalism

At the beginning of the twentieth century, a new wave of Anglo-American artists arrived in the Southwest. Trained in fine-arts traditions, they desired to live out their lives as artists serving as lenses through which the beauty of the physical world and human experience might be filtered.

The Taos and Santa Fe Artist Societies

Joseph H. Sharp (1859–1953) was perhaps the first Anglo-American artist to discover Taos and Santa Fe, New Mexico, in 1883, while on commission with *Harper's Weekly* magazine. His pictures and tales depicted the region, with its "exotic" people, enchanting landscapes, and beautiful light. In September 1898 two young artists prowling through the northern mountains of New Mexico in search of new themes for their paintings were stranded when one of their wagon wheels broke. Ernest L. Blumenschein (1874–1960) lost the flip of the coin with Bert G. Phillips (1868–1956) and had to ride into the nearest town on a draft horse with the wagon wheel in hand to seek aid. Blumenschein never forgot the breathtaking, beguiling setting he saw along that journey through the mountains. Phillips, too, must have been taken by New Mexico, since he moved there soon thereafter. After 1910, nearly a decade later, Blumenschein started to return to Taos each summer, finally moving there permanently in 1919. Others were inspired, and over time, through contacts and connections, more artists came to paint in the area, forming two artists' colonies: one at Taos and one at Santa Fe.

With Phillips and four other artists Blumenschein formed the original core of the Taos Society of Artists in 1913. The other Taos Society artists were Sharp, W. Herbert Dunton (1878–1936), E. Irving Couse (1866–1936), and Oscar E. Berninghaus (1874–1952). The Society artists pledged to consolidate their efforts to produce and exhibit a body of art work that reflected the inspiration attained from their unique and inspiring environment. Their goal was to meet the highest standards of fine art, not merely the popular tastes of mass-media markets. The Santa Fe artists were, for the most part, individuals with eclectic art styles who came to the area to enjoy the setting and soak in the ambience while creating their own artwork. Some integrated local themes and images into their work; others did not.

By contrast, the Taos artists were more united in a purposeful vision that was at its heart romantic. These artists were invigorated by the totally new scenery and culture that surrounded them, which was so unlike the urban environments they had come from. They reveled in the crystal-clear air borne of the high altitude, the open spaces of the high mesa regions, the complexity and contrasts in form, shape, and textures of the conifer forest juxtaposed against the deciduous aspens and cottonwoods, and the brilliantly colored wildflowers carpeting the jagged and undulating contours of mountain slopes and canyons. In the morning and evening, when the sun rose and set, the world all around them caught fire with every red, orange, golden yellow, and violet hue of their paint palettes. The Taos artists perceived in this place a primordial mysticism exuded by the noble savages (popularized by Jean-Jacques Rousseau) that surrounded them—the Taos Pueblo Indians. They felt as if they had stumbled on a world hidden in the mountains, away from the scrutiny of civilization and highly charged with eroticism due to the religious rituals suggestive of cosmic mysteries and supernatural forces that eluded their comprehension.

The Taos Pueblos continued to practice their ancient religious ways out of sight in their underground kivas, as they had done for centuries. Only glimmers of this secret life were revealed to the Anglo-American artists' eyes in above-ground ceremonies and dances. Compounding the sense of unalterable mystery, the Pueblos also embraced many tenets of Catholicism, the practice of which was overlaid like a metaphysical veil on the material aspects of their existence. The Taos artists regarded all of this with endless fascination. Although they were trained in European academic traditions, Sharp and Couse, rather than paint portraits of kings or wealthy society women, posed Indians in their studios instead. Rather than paint the pageantry and coronation of kings or bucolic farmers in their fields, Phillips and Blumenschein painted Pueblo Indians participating in their religious processionals and ceremonies. Only Dunton, a hunter, chafed at studio confinement and seemed to be more fascinated by the great out-of-doors, the physical geography of the land, and its quality of light and space than that which the others perceived to be the heart of darkness that lay buried beneath Anasazi ruins and was still beating as the pulse of Pueblo society.

Between 1917 and 1926 several artists who were attracted by news of Taos that had spread through the activities of the Taos Society were admitted as active members. These new members—Victor Higgins (1884–1949), Walter Ufer (1876–1936), Julius Rolshoven (1858–1930), Catherine C. Critcher (1868–1964), E. Martin Hennings (1886–1956) and Kenneth Adams (1874–1960)—brought with them fresh perspectives borne of a heightened sociopolitical conscience initiated by the Progressive movement in the United States, as well as the sweeping changes in artistic expression brought on by the influence of Modernism, which was imported to the United States with the New York Armory Show of 1913.

Georgia O'Keeffe

The Southwest lays claim to America's first great female contemporary artist of the twentieth century: Georgia O'Keeffe (1887–1986). Synthesizing the European and Anglo-American traditions of the fine art of easel painting with a Modernist sensibility, and inspired by the aesthetic qualities of the Southwestern landscape, she created a unique fusion that transcends traditional notions of what regional art might be.

O'Keeffe, originally from Sun Prairie, Wisconsin, had felt drawn to Texas and the Southwest ever since her mother had read bedtime stories to her children about Kit Carson, Billy the Kid, and the Wild West in general. In her early adulthood, after receiving fine-arts training in Chicago, New York, and Charlottesville, Virginia, and casting about for ways to earn her living thereafter, O'Keeffe accepted an art education position in Texas. During the academic school years of 1912 to 1913, she supervised drawing and penmanship in the public schools of Amarillo; and from 1916 to February 1918, she worked as head of the art department at West Texas State Normal College in Canyon.

On the High Plains, O'Keeffe experienced an epiphany of sorts. Unlike many newcomers to the region who were daunted by the vast arid plains and the arching vault of sky that was unrelieved by trees, she loved the plains and the sky, seeing in them a wonderful emptiness. The West Texas High Plains exerted a profound impact on her sensibilities and, in turn, her art. The simplicity of the land inspired an economy of means in her artistic expression. Then, in 1929 O'Keeffe stayed at a hotel in New Mexico with a friend and signed up for a Fred Harvey tour. She ran into Mabel Dodge Luhan (1879–1962), hostess of the Taos Society of Artists gatherings, who invited her to come and stay at her estate. Thereafter, O'Keeffe returned to New Mexico each summer, until her husband, photographer George Stieglitz (1864–1946), died in 1946. At that time she purchased a small place in the town of Abiquiu, fifty miles northwest of Santa Fe, and became a permanent resident of the Southwest until her death.

O'Keeffe uniquely distilled and simplified the forms illuminated in the light-filled unbounded space of the Southwestern landscape. Art critics now assert that in this she celebrated the transcendental spirituality to be discovered in landscape—and she was one of the first twentieth-century artists to do so by reducing the expression of an idea and feeling to the foundational artistic elements of line, color, and shape and artistic principles of emphasis, balance, repetition, and rhythm.

Although her work was always firmly grounded in what she observed in nature, she abstracted it to its simplest, most elegant essence, which made her one of America's first abstract painters of the Modernist era. However, unlike many Modernists, she never resorted to abstraction for art's sake alone, and this characteristic of O'Keeffe's work emerged dominantly only after her move to Texas. O'Keeffe's works also reflect a sense of Romanticism bordering on spirituality in a place where time seems to stand still, where, in her own words, she sought to "find the feeling of infinity on the horizon line."

Maynard Dixon

Artist Maynard Dixon (1875–1946) acquired a deep regard for the sparsely inhabited terrain and cultural heritage of the Southwest and for the intuitive, mystical bond Native Americans had with the land. Dixon came to the region to paint at a time when the entire country was gripped in the Depression and the plight of Native Americans was likewise steeped in poverty due to oppressive reservation policies. In his 1931 painting *Earth Knower* Dixon depicts the head of a Native American man shrouded in a blanket, his face lined like the craggy canyon behind him. Unlike his nineteenth-century predecessors, Dixon did not portray his subject as a savage, nor as many of the Taos artists did, romanticize him as "other" attired in exotic costume. Instead, Dixon confers a powerful, simple dignity on the man. It was Dixon's perception that Native Americans had long ago forged an enduring relationship with the land that exceeded the comprehension of most Anglo-Americans.

From Regional Romanticism to Social Realism

In the late nineteenth century, as the economy began to recover from the Civil War, several European artists trained in fine-arts traditions made their way to established cities in the Southwest. As they made contacts in the region by teaching and exhibiting their work, they passed along traditions of portraiture, history painting, and landscape art learned from their academic training back East and in Europe. Several of these painters brought sophisticated fine-arts techniques with them, such as the principles of observing and painting directly from nature and the contemporary world around them, painting *plein aire*, or out-of-doors, using a scientific basis for mixing color, and applying paint through loose brushwork—all associated with the Impressionist painters of France.

Regionalism and Romanticism of Place: The Texas Bluebonnet School

Several of the artists who settled in Texas became known as the "Texas Bluebonnet School," because they looked to their outdoor environment for inspiration, and they became famous for their paintings of Texas landscapes and fields carpeted with bluebonnets. Some of the Texas bluebonnet painters were Robert Onderdonk (1852–1917), Julian Onderdonk (1882–1922), José Arpa (1868–1952), Dawson Dawson-Watson (1864–1939), and Porfirio Salinas (1910–1973). Rather than paint studio reproductions of much-admired European scenery, their paintings celebrated the physical features of their adopted region. Their work began to establish pride of place for Southwesterners. The body of work of the Texas bluebonnet painters culminated in the Texas Wildflower Competitive Exhibitions of 1927–1929.

Regionalism and Romanticism of People: Tom Lea and Peter Hurd

At the beginning of the twentieth century, the American people became aware that opportunities to achieve economic success should and could be made available to all through education and hard work. However, these hopes were dashed with the stock market crash in 1929. The Southwest was doubly hit in the 1930s; both the Great Depression and the Dust Bowl brought economic misery to its inhabitants. The promise implied by the phrase "the American Dream"—coined in 1931 by James Truslow Adams to laud all things uniquely American, egalitarian, and devoid of European pretensions to class and status—seemed to elude everyone.

But from out of the cauldron of the social unrest that resulted emerged regional movements in art all across the country. In the long run, regional art, charged implicitly with the mission of representing the physical and cultural character of a locality, could not help but eventually became fused with social critique.

The rise of regional art in the 1930s and 1940s was fostered by the implementation in 1933 of President Franklin Roosevelt's federal Public Works of Art Project (PWAP), part of the constellation of Works Progress Administration (WPA) relief programs. To help provide economic relief to artists, the federal government commissioned them to bring art into the everyday life of people. One way this was done was to offer artists competitive opportunities to submit designs for painting murals in federal, state, and community buildings. Artists who needed to earn a living and wanted to secure a mural commission had to focus on using art to meet the preferences of the people—their audience—rather than merely to satisfy themselves. Their mission for art thus became externally rather than internally directed. The process of conceiving mural designs for submission opened up a dialogue about the role art plays in celebrating and fostering a sense of identity among people anchored to a local place. Artists further discussed what it means to be an American within the context of the cultural traditions and community values and how to express that visually.

Tom Lea (1907–2001) of El Paso, Texas, and Peter Hurd (1904–1984) of San Patricio, New Mexico, are regarded by some as the first purists of the regional tradition, partly because they were among the first Southwest regional painters who were, aside from Native Americans, actually *born* in the Southwest. Lea and Hurd saw the Southwest through eyes unclouded by romanticism but nevertheless with hearts filled with love for their region. They represent the antithesis of the romance of the Taos Society of Artists and the painterly brushwork and brilliant color palette of the Texas Bluebonnet School. By contrast, Lea and Hurd's view of the region is very American, in terms of their starkly realistic and simple portrayals, which may have been shaped by the fact that both Lea and Hurd were from pioneering families who had witnessed the hardship of carving out a life on the Western frontier. Both men developed art styles that are crisp and strongly linear, defining form through the use of contour lines and edges, as opposed to painterly in execution. In their work, color tones tend to contrast and shift abruptly, although Hurd's color palette generally is more subdued than Lea's. Hurd frequently used water-based tempera paint, which cannot be applied in translucent layers that trap light and glow with brilliance; thus, his color palette in some ways more accurately reflects those of West Texas and Eastern New Mexico, lands of little rain where colors are often sun-bleached by summer's end.

Lea and Hurd, among other noted regional artists, both painted murals for the United States post offices and federal courthouses of Texas, as part of the WPA program. Lea's *Pass to the North* mural, painted for the El Paso courthouse in 1938, honors the arrival in 1598 of the first European colonist to the Southwest, Spaniard Juan de Oñate. Lea portrayed all of the character "types" that forged the history of the area: two Native Americans, a Spanish conquistador, a Franciscan friar, a Mexican gentleman, a mountain man, a Texas revolutionary, a pioneer couple, a cowboy on horseback, a prospector with a pickax, and a lawman. All stand together along the same baseline as though a frieze and share as a common background a burnt umber landscape of a mountain range and basin region, with a steely blue sky giving rise to rain. As befits an artist's concern for visual accuracy, Lea obtained authentic costume pieces for each character portrayed in the mural to be able to render them accurately.

Hurd, born in Roswell, New Mexico, accepted commissions to paint murals in the post offices of Big Spring and Dallas, Texas, and Almagordo, New Mexico. His murals depict Southwestern life and history and exude the quality of the light and atmosphere of the area. Hurd's achievements as a regional artist brought him to the attention of William Curry and Francis Holden of Lubbock, Texas, who had been seeking an artist to paint a great fresco mural in the entry hall of the West Texas Museum building on the campus of Texas Tech University. Hurd executed the huge mural between 1953 and 1954.

In it he depicted sixteen pioneers from all walks of life who had helped to establish a city and its cultural institutions on the High Plains. As in a Gothic painting, each of the pioneers is shown standing in a full frontal pose, wearing the clothing and carrying tools of their trade. They are placed in the localized geography of the region, against the background of an unbroken horizon. The vast sky above and behind them shows the passage of the sun moving across the High Plains from sunrise to the end of the day, amidst the cloud formations of changing weather. Acknowledging the particular challenges that people faced in a region that receives less than seventeen inches of rainfall a year, Hurd depicted references to water in the mural—a windmill by a stock tank, an irrigation ditch, a well, and a thunderstorm off the caprock—alluding to the mystery and miracle of rainwater in a dry country and implying that in such a land, the presence of life-giving water was itself a subject worthy of art. Paul Horgan, a friend of Hurd's, explained the theme of the mural as the connection forged between land—the seemingly empty

Peter Hurd. *Pioneer Mural* (1953–1954). Courtesy of Joey Hernandez for Office of News and Publications, Texas Tech University.

High Plains space—and humankind. He noted that the figures stand squarely within the plains world that sweeps around them.

Regionalism and Social Realism: The Dallas Nine or Lone Star Regionalists

In Texas, the rise of regionalism, coalesced in the 1930s and 1940s when a group of painters, printmakers, and sculptors in the north central region of Texas came together to share their passion for art, their love for the Southwest, and to learn and benefit from association with one another. Thus came the formation of the Dallas Nine, or Lone Star Regionalists. The original impetus that brought the artists together: their desire to win the commission to decorate the walls of the Hall of State for the 1936 Texas Centennial Exposition, which was to be celebrated at Fair Park in Dallas. Of the original group of nine artists who joined together in this quest, those who later achieved the greatest notoriety were Williamson Gerald "Jerry" Bywaters (1906–1989), Thomas M. Stell, Jr. (1898–1981), Otis M. Dozier (1904–1987), Alexandre Hogue (1898–1994), and Everett Spruce (1908–). Their bid was unsuccessful. However, Bywaters, Stell, and Dozier successfully attained New Deal WPA commissions to paint murals throughout federal, state, and other public buildings in Texas. Their work appears today in Dallas, Paris, Trinity, Quanah, Graham, Farmersville, Houston, Corsicana, Longview, Teague, Fredericksburg, and Giddings. This suggests the breadth and depth of the artists' commitment to using art as a visual voice for telling the story of a region's people and to support themselves, as well.

Bywaters served as a pivotal leader, spokesperson, and conscience for the group through his positions as an art critic for the *Dallas Morning News* (1933–1939), director for the Dallas Museum of Fine Arts (1943–1964), and instructor of art history at Southern Methodist University (1943–1971). Under his guidance, and due to the economic circumstances that brought little relief to people until the outbreak of World War II, the Lone Star Regionalists gradually shifted their emphasis in subject matter. Their original arm had been to highlight and celebrate the land, wildlife, and people of the Southwest; eventually, their art became a tool used for social and political critique. For example, in the early 1930s, Hogue began a series of Dust Bowl paintings that starkly showed the desolation of erosion incurred by overgrazing and poor farming practices ill-suited to the Southwest region. Dozier painted images of ruined farmers and dispossessed families. The Lone Star Regionalists had absorbed the influence of the contemporary Mexican mural painters Diego Rivera (1886–1957) and José Clemente Orozco (1883–1949), who also used art to promote social and political conscience.

Alexandre Hogue. *Dust Bowl* (1933). © Smithsonian American Art Museum, Washington, DC/Art Resource, NY.

Similar to Lea and Hurd, the Dallas Nine adopted an earth-colored palette that mirrored the hues of the region and used a crisp, hard-edged style that seemed suited to art placed in the service of visual documentation and communication rather than sensuous pleasure. Although Modernism, with its emphasis on abstraction, had begun to influence them, most of this group of artists maintained a basic adherence to Realism. Their intent was to communicate content to an audience, so they did not want the message obscured by an overemphasis on innovative design that might only serve to obscure the message and bewilder the viewer.

Once World War II began, oppressed artists from Europe fleeing the tyranny of dictatorial governments began to arrive on the shores of America, bringing with them their training in Modernism. Once these artists were ensconced in leading positions in art schools throughout the United States, and the art world capital shifted from Paris, France, to New York City, the primacy of Regionalism as an art movement began to fade as it was supplanted by Abstract Expressionism. It did not resurface as a major force until the 1960s, when once again art was called upon to serve as a narrative of the people.

Syncretism

Contemporary art associated with the Southwest region uses strikingly different forms to emphasize the physical geography; for example, consider the neon light signs of Las Vegas, Nevada, and the earth art sited in all four states of the region. The rise of political consciousness among the formerly disenfranchised Native American and Hispanic peoples of the Southwest has, in turn, given rise to art that sometimes causes discomfort in its audience. Using art as a visual form of sociopolitical critique about the tensions enacted between the land and people of the region continues the Dallas Nine's traditions to this day.

Physical Geography: Light and Space

Light: Neon Signs, Las Vegas, Nevada

Travelers' guides note that the neon sign is the dominant icon of Las Vegas. A French inventor, Georges Claude (1870–1960), discovered in 1910 that an electric current passing through a glass tube of neon gas emitted a powerful, shimmering light. When, in 1931, the Nevada legislature legalized gambling and a six-weeks-only residency requirement for obtaining divorces, tourism boomed. In 1935 the completion of the Hoover Dam provided cheap electricity for the nearby city of Las Vegas. In the decades that followed, neon signs in Las Vegas proliferated, and the craft of neon signs assumed the status of art. Distinctive neon signs became signature logos for Las Vegas hotels, casinos, and restaurants. Collectively, they set one corner of the urban landscape of the Southwest ablaze with nighttime illumination as bright as the brilliant sunshine of the day. After the 1950s the trend in Las Vegas to tone down all things ostentatious to attract more family-oriented business resulted in removal of many neon signs along the Strip of Las Vegas Boulevard and in Glitter Gulch downtown on Fremont Street. However, in the 1990s neon-sign enthusiasts began to promote the idea of preserving the city's neon signs as its art legacy. They founded the Neon Museum, which is dedicated to acquiring old Las Vegas signs, refurbishing them, and putting them on display for Las Vegas visitors and residents to enjoy. Today, many of the neon facades belonging to some of the city's oldest casinos are on display there.

Space: Land Art

The Southwest contained the last lands of the American frontier and the last of the contiguous states admitted to the union (New Mexico and Arizona). Undeveloped tracts of this land attracted the attention and grandiose visions of earth artists of the 1960s. Earth artists create art works to invite contemplation of the natural forces that act upon the environment and the interaction of human beings within it. Walter de Maria's (1935–) 1980 creation, *The Lightening Field*, featured four hundred ten-meter-high stainless-steel poles that were placed in one square mile on a flat field in New Mexico to attract electricity from the sky. Another example is the work of James Turrell (1943–), who has, since the 1970s, been creating a celestial observatory out of an extinct volcanic cinder cone north of Flagstaff, Arizona. Inspired by the Hopi Indians' cosmogony, his visionary idea is to carve out of the cone various chambers that will be illuminated by natural light traveling through passageways. In addition, Michael Heizer (1944–) has been engaged since 1970 in carving an earthwork he calls *City* out of the floor of a central Nevada desert. It is a monumental structure the size, layout, and scale of which were inspired by the ancient ruins of Chichén Itzá, an Olmec ceremonial complex in the Yucatán. Heizer's goal is for his work to reflect the grandeur of ancient Mesoamerican cities.

Other Regional Artists

Native American: Roxanne Swentzell

The descendant of a long line of Pueblo women who made pottery, Roxanne Swentzell (1962–) is famous for her life-size clay figurines. Swentzell was born in

Santa Clara Pueblo, New Mexico, and she developed an interest in constructing clay effigy figurines like those created by the nearby Cochiti Pueblo women, who in generations past had constructed clay effigy figurines based on kachina characters and created caricatures of Spanish padres and Anglo-American colonists. Inspired by the cosmology of the ancient Pueblos, and aware of the social and political problems that today's Pueblos face in the attempt to interface with two worlds, she creates life-size clay figures who appear to be grappling with the dilemma of adjusting to two societies that adhere to such different values—Native American and Anglo-American. Their faces are often modeled with perplexed and grave expressions, as though contemplating the metaphysical dilemma of their situation.

Hispanic: Luis Jimenez

Emerging out of the barrios of El Paso, Texas, and funneled through the fine-arts traditions at the University of Texas, Austin, Luis Jimenez (1940–) rode the crest of the wave of sociopolitical awareness that crashed on the beaches of American consciousness in the 1960s. The incoming tide of the civil-rights movement swept across the country and brought with it the press for equal rights for all those previously disenfranchised by dominant Anglo-American society. Unlike many artists of the time, however, Jimenez deftly managed to drive home ironic commentary regarding ethnic and cultural heritage with humor and irony rather than outrage. With his innovative and monumental fiberglass outdoor sculptures, he fused Mesoamerican myth, Hispanic folk-art idioms, icons of the Anglo-American West, the Pop Art style, and the noble fine-arts traditions of public-monument sculpture, leaving as a legacy to the Southwest some of its most famous and original regional art works created in the twentieth century. Jimenez placed the men and women of his own ethnic heritage onto his sculptural pedestals, accompanied by symbols of the Southwest, such as prickly pear, cow skulls, coyotes, or armadillos. Sometimes satirical, sometimes ennobling, Jimenez's sculptures have showcased characters both heroic and humble, mythic and mundane, that inhabit the landscape of American visual culture in the Southwest: the Mesoamerican Aztec lord of the sky and queen of the earth, illegal immigrants making a border crossing in the style of Jesus and St. Christopher, cowboys and Indians, sodbusters and steelworkers, and most famously of all, the Mexican vaquero.

Native and African American: James C. Watkins

Of Native American and African American ancestry by way of Kentucky and Alabama, James C. Watkins' (1951–) art represents the syncretic experience of the new generations of Southwest regional artists. Trained in the art departments of Kansas City Art Institute and Indiana University, Watkins developed as a ceramicist and was transplanted to the Southwest in 1979. For over twenty years he has honed in his artwork a sensibility shaped explicitly by the region's geography. The platters, vessels, cauldrons, and lidded stoneware jars he has created, such as the ones in his Painted Desert and Rattlesnake Canyon series of ceramic works, echo glaze, in their color, form, and design the flowers, clay and sandstone earth, azure sky, and fiery sunsets around him. Like the Native American Pueblos, Watkins' work originates in the physical geography of the Southwest region—the very dirt of the land itself.

As seen in ancient Mesoamerican culture, Watkins' work incorporates cosmic symbols that represent a balance or a unification achieved between the forces of the sky and earth—all the universe—fused as one whole. This is reflected in combinations of bird and serpent motifs sculpted into his work. Like O'Keeffe, Watkins' identity as a regional artist is based on his sense of spiritual connection between his presence in a very unique land and the land's effect on him.

CONCLUSION

The main reason that the Southwest today is blessed with invigorated regional art derives in no small way from its physical geography as a borderland and the enriched confluence in cultural geography that resulted. Additionally, much of its Native American population survived the arrival of the Europeans in the nineteenth century. The foundation laid by people of diverse cultural backgrounds—those of Native American, Hispanic, or Anglo-American origins—provided the structure from which regional art of the Southwest evolved in the twentieth century. The formation of this base and the evolution in the arts that followed are a tribute not only to the resilience and diligence of the artists themselves but also because of those who worked hard to help save, support, and promote their art.

Throughout all the brilliantly illuminated lands of the Southwest, artists have always experienced an epiphany in their encounter with the majestic terrain, the sense of endless space, and dazzling light. In the midst of such beauty that lies within the boundless geographical and cultural borderlands, the possibilities for the human creative spirit seem endless.

RESOURCE GUIDE

Printed Sources

Bresenhan, Karoline Patterson, and Nancy O'Bryant Puentes. *Lone Stars, Volume I: A Legacy of Texas Quilts, 1836–1936*. Austin: University of Texas Press, 1986.

———. *Lone Stars, Volume II: A Legacy of Texas Quilts, 1936–1986*. Austin: University of Texas Press, 1990.

Bywaters, Jerry. *Seventy-Five Years of Art in Dallas: The History of the Dallas Art Association and the Dallas Museum of Fine Arts*. Dallas: Dallas Museum of Fine Arts, 1978.

Craver, Rebecca, and Adair Margo, eds. *Tom Lea: An Oral History*. El Paso: Texas Western Press, 1995.

Eldredge, Charles C., Julie Schimmel, and William H. Truettner. *Art in New Mexico 1900–1945: Paths to Taos and Santa Fe*. Washington, DC: Smithsonian Institution Press, 1988.

Giffords, Gloria Fraser. *Mexican Folk Retablos*. Albuquerque: University of New Mexico Press, 1974.

Goetzmann, William H., and William N. Goetzmann. *The West of the Imagination*. New York: Norton, 1986.

Graham, Joe S., ed. *Hecho En Tejas: Texas-Mexican Folk Arts and Crafts*. Denton: University of North Texas Press, 1991.

Hill, Tom, and Richard W. Hill Sr., eds. *Creation's Journey: Native American Identity and Belief*. Washington, DC: Smithsonian Institution Press in assoc. with the National Museum of the American Indian, Smithsonian Institution, 1994.

Hopper, Kippra D. *A Meditation of Fire: The Art of James C. Watkins*. Lubbock: Texas Tech University Press, 1999.

Horgan, Paul. *Peter Hurd: A Portrait Sketch from Life*. Austin: University of Texas Press, 1965.

Little, Carol Morris. *Outdoor Sculpture in Texas*. Austin: University of Texas Press, 1996.

Malotki, Ekkehart. *Kokopelli: The Making of an Icon*. Lincoln: University of Nebraska Press, 2000.

Newcomb, W. W., Jr. *The Rock Art of Texas Indians*. Austin: University of Texas Press, 1967.

O'Keeffe, Georgia. *Georgia O'Keeffe*. New York: Penguin Books, 1976.

Peterson, Susan. *Pottery by American Indian Women: The Legacy of Generations*. New York: Abbeville Press, 1997.

Reaugh, Frank. *Frank Reaugh: Painter to the Longhorns*. College Station: Texas A&M University Press, 1985.

Reaves, William E., Jr. *Texas Art and a Wildcatter's Dream: Edgar B. Davis and the San Antonio Art League*. College Station: Texas A&M University Press, 1998.

Spivey, Richard L. *The Legacy of Maria Poveka Martinez*. Santa Fe: Museum of New Mexico Press, 2003.

Stewart, Rick. *Lone Star Regionalism: The Dallas Nine and Their Circle*. Austin: Texas Monthly Press, 1985.

Tyler, Ron. *Visions of America: Pioneer Artists in a New Land*. London: Thames and Hudson, 1983.

Web Sites

Amon Carter Museum Online Photograph Collection. *Erwin E. Smith: Cowboy Photographer*.
http://www.cartermuseum.org/collections/smith/collection.php

Century Illustrated Monthly Magazine, April 1889. *Frederic Remington, A Scout with the Buffalo Soldiers*.
http://www.pchswi.org/oldwest/buffalosoldiers.html

Flury and Company. *Edward Curtis Gallery*.
http://www.fluryco.com/photos/southwest1.htm

Houghton Mifflin. *Encyclopedia of North American Indians: Art, Visual (to 1960)*.
http://college.hmco.com/history/readerscomp/naind/html/na_002900_artvisual.htm

Houghton Mifflin. *Encyclopedia of North American Indians. Art, Contemporary (since 1960)*.
http://college.hmco.com/history/readerscomp/naind/html/na_003000_artscontempo.htm

Klett, Mark. *Third View: A Rephotographic Survey of the American West*.
http://thirdview.org/3v/home/index.html

Peterson, Susan. *Women Artists of the American West: Pottery by American Indian Women: The Legacy of Generations: the Avant Garde Roxanne Swentzell*.
http://www.sla.purdue.du/WAAW/Peterson/Swentzell.html

Treasured Artworks at the Texas Capitol. *Visual Art*.
http://www.tfaoi.com/aa/1aa/1aa4c.htm

Festivals

Santa Fe Indian Market, Santa Fe, New Mexico

Held in August every year since 1922, it is the largest art market of its kind in the United States, providing a venue for Native American artists from more than eighty federally recognized tribes to display and sell their artwork to crowds of up to 70,000 collectors.

http://www.swaia.org/index_d.php

Spanish Colonial Arts Society's Spanish Market, Santa Fe, New Mexico

Held in July and December each year, it is the oldest and largest exhibition and sale of regional Spanish colonial art forms in the United States.

http://www.spanishmarket.org/

Museums

Texas

Amarillo Museum of Art, Amarillo
http://www.amarilloart.org/

Amon Carter Museum, Fort Worth
http://www.cartermuseum.org/

Blanton Museum of Art at the University of Texas, Austin
http://www.blantonmuseum.org/

Dallas Museum of Art, Dallas
http://www.dm-art.org/

Museum of Fine Arts, Houston
http://mfah.org/

Museum of Texas Tech University
http://www.depts.ttu.edu/museumttu/about.html#main

Panhandle-Plains Historical Museum, Canyon
http://www.panhandleplains.org/

San Antonio Art League Museum, San Antonio
http://saalm.org/about.html

San Antonio Museum of Art, San Antonio
http://www.sa-museum.org/

Sid Richardson Collection of Western Art, Fort Worth
http://www.sidrmuseum.org/

Stark Museum of Art, Orange
http://www.starkmuseum.org/

Texas Capitol Historic Art Collection
http://www.tfaoi.com/aa/1aa/1aa4.htm

Witte Museum, San Antonio
http://www.wittemuseum.org/

New Mexico

Blumenschein Home and Museum
http://www.taoshistoricmuseums.com/blumenschein.html

Georgia O'Keeffe Museum, Santa Fe
http://www.okeeffemuseum.org/indexflash.php

Harwood Museum at the University of New Mexico, Taos
http://www.laplaza.org/art/harwood/

Millicent Rogers Museum of Northern New Mexico, Taos
http://www.millicentrogers.org/

Museum of New Mexico, Santa Fe
http://www.museumofnewmexico.org/home.html

Taos Art Museum, Taos
http://www.taosnet.com/~simpson/tam/index.html

Wheelwright Museum of the American Indian, Santa Fe
http://www.wheelwright.org/

Arizona

Arizona State University Art Museum, Tempe
http://asuartmuseum.asu.edu/

Heard Museum, Phoenix
http://www.heard.org/

Museum of Northern Arizona, Flagstaff
http://www.musnaz.org/

Northern Arizona University Art Museum and Galleries, Flagstaff
http://www.artcom.com/museums/nv/mr/86011-60.htm

Phoenix Art Museum, Phoenix
http://www.phxart.org/

University of Arizona, Arizona State Museum, Tucson
http://www.statemuseum.arizona.edu/

University of Arizona Museum of Art, Tucson
http://artmuseum.arizona.edu/

Nevada

Neon Museum, Las Vegas
http://www.neonmuseum.org/pages/2/index.htm

Nevada Museum of Art, Reno
http://www.nevadaart.org/

Nevada State Museum and Historical Society, Las Vegas
http://dmla.clan.lib.nv.us/docs/museums/lv/vegas.htm

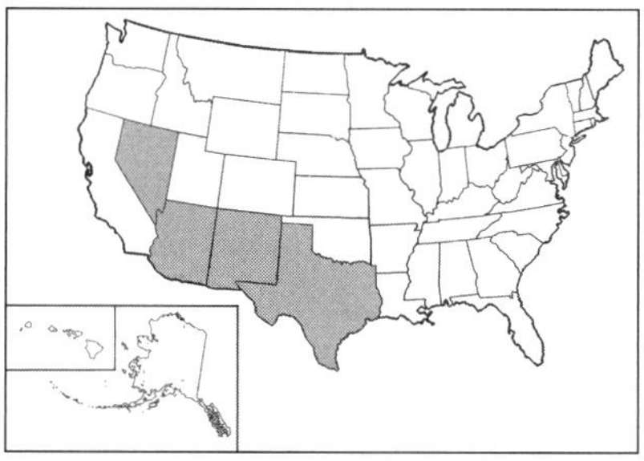

ECOLOGY AND ENVIRONMENT

Benjamin Johnson

In perhaps no other part of the United States is the natural environment more associated with regional identity than in the Southwest. Novelists and essayists write of the stillness and enormity of its vast deserts, artists struggle to capture the hues of its exposed rock, the camera records the passage of humans through this vast landscape. For many, the Southwest is a region defined by its environment's impact on humans. The author D. H. Lawrence wrote that his time in the Southwest "was the greatest experience from the outside world that I have ever had. It certainly changed me forever. . . . The moment I saw the brilliant, proud morning shine high up over the deserts of Santa Fe, something stood still in my soul, and I started to attend. . . . In the magnificent fierce morning of New Mexico one sprang awake, a new part of the soul woke up suddenly, and the old world gave way to a new."[1]

Indeed, from the Saguaro cactus on the license plates of today's Arizona SUVs, back to the cliff dwellings of the vanished Anasazi, the human and environmental histories of the Southwest have been virtually inseparable. The region's environment has clearly marked its inhabitants: for centuries its aridity limited the crops that could be grown and increased the relative value of raising stock, deeply marking both the area's cuisine and economy; the stark desert beauty now draws millions of tourists from all over the world; and during the cold war, federal officials saw the region's lightly populated expanses as a critical asset for the development of the nation's atomic weapons program.

Conversely, the human cultures of the region have left their own mark on the land. The horses, sheep, and cattle brought by the Spanish centuries ago became essential to the economies and cultures of native peoples, Hispanic frontiersmen, and Anglo-Americans alike. These centuries of grazing have transformed the landscape in ways that few contemporary Southwesterners are even aware of, allowing new grass and weed species to thrive, expanding the range of some native plants, and drastically curtailing that of others. Dams and reservoirs have allowed for the

OREGON
IDAHO
Humboldt River
Pyramid Lake
NEVADA
Reno
Virginia City
Carson City
Lake Tahoe
Great Basin
Walker Lake
UTAH
Rocky Mountains
COLORADO
Nevada Test Site
Lake Meade
Colorado
Grand Canyon Natíl Park
San Juan
Los Alamos
Taos
Santa Fe
Canadian
CALIFORNIA
Las Vegas
Paradise
Hoover Dam
San Francisco Mts.
Little Colorado
Chaco Canyon
Gallup
Grants
Amarillo
OKLAHOMA
Flagstaff
Bullhead City
Lake Havasu City
Verde
ARIZONA
Rio Grande
Albuquerque
NEW MEXICO
Red
ARKANSAS
Lubbock
Phoenix
Salt
Gila
Black
Roswell
Alamogordo
Sonoran Desert
Dallas
Yuma
Saguaro Natíl Park
Tucson
Las Cruces
Carlsbad
Midland
Abilene
Fort Worth
Tyler
Sierra Vista
El Paso
Guadalupe Mtns. Natíl Park
Pecos
Colorado
Waco
LOUISIANA
Chihuahuan Desert
TEXAS
Brazos
Trinity
Sabine
Austin
MEXICO
Houston
Port Arthur
Nueces
San Antonio
Big Bend Natíl Park
Galveston
Frio
Victoria
Laredo
Corpus Christi
GULF OF MEXICO
McAllen
Rio Grande Valley
Brownsville

planting of much land that was once not arable, as well as for the rise of cities too large for local water supplies alone to support. Environmental bureaucracies such as the U.S. Forest Service and Bureau of Land Management now administer much of the area's forests and deserts, and their decisions have, since the early twentieth century, shaped the landscape in often unpredictable ways.

From pre-Columbian times to the early twenty-first century, human and natural history have evolved in tandem to create the distinct region that we now recognize as the Southwest. Although much of the region is far removed from the centers of national power, it has nonetheless been a critical site for the wider relationship between humans and nature in the United States.

THE LAY OF THE LAND

The Desert

For many outsiders and natives alike, the environment of the Southwest is defined both by what is there and what is not. Mountains and large hills, whether the shorter ranges and basins in West Texas or the much larger and higher ridges of New Mexico, Arizona, and Nevada, are the most prominent geological features of the landscape. What is clearly in short supply over most of the region is water. The areas that are now the states of Texas, New Mexico, Arizona, and Nevada contain some of the continent's largest expanses of desert. Based on dominant plant communities, ecologists have identified four distinct desert ecosystems, three of which encompass most of the Southwest. The Chihuahuan desert covers West Texas and most of the nonmountainous portions of New Mexico, stretching down into the Mexican state whence it derives its name. Most of southwestern Arizona falls within the Sonoran desert, which also encompasses much of Baja California and the western portion of Sonora. Virtually all of Nevada is part of the much cooler desert of the Great Basin. The continent's fourth discrete desert, the Mojave, is found on the border of the Southwest, in California.

Those travelers accustomed to wooded and well-watered landscapes—including the Europeans and Euro-Americans who produced many of the first written descriptions of the Southwest—perceived little difference between these deserts. In fact, to the trained eye or to the deeply rooted native they are quite distinct. Rainfall patterns, altitudes, and salt concentrations differentiate these deserts. In the Chihuahuan desert, shrubs such as creosote, mesquite, and ocotillo depend on the summer to deliver most of the year's rain, which is as little as three inches in the lower areas and as much as sixteen in more elevated sites. This pattern provides a more generous growing season than do the other deserts. Numerous species of cacti, yucca, and agave provide this landscape with much of its distinct appearance. The Sonoran desert receives less rain—an average of as little as two inches, and fourteen at the most. Its rainfall is also less regular than that of the Chihuahuan desert, and ecologists' records indicate that large areas of this desert have gone for several years with no rain at all. Here the cacti with large water-storage capabilities, usually in the form of a barrel shape, comprise about half of all plants. The Saguaro (*Carnegiea gigantea*) is the most prominent of these, serving for some as a symbol of the nation's western deserts, though it often makes appearances in films and novels in regions in which it does not actually grow. The Great Basin desert of Nevada is similarly arid but significantly colder and higher than the others. Here sagebrush and shad scale dominate the landscape, often in large, nearly uniform stands. Juniper infiltrates the landscape at higher elevations, generally above 6,000 ft. Because the Great Basin does not drain to the sea, salt concentrations also exert a significant influence. Specialized plants, such as saltbush, supplant the relatively salt-intolerant sagebrush in highly saline areas.

More than Desert Land

Piney woods dominate the eastern edge of the region. Like the culture and economy of East Texas of the last century and a half, this ecosystem is more a part of the South than of the Southwest. Here rainfall is abundant, more than enough to support thick forests dominated by longleaf pines, white oak, and (in the wetter bottomlands), cypress. To the west, however, annual rainfall gradually tapers off, with attendant vegetation changes. A traveler heading in that direction would see that trees become shorter and less dense in the approach to present-day Dallas and then would observe that the trees give way to a mix of tall-grass prairie at higher elevations and to light forest in the bottomlands.

The prairie of central Texas stretches far down to the southern portion of the state, and before extensive European settlement and the reduction in fires that followed, it probably reached significantly farther east. Because average rainfall declines from west to east, the shorter grass species gradually become more common. (After the 100th meridian, average annual precipitation drops below twenty inches a year, which is the level needed to grow most crops without benefit of irrigation). After travers-

Desert Mammals

Although the most recognizable aspects of the Southwest's deserts are their distinctive shrub and cactus species, they also contain a remarkable set of mammals, including the kangaroo rat, the kit fox, woodrats, and numerous species of mice and voles. The three deserts of the Southwest offer their organisms a daunting combination of extreme heat, frequent temperature fluctuations, little water, and a shortage of edible vegetation. In deserts across the world, mammals have evolved similar features and behaviors to meet these challenges. The small mammals of the Sonoran desert and the deserts of Argentina, for example, share more characteristics in common with each other than with their nearby woodland relatives, with which they are evolutionarily closer.

In terms of physiology, desert mammals have adapted similar body shapes and kidney systems in order to keep water loss at a minimum. Their kidneys can store high salt concentrations, allowing them to use even extremely salty water, from desert streams or from plants, seeds, or animal prey. Many of these rodents' kidneys are so efficient in recapturing water that they excrete a paste rather than liquid urine. One animal, the chisel-tooth kangaroo rat, has evolved a body that allows it to consume even the saltbush plants of the Great Basin desert. The plants store massive amounts of salt in special cells on the surfaces of their leaves, thereby allowing them to retain water. This mechanism also protects against predation, as would-be herbivores spend more water digesting the salt on the plant than they gain from eating it. The chisel-tooth kangaroo rat, however, has chisel-shaped teeth that it uses to scrape the salt-filled cells off, leaving behind the moist parts of the leaf.[2]

Distinctive behaviors and foraging habits also help meet the challenges of desert life. Most desert mammals are nocturnal, which may account for why so few are well known to the general public. The regular kangaroo rat, whose teeth come to a sharp point effective at cracking open tough desert seeds, has an amazingly creative way of coaxing water from the desert. In fact, it has no need at all of standing water. This tiny rat, which weighs, on average, two to five ounces, cleverly uses seeds for both food and drink. Using its forefeet to separate miniscule seeds from sand, the creature deposits them in burrows for consumption later. It seals the openings in the heat of the day, increasing the burrow's humidity with its breath. This humidity is absorbed by the seeds and returned to the rat when the seeds are consumed.[3]

ing the anomalous cross-timbers, two strips of stunted oak forests that run north-south on either side of Fort Worth, Texas, our fictitious traveler would travel through more short-grass prairie and then see the landscape gradually shade into the Chihuahuan desert. However, the area of this transition has changed significantly in the last few centuries.

Although the Southwest is more arid than the continent as a whole, some of its most dramatic natural landmarks owe their creation to the action of water. The regular flow and the spring surges of rivers such as the Colorado, Rio Grande, Red, and Brazos have, for millenia, combined with continental uplift to create canyons, some extremely deep. The Grand Canyon, carved by the Colorado River in what is now northeastern Arizona, is the largest and most widely known. The sublime view from the rim and the mile-high drop to the river have made it a major national tourist destination since the late nineteenth century and more recently a place visited by international tourists.

The mountain ranges, which lie surrounded by deserts as if they were islands, are significantly cooler and moister than the deserts. Average summer temperatures decline three to four degrees Fahrenheit for each thousand-foot rise, with the result that frost-free periods are much shorter as elevation increases. More precipitation falls on mountains than in deserts of the same latitude, and the water available to plants is even greater in the draws and canyons that siphon it downward. As a result, vegetation changes with elevation and water availability, sometimes quite dramatically. Low shrubs and grasslands, often interspersed with oak, cover the lower foothills, though deciduous woodland can dominate better-watered stream courses. At higher elevations, juniper and piñon form coniferous forests, which are often nearly the only vegetation in the lower ranges of the Great Basin and which can be found interspersed with more shrubs and grasses in the rest of the Southwest. Higher still, Douglas fir and Ponderosa pine are the dominant species, although in places where fires have not been totally suppressed and overgrazing has not gone on unchecked, a thick cover of grass grows beneath them.[4]

The silence of vast deserts and the seeming timelessness of the mountains that divide them present a facade of unchanging nature. But in fact the environment of this part of North America has always been in flux, sometimes changing imperceptibly over centuries, but also dramatically from year to year. As recently as 15,000 years ago, glaciers covered large portions of what are now New Mexico and Arizona. The present landscape still bears the marks of past eras of glaciation. Many of the shallow lakebeds with no outlets, for example, are remnants of an enormous lake that covered thousands of square miles of what are now New Mexico, Texas, and Chihuahua at a period of heavy glaciation about 100,000 years ago. Long-term changes in precipitation have also wrought dramatic changes in vegetation cover. Pollen grains that remain trapped in pond sediments indicate that trees and shrubs used to dominate areas that are now grasslands or deserts, suggesting that much of the Southwest was once cooler and wetter. Isolated populations of maples deep in canyons and midway up mountain slopes bear characteristics that are a cross between eastern sugar maple and western bigtooth maple, hinting that sugar maples once spread westward and interbred with their larger western cousins.[5] By combining pollen sediments and sand-dune data, scholars have concluded that the region has gone through several long-term oscillations of temperature and moisture since the last glacial period. Around 7,500 years ago the Southern Plains entered one of their driest periods, one from which bison remains are extremely scarce, suggesting a widespread ecological reshuffling.[6]

Not all change is so gradual. Precipitation can vary dramatically between only centuries, decades or years. In 1851, for example, the U.S. surveyor of the boundary line with Mexico reported that a teamster drove mules in the bed of the Rio Grande for much of the distance between Presidio and El Paso, encountering only isolated pools of water. A person attempting the same feat in 1901 or 1978 would have had to contend with a raging torrent nearly a half-mile wide.[7] Droughts in the 1820s, 1850s, and 1860s, concluded paleoclimatologist, Connie Woodhouse, "may well have exceeded the severity of twentieth-century Southern Plains droughts" such as the well-known Dust Bowl.[8]

The flora and fauna are similarly dynamic. The armadillo, surely an iconic animal in Texas and the rest of the Southwest, has lived within the boundaries of the Lone Star State for a relatively brief 3,000 years. In the 1850s they were confined to a narrow strip along the Mexican border in southern Texas, but they had expanded their range northward to Austin by the twentieth century and into Oklahoma by the early 1950s.[9] Scores of less noticeable fish, bird, and small mammalian species have gone extinct in small mountain valleys or expanded into nearby areas. Rather than a changeless stage upon which the drama of human history is enacted, then, nature in the Southwest has itself always been changing, sometimes as the product of human actions, but at other times of its own accord.

ENVIRONMENT AND THE MAKING OF THE PRE-COLUMBIAN SOUTHWEST

One of the most important species in the contemporary Southwest arrived in the region after the last major ice age, probably between 10,000 and 11,000 years ago. *Homo sapiens* left evidence of their presence in the form of their own remains, campsites, trash heaps, and spear points. The large animals of the continent—many of which soon became extinct—were the most important food supply for these people. A distinctive type of fluted spear point was first discovered in 1932 near Clovis, New Mexico, by professional archaeologists. The point and the culture that used it both bear the name of the town.

Other resources besides large game were available to these people, even in the comparatively unproductive arid stretches of the Southwest. One of the continent's most important subsistence traditions, what has been called "Desert Culture," first developed some 10,000 years ago in the Great Basin. Here people formed small bands that constantly circulated within relatively fixed territories, taking seasonal advantage of a range of resources such as yucca, grass seeds, acorns, berries, pine nuts, and the fish of mountain streams. A distinctive material culture of fiber baskets, nets, grinders, traps, stone knives, and hammers undergirded this subsistence practice. Eventually this culture and its technology spread throughout the region and to much of the continent, supplementing large-game hunting with its reliance on a variety of plants and animals.

Outside the Great Basin, particularly in the river valleys of what later became New Mexico and Arizona, a more moderate and moist climate allowed for the possibility of agriculture and the denser sedentary populations that it can support. Systematic farming in the Southwest seems to have begun around 3,000 years ago near today's southern Arizona–New Mexico border. Here a people later named the Mogollon by scholars used digging sticks to cultivate the classic trinity of corn, beans, and squash first developed by the peoples of central Mexico. Another agricultural civilization emerged to the west of the Mogollon, in the floodplains of the Salt and Gila rivers in southern Arizona. Here the Hohokam constructed large and sophisticated irrigation systems to distribute river water to their crops, even to fields as much as fifty ft. above the level of the rivers. This was a powerful, creative, and long-lived adaptation to Southwestern aridity. The Hohokam maintained thousands of miles of irrigation ditches, some of which were as deep as seven ft. and as wide as seventy-five. (It is no accident that early scholars dubbed them the canal builders.) At the height of their culture Hohokam territory was as large as 25,000 square miles, with perhaps hundreds of thousands of acres under active irrigation.[10] Around 700 C.E., in what is now northeastern New Mexico, the Anasazi culture developed dense populations reliant on high-yield varieties of corn watered by rain and stored runoff. Although less elaborate than the Hohokam irrigation network, Anasazi agriculture was productive enough to support remarkable population densities. As many as 15,000 Anasazi may have lived in Chaco Canyon, and one building housed enough people to make it "the largest apartment building in North America until New York City surpassed it in the nineteenth century."[11] There can be little doubt that Anasazi agriculture was well suited to Southwestern soils and climate: at the height of their civilization, the Anasazi inhabited an area larger than present-day California.

The plains of eastern New Mexico and western and northern Texas provided natives with a critical resource that their western neighbors lacked: the bison. Even before the introduction of the horse, the Indian peoples in this part of the Southwest were able to derive much of their subsistence from the buffalo and therefore could maintain significant numbers without developing intensive irrigation agriculture. Many of the Jumanos, who ranged the area of present-day West Texas, were nearly full-time hunters, adding deer, snake, fish, birds, and antelope to the massive bison. The Apache, Kiowas, and Tonkawas planted corns, beans, watermelon, and other plants in river bottoms, becoming semi-sedentary during much of the growing and harvesting season. The Caddo peoples to their east settled in river valleys, taking advantage of the water and fertility these offered to become skilled growers of corn, beans, and squash and of numerous plants native to the area. Much more sedentary than their bison-hunting neighbors, the Caddos supplemented their diet with the meat of deer, bison, and bear but lived year-round next to their fields. The abundance of the Texas coast helped meet the dietary needs of the Karankawan and Coahuiltecan peoples. Relying neither on agriculture nor extensive hunting of the bison, their hunting and gathering techniques resembled those of Great Basin peoples in their reliance on regular migration to take advantage of the seasonal abundance of dozens of plants and animals. Pecans, mesquite beans, and prickly-pear fruit were important plant foods, and peccary, rabbits, birds, and shellfish joined an occasional bison to provide meat.

The extent to which the native peoples of the Southwest altered their environment in pre-Columbian times has been the subject of a scholarly and occasionally popular debate that shows no sign of letting up. Although contemporary Southwesterners are likely to associate environmental change with such recent developments as urban sprawl, modern agriculture, and the nuclear program, it is likely that pre-Hispanic natives dramatically altered the landscape. There is a strong consensus that humans helped Southwestern grasslands expand into areas that later became forested. Human-caused fires stimulated the growth of berries and grasses preferred by game animals. They helped prairie grasses triumph over trees and woody shrubs, thereby expanding the effective range of the bison—and presumably their numbers along with it.[12] *Homo sapiens* may also have aided the bison by killing other carnivores and their primary herbivorous competitors. Many scientists believe that the Clovis culture is responsible for hunting the so-called megafauna of North America—mammoths, mastadons, indigenous horses, giant bison, a camel, a large groundsloth, tapir, the sabre-toothed tiger, the superpredatory short-faced bear, a species of giant beaver, and flat-head peccary—into extinction. This theory is hotly disputed, with its opponents pointing to climate change or disease as more likely causes of the megafaunal extinctions. If humans did cause these extinctions, then they markedly changed the ecosystems and the very look of much of the Southwest many thousands of years ago. In particular, the enormous number of bison on the Great Plains may partly be the product of these extinctions. The disappearance of these animals left numerous grazing niches available, most of which were filled by a dwarf species of bison that was able to reproduce more quickly than its relatives.[13]

In the more recent past, the dense agricultural settlements of the Mogollon, Hohokam, and Anasazi may have caused even more dramatic local transformations. Their agriculture was productive enough to allow for high population densities, and local ecosystems may have been irrevocably changed as a result. Some areas were certainly deforested, such as the Anasazi heartland in Chaco Canyon, where scientists estimate that 200,000 trees were cut down to construct buildings. Devoting large areas to permanent agriculture led to further deforestation, at the very least, over the short term. Aridity makes for slow tree growth, and when combined with erosion this may mean that Southwestern agriculturalists permanently denuded the land.[14] Mogollon and Hohokam irrigation may have altered river valleys in a similarly dramatic manner. Across the globe, prolonged irrigation has often led to the salinization of soils, because the water leaves its mineral deposits year after year. This may have happened in the Hohokam territory. Some of the first Europeans to record their impressions of Arizona's Salt River noted the "sterile plains" and bottomlands that "appear as if they had been strewn with salt."[15]

If these cultures altered the environment to at least some degree, then natural changes also deeply affected them, perhaps even ending some cultures altogether. For example, a volcanic eruption in 1064 C.E., near what is now Flagstaff, Arizona, caused at least some shifts in settlement patterns. Heavy rainfall, particularly if it came on the heels of deforestation, could cause enormous flooding, enough to damage or even cripple complicated irrigation works and thereby threaten future agriculture.

Long-term fluctuations in average precipitation may have been the most influential way in which the rhythms of nature in the Southwest affected its cultures. They could either prompt people to rely more heavily on agriculture, as may have happened in the eighth century C.E. to the Anasazi, or could make intensive agriculture altogether unreliable. The Southwest entered a more prolonged period of drought in the twelfth century C.E. The Anasazi were hit hard, and despite what appear to be efforts to conserve water through terracing, mulching, and building more check dams and better canals, their agricultural system may have collapsed under the strain; perhaps these and other challenges they faced prompted their dispersion by the end of the fifteenth century from the Four Corners area. Many Anasazi settled in the less extreme upper Rio Grande valley, where they helped to form the villages of the Pueblo peoples. The same period of drought may have caused the decline of the Hohokam, who had abandoned most of their massive irrigation works by 1400.[16]

THE COMING OF THE SPANISH AND THE COLUMBIAN EXCHANGE

Much of our knowledge of the pre-Columbian environment of the Southwest rests on uncertain foundations. The lack of a written record necessitates a reliance on evidence unearthed by archaeologists or read by ecologists from pollen samples and tree rings. For some purposes this evidence is extremely reliable. Tree rings, for example, clearly show an intense drought from 1276 to 1293. But for others it is highly speculative. Those who argue that massive floods threatened the Hohokam agricultural system must rely on vegetative patterns from several hundred miles away on the Colorado plateau to identify the periods of heavy rainfall that caused these hypothetical floods, while those who assert a deep drought on the southern Great Plains base their assertions on tree-ring records from hundreds and even thousands of miles away.[17]

The arrival of the Spanish in the Southwest in the late sixteenth century inaugurated a documentary record that can be read alongside the evidence produced by other forms of inquiry. Although conquistadors, priests, and settlers dominate the popular images of the arrival of the Spanish, theirs was also a biological invasion of large dimensions. Other European organisms often preceded Europeans themselves. When Juan de Oñate entered New Mexico in 1598, for example, the Pueblos were already growing watermelons, originally a Eurasian species. Later European and American explorers consistently found European grasses and weeds thriving in parts of the Southwest that they had thought untouched by their cultures. The animals brought by the Spanish were similarly aggressive. Spanish hogs went feral in the Southwest early in the sixteenth century, spreading west as far as Texas as they evolved into the feral hogs later known as razorbacks. Thousands of cattle and horses already ran wild in Texas when the Spanish founded towns there in the eighteenth century.[18]

The Spaniards' greatest help came from microbes—particularly smallpox, bubonic plague, influenza, and dysentery—that wreaked havoc on the indigenous peoples of the Southwest, just as they did across the Americas. As Cabeza de Vaca recounted of his captors following his 1528 shipwreck on the Texas coast, "half the natives died from a disease of the bowels."[19] Europe's early urbanization, its connection to the enormous disease pool of the Eurasian land mass, and thousands of years of disease exchange with its numerous domesticated animals, meant that the Spanish were relatively unscathed by even the most severe of epidemics.[20] At the same time, the ecology of European diseases interacted in complicated ways with native cultures. More densely settled people tended to be hit harder than those who were nomadic and semi-nomadic, so groups such as the Pueblos and Caddos probably lost ground to the Apache and Navajo. On the other hand, high mortality could also reduce intertribal conflict by increasing the per capita resource base; the Pueblos, for instance, may have grown more unified as a result.[21]

Some of the environmental impact of Spanish settlement represented an intensification of the impact Native American populations may already have had. The Hispanic population and its buildings, for example, increased the local rate of timber harvesting in the upper Rio Grande valley but did not inaugurate a fundamentally different ecology. Whatever erosion Pueblo agriculture caused, the introduction of iron tools and the deeper plowing made possible by draft animals surely increased.

At the same time, however, some of the changes brought about by the Spanish were decidedly new in scope. The Spanish introduction of livestock was particularly important in this regard. Rapidly expanding numbers of cattle, sheep, and horses trampled vegetation and altered soil structure, particularly around sources of water. This not only directly changed vegetation and increased erosion, but it also increased runoff from rain, which further increased erosion. The relatively sparse ground cover and steep topography of most of the Southwest exacerbated this problem. Stock also caused more subtle but equally profound ecological changes. Because the seeds of many plants pass through the digestive systems of horses and cattle, they inadvertently spread numerous shrubs far beyond their previous range. The mesquite bean, for example, probably benefited from scarification in the guts of these animals. Deposited into areas disturbed by animal hooves, the mesquite also depressed the growth of grasses. The Texas cedar (*Juniperus ashei*) was similarly aided by livestock in its invasion of grasslands. Although many think of cedar and mesquite as iconic Texas trees, their abundance is an ecologically recent phenomenon.[22]

Perhaps the greatest testimony to the depth of the Spanish impact on the environment came from the ways in which new organisms altered life for Native Americans. On the one hand, environmental changes sometimes served the conquerors' cause of native subordination. In the late 1600s, for example, the lower portion of the Gila River impressed a Spanish priest as a lush oasis of green that provided the Pima (now Akimel O'odham) with "abundant fish and with their maize, beans, and calabashes [squash]."[23] Livestock herds consumed much of this vegetation and trampled what remained, so several centuries later the riverbed was a wide and barren gash. This degradation, and its analogues across the region, presumably made Pima subsistence strategies more difficult to perpetuate and thus made them more likely to accept the blandishments of mission life.

But in other respects the organisms that came with the Spanish became a cherished part of Native American life. Even when Indians turned decisively against Spanish political, religious, and cultural power, these new plants and animals proved more difficult to give up. In 1680 the Pueblo Indians rose against their Spanish rulers in an act of unprecedented political unity, killing nearly one-sixth of their colonizers and compelling the survivors to flee their century-old colony to El Paso. (Natural phenomena may have played a role in this upheaval, because a decade of drought had intensified Apache and Navajo raiding, which in turn increased Pueblo disdain for their rulers' inability to provide a decent life for them.) The rebellion's leader counseled the Pueblo to destroy images of Christianity, bathe in rivers to remove the taint of baptism, and return to their own practice of marriage. His insistence that the Pueblo were "to burn the seeds which the

Spaniards sowed and to plant only maize and beans, which were the crops of (our) ancestors" reflected a deep awareness of the ecological dimensions of conquest. It also mostly fell on deaf ears, for Spanish biological imports—wheat, cantaloupe, peach, pear, plum, previously unfamiliar varieties of corn and squash, sheep, goats, horses, mules, oxen, chicken, and others—remained appealing to many Pueblos. There was no going back to the old ways, either culturally or environmentally.[24]

Indeed, for other native peoples the environmental changes of this period made for more dramatic cultural transformations. The Navajo acquisition of sheep and horses in the seventeenth century prompted many to switch from being sedentary farmers or hunter-gatherers to being raiders and stock-herders. By the end of the century they had begun to weave the wool blankets that became so important to their own culture and to their trade with and perception by the outside world. The cultures of the Comanche and Apache were even more wholly transformed. By the 1690s, when the Spanish resumed effective control of Pueblo territory, the Apache had enthusiastically adopted the horse, becoming more nomadic, more reliant on the buffalo, and more militarily powerful. Their neighbors from the north, the Comanche, adopted the horse at about the same time and began to move into the Southwest in force, steadily driving the Apache southward into Texas and the rest of Mexico. No other people in the region were as marked by the power and mobility provided by the horse. Horses became a commodity of trade, a measure of wealth, and allowed their riders to exploit the buffalo and to control the trade of the southern plains. By the mid 1700s, the territory controlled by the Comanche stretched deep into central Texas. Simply by introducing the domesticated horse, then, the Spanish had created another empire, one that would deeply mark all those who called the Southwest home.

UNITED STATES SETTLEMENT AND ENVIRONMENTAL CHANGE

The Comanche were not the only expanding people of North America. To their east, the United States grew rapidly in population and by leaps and bounds in territory. With the U.S. victory over Mexico in 1848, the area lived in and often fought over by Spain, Mexico, and a host of native groups had become the southwestern portion of the United States. In some ways the advent of American rule simply marked the continuation of dynamics begun by the Spanish introduction of livestock and new crops or of even older trends. The year 1848 witnessed nothing as dramatic as the extinction of the megafauna, the advent of agriculture, or the introduction of Eurasian species, but Anglo farmers had to face the same environmental challenges—long droughts, unpredictable rainfall, occasional floods, the risk of salinization in some places—that had long bedeviled Hispanic and Indian horticulturalists. Mormon settlers in Arizona implicitly recognized the connection between the old and new Southwest when they adopted Hohokam canals for use in watering their own fields.[25]

But over time the incorporation of the Southwest into the United States did have an enormous impact on the face of the region. American sovereignty prompted an influx of new settlers and tied the region to a dynamic national market, one that would voraciously consume resources on its way to becoming the world's largest economy. Indeed, much as European plants and animals actually preceded the Spanish themselves, the agents of the North American market preceded the soldiers and settlers of the United States. By the early 1820s American trappers were sloshing through the mountain streams of northern New Mexico, harvesting thousands of beaver in order to ship their skins back east and ultimately to the European market. During the 1820s and 30s Taos was the largest fur-trading center for all of the southern Rockies. Demand for furs was high enough to ensure that beaver were becoming hard to find in the region by the late 1830s. In 1838 the Mexican government passed one of the first conservation measures in the Southwest, mandating a six-year pause on the harvest of beaver and otter in the Rio Grande.[26]

Livestock and the Southwest Environment

The incorporation of the Southwest into the United States also transformed older practices. The number of cattle in the Southwest skyrocketed as Anglo ranchers set up shop and generally adopted Hispanic cattle-ranching equipment and techniques, often even employing Hispanic cowboys. The new cattle industry differed from prior ranching in its focus on raising livestock as a commodity for the national market rather than as a source of food for ranchers and nearby residents. Antebellum Texas was the Goliath of this industry, exporting its cattle to markets and meatpacking centers such as New Orleans, California, Chicago, and the railhead towns of Kansas and Nebraska. By 1861 the Lone Star state boasted at least three million head of cattle intended for the commercial market.[27] Although nowhere near the scale of Texas, the ranchers of what became New Mexico and Arizona also dramatically increased their herds, in large part to meet the provisioning demand of the numerous U.S. Army forts.[28] Mining boomtowns in Nevada and Arizona also stimulated the development of local ranching, often in very environmentally fragile regions.

The expansion of the livestock industry had important effects on the landscape. If mission herds and feral longhorns had already begun to spread woody plants into what had been grasslands, then this trend accelerated rapidly in the second half of the nineteenth century. "Rapid and extensive demise of grassland," biologist Frederick Gehlbach wrote, "is the general outcome of Anglo settlement."[29] Sketches, travel accounts, and early photos all indicate that eastern New Mexico and much of western Texas were dominated by grass cover at the start of the American period, but over the decades much heavier use of the range by Anglo-run ranches converted these grasslands into deserts dominated by mesquite and creosote bushes. Because the previous soils have mostly been washed down arroyos or blown into dunes now covered with mesquite, there is no land-use or management technique that can restore these grasslands. Although scientists disagree as to the exact area that has been desertified—with some maintaining that there were no true deserts in New Mexico before the grazing pressure of the nineteenth century and others arguing for a more limited impact—it is clear that the American livestock industry has permanently transformed portions of the Southwest into desert.[30]

Even places not changed into desert saw their ecologies reordered. In the mountains of northern New Mexico, for example, booming sheep populations heavily grazed many mountain pastures in the 1880s. Grazing continued even as less productive grasses and forbs replaced the original native vegetation. Sometimes the combined effects of the animals' appetites and hooves denuded large territories. In 1898 the National Wool Growers' Association reported that sheep had so overgrazed areas of the Pecos Forest Reserve that they had to resort to denuding trees of their foliage in order to find further food.[31] The increased surface area free of vegetation was more vulnerable to loosening from rain and hail, and serious erosion soon ensued. The decreased ability of the range to hold water reduced the ground moisture, making reestablishment of dense grass cover all but impossible. The cover that did survive this period of intense grazing bore very little relation to the native flora. Eurasian plants, especially sheep fescue and the deceptively named Kentucky Bluegrass (which probably came from Europe), now dominate much of the southern Rockies' alpine grasslands and subalpine parks. "So thoroughly did domestic animals rework the flora of the high country," wrote William DeBuys, "that in many cases it is impossible to say with certainty what the original fauna actually was."[32]

Population Growth

If integration into the economy of the United States intensified long-standing practices like agriculture, cattle ranching, and sheep herding, then at the same time it also made the human impact on the environment more extensive. The human footprint grew larger and larger as the Southwest saw dramatic population growth in the second half of the nineteenth century. Not only did more people take a heavier toll on the land in terms of plowed land, domesticated animals, firewood, construction materials, and the like, but they also began living in more environmentally marginal areas. Prospectors and miners flooded into Nevada and Arizona. Virginia City, Nevada, for example, exploded from nothing before 1859 to perhaps 30,000 (the growth was too rapid to count) in a few years. Anglo farmers and ranchers found appealing lands in such previously lightly settled areas as the plains of eastern New Mexico and the Texas Panhandle, as well as in the river valleys and more moist uplands of Arizona. New Mexico's Hispanic population grew strongly during this period as well, founding numerous new villages in the northern portion of the territory and making greater use of timber lots, arable land, and pastures.

Logging in the timbered portions of the Southwest increased dramatically over the second half of the nineteenth century. The national railroad network provided a way to convey the region's large pines to the national lumber market, which was driven by house and railroad construction. Mines, including those in the Southwest, were also major consumers of timber. The square-set pattern of timbering, for example, was first implemented in Nevada's Comstock Lode, where it relied on enormous amounts of wood to provide greater tunnel stability. Mines used so much timber that many mining companies ran their own local logging and sawing operations. What was later called the bonanza era in Texas lumbering began in the early 1880s, when heavy cutting of the eastern pine forests began in earnest. By 1907 the Texas lumber industry boasted an annual production of more than 2.25 billion board feet, making it the third largest lumber-producing state in the union.[33]

The combination of expanded and intensified settlement, logging, grazing, farming, and erosion led to observable environmental damage by the end of the nineteenth century. Major rivers flooded more often and more heavily than before, since the land's ability to hold water had been so diminished. The upper Rio Grande, for example, after decades of intense agricultural and stock-raising expansion, flooded disastrously in 1884, 1904–1905, 1912, and 1920.[34] It was also in this period that arroyos—gullies that fill briefly with water during storms or spring melt-off, then return to their dry state—first became a common feature of the Southwestern landscape. Arroyos do much more environmental and social damage than even their stark appearance suggests. They drastically reduce the ecological (and potential agricultural or pastoral) productivity of land by lowering the water table, starving surface soils of much of their moisture. Moreover, they can quickly wash out roads, trails, and irrigation systems that took decades or even centuries of labor to construct and maintain.[35] Human-induced erosion and the collapse of montane pastures helped to force many Hispanics in New Mexico out of a purely subsistence economy and into the labor forces of the region's mines, large ranches, and Anglo-run commercial agriculture. Much like the mesquite, arroyos are assumed to be an essential part of the Southwestern landscape. But they do not capture the region's supposed timelessness so much as they reflect the dramatic changes brought to it by recent human history.

Abrupt and severe climate shifts, a fundamental feature of the Southwestern environment, continued to affect human cultures and people's efforts to coax a living from the land. The most dramatic came in the winter of 1886–1887, when cattle on the overstocked ranges all across the West died by the hundreds of thousands. A more localized but similarly drastic die-off took place in south-central Arizona from 1891 to 1893, in which somewhere from 300,000 to one million head of cattle perished in severe drought conditions.[37] Droughts also hit southern Texas in the late nineteenth and early twentieth centuries. Although all Southwestern cattle operations were hit hard by these episodes, the smaller owners with the fewest cattle and least capital were not as able to survive the lean years as larger, better-capitalized businesses. In the case of southern Texas, many of these smaller ranchers (all Hispanic) sold out to wealth-

Texas Fever

The scope of industries such as logging and grazing marked the late nineteenth century as a new period in the Southwest's environmental history. At the same time, however, nature and human cultures continued to interact in unpredictable ways, just as they had since humans first settled the area. This was clearly demonstrated in the piney woods of eastern Texas. The cattle tick, presumably brought to North America with Spanish cattle in the seventeenth century, caused "Texas fever" in cattle in the southeastern portion of the continent, where frost-free days and a relatively humid environment allowed the disease to thrive. It was endemic but not extreme, decreasing milk production and the rate of weight gain, but rarely killing livestock. The real threat it posed was to the cattle industry of the rest of the country, where livestock had evolved no resistance to the disease and could suffer up to 90 percent mortality when exposed to it. When the cattle drives of the 1850s brought significant numbers of Texas longhorns north, the cattle interests of the rest of the nation began to insist on a quarantine of southern cattle. After the restrictions they gradually put in place began to harm the commercial ranchers of the South, southern states ultimately implemented highly interventionist and very expensive measures to eradicate the tick, such as regular dipping in arsenic solutions. The numerous yeoman farmers who raised cattle not for market but as part of their subsistence economy could not afford these measures; thus, many had to give up their family's cattle. (But not without putting up a fight: disgruntled farmers in eastern and central Texas dynamited dipping tanks as late as 1919.) This loss joined other, more purely economic factors in pushing them out of independent farm ownership and, like many of their Hispanic counterparts in New Mexico, into wage work.[36] Environmental and social factors interacted in complicated but often important ways, just as they had since the arrival of humans.

ier Anglos.[38] One can thus hypothesize that the region's extremely variable precipitation and temperature patterns contributed to the ability of newly arrived Anglos to assert economic dominance over previous Hispanic settlers. These shifts may also have lulled newcomers into a false sense of security, however. Abnormally high rainfall in the first decade of the twentieth century helped convince tens of thousands of farmers that the Texas Panhandle and eastern New Mexico were places where conventional agriculture could easily be practiced. Later decades would not be so kind to these optimistic farmers.[39]

Bison Extinction

Perhaps the process by which the bison nearly went extinct in this period best captures the complexities of the Southwest's environmental dynamics in the late nineteenth century. In 1883 bison hunters fanning out onto the Great Plains, including the Llano Estacado (Staked Plains) of the Texas Panhandle, were shocked to find no animals to kill. Over the previous decade, there had been no shortage of targets. Buffalo had seemed to cover the plains, and many hunters were able to fire their guns successfully with such rapidity that they had to urinate on their barrels to keep them cool enough to function. The few animals that survived, barely more than a thousand, were all in Yellowstone or Canada. Much of the original bison population of some forty million had once lived on the southern portion of the Great Plains. Now none did.

As was acknowledged at the time, market hunters had much to do with this near-extinction. The construction of the transcontinental railroads in the 1860s and 1870s made it easier to transport buffalo to urban markets (and still easier for Southwesterners to do so when transcontinental railroads running through New Mexico and Arizona were finished in the early 1880s). In 1870, when tanners developed a process to turn buffalo hide into supple leather, they only increased the marketability of the species. Much as with the timber and grasslands of the region, the bison seemed to have been gobbled up by the hungry national market. In short, when the United States conquered the Southwest, it seemed to have inaugurated an era of rapid environmental destruction.

But it was more complicated than this. The bison actually began their decline before white market hunters began killing them by the thousands. In fact, by 1850 visiting Anglo-Americans noted that the Comanche were forced by starvation to begin eating their own horse herds. Evidence suggests that buffalo populations had already dropped to half of their historic heights by the 1840s, well before the start of heavy white hunting. So what caused this population decline? Older dynamics, predating the American conquest, seem to have been at work. Since their acquisition of the horse, Indian peoples on the southern Plains killed ten to twelve buffalo per capita, about half for their own use as food, shelter, and clothing and about half for trade in the form of robes and pemmican. Given the rate of natural mortality and wolf predation, even this native hunting may have consumed a large portion of each year's increase in bison population. The apparent Indian preference for killing young female bison, which had more tender meat and easily processed hides, disproportionately affected bison reproduction. As groups more exclusively dependent on the buffalo for subsistence (most notably the Comanche) displaced those who relied more on agriculture (particularly the Apache), the total native

George Catlin. *Buffalo Chase with Bows and Lances* (1932–1933). Courtesy of the Library of Congress.

harvest of buffalo would have increased steadily from the early eighteenth century onward. Expanded trade networks that predated the railroad—the same networks that led to overtrapping of beaver in the Southwest—likely increased this harvest.[40]

The mounts that the Comanche and the other horse-oriented peoples of the Southwest brought with them onto the Plains may have taken an even greater toll on the bison. Perhaps two million horses ran wild over the vast expanse of land from southern Texas to the plains of what is now Oklahoma, and Southern Plains Indians may have held another 500,000. These horses ate most of the same plants as the bison and thus decreased their total food supply. Moreover, Indians generally wintered in the shelter offered by river bottoms—the very same places that bison congregated when forage was scarce elsewhere on the Plains. So trampled did river bottoms of the southern Plains become that white settlers would often use their condition as an indicator for whether they were in territory routinely traveled in by Indians. A clear bottomland was reason for caution, whereas heavy cottonwood growth inspired greater confidence. Despite widespread popular notions of native American harmony with the environment, the horse culture of the Great Plains was only a few generations old, and there is no reason to assume that it had worked out a sustainable relationship with the animal that had become its lifeblood.[41]

Still more factors conspired against the hapless bison. Old-world animals, brought onto the Plains in ever-greater numbers by Americans, spread many of their diseases to the previously isolated bison. Anthrax was passed from cattle in Louisiana at the beginning of the nineteenth century. Tuberculosis and brucellosis, the latter of which causes spontaneous abortions in bovines, became endemic to remaining buffalo populations. They still afflict the wild herd of Yellowstone National Park. Finally, an old pattern in the natural history of the Southwest made itself present: drought. Droughts of more than five years in length struck the Plains at least four times in the nineteenth century, with exceptionally dry years from 1845 to 1852. Since archaeological data indicate that bison nearly disappeared from the southern Plains in previous episodes of severe drought, this short-term climatic oscillation could very well have sharply reduced the bison population even in the absence of other forces.[42]

As with many questions in environmental history, it is impossible to pinpoint a single cause for the elimination of the bison of the Southwestern plains. Perhaps the consumptive capacity of the rapidly industrializing United States was so enormous that market hunters would have nearly killed them off even had native hunting, habitat competition, climate change, and introduced diseases not added to the challenges they faced. But whatever its cause, the buffalos' scrape with oblivion illustrates the complexities of Southwestern environmental change from the 1840s to the end of the nineteenth century. The connection of the region to the nation's expansive market economy was indeed a transformative one, prompting Americans to introduce new industries and a more intensive use of the land and its products. But climate patterns, Native Americans, Hispanic settlers, and the environmental dynamics that they had introduced still continued to shape the landscape.

Conservation and the Making of the Modern Southwest

The accelerated rate of environmental change in the late nineteenth and early twentieth centuries prompted many Americans to reconsider whether putting land and natural resources in private hands as rapidly as possible was still sensible. Public fears that forests were being cut at an unsustainable rate prompted the rise of conservation, the effort to bring resource use under the management of professionals employed by the state. Conservation made the federal government a major factor in the ecology of the Southwest and, inevitably, one with a controversial impact on the inhabitants of the region.

Conservation of Forest Land

Early conservation measures were targeted at forests, including those in the Southwest, out of concern that deforestation was the most ruinous form of environmental damage and because forested lands were often unsuitable for and thus not needed for homesteading. The National Forest Reservation Act of 1891 allowed the president to withdraw timbered lands from homesteading use. Later that decade the lands that would become national forests in Arizona and New Mexico had been withdrawn. Subsequent measures brought small portions of Nevada and Texas into the national forest system. National policymakers, often backed by railroads and other economic interests that benefited from early tourism, similarly concluded that the nation's most sublime and dramatic natural features should be preserved as parks. The Grand Canyon, the Southwest's most notable such feature, became a national monument in 1908 and received formal park designation eleven years later. Millions of acres of Nevada, Arizona, and New Mexico that were not incorporated into the park and forest systems remained in the public domain, ultimately to be administered by the Bureau of Land Management. (Federal landholding in Texas was negligible, since the state had maintained ownership of its unsettled lands when it made the transition from sovereign nation to state.)

In part, the mission of these bureaucracies, particularly of the National Park Service, was to "preserve" these lands, in the sense of keeping them from chaotic and destructive use for private economic gain. A more fundamental purpose, however, was to make them more economically useful than they otherwise would have been. This was true even of national parks, where important tourism businesses such as hotels and outfitters sprang up. In forests and grazing lands owned by the government, federal agents set about the tasks of monitoring grazing, timber harvesting, building infrastructure—particularly roads.

Irrigation and Bringing Water to the Southwest

But it was the Bureau of Reclamation that most altered the landscape of the Southwest in the name of conservation. It took square aim at the region's major environmental feature: aridity. At less than twenty inches a year, the average rainfall west of the 100th meridian—the line that runs roughly north and south through the middle of the states of Texas, Oklahoma, Kansas, Nebraska, and the Dakotas—is just below the amount needed to grow wheat, and ten inches less than that needed by corn. Later settlers had followed native groups in turning to irrigation to surmount the challenge of aridity. Spanish and Mexican farmers in New Mexico created localized but quite sophisticated irrigation systems to support their own agriculture. Many of their villages and fields were actually built around an *acequia madre* (mother ditch), and they boasted well-articulated networks of authority and labor expectations to maintain the ditch. The Mormons developed a similar practice in Utah, bringing it with them to portions of Arizona and Nevada. They relied on the power and order of their church to allocate scarce water and to pool resources and labor for the construction of irrigation systems.[43]

A few influential Americans advocated developing a similar system across the nation's arid lands. Surveying the lands of the arid West in the 1870s, scientist and explorer John Wesley Powell came to the conclusion that they should be divided and governed according to watershed. Each watershed's farmers and ranchers would form a cooperative to raise the capital for the necessary irrigation network. Although Powell's vision failed for lack of political support, most private efforts to irrigate the arid areas of the Southwest also met with very limited success. Such projects were generally outside the reach of individual farmers because they required the control of large stretches of rivers and streams and the erection of sizable dams for storage. In the 1870s and 1880s, private land companies entered the irrigation business, constructing dams, building extensive canal systems, and then selling nearby lands to farmers who would remain dependent on the companies for their water. High capital costs, however, constrained these efforts. Only the most opportune sites were irrigated, the total acres under irrigation soon stagnated, and by 1900 nearly nine out ten of these irrigation companies were in financial jeopardy.[44]

Disturbed by these failures, in 1902 Francis Newlands, the aptly named congressman from Nevada, secured passage of the bill that created the Bureau of Reclamation, the federal agency charged with building dams, reservoirs, and irrigation canals for the benefit of private farmers. The government, in other words, was going to conquer aridity, making possible Eastern-style agriculture in the Southwest. Over the next few decades, the Bureau of Reclamation (and later the Army Corps of Engineers) built hundreds of dams in the Southwest, most notably Hoover Dam, which spans the Colorado River on the border between Arizona and Nevada. These often massive structures not only provided water for crops, but in some places they also produced electricity for farmers and urbanites alike. The politics of this highly interventionist form of environmental management proved irresistible, because dam construction created many jobs, and the lands that they opened up for agriculture swelled tax rolls and the bank accounts of real estate developers.

Irrigation and other conservation measures, however, did not have an even impact across the Southwest. Federal lands bureaucracies were powerful actors in New Mexico and Arizona, deeply shaping agriculture and livestock raising. They were even more influential in Nevada, for the simple reason that they owned 96 percent of the state. Farther east, however, the story was much different. The Bureau of Reclamation did little work on the plains of eastern New Mexico and the Texas Panhandle, although starting in the 1930s affordable pumps and low-cost electricity allowed farmers to pump groundwater from the Ogallala Aquifer and other sources. Federal conservation played the smallest role in Texas for the simple reason that the federal government owned virtually no land there. It was not until the 1930s, in the midst of the Depression, that national forests were established in the Lone Star State, after the Texas legislature voted to authorize the federal purchase of timbered lands for such a purpose. Until then, Texans worried that the depletion of natural resources could rely only on the modest power of state government, which in 1915 began to promote fire prevention and replanting efforts in the eastern piney woods.[45]

As with prior environmental changes, the coming of conservation to the Southwest had important human consequences. Foresters and other conservation professionals looked with great suspicion on many Southwesterns, particularly Indians and Hispanics. In part this suspicion reflected the social gulf between these Southwesterners and the primarily Eastern, well-educated professionals who staffed the

Hoover Dam, originally named the Boulder Dam, 2003. Courtesy of the National Archives.

public lands bureaucracies, and in part it was a consequence of the mission of public lands bureaucracies to make the Southwest economically productive in a way that private development alone had failed to do. U.S. Forest Service officials attempted to reduce the number of cattle allowed to graze on what had become government land and implemented similar measures with respect to the harvesting of timber. These steps were controversial across the region. The dispute became particularly heated in northern New Mexico, in part because there the national forests included lands that had traditionally been used by the Pueblo Indians and Hispanics as commons for grazing and firewood. For many New Mexicans, forest rangers were simply the newest agents of conquest by a hostile outside power with no respect for their traditions or their rights to make a living from the land. Early rangers were beaten and had their lodgings burned to the ground. They nonetheless persisted in their efforts, and over the decades the Forest Service maintained that it had made clear improvements in the quality of mountain ranges and timber lots, to the benefit of local residents.[46]

Native Americans objected even more vigorously to the effects of conservation. Residents of Taos Pueblo were enraged to find that the government had placed Blue Lake, high in the Sangre de Cristo mountains above them, into the national forest system. The site of an important annual pilgrimage, the lake was one of the holiest sites in their religion. The Pueblo demanded the return of the lake to their control after its 1906 incorporation into the forest. Although they won the right to use Blue Lake in 1927, the federal government continued to allow other Americans to use the site for recreation. It took until 1970 for the federal government to return the lake to their control. The Havasupai people, a small band who lived near the Grand Canyon, similarly found themselves at odds with conservation bureaucracies. In the fall of 1898 they began leaving their village in Havasu Canyon in order to hunt game and gather plants, as they had for many generations. The supervisor of the surrounding forest reserve was outraged, fearing that their presence would mar the scenic beauty of what was rapidly becoming a major tourist attraction. "The Grand Cañon of the Colorado," he wrote, "is become so renowned for its wonderful and extensive natural gorge scenery and for its open clean pine woods, that it should be preserved for the everlasting pleasure and instruction of our intelligent citizens as well as those of foreign countries. Henceforth, I deem it just and necessary to keep the wild and unappreciable Indian from off the Reserve and to protect the game."[47] Since the forest entirely surrounded the Havasupai reservation, it had effectively become impossible for them to live off the land.

The federal government's ambitious irrigation program also adversely affected Native Americans. Because of Francis Newland's leading role in establishing the Bureau of Reclamation, the first major irrigation project that the new arm of the government undertook was in Newland's home state, Nevada. Designed to bring some 350,000 acres under cultivation, what became known as the Newlands Project diverted about half of the Truckee River's flow. Since the Truckee fed Pyramid Lake, the result was dramatic: the lake's level dropped by seventy feet, and its surface area declined by a quarter. The Paiute who lived around the lake found their traditional reliance on its fish to be impossible to sustain, because the fish population collapsed.[48] Government-sponsored irrigation, intended to bring agricultural prosperity to the Southwest, had brought destitution and poverty to some of its longest-standing residents.

Irrigation may have been involved in a more prominent conflict between the federal government and a Native American group, the controversy over Navajo stock reduction. In the early 1930s, after the construction of the monumental Hoover Dam on the Colorado River on the border between Arizona and Nevada, federal officials became concerned that erosion from the Navajo reservation would rapidly fill the lake behind the dam with silt and therefore sharply limit its effectiveness in delivering irrigation water and electricity to the entire region. The Bureau of Indian Affairs and other federal offices believed that Navajo livestock were the culprit, pointing to gullying, a scarcity of grass, and the close cropping of juniper and pine trees to animal height as evidence that the range was overstocked. They then forcibly slaughtered tens of thousands of Navajo sheep, deeply scarring Navajo culture and destroying the economic life of thousands of herders and their families.[49]

Even apart from the ways in which it was clearly bound up with social conflict, conservation changed the environment of the Southwest, often unpredictably. Private ranchers and farmers joined government bureaucrats in a war on predators and "pest" species, one that used hunting, traps, and strychnine poisoning. The wolf was perhaps the most hated target. In 1924 ranchers killed the last wolf in the Texas plains, and by the 1930s breeding populations had been eradicated from the entire Southwest, though some wolves continued to slip into the country from the Sierra Madre in Mexico as late as the 1970s. Prairie dogs also provoked an extermination campaign.[50] The removal or near-removal of these species would cause a cascade of environmental consequences. Ferrets and other species dependent on prairie dogs, for example, were eventually pushed to the brink of extinction. The absence of predators such as the wolf allowed deer populations to explode in some places, most notably Arizona's Kaibab Plateau, a part of the Grand Canyon National Forest and Game Preserve. In the 1920s the deer population increased perhaps twenty-five-fold, eventually dying from lack of forage and convincing some ecologists that predator removal was not a sensible policy. Fire suppression, a major goal of the Forest Service, resulted in similarly complicated effects. Dense chaparral replaced open grass as the understory of many Ponderosa pine forests. The full impact of this policy could be appreciated by comparing "the open, park-like woods of Mexico," as one ecologist put it, "within a hundred miles of sapling-choked, brushy vegetation of a similar species composition in the same elevations across the Border."[51]

THE MODERN SOUTHWEST AND THE MAKING OF AMERICAN ENVIRONMENTALISM

The conservation measures that had such important consequences for the landscape and people of the Southwest were motivated by a desire to ensure that a rapidly industrializing United States did not irrevocably deplete its natural resources. And yet the Southwest remained more rural, more dependent on herding and agriculture, and significantly poorer than the nation as a whole. World War II changed much of this, bringing rapid population growth and new industries and government programs, as well as the environmental issues that often came with them. To be sure, parts of the region had already developed heavy industry even before the war. As early as the start of the twentieth century, mining companies in Nevada used enormous steam-powered shovels to strip large areas of surface soils in order to gain access to low-grade but still valuable mineral deposits that lay below. By the 1930s the Gulf Coast of Texas had become the nation's petrochemical center. Toxic by-products and pollutants from this industry have posed significant threats to human and environmental health alike, fouling coastal waters, creating numerous large hazardous waste sites on land, and causing elevated cancer rates in workers and nearby residents.

Postwar Development

World War II was the watershed for Southwestern urban and industrial development. The region's cities swelled in population during and after the war, as Southwesterners were pushed out of the countryside by a stagnant agricultural economy and drawn to urban life by military bases and private-sector employment, often in the defense industries. Houston, Dallas–Fort Worth, Phoenix, and Las Vegas grew most dramatically during this period, although Albuquerque, Reno, El Paso, and San Antonio also expanded substantially. Urban sprawl thus became a significant environmental issue, not only because of the rapidity and scale of urbanization, but also because most of it came in the form of low-density suburbs and much of it took place in the most arid parts of the continent. Urban development destroyed habitat for many species, particularly endemic fish and amphibian populations, and made urbanites significant consumers of the water once monopolized by farmers.

The postwar urban boom meant that enough people lived in the Southwest for the simple demands of daily existence to constitute a major force in altering its environment. The explosive growth of Las Vegas, Nevada, epitomized the extent to which the problems and quandaries of urban development had become pressing regional environmental questions. The metropolitan area's population reached one million in 1995 and may double that tally by 2010 if it maintains its rank as the fastest-growing city of the nation. Travelers who come expecting pure desert air are bound to be disappointed: only four American cities have more high pollution days, and its smog helps reduce visibility at the Grand Canyon. The city seems intent on defying the limitations of aridity. Hotel-casinos boast artificial canals, gondolas, and lakes large enough for jet-skiing, while one developer advocated transforming a major downtown thoroughfare into a grand canal modeled after Venice. As a result, Las Vegas' daily water consumption is 360 gallons per capita, far outpacing even other Southwestern cities such as Tucson (a mere 160 gallons, itself much more than the national average of around 100). While other cities demonstrated a willingness to reduce water use by such measures as encouraging cactus gardens in place of thirsty grass lawns, in the late twentieth century Vegas made aggressive moves on the water claims of Nevada's farmers and ranchers, threatening the stability of the region's most traditional industries.[52]

Less dramatically than the sprawl of Las Vegas or the arms race, dynamics long in place continued to exert their influence on the landscape. Irrigation altered natural river flows in ways that became impossible to ignore. The Colorado, for example, once mighty enough to carve the Grand Canyon, was so heavily drawn on for irrigation that it did not reach the Pacific from 1964 to 1983. Proposals to build further dams on the river sparked an environmental backlash as early as the

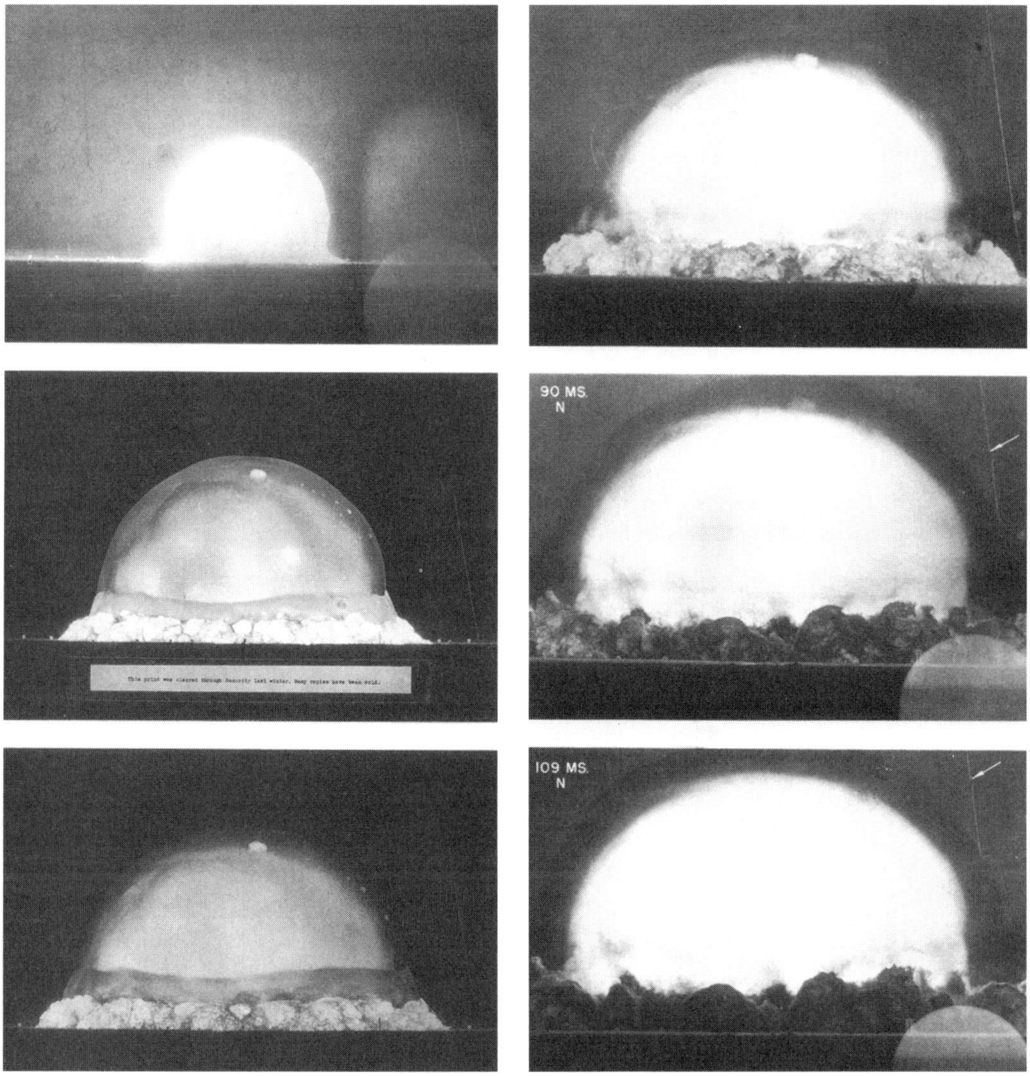

Photo sequence of the Trinity Nuclear Test, 1945. Courtesy of the Department of Energy.

1950s. The build-up of silt behind reservoir walls quickly became a problem; by 2000, most reservoirs built before 1945 had lost from 7 to 15 percent of their capacity. Salinization, possibly one of the oldest human environmental impacts, puts thousands of acres out of production each year. Groundwater pumping on the Great Plains seemed headed for extinction, with the aquifer predicted to dry up within a few decades. Drain-off from the Newlands irrigation project became so toxic and salty that in the 1980s it began killing millions of fish and waterfowl in Nevada's Stillwater Wildlife Refuge. Mining continued to be an environmentally critical industry. The extraction of such dangerous substances as mercury and asbestos declined in the latter decades of the twentieth century, and clean air and

American Ground Zero: The Nuclear Southwest

What is arguably the most dramatic environmental development in human history took place in the Southwest during this period: the development of nuclear weapons, which placed in humanity's hands the power to destroy all life. In the midst of World War II, as the federal government committed itself to trying to develop the atomic bomb, policymakers found themselves drawn to the Southwest. Then far removed from national centers of power and population, the region seemed secure from foreign spies and empty enough to test whatever weapons could be designed and still keep their existence a secret. They selected Los Alamos, New Mexico, as the site for the crash project. An atom bomb developed there was exploded near Alamogordo, New Mexico, on July 16, 1945.

The Southwest continued to play a critical role in the nuclear age after World War II. Much of the uranium used to build the United States' vast nuclear arsenal came from Arizona mines; the Nevada Test Site was where many of the nation's open-air explosions were staged; and the final assembly of the arsenal took place in the Texas Panhandle. And although they may not have had much power or influence over their government, there certainly were people in America's nuclear landscape. As many as 170,000 people may have been exposed to radioactive fallout from the Nevada Test Site.[53] Abandoned and poorly sealed uranium mines were scattered all over Navajo country. In the late twentieth century, cancer clusters could still be found in downwind communities. The author of one study of these areas writes of her dread of going to grocery stores and encountering "four- and five-year-old children wearing wigs, deathly pale and obviously in chemotherapy."[54]

water laws provided for further protections. Nonetheless, the development of new production methods ensured that mining would remain an environmentally risky industry. Spraying enormous piles of ore with a cyanide solution, for example, became the preferred method of gold extraction at modern gold mines. Tearing of the impermeable liners placed beneath the ore and flooding can release the cyanide into the local water supply, with potentially devastating consequences.[55]

Beauty of the Desert

Not all developments in postwar America had such ominous implications for the Southwest and its inhabitants. Many Americans learned to appreciate the beauty of desert environments in a way that they had not before. Mountains and forests had long been considered sublime places worthy of devotion and admiration, but deserts were something else entirely. Explorer John C. Frémont captured this perception in the 1840s as he crossed the Great Basin. "The whole idea of such a desert," he wrote, "is a novelty in our country. . . . Interior basins, with their own system of lakes and rivers, often sterile, are common enough in Asia . . . but in America such things are new and strange, unknown and suspected, and discredited when related." Not everybody felt this way, of course: earlier in the twentieth century, writers and artists such as John Van Dyke, Georgia O'Keeffe, and Mary Austin praised the virtues of the Southwest's open spaces, light, and color. But in the postwar period a group of influential nature writers extolled the virtues of the region's nature, finding particularly in its deserts wondrous landscapes of refuge and primal instincts. Edward Abbey was the most influential of these writers. Railing against the urban-industrial civilization that he felt threatened the best in humans and nature alike, Abbey proudly offered his own vision of the value of the Southwestern landscape:

> I am here not only to evade for awhile the clamor and filth and confusion of the cultural apparatus but also to confront, immediately and directly if it's possible, the bare bones of existence, the elemental and fundamental, the

> bedrock which sustains us. I want to be able to look at and into a juniper tree, a piece of quartz, a vulture, a spider, and see it as it is in itself, devoid of all humanly ascribed qualities. . . . I dream of a hard and brutal mysticism in which the naked self merges with a nonhuman world and yet somehow survives still intact, individual, separate. Paradox and bedrock.[56]

Pyramid Lake, Nevada, c. 1867. Courtesy of the Library of Congress.

Abbey's work found such a large audience in part because heightened prosperity dramatically increased the number of Americans who could afford to take a vacation from their jobs and homes and seek out the natural splendors of the Southwest. These nature enthusiasts expected to find clean air and water in pristine settings, not mine tailings, lakes sucked dry by thirsty cities, or over-grazed rangelands. Few people understood that even the places they thought

Pyramid Lake, Nevada, c. 1981. Notice the change in water level. Courtesy of the National Archives. © David Muench/Corbis.

Monument Valley Tribal Park in Arizona, an area where erosion has caused such natural beauty. Courtesy of Corbis.

of as wildernesses had in fact been substantially altered by thousands of years of human occupation or that such Southwestern icons as the mesquite and arroyos were so common because of the cattle that were so often held in contempt. Ironically, the visitors' very numbers could sometimes make them a threat to that which they professed so much devotion. By the 1990s, for example, the Grand Canyon attracted almost four million visitors annually, leading to traffic jams on parking lots near the rim, bumper-to-bumper boats on the Colorado River below, and helicopters constantly buzzing overhead.

Environmental tourists acted on the basis of their expectations, however, and environmental restrictions thereby gained a mass base among educated, prosperous urbanites within the region and beyond it. Propelled by such support from the 1960s forward, environmental groups made significant headway in such measures as limiting further dams on scenic rivers like the Colorado, restricting timber and grazing permits on public lands, and incorporating more territory into national parks and wilderness areas. In the 1990s the federal government committed itself to restoring the Mexican wolf to the region, a dramatic reversal of nearly a century of federal support for the extermination of the iconic predator.

Just as with the advent of conservation a century before, these heightened environmental measures have provoked enormous controversy in the Southwest, particularly in rural areas and most of all in ranching communities. Already pushed to the margin by low beef prices and the region's ever-fickle climate, ranchers complain that environmental restrictions, such as reductions in the number of cattle on federal grazing allotments, have made *them* the true endangered species. Many families have been in ranching for multiple generations and say that they will be forced out of the business and way of life entirely if wealthy, urban environmentalists have their way. For their part, environmentalists argue that they are simply forcing the Forest Service, Bureau of Land Management, and other public lands bureaucracies to finally live up to their mission to preserve and protect the areas under their supervision. Decades of over-grazing continue to harm the Southwest, they maintain, furthering erosion and runoff and threatening the riparian habitats of endangered species such as the Southwestern willow flycatcher. Moreover, according to these advocates, federal grazing rates are so low that the government in effect subsidizes this destructive activity. Often this dispute turns to violence. Prominent New Mexico environmentalist Tony Merten came under suspicion for shooting thirty-four cows and calves, killing himself before the investigation could come to a conclusion. Angry ranchers have threatened and assaulted environmentalists and Forest Service range conservationists who have expressed sympathy with environmentalists. In some places, however, environmentalists and ranchers have found common ground in open-space measures and private conservation easements. Private land trusts such as the Nature Conservancy have found willing buyers of ranchers' development rights. In such exchanges, ranchers get cash and reduced taxes—often enough to ensure the viability of their business—and environmentalists prevent open spaces from being wholly transformed by suburban development.[57]

Partisans in the debates over the proper relationship between humans and the environment in the Southwest often assume that nature is the mere subject of arguments, a timeless backdrop. But in fact nature is a dynamic force, in some sense an actor in these conflicts in its own right. At the beginning of the twenty-first century, Southwesterners were confronted with dramatic proof of this. Much of their forests went up in smoke as the entire West experienced some heavy years of burning. More than two hundred homes were devoured near Los Alamos, New Mexico, when a small fire set by the Forest Service to clear heavy underbrush blew out of control. In 2002 Arizonans saw two large fires merge into a single conflagration that burned nearly half a million acres, taking 465 homes and perhaps 300 million board-feet of timber with it. The fires were so destructive in part because of the burgeoning number of vacation homes built in the midst of once-secluded forests and in part because nearly a century of devoted fire suppression had let huge fuel loads build up. The ever-changing climate also played a role: 2002 went on record as one of the driest years ever recorded in many Western states, and some climatologists began warning of a megadrought caused by shifts in the global El Niño weather pattern, a climatic change potentially large enough to rival the culture-changing drought that may have sent the Anasazi packing centuries ago. Some argued that the fire problem would solve itself if the region's overburned forests were allowed to return to their natural cycle of regular fires, while others argued that only active logging and tree thinning could prevent future conflagrations so large that they threatened human lives, property, and the very survival of forests. Regardless of which side was right, it was clear that the story of humans and nature in the Southwest was still being written.

RESOURCE GUIDE

Printed Sources

Abbey, Edward. *Desert Solitaire*. New York: McGraw-Hill, 1968.

Baker, Will. *Tony and the Cows*. Albuquerque: University of New Mexico Press, 2000.

Davis, Mike. *Dead Cities*. New York: The New Press, 2002.

———. "Las Vegas versus Nature." In *Reopening the American West*, edited by Hal Rothman. Tucson: University of Arizona Press, 1998.

DeBuys, William. *Enchantment and Exploitation: The Life and Hard Times of a New Mexico Mountain Range*. Albuquerque: University of New Mexico Press, 1985.

Flannery, Tim. *The Eternal Frontier*. New York: Atlantic Monthly Press, 2001.

Flores, Dan. *Horizontal Yellow: Nature and History in the Near Southwest*. Albuquerque: University of New Mexico Press, 1999.

———. "Loving the Plains, Hating the Plains, Restoring the Plains." In *The Future of the Southern Plains*, edited by Sherry L. Smith. Norman: University of Oklahoma Press, 2003.

———. *The Natural West: Environmental History in the Great Plains and Rocky Mountains*. Norman: University of Oklahoma Press, 2001.

Gallagher, Carole. *American Ground Zero*. Boston: MIT Press, 1993.

Gehlbach, Frederick. *Mountain Islands and Desert Seas*. College Station: Texas A&M University Press, 1981.

Gutiérrez, Ramón. *When Jesus Came, the Corn Mothers Went Away*. Palo Alto, California: Stanford University Press, 1991.

Jacoby, Karl. *Crimes Against Nature*. Berkeley: University of California Press, 2001.

Jennings, Francis. *The Founders of America*. New York: Norton, 1993.

Krech, Shepherd. *The Ecological Indian*. New York: Norton, 1999.

Lawrence, David Herbert. *Phoenix: The Posthumous Papers of D. H. Lawrence*, edited by Edward D. McDonald. New York: Vintage, 1971.

Mares, Michael A. *A Desert Calling*. Cambridge: Harvard University Press, 2002.

Montejano, David. *Anglos and Mexicans in the Making of Texas, 1836–1986*. Austin: University of Texas Press, 1987.

Maxwell, Robert S., and Robert D. Baker. *Sawdust Empire: The Texas Lumber Industry, 1830–1940*. College Station: Texas A&M University Press, 1983.

Morris, John Miller. "When Corporations Rule the Llano Estacado." In *The Future of the Southern Plains*, edited by Sherry L. Smith. Norman: University of Oklahoma Press, 2003.

Smith, Sherry L., ed. *The Future of the Southern Plains*. Norman: University of Oklahoma Press, 2003.

Strom, Claire. "Texas Fever and the Dispossession of the Southern Yeoman Farmer." *Journal of Southern History* 66, no. 1 (2000): 49–74.

Weber, David. *The Spanish Frontier in North America*. New Haven, Connecticut: Yale University Press, 1992.

West, Elliott. "Trails and Footprints: The Past of the Future Southern Plains." In *The Future of the Southern Plains*, edited by Sherry L. Smith. Norman: University of Oklahoma Press, 2003.

White, Richard. *The Roots of Dependency*. Lincoln: University of Nebraska Press, 1988.

Wilkinson, Charles. *Crossing the Next Meridian*. Washington, DC: Island Press, 1992.

Woodhouse, Connie. "Droughts of the Past, Implications for the Future?" In *The Future of the Southern Plains*, edited by Sherry L. Smith. Norman: University of Oklahoma Press, 2003.

Worster, Donald. *Rivers of Empire*. New York: Oxford, 1992.

Web Sites

American Memory: The Evolution of the Conservation Movement. Accessed December 2003.
Part of a large project of the Library of Congress, this Web site features documents, chronologies, photographs, paintings, and reports relating to the conservation movement. A searchable index allows for the easy finding of southwestern places and topics.
http://memory.loc.gov/ammem/amrvhtml/conshome.html

Center for Bison Studies. Accessed December 2003.
The Web site of Montana State University's Center for Bison Studies. Features photographs, conference proceedings, and links and databases for numerous articles.
http://www.montana.edu/~wwwcbs/

High Country News. Accessed December 2003.
The online version of a weekly paper that covers the environmental and society of the American West. Excellent searchable archive going back to 1993.
http://www.hcn.org

Videos/Films

The Atomic Café. Prod./dir. Kevin Rafferty, Jayne Loader, and Pierce Rafferty. The Archives Project. 1982 [2002].

Entertaining yet chilling picture of America in the atomic age, particularly of Southwestern landscapes, compiled from news reports, government training films, and military footage.

The Return of Navajo Boy. Dir. Jeff Spitz. Chicago, IL: Jeff Spitz Productions, circa 2000.

A compelling documentary about a Navajo family and the troubled legacy of uranium mining in the Navajo Nation. Also see http://www.navajoboy.com for press coverage and links to other resources about nuclear issues in the Southwest.

Organizations

The Blue Ribbon Coalition
P.O. Box 5549
Pocatello, ID 83202
http://sharetrails.org/

An umbrella group for those who believe that environmental regulations have become excessive and harmful. Many local chapters and events in the Southwest.

Center for Biological Diversity
P.O. Box 710
Tucson, AZ 85702-0710
http://www.sw-center.org/swcbd/

A private environmental organization focused on endangered species and threatened places.

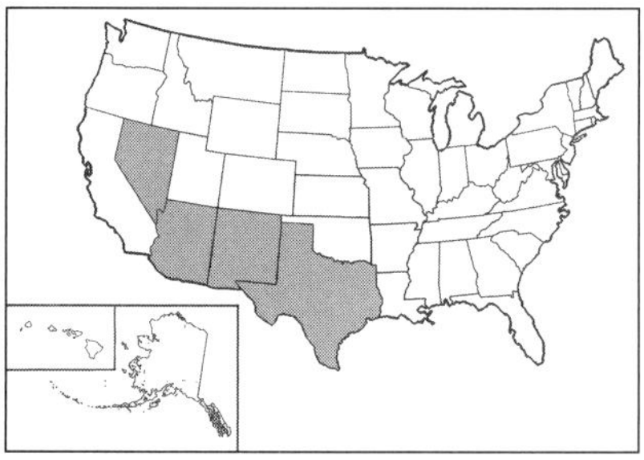

ETHNICITY

Ruben G. Mendoza and David L. Shaul

The American Southwest, as the saying goes, is the mother of many adopted children and as many widows, orphans, and outcasts as there are ethnic groups and immigrants in the region. Like her many children, she has adopted many place names along the way, not the least noteworthy of which is *deserte teribilius*, or terrible desert. Far from a desert of the human spirit, the Southwest conjures many images borne of both the antiquity and novelty of human adventure in so vast a region. Many other names have been proffered over the years, and many of those are attributed to scientists and scholars who have attempted to capture—by way of a singular moniker—the vast environmental and cultural diversity of the region that is the Southwest. Anthropologists, archaeologists, cultural geographers, and natural scientists have labeled this borderlands frontier the Greater Southwest, the Northern (Mexican) Frontier, and the Southwest Culture Area. Not surprisingly, such names hint at the geopolitical and geographical orientation of those scholars, explorers, colonists, and tourists who conjured the labels in the first place.

For many of the Hispanic and tribal peoples of the Southwest, a deeper and more sacred association with the land has been cultivated over the course of centuries. For the Native Americans, the Southwest is—like the *sipapu* openings in the floors of Anasazi and Pueblo *kivas*, or ritual enclosures—the place of emergence of the ancestors and all those who follow in the ways of the ancestors. For the Mexican-origin population, or Mexican American and Chicanos of the region, the Southwest is no less than the legendary Aztlán of Mexican/Aztec lore. No less revealing is that sense of loss seldom expressed but often experienced by those Hispanic and Mexican-origin peoples who come to see the region as the lost land or contested homeland where so many ancestors, be they Hispanic (Spanish), *mestizo* (mixed Hispanic), or *afromestizo* (mixed African American), toiled and bled for an elusive stake in the history of a place today simply referred to as the Southwest.

Ultimately, for archaeologists and ethnographers who have attempted to categorize and qualify the cultural diversity of the region, the Greater Southwest is seen to encompass that much broader expanse of terrain extending from Durango, Mexico, to Durango, Colorado, and from Las Vegas, Nevada, to Las Vegas, New Mexico. For those primarily concerned with simply characterizing the geopolitical landscapes of this vast borderlands frontier, inclusion of the contemporary U.S. states of Arizona, Utah, New Mexico, Colorado, and Texas will generally suffice. For this treatment, whose basic purpose is to identify and describe both cultural diversity and ethnicity on the borderlands frontier, we will limit this review to Arizona, New Mexico, Texas, and portions of Nevada. Although this essay will address the ethnicity of that portion of the Great Basin identified with the modern state of Nevada, it should be noted that the Great Basin lies outside of the purview of anthropologically informed definitions of what cultural and geographical areas constitute the Southwest.

An overview of those social and cultural dynamics that necessarily underscore the concept of ethnicity and the relative place of ethnic identity will assist efforts to conjure meaning from that cultural and geographic mosaic that constitutes the Southwest regional cultural tradition.

ETHNICITY DEFINED

An ethnic group consists of a group of people who—often by virtue of a common biological and linguistic inheritance, national or regional origin, or cultural heritage—maintain and perpetuate a common body of mutual interests, customs, beliefs, and traditions; and who perceive themselves as sharing a common cultural origin and identity. The term *ethnic* itself derives from the Latin *ethnicus* and the Greek *ethnikos*, which both signify a person or group borne of a national origin other than that of the nation-state in which said individual or group resides; and thereby, the condition of being an outsider to the national culture or patrimony. Secondary meanings for *ethnic* imply the status of being heathen, or "of or relating to large groups of people classed according to common racial, national, tribal, religious, linguistic, or cultural origin and background."[1] Ethnicity, in turn, is identified with those who maintain an "ethnic quality or affiliation."[2] In each instance, the identification of the term *ethnic* or *ethnicity* is consonant with a member or members of a "minority group who retains the customs, language, or social views" of such a group.[3]

Demography and Ethnicity

The census reports of the U.S. Census Bureau provide one particularly effective means by which to interpret the prevalence of ethnic groups and ethnic group identity in the Southwest. Although the U.S. Census makes a concerted effort with each new census to improve the body of data pertaining to the existence of cultural and ethnic groups, the reality is that ethnicity and identity are often mercurial and complex. A single respondent to the census may indicate identification with more than one ethnic group or cultural identity. While this presents some complications for the collection of U.S. Census data, and in turn, the efforts of some ethnic-group constituencies to use this data to address community needs, such information does, nevertheless, provide a basis for tracking the emergence and overall cultural and ethnic diversity of any given area of the state or region for which such data is collected.

For Nevada, for instance, Census 2000 provides a number of ways to interpret the data collected, including its relative breakdown by (a) sex and age, (b) race, (c) race alone or in combination with one or more other races, (d) Hispanic or Latino ethnicity and race, (e) relationship, (f) households by type, (g) housing occupancy, and (h) housing tenure. To use the race category as an example, of a year 2000 population for Nevada of 1,998,257, persons identifying with a single race amounted to 1,921,829, or 96.2 percent. Those identifying themselves as white constituted 1,501,886 persons (75.2 percent); Hispanic or Latino (of any race), 393,970 persons (19.7 percent); some other race, 159,354 persons (8.0 percent); those as black or African American, 135,477 persons (6.8 percent); Asian, 90,266 persons (4.5 percent); two or more races, 76,428 persons (3.8 percent); American Indian or Alaskan Native, 26,420 persons (1.3 percent); and Native Hawaiian and other Pacific Islander, 8,426 persons (0.4 percent).

When examined from the perspective of one of the least populated Southwestern states (i.e., Nevada), extant ethnic diversity—as measured by persons who self-identify with the categories listed in U.S. Census—is clearly far more complex than might otherwise be imagined for such a subregion. In a survey of the Southwestern states Texas, New Mexico, Arizona, and Nevada, one must bear in mind those ethnic groups that transcend specific environmental and political subregions and those that appear to represent a direct by-product of specialized regional adaptations and political identities. Where American Indian communities are concerned, internal dimensions of ethnic diversity are particularly pronounced among such groups as the Pueblos of the Rio Grande of New Mexico, whose language, cultural traditions, plastic arts, and sociocultural and political forms of organization and kinship reckoning may vary considerably from one community to another.

Finally, the 2000 census data for Nevada makes clear that persons of Hispanic and Latino ethnicity are the region's second largest group and that, unlike the Pueblos of New Mexico, Hispanics and Latinos are more often than not the by-product of transnational and inter-American heritage and affiliation. Moreover, within the Hispanic and Latino community in question, the Mexican, Mexican American, or Chicano population figures most prominently and is taken to represent a single ethnic group despite the fact that the Mexican-origin population itself varies significantly by race, ethnicity, language, and culture.

Native Americans of the Southwest

Much of the Southwest—including Arizona, New Mexico, Nevada, and much of Texas—was initially bypassed by Anglo and other Euro-American colonists who dubbed the region the "Great American Desert." But in the nineteenth century, many Euro-Americans were lured to the Southwest by land or gold. This resulted in virtually all Native American populations being resettled onto reservation lands, or near traditional tribal territories, by 1900. Despite the coerced mid- to late-nineteenth-century resettlement of Southwestern Indian populations onto government-allotted and -controlled land reserves, or reservations, each Native American group of the region nevertheless represents a complex whole that conjoins cultural, social, historical, linguistic, and ethnic dimensions and region-specific features and qualities. More often than not, tribal groups maintain their original language in concert with what can be construed as a postcontact-era cultural configuration or ensemble of ethnic traits and features. Rather than representing ethnic subcultures, Southwestern Indian tribes and communities often constitute what some anthropologists deem binational cultures: in this case, traditional societies that maintain a degree of cultural autonomy and a spirit of self-determination, from which a sense of political empowerment and continuity with ancestral cultures on par with the national culture may be inferred.

Ancestral Peoples and Archaeological Cultures

Some contemporary American Indian ethnic and tribal groups maintain traditions derived from the prehistoric Native American cultures of the core Southwest. This fact, the degree of cultural continuity that may be inferred from it, and the physical settings that the peoples occupy serves as a basis for linking the cultures of the past with the ethnic and tribal peoples of the present, and for creating an archaeological record.

Archaeologists and linguists have identified the Colorado River area as the heartland of the Patayan, or Hakataya, archaeological culture which has been identified with that of the Yumans. The Hohokam archaeological culture, thought to have been multiethnic, flourished from the latter half of the first millennium to the beginning of the second millennium, in a vast region extending across southern Arizona to the general vicinity of what is now El Paso, Texas. The Mogollon culture dominated the mountains extending between Arizona and New Mexico; the Mogollon cultural pattern was apparently a culture that fused the traditions of neighboring peoples to the north and west. Both the Pueblos of Zuni and Acoma claim ancestral ties to the peoples of the Mogollon archaeological culture. The Pueblo peoples of the Rio Grande and the Hopi Mesas can claim lineal descent from the Anasazi culture, which was situated in the Four Corners region.

Two prominent Southwestern archaeological cultures for which modern ethnicity may be inferred—include the traditions of the Anasazi of the Colorado Plateau and the Hohokam of the Basin and Range physiographic province of central and southern Arizona. Contrary to the mystique and popular explanations of Anasazi abandonment or ruin, the Anasazi did not simply disappear. The material culture of the modern Pueblos is an outgrowth of the prehistoric Anasazi culture, which archaeologists and linguists believe was multiethnic. The Pueblo cultural pattern, too, is multiethnic, encompassing some twenty ethnic groups represented in an equal number of Pueblo communities who speak a variety of languages that belong to four language families, including Uto-Aztecan, Tanoan, Zunian, and Keresan.

The Hohokam culture of central and southern Arizona could also represent a multiethnic complex. Using linguistic prehistory, kinship, and other nonmaterial cultural traits, linguist David Shaul and archaeologist John Andresen effectively showed that Yuman and Piman cultures (Tohono O'odham and Pima) maintained longstanding and intimate interactions in prehistory and that the most likely locus or interaction sphere for this relationship was that of the Hohokam regional system. Piman ethnohistory concurs with this idea. According to Piman tradition, the Hohokam killed the ancestor identified as Elder Brother, who, as a result, arose from the ground and brought forth the Pimans to defeat the Hohokam. The lat-

Anasazi ruins in Mesa Verde National Park. Courtesy of Corbis.

ter departed for the West and became the Yumans of the Colorado River, or, one of two moieties of the historic Piman culture.

AMERINDIAN CULTURE REGIONS OF THE SOUTHWEST

Colorado River and Sonoran Desert Peoples

The Colorado River divides Arizona and California and is at the core of the ancestral lands of the Yuman language family, which includes the Cocopa, Yuma (Quechan), Mojave, and Maricopa tribes. During the late eighteenth century, the Maricopa migrated eastward along the Gila River to the Phoenix area, where they joined the Pima, or Akimel O'odham (River People), who were allied with the Tohono O'odham (Desert People) of the Sonoran Desert of southern Arizona against most of the Colorado River Yuman peoples. It should be noted, however, that the Tohono O'odham were until quite recently known by their Spanish characterization, Papago (Bean Eaters), a name since abandoned by the Tohono O'odham nation. Tohono O'odham and Akimel O'odham (Pima) peoples are closely related linguistically and culturally.

Peoples of the Colorado Plateau

The Four Corners area—where Utah, Arizona, New Mexico, and Colorado converge—remains a geopolitical region imbued with significant symbolic and cultural meanings for peoples of the Colorado Plateau and beyond. Within a 250-mile radius of the Four Corners are to be found the material remains and

A Tohono O'odham woman collecting cholla cactus in Arizona, 1907. Edward Curtis. This cactus was an important staple to the Native Americans living in the area. Courtesy of the Library of Congress.

abandoned ruins of the ancestral Pueblo peoples, the Anasazi. Since just prior to the Spanish *entrada*, or initial Hispanic colonial exploration and contacts of the late 1500s, Puebloan peoples have settled and resettled along the Rio Grande drainage of New Mexico, as well as along those tributaries and places of refuge that dot the landscapes of northwestern New Mexico. Outside of the Rio Grande pueblos are the pueblos of Zuni, Acoma, and Laguna of northwestern New Mexico and the Hopi villages of northeastern Arizona. Zuni constitutes a language isolate with no known linguistic relatives. Hopi belongs to the broadly dispersed Uto-Aztecan language family.

To the west of the Hopi, in northern, western, and central Arizona, were the transhumant or hunter-gatherer Pai tribes, including the Havasupai of the Grand Canyon, the Walapai, and the Yavapai. These groups all communicated in closely related languages and dialects belonging to the Yuman language family.

The Pueblos of New Mexico speak languages belonging to the Tanoan language family, plus the Keresan language isolate. Keresan is spoken at seven villages (Acoma, Laguna, Santa Ana, Zía, San Felipe, Santo Domingo, and Cochiti). The Tanoan languages include Northern Tiwa, which is spoken at Taos and Picuris Pueblos; Southern Tiwa, spoken at Isleta and Sandia pueblos; Towa, spoken at Jemez Pueblo; and Tewa, spoken at San Juan, Santa Clara, San Ildefonso, Tesuque, and Nambe Pueblos. While each of these Pueblo Indian communities have been typified as tribal groups, they conform more closely to a town-centered, community tradition with ancient roots extending through to their Anasazi forebearers.

Peoples of the Mogollon Highlands

The vast Colorado Plateau mountain range dividing Arizona and New Mexico constitutes that region identified with the Mogollon Highlands. In the mountains of the Mogollon Highlands and in southern Arizona and New Mexico are to be found various tribal peoples identified as Apache, including the Mescalero, Chiricahua, and Western Apache. Related groups include the Jicarilla Apache of northern New Mexico and the Navajos (Diné) of the Four Corners area. The Apache and Navajo languages belong to the Athabascan language family. All other Athabascan languages are spoken in western Canada and Alaska, and it can be inferred that at some point in prehistory both the Apache and Navajos (or "Apaches de Navajo," according to Spanish colonial records) migrated into the Southwest. Archaeological evidence consisting of pit houses and related features indicates that Athabascan peoples entered the region nearly one thousand years ago.

The migratory hunter-gatherer lifeway of the Apache came into conflict with that of the Spanish colonists of New Mexico and the Pueblos who joined forces in the latter 1600s to defend agricultural lands and livestock from the Apachean pattern of raiding. Whereas the Navajo would in time be transformed—by way of subsequent conflict and subjugation by the U.S. Cavalry—into pastoralists dependent on introduced domestic livestock such as sheep and horses, the Apache would remain hunter-gatherers and engage in raiding activities against the Hispanic, Mexican, and Euro-American intruders who gradually swept up their ancestral Apache tribal lands during the nineteenth and twentieth centuries.

The Peoples of the Rio Grande Delta

The Native Americans who originally occupied the Rio Grande Delta of Texas were largely dispersed by the time Euro-American settlers entered the region in the early to mid-nineteenth century. In eastern Texas, Caddoan speaking tribes—the Wichita, Caddo, and Waco—along with the language isolate or group known as Atakapa, engaged in agricultural pursuits and sedentary village life prior to the arrival of the Euro-Americans. Southwestern Texas and adjoining New Mexico and northern Mexico constituted the original tribal territories of the Manso, Jumanos, and other lesser-known groups.

After 1700 a number of tribal groups introduced to the Southwest what is usually construed as the classic Plains Indian way of life, which included horses (originally introduced by the Spanish), tipis, and a buffalo-hunting economy to the plains of central, western, and northern Texas. These groups included the Lipan and Kiowa Apache (Athabascan language family), the Comanche (Uto-Aztecan), and the Kiowas (a Tanoan language related to some Rio Grande Pueblos), all of which ultimately overtook the nomadic Tonkawa tribal group and language isolate of central Texas.

Peoples of the Great Basin

The tribal peoples of Nevada and adjoining areas of Utah and California are speakers of Southern Paiute (closely related to Chemehuevi), Shoshone, and Northern Paiute, all of which are members of the Numic branch of the Uto-Aztecan language family (which also includes Comanche). The Ute tribe specifically and Paiute language and traditional culture generally once inhabited the physiographic province of the Great Basin, including much of what is today Nevada, Utah, and western Colorado. One last language isolate that bears mentioning is that of the Washo of the Lake Tahoe area. Tahoe, in fact, translates as *lake* in the Washo language.

Other Tribal Peoples of the Southwest

Many other tribal peoples and reservation communities may be found along the length and breadth of the U.S.-Mexican borderlands frontier, and these include people as diverse and linguistically distinct as the Tohono O'odham, Pima, and Havasupai of Arizona; the Paiute of Nevada, Utah, and Colorado; and the Caddo, Comanche, Kiowa, Lipan and Mescalero Apache, Cherokee, Kickapoo, Tigua,

Tonkawas, Wichitas, Creek, and Coahuilteca of Texas. Each of these groups has prospered or languished as the result of perennial patterns of conflict and accommodation with Hispanic, Mexican, and Anglo, or Euro-American, cultures, as well as with other Native American peoples.

Among these Native American peoples whose ancestries straddle the U.S.-Mexican borderlands frontier are groups not easily defined by any singular social and cultural tradition or by a single regional or national origin. These transnational peoples are the Yaquí and Tohono O'odham, or Papago, of southern Arizona and the Kickapoo and Isleta Pueblo of southern Texas. While the Yaquí and Tohono O'odham maintain closely guarded and vibrant, albeit Hispanicized, cultural traditions, the Kickapoo and Isleta del Sur Pueblo heritage has been largely attenuated and almost fully Hispanicized.

The Yaquí Indians of Sonora are a Mexican-origin group that survived a long-term pattern of persecution on the borderlands by migrating to southern Arizona and making use of their colonial acculturation as Hispanicized Indians to adapt to conditions in southern Arizona. In an effort to meld into the cultures and communities of Tucson and vicinity, the Pasqua Yaquí settled into existing Mexican and Mexican American *barrios* or *colonias*, where their status as hybrid Catholics, their proficiency with the Spanish language, and their Hispanicized lifeways made them invisible to their persecutors. Despite their Mexican-origin status, today the Yaquí are an acknowledged American Indian community whose closely guarded traditions and separate ethnic identities continue to be defined in terms of language, material culture, religion, and tribal territories.

HISPANIC- AND MEXICAN-ORIGIN POPULATIONS

Today, Mexican American or Chicano communities represent one of the largest and fastest-growing ethnic groups in the American Southwest. While the nation-state of Mexico represents the point of origin for many of the ancestral elements of this population, the reality is that a significant cohort of this Southwestern ethnic group or national-origin population has its roots in five primary periods of historically documented patterns of migration and colonization. The periods are as follows: (a) the colonial era, 1521/1602 through 1821, during which New Spain or Mexico undertook exploratory expeditions and colonial settlement programs in the Southwest, (b) the Mexican era, 1821 through 1848, during which antecedent Spanish colonial institutions such as the frontier mission system underwent secularization and dismantling, (c) the early American era, 1848–1875, during which repeated foreign interventions by the United States, France, and Spain generated instability in Mexico, resulting in population movements and displacements (d) the early period of Mexican modernization and development under the dictatorial and free-market mandates of Mexican President Porfirio Diaz (1880–84; 1888–1910) and the subsequent civil war that resulted in the long-term bloodshed of the Mexican Revolution (1910–1917) and its aftermath (for example, the Cristero Rebellion, 1917–1928), and (e) the pattern of twentieth- and twenty-first-century Mexican migration to the United States fueled by any number of U.S. and Mexican incentive programs and social and economic conditions that serve as push and pull forces operating to this day along the borderlands frontier. This latter long-term pattern of migration to the United States has been deemed the Fourth Wave insofar as the demographic scale and ethnic sources of the pattern are concerned.

Fundamentally, the contemporary Mexican-origin population of the U.S. Southwest represents a broad-based, diverse set of cultures, histories, and ethnicities; more generally, and as such, this ethnodemographic feature of the Southwest is largely a derivative of the patterns and processes that span the ancient, historical, and recent undercurrents that make up the shared cultural history of the U.S. Southwest and Mexico. But diverse European, African, and Asian cultural and linguistic origins and affinities, as well as Mexican and Southwestern Indian ethnic groups and tribal communities, also comprise part of the diverse backgrounds of extant Mexican-origin populations in the U.S. Southwest, a fact often overlooked. Whereas the Mexican-origin population is popularly characterized by the media and the general public as the result of recent in-migration to the U.S. borderlands region, the reality is that such groups as the *Manitos* or *Hispanos* of New Mexico, *Californios* of California, *Tucsonensis* of southern Arizona, *Norteños* of the Sonoran desert and borderlands, and the *Afromestizos* of Texas, all played an early historical role in the colonization and settlement of U.S. Southwest. Added to this is the growing admixture of other Latin American or Latina and Latino immigrants and Southwest Native American groups who have intermarried with, and melded into, the Mexican origin population of the region. Today, much of the pattern of migration that serves to reify the cultural and linguistic traditions of the Mexican and Chicano communities of the Southwest is in large part derived from northern and western Mexico, including the states of Michoacan, Colima, Nayarit, Jalisco, Chihuahua, Sonora, Tamaulipas, Guanajuato, and Queretaro. Other primary sources of migration to the Southwest include those specific to Zapotec and Mixtec Indian language speakers from the Mexican state of Oaxaca who are often recruited for the purposes of providing low-wage agricultural labor. These groups have added to the linguistic and ethnic diversity that is generally ascribed to the broader Mexican American or Mexican-origin population of the Southwest. Interestingly, the influx of Mexican Indian peoples from the aforementioned areas has added to the conflicting identities ascribed to the U.S. Indian population by demographers that seldom recognize such Mexican Indian groups as ethnically, biologically, culturally, or linguistically Indian. Chicano and Mexican American activists often interpret Mexican American or Chicano identity in terms of Hispanic or Indian ancestry, claiming Indian identity within the context of the politically charged arena of American Indian identity and culture.

Mexican origin or Mexican American ethnicity is essentially multicultural, with both Mexican Indian and Hispanic and European elements clearly apparent in social, linguistic, and material cultural sources. What is perhaps less apparent in the Mexican-origin population is the dimension of the cultural and biological substrate derived of West Africa, the Caribbean, and the afromestizos of Mexico and the U.S. Southwest. In her recent contribution to this dialogue, Martha Menchaca has produced a significant overview of the place and role of Africans and afromestizos in Southwestern and California culture history and ethnicity. According to Menchaca, a significant number of those early Hispanic settlers to Texas, New Mexico, Arizona, and California were in fact afromestizos who often remained unacknowledged due to proscriptions against recording their numbers as well as those of mestizos and Native Americans in colonial and postcolonial census lists and related documentary records.[4] Menchaca also cross-referenced both military and civilian census data and related records for the original Hispanic settlement of Santa Fe, New Mexico, in her efforts to determine the ethnic and cultural sources of eight hundred colonists who first settled that community. Menchaca determined that, despite the proscriptions and policies in effect at that time, only about two hundred of those settlers were specifically identified as ethnically or "racially" white. The vast majority of the original colonists were ethnically and culturally mestizo, mulatto, *vndio* (Mexican Indian; specifically, Tlaxcalteca and Otomí), afromestizo, and African-origin peoples. Clearly, the differential and often biased and exclusionary collection of census data continues to affect perceptions of the role of these groups in the Hispanic and Mexican origins, settlements, and colonization of the Southwest.

Cultural Contributions of Hispanic- and Mexican-Origin Peoples

Native American, Hispanic, and Mexican origin populations have had a profound impact on the aspects of the architecture, art, material culture, food, language, and religious beliefs that form the very foundations and most conspicuous dimensions of Southwestern culture and tradition. From Pueblo architecture, settlement, and art styles through to Hispanic and Mexican settlement patterns, architecture, foods, and agricultural traditions, the historical and cultural impact brought to bear by these two populations is generally unmistakable in modern Southwestern communities. While some architectural historians argue for the importance of the American-era emphasis on invention of the Santa Fe style of architecture, for instance, the underlying reality is that these architectural traditions are largely derivative or hybrid composites of both Hispanic and Southwest Indian traditional styles and settlement designs refined over the course of some four centuries of cultural interaction.

The so-called Mission style furniture tradition that is today widely reproduced and sold in furniture stores across the United States is but one reflection of the Hispanic and Mexican craft tradition first introduced into the U.S. Southwest during the Hispanic colonial, Mexican, and early American periods of settlement and interaction. Whereas the Native American tradition in the U.S. Southwest has been documented archaeologically as extending back 11,500 years, Hispanic or Mexican origin influences and interactions date to the period from A.D. 1540 with the initial *entrada* by Francisco Vasquez de Coronado, who first trekked the region from Arizona, through New Mexico, Colorado, and Kansas, and thereby made possible the subsequent, albeit belated, Hispanic settlement of Santa Fe by Juan de Oñate in 1602.

Anthropologist and ethnohistorian James E. Officer acknowledges the extent to which early American histories essentially excluded or minimized the much broader cultural, social, economic, and political impact of Hispanic and Mexican origin ethnic groups in the history of Arizona and the Southwest more generally.[5] In addressing this concern, Officer recognizes Hispanic contributions in Arizona beginning with the arrival at Hopi of Franciscan missionaries from New Mexico in 1629. The Jesuit Eusebio Francisco Kino is credited with the founding of the towns of Guevavi and Bac in 1700. However, recognition of the more permanent Hispanic- or Mexican-origin presence in Arizona materialized with the discovery in 1736 of silver mines at a location some seventy miles south of Tucson at a site then called Arizonac by Hispanic settlers. In his survey of what he terms Arizona's "Hispanic perspective," Officer makes specific reference to the considerable contributions of Hispanic- and Mexican-origin peoples in the region's exploration and settlement, architectural development, place names, and ranching, farming, mining, and civic-ceremonial traditions. Whether reflected in contemporary Mission style architecture, art, and furnishings, or through the impact of Hispanic and Mexican origin ranching traditions on the evolution of the American cowboy and his gear, the effect was considerable, and the presence remains pervasive.

Given that Hispanic peoples are credited with the initial exploration, settlement, and colonization of some thirty-eight of the fifty states within the United States, scholars now seem to be less reticent about acknowledging this growing preponderance of evidence for the immense Hispanic contribution to North American history and culture. Inevitably, this contribution is made more apparent in the place names of such major towns and cities as San Agustin and Pensacola, Florida; Los Angeles, Monterey, and San Francisco, California; Tucson, Arizona; Santa Fe and Albuquerque, New Mexico; El Paso and San Antonio, Texas; and in the many place names of the adjacent states of Nevada, Colorado, Louisiana, and, further afield, Alabama. And of course the Mexican and Hispanic presence in the Southwest is very pronounced: virtually every major city in the borderlands states of California, Arizona, New Mexico, and Texas was founded by Hispanic and Mexican origin settlers and explorers.

Ironically, however, despite such a legacy and the visibility of Hispanic- and Mexican-origin place names, the Hispanic contribution has been given less than its due in the American historical tradition. Much of the cultural and historical effacement and exclusion experienced by Hispanic- and Mexican-origin peoples in America's recorded histories, it may be argued, is largely the by-product of animosities and stereotypes born of the U.S. and Mexican War (1846–1848) and the subsequent displacement of Mexican-origin populations in the affected territories. Regional histories of the past that largely excluded mention of Mexican-origin and Hispanic contributions to the settlement and development of the Southwestern states were also hampered and limited by language barriers, problems with access to primary-source documents such as Hispanic census records, Spanish-language accounts and publications, and a predominately Anglo-American perspective. Today, the Hispanic and Mexican origin contribution has surfaced in literature, although some scholars and popular media sources refer to accounts that describe such contributions as "revisionist" histories, perceiving bias in a multicultural or implying an "ethnically" politicized agenda.

Conflict and Accommodation

One of the most persistent and entrenched ethnic political symbols of the Mexican-origin population in the Southwest concerns the ongoing struggle for a unified political identity and a modicum of cultural autonomy and self-determination. Spanning the period since the Battle of San Antonio de Valero (the Alamo) in 1836, and encompassing U.S. intervention and the Treaty of Guadalupe-Hidalgo of 1848; Mexican, Mexican American, and Chicano ethnicity and political and cultural activism continues to hinge on that historic turning point when

Mission San Jose De Laguna near Santa Fe, New Mexico. Courtesy of Corbis.

Mexico ceded its Northwestern frontier, the contemporary U.S. states of California, Arizona, Nevada, Utah, New Mexico, and Texas to the United States of America. One political refrain often heard among Chicano activists in the Southwest touts that "we didn't cross the border, the border crossed us!" Rodolfo Acuña's book *Occupied America: A History of Chicanos* provides an alternative treatment of Chicano history from a uniquely Chicano, or Mexican-origin, perspective. Needless to say, like so many artistic, cultural, and political statements anchored to the politics of the Mexican Cession of 1848, Acuña's book has elicited a significant—and largely antithetical—reaction from scholars concerned with Southwestern and American history. However one might perceive *Occupied America*, the reality is that Acuña's treatment brought to the fore the ongoing nature and extent of conflict, violence, and accommodation that has come to define Mexican-origin peoples and their interactions with both Anglos and other "outsiders"—that is, non-Hispanic peoples—in the Southwest.

At the same time, Anglo-American apologists are quick to note that the Hispanic mission system and those Mexican-origin settlers who followed, largely decimated the contact-era Indian populations of the U.S. Southwest. Recent studies by Martha Menchaca, Douglas Monroy, and a host of others now make clear that the dynamics of Southwestern cultural interaction and change was much more complex and complicated than that earlier historians described. Those earlier perspectives presented scenarios of predatory Hispanic or Anglo-American versus an otherwise peaceable Hispanic- or Mexican-origin peoples and Southwest Indians.[6]

The reality of Hispanic- or Mexican-origin and Anglo-American interactions along the borderlands frontier has been treated in a very broad and growing literature on ethnic conflict and accommodation. Whether the tumultuous ethnic identity of some elements of the Mexican-origin population has been characterized as the product of "Mexicano resistance" and the "sacred right of self-preservation" as in Robert Rosenbaum's treatise, or as the quest for the "Lost Land" or Aztlán, as discussed by John R. Chavez, Chicano identity and its youth counterculture often hearken to this fount of history for historical grounding and cultural meaning in the broader patterns of American history.[7] So the notion of the U.S. Southwest as the ethnic equivalent of the Chicano place of emergence and rebirth is still very much alive among activist Mexican origin youth who see reflected in the Mexica Aztec notion of Aztlán their own place of origin, or their "contested homeland."[8]

Such emotionally charged perspectives are part and parcel of a long and tumultuous history between Anglo-American, Indian, and Hispanic settlers, as well as African, Asian, European, and other Latin American groups and cultures. In Douglas V. Meed's account of border conflict, *Bloody Border: Riots, Battles and Adventures along the Turbulent U.S.-Mexican Borderlands*, the borderlands appears as little more than an oscillating frontier of conflict and violence in which soldiers of fortune, Texas Rangers, race wars, massacres, Mexican revolutionaries and social bandits are the order of the day. The characterization may well have fit the fluctuating fortunes that dominated the lives of those on the border during the mid- to late nineteenth and early twentieth centuries, and the U.S.-Mexico borderlands frontier remains a cultural, economic, political, and social frontier in every sense, though today's scenario is vastly different in scope and substance. The protagonists in this instance range from Billy the Kid to the Texas Rangers, Francisco "Pancho" Villa to Cesar Chavez, and African American U.S. Second Lieutenant Henry Ossian Flipper to Japanese rice farmer Seito Saibara, and many, many others.

The turbulent civil rights movements and actions of the 1960s and 1970s clearly hastened the introduction of state and federal legislation intended to safeguard the lives, property, and welfare of Hispanic, Mexican-origin, African American, and other peoples of color on the U.S.–Mexico borderlands frontier. The efforts by armed Hispanic landowners from 1889 to 1895 to protect their lands from Anglo-American encroachment via the formation of a vigilante group popularly known as the *Gorras Blancas* and the 1967 raid on the Tierra Amarilla, New Mexico, courthouse by civil-rights activist and land-rights advocate Reies López Tijerina show that Mexican and Hispanic resistance and civil-rights movements have responded time and again to both real and imagined encroachments on land and culture by those construed as "outsiders."

Where the question of intercultural accommodation and acculturation is concerned, once again the picture is as diverse as it is both individual and collective. The extent to which each group has sought to accommodate and/or tolerate the cultural practices and ethnic diversity of fellow Southwestern peoples varies according to the economic and social conditions and political agendas that affect each respective group. Whereas Hispanic and Native American land rights were once an overriding concern, today historic communities' demands for water rights and land-use treaties dominate the nature of formal relations and legal actions by Hispanic and Native Americans against other public and private concerns in areas like the state of New Mexico. Many of those sources of conflict that once framed the history of the region remain unresolved to this day. On the other hand, the recent emphasis on multiculturalism in public education and the celebration of diversity in public events and community programs has engendered a newfound respect and understanding for the traditions of ethnic groups and populations such as the Hispanic and Mexican-origin peoples of the Southwest. Long-term patterns of gerrymandering (exclusionary and discriminatory political redistricting), voting-rights violations, and poll taxes have all played a key role in undermining the extent to which Hispanic communities have been afforded the opportunity to represent their respective demographic dominance in some regions and counties of the Southwest.[9] But Hispanic and Mexican origin communities have increased their representation in the political, educational, and cultural arenas.

Community Participation and Celebrations

Despite the ongoing struggle for political and social empowerment in the Southwestern states, Hispanic and Mexican-origin peoples continue to maintain a relatively high visibility in the cultural life and civic affairs of many borderlands communities.[10] The creation of Hispanic Heritage Month (September 16–October 12) acknowledges the many and diverse contributions of Spanish-speaking, Hispanic, and Mexican-origin peoples in the United States. The month begins with very public displays and celebrations commemorating Mexican Independence from Spain, which was initiated by the heroic actions of parish priest in Dolores, Mexico, Miguel Hidalgo y Costilla, on September 16th 1810 (though it is celebrated on September 16), and culminates with Columbus Day, or *Día de la Raza*, which marks October 12, 1492, the date of Christopher Columbus' arrival in the Americas. The ceremonialism surrounding this latter acknowledgement is often challenged and celebrated in contrasting ways by Italian Americans and Mexican-origin peoples, the first of whom typically celebrate the life and explorations of this Genovese navigator and the latter sometimes as Día de la Raza in memory of those Native American forbearers lost in the European invasion of the Americas that began with Columbus' landfall in the Caribbean. For many Native Americans and some Chicanos, on the other hand, the date is not deemed worthy of celebration but censure.

Jovita Gonzales records her students while teaching at St. Mary's College in San Antonio. Ms. Gonzales was born near the Texas-Mexico border and became very involved with the Texas Folklore Society. Courtesy of the Library of Congress.

In remote Southwestern Mexican-origin communities like the Clifton-Morenci mining district of east-central Arizona, as well as in Mexico, the *dies y seis de septiembre*, or 16th of September, has been actively promoted and celebrated with considerable fanfare and a carnival-like atmosphere since the early part of the 1870s by Mexican patriotic and *mutualistas* (mutual-aid societies) such as *Alianza Hispano-Americana*. The centerpiece of the day is the reenactment of the so-called *Grito de Dolores* (The Cry of Dolores), in which Fray Miguel Hidalgo y Costilla called on the Mexican people to throw off the shackles of their Spanish overlords on September 16th of 1810. While the celebrations that open and close Hispanic Heritage Month are significant national Mexican-origin and Hispanic or Iberian-origin observances, neither is a direct by-product of Southwestern cultural history or Mexican American community histories; nevertheless, they serve to perpetuate a recognition of these historical events beyond the national-origin contexts within which each originated. Similarly, the continuing influx of *Sonorensis* (Sonorans) and other Mexican peoples into the U.S. borderlands reinforces and reinvigorates the vitality of each of these celebrations among the border peoples.[11] The 16th of September remains a very visible and particularly popular national celebration in Mexico, whereas in the U.S. Southwest its observance is largely restricted to places with significantly sized populations of first- and second-generation Mexican immigrants. For instance, in Tucson, Arizona, the 16th of September often brings on a carnival-like atmosphere, including Mexican food booths, mariachi musicians, and colorful parades that wend their way along the main boulevards of South Tucson.

In addition to the many moveable "feast days" of the *Santos* (saints of the Catholic Church), which remain a key *modus operandi* for promoting community solidarity and cohesion among Latina and Latino Catholics, another celebration key to the pride of Mexican-origin peoples is *Cinco de Mayo*, the 5th of May. The Cinco de Mayo proclaims and acknowledges the heroic exploits of a ragtag group of Mexican soldiers—under the command of Texas-born Mexican general Ignacio Zaragoza—who managed to fend off the invasion of the French imperial forces at the Battle of Puebla on May 5, 1862. The irony in this instance is that whereas the Cinco de Mayo remains little more than a regional celebration predominantly restricted to the Mexican state of Puebla, in the U.S. Southwest and its borderlands, the observance has been transformed into a major Mexican American cultural observance with a significant commercial aspect. During the Cinco de Mayo celebrations Mexican-origin peoples highlight the most colorful, culturally specific, and festive dimensions of the Mexican and Chicano traditions, and not unexpectedly, major product labels and manufacturers often target these celebrations to promote their products within the Southwest's Hispanic and Mexican-origin communities. So pervasive is this Mexican-origin celebration that it has emerged as a focal point of commercial and community celebrations beyond the Southwestern.

Whether manifested in the many mariachi bands and *conjuntos*, fiestas, speakers, and related cultural events that surface at such times or even the lowrider automobile "happenings" or car shows, these essentially Mexican cultural and historical traditions remain a visible aspect of Mexican-origin culturally oriented festivals in the U.S. Southwest and borderlands.

AFRICAN-ORIGIN AND AFROMESTIZO PEOPLES

The vast majority of the African-origin peoples who settled the Southwest in the period prior to the 1870s did so in concert with Spanish colonial expeditions, Mexican resettlement programs, and early American colonization. Spanish-colonial (1521–1821) and Mexican-era (1821–1848) African-origin colonists and settlers can be traced to West African and Caribbean or West Indian origins. African points of origin for European and early American slave trading—which resulted in the coerced relocation of some twenty million African peoples to the

Americas—is largely identified with the modern West African nations Benin and Ghana, where the precolonial and early colonial sub-Saharan African kingdoms of Ashanti and Dahomey held sway over the development of the slave trade in those regions. The slave raiders, influenced as they were by Muslim Arab traders, were mainly interested in those not of the Islamic faith and Arab tongue as fair game; only with the intensification of the European slave trade did more people of Islamic tradition find themselves caught up in the ever-broadening sweep for eligible slaves to be taken to the Americas.

In her book *Recovering History, Constructing Race: The Indian, White, and Black Roots of Mexican Americans,* Martha Menchaca presents a compelling synthesis of Southwest ethnicity and cultural diversity as pertains to the origins of the Mexican American people. A primary thrust of the Menchaca narrative is the extent to which Africans, afromestizos or (mixed-race blacks), and African American peoples played a role in the early colonization and settlement of the U.S. Southwest. As in other works about the role of blacks or African-descent peoples in the Southwest, Menchaca introduces the role of the African and afromestizos by describing the exploits of Estevan, also called Estevanico, who accompanied the explorer Álvar Núñez Cabeza de Vaca on the ill-fated expedition to Florida and subsequently trekked along the coastal margins of what today constitutes the Southeastern U.S. through to what later became Texas and New Mexico. After several years in captivity among Native American groups of the Southwest, Estevanico became proficient in the languages of the region. Having escaped his Native American captors, Estevanico eventually made his way back to northern New Spain, or Mexico. Given his demonstrated facility with Native American languages of the Southwest, Estevanico was subsequently recruited to lead Fray Marcos de Niza to the region in 1539. That latter expedition, which ended tragically for Estevanico at the Zuni Pueblo, nevertheless represents the first such Hispanic *entrada*, or encounter, between the aboriginal peoples of the Southwest and the Hispanicized African, or afromestizo cultures. By 1792 early Hispanic Texas, for instance, was populated by some 34 blacks and some 414 afromestizos or mulattoes. Given Martha Menchaca's previously cited analysis of that census data available for the earliest colonial settlement of New Mexico and the proscriptions set in place by the Spanish colonial military against counting nonwhites, it is likely that even the earliest figures from Texas for *afromestizo* settlers reflect an institutionalized undercounting of that population.

According to historian W. Marvin Dulaney, unlike those African-origin and afromestizo peoples who entered the region in the Hispanic colonial era, the vast majority of those who entered later did so as slaves.[12] Dulaney notes that from 1821 through 1836 slavery grew slowly in the Mexican province. According to Menchaca, in 1830, on the eve of Texan independence from Mexico, the slave population numbered 2,000.[13] Once free of Mexico's antislavery legislation, white settlers institutionalized slavery as a means of promoting economic development, and therefore, slavery and the slave trade grew to epic proportions in Texas. This fact is reflected in the census data. According to Dulaney, by 1840, 11,000 African-origin peoples were enslaved in Texas.[14] Menchaca indicates that by 1850 this number had grown to 58,161.[15] Ultimately, according the U.S. Census of 1864, by 1860 some 182,566 African origin peoples—or thirty percent of the population of Texas—were subjected to slavery.

The plight of African-origin peoples in the region that had once constituted the northern Mexican Republic worsened with Texas independence, in 1836. Whereas Mexican president Antonio Lopez de Santa Anna sought to enforce the antislavery legislation that in large part led to the conflict with Texas, Texan independence ultimately left former African-origin and afromestizo peoples vulnerable to exploitation and the loss of private properties. Such a deliberate subordination of African-origin peoples was facilitated by the actions of the Republic of Texas and subsequently by the U.S. Congress.

Shortly after independence, the Republic of Texas rapidly moved to nullify Spanish- and Mexican-era land grants and titles belonging to blacks and Indians. This wholesale dispossession of lands and the destruction of documents was subsequently reinforced in the courts of the American period, as most blacks had by this time little to no recourse where the verification of claims was concerned. In other instances, blacks were forced out of those communities and off those lands that they had in fact colonized and developed into the first black homesteads and communities in the state. This occurred in the case of the Aaron Ashworth family, whose ranch holdings and personal belongings were seized on May 15, 1856, by an angry mob of white neighbors intent on dispossessing any and all blacks of their homes and land holdings in Jefferson and Orange counties. Although Texas continued to perpetuate and advance new policies and legislation that were consistently adverse to the basic civil rights and newfound liberties of freedmen (liberated blacks) in the post–Civil War period (c. 1865–1885), a very few blacks managed to maintain land titles as the result of their ability to litigate their claims with substantial amounts of money and political capital. According to Menchaca, only nine black men are documented to have received an exemption to the loss of their land titles: Emmanuel J. Hardin, Robert Thompson, James Richardson, Samuel McMullen, John T. Weber, Greenborg Logan, Levi Jones, Samuel Hardin, and Hendrick Arnold.[16] All of the men in question were members of Stephen Austin's colony and had obtained their grants via Mexico's General Colonization Law of 1824. Their exemptions seem to have been based on the fact that each had been issued deeds as rewards for military service in the Texas War of Independence. Otherwise, the practice of dispossessing African-origin peoples of their land titles and civil liberties began with Texan independence and worsened through the course of the late nineteenth and early twentieth centuries.

The U.S. government intervened in the affairs of emancipated slaves via the creation of the so-called Freedmen's Bureau. Established in 1863, the Bureau of Refugees, Freedmen, and Abandoned Lands was the by-product of a congressional mandate to see through the effective transition of emancipated slaves from bondage to freedom. To that end, the War Department launched the American Freedmen's Inquiry Commission (AFIC) in an effort to determine the best course of action for assisting emancipated slaves. The American Union Commission (AUC) launched by antislavery advocates operated in concert with the AFIC in an effort to change southern attitudes toward slavery by seeking to aid southern white refugees. Historian Barry Crouch echoes the claims of others in asserting that the Freedmen's Bureau proved itself a resounding success in Texas by establishing a "sound foundation for Negro education" there.[17] Through its work and policies implemented, between 1865 and 1870, the Freedmen's Bureau, which was composed almost entirely of Union soldiers and Civil War veterans, could claim a legacy that included some 20,000 literate blacks. The significant cultural and educational role that the Freedmen's Bureau played in the successful transition of emancipated slaves has only begun to receive its due by way of supposedly revisionist reappraisals of its work.

Despite the early intervention of the U.S. government in ameliorating the plight of blacks in Texas and other Confederate states, much of the struggle was yet to be fought, and much of the struggle was left to blacks themselves to address. To that end, African-origin and afromestizo peoples responded to patterns of discrimination and institutionalized racism in a variety of ways, both formal and informal. For instance, in an effort to formalize and enforce sanctions protecting the rights of blacks, the National Association for the Advancement of Colored People (NAACP) and other African American groups established a foothold in Texas in order to protect and promote the rights still legally available to them in that state. Similarly, the role of black churches in promoting and protecting the rights of people in their congregations and communities cannot be overstated. Not surprisingly, then, African American church meetings ultimately became the venues within which the civil-rights movement was born. These same churches often became the targets of vandalism and arson by white southern extremists, ranging from the Ku Klux Klan to the Aryan Nation.

Despite the level of unfair treatment, outright discrimination, violence, or enslavement to which they were subjected throughout various areas of the U.S. Southwest, the fortunes of African-origin peoples varied significantly through time and between urban and rural settings. While many Southwestern urban communities maintained marginalized or core populations of blacks, in their efforts to seek their own fortunes in contexts free of discrimination and slavery, African-origin and afromestizo settlers established a number of all-black towns across the Southwest. Some of the "black towns" in Texas were Booker, Andy, Oldham, Shankleville, Board House, Kendleton, and Cologne. The black towns in New Mexico were Dora, Blackdom, and El Vado. Symbols of refuge from slavery and discrimination and colonies of the black experience, these communities remain a critical source of black pride in the African American historical and cultural enterprise.

Although earlier historical treatments relegated the history of African American presence and impact on the cultures and peoples of the Southwest to a marginal and demographically minor status—particularly because of their role as slaves and servants to Hispanic and American settlers—the reality is that African-descent peoples made an early and significant impact on the Southwestern economy, such as in the agricultural and cattle industries, from the Mexican era onward. Although they made early gains in their efforts to effect local, state, and federal legislation assuring their civil rights, African-descent peoples fared somewhat better in the 1870s than they did in the 1950s in the economic and political areas of, for example, Nevada. The collapse of the mining industry in Nevada served to undergird a heightened sense of tension and antiblack animosity there in the 1950s. This, coupled with the emergence and incorporation of Nevada's variant of the Ku Klux Klan, led to the state being dubbed the Mississippi of the West. Widespread discrimination in employment, suffrage, housing, and public accommodations persisted throughout the period from the 1880s through the 1950s.[18]

One particularly salient example of the collusion of the state and federal governments in institutionalizing public and private discrimination against people of color in the Southwest concerns the practice of what is referred to as redlining census tracts and real-estate markets in which larger numbers of either African American or Hispanic peoples of color represented an emerging majority. Redlining constitutes the practice of refusing to provide certain public and or commercial services within a particular geographical area because of the race or socioeconomic standing of that area's residents. Until this practice was outlawed by the passage of Title VIII of the Civil Rights (or Fair Housing) Act of 1968, the federal government actively encouraged the valuation or devaluation of real-estate markets on the basis of the racial composition of the residents of the affected area. In fact, the U.S. government provided mortgage lenders and state and federal agencies with the results of a nationwide housing survey in which entire communities were redlined. The Federal Housing Administration (FHA), which is an arm of the U.S. Department of Housing and Urban Development that insures mortgage lenders, reacted to racial change in both urban and rural contexts by literally drawing red lines on real-estate maps and urban zones so as to demarcate and further stigmatize minority neighborhoods. This practice was exacerbated when the GI Bill (Servicemen's Readjustment Act of 1944) opened access to higher education for millions of veterans of World War II and subsequent military conflicts. Along with increased incentives to complete an education afforded by the GI Bill, lenders and developers, along with the FHA, promoted the creation of vast housing developments in many suburban zones both in the Southwest and the rest of the nation.

The combination of redlining and housing discrimination in each new suburban development ultimately fueled the flight of whites from the cities into the suburbs. White flight in turn transformed formerly white neighborhoods into predominantly minority communities of color, and redlining played a significant role in depressing the real-estate markets within those towns and communities. This latter fact was due in large part to the hesitance of lenders to finance or refinance mortgages sought or held by African Americans and other peoples of color. At this same time, the mixing of European-origin and other whites of varying ethnicity within suburban zones that effectively permitted home purchases by whites only fueled the cultural acceptance of such groups as southern and eastern Europeans who had been the earlier subjects of discrimination within U.S. cities.

Today, African Americans represent a majority minority population in the U.S. Southwest. According to the U.S. Census Bureau's 2000 census, 33,000 currently call New Mexico home, 131,000 African Americans were found to reside in Arizona, Nevada recorded 118,000 inhabitants of African origin, and Texas registered an African American population of 2,436,000. These figures reflect the historical demographics of the early slave states, as well as the pioneering history, growing political clout, and increasing receptiveness to the cultural traditions and lifeways of the African American communities that have emerged in many Southwestern states in recent years.

Whereas the African Americans in the Southwest now enjoy a greater degree of visibility in the civic-ceremonial, legislative, and economic affairs of many contemporary Southwestern communities, many challenges remain. Though once largely invisible as a sociopolitical, economic, and cultural force—particularly given

Table 1. Census 2000 demographic summary and projected growth rates by ethnicity, for the Southwestern states, including comparisons with Utah, Colorado, and California

Native Americans	Arizona	New Mexico	Texas	Nevada	Utah	Colorado	California
1995	251,000	159,000	67,000	27,000	33,000	34,000	277,000
2000	285,000	181,000	65,000	31,000	39,000	36,000	276,000
2010	348,000	231,000	65,000	36,000	50,000	38,000	314,000
2020	415,000	288,000	68,000	39,000	59,000	41,000	362,000
Change: 1995–2020	65.30%	81.10%	1.50%	44.40%	78.80%	20.60%	30.70%

Hispanics	Arizona	New Mexico	Texas	Nevada	Utah	Colorado	California
1995	853,000	686,000	5,260,000	195,000	106,000	511,000	9,143,000
2000	1,019,000	792,000	6,173,000	264,000	127,000	595,000	10,584,000
2010	1,382,000	1,024,000	8,094,000	402,000	170,000	771,000	13,775,000
2020	1,810,000	1,295,000	10,302,000	559,000	220,000	975,000	17,489,000
Change: 1995–2020	112.20%	88.80%	95.90%	186.70%	107.50%	90.80%	91.30%

Blacks	Arizona	New Mexico	Texas	Nevada	Utah	Colorado	California
1995	123,000	32,000	2,251,000	100,000	14,000	156,000	2,512,000
2000	131,000	33,000	2,436,000	118,000	16,000	174,000	2,719,000
2010	143,000	35,000	2,817,000	144,000	18,000	200,000	3,245,000
2020	157,000	39,000	3,225,000	166,000	19,000	224,000	3,849,000
Change: 1995–2020	27.60%	21.90%	43.30%	66.00%	35.70%	43.60%	53.20%

Asians	Arizona	New Mexico	Texas	Nevada	Utah	Colorado	California
1995	91,000	25,000	461,000	70,000	54,000	89,000	3,908,000
2000	127,000	35,000	590,000	99,000	77,000	117,000	4,906,000
2010	204,000	56,000	839,000	148,000	122,000	166,000	7,169,000
2020	287,000	78,000	1,086,000	197,000	171,000	216,000	9,685,000
Change: 1995–2020	215.40%	212.00%	135.60%	181.40%	216.70%	142.70%	147.80%

Whites	Arizona	New Mexico	Texas	Nevada	Utah	Colorado	California
1995	3,606,000	1,460,000	15,814,000	1,281,000	54,000	3,431,000	25,701,000
2000	3,894,000	1,574,000	16,948,000	1,443,000	77,000	3,733,000	26,987,000
2010	4,379,000	1,760,000	19,130,000	1,609,000	122,000	4,090,000	30,357,000
2020	4,854,000	1,934,000	21,213,000	1,743,000	171,000	4,390,000	34,058,000
Change: 1995–2020	34.60%	32.50%	34.10%	36.10%	216.70%	28.00%	32.50%

Source: Adapted from Cheryl Russell's (1996) *The Official Guide to Racial and Ethnic Diversity: Asians, Blacks, Hispanics, Native Americans, and Whites.*

long-term patterns of racism, discrimination, and political and social exclusion, and the demographic dominance of other groups—the African American population has effectively negotiated a stigmatized and marginalized place for itself in its home of nearly four centuries.

Although not as demographically pronounced as Hispanic and Mexican-origin peoples within the Southwest, African Americans have nevertheless left a deep mark on the townscapes, industry, business, food, art, music, and dance of the region, well beyond their ethnic enclaves.

African American Community Celebrations

Like other ethnic and cultural groups of the Southwest, African-origin and African American peoples, or blacks, participate in broad variety of local and regional, formal and informal, and yearly celebrations and festivities. Kwanzaa—a Swahili term for "first fruit" and rooted in the tradition of the African harvest festival—is an annual African American celebration of black unity and ethnic pride that has gained national attention. Many African Americans of the Southwest and elsewhere partake of this weeklong holiday (December 26–January 1) that was first introduced in 1966 in the wake of the Watts riots in Los Angeles. Conceived by Dr. Maulana Ron Karenga of the Black Studies Department of the California State University, Long Beach, Kwanzaa centers around seven principles: acknowledgement of unity, self-determination, collective works and responsibilities, cooperative economies, purpose, faith, and creativity. Kwanzaa entails the use of a seven-branch candelabra, with the lighting of candle to commemorate and celebrate each of these seven principles. Each of these principles is also identified by its Swahili word, and the candelabra incorporates three red candles to signify the struggles of the African origin peoples, three green candles to symbolize hope, and one black candle to represent the African-origin peoples of the world. In the Southwest, the celebration involves commemorating ancestors, acknowledging deceased loved ones, participating in African naming ceremonies, communal feasting, the sharing of family mementos, and interfaith religious observances that include African and African American icons, foods, and beliefs.

School children learn about Juneteenth at the Altamira Elementary School in Arizona. Courtesy of Altamira Elementary School.

While the celebration of Kwanzaa has assumed national stature, Juneteenth—a contraction of June nineteenth—is a uniquely Southern holiday that commemorates the emancipation of African slaves on June 19, 1865. Juneteenth was for a time brought into question by black activists concerned that the focus was with the past and slavery, rather than with the defense of freedom, political unity, and the positive contributions of the African American community, but, interestingly, the celebration has only grown in popularity in the former Confederate slave state of Texas. Today,

Juneteenth vies with Kwanzaa and other African American celebrations, including Martin Luther King Day, for prominence among the yearly festivals of the African American community. While Martin Luther King Day was not officially acknowledged in many areas of the Southwest until relatively recently, it now commands the civic and commercial attention once denied it in, for example, the state of Arizona, where the celebration and acknowledgement of the civil-rights leader was resisted by Evan Mecham when he became governor in 1986. In response, the NAACP and many other African American and civil-rights organizations, boycotted the states that resisted the acknowledgement and celebration of the day devoted to Martin Luther King, Jr. Where Texas is concerned, the King holiday—which is celebrated annually on the third Monday in January—was not adopted as a state holiday until 1992.

EUROPEAN IMMIGRANT AND EURO-AMERICAN PEOPLES

Today, the demographically largest and most diverse pan-regional and multicultural immigrant population or subgroup of the Southwest is that generally identified with European and Mediterranean origins. While for the most part "racially" white, the European immigrants and European-origin Americans who settled the Southwest were from diverse backgrounds and included Portuguese, Germans, French, Basque, Italians, Slavs, and Czechs.[19] In fact, so many distinct European immigrant subgroups migrated to the Southwest, and subsequently intermarried, that it is often difficult to distinguish the ethnic cores of such Southwestern communities, and this is made more challenging because the hybrid by-product of European in-migration and intermarriage is largely perceived to represent a single-unit cultural epicenter of the American mainstream. Much of the influx of these groups into the Southwest occurred with the emergence of the early American period, which began shortly after the signing of the Treaty of Guadalupe Hidalgo in 1848. The treaty, which brought the U.S.-Mexican War (c. 1846–1848) to an end, paved the way for large-scale settlement in the region by Euro-American (in this use, non-Hispanic) and European peoples. The Anglos who settled the Southwest prior to 1848 did so as citizen converts to Catholicism and paid allegiance to the Mexican Republic (1821–1848) or, earlier yet, Spanish imperial (1810–1821) flags. Such was case with the American expatriates who staged the ill-fated 1836 rebellion against the Mexican Republic and the Presidency of Antonio de Santa Anna at the former Franciscan mission of San Antonio de Valero—today known as the Alamo.

The social and cultural transformation of ethnic enclaves, shifting economic and political fortunes, and the influx of new immigrant groups into preexisting Southwestern enclaves has created the push and pull factors that have resulted in the resettlement of Euro-American populations, and thus, the dispersal of second-, third-, and fourth-generation Euro-American enclaves.[20] Today, this ongoing pattern of ethnic dispersals sometimes referred to as white flight—from urban to suburban settlements—continues to affect landscapes and demographic makeup of the cities of the U.S. Southwest. However, some of the most demographically and culturally prominent, or ethnically visible, groups include English, German, Italian, Irish, Portuguese, French, Basques, Polish, and other Western and Eastern European peoples. The early visibility of the English and Irish groups, which today constitute a significant geographic majority in the

Southwest, was nevertheless challenged by the precocious and successful ethnic enclavement of such groups as the Germans and Czechs of South Texas (c. 1880s–1930s) and the Italian Americans of central Arizona.[21]

For the most part, however, distinct European ethnic groups in the present day Southwest have lost most traditional language and cultural practices, are of fairly recent arrival in the Southwest, and belong to the mainstream American culture. Some distinguish their European ethnicity in clubs that offer outlets for and sources of traditional culture in the form of traditional food, costume, and folk music and dance, but this does not pervade their daily lives. Some groups, however, have maintained a long-standing cultural presence and have persisted within the ethnic and social landscapes of the Southwest; among these are the Germans of South Texas and the Basques of Nevada and other parts of the Great Basin.

The Germans of South Texas

The Germans of South Texas produced one of the more ethnically distinctive and culturally conservative Euro-American enclaves of the region. Their migration to Texas—mostly from west-central Germany—was in large part fueled by the quest for fortunes in the ranching industry, and to that end, Germans made their way to those regions where they believed the cattle industry held the greatest prospects for success. Perhaps the largest influx of Germans into the Southwest began when the Adelsverein, or Society for the Protection of German Immigrants in Texas, organized willing émigrés near Mainz, Germany, for the newfound German settlements of New Braunfels and Fredericksburg, Texas. Germans constitute the largest ethnic group derived from Europe.[22] In 1850 they constituted 5 percent of the total population of Texas, and more recently, after generations of intermarriage, some 1,175,888 Texans claim "pure" German ancestry, whereas another 1,775,838 claim "partial" German ancestry. The vast majority of those who claim German ancestry today do not claim "ethnic" German identity. According to the *Texas Almanac (2004–2005)*, the German language was used widely in central Texas and continued in use until relatively recently. Most of the earliest German settlers colonized what has come to be called the German Belt, which lies in the south-central portion of the state, in a swath that spans the area extending from Galveston and Houston on the east to Kerrville, Mason, and Hondo on the west.

Only with the emergence of the hostilities that arose between Germany and America as a result of World War I did the Germans of Texas more decidedly adopt the English language and culture of their new homeland. World War I and World War II also led many to change their Anglicize their Germanic surnames and town names. Despite these adjustments, the German enclaves of south Texas retained and celebrated many ethnic, linguistic, and cultural traditions well into recent times, including the Wurstfest, and an earlier generation of Saengerfest and Volkfest events dating back to the 1850s. Today, the more prominent celebration of Oktoberfest is but one of many German traditions rooted in the early nineteenth century.

The relative social and cultural isolation of such communities through the latter half of the nineteenth and early twentieth centuries was what made possible the maintenance and persistence of significant elements of German traditional lifeways in south Texas. Other historians contend that the tendency of these well-financed and aristocratic early German settlers to limit interactions with outsiders was due in part to the mid-nineteenth-century colonial ambitions of the German state and its sponsorship and promotion of German emigration into the Texas territory. With the annexation of Texas by the United States, those ambitions were thwarted and the idea of fomenting an internal rebellion for the purposes of creating a German colony there became a distant memory. Irrespective of the veracity of this claim, the American Civil War stymied further German immigration, and much of that populations' expansion was the result of fertility and in-migration patterns.

The Basques of Nevada

The Basques originated in the Pyrenees Mountains, which straddle the intermontane regions separating France and Spain. Traditional occupations and lifeways in that region centered on a pastoral lifestyle, and in particular on the caring, tending, and herding of sheep. Basque peoples have settled in the Southwest mostly (California and Nevada) both before and since 1900. The Basques of Nevada continue to maintain their traditional language and an affinity for celebrating their cultural roots and homeland. The many Basque restaurants and ethnic enclaves of the Southwest attest to their presence in the region and also support their cultural and ethnic visibility in the eyes of visitors. In addition, Basques maintain a cultural inclination, largely derived from traditional customs originating in their ancestral homeland, to intermarry almost exclusively with other Basques, which reinforces and helps to perpetuate Basque traditions and cultural practices. So prominent is Basque language and culture in Nevada that an entire course of study has been established at the University of Nevada to acknowledge the Basque presence and to meet the demand of the enduring scholarly interest in this significant Southwestern cultural presence. Any study of the subject should make clear that while the vast majority arrived in the period after 1900, collectively, Basque peoples have occupied a place in Southwest cultural history since the first entradas into the region by the Spanish empire. In fact, Basques participated in the earliest Spanish entradas, or exploratory expeditions, into the area as early as the 1600s, and one explanation of the origin of the place name "Arizona" apparently originated with the Basque term for "good oak trees." Significantly, perhaps one of the most famous Basque pioneers of the Spanish colonial Southwest was Juan Bautista Anza, an eighteenth-century governor of New Mexico and the lead explorer and founder of the colony of San Francisco in Alta California. In that same region, the commander of the Tucson Presidio in 1791 was José Ignacio Moraga, whose Basque family heritage began in the Americas with an ancestor from the high Basque country of northern Spain who settled in New Spain (Mexico) in 1604. Clearly the Basque presence was not only quite early and significant to the development of region, it has also made an impact on the food, culture, ranching, music, dance, politics, economy, and place names of the Southwest.

The Jewish Presence in New Mexico

The Jews, or Jewish Americans, of New Mexico are yet another Southwestern ethnic group that has had a long and prosperous, albeit largely invisible, cultural presence mediated by way of religious and ethnic persecution.[23] Although ultimately of Southwest Asian or Middle Eastern origins, the earliest Jews and *conversos* (Jews who converted to Catholicism in an effort to avoid religious persecution during the colonial era [1492–1821]), arrived in the Southwest with other Spanish colonial settlers during the period extending from 1602 through 1821. The first Jews in the Southwest were predominently of Sephardic Jewish ancestry, the ethnic cohort with roots in the portion of the Mediterranean region that extends from Turkey to Spain. Subsequent émigrés made their way to the region via both Mexican and American settlement ventures. Conversos migrated to the Southwest from New Spain or Mexico with early Hispanic colonists of the New Mexico frontier. Their religious persecution led many conversos to adopt clandestine forms of Jewish religious practice, social customs, and related traditional observances. Because of this, the early Jews of New Mexico were largely invisible as an ethnic group population until relatively recent times, when a growing number of authors began seeking to reveal and document this group.[24]

Jews settled throughout New Mexico, Texas, Arizona, and Nevada. The Jewish communities of Texas, for instance, became significantly more visible with the establishment of the first Jewish synagogue in Houston in 1859. Today, the vast majority of Jews in the Southwest are of Ashkenazi affinity, that is, identified with the peoples of central and Eastern Europe; many reached the Southwest after the American Civil War.

The Jewish contributions to urban-based economic and commercial development (beginning in the 1880s), real-estate markets, food, cinema, synagogues, and ethnic enclaves in the region are by far the most visible dimensions of the Jewish contribution in the Southwest.

ASIAN IMMIGRANTS

According to University of Arkansas historian Shih-Shan Henry Tsai, nearly one million people from five Asian countries immigrated to the United States and Hawaii from the 1840s through mid-1930s. Of these, 7,000 Koreans, 8,000 Indians, 180,000 Filipinos, 300,000 Chinese, and 400,000 Japanese made landfall in the U.S. and Hawaii despite the highly restrictive anti-Asian immigration and naturalization policies that have limited their numbers.

The Chinese Americans

The earliest Asian immigrants to enter the American Southwest in appreciable numbers were the Chinese, largely Kwangtung province, and they entered California and the Southwest by way of the port of San Francisco as early as 1852. Many of those destined for Tucson and southern Arizona entered by way of northern Mexico during the 1870s and 1880s. Originally drawn to North America's Pacific Coast as free agents and by the prospects of wealth and opportunity in the form of gold in mid-nineteenth-century California, the vast majority of the Chinese males who trekked beyond the confines of San Francisco and into the vast reaches of the American Southwest did so in search of further opportunities working as miners or as low-wage laborers for the Southern Pacific Railroad. As the gold rush panned out with the heightened competition for mining claims and the diminishing returns that eventually beset the vast majority of independent miners, the influx into the Southwest of Chinese laborers seeking railroad work or their fortune was accelerated.

Most Chinese laborers were willing to undertake some of the most difficult and dangerous assignments available—including forest clearance, rail-bed grading, and tunneling—and did so despite the low wages afforded them as a result of a dual-wage system based on race and ethnicity. Mexican laborers were restricted to wages only a half to a third of the amount paid to Anglo workers for similar work, and the Chinese were paid far less than even their Mexican counterparts. As a result, Chinese workers in the Southwest quickly developed a reputation as diligent laborers—which, in this context, meant they willing to work long hours for low wages—and this in turn invited conflict and discrimination from diverse socioeconomic quarters and ethnic groups. Anglo and Mexican laborers who often found themselves at odds with one another over access to labor and opportunities nevertheless stood together to decry the invasion of "Orientals" that they believed stood to threaten their livelihoods. This pattern of hostility and discrimination against the Chinese met them on both sides of the borderlands frontier.

By way of the rail lines of the Southern Pacific that reached Tucson on March 20, 1880, Chinese laborers entered Arizona by the hundreds, and eventually their numbers would account for the largest concentration of Chinese people anywhere in the Southwest. According to author Lawrence Michael Fong, the 1880 United States Census enumerated the presence of some 1,630 Chinese residents, of which fully 1,153 resided in Pima County, and 159 lived in Tucson. Of these, 850 were identified as railroad workers. And just as readily as they arrived with the railroad, they departed when the availability of such work waned.[25] Eventually, many of those Chinese railway workers who did not depart Arizona after work with the railroads diminished settled into urban communities such as Tucson and Prescott, Arizona, where substantial Chinese enclaves, known as Chinatowns to outsiders, were established in the 1870s. Their increasing numbers through the late 1870s and early 1880s incited violence and anti-Asian sentiment in a number of communities of the American Southwest and northern Mexico. Such anti-Asian sentiment toward Chinese laborers often took on an ominous tone that frequently resulted in violence. This sad state of affairs would only intensify with the passage of the Exclusion Act of 1882, which essentially barred further Asian (read: Chinese) immigration in the United States and provisioned opportunities for the deportation of those deemed not legal immigrants. The xenophobic and anti-Asian sentiment that escalated throughout the latter part of the nineteenth and early part of the twentieth centuries was largely fueled by both labor and trade unionism and its concerns with inequities they perceived to be inherent in competing for work with such poorly paid Asian workers.

By contrast, the growing success of Chinese and other Asian businesses through the turn of the century spurred some non-Asians to support and patronize this growing sector of the business community. According to news reports in 1884, Chinese grocer Chan Tin-Wo was the "most prosperous groceryman" of Tucson at that time.[26] In 1882 Chan Tin-Wo, naturalized just the year before, voted in the Pima County elections for the first time. As noted by historian Lawrence Michael Fong, this suggests that for that era in Pima

County's history there were no social or political obstacles to any Chinese citizens who wished to participate in county or municipal elections and had the resources and wherewithal to do so.[27] The English language, however, was a significant prerequisite to inclusion in the American political system, and this, in part hampered political and social gains in the early years of Chinese immigration to the Southwest. The Chinese school of Prescott, the Chinese Mission School of Tucson, and the Chinese Evangelical Church were the result of Christian missionary programs that sought to teach Chinese the English language from within the context of the Bible and other Christian doctrinal literatures. However, the success of these English language programs left first- and second-generation Chinese parents concerned that their children would lose both the language and culture of their ancestral homeland.

Despite efforts to reintroduce Chinese language and culture to the youth, by the 1920s many Asian youth within the communities of southern Arizona had transitioned and or acculturated into a way of life that reflected mainstream Anglo customs and society. The vestiges of the Chinese way of life that survived discrimination, social and political isolation, undesirable working conditions, and the many hardships of the frontiers of southern Arizona have been sustained by means of Chinese fraternal and social organizations that have become a cornerstone of the way Chinese communities continue to communicate and convey their language and heritage from one generation to the next.

The Japanese-American Experience

In 1900 the U.S. Census documented the presence in Nevada of 10,093 foreign-born people of English, Irish, German, Italian, and Chinese origin. Whereas these groups were represented in roughly equal numbers, this same census count projected the presence of 35,405 Caucasian/white persons, 5,216 Native Americans, 1,352 Chinese, 228 Japanese, and 134 Negroes of non-foreign-born status within the state at that time. By contrast, the population of the state of Arizona for 1900 was 122,931 persons, including some 28,623 reservation-based Native Americans who had not been accounted for by way of previous census tallies. The Chinese and Japanese registered small numbers at that time, but their numbers would grow and they were subjected to a host of anti-Asian public policies, such as the Chinese Exclusion Act of 1882 which prohibited Chinese workers from working in the United States, the gentleman's agreement struck between Japan and the U.S. and much later, the humiliation and denial of basic human liberties that came with the establishment of the Japanese internment or relocation camps of the West Coast and Southwestern states during World War II.

The first Japanese-born immigrants, or *Issei*, to enter the United States in appreciable numbers were drawn first to Texas and Nevada by 1902. According to historian Edward J. M. Rhoads, Japanese consular official Sadatsuchi Uchida lured his countrymen to each of these regions as the direct result of a fact-finding tour of the Texas Gulf Coast and Southwest in that same year. The prospects for Japanese rice farmers were good as local officials and businessmen supported the idea of having the Japanese look into the feasibility of establishing rice crops in Texas, as well as other drought-resistant crops that might adopt to the varied, albeit harsh climatic regime of the Nevada desert. The early, innovative efforts at growing these crops were matched by similarly innovative farming methods in other areas of the Southwest, but the methods pioneered in the Las Vegas valley of Nevada are particularly noteworthy.

Perhaps one of the most notable Japanese American farmers and entrepreneurs of the Southwest was Nevada's Yonema "Bill" Tomiyasu, who diligently pursued the introduction of a host of crops and agricultural methods and schedules not known prior to his efforts in the Las Vegas valley. His innovative farming methods, developed in part from his experiences in California where the Japanese were not permitted to own or operate ranches, launched a veritable agricultural revolution in the Nevada of 1914. His pursuits allowed him to supply Nellis Air Force Base and a host of companies and produce outlets with fresh, locally grown fruits and vegetables previously unavailable in the region.

In Texas Japanese rice farmers made thirty separate attempts to establish rice agriculture in varying parts of the state; in 1903 Seito Saibara succeeded Webster in Harris County, near Houston, and Kichimatsu Kishi succeeded in Terry in Orange County, near Beaumont, in 1907. The success of these rice crops fueled the immigration of friends, relatives, and workers recruited by Saibara and Kishi to their rice fields, which was the chief cause for the Japanese population of Texas swelling from 13 people in 1900 to 340 in 1910. By 1990, Japanese Texans numbered 15,172 persons. According to the *Texas Almanac (2004–2005)*, the pioneering and early experimental efforts of Seito Saibara ultimately led to the doubling of rice production on the Texas Gulf Coast, and it is for this reason that Saibara is credited with establishing the Gulf Coast rice industry. Subsequent waves of Japanese immigrants arrived from California in 1920 as a direct result of their persecution there. Their contributions included the continuing development of Japanese vegetable and citrus crops in Mission, San Juan, and San Benito located within the Rio Grande Valley. Anti-Asian sentiment and hostility in Texas led to repeated attempts to enact legislation restricting the right of the Japanese to purchase or hold property in the state. To the credit of the Japanese Association, led by Houston entrepreneur Saburo Arai, the efforts to dispossess existing Japanese Americans of their lands failed.

The attack on Pearl Harbor by the Japanese imperial fleet on December 7, 1941, reawakened and fed anti-Asian sentiments. This culminated with the forced removal and relocation of Japanese and Hawaiian Americans and alien nationals who were suspected of posing a threat to U.S. security to internment camps in Manzanar, California; Moab, Utah; Leupp, Arizona; and Crystal City, Kenedy, and Seagoville, Texas. At these West Coast and Southwestern Wartime Civil Control Administration (WCAA) Assembly Centers or War Relocation Authority (WRA) camps held some 119,803 Japanese American men, women, and children who were stripped of all personal possessions and properties and coerced to submit to internment in any one or more of these facilities. Of the 6,000 or so detainees in Texas, many departed once the detention camps were closed; however, a significant number of former detainees stayed on and settled within the major urban centers of Houston, Dallas–Fort Worth, and San Antonio. Although Japanese Texans contributed significantly in such areas as medicine, art, and literature, it is their early development and improvement of rice farming that remain the achievements most heralded by fellow Texans.

Other Asian Immigration

Much of the Asian immigration since 1900 is the result of U.S. conflicts in Asian theaters of war and the lifting or liberalization of anti-Asian immigration laws in the United States. Whereas the Filipino populations of Texas, Arizona, and Nevada may be traced to the role of the U.S. military occupation of the Philippines as a result of the Spanish and American War, the influx of Koreans may be traced to the Korean War of the 1950s. Southeast Asians, particularly Vietnamese and Cambodians, sought refuge and opportunity in the United States as a direct result of the American conflict in Vietnam and Cambodia in the 1960s and 1970s. The liberalization of U.S. immigration laws in 1965 demarcates the point at which the population of some groups surged: for example, the number of Koreans in Texas was roughly 31,775 in 1990, up from 2,090 in 1970. Both natural fertility and the "war bride" phenomenon introduced a significant number of Asian females (who married U.S. soldiers) into Texas, New Mexico, Arizona, and Nevada, where there are military installations on which married GIs and their foreign-born wives reside.

Of course, while these are current trends and therefore accounts for the greater part of the recent influx of Asian peoples into the Southwest, it is clear that early Hispanic colonial transoceanic commerce identified with the Manila galleons introduced early Asian settlers into New Spain and North America. The early Filipinos known to have settled the Southwest—by way of Texas—in 1822, did so as a direct result of that trade. For example, Francisco Flores of Cebu, Philippines, made landfall in Texas and soon thereafter made Port Isabel his adopted home until his death in 1917.

CONCLUSION

This survey has attempted to represent the ethnic groups and enclaves and their respective cultures and traditions that have come to distinguish the Southwest from other regions in the United States. The emphasis has been on the earliest and most ethnically and culturally distinctive and dominant traditions that have come to define the Southwest for most Americans. Thus, the ancient Native American and Hispanic inhabitants of the region have received the lion's share of the narrative devoted to how ethnic groups have adapted to and embraced the environmental, social, cultural, and political diversity of the place understood to constitute the Southwest. Whether defined in terms of the region's ancient cultures or contemporary urban enclaves or understood from the standpoint of linguistic or traditional differences and similarities, ethnicity in the Southwest remains an oscillating frontier of hybrid cultures and recent immigrants, ancient pueblos and modern city-states that meld past cultural lifeways with modern global and transnational trends and influences.

RESOURCE GUIDE

Printed Sources

Arteaga, Alfred, ed. *An Other Tongue: Nation and Ethnicity in the Linguistic Borderlands.* Durham: Duke University Press, 1994.

Bahr, Donald, Juan Smith, William Smith Allison, and Julian Hayden. *The Short, Swift Time of the Gods on Earth: The Hohokam Chronicles*. Berkeley: University of California Press, 1994.

Bannon, John Francis, ed. *Bolton and the Spanish Borderlands*. Norman: University of Oklahoma Press, 1964.

Barr, Alwyn. *Black Texans: A History of African Americans in Texas, 1528–1995*. Norman: University of Oklahoma Press, 1996.

Boyd, Alex, Curt Idrogo, Lotsee Patterson, and Kenneth Yamashita, eds. *Guide to Multicultural Resources, 1997/1998*. Fort Atkinson, WI: Highsmith Press, 1997.

Carlyle, Shawn W., Ryan L. Parr, M. Geoffrey Hayes, and Dennis H. O'Rourke. "Context of Maternal Lineages in the Greater Southwest." *American Journal of Physical Anthropology* 113 (2000): 85–101.

Casey, Robert L. *Journey to the High Southwest: A Traveler's Guide*. 4th ed., Illustrated by Julie Roberts. Old Saybrook, CT: Globe Pequot Press, 1993.

Chan, Sucheng, Douglas Henry Daniels, Mario T. Garcia, and Terry P. Wilson, eds. *Peoples of Color in the American West*. Lexington, MA: D.C. Heath and Company, 1994.

Chavez, John R. *The Lost Land: The Chicano Image of the Southwest*. Albuquerque: University of New Mexico Press, 1984.

Chavez, Thomas E., ed. and anno. *Conflict and Acculturation: Manuel Alvarez's 1842 Memorial*. Santa Fe: Museum of New Mexico Press, 1989.

Cordell, Linda. *Archaeology of the Southwest*. San Diego, CA: Academic Press, 1997.

Crouch, Barry A. *The Freedmen's Bureau and Black Texans*. Austin: University of Texas Press, 1992.

Daniels, Roger. "The Incarceration of Japanese Americans During World War II." In *Peoples of Color in the American West*, edited by Suchen Chan, Douglas Henry Daniels, Mario T. Garcia, and Terry P. Wilson, 470–480. Lexington, MA: D.C. Heath, 1994.

D'Azevedo, Warren L., ed. *Handbook of North American Indians: Great Basin*. Vol. 11. Washington, DC: Smithsonian Institution Press, 1986.

Elliott, Russell R., and William D. Rowley. *History of Nevada*. 2nd ed. Lincoln: University of Nebraska Press, 1987.

Fong, Lawrence Michael. *Sojourners and Settlers: The Chinese Experience in Arizona*. Tucson: *The Journal of Arizona History*, 1980.

Foote, Cheryl J. *Women of the New Mexico Frontier, 1846–1912*. Niwot: University Press of Colorado, 1990.

Gonzales-Berry, Erlinda, and David R. Maciel, eds. *The Contested Homeland: A Chicano History of New Mexico*. Albuquerque: University of New Mexico Press, 2000.

Grayson, Donald K. *The Desert's Past: A Natural Prehistory of the Great Basin*. Washington, DC: Smithsonian Institution Press, 1993.

Gregory, Vicki L., Marilyn H. Karrenbrock Stauffer, and Thomas W. Keene, Jr. *Multicultural Resources on the Internet: The United States and Canada*. Englewood, CO: Libraries Unlimited, 1999.

Griffin-Pierce, Trudy. *American Indians of the Southwest*. Albuquerque: University of New Mexico Press, 2000.

Harris, Richard E. *The First Hundred Years: A History of Arizona Blacks*. Apache Junction: Arizona: Relmo Publications, 1983.

Jackson, Robert H., ed. *New Views of Borderlands History*. Albuquerque: University of New Mexico Press, 1998.

Jamail, Milton H., and Margo Gutiérrez. *The Border Guide: Institutions and Organizations of the United States-Mexico Borderlands*. 2nd ed. Austin: CMAS Books, Center for Mexican American Studies, University of Texas at Austin, 1992.

Jones, Siân. *The Archaeology of Ethnicity: Constructing Identities in the Past and Present*. London: Routledge, 1997.

Kearney, Milo, and Manuel Medrano. "The Development of Anglo-Hispanic Conflict." In *Medieval Culture and the Mexican American Borderlands*, 172–207. College Station: Texas A&M University Press, 2001.

Kertzer, David I., and Dominique Arel, eds. *Census and Identity: The Politics of Race, Ethnicity, and Language in National Census*. New York: Cambridge University Press, 2002.

Leiker, James N. *Racial Borders: Black Soldiers Along the Rio Grande*. College Station: Texas A&M University Press, 2002.

Lorey, David E. *The U.S.-Mexican Border in the Twentieth Century: A History of Economic and Social Transformation*. Wilmington, DE: A Scholarly Resources Inc. Imprint, 1999.

Martinelli, Phylis Cancilla. *Ethnicity in the Sunbelt: Italian American Migrants in Scottsdale, Arizona*. New York: AMS Press, 1989.

Meed, Douglas V. *Bloody Border: Riots, Battles and Adventures along the Turbulent U.S.-Mexican Borderlands*. Tucson: Westernlore Press, 1992.

Meier, Matt S., and Margo Gutiérrez. *Encyclopedia of the Mexican American Civil Rights Movement*. Foreword by Antonia Hernández. Westport, CT: Greenwood Press, 2000.

Meier, Matt S., and Feliciano Ribera. *Mexican Americans, American Mexicans: From Conquistadors to Chicanos*. Revised ed. New York: Hill and Wang, 1993.

Melendez, A. Gabriel. *The Multicultural Southwest: A Reader*. Tucson: University of Arizona Press, 2001.

Menchaca, Martha. *Recovering History, Constructing Race: The Indian, Black, and White Roots of the Mexican American*. Austin: University of Texas Press, 2001.

Mendoza, Ruben G. "Cruising Art and Culture in Aztlán: Lowriding in the Mexican American Southwest." In *U.S. Latino Literatures and Cultures: Transnational Perspectives*, edited by Francisco A. Lomelí and Karin Ikas, 3–35. Heidelberg, Germany: Carl Winter-Verlag, 2000.

Mendoza, Ruben G., and Cruz Torres. "Hispanic Traditional Technology and Material Culture in the United States." In *Handbook of Hispanic Cultures in the United States: Anthropology*, edited by Thomas Weaver, 59–84. Madrid, Spain: Instituto de Cooperacion Iberoamericana (ICI) and Houston, Texas: The University of Houston and Arte Publico Press, 1994.

Mithun, Marianne. *The Languages of North America*. New York: Cambridge University Press, 1999.

Nasatir, Abraham P. *Borderlands in Retreat: From Louisiana to the Far Southwest*. Albuquerque: University of New Mexico Press, 1976.

Newcomb, W. W. *The Indians of Texas: From Prehistoric Times to Modern Times*. Austin: University of Texas Press, 1961.

Nostrand, Richard L. *The Hispano Homeland*. Norman: University of Oklahoma Press, 1992.

Officer, James E. *Hispanic Arizona, 1536–1856*. Tucson: University of Arizona Press, 1987.

Ortiz, Alfonso, ed. *Handbook of North American Indians*. Vols. 9 and 10, *Southwest*. Washington, DC: Smithsonian Institution Press, 1979.

Rusco, Elmer R. "African Americans in Nevada, 1860s–1920s." In *Peoples of Color in the American West*, edited by Suchen Chan, Douglas Henry Daniels, Mario T. Garcia, and Terry P. Wilson, 323–327. Lexington, MA: D.C. Heath, 1994.

Russell, Cheryl. *The Official Guide to Racial and Ethnic Diversity: Asians, Blacks, Hispanics, Native Americans, and Whites*. Ithaca, NY: New Strategist Publications, 1996.

Shaul, David Leedom. *A Linguistic Prehistory of the Southwest*. Unpublished Manuscript, on file with author, 2003.

Shaul, David Leedom, and John M. Andresen. "A Case for Yuman Participation in the Hohokam Regional System." *Kiva* 54 (1989): 105–126.

Spicer, Edward H. *Cycles of Conquest: The Impact of Spain, Mexico, and the United States on the Indians of the Southwest, 1533–1960.* Tucson: University of Arizona Press, 1962.

Stoddard, Ellwyn R. *U.S.-Mexico Borderlands Studies: Multidisciplinary Perspectives and Concepts.* El Paso, TX: The Promontory, 2002.

Thernstrom, Stephan, ed. *Harvard Encyclopedia of American Ethnic Groups.* Cambridge, MA: Belknap Press, 1980.

Tobias, Henry J. *A History of the Jews in New Mexico.* Albuquerque: University of New Mexico Press, 1990.

Tonry, Michael, ed. *Ethnicity, Crime, and Immigration: Comparative and Cross-National Perspectives.* Chicago: University of Chicago Press, 1997.

Torrans, Thomas. *Forging the Tortilla Curtain: Cultural Drift and Change Along the United States-Mexico Border, from the Spanish Era to the Present.* Fort Worth: Texas Christian University Press, 2000.

Trimble, Stephen. *The People: Indians of the American Southwest.* Santa Fe: School of American Research Press, 1993.

Tsai, Shin-shan Henry. "Chinese Migration, 1848–1882." In *Peoples of Color in the American West*, edited by Suchen Chan, Douglas Henry Daniels, Mario T. Garcia, and Terry P. Wilson, 110–116. Lexington, MA: D.C. Heath, 1994.

Web Sites

African Native Americans: We Are Still Here. William and Anita Newman Library Digital Collections, Baruch College, CUNY, February 1999. Accessed October 10, 2003. http://newman.baruch.cuny.edu/digital/native/default.htm

Celebrate Hispanic Heritage Month with the National Register of Historic Places. National Park Service, September 15–October 15. September 12, 2003. Accessed October 22, 2003. http://www.cr.nps.gov/nr/feature/hispanic/index.htm

The Charlie Morrisey Research Hall. The African American Studies Program, University of New Mexico, Albuquerque. February 24, 2000. Accessed October 22, 2003. http://www.unm.edu/~afamstds/hall.htm

The Czech Heritage Society of Texas. The Czech Heritage Society of Texas Library and Archives, Houston, Texas. February 6, 2004. Accessed February 17, 2004. http://www.czechheritage.org/

The Descendants of José Ignacio Moraga: Commander of the Tucson Presidio. Compiled by Micaela P. Morales. The University of Arizona Library. June 24, 1998. Accessed January 19, 2004.
http://dizzy.library.arizona.edu/images/hispamer/moraga/

Dulaney, W. Marvin. "African Americans." *The Handbook of Texas Online.* Texas State Historical Association, December 4, 2002. Reviewed February 20, 2004. http://www.tsha.utexas.edu/handbook/online/articles/view/AA/pkaan.html

European Multi-ethnic Alliance of Tucson, Inc. Home Page, 2003. Accessed October 10, 2003. http://www.geocities.com/ematoftucson/

Institute of Texan Cultures at San Antonio Home Page. University of Texas, San Antonio, 2002. Accessed October 9, 2003.
http://www.texancultures.utsa.edu/public/index.htm/

Jordon, Terry G. "Germans." *The Handbook of Texas Online.* Texas State Historical Association, December 4, 2002. Reviewed February 20, 2004.
http://www.tsha.utexas.edu/handbook/online; sharticles/view/GG/png2.html

Native America Online. Native America Inc., Lacey, Washington, 2003. Accessed October 10, 2003.
http://www.nativeamericainc.com/

North American Indian Information & Trade Center Web Site. National Native American Cooperative, January 2000. Accessed October 10, 2003.
http://www.usaindianinfo.org/

Spanish Colonial Research Center. National Park Service and the University of New Mexico, Albuquerque. October 10, 2002. Accessed October 22, 2003.
http://www.cr.nps.gov/spca/Index.htm

Videos/Films

Cabeza de Vaca. Dir. Nicolás Echevarria. Perf. Juan Diego, Daniel Gimenez Cacho, and Roberto Sosa. New Horizon Home Video. 1993.

Chulas Fronteras. Dir. Les Blank. El Cerrito, CA: Brazos Films. 1994.

The Donner Party. Dir. Ric Burns. Perf. David McCullough. Steeplechase Films. 1992.

Lone Star. Dir. John Sayles. Perf. Chris Cooper and Kris Kristofferson. Columbia Pictures Corporation. 1996.

Salt of the Earth. Dir. Herbert J. Biberman. Perf. Rosaura Revueltas, Juan Chacón, and Will Geer. Independent Productions Corporation and the International Union of Mine, Mill, and Smelter Workers. 1954.

Spanish-Speakers and Bilingualism. Perf. Celso Martinez and Linda Cuellar. KLRN San Antonio; Alamo Public Telecommunications Council. 1992.

The Sun's Gonna Shine Blues Accordin' to Lightnin' Hopkins. Dir. Les Blank, with Skip Gerson. Perf. Lightnin' Hopkins, Billy Bizor, and Wendell Anderson. El Cerrito, CA: Flower Films. 1979.

Surviving the Dust Bowl. Prod. Chana Gazit and David Steward. Perf. David McCullough. Steward/Gazit Productions. 1998.

Tex-Mex Music of the Texas Mexican Borderlands. Dir. Jeremy Marre. Harcourt Films. 1990.

Tierra o muerte/Land or Death. Producer Carolyn Hales. Perf. Luis Valdez. KBDI-TV production. 1991.

Recordings

Borderlands from Conjunto to Chicken Scratch. Various musicians. Washington, DC: Smithsonian Folkways, 1993.

Creation's Journey Native American Music. National Museum of the American Indian. Washington, DC: Smithsonian/Folkways, 1994.

Conjunto Texas-Mexican Border Music. Various performers. Cambridge, MA: Rounder, 1988.

Country, the American Tradition. Sony, 1999.

4 Aces. The Texas Tornados. Warner Brothers, 1996.

Events

Campus Fusion
University of Texas, Austin
http://www.utexas.edu/student/txunion/students/sec/acc/events.html

This constitutes a campus student initiative celebrating diversity that brings together students from all walks of life, and features a host of cultural activities and ethnic group fashion shows, arts and crafts, and other educational and celebratory activities.

La Fiesta de San Ysidro
Las Cruces, NM
www.frhm.org

A tribute to New Mexico farmers that includes the traditional blessing of the fields, children's crafts and games, hands-on demonstrations, and a Hispanic art show and sale. The celebration includes mariachi music, a ballet folklorico, and flamenco dancers.

Matsuri: A Festival of Japan
Heritage and Science Park, Phoenix, AZ
http://www.azmatsuri.org

Celebrating the culture of Japan, this festival features Japanese exhibits, martial arts demonstrations, arts and crafts, children's activities, Bonsai displays, classical and folk dance, music, Taiko drums, comedic short skits, a traditional tea ceremony, lion dances, and Japanese food.

National Basque Festival
Elko, Nevada
http://www.rabbitbrush.com/anacabe/festival.html

A unique cultural gathering found only in Nevada, the annual National Basque Festival represents a weekend of music, dance, games, food, and fun each Fourth of July in Elko, Nevada. The Elko Convention and Visitors Authority host the celebration.

North Texas Irish Festival
Fair Park, Dallas, TX
http://www.ntif.org/

Billed as the largest Irish Celtic festival in the American Southwest, the celebration features Irish and Scottish entertainers and entertainment and includes world-famous musicians, award-winning dancers, enchanting storytellers, and educational workshops.

Santa Fe Indian Market
Downtown Plaza, Santa Fe, NM
http://www.swaia.org/market.php

Held annually in the month of August, the Santa Fe Indian Market features some 1,200 artists representing one hundred tribal groups who exhibit both traditional and contemporary arts and crafts in over six hundred individual booths.

Texas Folklife Festival
HemisFair Park, Bowie Street and Durango Boulevard, San Antonio, TX
http://www.texancultures.utsa.edu/tff/tff2003/index.htm

Touted as the premier "Bring Your Own Culture (B.Y.O.C.)" festival, this San Antonio celebration features ethnic music, games, entertainment, foods, arts and crafts, and an amusement park touting the cultures and contributions of some forty-five ethnic, cultural, and national-origin groups that today constitute the diverse cultures of the state of Texas.

Tucson Meet Yourself
El Presidio Park, Tucson, AZ
http://www.tucsonfestival.org

Established in 1973 and held annually on or about the month of October. A multicultural and multiethnic celebration of food, dance, music, art, and culture that reflects the diversity of thirty ethnic communities of Tucson and southern Arizona more generally.

Organizations

Arizona Jewish Historical Society
4710 N. 16th Street, Suite 201
Phoenix, AZ 85016
http://aspin.asu.edu/azjhs/azjhs@aol.com

A group dedicated to enhancing appreciation and awareness of the Jewish experience in Arizona and the Southwest via the collection and preservation of a record of Jewish contributions to Arizona's political, economic, social, and cultural development.

Dallas Jewish Historical Society
7900 Northaven Road, Dallas, TX 75230
http://www.djhs.org/index.php?menu=1

This Dallas-based historical society actively collects and preserves the history of the greater Dallas Jewish community, and its repository houses more than two hundred linear ft. of materials, including some 4,000 photographs and images.

The Heard Museum
2301 N. Central Avenue
Phoenix, AZ 85004–1323
http://www.heard.org

This regional museum contains more than 35,000 items of fine art, basketry, jewelry, textiles, and other work by precontact and modern native peoples of the American Southwest.

Hopi Cultural Center
P.O. Box 67
Second Mesa, AZ 86043
http://www.hopiculturalcenter.com/

The Hopi Cultural Center consists of a restaurant, inn, and gift shop located on the Hopi Second Mesa, whose ancient villages are noted for their production of coiled baskets and kachina images.

Institute of Texan Cultures at San Antonio
801 S. Bowie Street
San Antonio, TX 78205
http://www.texancultures.utsa.edu/public/index.htm/

The Institute of Texan Cultures features a state of the art museum and cultural center devoted to the history, culture, and traditional ethnic arts of the many and diverse cultures of the state of Texas.

Museum of Indian Arts & Culture/Laboratory of Anthropology
710 Camino Lejo
Santa Fe, NM 87504
http://www.miaclab.org/indexfl.html

The premier repository and archive of Native art and material culture in New Mexico, the museum features collections from throughout the Southwest that span the period from prehistory to the modern era.

National Hispanic Cultural Center
1701 4th Street S.W.
Albuquerque, NM 87102
http://www.nhccnm.org/

This cultural center showcases historic and contemporary Hispanic arts, humanities, and contributions spanning the past four hundred years and features art exhibits, dance, music, theater, and a state-of-the art genealogy center.

Nevada Historical Society
1650 N. Virginia Street
Reno, NV 89507
http://dmla.clan.lib.nv.us/docs/museums/reno/his-soc.htm

This facility constitutes the state's oldest museum and serves as the repository and research library for more than 15,000 artifacts and works of art, 2,700 manuscripts, and approximately 300,000 photographs.

New Mexico Heritage Preservation Alliance (NMHPA)
Box 2490
Santa Fe, NM 87504
http://www.nmheritage.org/

The New Mexico Heritage Preservation Alliance is a statewide, private nonprofit organization that promotes, protects, and provides advocacy on behalf of New Mexico's cultural and historic heritage.

Pioneer Arizona Living Historical Museum
3901 West Pioneer Road
Phoenix, AZ 85086
http://www.pioneer-arizona.com/index.htm

This living-history site and museum consists of a ninety-acre historic village that includes both original buildings and historically accurate replicas enhanced with the addition of costumed interpreters.

Southwestern Association for Indian Arts, Inc.
P.O. Box 969
Santa Fe, NM 87504–0969
http://www.swaia.org/intro.html

This organization is devoted to developing, sponsoring, and promoting the Santa Fe Indian Market and related events that encourage cultural preservation, intercultural understanding, and economic opportunities for American Indians.

Texas Folklife Resources
1317 S. Congress Avenue
Austin, Texas 78704
http://www.texasfolklife.org/

A nonprofit organization dedicated to documenting, interpreting and presenting the many cultures and folkways of Texas.

White Mountain Apache Heritage Program
Near Intersection of Route 73 & Ind. Route 46
(about five miles south of Whiteriver)
http://www.wmat.us/wmaculture.shtml

The White Mountain Apache Heritage Program consists of a cultural center that serves as a repository for the tribal heritage of the White Mountain Apache.

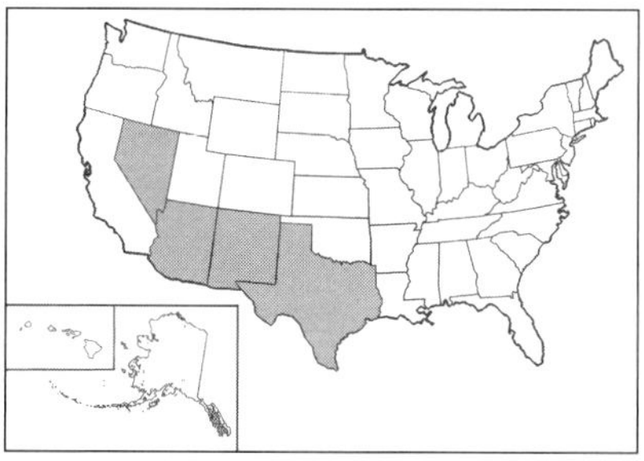

FASHION

Brenda Brandt

Cowboys and Indians—these images have become national icons and are what come to mind when conjuring up a view of people who have inhabited the semiarid to arid regions of the American Southwest. From this image, their dress—in the form of outerwear, hats, shoes and adornment, such as hairstyle—immediately comes to mind. While these images may be authentic or stereotypical, the dress they reveal has changed over time due to a phenomenon known as fashion.

For this discussion, *dress* is identified, by using definitions from classification systems developed by both costume historians and anthropologists, as body coverings and adornment. Dress is what we see—the arrangements, elements (line and shape) and details of coverings and adornment—when we observe what someone is wearing. The manner in which the elements and details of clothing are arranged is referred to as *style* and is a important part of dress. Style of dress consists of the overall silhouette, neckline or collar shape, sleeve shape as well as length and width, and applies to both men's and women's clothing. *Fashion* is defined as a form of human behavior and a product of behavior, which is widely accepted for a limited time and is replaced by another fashion that is an acceptable substitute for it. This definition recognizes that fashion occurs in many aspects of life—dress, cars, home décor, food, music—and that change is an implicit element in the process. Fashion includes styles that are classic and change very slowly or styles that are very short lived. In societies where fashion as a form of dress is not operative, custom is in control of what people wear and how they adorn themselves.

There are many reasons as to why fashion exists and changes, including influences of environment, technology, culture contact/trade, social structure, age, gender, and occupation, to name a few. People, events, and historical issues such as conflict, settlement and community formation also influence fashion and create either subtle or radical changes in dress in a matter of weeks, years, or centuries. As a result, fashion is today considered an integral part of the human experience, with dress and body adornment studied as material culture. Clothing/dress is one of the most personal of all artifacts, reflecting one's ideas, beliefs, values, and practices.

This chapter traces the history of fashion in the Southwestern states of Texas, New Mexico, Arizona, and Nevada. Identification of certain iconic elements of fashion that immediately signify Southwestern dress to outsiders is provided, as well as ethnic and socio-economic influences on dress from prehistory to contemporary time periods. The unique climate and physical environment of the region is also considered in this discussion as significant influences on Southwestern dress over time, and although fashion today in the Southwest is similar to other regions throughout the United States, certain enduring images of iconic stature still exist.

PREHISTORIC NATIVE AMERICAN FASHION

Tracing fashion history in the American Southwest begins with evidence in the form of material culture (physical artifacts) discovered during archeological research, which has been carried out in this region for more than one hundred years. Textiles supply the information needed to understand what influences impacted the clothing prehistoric peoples designed and wore in the regions today known as Arizona, New Mexico, Nevada, and Texas.

In Arizona and New Mexico, the Hohokam (assumed to be ancestral Piman speakers), Mogollon (ancestors to the present-day Pueblos) and the Anasazi (now more commonly referred to as the Ancestral Pueblo) were the three major sedentary cultures that lived in Arizona and parts of New Mexico just prior (300 B.C.E.) to and after the Common Era (1 C.E.) to the end of the prehistoric period, 1450.

The Anasazi lived in the high plateau country of Arizona and New Mexico, the Hohokam in the southern Arizona desert area, and the Mogollon in the mountainous areas of eastern Arizona and southwestern New Mexico. All were dry farmers who either diverted rain collected in washes to their fields or, in the case of the Hohokam, developed irrigation canals. They produced everything they needed, including their pots, implements, weapons, clothing, tools, and jewelry and occasionally traded with others for additional raw materials or finished products. Hohokam jewelry consisted of bracelets, rings, earrings, necklaces, and nose plugs, all worn for personal adornment. Materials used included seashells, semiprecious stones, pieces of pottery, and bone. The Hohokam probably painted themselves as well.

The physical environment in which these native peoples lived was semiarid or arid, and these conditions proved to be beneficial in preserving the textiles that today provide a prehistory of fashion. Most information about this prehistoric clothing comes substantially from the actual woven pieces themselves; most have been found in the Anasazi area, due to preservation in protected sites and the dryness of the climate. These uncovered textiles run the gamut from very small fragments, which are important in revealing technology and design, to complete belts, blankets, aprons, breechcloths, kilts, shirts, ponchos, and robes, which "tell all," about color, raw materials, construction, and how the item was worn.

Prehistoric Southwesterners were well equipped technologically to create both functional and fashionable clothing items. Simple looms for creating transitional textiles (sandals, mats, bags) evolved into horizontal looms on which weavers created dress and related items for physical protection and/or symbolic communication. Almost all weaving was directed toward the production of clothing, and every form of textile fabric was a square or rectangle, with the latter ranging from short to very long. Cutting and fitting garments was done rarely, if ever. Clothing was limited to a few types of garments in the early years and less so in later times; more garments appeared in the Pueblo IV and Pueblo III periods. Some specialization in creating clothing was evident; for example, beautifully decorated robes were probably worn in ritual situations. Variation in weaving was quite common among the native peoples. Elaborate weaves incorporating embroidery and brocading were common in southern Arizona and New Mexico, whereas fine weaving with about 80 warp and weft per inch was common in the north and south. In form, there was a trend toward a more nearly square textile fabric in the north, and a more rectangular shape in the south.

The semiarid to arid environment provided several vegetal/plant fibers for use in dress. Whether cotton or yucca leaf was used depended on the availability of water or irrigation for cultivation. Preference for certain fibers may also have been due to traditional usage; for example, this might explain the use of yucca in women's aprons in the Anasazi regions, where cotton was available.

Traders from Mexico introduced cotton into the Southwest. The species grown was *Gossypium hopi* which was related to a southern Mexican and Guatemalan species. There is evidence of cotton usage in the Southwest beginning in 700 C.E., and by 1000 C.E. it had spread throughout the entire region. Yucca leaves and the Apocynum (Indian hemp) stem were typically used before cotton for transitional textiles. Wool was not used in Southwestern textiles until the Spaniards brought sheep to the New World after 1540. More unusual materials for weaving included human hair, as well as dog, goat, bear, and buffalo hair.

Textile decorative design among the Hohokam, Mogollon, and Anasazi, which has achieved iconic status today, is essentially an arrangement of angular geometrics. Basic elements included lines, triangles, squares, zigzags, chevrons, barbed lines, checkers, hooked triangles, frets, and cross-hatching. Despite the relatively few elements and units, no two designs were alike. Weave played a major role in many details of the design; plain, twill, and tapestry weaves gave the fabric pattern, texture, and dimension. These basic decorative design elements also appeared in these native peoples' pottery and painted cloth.

Some textile decoration was regional and reflected trends over time. While Mexican influence is unclear, the Hohokam may have been affected by Mexican textile design more than the Anasazi. Stripe twills became distinctive to the Anasazi and remain so to this day among their descendants. The finishing of a woven fabric was important to the prehistoric weaver, and several techniques were used, including fringe, tassels, cord selvages, or adding a woven border.

The first inhabitants of modern-day Nevada were the Anasazi, the same native peoples living in Arizona and New Mexico, but a variant of that culture. Evidence indicates that they constructed large villages.

Basic clothing items found in the Great Basin, which includes all of Nevada, can be traced back 9,400 years. Rabbit-skin blankets and robes and sagebrush bark sandals underwent changes in production techniques during the prehistoric period and continued to be worn just prior to the historic period. Basketry caps, either coiled or twined from willow and sometimes feathered, have also been determined to have been worn by native peoples. Use of moccasins was limited; however, during the Fremont culture, which thrived from 400 to 1400 C.E., "hock moccasins" were worn.

During Texas prehistory (Archaic period, 6,000 B.C.E.–500 C.E.) native peoples collected edible wild plants and hunted game animals. A shallow archaeological record and limited artifacts have yielded precious little other information about these cultures, but it is known that they used stone tools and harvested yucca plants for both food and fiber. Baskets, sandals, mats, and other useful artifacts provide evidence that peoples of this area wove simple items, both fashionable and functional. One dry-rock-shelter archeological site in southwestern Texas contained a pair of well-preserved woven sandals. Although these hunting tribes left stories in the form of pictographs on rock shelter walls, tribal activity rather than clothing is depicted.

The appearance of the bow and arrow and pottery marked the end of the Archaic period and the beginning of the Late Prehistoric period of Texas Indian culture. Two main groups of native peoples are identified as living in Texas at the time, the Caddo, who resided in what is now the northeastern part of the state, and the Jornada Mogollon, who made their home in West Texas, near El Paso. Both were agricultural people, living in one place for long periods of time, then in larger groups and in more permanent houses. Evidence shows that these native peoples developed the technology for weaving and used indigenous materials such as plant fibers, and also that they traded for turquoise and obsidian from New Mexico's native peoples. By 1400 C.E. the Jornada Mogollon people and their culture had disappeared.

FASHION DURING SPANISH SETTLEMENT, 1540–1848

Spanish missionaries and explorers began their expeditions into what is now the U.S. Southwest in 1540. The native peoples they encountered were quite different from the Aztecs and other peoples of Mexico with whom they were familiar. Indian settlements varied widely, ranging from permanent, compact villages to temporary places lived in for a brief periods once a year. The first wave of Spanish settlement began in the mid-sixteenth century, when Spaniards moved quickly to add what is now New Mexico to their New World land holdings and, later, Texas and Arizona. Little is known about Spanish fashion from this time period, other than men in European military uniforms. In the seventeenth century, from the area of what is now New Mexico, Spanish of Basque origination moved into southern Arizona to gain a foothold to establish a Christianizing program among the Hopi Indians and to mine silver at a location near Tucson. Missionary activity and the push to move the frontier northward occurred in Texas at the same time as in New Mexico and Arizona.

Native Peoples

In present-day Arizona and New Mexico, the prehistoric craft of weaving textiles discussed earlier continued into the historic period for native peoples, but during this latter time, older weaving traditions were replaced by types of embroidery, colors, and materials. By 1000 C.E. Hopi and Acoma pueblos were well established, but by the thirteenth century the Hohokam peoples had declined in number due to a great drought. Pimas were among the other native tribes that the Spanish encountered.

Sixteenth-century Spaniards encountered these and other native peoples and observed that they lived in compact villages, practiced agriculture, and were skilled in many crafts, especially pottery making, basketry, and weaving. In marked contrast to the generally naked peoples the Spanish had previously met in Texas and Mexico, Pueblo Indians, who were descended from earlier peoples and lived in New Mexico and the Hopi country of northeastern Arizona, were well clothed in cotton textiles. Spanish accounts mentioned embroidered and painted shirts, *mantas* (shawls), sashes, and breech clothes, although they gave little information about technical processes or design styles.

Zuni villages at this time were at the crossroads of major trade routes running to the south and southwest, northwest toward the Hopi country, and north and east to the Rio Grande valley, Pecos Pueblo, and the southern Great Plains. Cotton clothing was among the goods carried along these routes. Turquoise came from New Mexico, shell and coral from the Gulf of California and the Pacific Coast, feathers from Mexico, and hides from the Great Plains. Other indigenous clothing of the Pueblos included blanket-dresses, open work shirts, leggings, woven belts, and braided sashes. These items were considered daily wear in prehistoric and early historic times but survive today mainly in ritual use.

Native American cultures present in Texas when the Spanish arrived in the 1500s included the Caddos, Tonkawas, Atakapans, Karankawas, Coahuiltecans, Jumanos, and Apache. Groups of Native Americans that had migrated to Texas by the sixteenth century included the Kiowas, Comanches, Wichitas, Wacos, Tawakonis, Cherokees, Alabamas, Coushattas, Kickapoos, Delawares, Shawnees, and Tiguas.

Climate, the availability of raw materials, and the clothing of the Plains Indians influenced native peoples' dress in Texas. Much of what is known about the Indians of southern Texas comes from the accounts of explorer Cabeza de Vaca, who was shipwrecked on the Texas coast and traveled through southern Texas and Northern Mexico for eight years, from 1528 until 1536.

Spanish records provide descriptions of the physical appearance of the people as well as their manner of dress, subsistence, and material culture. What many of these tribes had in common was the use of skins or hides as protective clothing and tattooing as body adornment for both men and women, which denoted tribal affiliation as well as symbolizing age and sex categories. Face painting in the form of stripes or animal patterns was also a common practice, and the *Caddos*, in particular, practiced artificial cranial deformation, in which their heads were elongated and made to taper off toward the top. This custom dated back to prehistoric times; human skulls with strong frontal deformation have been found in multiple burial sites in Texas.

Spanish accounts made during expeditions mention that little clothing overall was worn; for example, men wore a loincloth in warm and hot seasons, and in inclement weather, a cloak or robe was added. The loincloths of Coahuiltecan men were decorated with animal teeth, seeds, and other ornaments. Rabbit skins were cut, twisted into ropelike strands, and sewn together to make blankets or robes. Cloaks were made from coyote hides and probably other hides they were able to obtain. Nipple and lower-lip piercing was a way of decorating one's body. Women typically wore more clothing than men did, an example being a skirt of Spanish moss and deerskin worn by a Karankawa woman. Both sexes parted their hair in the center and wore moccasins.

Plains Indian clothing and ornamentation influenced the dress of the Kiowas, Kiowa Apache, and Comanche. Deerskin was the material of choice for moccasins, loincloths, and shirts for men, and of dresses and high moccasins for women. As did the Plains Indians, these tribes made buffalo robes that served as protection from winter storms. War-party clothing was elaborate; colorful bird-feather (crow and owl) headdresses combined with heifer or buffalo horns were popular.

For the Tonkawas, ornamentation in the form of shells and bone and feather earrings, necklaces, and bracelets was an important part of their appearance. Comanche men pierced their ears in a number of places for shell earrings or rings of brass or silver. Warriors cut off their hair on the left side above the top of the ear and allowed the hair on the right side to grow long. Feathers and other trinkets adorned their hair, and for dress occasions six to eight earrings were worn, in all the pierced holes. Some tribes also practiced nose piercing, and men typically removed their eyelashes, eyebrows and facial hair through plucking.

FASHION DURING ANGLO SETTLEMENT, 1848–1900

Dates for Anglo settlement vary depending on what area of the Southwest is being discussed. The Anglo settlement of Texas began in the 1820s, with the search for land. Gold and silver rushes, including those in present-day Arizona and New Mexico, brought adventures westward to seek new opportunities. Nevada was sparsely populated until the discovery of silver (the Comstock Lode) in 1859. After the Civil War, the U.S. Army was called to areas of the Southwest to protect settlers from raiding Indians. In addition, the first transcontinental railroad, which was largely completed in 1869, brought hundreds of thousands of Americans and overseas immigrants into the Southwest and West, creating one of the largest mass movements of people in history, and towns began to grow up rapidly along railroad lines. What helped create the Southwest's distinctive, unique identity, though was the continuation of the Native American/Indian and Mexican American/Hispanic peoples and cultures. All aspects of life, including fashion, were marked and influenced by both the separateness, and therefore the intactness, as well as the intermingling of these cultures, and during the twentieth century the dominant Anglo-American culture was the recipient of the spread of ethnic fashions.

Anglo-American Dress

Dress was a portable commodity that early settlers brought with them from their home communities elsewhere in the United States or in Europe. This meant that whatever was fashionable dress at their time and place of origination was what they brought with them and wore on the frontier.

Clothing in the nineteenth century was specific to gender, social class, and age. In addition to these restrictions, fashionable clothing for women was tied to the activity they were engaged in and to the time of day at which it was being worn. There was clothing worn in the morning and the afternoon at home, as well as dress specifically designated for visiting, walking, dining, attending balls and receptions, and for mourning. Men's clothing was also prescribed, but since there were fewer items in their wardrobes, town suits did double duty for many activities.

Anglo men's and women's styles of clothing worn in other parts of the United States and brought to the Southwest were based on European styles; for women of the 1850s and 1860s, this included a two-piece dress with a tightly fitting bodice and full hoopskirt. Clothing worn underneath the dress consisted of drawers and a short-sleeved chemise. Corsets, which were tightly drawn, shaped the upper torso of the woman's body and were worn over the chemise. Lastly, stockings fastened with knee garters, two or more full-length petticoats, and a second corset were all worn over the first corset. Dress silhouettes underwent changes 1870–80, with bustles appearing and disappearing and corsets making changes to a women's upper body according to the dictates of fashion. Necklines and sleeve shapes and lengths changed decade by decade, as did the styles of hats and the frontier sunbonnets that covered the head and face.

Men idling on the steps of a general store in Chacon, New Mexico, 1943. Courtesy of the Library of Congress.

Men also wore drawers, with a long-sleeved undershirt added to the upper body. Their outer clothing included a collarless shirt, to which was added a stiff starched removable collar buttoned to the collar band. Braces (suspenders) held up woolen pants, and a matching vest was added over the shirt. Frock, or sack, coats, which matched the pant and vest fabric, completed the look. Neckties, shoes, and hats were added either as a necessity or an accessory.

Ready-to-wear clothing for men was not readily available until after the Civil War, and women waited until the early twentieth century to purchase machine-made clothing in retail stores. Due to the complex designs of women's clothing in the nineteenth century, many women brought fabric wherever it was available and used patterns to make their own, their husband's, and the children's clothing. Women designed, fitted, and constructed clothing, as well as doing the washing, ironing, and mending. Most children's clothing was made from partially worn out adult garments or even empty flour sacks and patterned after adult clothing, only looser. Early settlers in Nevada circa 1860 traded with peddlers for fabric and Indians for blankets.

Textiles

During the early territorial days in Arizona (1870s), steamers brought fabric from San Francisco. These fabrics were available for purchase in grocery or dry-goods stores. Clothing patterns sent by family and friends back East were used for cutting and sewing garments in the home. Custom clothing made by tailors and dressmakers was also available during the last two decades of the nineteenth century, and mail-order catalogues offered another outlet for clothing and accessory purchases. A ready-to-wear dress was considered unique in the Arizona territory in the 1880s. By the beginning of the twentieth century, merchants sold men's clothing and some women's, usually outerwear and underclothing. Phoenix, Tucson, and Yuma all had one or more retailers of ready-made garments. In Reno, Nevada, a prominent dry-goods store was Palace Dry Goods, which began in Virginia City, Nevada, under another name and moved to Reno in 1907, remaining in business until 1932. The stores were stocked with practical, functional clothing items and accessories for all family members. A newspaper advertisement for Compton's store in Houston featured men's and women's leather shoes, gloves, and stockings as accessories and a variety of fabrics, including cottons, merino wool, calicos, gingham, and silk crepe.

Evidence indicates that the raw materials used in making yarns and fibers were available in several regions of what now makes up the Southwest. Wool was introduced into New Mexico via the Spanish (the early Albuquerque wool industry), who traded with Mexico for woolen products. Wool was available in the Arizona territory in 1881. One Arizona commissioner, while trying to lure European immigrants to Arizona, expressed the need for a woolen mill in the territory. Despite his soliciting, cotton mills for making wool fibers into yarns and fabrics did not become a reality in Arizona. However, extra-long staple Pima and Upland varieties of cotton were produced in Arizona beginning in 1902, and garments now held at the Arizona Historical Society reveal that a variety of wool fabrics, as well as wool-cashmere blends, were found in men's and women's suits and outerwear in Arizona from 1880 to 1910 (the years from which the garments date). More common was clothing made of cotton (underclothing, women's blouses and dresses, and men's shirts), silk (women dresses), linen, and cotton-alpaca blends.

Army Wives

Owning a sewing machine and knowing how to sew was a great asset for any woman and especially for army wives who lived on military posts in the Southwest and West during the nineteenth century. Because of their backgrounds, army wives were accustomed to such amenities as dry-good stores and dressmakers. In contrast, the army considered any females, even wives of officers, to be camp followers and made little official allowance for them. Officers' wives socialized only with each other if there were a group of them at the post. The laundresses and enlisted men's wives were not considered to be of the same social class, and sometimes these individuals were hired as domestics by officers' wives.

The expense of obtaining clothing on the frontier and constant relocation were always a worry for military wives. Women, in published diaries, memoirs, and letters, told of losing clothing to fire, mildew, and family pets, who chewed up hats and socks. Replacement of clothing items through sharing and borrowing from other wives helped the women cope, and owning a sewing machine and knowing how to operate it was an indispensable skill. Women without machines sewed clothing by hand.

Banding together and forming groups to share sewing knowledge, military wives established sewing bees, which allowed them to work together as a unit, with each person performing a specific construction process—fabric cutting, straight stitching, and fancy hemming and ruffling. Sewing comfortable shirts for a husband to wear under his uniform, as well as making trousers for one's boys were tasks that many women were called on to perform. Altering dress patterns received from fashion magazines such as *Mme. Demorest's Mirror of Fashion* also presented a challenge for many army wives. These women had grown up in a society where they were accustomed to selecting and purchasing clothing based on fashion, and this persisted on the frontier, so wearing badly fitting and poorly sewn clothing was not acceptable to them. Some, however, eventually learned the skills and expertise to do everything from making a beautiful French organdy dress to inserting pockets into a boy's trousers. After all, the women had reached a land with no seamstresses and no ready-made clothing.

Texas's textile industry can be traced back to the 1830s, when James Bowie proposed establishing a cotton mill in the Mexican state of Coahuila and Texas. He, along with several other entrepreneurs, purchased charters for other textile production companies, but none of these early ventures was successful. According to the *Texas Almanac* for 1868, the Waco Manufacturing Company, the Eureka Mills in Houston, and the Houston City Mills Manufacturing Company began producing cotton and wool fabrics. These mills were similar to textile mills in England and in the eastern United States. A slight decline in the textile industry occurred immediately after the Civil War, but production gradually expanded in the years that followed. The most important single mill was the Slayden-Kerksey Woolen mill built in Waco in 1888 for producing fabric for men's suits. In addition to textiles, clothing manufacture was also a small but growing industry in Texas, with five companies manufacturing clothing at the beginning of the Civil War. During the war, uniforms for Confederate troops were made at the Texas State Penitentiary at Huntsville. Numbers of manufacturers rose and fell until the end of the nineteenth century, and all clothing production in Texas until 1910 was men's, with a focus on pants and work clothes.

In Texas and Nevada, men and women stepped out of their log cabins or exited mining-camp buildings wearing fashionable dress. Although modern, popular images are of buckskin jackets and calico dresses with sunbonnets, keeping up appearances was very important in new communities in the Southwest where a person's background was unknown, and newcomers were judged as individuals. In the backwoods areas of Texas, frontier men did wear buckskin, and their wives spun yarns and produced hand-woven fabrics for all their clothing and household linens. But in the years prior to statehood in 1846, men living in the growing cities of Houston and Austin were described as wearing clothing brought from New York in the newest fashion, and women who attended the many balls held for various occasions dressed in fashions similar to ones designed by the famous dressmaker Worth. This was possible due to the Texas' proximity to New Orleans and the port city's close ties with Paris, the fashion capitol of the world during the nineteenth century. Nevada's closeness to California meant that San Francisco was its fashion center.

Women's Clothes 1848–1900

Diaries, memoirs, and photographs give some indication as to how men, women, and children adjusted their dress to adapt to the physical environment of the Southwest. In settled Arizona communities, businessmen would simply remove items of clothing worn as town clothes, such as the suit coat, and wear an opened vest, a shirt with rolled-up sleeves, and tie as outerwear. Women were not as fortunate in adapting their clothing to the environment. In the hot, arid summer climate, women suffered by wearing multiple layers of clothing that extended from head to toe and could weigh several pounds. Some women rebelled by staying indoors and striping down to their underclothes, and others, such as Martha Summerhayes, an army officer's wife, suffered but longed to adopt the clothing of the Mexican women while living in Arizona. Victorian conventions, which extended to dress, and her husband's adherence to these standards kept Martha and other women from adopting more suitable clothing for the desert environment. Summerhayes wrote of her envy of the dress of the modest and clean Mexican women:

> The women always wore, when in their *casa*, a low necked and short sleeved white linen *camisa*. . . . Over this they wore a calico skirt. . . . Their necks and arms do look so cool and clean. . . . I have always been sorry that I did not adopt their fashion of house apparel. Instead I yielded to the prejudices of my conservative partner, and sweltered during the day in high necked and long sleeved white dresses.[1]

But some women seemed to lack even the will to adjust their style of dress to the hot, arid climate in many areas of the Southwest, maintaining a preoccupation with their former lives in "civilized" parts of the United States and continuing to wear clothing appropriate to Eastern or Midwestern locales. One second-generation Arizonan commented on her mother's tendency to continue to wear clothing from a previous location. She said that her mother, despite living in Arizona for forty years, never became Westernized; she remained a New Englander all her life. Adjustment for the younger woman was much easier because she was born and raised on the desert frontier.

Overall, evidence indicates that being fashionably dressed was very important to women in established communities in the Southwest, although the extent of this seemed to be determined by the individual's lifestyle. Letters from women living in the established communities provided great detail about women's dresses and menswear worn at parties and weddings. For those living in rural areas and pioneers on route to the Southwest, clothing was strictly functional. For women, this might include a house dress called a Mother Hubbard, a style of dress that had no waistline seam (a belt was worn to adjust the size) and a gathered yoke as the neckline. Whether corsets were worn or loosened when this dress was worn is not known. This more functional form of women's clothing was not to be worn in public, only among friends and family.

One example of the importance and value of clothing comes from Virginia City, Nevada. The May 1868 newspaper announcement of the tragic murder of a renowned prostitute described what was stolen from her house; among the items were money, jewelry, a set of valuable furs, and silk dresses. The murderer/thief was later caught when trying to sell her valuables. The power and significance of fashionable dress was also evident when well-to-do families gave hired domestics their discarded clothing as partial payment for services, as indicated in a quote from an 1870s Virginia City resident.

Communications with family and friends living in "civilized" areas of the United States and the sharing of fashion magazines such as *Harper's Bazaar* and *Godey's Ladies Book*, which contained colored drawings of the latest clothing styles, helped link women with other women and, most importantly, spread the word about fashionable dress. In addition, new arrivals who came by railroad brought fashion information and fabric to the frontier.

Ranching Clothing

The opportunities that initially brought settlers to the Southwest—mining, ranching, and agriculture—led to the development of occupational dress that in some cases withstood the test of time and became classic and in others fell victim to fashion. Cowboy dress is an example of one iconic image of the Southwest that

A group of vaqueros in Texas. Courtesy of Corbis.

has developed over time and has a history. Cowboy clothing is also recognized worldwide, with its stereotypical images primarily resulting from staged photographs, postcards, dime-store novels, movies, and wild-west shows.

Ranching in all four states required a type of work clothing that was generally protective in nature in the beginning and later became symbolic. The earliest cowboys in America, dating back to the eighteenth century, were the Mexican *vaqueros*, who lived in the Southwest and needed protection from desert vegetation, the hot sun, and a hot, dry, dusty climate. These were Spanish and Mexican ranchers who raised cattle on land granted from the Spanish government. In Arizona and Texas, Anglo ranch owners depended heavily on Mexican cowboys to handle their cattle.

The term *cowboy* did not come into common use until the 1880s, and they were called buckaroos in Nevada. The most important, practical parts of what would become Anglo-American cowboy dress were leather leg coverings, which can be traced back to vaquero leggings; spurs, which Anglo-American cowboys purchased from retailers; and a hat with a wide brim to shield the wearer's face from the hot sun, also an important vaquero contribution. Wool vests, usually a part of a town suit, were worn in place of the vaquero's short jacket, and bandannas, which had long been used by men working outdoors, were occasionally worn. Edith Kit, who grew up on several ranches in southern Arizona, described the clothing of a typical cowboy as including a blue shirt, Levi's, a dark vest, and a hat with a high, round crown and a broad, straight brim. One Western historian observed that everything that characterized the American cowboy was taken over from the Mexican vaquero, including utensils, language, methods, and equipment. For certain, the vaquero is the source of the American cowboy's lasso, cinch, halter, chaps, spurs, bridle, and bit.

Written accounts by cowboys provided evidence to indicate that fashion had an

Cowboys at dinner—scene at noon hour in a typical cowboy camp of the "wild and wooly West," Arizona, 1907. Courtesy of the Library of Congress

Levi's Jeans

Levi's were created in Reno, Nevada, the result of a need for clothing that was suitable for the rugged lifestyle in the Sierra Nevada mountains. Laborers complained that ready-to-wear pant seams came apart, especially where the pockets were sewn to the trousers. In 1871 local tailor Jacob Davis was asked by one wife to make a sturdy pair of pants for her husband, who was a woodcutter and whose large size was outside the range of what was available at the local dry-goods store. Davis came up with the idea of putting copper rivets on to the pockets of his trousers. He made the pants out of a ten-ounce beige duck fabric, because he thought the fabric would withstand the rigors of working in the mountains, and charged the women $3.00 for the pair. The durable pants were a success, and Davis had orders for ten pairs the next month. For these trousers, he used nine-ounce denim fabric he purchased from the dry-goods firm, Levi Strauss, in San Francisco. The next year, Davis approached Levi Strauss with a partnership proposal for obtaining a patent on the riveted pants. Strauss agreed, and in 1873 Davis left Nevada and moved with his wife and family to San Francisco, where he supervised the manufacturing of the durable denim pants.

impact on their clothing. They mentioned that style changes in hats, boots, spurs, chaps, and horse gear occurred not only from decade to decade but year to year. Charles M. Russell, a cowboy, author, and artist provided this description of a cowboy who followed fashion, "Cowpunchers were mighty particular about their rig, an' in all camps you'd find a fashion leader. . . . Of course a good many of these fancy men were more ornamental than useful, but one of the best cow-hands I ever knew belonged to this class."[2]

Mining Clothing

The lure of gold, silver, and, later, copper brought many miners to the Southwest in the nineteenth century. Although mining frequently brought quick wealth to an area, economic disaster often followed once the deposits played out. This pattern repeated itself many times in Arizona and Nevada. The solitary prospector and his burro heading out in search of gold was the image of Southwestern mining in the early decades; however, by the 1860s mining camps were established, as were the saloons, brothels, dry-goods stores, and almost everything else found in small towns, except, in some camps, a church or jail.

Mining was hard work that required clothing durable enough to last through its rigors. In most of miners' nineteenth century photographs men are shown wearing some type of hat and typical laborer or work clothes consisting of Levi's or sturdy trousers held up by belts or suspenders, undershirts, outer shirts with or without collars, and shoes or boots. Men were also photographed in loose-fitting suit coats, which may or may not have been worn in the mines, depending on the climate or mine location; or perhaps they were worn only for the camera. Miners working by candlelight underground at the Tombstone Consolidated Mine are observed wearing clothing that included a wide-brimmed hat stiffened with resin, an undershirt, union drawers, woven shirt, baggy trousers, and boots or ankle-high brogans. Many of these men were from Cornwall in England, and they worked alongside Irishmen and refugees from Pennsylvania oil fields. Mexicans were also represented in photos wearing Anglo dress when doing this type of work. As the demand for skilled miners developed throughout the West, company demands for production and competition for jobs soon led to a hierarchy within mining camps. Cornishmen known as "Cousin Jacks" were easily identified by their lunch pails. Mexican laborers were only tolerated in most camps, eagerly sought out in some, and pushed into lower-paying, inferior positions in yet others.

Stetson Hats

The Stetson hat, whose history dates back to the 1860s, was the contribution of John B. Stetson of Philadelphia, who went west to regain his health. While there, he fashioned for himself a large hat that would protect him from the rain, sun, and wind. Upon his return to Philadelphia, Stetson made a hat that he called the "Boss of the Plains" and sent samples to Western retailers. This prototype eventually became known as the Stetson hat. Texas Rangers adopted it and soon found that it could be used in many ways: to drink from, fan a campfire, blindfold a stubborn horse, slap a steer, smother grass fires, and serve as a target in gunfights. It could also be brushed and made ready for dress wear. The hat's durability and versatility became a distinguishing feature for the real cowboy as well the popular, stereotypical fictional ones.

Military Clothing

Conflict between Native Americans and settlers in the West was the primary reason why the military came westward after the Civil War. As more and more Anglos and European immigrants established settlements, forts were built to keep Native Americans from attacking whites on ranches, farms, and towns. Military dress for those soldiers coming West was basically the same as what was worn during the so-called War between the States. The War Department was hesitant to make changes in the uniforms because there was so much surplus after the war. These uniforms consisted of a coat, trousers, a cap and cap covering, neck cravats or stocks depending on rank, boots, spurs, and an overcoat. Underneath, soldiers wore shirts, drawers, and stockings that were identified in the uniform regulations. Unfortunately these uniforms were not suited to the environmental conditions experienced in the Southwest, so men on duty wore the regulation uniform at the fort but were free to choose clothing for the conditions they found in the field. Cotton shirts replaced wool shirts (called campaign blouses) when temperatures went above 100 degrees during the hot, dry summer days and nights.

During the 1870s, new uniforms were authorized and distributed to enlisted men; these were basically the same as the previous ones but had some changes in the shirt, trousers, and hats. One of the more interesting innovations was the issue of "unmade trousers" as well as "unmade blouses" that were precut and sent with all the materials and equipment—the thread and needles—needed to assemble them. However, complaints continued from soldiers serving on the frontier because no new underwear designed for conditions in the West was included with the new uniforms. Army wives and their sewing machines were often enlisted to create more suitable items of clothing.

Mexican/Hispanic Fashion

As more and more Anglos settled in Texas in the 1830s, Hispanics became the minority in this region. As already mentioned, many Mexican articles of dress—leggings, spurs, and hats—were adopted by Anglo cowboys because these items were well suited to their occupation. While Anglos and wealthy Mexicans wore fashionable dress based on European styles, the typical Mexican man and woman wore more practical styles of dress that expressed their ethnic identity and were appropriate to the climate and physical environment.

Mexican women commonly wore a short-sleeved blouse with a long skirt and several petticoats. The blouse was pointed at the waist in the front and back and hooked up the back if the neckline was low. For long-sleeved blouses, the closing was in front with buttons or hooks, and the high neckline was finished with a roll collar and fastened with a brooch. Even though Anglo women during this same time period wore bodices with low necklines for formal evening wear, Anglos failed to understand the appropriateness and propriety of the everyday, low-neckline blouse for Mexican women. The skirt was generally shorter in length than the Anglo woman's and full, with more petticoats worn for dances. Skirts were decorated with ruffles, flounces, or diagonal stripes of contrasting fabric as trim along the bottom. Colorful sashes were tied at the waist and allowed to fall over the skirt.

In place of a bonnet or hat, a Mexican woman usually wore a *rebozo*, a *mantóne de Manila* (shawl of Manila), or less often, a *mantilla*. Women wore a *sombrero* (a broad-brimmed hat) only on horseback. The rebozo was a silk or cotton scarf seven ft. long and one yard wide, with fringed ends. It was worn over the head and drawn across the shoulders, sometimes covering all but the facial features. A shawl of Manila, which was embroidered (manufactured in China) and fringed, was worn in a manner similar to the rebozo. The delicate and costly lace mantilla was triangular in shape and attached to the hair above the forehead, so that it fell over the shoulders. Most were black in color and were sometimes worn like the rebozo. Due to their value, mantillas were often saved and worn for fiestas and holy days.

Mexican men's dress was influenced by the social status of the wearer. Most men wore a sombrero, with crown shapes varying from high and conical to low and flat, and often trimmed with gold or silver bands, tassels, braid, or chains. Color and raw material denoted social class; black or white felt sombreros were considered the best; poorer men wore straw versions. A colored scarf, tied around the head, was often worn under the hat. The *serape* was an item of Mexican dress that was worn by almost all classes. Made of wool dyed in bright colors and woven either in geometric patterns or plain with borders, a serape was a blanket used as a wrap, and due to the fabric's texture and tight weave, it was almost waterproof. There were various ways of draping the blanket over the body, each resulting in a very graceful appearance, even while on horseback. A serape was also used as a pillow, mattress, or cover, as well as a saddle blanket. Another body covering, the *poncho*, was similar to the serape but more rounded and not necessarily woven of wool.

Mexican laborers typically wore the poncho, as well as simple pants and shirts made of cotton muslin. The pants were snug around the thigh and wider near the ankle. Shirts were of a pullover style with wide sleeves and colored sashes at the waistline, and sandals completed the appearance. Many of these laborers worked for Anglo-American settlers as agricultural wage-workers in the southern parts of the Arizona territory and also played an important role in the development of Arizona's mining industry.

In contrast, the dress of the *caballeros* (gentlemen riders) consisted of a hat that was decorated with silver ornaments; a short jacket that, when made of buckskin, had sleeves open to the elbow and embellished with silver buttons; *calzoneras* (pants) decorated with silver buttons and made of buckskin or blue and black velvet; a sash of blue or red fringed silk circling the waist; and boots with large silver spurs that clanked at the caballeros' heels.

Many eminent male Anglo citizens in Texas wore Mexican blankets over their Anglo clothing. Serapes and ponchos were very popular in Texas, worn for protection against the cold and rain. In addition, certain components of Mexican dress such as the sombrero or sash were worn to suit the "capricious" taste of the individual.

Native American Fashion

The Native Americans living in Texas during Anglo settlement in the mid-nineteenth century dressed and adorned themselves in a manner not unlike their ancestors when they were first observed by the Spanish. These native people consisted of nomadic plains men and horsemen of western Texas, the agricultural Plains Indians of the Wichita group, the desert-dwelling Coahuiltecans of the Rio Grande valley, the Karankawan fishermen of the Gulf Coast, the native agricultural peoples of the eastern interior, and the tribal people who migrated from the southern and eastern United States into eastern Texas after 1800. However, by the mid-nineteenth century, changes had occurred: less body covering was worn, wool and cotton fabric supplemented skins and hides as clothing, and Anglo items of clothing were worn along with traditional Indian clothing.

By the nineteenth century, Lipan and other tribal women had added a Mother Hubbard–type blouse fashioned from a complete doeskin to the short skirt that covered the lower portion of the body. A hole was cut in the middle of the skin for the head to slip through, and the deer's tail with the hair left on hung down the back. The blouse was elaborately beaded, and fringe consisting of brass or tin ornaments was added. For Lipan men, a shirt and blanket were added to the loincloth for winter wear.

Woven wool fabric was introduced to the native peoples of Texas from the Navajo of New Mexico and the Cherokees from Arkansas and Tennessee. These eastern tribe transplants came to Texas and brought with them looms they had copied from Anglos, along with coarse, particolored cotton fabric for their own and their families' use. Cherokee women dressed simply and added red sashes and turbans to complete their appearance. Women of the Carissos tribe wore worn-out cotton dresses that were given to them by Anglo-Americans to cover their seminaked bodies.

Nineteenth-century visitors to Texas, such as Jean Louis Berlandier, described in his writings that he had observed Comanche, Lipan, and Tonkawa men wearing caps and military uniform coats, but lacking shirts and trousers. He reported that such whimsies in dress were rare and were never seen except among tribal chiefs who had acquired the items during visits to the state capitol. In the process of adopting Anglo clothing, the last traditional items to be given up were soft-skin moccasins in favor of leather shoes.

In addition to his written account of the Indians of Texas, Berlandier complemented his manuscript with a unique graphic record consisting of eighteen watercolor drawings of sixteen tribes. The artwork was a representation of native peoples' dress in the tradition of the European fashion plate. The emphasis was placed on clothing and adornment typical of the particular tribe; the settings were of secondary importance. Unfortunately, by 1875 all the original Indians groups of Texas had been killed or forced onto reservations in Oklahoma.

The Northern Paiute Indians in Nevada were traditionally hunters and gathers; in Virginia City during the nineteenth century men worked as laborers on the Comstock placer claim, while women were employed as wage laborers—laundresses, seamstresses, and housekeepers—as well as in the more traditional task of food collection. Northern Paiute women in Virginia City, Nevada, during the 1860s continued the aboriginal practice of face painting by adding red, white, and blue lines to their chin and cheeks and sometimes red pigment over the entire face. Ornamentation consisted of glass trade beads, "pony" beads, and abalone shells. Their dress was made of Anglo-American fabrics, but the style was definitely Native American. Women wore a distinctive loose-fitting, high waisted calico-print cotton dress with two or more flounces. Accessories included a fancy shawl, a silk scarf worn on top of the head, and, rarely, hoop skirts. Washo Indian women also wore this style of dress.

A Paiute basket maker, dressed in Western clothes, 1902. Courtesy of the Library of Congress.

In New Mexico the Comanche men around Santa Fe dressed in a shirt that fell to the knee, leggings of softened deerskin, and shoes of the same material. Women wore a longer dress with their stockings, which also served as shoes and were made of specially prepared deerskin. These items were trimmed with painted borders of their own design.

During the mid-nineteenth century, as more and more settlers moved to New Mexico and Arizona, more encounters occurred between Anglos and those tribes whose land was being taken away. These tribes included the village farming tribes (Pueblo, Hopi, Zuni), the *rancheria* farming people (O'odham, Yaqui, River Yumans), and the foraging and farming groups (upland Yumans, Navajo, Apaches, southern Paiutes). Photographs of Native Americans depicted many different ways of dressing; the clothing was as diverse as the many languages the people spoke. Items of clothing common to Pueblo women included a one-piece belted *manta* (dress)

Navajo children wrapped in blankets, 1908. Courtesy of the Denver Public Library.

adorned with turquoise or coral jewelry, as well as high-wrapped, hard-soled moccasins, whereas Apache women favored cotton over blouses and full skirts, known as camp dresses, that were patterned after the calico dresses of the Anglo women living on Army posts. Navajo velvet blouses and skirts were accentuated with silver and turquoise jewelry and concha belts, reflecting the high quality and simplicity of their silversmithing design. Men's clothing varied from breech cloths worn by Apache hunters with headbands and high moccasins to the shirts, trousers, hats, headbands, vests, and military coats that made up the clothing of Apache scouts at Camp Apache in Arizona in 1871. Loose-fitting trousers, shirts, moccasins, and blankets were observed in photos of Navajo silversmiths outside a mud home in northern Arizona.

Government policy until the late 1880s favored removal of Native Americans to remote regions in response to the fear felt by most Anglo-American settlers. Although settlers and ranchers pressured the government to control the Indians and to isolate them on reservations, with only a few exceptions, such as the Chiricahua Apache who were relocated from Arizona to Fort Sill, Oklahoma, Southwestern native peoples were not forced to relocate in areas far removed from their homelands. They were able to remain on their sacred lands and did not experience the major population losses suffered by the eastern tribes. This meant that native peoples in the Southwest were able to retain much more of their culture over time.

For Native Americans one beneficial effect of the railroads bringing people to the Southwest was the tourism industry that developed. Railroads beginning in Kansas City, Missouri, and traveling through Texas, New Mexico, and Arizona to Los Angeles brought tourists fascinated by a romanticized vision of Indian peoples. At the same time, many people in the late nineteenth century, primarily followers of the aesthetic movement, were reacting to growing industrialization and developing a deeper sense of appreciation of handmade objects. This transformed the cultures of Southwestern native peoples into a marketable commodity. Enterprising individuals such as Fred Harvey arranged for Indian women to sell their pottery, silverwork, baskets, and rugs in railroad stations and restaurants, with employees of his company—Harvey Girls and Indian Detours drivers—present to explain Indian culture.

FASHION IN THE TWENTIETH CENTURY

Settlement in the American Southwest didn't end at the beginning of the twentieth century; rather, it was just getting started. Despite the introduction of the railroad, the region continued to be underpopulated in comparison with the rest of the country. Before World War II and the postwar boom, the region remained sparsely settled, an area still devoted primarily to mining, agriculture, and ranching. Each present-day state became a study in contrast between its isolated urban centers and the vast countryside that surrounded them. Thus, the label "metropolitan frontier" was the name coined by an historian and used to describe the Southwestern region of the United States in the twentieth century. World War II became the important turning point in the growth of the region and its cities, launching the entire Southwest and West into a half century of urbanization.

Early Years

While the Southwest grew in population, so did changes in fashion. Women's dress changed more frequently and dramatically than men's, beginning early in the century and continuing decade by decade. One of the reasons for the change was the new thinking about clothing and the improved position of women in American society. This thinking actually dates back to the late nineteenth century, when a dress-reform movement surfaced, proposing the need for healthful dress for women which afforded them the freedom of movement and activity. Attention was given to how the dress of women symbolized their subservient relationship to men and limited their roles and activities in society. As a result, and because of mass production, during the first decade of the twentieth century clothing became looser, styles less complicated, and hemlines shorter and silhouettes straighter and tubular. This gave the wearer increased comfort and physical freedom.

World War I is the event that freed woman from many previous traditional roles, but the 1920s marked the emergence of the "modern" woman. Dress styles reflected the fact that women were now able to conduct business on their own account, hold separate property, will their property, and share in the control of their children. In 1920 women received the right to vote nationally, with Nevada and Arizona being two of several Southwestern states to support this important issue. Changes did not come without protest, however, and attempts were made in several states to regulate the length of women's dresses and the brevity of bathing suits.

Sportswear

The category of dress known as sportswear, which was introduced to the public in the later part of the nineteenth century, became very popular in the twentieth century and eventually evolved into the more casual clothing separates labeled as sportswear today. Initially, the clothing worn by early athletes was based on the traditions of male and female fashionable dress. Women wore floor-length skirts and corsets to ride horseback, bicycle, and play tennis, and men remained in their formal town suits, without jackets, to play golf so as to adhere to the nineteenth-century standards of propriety. However, increased interest in leisure during the turn of the century was an important catalyst for clothing change in sportswear and more general dress. Not surprisingly men were the first to adopt special-function sportswear. Gym suits, football helmets, and baseball uniforms were developed that offered freedom of movement, protection, and team identification. At the present time, even nonathletes in Southwestern urban areas having sport

A woman riding astride a horse in Texas, c. 1920s. Courtesy of the Library of Congress.

teams—Dallas, Houston, Phoenix—choose to wear athletic shirts for team-allegiance purposes. And, with today's trend toward fitness for both health and appearance, along with increased time for recreation and leisure, men's, women's, and children's sportswear marketed as active wear is worn for every day.

It took longer for feminine active wear to gain acceptance. But women were able to modify their clothing by choosing a simpler, shorter, and less decorative version of fashionable dress, and some daring women enjoyed the freedom of divided skirts; these were worn in the West and Southwest by women who lived on ranches and rode astride rather than side-saddle for both transportation and leisure.

Along with style changes came changes in the technology that in turn affected both textile availability and clothing manufacture. Ready-to-wear became increasingly popular and mechanized. Twentieth-century textile-fiber technology created numerous manufactured fibers, and designers and their collections became the starting point for fashion.

Dallas's Fashion Industry

Of all the present day states in the Southwest, Texas is the one area that boasts a fashion industry, which includes textile production, clothing manufacture, and designing. The manufacture of clothing and related products by Texas producers in the twentieth century became a "rags to riches" tale in both the literal and figurative sense. Texas producers and designers have challenged the hegemony of the New York and California fashion industries.

By the late 1920s more Texas companies had emerged that manufactured clothing better suited to the regional tastes and seasonal demands of the Southwest. Several companies, including the Haggar Company in Dallas, produced men's work clothes and pants, ladies' cotton dresses, and children's play clothes. During the 1930s Dallas companies capitalized on the marketability of the low-cost cotton house dresses and produced distinctive lines of sportswear, especially ladies' pants, for national consumption. The receipt of federal contracts during World War II to manufacture large quantities of military uniforms enabled Texas firms to modernize plant machinery and expand national sales contracts. In 1942 manufacturers formed the Dallas Fashion and Sportswear Center, now the Southwest Apparel Manufacturers Association, to advertise in national fashion magazines and promote apparel markets held in Dallas. Fashion-minded retailers such as Neiman Marcus, also in Dallas, produced a favorable fashion climate for the expansion of Texas apparel producers.

Growth in the importance of fashions designed and produced in Texas continued in the postwar period. Many of the early firms moved manufacturing operations from large urban centers to factories in smaller communities throughout the state, especially along the border with Mexico. By 1963 clothing manufacture was, in number of employees and size of payroll, the fourth largest manufacturing industry in Texas. Along with this came the opening of an Apparel Mart building in Dallas in 1964, which attracted approximately 80,000 buyers annually. Competition from imports produced with low-cost labor began to alarm clothing manufacturers nationwide, as well as Texas producers, in the mid 1980s. However, niche marketing and an emphasis on private corporate ownership brought about a longevity among many Texas companies that has not occurred in the national apparel industry.

Texas (in addition to Arizona) was also recognized in this century as a producer and supplier of cotton, wool, and mohair natural fibers. By 1971 the state pro-

Neiman Marcus

The Neiman Marcus Company was established in 1907 and grew up along with Dallas and with Texas. It was first recognized as a local specialty store (high-quality women's ready-to-wear clothing) and has now become an internationally recognized innovator in fashion and merchandising. Its founders—members of the Neiman and Marcus families—formed a partnership and identified personal service and customer satisfaction as their merchandising objectives. The store developed a reputation for high prices as well as high quality, even though its founders depended primarily on the sale of medium-priced items.

The store survived the Great Depression; an important factor affecting its survival was the discovery of an East Texas oil field in 1930, which produced a new group of millionaires and potential Neiman's customers. World War II led to a general economic boom in Texas and expansion of the store. Branch stores were opened in Fort Worth and Houston in the 1950s, and mergers with other retailing groups occurred in the 1960s and 1980s. Neiman's opened outlets across the nation, including those in Phoenix and Las Vegas, and became part of the specialty-store division of its parent company, Carter Hawley Hale.

Several innovations in merchandising and fashion, including being the first retail store in Texas to launch a national advertising campaign, added to Neiman's success and reputation over the years. The store also followed a liberal credit policy, dating from the earliest days of the store, when cotton producers were permitted to defer payment until after their crops were harvested. Annual fashion shows honoring outstanding designers, presenting cultural exhibits and merchandise from other nations in the stores, and mailing out its Christmas catalog also promoted the store. The concept of "selling the store," and not a particular item of merchandise made Neiman Marcus a Texas institution with an international reputation.

duced 25 percent of the nation's cotton, 97 percent of the nation's mohair, and 20 percent of its wool, with mills in Texas selling their fibers in both national and international markets. These fibers were often used in combination with synthetic fibers, depending on the design, color, and purpose of the fabric. Domestic companies used wool and mohair in the production of drapery fabric, neckties, scarves, blankets, upholstery fabrics, uniform goods, coating materials, and flannels. Burlington Industries, Inc., an internationally known textile manufacturer, had plants in three cities in Texas and produced bed sheets and pillowcases from the cotton and cotton blends. Alongside production of woven fabric, Texas added knitted machines in their plants to capitalize on the importance of knitted fabrics in the 1960s, popular because of the fabric's elasticity, its virtually wrinkle-free appearance, and aesthetic appeal. Prior to this point in time knit fabrics were mainly used as underclothing, with the exception of when Coco Chanel's use of jersey knits in fashionable women's dress in the 1920s. Woven-fabric producers also added stretch woven fabrics to their repertoire to meet fashion demands.

Midcentury Fashion in the Southwest

World War II and the postwar period stand as important turning points in the growth of the Southwest and its cities. New Mexico, Arizona, Texas, and Nevada became prime locations for defense and military bases sites due to the expanse of land available in the region. Planners for the U.S. Army Air Corps decided as early as 1940 that future training bases should be located in the southern third of the country. New or expanded bases appeared in such cities as El Paso, Tucson, and Albuquerque. And as a result, many servicemen and their families who were stationed at these bases returned to the Southwest to establish residence after the war. The "sunbelt" became an area alive with new technologies of production (such as computers) and consumption (such as fast food) as well as with new ideas, ethnicities, and national trends.

Southwestern Style

Fashion was also experiencing a postwar change in 1947, and locally owned shops and department stores all across the United States were tuned in to this phenomenon. The Southwest was no exception, with Albuquerque being an example of a city that was following the national and international trend of the "New Look" in fashion for women.

Prior to the New Look, created by the French designer Christian Dior, wartime fashion, which featured minimum fabric and little decoration, was loosely based on the look of men's military uniforms. Padded shoulders and knee-length hems were typical for women, and restrictions also extended to leather, which affected shoes, gloves, and handbags. Men's clothing was also restricted, with single-breasted suits with narrow lapels and cuffless trousers worn as the accepted style. In contrast, the "New Look" enhanced the lines of the female body. Shoulders became more natural and rounded, the bust and waistline were emphasized, and hips were curved. In addition, hemlines dropped and numerous yards of fabric were used in skirts and dresses.

After the war, Albuquerque's population steadily grew to over 95,000 as new-

Bola Tie

The bola (or bolo) tie, which originated in Arizona, is considered to be a symbol of the American Southwest and West. It was created in the 1940s in Wickenburg, Arizona, by a silversmith and considered the Western version of the necktie. The bola became the official Arizona state neckwear in 1971 and is worn all over the region. Usually crafted by silversmiths and leather makers in many shapes, sizes, and types, it is an appropriate accessory for Western as well as business wear.

comers from other regions of the United States moved to the Southwest. Many people couldn't afford Christian Dior clothing, so they created their own by using Vogue, McCalls, Simplicity, and other patterns. One of most enduring local fashions in the 1950s, inspired by Mexican dress in Albuquerque, was the "fiesta" dress, which was either purchased or sewn by hand and worn for fiestas or other celebrations. These dresses featured solid-colored cotton fabrics decorated with bright rick-rack trim and metallic braid trim, and they were usually worn with high heels. In Phoenix, during this same time period, the "squaw" dress was worn and featured a look adapted from Native American culture; soft suede squaw boots in bright colors completed the look. The skirt was gathered with three tiers and was designed to look like a broomstick, this effect being created by washing the skirt, squeezing it, and finally tying it with a string or rubber band while it dried. A concha belt was added at the waistline.

Continuing in the 1950, designers in New Mexico were inspired by the blending of traditional Native American, Hispanic, and Mexican fashion to invent its own look which included the long, full skirt and small waist of the originals. The key elements included the twisted broomstick skirt, with pleats and tiers, a fitted blouse, an abundance of Native American jewelry, fringed woven jackets, cowboy boots, hats, bola ties, and blue jeans.

Today this look is labeled as "Southwestern" or "Santa Fe" style. American designer Ralph Lauren has promoted and exported this style internationally in many of his collections during the last three decades. Lauren's contributions to the modern Southwest look certainly helped the style cross over into high fashion. The 1960s ushered in a more casual, youth-oriented, nonconforming look, with U.S. and British rock groups and the hippie generation changing fashion forever with T-shirts, bell-bottom jeans, love beads, long hair, and a unisex look for men, women, and children. In contrast, the 1970s and 1980s brought back a more adult style as more women entered the work force and adopted the pant and skirted business suit as professional wear.

Occupational Clothing

Occupational clothing in the Southwest underwent changes during the twentieth century, with cowboy dress evolving into Western wear and miners pushing for safety and protection in their work clothes.

The safety and protection of miners came to the forefront in the early 1920s, with miner's strikes in the Southwest occurring to secure better and equal working conditions for both Anglo and Hispanic workers. Miners continued to wear basic work clothes, and changing rooms were added to the mines to allow miners to shower before leaving work and as a check for theft in gold mines. Miners safety was an important issue from the 1920s to 1940s; safety shoes with hard toes were issued, and leather hard hats were replaced by the carbide lamp hat, which in turn was replaced by battery operated and eventually electric lamps. In the 1950s and 1960s, Arizona mining codes specified that long-sleeved shirts, work pants or jeans (no shorts), eye protection, and hard hats be worn. These codes formed the basis of what OHSA (Occupational Health and Safety Administration) and MOHSA (Mining Occupational Health and Safety Administration) adopted as requirements for protective clothing in the 1970s.

Cowboy style gained significant attention in the United States and worldwide as more and more tourists spent time in each of the Southwestern states while vacationing on dude or divorce ranches in Nevada in the early years of the century as well as in the years since. Cowboy dress was adopted and became known as Western wear by those visiting and vacationing, and custom or ready-to-wear Western clothing stores were well positioned in large cities and small towns to provide what was needed—boots, hats, Levi's, belts, bola ties, skirts, and shirts with decorated yokes and pearlized gripper snaps—to both men and women.

Movies during the 1940s and 1950s were also a motivating force in bringing cowboy dress to the national consciousness. John Ford (1895–1973) movies featured handsome heroes who dressed for show rather than wearing the practical, durable styles that actual cowboys wore. In 1980 the movie *Urban Cowboy* opened to mixed reviews; however, it launched a renewed national interest in all that was cowboy fashion and introduced a new generation to a style of clothing and accessories that could be worn by everyone in urban and rural America. In addition, during these same years Nashville recording groups, rock artists, and country bands discovered the glitter and glitz of Western wear for live and video performances.

Ethnic Clothing

During the twentieth century Native Americans continued the gradual progression from traditional to Anglo clothing. Mixing of both cultures' dress remained common as well. There is no exact date when Indian tribes became assimilated as to their dress; older generations in both Apache tribes and the Navajo Nation continue to this day to wear either the ribbon-decorated camp dress (Apache) or the velvet overblouse and skirt (Navajo) combination. Moreover, all generations wear traditional dress today when they participate in ceremonies; for example all women who participate in the Apache Girl's Puberty Ceremony wear the camp dress, while those watching the event might wear jeans or other current styles. Traditional men's dress is also worn when the Heard Museum in Phoenix sponsors an intertribal hoop dance contest, an annual event for the past fourteen years. Today, one can also visit the Heard Museum for a fashion show, held to highlight the creations of local fashion designers who are creating contemporary fashion inspired by and incorporating elements of Native American culture and traditional dress.

Increases in the Hispanic population of the Southwest have brought what was once minority fashion into mainstream American culture. Many styles associated with early Western wear reflect Mexican influence. Early in the twentieth century, wool jackets of Mexican origin were often made and sold specifically for the tourist trade. For example, imported Mexican felt jackets with embroidered and appliquéd motifs, sometimes called Rio Grande jackets, were available in an assortment of bright colors for women. Another popular item, Chimayo jackets, came from the

Native American performing a hoop dance. Courtesy of the Library of Congress.

Chimayo Valley near Santa Fe, New Mexico. This item was made from fabric from Rio Grande weaving and was adopted from the Spanish and Mexican styles into Southwestern fashion.

In the 1930s to 1950s *pachucos* (Mexican American adolescents in urban areas who belonged to juvenile gangs) created a look that featured baggy trousers worn high at the waist and tightly cuffed at the ankles. A sport coat that had wide shoulders and hung to mid thigh, as well as Florsheim shoes pointed at the toes, completed the style. The American media referred to them as "zoot suiters." Accessories included tattoos on the arms and hands, long decorative chains, and perhaps a concealed weapon such as a knife. Some pachucos engaged in criminal activity that included gang rivalry, while others were imitators or sought to emulate the antiestablishment attitude. The look had declined by the 1960s, when the youth-movement style provided a new way of displaying nonconformity. Today, gang members and rap artists have created a baggy style that began as being unique to their particular ethnic group but has now gone almost mainstream. Also, while not originating as an ethnic style, lower socioeconomic groups have in the last decade adopted the "wife beater" tank top as fashion.

Climate and Environment and Southwest Fashion

The impact of the Southwestern climate and environment on fashion became an issue to be debated in contemporary literature in the mid-twentieth century and was discussed as popular culture in the 1970s. In Arizona and elsewhere in the Southwest, mechanized, evaporative swamp coolers (1920s) and air-conditioners (1950s) made living much more comfortable, especially indoors. This removed climate as a primary factor in influencing fashion. In 1955 one author observed that both men and women dressed to accommodate the desert; whereas in 1978 it was reported that the desert climate did not dictate a particular form of dress. However, many Southwesterners today would probably agree that when facing a 107-degree day in Phoenix, Las Vegas, Albuquerque, or Houston, dress does matter! In addition, the wide variety of fashionable clothing available today for both sexes has made dressing for the climate much easier because of the wider range of choices. Furthermore, a more informal and casual Southwest lifestyle than in the past has created a social environment in which comfort can be a priority in dressing, in either work or weekend casual fashion.

FASHION IN THE TWENTY-FIRST CENTURY

Today, the images of cowboys and Indians live on in the iconography of the Southwest; these are enduring, nationally known images that reflect the region's cultural roots. Each new generation coming of age, often along with the help of a fashion designer, reinterprets the look, style, and image and captures the attention of those seeking something new to replace the old, thus experiencing—and creating—fashion.

Bonafide Southwesterners continue to embrace the subtleties of regional styles, adapting elements into their daily dress that are identifiable both within and outside the region. One of the most visible signs is the wearing of Indian jewelry. Another is the use of the now-iconic decorative designs adapted from prehistoric Southwest peoples and added to almost everything from clothing to tote bags. And the entire Western-wear phenomenon lives on in vintage and retro clothing stores, as well as antique shows, which many American and international enthusiasts visit regularly.

RESOURCE GUIDE

Printed Sources

Abbott, Carol. *The Metropolitan Frontier: Cities in the Modern American West.* Tucson: University of Arizona, 1995.

Balchin, W. G., and Norman Pye. "Climate and Culture in Southern Arizona." *Weather* 9–10 (1955): 399–404.

Berlandier, Jean Louis. *The Indians of Texas in 1830.* Washington, DC: Smithsonian Institution Press, 1969.

Brandt, Brenda. "Arizona Clothing: A Frontier Perspective." *Dress* 15 (1989): 65–78.

Campbell, Julie A., and Brenda Brandt. "No Steamstresses, No Ready-Made Clothing Consumption on the American Frontier, 1850–1890." *Clothing and Textiles Research Journal* 12 (1994):16–21.

Cordell, Linda S. *Prehistory of the Southwest.* Orlando, FL: Academic Press, 1984.

Dary, David. *Cowboy Culture.* Lawrence: University Press of Kansas, 1987.

Foner, Eric. *The New American History*. Philadelphia, PA: Temple University Press, 1997.

George-Warren, Holly, and Michelle Freedman. *How the West Was Worn.* New York: Harry N. Abrams, 2001.

Griffin-Pierce, Trudy. *Native Peoples of the Southwest.* Albuquerque, NM: University of New Mexico Press, 2000.

Hecht, Melvin. "Climate and Culture: Landscape and Lifestyle in the Sunbelt of Southern Arizona." *Journal of Popular Culture* 4, no. 11 (1978): 928–947.

Holman, David, and Billie Persons. *Buckskins and Homespun: Frontier Texas Clothing*. Austin, TX: Wind River Press, 1979.

James, Ronald M. and Elizabeth Raymond, eds. *Comstock Women: The Making of a Mining Community*. Reno/Las Vegas: University of Nevada Press, 1998.

Kent, Kate Peck. *Prehistoric Textiles of the Southwest.* Albuquerque: University of New Mexico Press, 1983.

———. *Pueblo Indian Textiles, A Living Tradition*. Santa Fe, New Mexico: School of American Research Press, 1983.

Kidwell, Claudia, and Valerie Steele. *Men and Women: Dressing the Part*. Washington, DC: Smithsonian Institution Press, 1989.

Langellier, John P. *Sound the Charge: The U.S. Cavalry in the American West, 1866–1916*. Philadelphia, PA: Stackpole Books, 1998.

Malone, Michael P., and Richard W. Etulain. *The American West: A Twentieth-Century History*. Lincoln: University of Nebraska Press, 1989.

Marcus, Stanley. *Minding the Store*. Boston, MA: Little, Brown, 1974.

McBride, James. *The Mission, Means and Memories of Arizona Miners: A History of Mining in Arizona from Prehistory to Present*. Phoenix: Arizona Mining Association, n.d.

McChristian, Douglas C. *The U.S. Army in the West, 1870–1880: Uniforms Weapons, and Equipment*. Norman, OK: University of Oklahoma Press, 1995.

Mills, Betty J. *Calico Chronicles*. Lubbock: Texas Tech Press, 1985.

Newcomb, W. W., Jr. *The Indians of Texas: From Prehistoric to Modern Times*. Austin: University of Texas Press, 1961.

Officer, James E. *Hispanic Arizona*. Tucson: University of Arizona Press, 1989.

Polling-Kemptes, Lesley. *The Golden Era 1922–27; West By Rail With the Harvey Girls*. Lubbock: Texas Tech University Press, 1997.

Reid, Mary. "Fashions of the Republic." *Southwestern Historical Quarterly* 45 (1942): 244–254.

Roach, Mary Ellen, and Kathleen L. Musa. *New Perspectives on the History of Western Dress*. New York: NutriGuides, 1979.

Rollins, Philip Aston. *The Cowboy: An Unconventional History of Civilization on the Oldtime Cattle Range*. New York: Charles Scribner's Sons, 1922.

Shafer, Harry. *Ancient Texans*. Austin: Texas Monthly Press, 1986.

Slatta, Richard W. *Cowboys of the Americas*. New Haven, CT: Yale University Press, 1990.

Tanner, Clara Lee. *Prehistoric Southwestern Craft Arts*. Tucson: University of Arizona Press, 1976.

Teague, Lynn. *Textiles in Southwestern Prehistory*. Albuquerque: University of New Mexico Press, 1998.

Tinkle, Lon, and Allen Maxwell, eds. *The Cowboy Reader*. New York: Longmans, Green and Company, 1959.

Tuohy, Donald. *To Clothe Nevada Women, 1860–1920*. Carson City: Nevada State Museum, 1990.

Web Sites and Special Collections

The Albuquerque Museum
2000 Mountain Road NW
Albuquerque, New Mexico 87104
http://www.cabq.gov/museum

Arizona State Library, Archives and Public Records
1700 W. Washington Street
Phoenix, AZ 85007
http://www.lib.az.us

The Handbook of Texas History
General Libraries at the University of Texas at Austin and the Texas State Historical Association
http://www.tsha.utexas.edu

Heard Museum
2301 N. Central Avenue

Phoenix, AZ 85004-1323
http://www.heard.org

Nevada State Museum
600 N. Carson Street
Carson City, NV 89701-4004
http://dmla.clan.lib.nv.docs/museums/cc/carson.htm

Witte Museum
3801 Broadway
San Antonio, TX 78209
http://www.wittemuseum.org/main.html

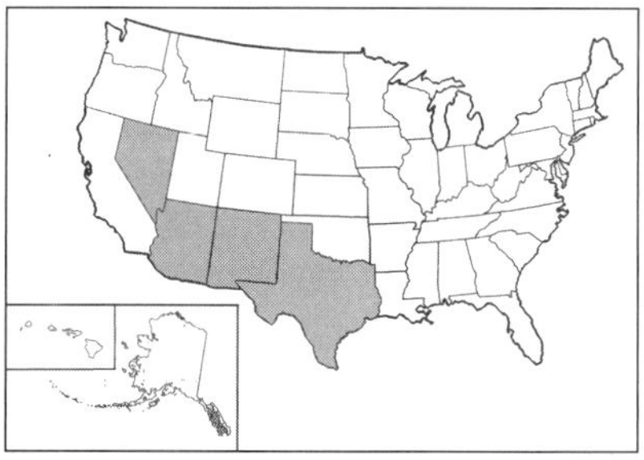

FILM AND THEATER

Mark Busby

The American Southwest became a dominant American place in the last hundred years largely because of the power of the images associated with the West and the Southwest. Among the most significant producers and suppliers of these images are Southwestern theater and film, both of which evolved from literature and other forms of entertainment such as Wild West shows and rodeos.

WILD WEST SHOWS AND RODEOS

Although these two types of entertainment share a connection to the American West, they have very different histories, influences, and effects. The two merge at several important points that highlight their relationship. Wild West shows draw from several sources, including circuses, minstrel shows, and traveling displays that focused on aspects of the American West. Like the circus—which can be summed up as large traveling entertainments in tents pitched in large open fields and featuring animals and performers—Wild West shows typically took place in large, open fields, set up temporarily with bleachers and tents. And the shows usually featured bronco-riding cowboys doing tricks and roping, events that later became part of the rodeo, as well as sharpshooting, American Indian ceremonies, and dramatic presentations of life on the frontier, including Indian attacks and historical reenactments.

Wild West shows began in a rudimentary way with painters like George Catlin (1796–1872), who traveled the American West. Along the way he painted the realistic details of the people, views, plants, and animals, collected artifacts; and then returned East to display them, lecturing about the exotic things he had seen. While Catlin laid the groundwork for the Wild West show, former cavalry scout William F. "Buffalo Bill" Cody (1846–1917) and his partner, W. F. "Doc" Carver, are usually credited with having begun it. After a modest career as a scout and buffalo hunter, Cody was plucked from obscurity by Ned Buntline, pseudonym for E.Z.C.

Judson, who made Cody the hero of a series of dime novels and then a play, *The Scout of the Plains*, in which Cody began playing himself on stage in Chicago in 1872.

Cody began his own "Wild West & Congress of Rough Riders of the World" in 1883, and in 1887 he opened the show in Madison Square Garden, New York City, with a cast that included sharpshooter Annie Oakley, Texas Jack Omohundro and other trick riders, shooters, ropers, and over 100 Indians. Drawing its inspiration from the circus, the show included displays of animals such as longhorn cattle, buffalo, elk, bear, moose, and deer. Cody took his show abroad successfully from 1887 to 1893, playing before the European crowned heads, including Queen Victoria. Cody extolled the virtues of the American West in patriotic skits about the settlement of the country, and he continued to pit American abilities against the decadence of Europe, having Annie Oakley match her skills against those of Grand Duke Michael of Russia. She won easily. Cody angered the Spanish by claiming that bulls were not dangerous, which the Spanish took as a slap in the face of their national sport.

As Cody aged, he tried to hold on to his influence, but others began to adopt his techniques. Among the most important of these was the Miller Brothers 101 Ranch Real Wild West Show, started in 1893 by Colonel George Washington Miller on the 110,000-acre 101 Ranch, which was spread over four counties in northeastern Oklahoma. Miller's fours sons recognized Cody's brilliance, bought some of Cody's equipment that he was forced to sell, and began to compete. The history of the 101 brings together Wild West shows, rodeos, and movies—all the most influential popular culture media associated with the American West.

Cody himself appeared in the Millers' shows, along with Geronimo, Will Rogers, Yakima Canutt, and Tom Mix, as well as Lucille Mulhall, called the first cowgirl and ladies' world champion roper. One of the most interesting figures to make his name with the 101 was the African American cowboy William (Bill) Pickett (1870–1932) from Travis County, Texas. After watching bulldogs bring down cattle by grabbing their lips or ears with their teeth, Pickett started a method of bulldogging by taking the steer's lip in his teeth. Now known as steer wrestling, it is one of the established rodeo events.

The modern rodeo is a sporting event that showcases skills developed by cowboys during the golden days of the cattle industry in northern Mexico and the American West in the latter half of the nineteenth century. There are five standard rodeo events—calf roping (which was a Wild West show feature), bull riding, steer wrestling (bulldogging), saddle bronc-riding, and bareback bronc-riding—and two other recognized championship events—single-steer roping and team roping. Rodeos often include specialty exhibitions such as trick riding and fancy roping. A popular contest for cowgirls is the barrel race, where a cowgirl races a horse around a series of barrels, and the fastest time wins.

Rodeo looks back to the Spanish influence in the Southwest. The Spanish introduced horses and cattle and even much of the terminology: *rodeo* (roundup) and *vaquero* (cowboy). When Civil War veterans returned to Texas after the war, with the economy and much of their livelihood in chaos, they discovered that their cattle had multiplied and that a market for them existed if they could round them up and drive them up the trail to railheads in the north. Cowboying skills were valued, and bucking-bronco-riding and roping competitions began on ranches and at the end of cattle drives. Those events became part of Wild West shows, competing with theater for audiences and later influencing film.

THEATER HISTORY IN THE SOUTHWEST

English-language theater arrived in the Southwest after 1821, but various types of performance existed before then. Indian bands' religious rituals included such performance elements as dance, costume, and impersonation. The Spanish brought European theater with them. Soon, the missionaries learned that the native people's lives revolved around ceremonies and were therefore open to lessons learned through performance. Spanish missionaries presented religious dramas, which were integrated with native dance to create a synthetic type of presentation. These folk dramas evolved early on in the Spanish colonial era and survived into the twenty-first century in holiday productions of such plays as *Los Pastores* (The Shepherds) short for *El Segundo Colóquio de los Pastores* (The Second Colloquy of the Shepherds), the most widespread of the Nativity Plays; and *Las Posadas* (The Inns), in which processionals lead Joseph and Mary through the streets as they beg for lodging; *Los Tres Reyes Magos* (The Three Kings); as well as performances about appearance of the Virgen de Guadalupe. The latter ranged from brief tableaus of Guadalupe revealing herself to the humble Aztec Juan Diego, to costumed *Comanche* and *Azteca* dances, to a complete performance of *Las Cuatro Aparíciones de Nuestra Señora de Guadalupe* (The Four Apparitions of Our Lady of Guadalupe). Performances occurred in 1598 near El Paso, in 1721 at Los Adaes, and during the 1770s in San Antonio.

Anglo Southwesterners—soldiers, farmers, trappers, miners, and cowboys—also sought theatrical performances, initially through amateur productions, but soon itinerant traveling troupes arrived. Houston obtained a theater before constructing a church, first with amateurs such as the future Texas presidents Sam Houston and Mirabeau B. Lamar. By the late 1830s professionals arrived at the port of Galveston, which became an attractive addition to the New Orleans–based touring circuit. Inland towns had amateur dramatic societies. By 1845 strolling players traveled the towns along accessible trade routes, such as Matagorda, San Augustine, and Jefferson. During the U.S.–Mexican War, actors performed for U.S. troops in the Rio Grande Valley. In 1845 troops in the Fourth Infantry Regiment stationed at Corpus Christi staged a performance of *Othello* with Lt. Ulysses S. Grant as Desdemona.

During this time Texans produced a few original plays, including several about the Texas Revolution, such as *The Storming of the Alamo*. In the 1840s San Antonio audiences could find plays performed in English, Spanish, and German, many in Casino Hall. The Menger Hotel, across from the Alamo, hosted German theatrical productions. German towns Fredericksburg and New Braunfels offered sophisticated German-language theater and opera through social clubs after 1850. New Braunfels presented Schiller's trilogy, *Wallenstein*, in 1850. In 1877 the railroad reached San Antonio, soon bringing touring companies that attracted large audiences for productions in English. In El Paso, Myar's Opera House offered operas and classical plays, including, in 1887, *The Count of Monte Christo* starring James O'Neil. Other theaters there presented plays, musicals, and vaudeville, and provided a venue for repertory players.

Other theater experiences existed elsewhere in the Southwest. Venues for theater were found in Las Vegas in New Mexico territory and in Tombstone and Tucson in Arizona territory. Las Vegas, New Mexico, had eight local theatrical groups and five opera houses operating in the 1880s. Nearby Fort Union offered a drama society, La Sociedad Dramática, which presented plays in Spanish that featured

Spanish-Language Theater

Spanish-language theater in Texas and the Southwest has also had a marked effect made more pronounced by touring companies. Touring companies from Mexico probably established a regular route in Texas by 1900, performing opera, operetta, *zarzuela* (Spanish operetta or musical comedy), or drama. The best known was probably the Compañía Dramática Solsona. After 1900 the number of theatrical companies performing in Texas increased. The Mexican Revolution (1910–1920) forced many Mexicans to journey north to the United States; among these were many of Mexico's greatest artists and theatrical companies, such as the theater troupe that arrived and stayed, the Compañía Villalongín. Originally formed by Encarnación Hernández in 1849 in Guadalajara as Compañía Hernández, it was mainly composed of family members who toured northern Mexico until 1900. From 1900 to 1911, Hernández's son-in-law, Carlos Villalongín, was the leading man, and the ensemble performed throughout the Southwest. After the Mexican Revolution began, Compañía Villalongín, renamed for its star, moved to San Antonio and first leased the Teatro Aurora in 1911, moved in 1912 to the Teatro Zaragoza, at the center of the Mexican American community, and still toured occasionally until 1924, when Compañía Villalongín disbanded. Resident stock companies also contributed to the Mexican American theater, including the Compañía Dramática Mercedes Navarro and the Gran Compañía Dramática Mexicana de Rosita Arriaga in El Paso, and the Compañía Virginia Fábregas performed in Laredo, El Paso, and San Antonio.

Mexican American theater declined during the Depression and World War II, but it was revived in 1965 with the founding of El Teatro Campesino, whose success stimulated the rise of a generation of Chicano theater groups. Luis Valdez established El Teatro Campesino as a traveling company that played to California farm workers. In 1981 Valdez moved into a permanent structure in San Juan Bautista, California, and opened with David Belasco's *Rose of the Rancho*. As a traveling company, El Teatro Campesino's most significant work was Valdez's *Zoot Suit*, originally commissioned by Gordon Davidson, director of the Mark Taper Forum. After its success at the Mark Taper, *Zoot Suit* moved to New York in 1979 and was filmed in 1981. The play is based on the Sleepy Lagoon murder trial of 1942, in which seven teenaged Mexican Americans were tried for the murder of another Mexican American in Los Angeles. The trial and its aftermath, riots by American servicemen who began beating and stripping zoot-suited Hispanics, allowed Valdez to dramatize the treatment of Mexican Americans in the West and to examine the difference between a mythic Western hero—in this case, the *pachuco*—and his modern follower, Hank, the leader of the gang. Valdez furthers his search into the Chicano past in *Bandito!* (1981), a play about Tiburcio Vasquez, a Mexican American Robin Hood hanged in 1875. Following Valdez's success, several significant groups emerged in Texas. Teatro Chicano de Austin presented *actos*, short skits similar to the ones that Valdez originated. Teatro de los Barrios began in 1970 in San Antonio, and in 1973 presented *El Alamo: Our Version of What Happened*.

leading citizens such as the future governor Ezequiel C. de Baca. Tombstone miners viewed the classics and contemporary plays at Schieffelin Hall and saw Gilbert and Sullivan operettas or vaudeville shows at the Birdcage Variety Theater including Eddie Foy. In Tucson the amateur group the Thespians performed plays, as did Spanish-language companies from Mexico.

In the 1890s entrepreneurs across the Southwest began to build theaters to book traveling companies. In Texas, Henry Greenwall of Galveston managed an important touring circuit. After 1905 theaters also began showing films, first as novelties. Karl Hobliztelle of Dallas built large theaters that alternately presented movies, vaudeville, and plays. Soon the growing popularity of these films led to the decline of commercial theatrical tours, with the exception of the Spanish-language troupes that fled to southern Texas during the Mexican Revolution and toured until the 1930s. Around the Southwest, many grand theaters alternated between live performances and film: the Palace and the Lakewood in Dallas, the Paramount in Austin, the Majestic in San Antonio, the Grand in Galveston, the Fountain in Mesilla, New Mexico, the Rio Grande in Las Cruces, the KiMo in Albuquerque, the Lensic in Santa Fe, the Grand in Douglas, Arizona, the Rialto and the Fox in Tucson, the Birdcage in Tombstone, the Orpheum theaters in Phoenix and Flagstaff, the Eureka Opera House in Eureka, Nevada, Piper's Opera House in Silver City, and many others.

Although the popularity of movies led to a decline in theater, it didn't lead to its demise, and throughout the twentieth century the Southwest saw the growth of little, community, and university theater programs. After the San Antonio Little Theatre began in 1912, amateur little theaters sprang up around Texas and the Southwest by the 1920s. The Dallas Little Theatre, founded in 1921, presented new plays, including those of Paul Green (1894–1981), author of the outdoor drama *Texas* still produced in Palo Duro Canyon, and through subscribers, built a theater in 1924 that seated over 200 people. That same year the Dallas Little Theater won the Belasco Cup of the National Little Theater League in New York for its production of *Judge Lynch* by John William Rogers. The Albuquerque Little Theater began after the Great Depression and flourished, mainly through the help of Broadway actress Kathryn Kennedy (n.d.), who moved to New Mexico for her health and then met and married the Irishman James O'Connor. With an Albuquerque journalist, Irene Fisher, Kathryn O'Connor established the Albuquerque Little Theater in 1930. Their first play, presented at the KiMo Theater, was a comedy whose cast included the young actress Vivian Vance. Then O'Connor began bringing Broadway hits to the Southwest. With WPA funds and with the aid of future senator Clinton Anderson the group began to build a theater, designed by architect John Gawk Meem. In 1936 WPA Director Harry Hopkins traveled from Washington, D.C., for the first performance, Lynn Riggs' *Russet Martle*. By the 1970s the Albuquerque Little Theater had more than 10,000 season subscribers.

At the University of Texas in Austin in 1907, Stark Young (1881–1963), later a well-known scholar, began the Curtain Club, a drama society that was active into the 1950s. Other drama clubs at Texas universities soon followed. Soon, academic programs across the region also contributed to Southwestern theater. One program that increased the interest in theater was the first University Interscholastic League's play contest, initiated in 1927, which led secondary schools to institute

The KiMo Theater in Albuquerque, c. 1980. Courtesy of the Library of Congress.

drama programs and arguably became the most significant institution in Texas theater. The University of Texas in Austin began its curriculum in 1938. At the University of New Mexico in Albuquerque Professor Edwin Snapp (n.d.), who had attended UNM and later taught playwright Preston Jones (1936–1979), began the theater program there in the late 1930s. During the 1940s, director and educator Paul Baker (1911–) began applying his theory of what he referred to as the integration of abilities at Baylor University, and he later collaborated with the Dallas Theater Center, which opened its Frank Lloyd Wright–designed facility in 1959. After a falling-out with Baylor over a production of Eugene O'Neill's *A Long Day's Journey into Night* in 1963, Baker moved his company (which included playwrights Preston Jones, Robert Flynn, and Eugene McKinney) and his collaboration with the Dallas Theater Center to Trinity University in San Antonio. Mark Medoff (whose plays will be discussed below) joined the theater program at New Mexico State University in Las Cruces in 1966 and later became the school's dramatist-in-residence and drama department chairman. He won a Tony Award for his play *Children of a Lesser God*, later made into an Academy Award-nominated film.

The little theaters and academic programs sometimes collaborated with professional theater, such as Paul Baker's program at the Dallas Theater Center, but some successful professional theaters began in the mid-twentieth century. While the WPA Federal Theatre Project had little success employing theater artists in Texas, it provided a start for Margaret Jones (1912–1955) in Houston, who later, as Margo Jones, became one of the major figures in the American regional theater movement. Jones created the first nonprofit professional theater in the country and later, through her book *Theater-in-the-Round*, promoted the intimate kind of staging that became popular throughout the country. After working in the WPA project, traveling around the world, directing at the Pasadena Playhouse, founding and directing the Houston Community Theater, and teaching theater at the University of Texas, Jones began Theatre '47 in 1947 in the stucco-and-glass-block Gulf Oil Building at the State Fair of Texas in Dallas. The theater's name changed annually to correspond to the year, and they performed such new plays as William Inge's *Farther Off from Heaven* (later *Dark at the Top of the Stairs*) and Tennessee Williams' *Summer and Smoke*. Theater '55's schedule included the first production of Jerome Lawrence and Robert E. Lee's *Inherit the Wind*, which, like *Summer and Smoke*, then moved to Broadway. Jones died in a tragic accident in 1955, poisoned by carbon tetrachloride used to clean her carpets. While Jones' program collapsed after her death, her success had demonstrated that resident, regional theaters could flourish; the Dallas Theater Center's collaboration with Paul Baker was partially the product of that success.

At about the same time that Jones began her program in Dallas, Nina Vance (1914–1980), who had worked with Jones at the Houston Community Theater, began to develop the Alley Theater in Houston. Vance started in 1947 by mailing 214 penny postcards (all the change she had) asking for contributions to create a theater. With $740 from twenty donors and hundreds of volunteers, she staged the first production six weeks later. The company moved to an old fan factory in 1948. In a controversial move in 1954, Vance insisted on hiring professional actors, and by 1961 the company was purely professional. Through grants from the Ford Foundation, in 1968 the Alley Theater moved into a new building designed by Ulrich Franzen. When Vance died in 1980, the Alley Theater had 30,000 subscribers and a yearly budget of almost $4 million. Later the Alley, along with the University of Houston, became the artistic home for Edward Albee. In the 1990s, visionary artist Robert Wilson, originally from Waco, returned to Texas to direct at the Alley and the Houston Grand Opera.

While the Dallas and Houston theaters dominated the region, theater groups elsewhere continued. The Phoenix Little Theater began before the Depression and continued to operate during it, later becoming part of a cultural complex that included a new public library and art museum. The Tucson Little Theater was first named the Tucson Community Theater and then the Arizona Civic Theater. Many of these theater programs contributed directly to the success of playwrights and plays that have come to define the Southwest.

SOUTHWESTERN DRAMA

Southwestern theater looks back to numerous theatrical productions about the American frontier dating from shortly after the end of the Civil War to the beginning of cinema. Because interest in the West and Southwest increased after the Civil War, American frontier plays gained audiences. Roger Hall (1939–) in *Performing the American Frontier, 1870–1906* identifies eleven elements of most early frontier plays: distinctive lead characters; varied ethnic supporting characters, often portrayed as comic caricatures; frontier costuming; frontier weapons; frontier occupations; idiomatic border language; specific references to primal elements such as weather and animals; rudimentary social institutions; frontier modes of transportation; importance of the land; and traditional melodramatic elements adapted to the frontier.

Many of these plays take place in some generic West or are about Western but not Southwestern figures, such as Buffalo Bill Cody, the James Brothers, Calamity Jane, Custer, and Sitting Bull. But a significant number of the plays are about Southwestern historical figures, including Davy Crockett, Kit Carson, Sam Houston, John B. "Texas Jack" Omohundro, and, later, Will Rogers.

William F. Cody, popularly known as Buffalo Bill, frontiersman, actor, and Wild West show entrepreneur, is important because he served as the subject of plays in which he played an exaggerated and fictitious version of himself. But it was only upon returning to the West that, ironically, his exploits came true: the day he arrived at War Bonnet Creek in northwest Nebraska, Cody killed a minor Cheyenne chief, Yellow Hair (Yellow Hand). At the time, Cody was wearing a theatrical costume that was decidedly Southwestern, that of a Mexican *charro* (rodeo performer)—black velvet with scarlet slashes, silver buttons, and lace.

At the beginning of the twentieth century such American frontier plays as Augustus Thomas' *Arizona* (1900), David Belasco's *The Girl of the Golden West* (1905), and William Vaughn Moody's *The Great Divide* (1906, set in Arizona) became almost mainstream and a dominant force in American theatre, pointing the way toward the characters, plots, and themes adopted by film, radio, and television.

Shortly thereafter, Southwestern drama receded. The most important Southwestern playwright of this period was Lynn Riggs (1899–1954), whose *Green Grow the Lilacs* (1931) later became the popular American musical *Oklahoma!* Another significant regional playwright of the early and mid-twentieth century was Ramsey Yelvington (1913–1973). Yelvington studied with Paul Baker at Baylor in the 1930s. After World War II Yelvington, encouraged by Baker, began writing plays, and in the early 1950s Baker produced *Home to Galveston*, *Cocklebur*, and *The Long Gallery* at Baylor. *The Long Gallery* was also produced off Broadway in 1958. Yelvington's *A Texian Trilogy* includes *Women and Oxen*, *A Cloud of Witnesses* (published in 1959), and *Shadow of an Eagle*.

But Southwestern theater became much more prominent after 1960, primarily the result of two developments: the growth of powerful regional theaters and the emergence of Off and Off-Off-Broadway playhouses. These changes lessened the Broadway clawhold on American theater and allowed several Southwestern playwrights—in particular, Preston Jones, Sam Shepard, Lanford Wilson, and Mark Medoff—to gain national prominence from the 1960s to the 1980s. Minority Western writers such as Luis Valdez, Hanay Geiogamah, and Frank Chin also influenced the look of Southwestern drama. However, Southwestern drama, like American drama in general, began to wane after this important period. Beginning in the 1990s, big-budget musicals and revivals of classic plays dominated Broadway; new plays declined as playwrights turned to film and television to reach audiences.

Preston Jones (1936–1979) and Sam Shepard (1943–) represent the extremes of Southwestern drama since 1960. Jones' plays are generally comic examinations of small-town Southwestern life presented realistically, with stock characters speaking recognizable dialect. Shepard's magical realism is peopled with mythic figures who often float off into incantatory monologues. Jones got his start with Paul Baker at the Dallas Theater Center; Shepard began Off-Off-Broadway. Despite these differences, both Jones and Shepard wrote plays that concentrated on themes central to much Southwestern American literature. Both, for example, demonstrate a deep ambivalence toward the impermanence of the values of the mythic Southwest and the heroic images it has spawned.

Jones' three plays comprising *A Texas Trilogy—The Last Meeting of the Knights of the White Magnolia*, *The Oldest Living Graduate*, and *Lu Ann Hampton Laverty Oberlander*—began at the Dallas Theater Center, where Jones had been an actor since 1960, in the 1973–1974 season. Their Texas performances were successful, and in 1976 the three plays were presented at the Eisenhower Theater at the Kennedy Center in Washington, D.C., to receptive audiences. However, when they opened in repertoire on Broadway, they received tepid reviews. Jones went back to Texas, continued to write plays, and died in 1979 of complications from bleeding ulcers at age 43.

Sam Shepard followed a different trail, leaving California for New York in 1963. Shepard was born in Ft. Sheridan, Illinois, in 1943, but he grew up in South Pasadena, California. In New York, he became a waiter at the Village Gate, a popular jazz club, where he met Ralph Cook, the founder of Off-Off-Broadway's Theater Genesis. Cook encouraged Shepard to write, and in 1964 Theater Genesis presented Shepard's two one-act plays, *Cowboys* and *The Rock Garden*. Since that time Shepard has written over forty plays and won ten Obie awards and a Pulitzer Prize for *Buried Child* (1978). Other important Shepard plays are *Cowboys* (1964) and its revision *Cowboys #2* (1967), *The Unseen Hand* (1969), *Operation Sidewinder* (1970), *Cowboy Mouth* (1971), *The Tooth of Crime* (1972), *Geography of a Horse Dreamer* (1972), and *True West* (1980). Although Sam Shepard has written numerous plays and over five film scripts, including Michelangelo Antonioni's *Zabriskie Point* (1970) and Wim Wenders' *Paris, Texas* (1984); directed two films based on his scripts, *Far North* (1991) and *Silent Tongue* (1993); and won prestigious prizes for his writing, he is probably far better known for his lean good looks and as an actor in movies. These include *Days of Heaven* (1978), *Resurrection* (1980), *Raggedy Man* (1981), *Frances* (1982), *The Right Stuff* (1983), *Fool for Love* (1985), *Baby Boom* (1987), *Crimes of the Heart* (1987), *Thunderheart* (1992), *Streets of Laredo* (1996), *All the Pretty Horses* (2000), and *Black Hawk Down* (2001). Between 1986 and 2004 Shepard wrote only a few new full-length plays, *States of Shock* (1991), *Sympatico* (1994), *When the World Was Green* (1996), *Eyes for Consuela* (1998), and *The Late Henry Moss* (2000). Shepard has also published four collections, *Hawk Moon* (1973), *Motel Chronicles* (1983), *Cruising Paradise* (1996), and *Great Dream of Heaven* (2003), gatherings of fiction, vignettes, tales, poems, songs, and autobiographical musings.

Where Jones' strength was the realistic Southwestern comic language of his characters, Shepard's vitality stems from his mythic imagination. Both writers, though, have been concerned with the loss of heroic ideals and coherent values the American West. In Jones' plays the contemporary Southwest is often effete, enervated, and materialistic, and old patterns embracing racism, sexism, and corrupted individualism hang on in unsympathetic ways. Shepard, often in dazzling, absurdist fashion, presents a similar world that has fallen or is falling away from something valuable. But whereas Jones' plays concentrate on the ennui of small-town Southwestern life, Shepard's emphasize the fragmentation of a world searching for characters that can continue to embody positive ideals in new ways.

Horton Foote (1916–), who has become one of our most acclaimed writers about small-town America, especially Wharton, Texas, his hometown, influenced Jones' emphasis on small-town Texas. Foote wrote about Wharton in a nine-play series about four generations of his Texas ancestors. Several of these plays have been made into films: *1918* (1985), *On Valentine's Day* (1986), and *Convicts* (1991). Besides adapting his own work for the screen, Foote has written screen adaptations of *To Kill a Mockingbird* (Harper Lee; film, 1962), *Tomorrow* (William Faulkner; film, 1972), and *Of Mice and Men* (John Steinbeck; film, 1992). He won his first Oscar for Best Screenplay for *To Kill a Mockingbird*. He added a second Academy Award for his only original feature screenplay to date, *Tender Mercies* (1982), the portrait of a country singer; Robert Duvall won a Best Actor Oscar for his performance in the film. The Signature Theater Company in New York City honored Foote by devoting its 1994–1995 season to him. One of those productions, *The Young Man from Atlanta*, won the 1995 Pulitzer Prize.

Mark Medoff (1940–), a long-time faculty member at New Mexico State University in Las Cruces, took both the regional theater and the Off-Off-Broadway routes. The Southwest provides the setting for several of his plays, including his first, *Doing a Good One for the Red Man: A Red Farce* (1969), which was first produced in San Antonio, Texas, by the Dallas Theater Center. His first popular success, *When You Comin' Back, Red Ryder?* (1973), was originally produced Off-Off-Broadway by the Circle Repertory Theater Company. Like Shepard, Medoff dramatizes a contemporary Southwest where traditional heroes have vanished. In a quiet New Mexico diner a marijuana smuggler headed to California menaces the patrons and the night attendant, Stephen Ryder. Stephen cannot transform himself into the cowboy hero, Red Ryder, nor can he summon Red's faithful Indian companion, Little Beaver. To confirm his point about lost heroes, Medoff uses Paul Simon's famous line from "Mrs. Robinson" as an epigraph, asking where Joe DiMaggio has gone.

With *Firekeeper* (1978), Medoff resumed his relationship with the Dallas Theater Center. The play revolves around the activities of a priest, a mentally disturbed Hispanic girl, a local sheriff (played by Preston Jones at the DTC), and an old Indian. The Indian at one point recalls the legend of the firekeeper, the shaman who could determine the right path for men to follow. Neither law nor religion seems to be able to provide this information in Medoff's contemporary Southwest. (Medoff's most commercially successful play, *Children of a Lesser God* (1979), does not have a Southwestern setting.)

Other Western and Southwestern playwrights began to find greater acceptance for their work in the seventies. In *Vanities* (1977) Jack Heifner (n.d.) focuses on three Texas girls at various times of their lives. His two one-act plays about Texas women—sisters in *Patio* (1977) and mother and daughter in *Porch* (1978)—achieved moderate success. James McLure, trained at Southern Methodist University in Dallas, received acclaim for *Laundry and Bourbon* (1979), *Pvt. Wars* (1980), and *Lone Star* (1979). *Lone Star*, first presented by the Actors Theater of Louisville, combines light, folksy humor with a weightier analysis of the effects of the war on a Vietnam veteran. D.L. Coburn, a Dallas friend whom Preston Jones encouraged to write, won a Pulitzer Prize for *The Gin Game*, an unsentimental play about elderly people in a nursing home that could be anywhere.

Texas chic aided Larry King's (1929–) and Peter Masterson's (1934–) *The Best Little Whorehouse in Texas* (1978). *Whorehouse* grew out of a *Playboy* article that

Texas journalist King had done about the closing of the legendary Chicken Ranch, a brothel outside LaGrange, Texas. Using the traditional Western theme of individual freedom versus the constraints demanded by civilization (represented by a meddling television journalist), this musical, with songs by Carol Hall, enjoyed an extended Broadway run and a less successful film version with Dolly Parton and Burt Reynolds. Buoyed by the success of his first play, King went on to write several other plays, including *The Night Hank Williams Died* (1989), *The Kingfish* (1990), *Golden Shadows Old West Museum* (1993), and *The Dead President's Club* (1995). A sequel to the *Best Little Whorehouse in Texas*, called *The Best Little Whorehouse Goes Public* (2000) was savaged by the critics. King also published several noteworthy nonfiction collections, earning a National Book Award nomination for *Confessions of a White Racist* (1972).

Carlos Morton (1947–) is an important and prolific Chicano playwright. His works include *Johnny Tenorio* (1983), *The Savior* (1986), *The Miser of Mexico* (1989), and *Pancho Diablo* (1987). Known for his humorous, satirical characters, Morton's plays include a modern-day version of Don Juan, of Moliere's miser, and of the Devil himself. His *El Jardín* (1974) presents a comic creation story. Another Mexican American playwright, Denise Chávez (1948–), studied with Mark Medoff at New Mexico State University. Chávez began writing plays in the early 1970s, focusing on Chicano culture, before turning to fiction. Her plays include *Novitiates* (1973), *The Flying Tortilla Man* (1975), *Adobe Rabbit* (1980), *Nacimiento* (1980), *Santa Fe Charm* (1980), *Sí, Hay Posadas* (1981), *El Santero de Córdova* (1981), *The Green Madonna* (1982), *La Morenita* (1983), *Novena Narratives* (1987), and *Women in the State of Grace* (1989).

The most significant Southwestern American Indian playwright in recent years is Hanay Geiogamah (1945–), a Kiowa-Delaware who established the American Indian Theater Ensemble in the 1970s, now based at UCLA. Later called the Native American Theater Ensemble, the company toured America and Europe, presenting Geiogamah's and other writers' plays. Although oral performance is central to Indian tradition, theater is a European literary form; thus, Geiogamah combines the two as he, explores Indian culture and history. Most of his plays focus on contemporary Indian life but include glimpses into the past. *Body Indian* (1972) examines the way the Indian body politic undermines itself. Bobby Lee is an alcoholic who has lost his legs to the archetypal American machine in the garden—the train—and when he gets drunk in some friends' apartment, they steal his lease money. *Foghorn* (1973) takes its title from the foghorns used to harass the Indians who occupied the island of Alcatraz in 1969. It presents a variety of Indian stereotypes, from Pocahontas to activists at Wounded Knee, in an effort to exorcise them. In *49* (1975) the subject is an Indian celebration broken up by police.

Other notable Indian playwrights include Diane Glancy (1941–), a Cherokee, author of such plays as *The Lesser Wars*, *Jump Kiss*, *The Woman Who Was a Red Deer Dressed for the Deer Dance*, and *The Best Fancy Dancer the Pushmataha Pow Wow's Ever Seen*; and LeAnne Howe, a Choctaw, author of *Indian Radio Days* and *Big Pow Wow* (with Roxy Gordon). Both Glancy and Howe have also published fiction and nonfiction.

The Chinese-American experience in the Southwest has been explored by Frank Chin (1940–) in *The Chickencoop Chinaman* (1972) and *The Year of the Dragon* (1974). Another play with a Southwestern setting, presented by Douglas Turner

Ward and the Negro Ensemble Company, was Charles Fuller's (1939–) *The Brownsville Raid* (1978), based on a 1906 incident. When the town of Brownsville, Texas, was shot up, white townspeople charged that members of a black regiment were responsible. Eventually the entire regiment was dishonorably discharged. Fuller, who grew up in Philadelphia, won the Pulitzer Prize for *A Soldier's Play*. African American playwright Ntozake Shange (1948–) lived in Houston for many years. Shange's work *for colored girls who have considered suicide/when the rainbow is enuf* played on Broadway and toured the country for several years. J. California Cooper (n.d.), originally from Marshall, Texas, gained acclaim for her short stories in *A Piece of Mine* (1984), but she began as a playwright and still performs her own works.

Houston playwright Celeste Bedford-Walker's most successful play is *Camp Logan* (1991) based on a true story of the all-black 24th Infantry, which was sent to Houston in 1917 to construct Camp Logan. The soldiers had expected to be sent to France in World War I, but Houston police used them as laborers instead and subjected them to racial attacks, harassment, and beatings. After one soldier died at the hands of a Houston policeman, the soldiers marched on the town, killing and wounding more than 30 people. The production focuses on the soldiers' court-martial proceedings. Bedford-Walker's *Distant Voices* (1998) includes the voices of some of the 60 people buried in College Memorial Park Cemetery in Freedman's Town, Houston's Fourth Ward. Similarly, Eugene Lee had success with his touring play *East Texas Hot Licks* (1994), which concerns Texas in 1955, when the Klan were active and young black men were disappearing or turning up dead.

SOUTHWESTERN FILM

The iconography of this genre is immediately recognizable. A lone rider appears silhouetted against a high sky.[1] A brilliant sun shines mercilessly on the solitary horseman riding across the screen amidst a rocky, dusty landscape of buttes and mesas, the massive arms of the distinctive Saguaro cactus, looming almost humanlike in the background. Yet these images intermingle fact and fiction: for example, though the Saguaro is decidedly Southwestern, it grows only in a small portion of the Sonoran desert in southern Arizona and northern Mexico.

Although the Library of Congress includes hundreds of books on Western film, almost nothing turns up on a genre called "Southwestern." However, because definitions of the Southwest often include Texas, New Mexico, Arizona, and Nevada, plus parts of Oklahoma, Colorado, Utah, Southern California, and northern Mexico, and almost every recognizable Western trait is more truly Southwestern, the label *Southwestern* is more accurate.

As well as covering a rather broad area, the region's prehistory and history reflect the lives and interaction of diverse peoples. Its compelling prehistory has often been the subject of documentaries about native bands that populated the region. The Anasazi, builders of cave dwellings at Mesa Verde in the Four Corners region and at Chaco Canyon in New Mexico, have been evaluated effectively in *The Anasazi* (1985) and *The Anasazi and Chaco Canyon* (1994).

Álvar Núñez Cabeza de Vaca (c. 1490–1557) was the first European to contact the many native peoples and to travel the Southwest after he was shipwrecked and washed up on the shores of present-day Galveston, Texas, in 1528, exploring

Texas, New Mexico, and Mexico before returning to Spain in 1536. His stories of golden cities to the west led Coronado to search for the seven cities of gold in 1540. The explorer's story was dramatized in a feature film, *Cabeza de Vaca* (1991), by Spanish filmmaker Nicolás Echevarría (1947–). The film is unsatisfying partly because the lush river scenes make Texas look like the Amazon valley and because the film transforms Cabeza de Vaca's *mala cosa* (evil spirit) into a malicious dwarf.

When Juan Oñate (1595–1614) settled New Mexico in 1598, he brought cattle and horses, animals that would eventually transform the natural environment through overgrazing and alter the human landscape when the Plains Indians—particularly the Comanche and Apache—became lords of the plains on horseback. Filmmakers have found little in this time period of interest, except for the often-told story of Zorro in colonial California, most recently in Martin Campbell's *The Mask of Zorro* (1998) with Antonio Banderas.

After Mexico won its independence from Spain in 1821, the Mexican government offered land grants in Texas to Anglo settlers such as Moses Austin (1761–1821) and his son Stephen (1793–1836); thus, the Anglo migration into the Southwest began and led to the major events that shaped the region in the nineteenth century: Texas independence, the U.S.-Mexican War, the discovery of gold in California, the Civil War, Indian wars, and the growth of the cattle industry. One of the signal events, of course, was the massacre at the Alamo, dramatized in an early film, *Martyrs of the Alamo* (1915), which was directed by Christy Cabanne and featured Douglas Fairbanks, and, most famously, in *The Alamo* (1960), a long, talky epic directed by and starring John Wayne. A new version, directed by John Lee Hancock and starring Billy Bob Thornton as Davy Crockett, Dennis Quaid as Sam Houston, and Jason Patric as Jim Bowie, was released in 2004. Two notable sendups of the Alamo story are director Jerry Paris' *Viva Max!* (1970), starring Peter Ustinov, script by newsman Jim Lehrer, about a Mexican general who recaptures the Alamo in the twentieth century, and Tim Burton's *Pee Wee's Big Adventure* (1985), which features Pee Wee Herman searching for his lost bicycle in the "basement" of the Alamo.

The Southwest's diverse landscapes, uncommon light, and appealing history began attracting filmmakers early in the history of film. There were public demonstrations of Thomas Edison's (1847–1931) Vitascope in Dallas in February 1897, probably the first instances of projected film in Texas. The program included scenes of a Mexican duel, a lynching, a fire rescue, and Niagara Falls. In January 1900 projected film debuted at a tent show in Austin. The first movie made in Texas documented the aftermath of the Galveston hurricane of 1900. D. W. Griffith's (1897–1954) cameraman G. W. "Billy" Bitzer (1872–1944) shot eight scenes of the destruction. Bitzer probably shot other short Texas scenes at that time—a passing train and oil wells at Beaumont. Nevada film history began in Carson City in 1897 with the filming of British challenger Bob Fitzsimmons' heavyweight title fight with America's James J. "Gentleman Jim" Corbett. In 1898 Thomas Edison sent camera crews to Isleta Pueblo in New Mexico to shoot a short film entitled *Indian Day School*. In the 1910s film companies in New Mexico and Texas produced scores of silent films; among the companies were Tom Mix and Selig Polyscope Films in Las Vegas and Star-Film, established in San Antonio in 1910 and operated by Gaston Mélies, brother of pioneer French filmmaker Georges Mélies.

The Alamo (1960). Courtesy of Photofest.

Gaston Mélies made approximately seventy films at the Star-Film Ranch before moving to California in 1911. With companies established on the East and West coasts by the 1920s, most regional film companies disappeared, but since that time, hundreds of movies have been made in the Southwest, many of which have nothing to do with the region. Among the important early films made in the Southwest are *North of 36* (1924), the first major cattle-drive movie, and one of its two remakes, *The Texans* (1938), as well as *Sundown* (1924) and *The Big Show* (1936), all shot in Texas; *Billy the Kid* (1930), *Way Out West* (1930), and *The Grapes of Wrath* (1940) in New Mexico; *The Iron Horse* (1924) and *The Call of the Wild* (1935) in Nevada; and *Red River* (1948) in Southern Arizona.

An important Southwestern studio began in 1939 when Columbia Pictures selected a Pima County site on which to build a replica of 1860s Tucson for the movie *Arizona*, starring William Holden and Jean Arthur. The set included more than fifty buildings made from more than 350,000 adobe bricks. Other films made there include *The Bells of St. Mary's* (1945), starring Bing Crosby and Ingrid Bergman; Gene Autry's *The Last Roundup* (1947); *Winchester '73* (1950), starring Jimmy Stewart; *The Last Outpost* (1950), starring Ronald Reagan; *Gunfight at the OK Corral* (1956), with Burt Lancaster and Kirk Douglas; and *Cimarron* (1959) with Glenn Ford. The 1950s were an especially prolific time for filmmaking at the Old Tucson and elsewhere in the Southwest. In 1960 Old Tucson Studios was renovated and reopened as a film studio and a family fun park. John Wayne starred in four movies made at Old Tucson Studios: *Rio Bravo* (1959), *McLintock!* (1963), *El Dorado* (1967), and *Rio Lobo* (1970).

In the 1990s alone more than 100 movies and television series were filmed in New Mexico, which was the first state to form a film commission. Over 600 films have been shot in Nevada, and Texas now boasts that it is the "third coast" for filmmakers. Most of the major cities in the Southwest now have film commissions ready to assist filmmakers looking for locations.

The Western, perhaps the major American film genre, is identified by its nineteenth-century setting, by cattle, horses, Indians, and outlaws, and, of course, by cowboys. The cowboy is primarily a Texas and Southwestern figure. As Henry Nash Smith (1906–1986) points out in his major study, *Virgin Land*, the term *cowboy* had no heroic overtones when it first entered the lexicon and referred instead to those rowdies who followed ranch life and frequently disturbed the peace in town. After the Civil War, when Texas veterans returned to their homes, some enterprising vets began to round up their expanded herds of roaming cattle and began the trail drives that are at the heart of cowboy legend. That life lasted about twenty-five years, from 1870 to 1895, when barbed wire, the opening of train service, and economic downturns ended the golden days of trail driving. Still, the cowboy is internationally recognizable as an American symbol of frontier freedom and independence.

In the twentieth and twenty-first centuries, Southwestern history reveals a schism between urban and rural life, particularly the transitions from ranch to farm to oil to computers to tourism, all within the context of the clash and cooperation of the region's diverse cultures.

The Classic Southwestern: *Stagecoach*

Just as famed historian Frederick Jackson Turner (1891–1932) proclaimed the closing of the West in 1893, pondering the impact of the end of the frontier on the American character, frontier life burst onto the scene of American popular culture. It came through Buffalo Bill's Wild West Show, through dime and half-dime novels, and through the first Western film, Edwin S. Porter's *The Great Train Robbery* in 1903, a year after the first serious Western novel, Owen Wister's *The Virginian*. Also in 1903 the first major trail-drive novel, Andy Adams' *The Log of a Cowboy*, was released.

As many commentators, such as Jim Kitses and Will Wright, have noted, the classic Western and Southwestern film turns on a series of oppositions about characters who are either inside or outside of society; good or bad; strong or weak, and, perhaps more importantly, on characters, symbols, and events that point to the opposition between wilderness and civilization. Frontier mythology that permeates Southwestern fiction and film includes a cluster of images and values that grew out of the confrontation between what Turner called the "meeting point between savagery and civilization," which was his definition of the frontier. In the classic Southwestern narrative, civilization has generally been associated with the past and with European society—its institutions, laws, and restrictions, its demands for cultural refinement, emphasis on manners, and class distinction, and its focus on industrial development. The wilderness that civilization confronts suggests a number of binary ideas. Rather than the restrictive demands of society, the wilderness offers the possibility of individual freedom, where individuals can test their sense of self against nature without the demand for social responsibility. Cultural refinement and emphasis on manners give way to empiricism. Class distinctions seem to disappear. Pastoralism or living with the earth is the dominant force; in the wilderness, Indians, Transcendentalists, Naturalists, and cowboys worship nature like a deity.

The classic plot, as identified by Will Wright in *Sixguns & Society: A Structural Study of the Western*, involves a series of actions where the hero enters a social group to which he is unknown and reveals special abilities that confer on him a distinct status.[2] After villains threaten the society, the hero fights and defeats them, making the society safe so it accepts and reveres the hero. A variation on the classical plot involves the hero's relentless need to avenge some past wrong. The hero, a member or former member of society, seeks vengeance against villains who threaten the society and have done him harm. The hero plans to use his special abilities and must go outside society, but first his quest for vengeance is challenged. Finally, he fights and defeats the villains, gives up his special status, and enters society fully.

The preeminent Southwestern film classic, John Ford's (1894–1973) *Stagecoach* (1939), adheres to that variation of the classic plot line. This is the film that lifted John Wayne from B-Western obscurity and set him on the path to becoming America's favorite movie star. The Ringo Kid (Wayne) has broken out of prison so that he can seek revenge against the Plummer brothers, who are supposed to be in Lordsburg, New Mexico. Wayne's initial appearance in the film takes place along the trail after the stagecoach leaves Tonto, Arizona, for Lordsburg. The way Wayne's image fills the screen as the camera tracks up to him as he stands with his rifle and saddle suggests his character's mythic stature. Against the spectacular backdrop of Monument Valley and in a post–Civil War, nineteenth-century setting, Ford has the coach and its passengers journey into the wilderness, where the confrontation with the forces of nature and savagery will bring out the best qualities in characters who represent a microcosm of American society.

Stagecoach seems to include almost every recognizable Western type, from Wayne's outlaw–former cowboy hero; Indians; Mexicans; the comic sidekick stagecoach driver, Buck (played by Andy Devine); the whore with the heart of gold, Dallas (played by Claire Trevor); the dandy-gambler, Hatfield (John Carradine); and the drunken philosopher-physician, Doc Boone (Thomas Mitchell). Dallas ignores the insults from the Southern lady to nurse her and care for her baby, the Southern lady loses her prejudices and acknowledges Dallas's humanity, the gambler sacrifices himself for the Southern lady, and the doctor sobers up and delivers the baby. Even the mild-mannered whiskey drummer exhibits a certain amount of courage.

Ford saves his censure for the banker, Mr. Gatewood (played by Berton Churchill), who is attempting to escape from his pinched-face wife back in Tonto (which means *stupid* in Spanish). She is the leader of the Ladies of the Law and Order League that expels Doc Boone and Dallas from the society. Thus, *Stagecoach* clearly turns on the civilization/savagery dichotomy, as the restrictive and hypocritical representatives of civilization counterpoint the agents of savagery, Geronimo and his Apaches and the Plummers. The mediating figure is Ringo, who sits symbolically on the floor of the stagecoach and talks of borders.

Stagecoach (1939). Courtesy of Photofest.

Ringo, the vengeance hero, saves three shells to use against the Plummers, ultimately achieving his revenge on the dark streets of Lordsburg. Ringo's special status leads Curly, the sheriff (played by George Bancroft), to set him free to leave with Dallas, even though he should arrest him as an escaped convict. Curly and Buck proclaim that Dallas and Ringo are "free from the blessings of civilization," as they set off for the real and symbolic border where they will begin a new life. Ford's Southwest in *Stagecoach* is one in which fate plays a large part; it is a fate that plays the right cards for the chosen ones.

The Ringo Kid's outlaw status and name suggest the most durable Southwestern figure, Billy the Kid, who has been the subject of numerous films over the years, including Kurt Neumann's *The Kid from Texas* (1950) with Audie Murphy; Arthur Penn's *The Left Handed Gun* (1958) with Paul Newman; Sam Peckinpah's *Pat Garrett and Billy the Kid* (1973) with Kris Kristofferson; Christopher Cain's *Young Guns* (1988); and Geoff Murphy's *Young Guns II* (1990), both with Emilio Estevez. And the list goes on.

The Trail-Drive Film: *Red River*

Another recognizable Southwestern subgenre, one that draws from the history of the cowboy, is the trail-drive film. Among the most notable examples of this are the several versions of Emerson Hough's (1857–1923) novel, *North of 36*, that were adapted for the silver screen, including an eponymous version released in 1924, a year after the novel was published. It was remade in 1931 as *The Conquering Horde* and again in 1938 as *The Texans*, with Randolph Scott and Walter Brennan. The actual trail drive lends itself to narrative since it includes a journey with a clear beginning, middle, and end, with intervening obstacles such as river crossings, thunderstorms, sandstorms, hailstorms, wind, lightning, stampedes, Indians, quicksand, drought, rustlers, and snakes. The ultimate trail-drive film, critic Don Graham makes clear in *Moo-vie Cows: The Trail to Hollywood*, is Howard Hawks' (1896–1977) *Red River* (1948), with its ambiguous melding of history, legend, and region.[3] The title suggests the variety of approaches to the film. The film was based on the story "The Chisholm Trail," but Hawks decided to change the title to *Red River* partially because the Red River actually serves as the boundary between Oklahoma and Texas and becomes the defining point for Tom Dunson (John Wayne) to break free from the wagon train heading west and travel south deep into Texas, where he can begin the empire he will call the Red River D (based loosely upon the King Ranch). But Hawks wanted to evoke the Biblical overtones that the Red River (Red Sea) might elicit so that the echo of epic activity and empire-building sloganeering would hover over the film.

Recently, the title has led to some unusual viewings of this film. In her 1992 study of the Western, *West of Everything*, Jane Tompkins interprets the title as a symbolic reference to the river of blood that will result from the slaughter of the cattle at the end of the trail, asserting that the "sacrifice of their lives underwrites everything. *Red River* ends with the prospect of a gigantic river of blood, but that river is kept off screen because it has no place in the consciousness of filmmakers or of the society they cater to."[4]

Taking his cue from Tompkins, with tongue slightly in cheek, Don Graham writes in *Giant Country: Essays on Texas* that "if red can refer to the cattle's blood, why can't it refer to menstrual blood?" Graham points out that women are questioned throughout the film, with male characters with feminine names such as Nadine Groot (Walter Brennan) and Cherry Valence (John Ireland). And Lee Clark Mitchell in *Westerns: Making the Man in Fiction and Film* (1996) asserts that Westerns are always examining gender, especially questions of masculinity.

The Trail Drive film returned in the 1990s as the source of humor in Don Underwoods' *City Slickers* (1991), featuring Billy Crystal, Daniel Stern, and Bruno Kirby, with a star turn by Jack Palance and then in Paul Wieland's *City Slickers II: The Legend of Curly's Gold* (1994), with Jon Lovitz replacing Bruno Kirby.

Transitional Films: *High Noon*

In the 1950s the classic Southwestern film moved beyond traditional plots and characters toward allegorical statements about contemporary concerns. A major transitional film is Fred Zinnemann's (1907–1997) *High Noon* (1952), starring Gary Cooper as Will Kane and Grace Kelly as his wife, which has many of the traditional plot elements, but it reverses Wright's classic pattern: the hero begins inside society and ends outside of it. For a traditionalist like John Wayne, the changes were unacceptable. In a 1971 *Playboy* interview Wayne described *High Noon* as "the most un-American thing I've ever seen in my whole life. The last thing in the picture is ole Coop putting the U.S. Marshal's badge under his foot and stepping on it."[5] Wayne recalled the final scene with a creative memory, for Will Kane only drops his badge.

Still, Gary Cooper's Will Kane displays traditional and nontraditional elements of the Western hero in this transitional film. Like other heroes, he is resolute and determined, strong-willed and capable. He is a "man" in contrast to his youthful deputy Harvey (Lloyd Bridges, 1913–1998). Screenwriter Carl Foreman (1914–1984), blacklisted as a result of the House Committee on Un-American Activities (HUAC) hearing, later explained that he had adapted the town of Hadleyville from Mark Twain's Hadleyburg to attack the cowardice of Hollywood. He also said that he had written the film as an explicit attack on the country's fear of Sen. Joseph McCarthy's (1908–1957) anti-Communist bullying. But it can be viewed in the exact opposite light (Kane as McCarthy, the strong protector), or it can even be interpreted as an allegory about the need for the country (Kane) to act against aggression (North Korea) after the threat returns when it had been banished five years earlier (World War II).

A classic Western, *High Noon* is rarely viewed as a Southwestern film, although numerous clues support such a description. As the movie begins, a dark-skinned woman crosses herself when Frank Miller's men ride into town. Another dark-skinned Mexican woman, Helen Ramirez (Katy Jurado), is Miller's, then Kane's, then Harvey's ladyfriend. A native woman cares for Lon Chaney Jr., the arthritic former marshal. Finally, the dusty and arid landscape in which *High Noon* takes place is a Southwestern landscape where violence must meet violence to overcome chaos. The real evil here is the complacency of the town, with its sham democracy and craven boosterism, conveyed forcefully by Thomas Mitchell's character, the mayor.

High Noon ultimately dramatizes a series of principles that often underlie American life: good will prevail over evil; civilization will prevail over savagery. Intelligence, physical skills, and inner resourcefulness will be rewarded. Violence is regrettable but necessary to extend the forces of good and peace. Nonviolence is unworkable. If we don't fight here and now, we'll fight later somewhere else. The hero is resolute, despite strong voices urging compromise. One must act at a given moment; to waver from the course is an act of cowardice. Self-interest, as in the case of the mayor, is despicable. The errors of a previous generation must be avoided.

High Noon signaled that the Southwestern film was changing, and other Texas and Southwestern films of the 1950s echoed the changes. Delmar Davies' *Broken Arrow* (1950) presented Indians in a new and sympathetic light and changed the long-standing representation of Indians as simply savages. John Ford's *The Searchers* (1956) offered a new variation on the vengeance hero, with John Wayne on a monomaniacal quest to find his niece who has been captured by the Comanches. His vicious racism saps his humanity and renders him a mirror image of the savagery he seeks to destroy. Ford uses a number of plot and visual devices to indicate how Wayne's character, Ethan Edwards, mirrors the "savage" Comanche Chief Scar (Henry Brandon): Ethan reproduces Comanche ceremonies by shooting the eyes out of an Indian corpse so its spirit will wander, and then in the most brutal onscreen violence in the film, he scalps Scar. As the Texan searchers ride across Monument Valley in the foreground, with the Comanches riding parallel in the background, Ford establishes a visual image of the identification between savagery and civilization. In 2003 an updated version of *The Searchers*, titled *The Missing*, was directed by Ron Howard (1954–), with Tommy Lee Jones and Cate Blanchett, and was released to mixed reviews. Set in southwestern New Mexico in 1885, just as the last of the Apache conflicts were ending, the plot turns on Jones' granddaughter, Blanchett's daughter, who is abducted by a ragged band of American Indians and whites who sell women into slavery in Mexico.

Another important film of the 1950s that concerns the sweep of Texas history is George Stevens' (1904–1975) *Giant* (1956), an epic tale of the shift from a cattle to an oil economy. In *Cowboys and Cadillacs: How Hollywood Looks at Texas*, Don Graham asserts that "*Giant* is the archetypal Texas movie: it contains every significant element in the stereotype: cowboys, wildcatters, cattle empire, wealth, crassness of manners, garish taste, and barbecue."[6] Bick Benedict (Rock Hudson) owns the sprawling south Texas ranch, Riata (based on the King Ranch), and, after marrying a wealthy Eastern woman (Elizabeth Taylor), he begins to establish a dynasty. The discovery of oil changes their lives, especially the life of Jett Rink (played by James Dean in his last movie role), who is based on Texas wildcatter Glenn McCarthy. Dean's JR becomes wealthy when he strikes oil on the small bit of Riata left to him when Bick's sister died. The film examines attitudes toward sexism and racism, issues that would become more prominent in the next decade.

Southwestern Farm Films

While *Giant* is the ultimate ranch film, other Southwestern films examine farming in the Southwest. Famed French filmmaker Jean Renoir (1894–1974) adapted George Sessions Perry's Pulitzer Prize–winning novel, *Hold Autumn in Your Hand*, about a year in the life of a central Texas sharecropper, into *The Southerner* (1940). The story explores the demise of small family farms in the Southwest, documenting an era in American history when many people led rural lives in constant contact with—and at the mercy of—changing climates. A year later John Ford filmed *The Grapes of Wrath*, John Steinbeck's famous novel about uprooted Okies forced off their farms who traveled west on Highway 66. Terrence Malick's (1943–) *Days of Heaven* (1978) studied new immigrants and the American dream in the Texas Panhandle in 1916, where the possibility of realizing the dream is palpable, but the reality of violence and a plague of grasshoppers intrude. This film dramatizes powerful feelings of ambivalence toward the natural: both good and bad fortune are linked essentially with natural conditions and natural events, and the characters' fates are determined by the whims of nature rather than by human action. Similarly, Robert Benton's (1932–) *Places in the Heart* (1984) explores the vicissitudes of cotton farming in the 1930s near Waxahachie in north-central Texas.

The 1960s: Anti-, Spaghetti, Transformed, Professional, and Border Films

The 1960s ushered in a decade of new Westerns, with John Huston's *The Misfits* in 1961 and then three releases in 1962: David Miller's *Lonely Are the Brave*, John Ford's *The Man Who Shot Liberty Valence*, and Sam Peckinpah's *Ride the High Country*. These end-of-the-West narratives signaled a movement from the classic Western's glorification of the hero to an interest in antiheroes and outsiders. For example, *Hud* (1963), based on Larry McMurtry's first novel, *Horseman, Pass By*, shifts from the book's focus on the initiation of its narrator Lonnie to the amorality of Hud and examines how the frontier world represented by Granddad, Homer Bannon, is being replaced in 1950s Texas. With Paul Newman as Hud, Melvyn Douglas as Granddad, Patricia Neal as Alma (in the novel Halmea is black), and Brandon de Wilde as Lonnie, the strong cast helped ensure the success of the film.

Newman dominates the screen, making the amoral Hud a heartthrob. On the posters a smirking Newman dressed in boots and jeans gazes out of those eyes that have caused four generations of moviegoers to swoon. As Alma, Patricia Neal's compelling performance earned her the Academy Award for Best Supporting Actress. Melvyn Douglas' performance as Granddad was another winning one, receiving the Academy Award for Best Supporting Actor. Douglas' raspy voice and flinty acting made him seem like everyone's grandfather.

The Misfits, *Lonely Are the Brave*, and *Hud* point to a continuing trend in Southwestern film, the anachronistic Southwestern, where films with post-1940s settings look back to a frontier past. More recent films, like Stephen Frears' *The Hi-Lo Country* (1999) and especially Billy Bob Thornton's (1955–) *All the Pretty Horses* (2000), follow this trend. Thornton's film, based on Cormac McCarthy's highly celebrated novel, was long anticipated but disappointing to many reviewers. Thornton's original four-hour film was cut by almost two hours, which left out the depth and ambivalence of McCarthy's look at the changing Southwest.

The 1960s saw other new types of Southwestern films. Sergio Leone's "Spaghetti Westerns" featuring Clint Eastwood, *A Fistful of Dollars* (1964), *For a Few Dollars More* (1965), and *The Good, the Bad, and the Ugly* (1966), are set in some unspecific—but iconical Southwest—places, usually hot, dry, and peopled with brown-skinned characters, with Eastwood wearing his trademark *serape*. The Spaghetti Westerns, inexpensive productions filmed in Spain helped rejuvenate the Southwestern genre in the 1960s, and their emphasis on violence clearly reflects a major issue of the Vietnam era.

The Good, the Bad, and the Ugly (1966). Courtesy of Photofest.

Arthur Penn's (1922–) *Bonnie and Clyde* (1967) transformed the outlaw tale into the ultimate film for the 1960s counterculture, using historical Texas bank robbers Clyde Barrow (Warren Beatty) and Bonnie Parker (Faye Dunaway) as its antiheroes. The young outlaws are opposed by a stiff, moralistic older generation. Penn, drawing from French New Wave films, notably Jean-Luc Godard's *Breathless*, includes psychosexual themes, mixes the comic and tragic, and brings film violence to a different level, especially in the concluding, graphic, slow-motion scene in which Texas Rangers riddle Bonnie and Clyde with hundreds of bullets.

Another important film is Dennis Hopper's (1936–) now classic *Easy Rider* (1969), which reverses the traditional westward movement; in this "road film" the anti-hero bikers, played by Dennis Hopper and Peter Fonda,

Bonnie and Clyde (1967). Courtesy of Photofest.

travel east. They leave Los Angeles and travel on Harleys across the American Southwest to New Orleans, encountering a violent, bigoted, and corrupt America. Their characters' names, Wyatt and Billy, recall Wyatt Earp and Billy the Kid. The film won the 1969 Cannes Film Festival award for the Best Film by a new director. It represents the 1960s counter-cultural world of sex and drugs, and a rock and roll soundtrack reinforces the film's themes. This film gave Jack Nicholson his first major role.

Another change in the traditional Western pattern that began at the end of the 1950s and continued into the 1960s was what Wright calls the Professional Plot, seen in such films as Howard Hawks' (1896–1977) *Rio Bravo* (1959), Richard Brooks' *The Professionals* (1966), and Peckinpah's *The Wild Bunch* (1969). In this formula variant, the heroes are hired to protect a society incapable of defending itself. The heroes band together into a group with special abilities, affection, and loyalty. Ultimately they fight the villains and either settle down or die together.

The most significant Southwestern film at the end of the 1960s was *The Wild Bunch*, which draws carefully from a specific historical era. Peckinpah worked with the Western genre throughout his tempestuous career. *The Wild Bunch* foreshadows the novels of Cormac McCarthy by focusing on a specific historical moment along the border between Texas and Mexico. Set in 1913, the film suggests how the older world is about to be irrevocably changed against the backdrop of the Mexican Revolution, the legislated morality of Prohibition, the looming World War I conflict, the disappearance of the older world of horses and outlaws, and concomitant imminent industrial transformation of the Southwest.

The Wild Bunch acknowledges that the basic appeal of the Western has been its emphasis on violence, and it dramatizes explicitly, in repeated slow-motion scenes of gunfire and blood, the reality of that assumption. The plot hinges on the aging leader of the Bunch, William Holden, plagued by the knowledge of his past mistakes and aware of the changing world ("We've got to start thinkin' beyond our guns. Those days are closin' fast"), who realizes that the only redemptive possibility in a world of violence is the existentialism of a dramatic exit in a final, flaming, brutal act based on the only principle that they have learned to live by, that the band must act together. This furious scene, when the band fatalistically attacks General Mapache's troops, is in counterpoint to the film's famous opening sequence where the Bunch rides into an ambush in San Rafael, Texas, but escapes as delighted children burn a mound of ants attacking a scorpion. (Much of Peckinpah's social vision in this landmark film is explored in Paul Seydor's 1996 documentary *The Making of "The Wild Bunch,"* with Ed Harris reading Peckinpah's comments about the film. Seydor interviews other principals, such as Edmond O'Brien and Peckinpah's daughter.)

The Wild Bunch emphasizes how the Southwestern is a Border film, a strong subgenre reflected in a number of other productions about the region: Robert Montgomery's *Ride the Pink Horse* (1947); Orson Welles' (1915–1985) *Touch of Evil* (1958); Jack Nicholson's *Goin' South* (1978); Australian director Fred Schepisi's *Barbarosa* (1982), from a script by the Texas-born William D. Wittliff; Tony Richardson's *The Border* (1982), with Jack Nicholson, about drug trafficking, a special concern of Border films; William Tannen's *Flashpoint* (1984), also a JFK conspiracy film; Walter Hill's *Extreme Prejudice* (1987), another Border drug film; and John Sayles' *Lone Star* (1996). Another interesting Border film is *And Starring Pancho Villa as Himself* (2003), a film made for the Home Box Office cable channel, directed by Bruce Beresford from a script by Larry Gelbart and starring Antonio Banderas (1960–) as Mexican revolutionary Pancho Villa, who actually made a deal with American filmmakers to film his war and recreate his life. Earlier, Marlon Brando plays Villa's revolutionary counterpart in Elia Kazan's (1909–2003) *Viva Zapata!* (1952).

The 1970–2000s: Failed, Parodic, Rodeo, Small-Town, and City Films

In the 1970s and 1980s Southwestern films set in the traditional nineteenth-century Southwest were in decline, partially because of the colossal failure of Michael Cimino's *Heaven's Gate* (1980), which investors, shying away from the genre, cited as a clear example of Hollywood excess. Earlier, Elliot Silverstein's (1927–) *Cat Ballou* (1965), with Jane Fonda (1937–) and Lee Marvin (1924–1987); John Huston's *The Life and Times of Judge Roy Bean* (1972), with Paul Newman (1925–); Mel Brooks' (1926–) *Blazing Saddles* (1974); and Robert Altman's *Buffalo Bill and the Indians* (1976), also with Paul Newman, sent up the traditional genre. However, several Southwestern films set in the twentieth century examined small-town Southwestern life. Peter Bogdanovich's *The Last Picture Show* (1971) softened the harsh satire of Larry McMurtry's novel but still treated small-town life critically. The film's success was partially the result of the success of *Easy Rider* (1969), which made the small film with unknown actors acceptable. *The Last Picture Show* also benefited from brilliant casting, and the entire production was first-rate. For many of the cast members, it was a career-launching film: Cybill Shepherd as Jacy, Jeff Bridges as Duane (whose last name is changed from Moore to Sanders in the film), Timothy Bottoms as Sonny, and Randy Quaid as Lester Marlow. The seasoned actors also were excellent: Ellen Burstyn as Lois Farrow, Clu Gullagher as Abilene, Eileen Brennan as Genevieve, and particularly Ben Johnson who won the Academy Award for best supporting actor, as Sam the Lion. Although Cloris Leachman had been acting for over ten years when she was cast as Ruth Popper, it became her most important role, because her performance earned her an Academy Award for best supporting actress, and her career moved to a new level.

Director Peter Bogdanovich's decision to tone down the satire of the novel and attempt to present the story as a realistic portrayal of small-town Texas life was significant: it led him to shoot the film in black and white, to use McMurtry's own home town as the location, to employ locals as bit players, and to attempt to make the film as gritty as the actual town in the early 1950s. To accomplish the latter Bogdanovich used realistic costumes, props, and music that included Hank Williams, Bob Wills, and other country singers of the time, and his scenes emphasized dust, wind, and blowing tumbleweeds. The result was a film that captured the essence of growing up in a northwest Texas town, with a feeling of longing, and with the film's town, Anarene, playing the role of "anytown." (Called Thalia in the novel, this change was perhaps to distinguish it from the Thalia of *Hud* or the real Thalia, Texas. Anarene was a small settlement in Archer County.)

Other small Southwestern films of the period include Jack Hicks' *Raggedy Man* (1981); Robert Benton's *Tender Mercies* (1983), *Places in the Heart* (1984), and *Nadine* (1987), set in 1954 Austin, when it was a small town; and Kevin Reynolds' *Fandango* (1985), with a young Kevin Costner (1955–) visiting Marfa, Texas, where *Giant* was filmed. Sam Peckinpah's (1925–1984) *The Getaway* (1972), with Steve McQueen and Ali McGraw (1938–), and Steven Spielberg's (1946–) *The Sugarland Express* (1974), with Goldie Hawn (1945–), use small-town Texas crimes as the basis for flight and chase stories. An ironic film with a small-town Texas title is Wim Wenders' *Paris, Texas* (1984), whose screenplay was by Sam Shepard. This film uses the Southwestern desert landscape around Terlingua as a sardonic mirror of the bleak, urban sprawl of Houston. Wenders and Shepard reunited in 2004 with *Don't Come Knockin'*.

In 1990 Peter Bogdanovich directed *Texasville*, the sequel to his earlier triumph, *The Last Picture Show*. *Gas, Food, Lodging* (1992), directed by Allison Anders, concerns a truck-stop waitress and her two daughters, who live in a Laramie, New Mexico, trailer park. Clint Eastwood's *A Perfect World* (1993) stars Eastwood and

Paris, Texas (1984). Courtesy of Photofest.

Kevin Costner and uses murder, Texas Rangers, and car chases to explore the familiar issue of violence. Lesser-known independent films set in small-towns were also produced in the 1990s and since 2000, including Tim McCanlies' *Dancer, Texas Pop. 81* (1998) and *Secondhand Lions* (2003) and Mark Illsley's *Happy, Texas* (1999). *The Good Girl* (2002), directed by Miguel Arteta from Mike White's screenplay, features Jennifer Aniston as a bored wife who works at the Retail Rodeo in a small Texas town whose life is turned upside down after she gets involved with a young clerk who calls himself Holden. A locally popular documentary with a similar focus on the small town is *Hands on a Hard Body* (1998), which sympathetically captures the spirit of a contest held in Longview, Texas, in which the last person standing with his or her hand on a pickup truck wins the truck. One rural Texas film that stands apart because of its allegorical qualities is Andrew Davis's *Holes* (2003), based on a best-selling young adult book by Louis Sacher, who also wrote the screenplay. *Holes* takes place in a West Texas desert area where delinquents are forced to dig holes in a Sisyphus-like parable.

Rural Arizona is a partial setting for Joel and Ethan Coen's *Raising Arizona* (1987), a high-energy "film school" movie filled with zany technique and in-joke references to other films. Nicholas Cage and Holly Hunter play a trailer-trash couple living near Tempe who decide to kidnap the young son of Nathan Arizona Sr., the scion of a statewide empire of unpainted-furniture and bathroom-fixture outlets. The Coen brothers have an affinity for the Southwest, setting their first film, *Blood Simple* (1984), in Texas and patching together elements of Pappy Lee O'Daniel's dubious tenure as candidate and governor of Texas for their hugely successful *O Brother, Where Art Thou?* (2001), which is set in a mythic South.

A special subset of Southwestern films concerns rodeo performers or the power of the rodeo as a spectacle and dangerous sport. From the 1930s to the 1950s dozens of B movies used rodeo or rodeo performers, including several with Gene Autry, Roy Rogers, and Rex Allen. Later significant films about the rodeo or rodeo performers include George Axelrod's *Bus Stop* (1956), with Marilyn Monroe and Don Murray; Burt Kennedy's *The Rounders* (1965), with Glenn Ford and Henry Fonda; Sam Peckinpah's *Junior Bonner* (1972), with Steve McQueen; *J. W. Coop* (1972), directed by and starring Cliff Robertson; Sydney Pollack's *The Electric Horseman* (1979), with Robert Redford and Jane Fonda; and Gregg Champion's *The Cowboy Way* (1994), with Woody Harrelson and Keifer Sutherland, from a script by William Wittliff. A related subset is the Wild West show film, more broadly Western than Southwestern. These include Robert Altman's *Buffalo Bill and the Indians, or Sitting Bull's History Lesson* (1976) and Eastwood's *Bronco Billy* (1980).

Raising Arizona (1987). Courtesy of Photofest.

Southwestern City Films

Although small Southwestern towns have perhaps gotten the most film treatment, some of the major cities have been important settings, such as James L. Brooks' *Terms of Endearment* (1983), based on another McMurtry novel, which is set Houston. This major Hollywood production's slick combination of humor and melodrama captivated audiences, and the film won five Academy Awards, including Best Picture. A sequel, *The Evening Star* (1996), directed by Robert Harling (1951–), also is set in Houston and featured Ben Johnson's (1918–1996) last performance. James Bridges' (1936–1993) *Urban Cowboy* (1980) takes vestiges of the old world inside Houston honkytonks; John Travolta's (1954–) performance created a neocowboy clothing craze and made riding mechanical bulls popular.

No film has influenced the popular image of Dallas as much as the television series about oilman J. R. Ewing called *Dallas*, but its setting for a number of films is important. The Dallas Cowboys' football team yielded Ted Kotcheff's (1931–) *North Dallas Forty* (1979), an examination of the macho world of Texas football. Errol Morris' acclaimed documentary, *The Thin Blue Line* (1988), examines the killing of a Dallas policeman in 1976. Likewise, the city of John Kennedy's (1917–1963) assassination is important to Oliver Stone's *JFK* (1991), Jonathan Kaplan's *Love Field* (1992), and John Mackenzie's *Ruby* (1992), with Danny Aiello. Austin's post-1960s dropout culture permeates Richard Linklater's *Slacker* (1991), while the multiculturalism of San Antonio is featured in Gregory Nava's *Selena* (1997).

Another important Southwestern city's history is explored in Barry Levinson's *Bugsy* (1991), with Warren Beatty dramatizing "Bugsy" Siegel's role in building Las Vegas. Las Vegas offers a special subset of Southwestern films and includes *Boulder Dam* (1936); *Las Vegas Nights* (1941); *The Lady Gambles* (1949); *The Atomic Kid* (1954); *Ocean's Eleven* (1960), starring Frank Sinatra and the Rat Pack, and the 2001 remake starring George Clooney and Brad Pitt; *Viva Las Vegas* (1963); *The Professionals* (1966); *The Grasshopper* (1970); *Diamonds Are Forever* (1971); *Play It As It Lays* (1972); *Going in Style* (1979); *The Electric Horseman* (1979); *Melvin and Howard* (1980); *Desert Bloom* (1986); *Rain Man* (1988); *Honeymoon in Vegas* (1992); *Indecent Proposal* (1993); *Casino* (1995); *Leaving Las Vegas* (1995); *Independence Day* (1996); *Con Air* (1997); *Hard Eight* (1997); *Truth or Consequences, N.M.* (1997); *Vegas Vacation* (1997); *Very Bad Things* (1998); *Fear and Loathing in Las Vegas* (1998); *Play It to the Bone* (1999); and *The Mexican* (2001).

Phoenix appears almost as a Southwestern city film footnote in Joshua Logan's *Bus Stop* (1956) and Alfred Hitchcock's classic *Psycho* (1960). Marian Crane (Janet Leigh) takes $40,000 from her Phoenix employer and heads to California, where she ends up in the shower at the Bates Motel. Other Phoenix-based films include Martin Scorsese's *Alice Doesn't Live Here Any More* (1974), Clint Eastwood's *The Gauntlet* (1977), Forest Whitaker's *Waiting to Exhale* (1995), and Bob Dolman's *The Banger Sisters* (2002).

North Dallas Forty points to another subgenre of Texas films, sports films, especially those about football. These include Stan Dragoti's *Necessary Roughness* (1991), a humorous look at college football; Brian Robbin's *Varsity Blues* (1999), an examination of the "win at any cost" mentality in a small Texas high school; Peter Berg's *Friday Night Lights* (2004), with Billy Bob Thornton; and an infamous X-rated film,

Debbie Does Dallas (1978). Ron Shelton's *Tin Cup* (1996) is about a seedy West Texas golf pro played by Kevin Costner; John Lee Hancock's *The Rookie* (2002) stars Dennis Quaid as a high school baseball coach who tries out for and makes it to the Big Show.

Diverse Southwesterns

In the early 1970s Southwestern Native Americans were portayed in a new light in a series of films about an Indian Vietnam vet in the Arizona-New Mexico area in Tom Laughlin's *Billy Jack* (1971), *The Trial of Billy Jack* (1974), and *Billy Jack Goes to Washington* (1977). These amateurish films combine karate action sequences with late-1960s multiculturalism that celebrated a Native American outsider as the hero. The films achieved a cult status.

In the late 1980s and 1990s, Western and Southwestern films were adapted as a means of presenting Native American, feminist, African American, and Mexican American issues. One film, Louis Malle's *Alamo Bay* (1985), extends the concerns to the conflicts over shrimp harvests that occasionally led to violence between Texas and Vietnamese-American fishermen along the Gulf Coast. Jonathan Wacks' *Pow Wow Highway* (1989) follows two contemporary Cheyenne men from Montana to New Mexico, merging the road movie with a poignant quest for racial heritage. Similarly, Chris Eyre's (1969–) *Smoke Signals* (1998) follows two Coeur d'Alene Indians as they travel from Idaho to Arizona to retrieve the remains of the father of one of them. Walter Hill's *Geronino* (1994) takes a new look at the title figure.

Ridley Scott's (1937–) *Thelma and Louise* (1991) begins in Arkansas and then becomes a feminist Southwestern buddy road-film as Susan Sarandon and Geena Davis (1956–) travel through Oklahoma, heading for Mexico. Maggie Greenwald's (1955–) *The Ballad of Little Jo* (1993), Sam Raimi's (1954–) *The Quick and the Dead* (1995), and Jonathan Kaplan's (1947–) *Bad Girls* (1994) revise the Western from a feminist perspective. These 1990s feminist films seem indebted to the earlier *Alice Doesn't Live Here Anymore* (1974), set in Phoenix.

Smoke Signals (1998). Courtesy of Photofest.

Some significant films treat African Americans in the Southwest. *Waiting to Exhale* is based on the best-selling 1992 novel by Terry McMillan (1951–), who was born in Port Huron, Michigan, but lived in Tucson, Arizona, for a number of years, and served on the faculty at the University of Arizona. The novel and film follow four black women who live in Phoenix. Mario Van Peebles' (1957–) *Posse* (1993) adapts the Western for African Americans. Earlier Southwestern films that are concerned with African American characters and themes include John Ford's (1894–1973) *Sergeant Rutledge* (1960) about a black soldier in the Southwest and *Black Like Me* (1964), based on Texas writer John Howard Griffin's

(1920–1980) book about darkening his skin chemically and then traveling through the South and back to Texas. Other films trace the lives of important African American Southwesterners: Gordon Parks' (1912–) *Leadbelly* (1974) traces the life of the famous bluesman Huddie Ledbetter (1885–1949), who spent years in Texas and Louisiana prisons until he was brought to national prominence by Texas folklorist John Lomax. Similarly, Jeremy Kagan's (1945–) *Scott Joplin* (1977) follows the life of ragtime's most famous practitioner, born in Texarkana, Texas.

Films that focus on Mexican American life include Robert Young's (1907–1998) *The Ballad of Gregório Cortez* (1982), based on a ground-breaking book by Chicano scholar Américo Paredes (1937–), Robert Redford's *The Milagro Beanfield War* (1988), which dramatizes the politics of water rights and the tensions between Anglo newcomers and Hispanic residents specifically in late twentieth-century northern New Mexico, but—by implication—throughout the Southwest; Severo Perez's *And the Earth Did Not Devour Him* (1994), based on Tomás Rivera's (1935–1984) story of a young south Texas migrant worker and his family in the 1950s; and Gregory Nava's (1949–) *Selena* (1997), based on the life and death of the enormously popular Tejana singer of the same name. Robert Rodriguez's $7,000 student project *El Mariachi* (1991) was remade with a large budget as *Desperado* (1995). The third film in the series, *Once Upon a Time in Mexico* (2003), also starring Antonio Banderas and Salma Hayek, with a brief appearance by Johnny Depp, was released in 2003. Rodriguez's *From Dusk Till Dawn* (1996) is in a special category, a Border horror film complete with bats and vampires. Rodriguez's films are characterized by the clear homage they pay to Sergio Leone's Spaghetti Westerns, their focus on Hispanics, their violence, and their desire to be action films rather than examinations of culture.

Probably, the most significant Southwestern film of the 1990s is John Sayles' *Lone Star* (1996). Like novelist Cormac McCarthy, Sayles uses the border between Texas and Mexico both as a physical setting and as a metaphor for the *mestizo* world that characterizes the Southwest, a mixture of cultures, histories, motives, hopes, and desires. The film crosses borders between Texas and Mexico, parent and child, past and present, African American and Indian, even sexual relations between brother and sister. True to its revisionist nature, the film ends not by remembering the Alamo but with "Forget the Alamo"—language that banishes the single symbol of cultural confrontation from collective memory.

Special Southwestern Places

Some specific Southwestern places and events have been the subject of several films, such as those about the Alamo, the JFK assassination, and NASA noted earlier. Perhaps the most significant American and Southwestern site is Monument Valley in northern Arizona and southern Utah. John Ford transformed these sandstone monoliths into iconic expressions of the mythic West. Besides filming *Stagecoach* (1939) there, Ford filmed his post–Civil War cavalry trilogy—*Fort Apache* (1948), *She Wore a Yellow Ribbon* (1949), *Rio Grande* (1950)—there, as well as *The Searchers* (1956), *Sergeant Rutledge* (1960), and *Cheyenne Autumn* (1964).

Ford's many movies filmed there made Monument Valley's expansive space the archetype of the Western, even though the actual settings may have been somewhere else. Much of Ford's *My Darling Clementine* (1946) with Henry Fonda

The Return of the Western

Over the years the Western has been declared dead, only to arise in some new form. In 1989 the television miniseries *Lonesome Dove*, based on Larry McMurtry's novel, blazed the trail for the big Westerns of the 1990s—*Dances with Wolves* and *Unforgiven*, the only two Western films to win Academy Awards for Best Picture. When Bill Wittliff wrote the screenplay for the television miniseries, his first goal was to try to keep the planned six-hour miniseries faithful to the novel, believing that "*Lonesome Dove is the star*. If we take care of *Lonesome Dove*, it will take care of us."[7] Wittliff's connection with the material, his background as a screenwriter, producer, director, book collector, and publisher, and his friendship with McMurtry made him the perfect choice to transfer the large novel to the small screen. Wittliff, who grew up in central Texas, in Blanco, was the publisher of McMurtry's *In a Narrow Grave* from his Encino Press in 1968. Wittliff's film credits also include *The Black Stallion*, *Barbarosa*, *The Red Headed Stranger*, and *The Cowboy Way*. And as the film's writer and coproducer, Wittliff ensured that it had the authentic feel of Texas trail drives, since the director, Simon Wincer, had little Texas or Southwestern background. Wincer, an Australian, did have experience working on a large scale with large groups of people and animals in *Pharr Lap* and *The Light Horsemen*.

With a strong screenplay by a committed coproducer, a seasoned director, a $20 million budget, and a pledge to produce a television miniseries that was both faithful to the original and more like a movie epic than a TV production, the next major decision was the cast, and those decisions also proved to be fortunate. With Academy Award winners Robert Duvall (Augustus McCrea), Tommy Lee Jones (Woodrow Call), and Angelica Houston (Clara Allen), it was one of the most successful miniseries in recent years, perhaps signaling that the American public was ready to return to the American Southwest for its popular culture. The other members of the cast were equally strong: Robert Urich (Jake Spoon), Danny Glover (Deets), Diane Lane (Lorena), Tim Scott (Pea Eye), Ricky Schroder (Newt), and D. B. Sweeney (Dish Boggett). At the Southwestern Writers Collection at Texas State University–San Marcos, the miniseries memorabilia remains one of most popular exhibits, especially the prop representing Gus McCrea's dead body.

As Wittliff intended, the screenplay and the production were extremely faithful to the original. One major change concerns the conclusion, but it is true to McMurtry's vision and probably strengthens the story. Wittliff decided to have Call repeat Old Man Goodnight's famous line when asked if he were a man of vision. "Yes, a hell of a vision," he replied. McMurtry uses the line earlier in the novel and as an epigraph in *In a Narrow Grave*. The line's ambivalence captures the story's doubleness and provides a final ironic statement.

In 2003 Kevin Costner released *Open Range*, a Western set in some unnamed range territory that could be West Texas, New Mexico, Oklahoma, Kansas, Colorado, or Wyoming, but it was filmed in Canada. Set in 1882 as the Old West is disappearing, the film turns on the recognizable conflict between a wealthy, unscrupulous rancher (Michael Gambon) and a few free grazing cattlemen led by Costner and Robert Duvall. Duvall's character, Boss, introduces the stuff of the traditional Western, which is an emphasis on the kind of human values that define a life and that lift a traditional story into the realm of the archetype.

(1905–1982), Victor Mature, and Walter Brennan was filmed there, even though the actual setting for the famous fight between the Earp brothers, Doc Holliday, and the Clanton gang is Tombstone in southern Arizona. The famous shootout at the O.K. Corral has given rise to several films, including John Sturges' (1911–1992) *Gunfight at the O.K. Corral* (1957), with Burt Lancaster (1913–1994) and Kirk Douglas (1905–1982); Sturges' *Hour of the Gun* (1967), with James Garner, Jason Robards, and Robert Ryan; George Cosmatos' *Tombstone* (1993), with Kurt Russell, Val Kilmer, and Sam Elliott; and Lawrence Kasdan's (1949–) *Wyatt Earp* (1994), with Kevin Costner and Dennis Quaid. Also in Arizona, the Grand Canyon has provided a spectacular backdrop for several films, including the last scene in Lawrence Kasdan's *Grand Canyon* (1991), about six Los Angeles residents. Elsewhere in the Southwest, the nuclear testing sites, especially Los Alamos, New Mexico, and the Trinity Test site near Alamogordo south of there, provide a distinctive venue. Los Alamos was called *The Atomic City* in a 1952 film, was treated in a popular documentary called *The Atomic Café* (1982), and was the subject of feature films about the making of the atomic bombs dropped on Japan in Roland Joffe's (1945–) *Fat Man and Little Boy* (1989) with Paul Newman and Matthew Broderick's (1962–) *Infinity* (1996) about physicist Richard Feynman (1918–1988).

CONCLUSION

American theater and film have often looked to the Southwest, frequently harkening back to the cultural experiences of the region—Indian, Mexican, African American, Asian, and Anglo, but chiefly the cowboy tradition—adapting the familiar elements for contemporary circumstances or examining a world where the older values have been altered or forgotten. Even if the actual region seems endangered by parking lots and megamalls, the Southwest of buttes, mesas, and Saguaro cactus will live forever in the imagination.

RESOURCE GUIDE

Printed Sources

Allen, Paula Gunn. *Grandmothers of the Light: A Medicine Woman's Sourcebook*. Boston, MA: Beacon Press, 1991.

———. *Shadow Country*. Los Angeles: Native American Series, UCLA, 1982.

———. *The Woman Who Owned the Shadows*. Albion, California: Spinsters Ink, 1983.

Bryant, Keith L. *Culture in the American Southwest: The Earth, the Sky, the People*. College Station: Texas A&M University Press, 2001.

Busby, Mark. "Contemporary Western Drama." In *The Literary History of the American West*, edited by J. Golden Taylor, 1222–1234. Fort Worth: Texas Christian University Press, 1987.

———. *Larry McMurtry and the West: An Ambivalent Relationship*. Denton: University of North Texas Press, 1995.

———. *Preston Jones*. Western Writers Series #58. Boise: Boise State University, 1983.

———. "Sam Shepard." In *Twentieth-Century Western Writers, Second Series*, edited by Richard H. Cracroft, 259–268. Detroit: Gale, 2000.

———. "Texas and the Great Southwest." In *A Companion to the Regional Literatures of America*, edited by Charles Crow, 432–457. New York: Blackwell, 2003.

———. "Texas and the Southwest." In *Columbia Companion to American History on Film*, edited by Peter Rollins, 488–496. New York: Columbia University Press, 2004.

Cabeza de Vaca, Álvar Núñez. *The Account: Álvar Núñez Cabeza de Vaca's Relación*. Trans. Martin A. Favata and José B. Fernández. Houston: Arte Publico Press, 1993.

Chin, Frank. *The Chickencoop Chinaman, The Year of the Dragon: Two Plays*. Seattle: University of Washington Press, 1981.

Coburn, D. L. *The Gin Game*. New York: Samuel French, 1978.

Geiogamah, Hanay. *New Native American Drama*. Norman: University of Oklahoma Press, 1980.

Graham, Don. *Cowboys and Cadillacs: How Hollywood Looks at Texas*. Austin: Texas Monthly Press, 1983.

———. *Texas: A Literary Portrait*. San Antonio, Corona, 1985.

Graham, Don, James W. Lee, and William T. Pilkington, eds. *The Texas Literary Tradition: Fiction/Folklore/History*. Austin: College of Liberal Arts, University of Texas, 1983.

Harrigan, Stephen. "The Making of *Lonesome Dove*." *Texas Monthly* 16, no. 6 (June 1988): 82–86, 156–159.

Heifner, Jack. *Patio/Porch*. New York: Dramatists Play Service, 1978.

———. *Vanities*. New York: Samuel French, 1977.

John, Elizabeth A. H. *Storms Brewed in Other Men's Worlds: The Confrontation of Indians, Spanish, and French in the Southwest, 1540–1795*. Norman: University of Oklahoma Press, 1996.

Jones, Preston. *Santa Fe Sunshine*. New York: Dramatists Play Service, 1977.

———. *A Texas Trilogy*. New York: Hill & Wang, 1976.

King, Larry L., and Peter Masterson. *The Best Little Whorehouse in Texas*. New York: Samuel French, 1981.

King, Larry L. *Of Outlaws, Con Men, Whores, Politicians, and Other Artists*. New York: Viking, 1980.

Lamadrid, Enrique R. *Hispano Folk Theater in New Mexico.* http://memory.loc.gov/ammem/rghtml/rgtheater.html.

Lavender, David Sievert. *The Southwest.* Albuquerque: University of New Mexico Press, 1984.

McCarthy, Cormac. *All the Pretty Horses*. New York: Alfred A. Knopf, 1992.

———. *Cities of the Plain*. New York: Alfred A. Knopf, 1998.

———. *The Crossing*. New York: Alfred A. Knopf, 1994.

McLure, James. *Lone Star*. New York: Dramatists Play Service, 1980.

———. *Pvt. Wars*. New York: Dramatists Play Service, 1980.

Medoff, Mark. *Children of a Lesser God*. New York: Dramatists Play Service, 1981.

———. *The Wager: Two Short Plays*. Clifton, NJ: James T. White, 1976.

———. *When You Comin' Back, Red Ryder?* Clifton, NJ: James T. White, 1974.

Meinig, D. W. *Imperial Texas: An Interpretive Essay in Cultural Geography*. Austin: University of Texas Press, 1969.

Mitchell, Lee Clark. *Westerns: Making the Man in Fiction and Film*. Chicago, University of Chicago Press, 1996.

Paredes, Américo. *"With His Pistol in His Hand": A Border Ballad and Its Hero*. Austin: University of Texas Press, 1958.

Pilkington, William T. *Imagining Texas: The Literature of the Lone Star State*. Boston: American, 1981.

———. *My Blood's Country*. Fort Worth: Texas Christian University Press, 1973.

Rivera, Tomás. *. . . y no se lo tragó la tierra/ . . . And the Earth Did Not Part*. Berkeley: Quinto Sol, 1971.

Rose, Wendy. *Academic Squaw—Report to the World from the Ivory Tower*. Marvin, SD: Blue Cloud Quarterly, 1977.

———. *Hopi Roadrunner Dancing*. Greenfield Center, New York: The Greenfield Review Press, 1973.
Shepard, Sam. *Buried Child*. New York: Urizen Books, 1979.
———. *Five Plays*. Indianapolis: Bobbs-Merrill, 1967.
———. *Four Two-Act Plays*. New York: Urizen Books, 1980.
———. *Seven Plays*. New York: Bantam Books, 1981.
Valdez, Luis. *Actos*. San Juan Bautista, CA: Centro Campesino Cultural, 1971.
Wright, Will. *Sixguns & Society: A Structural Study of the Western*. Berkeley: University of California Press, 1975.

Web Sites

Film Information

International Movie Database
http://www.imdb.com

Play Information

Interplay
http://www.lib.pdx.edu/systems/inteprlay/

State Film Commissions (with Filmographies)

Arizona
http://www.commerce.state.az.us/Film/default.asp

New Mexico
http://www.edd.state.nm.us/FILM/

Nevada
http://www.nevadafilm.com/home/index.php

Texas
http://www.governor.state.tx.us/film/

Handbook of Texas
http://www.tsha.utexas.edu/handbook/online/

Organizations

See in particular:
Abernathy, Elton. "Yelvington, Leonard Ramsey."
Barnes, Michael. "Theater."
Ramírez, Elizabeth C. "Carlos Villalong in Dramatic Company" and "Mexican-American Theater."
Sheehy, Helen. "Jones, Margaret Virginia."
Stanley, N.J. "Vance, Nina Eloise Whittington."

Albuquerque
http://www.digifestsouthwest.com/

American Indian Film Institute
http://www.aifisf.com/

Austin Film Festival
http://www.austinfilmfestival.com/

Deep Ellum Film Festival
http://www.def2.org/

Las Vegas
http://www.cinevegas.com/films.html and http://www.bsiff.com/

Native American Film
http://www.lib.berkeley.edu/MRC/IndigenousBib.html

Native American Playwrights
http://www.haskell.edu/academic/art_sci/playwrights/playwrights.htm

The Native American Women Playwrights Archive
http://staff.lib.muohio.edu/nawpa/

Phoenix Film Festival
http://www.phoenixfilmfestival.com/

Santa Fe Film Festival
http://www.santafefilmfestival.com/

South by Southwest
http://www.sxsw.com/

Southwest Regional Humanities Center
http://swrhc.txstate.edu

Southwestern Writers Collection, Texas State University
http://www.library.txstate.edu/swwc/

Tucson Film Office (with filmography)
http://filmtucson.com/

Women of Color, Women of Words
http://www.scils.rutgers.edu/~cybers/home.html

Films

Border Films

Barbarosa (1982)
The Border (1982)
Extreme Prejudice (1987)
Flashpoint (1984)
Goin' South (1978)
Lone Star (1996)
Ride the Pink Horse (1947)
And Starring Pancho Villa as Himself (2003)
Touch of Evil (1958)
Viva Zapata! (1952)

Diverse Southwesterns

Alamo Bay (1985)
. . . And the Earth Did Not Devour Him (1994)
Bad Girls (1994)
The Ballad of Gregorio Cortez (1982)
The Ballad of Little Jo (1993)
Billy Jack (1971)
Billy Jack Goes to Washington (1977)
Black Like Me (1964)
Desperado (1995)
El Mariaci (1991)
From Dusk Till Dawn (1996)
Geronimo (1994)

Leadbelly (1976)
The Milagro Beanfield War (1988)
Once Upon a Time in Mexico (2003)
Posse (1994)
Pow Wow Highway (1989)
The Quick and the Dead (1995)
Scott Joplin (1977)
Selena (1997)
Sergeant Rutledge (1960)
Smoke Signals (1998)
The Trial of Billy Jack (1974)

Early Southwestern History

The Alamo (1960)
The Alamo (2004)
The Anasazi (1985)
The Anasazi and Chaco Canyon (1994)
Cabeza de Vaca (1991)
The Great Train Robbery (1903)
Martyrs of the Alamo (1915)
The Mask of Zorro (1998)
Pee Wee's Big Adventure (1985)
Viva Max! (1970)

End-of-the-West Southwesterns

All the Pretty Horses (2000)
The Hi-Lo Country (1998)
Hud (1963)
Lonely are the Brave (1962)
The Man Who Shot Liberty Valence (1962)
Ride the High Country (1962)

Las Vegas Films

The Atomic Kid (1954)
Boulder Dam (1936)
Bugsy (1991)
Casino (1995)
Con Air (1997)
Desert Bloom (1986)
Diamonds Are Forever (1971)
The Electric Horseman (1979)
Fear and Loathing in Las Vegas (1998)
Going in Style (1979)
The Grasshopper (1970)
Honeymoon in Vegas (1992)
Hard Eight (1996)
Indecent Proposal (1993)
Independence Day (1996)
The Lady Gambles (1949)
Las Vegas Nights (1941)
Leaving Las Vegas (1995)
Melvin and Howard (1980)
The Mexican (2001)
Ocean's Eleven (1960) *remake* (2001)
Play It As It Lays (1972)
Play It to the Bone (1999)
The Professionals (1966)
Rain Man (1988)
Truth or Consequences, N.M. (1997)
Vegas Vacation (1997)
Very Bad Things (1998)
Viva Las Vegas (1963)

Parodic Westerns

Blazing Saddles (1974)
Cat Ballou (1965)
The Life and Times of Judge Roy Bean (1972)

Return of the Western

Lonesome Dove (1989)
The Missing (2003)
Open Range (2003)

Rodeo and Wild West Show Films

Bronco Billy (1980)
Buffalo Bill and the Indians, or Sitting Bull's History Lesson (1976)
Bus Stop (1956)
The Cowboy Way (1994)
The Electric Horseman (1979)
J. W. Coop (1972)
Junior Bonner (1972)
The Rounders (1965)

Small-Town Southwestern Films

Blood Simple (1984)
Dancer, Texas Pop. 81 (1998)
Fandango (1985)
Gas, Food, Lodging (1991)
The Getaway (1972)
The Good Girl (2002)
Hands on a Hard Body (1998)
Happy, Texas (1999)
Holes (2003)
The Last Picture Show (1971)
Nadine (1987)
Paris, Texas (1984)
Places in the Heart (1984)
Raising Arizona (1987)
Secondhand Lions (2003)
The Sugarland Express (1974)
Tender Mercies (1982)

Southwestern City Films

Alice Doesn't Live Here Any More (1974)
Apollo 13 (1995)
The Banger Sisters (2002)
The Evening Star (1996)
The Gauntlet (1977)
JFK (1991)
Love Field (1992)
Necessary Roughness (1991)
North Dallas Forty (1979)
Psycho (1960)
The Right Stuff (1983)
Selena (1997)
Slacker (1991)
Space Cowboys (2000)
Terms of Endearment (1983)
The Thin Blue Line (1988)
Urban Cowboy (1980)
Varsity Blues (1999)
Waiting to Exhale (1995)

Southwestern Farm Films

Days of Heaven (1978)
The Grapes of Wrath (1940)
Places in the Heart (1984)
The Southerner (1940)

Southwesterns

The Kid from Texas (1950)
The Left Handed Gun (1958)
Pat Garrett and Billy the Kid (1973)
Stagecoach (1939)
Young Guns (1988)
Young Guns II (1990)

Spaghetti Westerns

A Fistful of Dollars (1964)
For a Few Dollars More (1965)
The Good, the Bad, and the Ugly (1966)

Special Southwestern Places

Atomic Café (1982)
The Atomic City (1952)
Cheyenne Autumn (1964)
Fat Man and Little Boy (1989)
Fort Apache (1948)
Grand Canyon (1991)
Gunfight at the O.K. Corral (1957)
Hour of the Gun (1967)
Infinity (1996)
My Darling Clementine (1946)
Rio Grande (1950)
The Searchers (1956)
Sergeant Rutledge (1960)
She Wore a Yellow Ribbon (1949)
Stagecoach (1939)
Tombstone (1993)
Wyatt Earp (1994)

Transitional Western Films

Bonnie and Clyde (1967)
Broken Arrow (1950)
Giant (1956)
Heaven's Gate (1980)
High Noon (1952)
The Searchers (1956)

Trail Drive Films

City Slickers (1991)
City Slickers II: The Legend of Curly's Gold (1994)
The Conquering Horde (1931)
North of 36 (1924)
Red River (1948)
The Texans (1938)

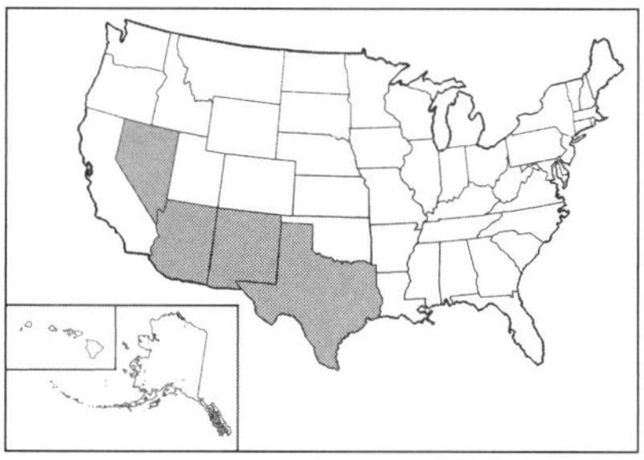

FOLKLORE

J. Rhett Rushing

The folklore of the Southwest is an easy topic to embrace but somewhat more difficult to fix in time and space. Approaching folklore study from a regional standpoint depends on (and derives from) an understanding that the folk performances of one area are distinctly different from those in other areas. In an era of mass and instant communication, time and distance have been rendered moot. How can regional identities and distinctions be maintained in the face of national news, restaurant chains, and global e-mail?

The answer to this question goes to the heart of what folklore is and how it is performed. Folklore is fundamentally a response—humans responding to their physical, cultural, or spiritual environments—and those responses are guided and governed by a shared aesthetic. Any claim to a region-specific body of folklore accepts that the environments of the Southwest can produce responses significantly different from those of any other region in America.

Operating within this region are innumerable human groups drawn along an infinite variety of lines—ethnic, religious, occupational, age, location, and so forth—all shaping their own sense of the aesthetic and creating the foundation for tradition. Since many conditions are common to all humans—love, death, the search for identity, or the innate desire to belong—folklore performances have often been grouped and studied by form or by genre. Though people in both Albuquerque and Anchorage get hungry and prepare food as a response, what they prepare frequently differs due to regional resources and traditions.

It is quite easy and common to reduce folklore to a comparative study of its forms, but folklore is nothing if not dynamic and interactive. A legend does not exist in the "ether" or on paper. It exists entirely within the context of each telling and hearing and interpretation. A morality tale does not float along in cultural space. It is drawn upon and performed when there is a cultural need for it.

SOCIAL INEQUALITIES AND SOUTHWEST FOLKLORE

Perhaps the greatest examples of this sort of cultural response come about in conditions of social and economic stratification. The history of the Southwest is filled with social disequilibrium, and this often produces folklore performances as a response. In the late 1800s and early 1900s the ballad style known as the *corrido* was enormously popular throughout the Southwest. Often pitting the poor, underdog local hero against the hegemonic and powerful forces of some religious, ethnic, or economic "other," the corrido was a masterful form of social protest.

Corridos are not disappearing. Where once people sang of tequila smugglers outwitting the G-men during Prohibition, there are now narco-corridos glorifying the exploits of local boys against the DEA. These fall naturally into the tradition of corridos as social commentary, cultural heroics, and a version of local history. Folklore forms will change with time, but the basic meanings, messages, and contexts seem to be forever fixed in human behavior.

Although over time certain genres will increase or decrease in popularity, there is no shrinking or disappearance of folklore on the whole—if anything, instant communication has increased folklore performances a hundred-fold. For a hundred years the mantra of early folklorists was to "collect and preserve" disappearing folklore forms. As technology allows for new manners of exploitation, humans continue to find a way. Hobos and drifters did not tag railroad trains with graffiti until after the train was invented. There was no copy machine lore until after the copy machine became readily available. It should be no surprise that folklore transmission has skyrocketed with the Internet.

One caution with computer technology is that it has a tendency to "normalize" expression across boundaries that do not exist for it. The Internet does not stop at mountain ranges or oceans, leaving peoples on either side isolated and unique. Folk speech in the form of emotions (the pictographic use of a keyboard's punctuation keys to convey emotion [:-) for happy or :-(for unhappy]) is a natural folkloric adaptation to technology, but the community with access to this is global, not local.

Another concern with technologically distributed folklore is that since computers became a routine office machine and networks are maintained, serviced, and run by employers, there is an ever-present sense of Big Brother watching. It is estimated that 65 percent of all employers monitor employee e-mails and Web interactions. The ethical jury is still out on this one, but one

El Corrido de Gregorio Cortez

In the county of El Carmen
A great misfortune befell;
The Major Sheriff is dead;
Who killed him no one can tell.
At two in the afternoon,
In half an hour or less,
They knew that the man who killed him
Had been Gregorio Cortez
They let loose the bloodhound dogs;
They followed him from afar.
But trying to catch Cortez
Was like following a star.
All the rangers of the county
Were flying, they rode so hard;
What they wanted was to get
The thousand-dollar reward.
And in the county of Kiansis
They cornered him after all;
Though they were more than three hundred
He leaped out of their corral.
Then the Major Sheriff said,
As if he was going to cry,
"Cortez, hand over your weapons;
We want to take you alive."
Then said Gregorio Cortez,
With his pistol in his hand,
"Ah, so many mounted Rangers
Just to take one Mexican!"[1]

hundred years ago if the ranch foreman said it was time to brand cattle and yet one cowboy chose to sit out and write letters to his girlfriend instead, that cowboy would be looking for work quickly.

First Amendment rights notwithstanding, company time and company resources are by volume most often the vehicles of folkloric transmission. Knowing that the boss might be monitoring performances, and operating in a climate of political correctness, employees often sanitize jokes, urban legends, and other folklore forms of their insider/outsider functions. Ethnic jokes are often dropped or altered beyond intent, gender jokes have become balancing acts, and most folkloric performances have become diatribes against the outsider du jour.

Folklorist Bess Lomax Hawes, daughter of famed folk music collector John Lomax, once decried the graying of American culture—that a restaurant chain's hamburger in Boston was identical to its hamburger in Las Vegas—but a closer look at folklore performances discovers just the opposite. Inextricably bound up with the human need for acceptance and community is the equally powerful human desire for identity. Folklore will always be a community response to the threat of chaos, and if the national chain's hamburgers are identical, then the local picnics and backyard cookouts will offer proof of uniqueness.

There are certain markers—particular elements from the environment—that give regional folk performances their uniqueness and flavor. Chiles, corn, and beans have been cultivated throughout the Southwest for millennia, and it is little surprise that those elements are considered staples in indigenous cuisines. Analogously, language, religious beliefs, costume, ethical codes, and architecture all shape and are shaped by the folklore performances within a region, and these have become synonymous with their host cultures.

Folk identity is inextricably tied to familiar folk performances (*menudo* as a hangover cure, specific woven blanket designs, *y'all* as a second-person pronoun, or adobe bricks as a building material). Though these cultural familiarities can become fodder for stereotyping (terms like *limey*, *kraut*, *beaner*, *greaser*, *dog-eater*, and so forth have all been slung as insults in the Southwest), they can also help individuals find comfort and order and locate their place amid the imposed chaos of multiculturalism. Simultaneously folk identity is an issue of defining oneself by what one is not. It is far easier to point out behaviors and responses that are unattractive and unacceptable than to enumerate all that is acceptable. When groups come into contact (and conflict), it is far easier to recognize the outsider.

Once, while president, Gerald Ford spoke in the Southwest and was offered a tamale after his speech. Before anyone could stop him, he attempted to bite it with the husk still on. This is a glaring example of otherness and outsider behavior, and the message did not go unnoticed in the next election.

Folklore in the Southwest is often about borders as well. With so many cultures moving through time over a broad but finite space, conflict is inevitable. Often the first to arrive chose the best places to settle, but when a more powerful group came along, the original settlers were forced to fight or flee. Strangers became enemies and conquerors, and everyone not a recognized member of the culture came to be understood as the "other."

Borders are not always physical, and the folklore of the Southwest reflects this. Religious differences, economic opportunities, ethnic heritage, and even age can be used to delineate the differences between insider and outsider. Experiential space is claimed and held for a group by virtue of tradition and expectation. Sunrise at Dairy Queens across the rural Southwest finds tables daily filled with very old men. These are men of the land who have given their patriarchy and responsibilities over to their sons, lost them to banks, or just gotten too tired to continue.

Every morning these men gather in a community not entirely of their own making. They are age mates, occupational equals, or just survivors, but they gather with a purpose, because they are daily defying the nursing home, the grave, and a sense of uselessness. They tease and joke with each other, complain about the sorry state of the world, tell how they would solve current problems if it were up to them, and generally stake their claims among the living and the purposeful.

Communities like these exist in places most do not realize. VFW halls, homeless shelters, adult day-care centers, church choirs, barber shops, whittle-and-spit benches around the courthouse, the periodical sections of public libraries, museums, beer joints, and domino parlors—all places where the formerly powerful can claim space and time on their own terms among peers. This is a claiming of space within a certain time by a folk group.

Of course the same Dairy Queen becomes the teen hangout on Friday and Saturday nights. It is the same space but in a different time. On Saturday afternoons the restaurant is swamped with soccer moms and Little League dads buying team ice creams or grabbing supper on the run. Borders become flexible and permeable over time as folk groups move across the landscape, but they can also be fiercely defended.

Many communities in the Southwest are "dry"—banning by law the sale of alcoholic beverages. For each of these communities there is a liquor store just beyond the defined border. Just beyond many established suburban subdivisions there are apartment complexes. Beyond that, trailer parks. Neighborhoods claim status and space according to wealth and image, urban or suburban or rural. There are homeowners' associations with legal status and citizen groups and PTAs and church deacons all meeting to protect the interest of their communities—to identify what behaviors and performances are explicitly "not them," thereby defining themselves in opposition.

Folklore in the Southwest is all about borders and identity and community. It is a dynamic interplay as alive as the people who maintain their traditions and aesthetics and expectations. Folklore is about insiders and outsiders, esoteric and exoteric, the emic and the etic. It is about perceptions and performances and perpetuating order in the face of terrifying chaos. Folklore is foremost a product of and a response to a perceived threat to order, and it is the very best and the very worst of us.

TYPES OF FOLKLORE IN THE SOUTHWEST

Narrative Folklore

By its most fundamental definition, folklore is oral: it is the orally performed knowledge of the people. This is rudimentary and inadequate for scholars, but it is a good stepping stone for the novice. If the oral nature of folklore defines its character, then there are a number of forms that need to be discussed.

There is a hierarchy of believability and acceptance that legitimizes all folk narrative, from the most believable (sacred narrative or mythology) to the least believable (jokes); categories fall all along the spectrum: first-person personal experience narrative (the *caso*), urban legends, ghost stories, historical legendry, and so forth. What matters most are the contexts in which the narrative is performed and the cultural and contextual legitimacy of the performer.

Supernatural Narratives

It was never man's lot to stay in the dark when it comes to the bigger questions of the cosmos. Is there life after death? A benevolent creator? An intelligent design? Ghosts, spirits, wraiths, or saints that interact with the living? How about the Devil and other supernatural manifestations of evil (*Lechusa*, *El Cupacabra*, *El Cucui*, or Skinwalkers for example)?

In the Southwest these uncertainties are explained and maintained narratively, and in narrative tradition everyone is allowed to participate. Folk cosmology does not come from the "top down" like formal religious canon, but is generated and spread through traditional narrative communities and performances. Imagine it as a product of "cultural faith" or a syncretism of doctrine and daring. In situations of chaos or disorder, humans will create order. When there are no ready answers or explanations, humans will always try to find them.

Since the beginning of Catholicism, the church has dealt with one form of public or folk interpretation of dogma or another. The church is hesitant to give credence to miracles, apparitions, and images that appear outside of a church building or, and especially, outside the church's doctrine largely because they are beyond the control of the clergy. Religion in the hands of the people is frightening to some, yet the church has adopted a wait-and-see policy of examination and investigation to deal with centuries of supernaturalism.

Religious-studies scholar Sandra Zimdars-Schwartz has studied religious apparitions (particularly various manifestations of the Virgin Mary) in places such as Lourdes, Medjugorje, Fatima, Mexico City, and Conyers, Georgia. Usually only one person is the percipient of the apparition and messages, but on occasion others have claimed divine guidance at these apparition sites.

For others wishing to personalize the supernatural phenomenon, narrative fills the void. There are tales of rosaries turning into gold as people prayed, miraculous healings, images of the Virgin or of Jesus in Polaroid photos of the sun, on trees, hospital doors, mailboxes, and even tortillas. Each, within the constructs and traditions of the narrative community, is called a personal miracle, and the telling and retelling of these miraculous narratives form a community of folk belief well beyond the reach of church canon.

Native American folklore in the Southwest is often an awkward topic until students and readers can understand that every human being on the planet participates in a myriad of folk groups, each with their own traditions and customs and beliefs. The Hopi or the Navajo are no more prone to folk beliefs than Presbyterians or accountants. By the same token, they are exactly as prone to folk beliefs and expressions as Presbyterians and accountants. Historically, ethnographic writing has characterized the mythologies and cosmologies of many Native Americans as primitive, savage, and heathen. With little awareness of the interconnections between folkloric performance and cosmology, few understood the similarities between the Corn Dance and a prayer meeting, between Coyote tales and biblical parables. Native Americans in the Southwest combine the same variety of folkloric forms and performances as any other peoples of the region. With this understood, there is an incredible wealth of Native American folklore to explore.

Native American Creation Mythology

There are two major forms of Creation mythology prevalent among Native Americans in the Southwest: Emergence and Earth Diver. Creation mythology serves to explain the origins of all things, and though set in the distant past, it is ongoing and performed as part of the immediate reality.

In the Emergence series, the beginning is always a void. Into that void the creator brings forth water, land, light, and life. Through a number of trials and errors, humans eventually emerge from a lower world into the present world. What follows is a small sampling of Southwestern Native American cosmological components compared to each other:

Zuni—A wonawilona creates water. Life emerges from the earth (all-Father) land, and life. The Ashiwi lead the way into the middle world, followed by all the other people (Hopi, Mexicans, Cocinino, Pima, Navajo, and the other Apaches).

Hopi—Taiowa creates four worlds as well as Sotunknang and Spider Woman who help humans overcome faults and emerge into each new world. The third world is destroyed by flood after humans became preoccupied with their own earthly plans. They enter the fourth world, Tuwaqachi, or World Complete.

Navajo—First Man and First Woman lead humans through four worlds and then up a reed from the bottom of the lake into the world.

Tewa—The people were underground in darkness and followed Mole up to the daylight and the Middle World.

The Earthdiver cycle diverges from emergence myth somewhat in that the world is all water and darkness until a culture hero dives down deeply enough to bring up mud. The mud is formed into a ball and placed upon Turtle's back as it grows and grows and becomes Earth.

Other origin mythologies explain how people came to eat what they eat, believe as they believe, or comport themselves as proper people should. These tales tell of how the deer, buffalo, corn, or other food staples came to the people and abound in each culture, although they differ from tribe to tribe. These tales explain why Bear walks the way he does or why Raven is black or how horses came to the people. Everything from planting practices to funerary rites are passed down in an oral tradition reaching back farther than any historian, archaeologist, or anthropologist could possibly ascertain.

The most heavily researched and scrutinized of all the Native American oral genres are the Coyote stories. Coyote, throughout the Southwest and much of North America, is understood as a trickster, both fool and hero. Coyote acts upon impulse and whim; he responds immediately to his desires and is often held up as a foil for teaching morality. Like all trickster/heroes, Coyote is often too clever for his own good, completely unable to resist temptation, extreme in every thought and action, and a supernatural character. Coyote both models and mocks human behavior, but he establishes cultural limits on both sides of behavioral acceptability.

Native American narratives often have rigid rules that govern their performances. Several tribes will not tell Coyote stories during the summer months because to do so invites rattlesnake bites as retribution. Other tribes will refuse to speak the name of the deceased for fear of distracting its ghost along its path to the other world.

Perhaps the most striking and magnificent aspect of Native American folklore in the Southwest is its integral relationship with all imaginable realms simultaneously. There is a marked relationship with the physical and the natural environment, an interdependence among the landscape and the living that is not determined or encumbered by a hierarchy of being. Animals are referred to as Brother, and the mountains are the sacred homes of the spirits. The earth is Mother and the sun is Father. Those gone before, whether human or spirit or animal, are considered to be ancestors, and all are treated with reverence.

Perhaps the greatest testament to this timeless integration is when folklorist Barre Toelken collected tales from the Navajo, Yellowman. As a pioneering folklorist, Toelken opened the world's eyes to the Navajo worldview and hinted at their spirituality but maintained a very respectful distance between insiders and outsiders. Recently Toelken opted to destroy all his fieldwork tapes with Yellowman because the tales belonged neither to Toelken nor to Yellowman but to the timelessness of the Navajo. Any social scientist who views such a response as wasteful or irresponsible is still viewing Native Americans as an other and as merely a subject of study undeserving of privacy and respect. If archaeologists suddenly decided to dig up Anglo ancestors in Arlington Cemetery, would it garner more or less publicity than any dig on tribal grounds?

Line drawing of an old Native American woman by James R. Snyder, published by the Texas Folklore Society. © Texas Folklore Society.

Ghost Stories

Ghost stories are essential to the Southwest. Objections to ghost stories surface occasionally, largely from fundamentalist religious groups erroneously afraid that these stories promote Devil worship and illicit sex, but they are an integral part of the human experience. They cover all subjects: lost love, lost fortunes, unfinished business, revenge, injustice, undying loyalty, and even pure evil. As a narrative genre, ghost stories are

Pen and ink illustration of La Llorona by Jose Cisneros, published by the Texas Folklore Society. © Texas Folklore Society.

the most prolific and the most recognizable folklore form. They cover everything because they are products of the connection between human fantasy and reality, a venue for narrative exploration of all social ills, and perhaps, an outlet or pressure-release valve for human concerns.

There is no culture on the planet that does not have a ghost story in its folktale repertoire. For that reason alone they belong at campfires and slumber parties and in the public school classroom, taught as part of the narrative tradition. Ghost stories are usually secular; they rarely promote specific forms of religious expression. They are a fundamental part of childhood that stays with us through adulthood.

In the Southwest ghost stories are all the richer because of the confluence of cultural contributions. Anglo, Hispanic, Black, Asian, and Native American cultures tend to borrow from each other's ghost stories, and the logical explanation is that good ghost stories are so compelling that everyone will retell them. Ghost stories cross cultural borders with greater ease than recipes or religion simply because they are captivating and entertaining.

The vast majority of ghost stories in the Southwest deal with injustice and unresolved issues, since, like any traditional narrative, they will reflect the concerns of the particular culture. In a region of such cultural, religious, and socioeconomic variety, however, the stories will run the gamut of societal ills and fears. While the cautionary legend "La Llorona," for example, warns of ethnic and class boundaries, it also enforces religious messages against having children out of wedlock and infanticide:

La Llorona (The Wailing Woman)

Back in the days when the Southwest was part of Spain there was a beautiful young Indian woman who fell in love with the son of a wealthy Spanish governor. The young man bought her a house on the edge of town, paid her a monthly allowance, and fathered three children by her outside of the bond of marriage.

One day the money stopped coming, the young man stopped visiting, and the woman was wondering what might have happened to her true love. Against all societal rules, she went to the grand hacienda and asked to speak to the young man. The household servants refused to allow her entrance, but the cook whispered that she ought to go over to the church. Angry and confused, the Indian woman made her way over just in time to see her lover emerging from the church with his new bride.

Blind with rage, the woman went home and began to destroy everything that reminded her of her Spanish lover. In a fury she broke plates, furniture, and gifts—everything that had come from him. And then she turned on the three children. Methodically, she took them down to the river and held them under the water until they drowned and floated away.

Snapping out of her rage, the woman realized what she had done and threw herself into the river and drowned, but her sins were so great that she was denied admittance into heaven. Instead, she was doomed to wander the earth forever as a wandering ghost in search of her children along the waterways of the Southwest.

Other ghost stories serve other functions. The legend of the children of the tracks is largely a horror story with a sympathetic twist at the end. This story about the tragedy of a busload of children being killed has been used to explain everything from railroad crossing lights to rear emergency exit doors on school buses. The continued testing of the legend by local high school and college students who try to reinact the story only strengthens the story's message by making it personal. But it is the telling of the narrative that weaves it into folk tradition and cements it into our minds.

The Children of the Tracks

Many years ago in San Antonio a school bus full of children approached a railroad crossing on the south side of town. A train whistled in the distance as the bus pulled up and onto the tracks, but for some reason the bus got stuck—"high-centered," they called it—and the rear wheels could find no traction. The train was upon them in an instant, and before the frantic driver could evacuate the children, one of the Southwest's worst traffic disasters was history . . . or perhaps legend?

To this day, hundreds of curious drivers each year go to the same railroad crossing, ease their cars to a stop on the tracks, put the car in neutral, and wait. Some say you can hear a train whistle in the distance, but all agree that after a while the car will experience a slight bump and begin to roll forward off the tracks, away from danger.

For those who sprinkle baby powder on their rear bumpers, once they are off the tracks and climb out to inspect, they usually find dozens of tiny little hand prints in the powder: evidence of the Children of the Tracks trying to save them.

There are myriad cautionary tales used to frighten children and drunken husbands back into acceptable behavior. "La Llorona" is frequently spotted near waterways by men looking for a little adventure, yet they are horrorstruck when they see her face, which has been said to take the form of either a skull or a horse's head. El Cucui is the Mexican American equivalent of the Boogeyman who lurks after misbehaving children. Even the Devil visits dance halls in Southwestern legendry, seeking out vain and improper young women to defile and disfigure.

The Devil in the Dancehall, or Pato de Gallo

Once there was a very beautiful but very vain girl named Florita. At thirteen years of age, her father insisted she was too young to attend the dances in town alone and forbade her to leave the house. Florita pretended to obey but secretly dressed in her finest clothing and sneaked out of the window for the dance.

Once there, many young men begged the beautiful Florita for a turn on the floor, but the haughty girl just raised her nose in the air and refused them all. None of these local boys was good enough for her. Then a stranger appeared in the doorway, tall and handsome and dressed in the finest of clothes. He locked eyes with the beautiful Florita, and her heart melted.

From then on the couple danced every dance, and as the tempo increased the magnificent couple spun faster and faster around the floor. As they accidentally bumped into another couple, the offended local girl looked down and began screaming. Florita's handsome partner had, instead of two human feet, one human foot and another of a rooster!

Immediately everyone in the room stared in horror at what could only be the presence of the Devil himself. Then all the lights went out, and one young scream was heard above all others. When people began lighting candles and lamps everyone saw poor, vain Florita lying in a pool of blood in the middle of the floor. Her once beautiful face was horribly clawed from eyes to chin—never again to be the source of her pride and vanity.

Using narrative to establish socially acceptable behavior is a worldwide tradition. Native American Coyote stories often illustrate what is acceptable by relating the extremes of what is not acceptable. Mexican American revenant tales bring back the dead to right wrongs, repay debts, or help loved ones. African American Dog Ghosts model loyalty and devotion, whereas fool's tales, though not always supernatural, honor cleverness by telling exaggerated tales of ignorant heroes. In some tales enormous ghost deer lead greedy hunters to their deaths, and in others the magnificent Pacing White Stallion has caused many Southwestern cowboys to go insane trying to capture it. There are tales of nuns turned to stone to prevent them from breaking their vows of chastity and tales of mysterious ghost nuns making predictions or warning sailors about the horrors of war.

Individual behavior—perhaps even conformity—is a cultural concern. Pick any of the seven deadly sins and a supernatural story can be found to serve as warnings against such behavior. There will always be allowable latitudes beyond the norm, but without a group expectation of what is right and wrong—enforced through traditional narrative—there can be no sense of community.

This gets incredibly complicated in the religious narratives of folk Catholicism because the Virgin Mary is impossible to emulate. For all the young women desiring to be both virgin and mother, life is a constant disappointment. With Coyote stories the magic invoked separates the audience from the narrative—few listeners can turn themselves into logs or return from the dead at will—but supernatural narratives work because their characters exhibit behaviors that mere mortals can control in themselves: there are no role models in supernatural narratives, just models of behavior.

Other Southwest Legendry

Legends, whether supernatural, historical, or even "urban" have long been hallmarks of the Southwest. In a region where heroes get bigger and tougher and faster with each telling, legendry has gone hand in hand with the concept of the frontier. Legends differ from myths (sacred narratives) and tales largely in that they are set in historic time, usually include real people and places, and are, on occasion, believed to be true.

Author and folklorist J. Frank Dobie made a career out of collecting and publishing legends from all over the Southwest. As longtime steward of the Texas Folklore Society, Dobie used the society's publications to showcase and preserve legends ranging from Robin Hood types, featuring Billy the Kid, Sam Bass, or Bonnie and Clyde, to stories about hidden treasure and lost gold mines. Other collections explored historical battles and heroes, fantastic animals, feuds, hunting and fishing exploits, and even music. The Texas Folklore Society dutifully continues to collect and preserve Southwestern legendry, and with the publication of over sixty volumes at last count, the stories will endure.

Good Guys/Bad Guys

The figure of the bad man (or woman) is not unique to the Southwest, but the lawlessness and the legendry of the nineteenth century fixed the image in time and space. In an open, ungoverned land like the early Southwest, the lines between right and wrong—between hero and villain—were never clearly drawn. Oral tradition retains only those parts of the story that are meaningful to the teller, and the character of the bandit hero was often a question of perspective.

Southwestern Folklore is filled with heroes and villains that are often juxtaposed in legendry. Billy the Kid, (William Antrim? 1859?–1881) historically depicted as a mentally-retarded, cold-blooded killer may very well have been a literate ne'er-do-well that began life as an abused child. Popular narrative at the time hailed him as both evil and handsomely daring—complete with folksongs (*corridos*) extolling his virtues. Billy the Kid's exploits in the famous Lincoln County wars in New Mexico and his death supposedly at the hands of Sheriff Pat Garrett have entered into Southwestern legend and numerous films over the years including Kurt Neumann's *The Kid from Texas* (1950) with Audie Murphy, Arthur Penn's *The Left Handed Gun* (1958) with Paul Newman, Sam Peckinpah's *Pat Garrett and Billy the Kid* (1973) with Kris Kristofferson, Christopher Cain's *Young Guns* (1988), and Geoff Murphy's *Young Guns II* (1990), both with Emilio Estevez, and many others.

Sam Bass (1951–1878) came to Texas from Indiana and fixed himself in local legendry as a Robin Hood character that stole from the rich (the banks) and gave to the poor. There are still tales around Round Rock, Texas, of $20 gold pieces (double eagles) paid by Sam Bass to a farm wife for a meal or a night's refuge in a barn while he was on the run.

Western figures like Wyatt Earp (1848–1929) or Kit Carson (1809–1868) became larger than life through the repeated tellings of their exploits and adventures. The popular press back East gets credit for many of the exaggerations, but oral tradition needed little help creating heroes. Kit Carson was a straight arrow. He left his boyhood home Boone's Lick, Missouri, and became the first truly recognized mountain man of the early nineteenth century. Upon Carson's exploits the stereotype took shape—the lone trapper making friends with the Indians, leading the wagon trains over the mountains, scouting for the army, and eventually betraying the Indians in our nation's campaign of relocation and genocide. To Carson's credit, both history and legend portray him as honest and moral, and after his planned attacks upon the Navajo, he became an Indian agent and trader with a remarkable reputation. His home in Taos, New Mexico, is still open as a museum.

Wyatt Earp and his brothers were a wanderlust bunch that worked as saloon keepers, gamblers, and sometimes lawmen. Their crowning moment—the shootout at the O.K. Corral—quickly departed from historical fact and elevated them into legends. Various accounts of the Earp legend claim that the famous gunfight in Tombstone, Arizona, was a noble and fearless bit of lawmanship, yet other versions claim the Earps hunted their adversaries down and killed them in cold blood. Hollywood has made a fortune from the Earp stories in several films, including John Sturges' *Gunfight at the O.K. Corral* (1957) with Burt Lancaster and Kirk Douglas, Sturges' *Hour of the Gun* (1967) with James Garner, Jason Robards, and Robert Ryan, George Cosmatos' *Tombstone* (1993) with Kurt Russell, Val Kilmer, and Sam Elliott, and Lawrence Kasdan's *Wyatt Earp* (1994) with Kevin Costner and Dennis Quaid, but no one seems to be able to pin down the whole truth.

Bonnie and Clyde (Bonnie Parker 1910–1934 and Clyde Barrow 1909–1934) benefitted from the Robin Hood legendry to a point, but their status in Southwestern stories is truncated somewhat by their brutality. Bonnie Parker did wait tables in north Texas and Clyde Barrow did pay a fellow prisoner to chop off two of his toes to avoid hard labor, but reality and historical fact (they were fully paid up on their car insurance when they died) pale to the tales of their manners and decorum while on the run from the law. When Frank Hamer (a Texas Ranger) ambushed them in Louisiana and then paraded their corpses for days, everyone in the region developed a tale about near-misses and casual acquaintences, and they became the subject of the famous Arthur Penn film, *Bonnie and Clyde* (1967).

HOLIDAYS, FESTIVALS, AND CELEBRATIONS

Holidays in the Southwest reflect the mix of cultures in the region. Anglo imposition of a largely Protestant calendar on the region and its institutions have determined bank holidays, school calendars, and most vacation times. Preconquest ceremonialism in the Southwest reflected the needs and concerns common to most of the world's peoples: summer and winter solstices, planting and harvest guidelines, and special astrological appearances marking an affirmation of the human place in the cosmos. If humans could predict when different constellations would appear each year in the sky, it linked them with greater powers and larger concerns. This possession of knowledge led to the development of an aristocracy, a priestly class, and eventually the concept of scholars with specialized knowledge.

The celebration of calendrical events and commemorations led to festivals and ritualized religious performances. Initially wedded to sacred events, many festivals became feasts and performances of communal excess—too much dancing, eating, drinking, and bravado. Ritual sacrifices were replaced by semiwilling participants sacrificing their bodies (and even lives) in ritualized combat with bulls, demons, or other symbolic manifestations of nature or evil.

Festivals and celebrations normally center on a particular item or function. Whether properly ushering in the new year, marking religious devotion, or glorifying the harvest (and in some communities, all three are related), most festivals began with a higher purpose than providing beer and fried dough. At the extreme, some communities create festivals simply for the revenue.

So many festivals have lately become creations of chambers of commerce—tourist traps only remotely connected to original meanings and intentions. As the tide of cultural and heritage tourism rises, more and more groups are reevaluating their traditional celebrations as ticketable venues. (Of note, the Texas Historical Commission has instituted a program whereby agents will meet with interested groups and conduct workshops that help communities to share resources and draw a greater number of tourists.) The almighty dollar reigns supreme, and although deeply religious or traditional performances still hang on in the Southwest, many are merely vestiges maintained by the pure stubbornness and dedication of their participants.

Religious Drama

As folklorist John West noted, Christmas in the Southwest usually begins on December 12 with the feast day of the Virgin of Guadalupe and ends on January 6, Kings Day. The season is all the more splendid due in part to the panoply of traditional folk dramas, dances, and religious celebrations across the region. Derived from the passion plays and other performances of religious instruction in Spain, many of these dramas depict Old World conflicts transferred to New World settings.

Perhaps the best known of these religious dramas is *Los Pastores* (The Shepherds). Characters that include the Hermit, the shepherds, the Devil, and the angel Michael interact and eventually do battle on the eve of Christ's birth. Once Good has defeated Evil, the shepherds are free to learn of the Nativity and travel to visit the holy family.

Some versions of *Los Pastores* can last for many hours and even stretch over the course of days. Each drama is based on a script, often handwritten, that has been passed down through generations of performers. These performances can range from reverent to ribald and are most commonly staged away from church grounds.

Another folk drama, *Las Posadas*, is quite popular across the Southwest and tells the story of Mary and Joseph seeking shelter in Bethlehem. Usually children portray Mary and Joseph, with friends, family, and neighbors taking the parts of townspeople, cruel innkeepers, and the mobile choir. The procession is usually candlelit and quite spectacular on dark December nights. Depending on community tradition, some performances of *Las Posadas* are scheduled over a period of nine nights (a novena), but many groups will perform just once, on Christmas Eve.

Still another regional drama is *Los Matachines*, which combines morality play, folk dance, and the boogeyman and is usually performed on Christmas Eve and Christmas morning. A cast of New World characters plays out this Old World form: El Monarca (Montezuma), La Malinche (translator and mistress of Cortés), El Abuelo (the old boogeyman character that carried a whip and often terrorized children by asking if they had been "good"), and the comic El Torito (little bull).

The malinches dance in two lines as the main characters act out a centuries-old drama of good versus evil. The characters fight and argue and do their best to disrupt the dancers' order and rhythm, but eventually the characters conquer the stage and slay the little bull. It is arguable how clearly the modern versions reflect the ancient sword dances that depict the conflict between the Moors and the Spaniards, but audiences love the dramas and perpetuate the tradition nonetheless.

On the more extreme side, there are four communities documented in New Mexico and Arizona that still enact the passion of Christ quite literally, complete with nails driven through the actor's hands and feet. There are also designated days when the devout will strip off their shirts and make a pilgrimage while flagellating themselves with leather whips until their blood runs down them in streams. These performances, though endorsed within their sect, are not part of the mainstream, endorsed by the church, or tolerated publicly. There is a line in the communal ethos that these devotions overstep, and it would be difficult to locate them folklorically as acceptable performances within the larger tradition.

The festival schedule of the Southwest generally follows the Catholic calendar of feast days and religious celebrations, or the dominant Anglo (here meaning Euro-centric conquerors of America) calendar of military holidays and updated pagan celebrations. By far the most significant of the calendrical festivals in the Southwest is El Dia de los Muertos (the Day of the Dead), but its location between the Anglo Halloween and the Catholic All Souls Day has hidden it from public recognition until relatively recently.

El Dia de los Muertos is a time for the families of the deceased to commemorate the dead, commune with ancestors through the serving of a symbolic meal, and tend to grave sites. Family members will clean and decorate the graves of their ancestors during the day and then return to local cemeteries after dark, carrying the favorite foods of the deceased for a shared meal and a system of offerings. Many believe that the souls of the dead are free to wander the earth at this time, and if the families are there in the *campo santo* (sacred place, cemetary), the deceased are appeased.

Rites of Passage

According to anthropologists Arnold Van Gennup and Clifford Geertz, human ritual celebrations peak around rites of passage—the movement of humans from one social stage to another. Clearly birth, puberty, marriage, childbearing, old age, and death are hallmarks of the human progression through life's experiences, and the varied cultures of the Southwest celebrate or mark each stage.

Prior to the birth there are corn pollen ceremonies, ritual cleansings, or baby showers. The mother-to-be is instructed in the strangeness of status change and the responsibilities of parenthood. Her social network is reestablished so that she can call on those it includes in times of need. Her husband is similarly trained in the duties of fatherhood and advised of the limits of his activities. The community pulls together to instruct the soon-to-be parents in their expected roles and has done so for thousands of years, well before Lamaze classes came to be.

Both the Hopi and Navajo have elaborate birth ceremonies, including the isolation of the birth mother and the dressing and ceremonial treatment of the newborn. Black, Asian, Anglo, and many Hispanic cultures do much the same by shuffling the birth mother off to a hospital and isolating her in a maternity ward and removing her from friends and family and traditional caregiving networks. The birth is attended by a cultural stranger with complete authority, and the presence of family is allowed or disallowed by hospital personnel. There are obviously stories aplenty of babies born in unexpected places like taxi cabs, restaurants, or rest rooms. Outwardly these are hilarious cautionary tales, but inwardly they are stern reminders to follow cultural norms and to be dutiful. Childbirth is the renewal (and ergo, preservation) of the culture, and it is attended to with the utmost of concern.

In another vein, there are as many cautionary tales about mothers delivering "inappropriate babies" of mixed race or features. Popular legendry locates the inebriated mother at the bachelorette party when the beautiful but other-raced male stripper puts on an incredible show culminating in "one last fling" before marriage. Nine or so months later a baby is born that is obviously not the husband's.

Curiously, and not surprisingly, few such tales exist for potential fathers. This is blatant gender and racial inequality, but its impact is rendered all the more significant because the mother literally internalizes the taboo and carries the child to term, to the horror of all the relatives and in-laws. At birth there is no hiding that the social restriction has been violated, and at a time set for celebration, the family and society goes into group shock.

Puberty is another time for family shock, and every established culture has devised means to deal with it in ritualized ways. The Hopi puberty ceremony for girls is elaborate, somber, and formal. Ritual separation, instruction, and eventual reincorporation mark their change in status. Anglos, if they are wealthy enough, have devised cotillions, high school proms, and middle school maturation classes to mark the changes in their young women.

Few rituals exist for male maturation or transition into manhood anymore. In days of yore young males were considered men with their first kill or their assumption of adult duties. The modern state has largely taken control of marking male passages through normalized high school graduations, drivers licenses, military selective service, and drinking and voting ages. There are voluntary rites like achieving Eagle Scout rank, getting a job, or going to college, all of which mark a change in status for young men, but these are not universal.

Among Hispanics in the Southwest there remains a pivotal pubertal hallmark for young women, the *quinceanera* (fifteenth birthday). Akin to the coming out party, the *quinceanera* calls on every possible family member, friend, and neighbor to finance the elaborate and expensive function and to recognize the young woman's change in status. Although usually accompanied by a special mass for the honoree church officials recently have attempted to normalize the *quinceanera* into more of a religious occasion (similar to confirmations, bar mitzvahs, and bat mitzvahs); however the community has come to expect a grand show.

Gowns, attendants, bands, and caterers for a *quinceanera* rival the most exclusive weddings, and several families can go deeply in debt for this. This is a culture's investment in its own continued existence, but it depends entirely on the customary system of *compadrazgo* (ritual co-parenthood) that supports almost every social function in the Hispanic Southwest.

Compadrazgo is a system of social interdependence somewhat akin to godparenthood, but with deeper roots and a far more binding commitment. With the birth of a child, the parents will seek out potential *compadres* who can be called on to assist (spiritually, physically, and often financially) with the raising of the child. There are status concerns with the selection of the *compadres* but more important is the binding together of families with a sense of mutual obligation. *Compadrazgo* ties, over time, will connect the entire community and thus put the responsibility of communal success on everyone's shoulders.

Marriages certainly signify a status change, but they have undergone a normalization of late not unlike fast-food menus. As national television broadcasts "reality" show ceremonies and morning news shows let America plan weddings for a lucky couple, viewers lose ethnic and community uniqueness in favor of homogenized fashion. Bridal magazines, elaborate trade shows, and even talk shows now dictate what most of America wears and eats and dances at their weddings.

Occasionally the Czech wedding still features beer and BBQ, guests at a Jewish wedding are hoisted aloft in a chair, the color red is in evidence in the Chinese wedding, and the Greek wedding features dancers with handkerchiefs, but for the most part American weddings have grown wearily familiar. The bride wears white, the groom wears black, and the mother of the groom wears beige and sits on the right.

Some receptions vary by the amount of liquor or food served, whether or not dancing is allowed, or if the guests collect money for the bride and groom at any point. There are usually pranks associated with the couple's car—tying cans to the bumper, lewd slogans written in shoe polish, petroleum jelly on door handles and gearshifts—all designed to mildly annoy or inconvenience the couple. In some areas it is considered great fun to try and steal the couple's luggage or to gain access to the honeymoon bedroom (to delay the newlyweds from consummating the marriage). In many parts of the Southwest this ritualized annoyance is called a Shivaree (or *charivari*) and can last all night if allowed to continue.

And finally, there is death. Funeral customs have undergone much the same mainstreaming that weddings have since death became an industry. With powerful political lobbyists influencing legislators to pass laws making home burials illegal in most states, the deceased literally becomes the property of the state. Death is now "pronounced" and declared by professionals. The deceased is handled only by a licensed facility (for autopsy, funeral preparation, or cremation), and the family is kept at a secure and sterile distance.

Mourning customs still exist, but their performance and duration have been altered by death's institutionalization. Some widows will wear black for a respectful period, some households still turn clocks and mirrors around to face walls, and some families will close all the windows and draperies in the home. Most Navajo still refuse to touch a dead body or enter the *hogan* (dwelling) where the person died. Most Catholics will attend a funeral mass and light candles for the departed soul. Many Irish will still hold a wake for the deceased.

The funeral is frequently handled by the mortuary company—from viewing and visitation to memorial service to graveside ceremonies. Flowers are still common but are losing popularity to charitable donations made in the name of the deceased. Church services and the inevitable bringing of food to the family are still quite prevalent, as are obituary notices in the local paper and funeral processions to the cemetery.

Perhaps the only folk performances of grief allowed anymore are the public displays beyond the reach of the state. Something as simple as putting fresh flowers or decorations on the grave is one public display, but *descansos* (roadside crosses), *altarcitas* (small altars), memorial poetry in the classified section of the newspaper, and a ritualized scattering of cremated remains involve more elaborate performances.

MATERIAL CULTURE

Material culture refers to the built or created environment, which is the human response to a sense of lack. If humans are cold, they construct shelter and clothing. If they are hungry, they fabricate tools to gather food. Humans have manipulated their environment since before they could be called humans, and over time certain patterns in their manipulations evolved. This emergent sense of an aesthetic helped guide human efforts and served to normalize responses. A house is recognizable as a house because it exhibits culturally acceptable qualities of house-ness.

It is important to a discussion of folklore to at least mention how the folklorist views human material performances. Each time an object is intentionally altered from one form into another by humans, art is performed at some level. When the woodcutter takes a chainsaw to a tree stump and finishes with a likeness of a bear or an eagle or anything at all, art is at work. When the welder welds each link of a chain together to support a mailbox in the front yard, art is at work. Whether nailing crushed beer cans to the outside of a house or burying tires halfway into the ground along the sidewalk and painting them white, art is at work.

Defining art is an argument for the ages and a proprietary battle royale but perhaps the only constant in the conflict is the concept of how aesthetics determine whether an object is art or folk art or garbage. Because of potential commercial interests, all definitions become skewed when there is a "buyer" present. What is significant to the study of folklore is the relationship between the object and its creator, with a strong focus on the creator's community.

Any artist, whether folk or formal, makes decisions on the basis of what is allowable as art in his or her community. The Taos artist might decide to break convention and mix media and metaphors in ways that the community is not used to or is even shocked by. Folk art, often closely tied to function, tends to hold more closely to traditional expressions because that is what the community expects. Community expectation often determines form and expression, and if a folk artist wishes her work to be acceptable to or understood by the community, then he or she must conform—somewhat—to traditional expectation. Rearranging traditional stone settings in a turquoise squashblossom necklace may still be acceptable within the larger tradition, but soldering a toaster to silver is simply beyond the allowable standard. It may still be art, but it is no longer folk art.

For many the distinction between art and folk art lies in the extent of the artist's training and in an adherence to form and function. For folk artists, training is largely a life spent within the community aesthetic. A chair is recognized as a chair due its chairlike qualities. A hand-thrown water jug may have an experimental glaze or nontraditional design on the outside, but it cannot have a gaping hole in the bottom and expect to be recognized within the tradition.

Folklorist John O. West spent a lifetime documenting traditional arts along the Rio Grande from source to sea, and he recognized motive over money in every folk-art expression. From *grutas* (religious yard shrines) to grave decorations, West discovered that devotion was at the heart of each performance. Even in the case of the New Mexico *santeros* (saint makers) who carve or paint depictions of saints, religious devotion is at the center of their craft.

There will always be outside collectors who inflate the monetary value of folk art and remove it from its original context, but few artists within the tradition cater to their whims. Obviously there are artists who will cater to the collector trade, but they have moved too far beyond the acceptable parameters of the community aesthetic to be considered folk. Of course there are other folk-art forms that dwell in this liminal zone between tradition and consumerist cooptation—foodways, architecture, clothing, and so forth—and they each have undergone peaks and valleys of popularity at the hands of monied outsiders with no knowledge of the community expectation from which they were born.

FOLK MEDICAL SYSTEMS

Every group in human history has developed its own responses to ill health. Some cultures have developed elaborate pharmacopia and belief systems designed to maintain both body and spirit. Several Native American groups with shamanistic traditions such as the Apache understand disease as a spiritual ill. A sick individual is a potential threat to the whole community, so healing becomes a communal affair. Many disease etiologies are considered the consequences of social violations: improper observation of ceremonial proscriptions, gender taboos, and even self-abuse are cause for disruption in the social order.

For several Asian communities in the more urban areas of the Southwest such as the Texas Gulf Coast, medical responses often begin with traditional healing methods. Herbal shops, acupuncture and acupressure clinics, and practitioners of healing massage can be found in areas of concentrated Asian populations.

On a somewhat more sinister side, two versions of *vodou* (voodoo) operate in the region. Though vodou and *Santeria* (a syncretistic Caribbean religion) deal less with maintaining good health and more with manipulating people and outcomes, they utilize ritual and belief systems to affect health. *Brujeria* (witchcraft) is a similar response with decidedly New World origins. In Brujeria there are three distinct types of magic: red, white, and black. Red magic is intended to cause harm, black magic to cause death, and *Curanderismo* (white magic) to restore health.

Curanderismo is a much more complicated and dynamic system than many scholars and most outsiders give it credit for. What some have termed folk psychiatry, Curanderismo is simultaneously herbalism, pharmacology, drama, social work, psychology, and religious instruction.

To understand Curanderismo in its cultural context, it is important to understand the hierarchy of healing at work in the traditional Mexican American Southwest. Primary care of most ills usually begins in the home, with the mother providing the initial diagnostics and treatment. If the ailment persists, then the mother may seek the advice and intervention of someone more experienced, her mother or grandmother, perhaps. If this is ineffective, there are usually neighborhood healers (almost always older women) and skilled *parteras* (midwives).

At the top of this hierarchy is the regional curandero, made famous by low-status birth, enduring a near-death experience and religious conversion, physical disfigurement, celibacy, miraculous cures, and poverty resulting from the utter refusal to accept payment for services. Healing is understood to be a gift from God and to openly charge for healing services would threaten the gift. Two healers who earned folk-saint status as curanderos—El Nino Fidencio and Don Pedrito Jaramillo—became so famous that cults of their faithful developed to continue petitioning them even after their deaths. The grave sites of each of these men are nothing less than shrines to their efficacy and prowess.

The success of any curandero is maintained narratively, either through personal testimonies or local legendry. Frequently Curanderismo is legitimized in opposition to Western medical practices. Hundreds of stories circulate where the gringo doctor charges thousands of dollars and tries many different cures before giving up. The desperate patient finally goes to the curandero who prescribes something simple and ingenious, affecting an immediate cure at no cost.

Perhaps the most intriguing aspect of Curanderismo is that it involves maladies unique to its cultural context and performance. Diseases such as *caida de la mollera* (fallen fontanel) and *empacho* (improper eating) may have some Western medical parallels, but *mal de ojo* (evil eye; literally, "evil from the eye"), *susto* (extreme fright or shock), and *mal puesto* (curse or witchcraft) offer explanations and demand treatments that only the host culture can provide.

Mal de ojo might translate best as *envy*. According to custom, if one person covets something belonging to another and gazes at it longingly, all the negative energy from envy and jealousy can be transferred to the object of desire or admiration. To prevent such a tragedy, the admirer must touch the object and release any tension between them. Though this involves elements of con-

Pen and ink illustration of Don Pedrito walking with a staff by Jose Cisneros, published by the Texas Folklore Society. © Texas Folklore Society.

tagious magic as ancient as all life on earth, it also enforces a sense of communal access and sharing. Just like the *maerchen* (fairy tale) of Sleeping Beauty when the one witch excluded from the princess' birthday party causes all the harm, guarding against *mal de ojo* is a social act of inclusion.

Curing *mal de ojo* (characterized by a general listlessness and malaise) is most often done with a combination of divination with a raw egg and the sweeping of the body with branches to cleanse the evil. The raw egg is rubbed over the patient's body before it is cracked open into a glass of water. Though diagnostics vary by region and household, generally the egg yolk floating in the glass will develop a spot, or eye, after some time, thereby confirming the malady and prompting the proper treatment of sweeping and prayer.

A victim of *susto* is believed to have undergone a traumatic experience beyond the pale of social convention. Victims of abuse, witnesses to crimes or tragedies, or those experiencing a sudden personal loss are extremely susceptible. With *susto*, the patient appears as if in shock, and the egg diagnostics can often produce a picture of the shock's source. Treatments usually involve ritual cleansing and prayer, but certainly the attention and concern of the community helps the cure along.

Among the *males naturales* (natural evils) that are unique to *Curanderismo*, *caida de la mollera* (fallen fontanel) is perhaps an affliction of attention, or lack thereof. Health departments in Mexico treat *caida* as dehydration, but the folk remedy requires the mother to spend countless hours in meticulous ritual with the baby involved. It is difficult to say if the cure is treating the symptoms or the caregiver, allowing her socially prescribed time to spend with the

Don Pedrito Jaramillo: Benefactor of Humanity

Perhaps the most famous curandero and folk healer in the Southwest, Don Pedrito Jaramillo began life in Guadalajara, Jalisco, Mexico, and enjoyed a rather scandalous youth. Offered a job in 1881 with a mule train headed north into Texas to deliver liquor to a large hacienda for a party, Pedro accepted, expecting to "see the world." He liked the country, and after a brief return trip to Mexico, Pedro Jaramillo moved to the Los Olmos Ranch near present-day Falfurrias, Texas.

Pedro, perhaps as a consequence of his misspent youth, endured a horrible affliction of the nose, and according to biographer Ruth Dodson, was in so much pain one night that he fell headlong into a pond and used the mud to treat his pain. After a time his nose healed, leaving but a disfiguring scar. One night as he slept, Pedro received a message from Heaven that he had been given the gift of healing to serve all humanity. He was instructed that his master at the ranch was in pain, and Pedro got up to prescribe the first thing that came to his mind—a tepid bath over the course of three days. His master was cured, and Pedro's career as a healer had begun.

Essential to Don Pedro's cures was his incredibible humility and refusal to accept payment for his God-given gift. He never asked for payments, but frequently patients would leave money of gifts of food behind. These, in turn, he redistributed to the next patients. The grocery store in Alice reported that Pedro would often order $500 worth of groceries at a time (1890s). According to Dodson, one wealthy benefactor deeded Don Pedro one hundred acres of land, which Pedro turned into a farm to grow produce and herbs he needed for cures and for feeding his patients. When he would have to travel to heal someone, he always left groceries for those pilgrims who were bound to arrive while he was gone.

During the cataclysmic drought of 1893 that lasted several years, many agree that Don Pedrito personally fed and kept most of northern Starr County, Texas, alive. When they built a post office nearby and named it Paisano, Don Pedro began conducting the majority of his healings by mail. Everyone knew he was clairvoyant, and postal carriers reported over 500 patients waiting outside Don Pedrito's *jacal* on any given day.

Don Pedrito Jaramillo died on July 3rd, 1907, in Starr County, Texas. His gravesite is a shrine to this day. His power and sacrifice will be remembered.

newborn and forcing others in the family to deal with housework and cooking and the innumerable chores that might detract from infant care.

Empacho is really a matter of what John West termed *surfeit*—eating beyond reason, whether in terms of amounts or food choices. Too much of a good thing or even a bit of the wrong thing could lodge itself against the stomach or digestive tract and cause problems. Treatments are often manipulative and painful and perhaps designed to teach the sufferer a lesson about food choices. In many ways, *Curanderismo* serves as behavior modification, health care, and social correction simultaneously.

The continued popularity of *Curanderismo* is not hard to explain. With ancient origins and persisting due to its efficacy, *Curanderismo* addresses the physical, the cultural, and the spiritual simultaneously. It is both holistic and comprehensive. Approximately 4,000 years before the American Medical Association began doing battle with HMOs, peoples of the Southwest enjoyed an effective medical system that made sense.

Don Pedrito's Cure-All

Once a rich man became very ill in his stomach. He refused to go to the curandero, claiming that he could afford the "real doctors" in town. He tried doctor after doctor, but all they could do was run tests, write prescriptions, and give him bill after bill for their services.

For a very long time the rich man went to the doctors in town, but he never got better. Finally, one day, his gardener found him near-death on the patio and took him to see Don Pedrito Jaramillo, the curandero.

There was a long line of sick and poor people in front of Don Pedrito's *jacal*, but the rich man shouted that he was rich and important and should be taken care of first. Don Pedrito motioned him in and began to examine him. After a lengthy exam and careful diagnosis, Don Pedrito told the rich man to buy a goat.

"A goat?" the man exclaimed. "Why a goat?"

"Because I need you to collect seven goat pellets from your yard every day and brew them in a tea. Drink this tea three times a day with every meal. If you to do this for seven days without fail, I promise you will be cured."

The rich man thanked Don Pedrito and instructed his gardener to give him a great sack of money. Since Don Pedrito never accepted payment for his cures, he in turn gave that money to all the poor people waiting to see him.

A week later the gardener came back to visit Don Pedrito and to tell him that his cure worked—the rich man was in fine health.

The gardener laughed, "I enjoyed your little joke on my employer—making him drink tea made from goat pellets. I think it humbled him a little."

Don Pedrito replied with a wry smile, "No my friend, I was not trying to humble him very much. I knew that one of the *yerbas* around here would cure him, but I couldn't remember which one. I knew the goat would eat a little of everything, so a tea made from his pellets would certainly work."

CONCLUSION

Folklore in the Southwest, like folklore everywhere, is the product of human interaction—folk performances in a particular time and place that respond to immediate circumstances. Although mass and instant communication seem to blunt the importance of time and space, folklore remains distinctly regional as humans react to their physical, cultural, or spiritual environments. Southwestern folklore evolves from ethnic, religious, occupational, age, and other human factors—all shaping people's own sense of the aesthetic and creating the foundation for tradition. So Southwestern humor, ballads, folk medicine, ghost stories, legends, holidays and celebrations, material culture (folk arts, dress), and folk medicine all demonstrate strong connections to the long prehistory and history of the varied peoples of the Southwest. Despite the homogenizing power of technology, they will continue to do so.

RESOURCE GUIDE

Printed Sources

See also most all of the Texas Folklore Society Publications for an enormous collection of myths, legends, and tales.

Abernethy, Francis Edward, ed. *Folk Art in Texas*. Publications of the Texas Folklore Society, Number XLV. Dallas: Southern Methodist University Press, 1985.

Anderson, John Q., ed. *Texas Folk Medicine: 1,333 Cures, Remedies, Preventives, and Health Practices*. Austin: The Encino Press, 1970.

Barrera, Alberto. "Mexican-American Roadside Crosses in Starr County." In Hecho En Tejas: *Texas-Mexican Folk Arts and Crafts*, ed. Joe S. Graham. Publications of the Texas Folklore Society, Number L. Denton: University of North Texas Press, 1991.

Basso, Keith H. *The Cibecue Apache*. New York: Holt, Rinehart and Winston, Inc., 1970.

Boatright, Mody C., ed. *The Healer of Los Olmos and Other Mexican Lore*. Dallas: Southern Methodist University Press, 1951.

Boatright, Mody C., Wilson M. Hudson, and Allen Maxwell, eds. *Texas Folk and Folklore*. Dallas: Southern Methodist University Press, 1954.

Bright, William. *A Coyote Reader*. Berkeley: University of California Press, 1993.

Brunvand, Jan Harold. *The Choking Doberman and Other "New" Urban Legends*. New York: W.W. Norton and Company, 1984. See also by Brunvand: *The Vanishing Hitchhiker*, *The Baby Train*, *Curses! Broiled Again*, and *The Mexican Pet*.

Coffin, Tristram P., ed. *Indian Tales of North America: An Anthology for the Adult Reader*. Austin: University of Texas Press, 1961.

Dodson, Ruth. "The Curandero of Los Olmos." In *Texas Folk and Folklore*, ed. Mody C. Boatright, Wilson M. Hudson, and Allen Maxwell. Dallas: Southern Methodist University Press, 1954.

Dozier, Edward P. *Hano: A Tewa Indian Community in Arizona*. New York: Holt, Rinehart and Winston, Inc., 1966.

———. *The Pueblo Indians of North America*. New York: Holt, Rinehart and Winston, Inc., 1970.

Everett, Holly. *Roadside Crosses in Contemporary Memorial Culture*. Denton: University of North Texas Press, 2002.

Farrer, Claire R. *Thunder Rides a Black Horse: Mescalero Apaches and the Mythic Present*. Prospect Heights, IL: Waveland Press, Inc., 1994.

Giddings, Ruth Warner. *Yaqui Myths and Legends*. Tucson: University of Arizona Press, 1978.

Glassie, Henry. *Material Culture*. Bloomington: Indiana University Press, 1999.

Graham, Joe S. "The Role of the Curandero in the Mexican American Folk Medical System in West Texas." In *American Folk Medicine*, ed. Wayland D. Hand. Los Angeles: University of California Press, 1980.

———, ed. *Hecho en Tejas: Texas-Mexican Folk Arts and Crafts*. Publications of the Texas Folklore Society, Number L. Denton: University of North Texas Press, 1991.

Hackett, David G., ed. *Religion and American Culture: A Reader*. New York: Routledge, 1995.

Hymes, Dell. *"In Vain I Tried to Tell You": Essays in Native American Ethnopoetics*. Philadelphia: University of Pennsylvania Press, 1981.

Kiev, Ari. *Curanderismo: Mexican-American Folk Psychiatry*. New York: The Free Press, 1968.

Kluckhohn, Clyde. *Navajo Witchcraft*. Boston: Beacon Press, 1944.

Kroeber, Karl, ed. *Traditional Literatures of the American Indian: Texts and Interpretations*. Lincoln: University of Nebraska Press, 1981.

Leslie, Charles, ed. *Asian Medical Systems: A Comparative Study*. Los Angeles: University of California Press, 1976.

Marriott, Alice, and Carol K. Rachlin. *American Indian Mythology*. New York: Thomas Y. Crowell Company, 1968.

Rothenberg, Jerome, ed. *Shaking the Pumpkin: Traditional Poetry of the Indian North Americas*. Garden City, New York: Doubleday and Company, Inc., 1972.

Santino, Jack. *All Around the Year: Holidays and Celebrations in American Life*. Chicago: University of Illinois Press, 1994.

Simmons, Marc. *Witchcraft in the Southwest: Spanish and Indian Supernaturalism on the Rio Grande*. Lincoln: University of Nebraska Press, 1974.

Spicer, Edward H., ed. *Ethnic Medicine in the Southwest*. Tucson: The University of Arizona Press, 1981.

Sproul, Barbara C. *Primal Myths: Creation Myths Around the World*. San Francisco: Harper San Francisco, 1979.

Tedlock, Dennis, and Barbara Tedlock, eds. *Teachings From the American Earth: Indian Religion and Philosophy*. New York: Liveright Publishing Corporation, 1975.

Toelken, Barre, and Tacheeni Scott. "Poetic Retranslation and the 'Pretty Languages' of Yellowman." In *Traditional Literatures of the American Indian: Texts and Interpretations*, ed. Karl Kroeber. Lincoln: University of Nebraska Press, 1981.

Toor, Frances. *A Treasury of Mexican Folkways*. New York: Crown Publishers, 1947.

Waters, Frank. *Masked Gods: Navajo and Pueblo Ceremonialism*. Athens, Ohio: Swallow Press, 1950.

West, John O., ed. *Mexican-American Folklore: Legends, Songs, Festivals, Proverbs, Crafts, Tales of Saints, of Revolutionaries, and More*. Little Rock: August House, 1988.

Zimdars-Swartz, Sandra L. *Encountering Mary: Visions of Mary from La Salette to Medjugorje*. New York: Avon Books, 1991.

Web Sites, Museums, and Collections

General

American Folklore: Tales by Region
http://www.americanfolklore.net/rr.html#five

American Folklore Society
http://afsnet.org/

American Studies Electronic Crossroads
http://crossroads.georgetown.edu/index.html

Festivals by State
http://www.festivalusa.com/festivals.htm

Fife Folklore Archives, Utah State University
http://library.usu.edu/Folklo/index.html

Internet Sacred Text Archive
http://www.sacred-texts.com/nam/sw/

J. Frank Dobie's Guide to Life and Literature of the Southwest online
http://users.erols.com/hardeman/lonestar/olbooks/dobie/dobie29.htm

Mexican American Folklore
http://www.lasculturas.com/lib/libFolklore.php

Southwest Regional Humanities Center
http://swrhc.txstate.edu

Urban legends
http://www.urbanlegends.com/

Arizona

Arizona Folklore Preserve
http://www.arizonafolklore.com/

Arizona State Museum
http://www.statemuseum.arizona.edu

Heard Museum
http://www.heard.org/

Navajo Nation Museum
PO Box 1840
Window Rock, AZ 86515

Pioneer Living History Village
http://www.Pioneer-Arizona.com/

Prescott Folklore Center
http://www.thefolklorecenter.com/

Southwest Folklore Collection, University of Arizona
http://www.library.arizona.edu/branches/spc/homepage/Manu6.htm

Superstition Mountain Museum
http://www.superstitionmountainmuseum.org/

White Mountain Apache Tribe
http://www.wmat.nsn.us/

Nevada

Nevada Native American Culture Society
HC 10 Box 10795

Nevada Yesterdays
http://www.knpr.org/nevadayesterdays/list.cfm

Western Folklife Center (Elko, NV)
http://www.westernfolklife.org

New Mexico

Acoma Pueblo
P.O. Box 309
Acoma Pueblo, NM 87034
http://www.puebloofacoma.org

Fort Burgwin Libary, SMU in Taos
http://www.smu.edu/cul/FBL/religion.htm

Indian Pueblo Cultural Center
http://www.indianpueblo.org/

Museum of Internatonal Folk Art, Santa Fe
http://www.moifa.org/home.php

Native Rhythm and Roots Festival
http://www.santafe.net/nativerootsnrhythms/overview.html

Texas

Handbook of Texas
http://www.tsha.utexas.edu/handbook/online/index.html

Sam Houston Folk Festival
http://www.samhoustonfolkfestival.com/

Southwestern Writer's Collection
http://www.library.txstate.edu/swwc/

Texas Folklife Festival
http://www.texasfolklifefestival.org/

Texas Folklife Resources
http://www.texasfolklife.org/

Texas Folklore Society
http://www.texasfolkloresociety.org

The University of Texas Institute of Texan Cultures at San Antonio
http://www.texancultures.utsa.edu/public/

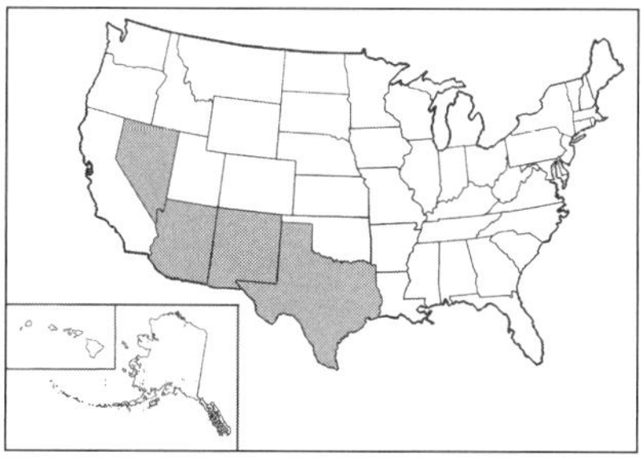

FOOD

Jay Cox Hayward

Anthropologist Claude Lévi-Strauss wrote that the "cooking of a society is a language in which it unconsciously translates its structure—or else resigns itself, still unconsciously, to revealing its contradictions."[1] The Southwest is no different—in its foods and recipes, one can see all the structure and contradiction inherent in the culture of the region.

In many ways, Southwestern food is a foreign language. Dishes bear names from Spanish or native words, incorporate foods that seem exotic or spicy to outsiders, or are prepared in unconventional ways. In this very fact, one can see the diversity and conflict that epitomizes Southwestern culture.

To unravel the secrets of Southwestern food, one must examine the movement of people into and out of the region since contact shortly after 1492. Many of the culinary influences in Southwest cuisine can be traced, of course, to indigenous cultures, but overwhelmingly today's barbeque, chili, tacos, and Mexican food are influenced by the outsiders who came to the area from somewhere else–conquerors, missionaries, travelers, settlers, and tourists. What is now considered typical "Southwestern" food has shifted toward introduced foods, due to their portability and the adaptability.

Of course, the demand for familiar foods from the white and European settlers flocking to the area has introduced a lot of northern and European dishes into the mix. Many of these foodways remain intact in the region. For example, the German, Czech, and Polish cuisines in central Texas have little in common with more commonly recognized barbeque and Mexican foods. Yet for many, these are a big part of Southwestern cuisine. Likewise, the Basque food in Nevada or the Thai and Vietnamese food in urban centers such as Phoenix, Albuquerque, El Paso, Dallas, and Houston are an essential part of Southwest foodways.

In fact, it might be appropriate to say that there is no one Southwest cuisine since it is a large region populated by a patchwork of people and cultures, some native, some long-settled immigrants, some recently arrived. Drawn from sources as diverse as its indigenous people, earliest Spanish settlers in the time of Cortés and Coronado, missionaries, Mexican residents, and the wave of white miners, cattlemen, and settlers in the Nevada, New Mexico, and Arizona territories, food in the Southwest is a language full of borrowed words and secret idioms. However, translating Southwest cuisine(s) requires a map, a working knowledge of the geography and history of the region and a sense of adventure, for the story of this language is the story of the Southwest itself.

HISTORICAL NOTES ON SOUTHWEST FOODWAYS

Early Native Foods

Before the conquest of the Southwest, chiles, corn, and a variety of lesser-known foods were staples in the diets of the indigenous people, with wild animals providing fresh meat. Depending on the locale, altitude, and available water, tribal groups used their resources to produce crops, save seeds, raise animals, and live off wild animals and plants as well.[2] Meat was added to the diet when hunting was good, but the staples were nut and seed flours, beans, vegetables, and fruit, including the pads and fruit of cacti such as the *nopal* (prickly pear). Daily life was structured around the preparation and gathering of food, and food was also an integral part of the religious and social life of a tribe. Among the Hopi of Arizona, for example, when a child is presented to the sun and named on the twenty-first day of its life, they put a dab of sacred cornmeal on the baby's tongue and say they have planted the seed of the Hopi culture, which in time will grow in the child and make him or her a Hopi.

Corn masa for gorditas is prepared in mass quantities at the Texas Folklife Festival; the recipe is a thousand years old. Courtesy of Jay Cox Hayward.

Timeless Tools

Many of the tools used by native people throughout the Americas are still used today, unable to be improved on except by electricity-fed machines. Usually made of volcanic stone, the *metate* is an elegantly simple food processor—a large, sometimes sloping piece of stone used with a *mano* (stone bar) that grinds the grain, corn, and seeds against it. The bar is made of the same stone as the metate and is nearly as long as the metate is wide. Dry seeds and small beans were ground as is, but larger kernels were softened. Corn, for example, was treated with ash or lime to make *nixtamal* (slaked corn). Lime makes the corn's amino acids more available to metabolize, a process that, mysteriously, has not been exported along with corn. Ground on a metate, the corn becomes the soft corn dough called *masa* that is used in numerous recipes—in *piki* and *atole*, which are porridges, and more commonly today, in tortillas, tamales, or gorditas. Even today, masa is often kneaded by hand for the right consistency.

A *molcajete* is similar but is smaller and bowl-shaped; it, too, is made of volcanic stone and used with a mano. It resembles a mortar and pestle. Nearly any food to be roughly chopped, mashed, or pureed can be prepared in a molcajete.

A more recent addition, the *comal*, is a flat sheet of metal, sometimes cast iron, that sits on top of a heat source. The comal is used for cooking tortillas or anything that cannot be placed on a grill. It is extremely versatile, portable, and lightweight.

Pioneers in the Southwest

Lewis and Clark's expedition raised the interest of many people in the vast wilderness west of the Mississippi. Those who came from the northeastern United States to the Southwest found hard living but abundant natural resources. Native fruits, vegetables, animals, and grains were all cultivated and harvested to sustain the settlers, and the traditional crops of Europe and the eastern United States were adapted for these climates. Trappers, buffalo hunters, and miners all came to see what riches they could take back home.

After the U.S.-Mexican War (1846–1848), the U.S. Army began establishing outposts and sending men, sometimes families, to live in this wild land. On the heels of these settlements, others soon followed to stake a claim and start a new life. These people brought with them their cooking methods and preferences, which left a legacy of wresting sustenance from the wilderness.

Army food was characterized by hard bread, hard dried meat, and coffee so black one could reputedly cut it with a knife. There were no fancy kitchens or cooking methods; soldiers and their families ate whatever the Army could provide and what they could harvest or hunt out of the way of the Native Americans, who viewed them as an invasion force and were, for the most part, set upon vanquishing them.

Cooking with Cacti

Not many would willingly eat these prickly plants, but in fact, dwellers of the desert Southwest—native and non-native, two- and four-footed—do eat them, with great relish. Prickly pear offer two sources of food. The fruits, called *tunas*, yield a ruby red juice suitable for drinking or making jam. The pads, called *nopales*, are sliced and either cooked or pickled. Boiled and eaten plain by native tribes in the past, these days, nopales are often combined with eggs or in Mexican dishes.

The Tohono O'odham are known for their annual harvest of the fruit of *Cereus gigantus*, or the Arizona state tree, the Saguaro (sah-WAHR-oh). Growing upwards of forty ft., these desert giants blossom in the spring and yield a rich, ruby-red fruit that has a tough rind and hundreds of tiny black seeds inside. The fruit is respectfully knocked off the plant using long poles often made of Saguaro ribs. Both the seeds and the fruit pulp of the Saguaro are used. The pulp is sometimes made into a wine called *navai't*. The rituals associated with the Saguaro harvest celebrate the advent of the much-welcomed summer rainy season.

Careful handling is required when harvesting and preparing cacti, for the spines can be microscopic but unpleasant if lodged in one's gums. Cacti are quite versatile and can be used in many recipes calling for fruit, including ice cream and sherbets.

Other cacti are good to eat as well, but they are only one of the desert plants that native peoples gathered and prepared. There are also wild gourds and pumpkins, greens, berries, nuts, seeds, and melons (the Spanish word for watermelon is *sandia*, which is also the name of the mountain range near Albuquerque, New Mexico).

Succulents such as agave and yucca are used for many food and nonfood products. Yucca can be harvested for its edible flowers, its soap-bearing leaves, and its fibers, which can be made into ropes and baskets. The agave plant, too, provides food, juice, medicine, cosmetics, and textiles. The larger agave plant in Mexico is the source for tequila and mescal.

Carolyn Niethammer's recipe books explain the lore of these foods and give practical tips for preparation and recipes (see Resource Guide at the end of this chapter).

The Southwest as a region was more thoroughly affected by another influence. Soon after the conquest of Mexico in the 1500s, the Catholic church and the missionary priests followed to build churches all across Mexico and up into what is now the U.S. Southwest—California, Arizona, Nevada, Colorado, New Mexico, and Texas.

Catholic missionaries were inclined to learn about the indigenous people in order to win them over to Christianity. Living among the people for much longer than settlers from the United States, the friars brought much more than biblical teachings to the Southwest.

Born Eusebius Chinus in Segno, Italy, as a young boy Father Eusebio Kino studied in Tirol, Austria, under Jesuits and became a Jesuit priest himself after a life-threatening illness that led him to vow allegiance to the priesthood. His education was first-rate and included astronomy and mathematics. He hoped for a mission to China but complied with the wishes of his superiors and went to New Spain, eventually arriving there in 1681. He changed his name to Kino because of this change in destination, *chino* meaning "Chinese man" in Italian and Spanish.

He first visited Baja California and then traveled to Sonora and the Pimería Alta, as the region is known. Kino became fluent in the Piman languages and seemed to be a fatherly and popular figure with them.

During his influence, he introduced cattle and wheat to the area. These foodstuffs are evident today in the Sonoran-style foods that rely heavily on beef (*carne seca*, *carne asada*, *birria*) and dairy products, such as cheese and sour cream. The large, translucent, and delicious flour tortillas used even today and that replaced somewhat the use of soft corn masa for tortillas and tamales reflect his influence.

The "Bean Eaters"

On his first visit to the U.S. Southwest (then Mexico) in 1694, Father Eusebio Kino encountered a southern Arizona tribe numbering in the thousands—the Tohono O'odham. Formerly known as the Papago, which means "bean eaters," this tribe was known for its ability to sustain itself in the seemingly meager surroundings of the arid desert lands. In the 1980s, the tribe officially changed its name to Tohono O'odham, which means "Desert People" in their language.

Father Kino was the first white person to travel to this region on a Catholic mission. He helped establish missions through Sonora, the desert region that extends up from Mexico into Arizona. With him, he brought wheat and cattle, and subsequently, cheese, flour, and beef were introduced into the native diet. Still, the O'odham relied heavily on their ages-old agricultural practices, making the best of intermittent rains and seed saving. This diet consisted of beans, both wild and cultivated, and bean flours, corn, cactus and cactus fruits, chiltepins, melons, various squashes and gourds, and wild meat from birds, rabbits, and javelinas.

When water resources began to be depleted by the pumping of groundwater for the emerging cities and towns in the region, the O'odham's agrarian culture was disrupted, and they began to adopt the "junk" foods of the settlers. As a result the incidence of obesity and Type II diabetes steadily climbed. Studies done by medical researchers and ethnobotanists have revealed that a return to the traditional diverse, high-fiber, low-cholesterol diet diminishes and even reverses the effects of these modern-day diseases in the Tohono O'odham.[3]

In the 1980s an initiative to reclaim this agricultural past was born. Native Seeds/SEARCH (Southwest Endangered Arid Lands Resources Clearinghouse) endeavors to harvest and save heirloom seeds of varieties and species that are native to this region and its people. Gary Paul Nabhan's work in ethnobotany and conservation has been hugely instrumental in raising awareness of this cause and in building the nonprofit organization that continues today.

The Native Seeds/SEARCH community has a catalog, store, and Web site. The work to revive and preserve these important traditions encompasses everything from storytelling to seed saving to teaching farmers how to grow native crops.

The Mexican cheeses run the gamut from *queso blanco*, a soft cheese not unlike mozzarella, to *queso cotijo*, a hard, crumbly cheese that resembles feta.

A good history of Kino's missions in the region can be found in Charles Polzer's *A Kino Guide: A Life of Eusebio Franscico Kino and a Guide to His Missions and Monuments* (see Resource Guide at the end of this chapter).

Advent of Cattle and Wheat

Two food elements introduced after contact had a subtle but widespread influence: beef and dairy cattle and wheat. The presence of beef, milk, cheese, and wheat flour in regional dishes and recipes is the culinary archeological time stamps of postconquest cuisine. From corn, beans, fruits, wild game, and teas from native plants, the more readily available foods gradually shifted to bread, beans, beef, coffee, and sugar.

The vast, unfenced plains were tall with grasses. Beef and dairy cattle were domesticated (even the wily longhorns of Texas and Mexico could eventually be rounded up and driven to market), thus they were easier to raise, slaughter, and eat. The horses introduced by the Spaniards changed the way of life as well and made driving the cattle to markets profitable.

Besides beef's influence in the diet of those living in the Southwest, an entirely new way of life for this region began and changed how the land was used. Cattle raising and ranching turned large expanses of sparse grassland into a portable commodity—money on the hoof.

Circle the Chuckwagons

Though not unique to the Southwest, ranch cooking is marked by grilling, rotisserie-cooking over an open flame, slow cooking in fire pits, and cast-iron pots buried in hot coals or hung from a hook over the fire. For a large group, for example the entire feudal community of a *rancho* celebrating a festival or wedding, a calf or two were slaughtered and nearly six hundred pounds of meat had to be cooked in a few days, or it would begin to spoil.

Gary Paul Nabhan: Sustaining Native Foods and Research

Currently the Director of the Center for Sustainable Environments at Northern Arizona University in Flagstaff, Gary Paul Nabhan is a prize-winning author, conservationist, ethnobotanist, and MacArthur fellow. Among his many accomplishments is Nabhan's cofounding of Native Seeds/SEARCH, a grassroots heirloom-seed preservation and education initiative. He also spearheaded the Ironwood Alliance, which advocated for and succeeded in the establishment of the 120,000-acre Ironwoods Forest National Monument, and initiated the Traditional Native American Farmers' Association. In addition to the MacArthur Foundation "Genius" Fellowship, he has also received a Lifetime Achievement Award from the Society for Conservation Biology.

Nabhan is a first-generation Lebanese-American, an avid gardener and "subsistence hunter-gatherer," and actively involved in reinstituting native food traditions. Nabhan's writing is widely anthologized and translated and has won him the John Burroughs Medal for Nature Writing, a Western States Book Award, and a Lannan Literary Fellowship. In an effort to explore sustainable ecology, Nabhan spent a year eating only foods gathered, grown, or fished within 250 miles of his desert home.

About this year-long project, he wrote in *Coming Home to Eat*, "We have become a nation of food worriers more than food savorers. We fatalistically concede that we hardly know anything about who grew our food and how, but we are fixated on whether today's fare is more nutritious or less so, more tasty or more toxic, higher in fiber, folic acid, fat, and antioxidants or less so. . . . What do we want to be made of? What do we claim as our tastes? And what on earth do we ultimately want to taste like?"

Nothing of the slaughter went wasted. The prime cuts were prepared for the rancher's family or the feast, but the head was often prepared and buried in ashes at the barbeque. A scene from the epic Texas movie *Giant* depicts a big welcome barbeque for Elizabeth Taylor's character. At that party, they show the roasted head on the table, at which point Taylor's character faints. This delicacy is known as *barbacoa*. Traditionally, a calf's or steer's head is wrapped carefully to prevent drying out, and it is cooked in a pit of coals or over open flames. The result is tender bits of slow-cooked meat and brains, which some find delicious.

Carne asada simply means "roast beef," but it's a particularly tasty version of it. Usually carne asada is grilled or spit-roasted and basted or seasoned during cooking. This meat can be shredded, sliced, or cubed for use in anything from a tortilla to a stew.

Fajitas were first eaten in ranch communities by the undoubtedly poor hired hands. *Fajita* means "belt," a fancy term for the diaphragm muscle, which is not a prized cut of meat. The highly seasoned and thin strips of today's beef fajitas would have come from the tough meat, sliced to tenderize it and highly spiced to mask the taste of meat going bad.

Parts of meat that were not eaten right away were smoked or dried. The ranch culture along both sides of the border has given Southwestern cuisine many different forms of beef, with subregional differences in preparation from Texas to Arizona.

Carne seca is dried beef. Often, what wasn't eaten in the first week after a slaughter was set out to dry. In this way, the meat would keep indefinitely. It could be shredded, seasoned, and stewed to moisten it. Wrapped in a tortilla or stuffed into an enchilada or a burrito, carne seca is still eaten today. In the sunnier parts of the Southwest's cattle country, namely southern Arizona, it's called carne seca, and in other parts of ranch country it's known as *machaca*. The meat is marinated and seasoned, dried, and then pounded or shredded for use in various dishes.

Another food artifact from the early cattle ranch days is *menudo*. This stew is made from the honeycombed stomach of the calf or steer, also called *librilla* because its folds resemble the pages of an intricate book. It requires laborious cleaning and is combined with chiles, onions, and a small quantity of meat and spices. Mexican Americans in the Southwest still eat menudo for its hearty helping of protein and as a hangover remedy. Most small restaurants and taco stands make menudo only once a week because it is so labor intensive. In Arizona white menudo is more prominent, whereas red menudo, made red by the addition of chiles, is more prominent in Texas. However, one can find both types throughout the Southwest.

The cattle drives from Texas to railhead markets in Kansas, Colorado, Nebraska, and expanding ranches all over the West led to an interesting invention. The chuckwagon, very much a portable kitchen and larder in one, is perhaps the very first form of American fast food. The camp cookie was the alchemist who had to provide meals for anywhere from five to twenty men twice a day, usually ten to twenty miles apart. Relying heavily on dried and smoked meat, dried beans, white flour, sugar, and coffee, the basic diet for trail drivers was some kind of stewed, reconstituted beef mixed with beans, accompanied by sourdough biscuits or cornbread and coffee. The chuckwagon cook could not afford to waste anything and so would toss remnants of various vegetables foraged along the way, dried beans, tag ends of jerky and bacon, and lots and lots of the ubiquitous dried chile peppers to make this mélange, or "mess of beans," palatable.

In later years, as the trail drives prospered, the cookies would carry canned fruit and tomatoes along as well. One drover recalled that he could see how well-traveled a trail was by how many discarded cans were strewn along it.

Westward Expansion

After the California Gold Rush of 1849–1850, the West seemed to the world to be an untapped treasure trove of natural resources. The railroads were being extended and opening up more opportunities for a new life and prosperity. By coach, by rail, by sea, by horse, on foot, colonists flocked into the region. Among them were the Chinese, the Basques, and the Mormons, who have left an indelible mark on the landscape and the cuisine.

The Basques: Old Ways in a New Land

While cattle raising dominated the economy and menu in the Southwest, many groups of Europeans looked to the American West for gold to solve economic problems. Specifically, the Basque of northern Spain had been lured to the gold fields of California, but when the gold started to peter out, they ventured into the high plains of Nevada, finding a terrain amenable to their former way of life. In the old country between the Pyrenees and Cantabrian mountains along the Spanish and French border, the Basque were known for their resourcefulness and close-knit community. However, many became American colonists because of the necessity of finding food as the population of the old country became more and more congested.

The Basque sheepherders of northern Spain entered the mountains and high plains of Nevada and southern Idaho in the 1850s, applying their skills for both subsistence and market production in a market that was just developing. The Indians had by then begun to rely on sheep and goats for meat and wool, and the Basque realized that they could raise sheep and remain in the New World.

At first, the land was wide open for their sheep, but the cattle ranchers soon saw the Basque as rivals, both for the grazing and in the emergent markets for meat. But the Basque were not easily intimidated—or assimilated. They were seminomadic and used the unfenced range to roam wherever the grazing was good. For the most part, the Basque lived communally, many taking rooms in boarding houses run by or frequented by other Basques. These so-called Basque hotels were pockets of home, complete with the family-style tables and the delicious foods that were familiar to them.

As did many of the pioneers, the Basque also ended up living on remote ranches and farms, where adaptation of traditional recipes was required. Use of dried, rather than fresh, fruits in their desserts and substitution of beef for pork or lamb are evident in the memoirs and recipes of Basque settlers. But these variations were minor, and the basic character of the dishes remained intact.

Because of their strong cultural identity and their isolation in enclaves, the Basque community maintained its distinctiveness and continues to be an identifiable folk group in Nevada. Much of their cuisine can be found in that state. Restaurants still extant in Sparks, Gardnerville, Elko, and Reno serve distinctive Basque dishes such as steaks smothered in fresh garlic cloves, lamb chops, egg-dipped fried chicken, and seafood dishes.

Basque cookery seems like a blend of Spanish, Portuguese, and even French foods, yet some scholars believe that Basque cooking is much older, and thus influenced those neighboring cuisines. Particularly identifiable meals in the Basque cuisine are the Basque omelet, *piperrada vasca*, which is made of eggs, chiles, salt pork, ham, tomatoes, and parsley, and *porrusalda*, a vegetable stew based on potatoes and leeks. Cabbage and bell peppers are also prominent.

Because the Basques lived close to the Bay of Biscay, many of their traditional recipes incorporate fish and seafood, including mussels, squid, cod, and trout (in fact, another wave of colonists went to Northeastern waters to fish for cod). The abundant freshwater fish in the West lent itself well to Basque cooking early on, and now, with the ease of air freight, Basque restaurants in Nevada offer fresh paella, salt cod, and shellfish dishes very little changed from nineteenth-century European recipes.

Besides a rich variety of recipes for lamb and mutton, traditional Basque dishes also incorporate pork, beef, and poultry. Methods of cooking include baking, roasting, and *en cazuela* (slow cooking in an earthen casserole). Basque bread resembles the Dutch-oven cooking of the trail-drive cook—it is a crusty, quick-rising yeast bread cooked over coals or on the top of a pot in an open fire.

Most of the Basque in the United States were herders but not owners. After a butchering, the meat was dressed and sent to market, and the innards were left to the herders. The Basque cooked these parts of the animal, be it sheep, pig, or cow. From these came oxtail soup; *choriak* (sweetbreads) in a tomato sauce or fried in oil, garlic, and bell peppers; beef-tongue stew; heavily spiced *chorizos* (sausages), made with or without blood; and a dish of stewed entrails, called *tripoches*.

Among the long-time Basque restaurants in Nevada that still offer Old World food and hospitality are the Overland Hotel, Bar and Basque Restaurant in Gardnerville and the Restaurante Orozko in Sparks, but the most acclaimed as quintessentially Basque is Louis' Basque Corner in Reno, established in 1947.

The Chinese: From East to Old West

The Chinese came to America with the desire for riches and then stayed, quickly becoming a fundamental part of the economy of the Old West. Their cheap labor built cities and railroads and cleaned the clothes and houses of the newly rich.[4] It is believed that the railroad crews were 80 to 90 percent Chinese men, which is rarely emphasized in histories of the West.

In 1882 Congress enacted the Chinese Exclusion Act, which expressly forbade the immigration of Asian groups—Chinese, Japanese, Korean—into the United States. This law was not overturned until sweeping immigration reforms in the 1960s and 1970s. Despite this intense and systematic discrimination, the Chinese persisted, using the courts to settle their disputes, moving often to less populated areas in the territories, or banding together in urban centers in their own Chinatowns.

Many Chinese immigrants learned English, and they worked in a wide variety of occupations: as miners, railroad repairmen, barbers, cooks, waiters, house servants, doctors, store owners, launderers, and proprietors. Jobs were plentiful in a region that lacked women for traditionally female roles; the Chinese newcomers filled these gaps.

In the face of appalling working conditions, the Chinese made efforts to maintain their cultural identity through their festive dress and their food. They imported the dried and pickled foods characteristic of Chinese cooking, to the disgust of the Americans. Compared to the red meat, potatoes, eggs and boiled coffee that the Euro-Americans ate, the foods of the Chinese were "queer messes" and "loathsome to look at and taste."[5] Their staples—soy sauce, bean sprouts, pickled duck eggs and cabbage, dried seaweed and fish, green tea, and rice—were easily shipped from China or even made or grown in their new home. Additionally, their cooking tools were decidedly different from those used in Euro-American kitchens: the wok, the razor-sharp cleaver, chopsticks, and cups with no handles.[6] The railroad camps were soon well stocked with these Chinese groceries in addition to the beef, beans, and coffee.

In a description of Chinese New Year, territorial newspapers in Arizona and Nevada referred to the Chinese celebrating and then retiring to "noodle joints" where they could get a Chinese meal. In addition to taking in laundry, many Chinese businessmen rented dining rooms and sold dinners.[7] Many of the older neighborhoods in Tucson have corner grocery stores that were run by Chinese families, who also raised and sold chickens for the public. As late as the 1970s, before highways were constructed through and divided these neighborhoods, many Mexican American and Chinese families lived side by side, raising goats, ducks, and chickens in their backyards.

Because of these domestic duties, it is quite likely that a good deal of Chinese cooking has filtered into Southwest cuisine uncharted. In *Bonanza*, the popular television show of the 1960s, Hop Sing was the Cartwrights' butler, cook, servant, and comic relief. But what he represented is the presence of the ubiquitous "Chinaman" in a subordinate but trusted position.

Like the ubiquity of the Chinese on the frontier, Chinese restaurants are a mainstay of dining out across the Southwest. Every community of any size has at least one, and many of them are run and owned by Chinese Americans who can trace their families back to those railroad workers and frontier settlers from the Old West.

The Chinese restaurants in predominantly Mexican-American neighborhoods in Tucson and other Southwestern communities appear to thrive and suffer less of the usual attrition than in mixed neighborhoods. For example, on the southside of Tucson, aside from a few franchise restaurants, Chinese buffet restaurants are as busy on evenings and weekends as their counterparts that serve Mexican food. Conversations over the past 30 years with Hispanics have led me to believe that Mexican Americans select Chinese food as one of their top choices when dining out.

Putting Food By: The Mormons in Arizona and Nevada

Self-reliance and emergency preparedness are basic tenets of the Church of Latter Day Saints (LDS), also known as the Mormons. It is not enough to ward off evil; a believer must engage in a program of "positive preparation." This program includes putting by a year's supply of food, learning recipe substitutions in case fresh foods become unavailable and using methods of cooking for dry storage, such as canning and dehydrating. Based on the Old Testament stories of God calling for his children to prepare for the famines that would destroy evildoers, food storage is raised to a fine art in the Mormon tradition.

Additionally, LDS beliefs call for abstinence from caffeine, alcohol, and tobacco, which redirects their attentions to a wide range of culinary delights and sweets. In the West, predominantly LDS communities are well known for their church suppers and restaurants that feature rich desserts, hearty casseroles, and jams and jellies.

In Arizona and Nevada there are many Mormon settlements, which are divided equally among rural, suburban, and urban locations. Mormons first settled in Nevada in 1855, in the Las Vegas valley and environs. Today, Las Vegas has a sizeable LDS contingent and a temple east of the city. In Arizona there were Mormon settlements along the Little Colorado River plateau beginning in the 1870s. By 1890 the towns of Snowflake, Woodruff, St. Joseph, and Taylor were thriving.

Not only do the local cafes have typically "Mormon" food on their menus, but because the LDS population is well distributed throughout these states, one can find a treasure-trove of Mormon-inspired foods—for example, both sweet and savory pies—at mainstream restaurants and cafeterias. Franchise cafeterias and restaurants such as Marie Callender's and the Golden Corral Buffet serve the homestyle cooking that mirrors what one might find at a church supper, complete with a dessert selection as plentiful as the main dishes, salads, and vegetables combined: hot berry, cherry, and apple pies, coconut and chocolate cream pies piled high with meringue; carrot, chocolate, coconut, and red-velvet cakes; brownies, cookies, gelatin, and ice cream with all the sprinkles, candies, and jimmies a sweet tooth may crave. Some have jokingly called the area from Idaho to northern Arizona "the Jell-O Belt," because no proper LDS church supper is complete without a molded gelatin salad. But of course, these concoctions can also found in church basements of many denominations across the country.

The recipes in the many Mormon cookbooks currently available are an artifact and testament to the resourcefulness of many generations of families and offer clues to the way this community continues as a distinct sub-culture in the Southwest but still adapts to mainstream, modern-day convenience.

HOW THE WEST WAS WON

In the late nineteenth and early twentieth centuries, tourism to this last "wild" territory of the continental United States was extremely popular, even though it required days of arduous travel. Some would argue that the horse, the iron horse (the steam locomotive), or the six-shooter won the West. But those who live in the region know the real answer: it was refrigeration and the internal combustion engine that opened up and conquered the Wild West.

The mild winter climate that attracted visitors could be extended with the use of air conditioning. Refrigerated trucking extended the reach of the railroads for distributing goods from all over the country. This meant that agricultural products could then be exported out of the area to new markets, without the need for an individual consumer to visit the region. As the country became more mobile, the Southwest became, despite the sometimes inhospitable landscape and extreme temperatures, accessible through its foods, its image in the burgeoning movie industry, and its reputation as a land of enchantment and exotic playplace for the rest of the country.

Las Vegas developed a brash casino/vacation culture, becoming much more than a desert oasis. Cities in Arizona—Phoenix, Tucson, and Sun City—and in New Mexico—Santa Fe, Taos, Silver City, Albuquerque, and Truth or Consequences—now made big business out of their golf courses, swimming pools, and resorts. El Paso, always a key avenue for commerce, became increasingly important as a gateway to and from Mexico. Business and tourism increased in the Southwest because of its natural resources, which tourists admired the beauty of and business people tapped for their wealth. This economic development served to expose the rest of the country to the Southwest's unique foodways, and vice versa. Many more people moved to the area, bringing with them their foods, cooking, and tastes.

CONTEMPORARY FOODWAYS

One sign that Southwest regional and ethnic food is no longer the "loathsome mess" that tourists and outlanders disparaged is that you cannot turn around in a restaurant, cookbook aisle, or grocery store without encountering some take on Southwestern cuisine.

Now that the world comes to us via television, interstate trucking, and computers, the United States and the world have been engaging in gastronomic tourism—taking trips to the Southwest in order to discover and eat the region's foods, though of course now one can simply buy and prepare packaged versions of "authentic" foods.[8] Many of these products are being exported to the corners of the world. Reports of mistakes in the duplication of dishes—green-bean burritos, deli-sliced roast beef in an enchilada, chili made red with ketchup—are also signs that Southwest recipes are on the move. In a medium like food, mistakes are fleeting but telling, and translation errors might be taken as variations. In fact, as recipes and dishes cross cultural and geographical borders, originally spicy dishes may begin to taste bland enough to appeal to many more and uninitiated palates.[9] These borrowed foods began to flood the American culinary lexicon in the 1960s and 1970s; in particular, taco, burrito, margarita, salsa, tortilla, enchilada, chili, fajita. As the economy boomed, people moved into and out of the Southwest, learning to make regional dishes and demanding the ingredients in their local stores, or they improvised and adapted.

Salsa fresca (left) is usually uncooked and homemade, though there are salsas frescas available in the refrigerated section of grocery stores. (Also popular are salsas made from mango, jalapeños, onions and cilantro, or avocado and jalapeños.) Because it is cooked, salsa picante (right) can be jarred or canned and shipped around the country. Courtesy of Jay Cox Hayward.

In Mexico, ketchup is simply a "salsa," i.e., a sauce, as this bottle, purchased in the border town of Nogales, shows. Courtesy of Jay Cox Hayward.

Today, enter into any grocery store across the nation, and you will see the results of mainstream adoption of Southwestern cuisine on the shelves.[10] Salsa outstripped ketchup as the number-one condiment in the 1990s, and now, in the early twenty-first century, the tortilla is believed to be taking the lead from the humble and ubiquitous loaf of Wonder Bread. In addition to salsa and tortillas, one can find a huge range of chile products and taco seasonings. In restaurants as well, look for Mexican pizza, nachos, chile-and-lime-flavored tortilla chips, tequila marinades for chicken, beef fajitas, and almost anything stuffed and wrapped into a burrito. Advertising and the fast-food industry rely on Southwest-influenced cuisine to boost sales. A quick look at book shelves reveals, among the Mediterranean, French, and Asian offerings, many cookbooks filled with recipes originating in Texas, New Mexico, Arizona—all heavily influenced by the zesty, vibrant flavors of Southwest cuisine.

The rise of restaurants, including national chains and franchises such as Taco Bell, Chi Chis, and Chili's, attests to this "globalization" of Southwest foodways, as does the proliferation of brand-name products brands exported from the Southwest, such as Fritos, Old El Paso, Pace Picante Sauce, and El Chico frozen foods.

THE FUTURE: EAST MEETS SOUTHWEST

With chiles as the common denominator, the Asian influence on Southwestern cuisine has become the latest trend and will probably be a huge influence on further cross-cultural blending, both at the national and regional levels. *East Meets Southwest* written by Michael Fennelly, chef at the chic Santacafé in Santa Fe, is the title of a cookbook that heralded this trend. Other signs that the chile is bridging the gap between borders and cultures is the preponderance and popularity of Asian food, specifically the chile-dependent Thai and Vietnamese cuisines, and wasabi, that hot horseradish paste in Japanese food.

Chiles have circumnavigated the globe a few times. It is believed that chiles began as wild plants in the hot climates in Central America, especially southern Mexico, but that seeds were spread by birds across the Caribbean and into South America. Some believe it was the other way around, that South American plants were spread northward, by birds, Indian trade, and the Spanish conquest. Columbus encountered a fiery pepper, called *ahí*, in the West Indies. He thought it was the black pepper he had intended to find. Nonetheless, he took chiles to Europe (along with corn and a host of other foods), where their popularity spread so quickly that some say they outstripped historical records, which may be why their origins are always disputed.[11]

Another point of contact between Asian and Southwestern, specifically Mexican, food, is rice. Whether it's Spanish rice from New Mexico or steamed rice from China, rice is now a staple in both cuisines and has found its way inside the very mainstream burritos at Taco Bell.

There are also the wonderful beverages such as *horchata* (made with almonds, rice, cinnamon, lime, and sugar), *jamaica* (made with hibiscus flowers), and *tamirindo* (made from tamarind ponds), alcoholic beverages such as tequila and mescal from Mexico, the wonderful range of regional beers such as Shiner, Celis, Nimbus brews, and the Southwest's burgeoning wine industry. Also relatively undiscovered are the delicious pastries—*kolaches* (jam-filled Czech breakfast pastries), *cochitos* (gingerbread in the shape of pigs), strudel from central Texas and *pastel de tres leches* which is sometimes known as Mexican wedding cake.

There is so much more of Southwestern cooking to discover. The region is geographically huge, its people diverse and dynamic, and its foods and beverages varied and delicious. Food itself is such a plastic medium that endless combinations exist, so it is difficult to fully encompass all of the foods the Southwest has to offer. The key to understanding Southwest food is eating it, and one is encouraged to continue further study—at least three times a day.

A third type of sauce is prepared and bottled differently, to be sprinkled on food in very small quantities because of its intense heat. These thin Tabasco-like sauces are made almost entirely from chiles. Courtesy of Jay Cox Hayward.

Chiles and Chili: Is There a Difference?

When words are borrowed into the language, some distortion and garbling is bound to happen. From time to time, there has been a tempest in a teapot over whether there is a difference (beyond the spelling) of *chile* and *chili.* Some say firmly that *Chile* is

For the unfamiliar (read: non-Mexican) buyer, the appeal must borrow from the buyer's stereotypical images of the Southwest—cartoon images of coyotes, Mexicanos, cacti and bilingual wordplay. Often, a temperature gauge or rating for the heat of the salsa will be included on the label. Courtesy of Jay Cox Hayward.

The spiciness of chile peppers is often associated with gunfire or dangerous women—and in this case, with both. Images of the Old West's lawlessness are often associated with spiciness on salsa labels. Not pictured are two brands, Ass Kickin', showing a cartoon mule under the effects of hot sauce, and Mad Dog Salsa, which depicts a desperado whose eyes have bugged out because of the salsa. Courtesy of Jay Cox Hayward.

a country, and *chili* is the food. Others hear "chile" and then ask, "red or green?"

In fact, the dish *chile con carne*, which is a stew of meat, chile peppers, and spices among other ingredients can be found spelled both ways—*chili* or *chile*—throughout an assortment of reputable cookbooks. In addition to the spelling difference, one New Mexican cook observes that in Tex-Mex cooking, the chiles are a seasoning; in New Mexico, chiles are a vegetable.[12]

So which is right? *Merriam-Webster's Collegiate Dictionary* acknowledges both spellings (as well as *chilli*), though *chile* is originally a Spanish word. So then, *chili* could be construed as an English adaptation, since *Webster's* also lists "chili dog," "chili sauce," and "chili powder."[13]

Whatever you call it, chili con carne (usually abbreviated simply as "chili" in the Southwest and elsewhere) is not strictly Southwestern food anymore. Originating probably along the cattle drives in ranch country in Mexico and Texas, this dish has "translated" across state borders, and nearly everyone now has a favorite recipe. Cincinnati has even become rather famous for its three-way, four-way, and five-way versions, served over pasta.

The circle was completed in 1986 when Skinner Pasta put its Lone Star Pasta on the market. The fact that a Texas "bowl of red," as chili is commonly called, has no original relationship with pasta didn't matter, but Texas' sesquicentennial presented a good marketing opportunity.

The Chili Queens

Chile con carne was one of the first fast foods in Texas, thanks to the Chili Queens. Around 1880, women who were trying to supplement their family's income set up their fires and cookpots around Military Plaza in San Antonio to cook and sell chile con carne. The scene was quite festive, with street musicians and the queens all attempting to attract business and compete with each other.

Today, it is hard to find a family restaurant in Texas that does not have its version of a "bowl of red," though unfortunately many smaller, more homegrown establishments have been squeezed out of a highly competitive restaurant market.

Competition Chili

In the world of the chili cookoff, there is meat and there are spices. And that's about it. Diehard chili cooks believe that beans, tomatoes, or any other such fillers dilute the purity of chili. Some believe that the only recognizable food in chili should be the meat and that the meat should be beef. Claims of using possum, rattlesnake, armadillo, or jackalope in these competition concoctions tend to be exaggerations in keeping with the lore of these events.

Some claim a different metaphor for the exquisite pain caused by chile peppers. Such pain is often associated with "religious experiences." The heat of this salsa must be high, as its label indicates one will experience "wrath" by eating it. Another brand (not pictured) is the Hotter Than Hell line of salsas. Courtesy of Jay Cox Hayward.

Chiles: La Reina Del Valle

Most Southwesterners would classify chiles are vegetables—hot, spicy, and saucy staff of life. Current debate centers around whether the chiles were introduced from China to the New World via Marco Polo and the conquistadors, or if chiles were native to the Americas and the conquerors took them back to Europe as something mislabeled as "spice." Chiltepines are tiny, fiery peppers that grow in wild bushes in Arizona and New Mexico, but they are unrelated to the currently cultivated crops of capisicum.

The largest producer of chile peppers in the United States is New Mexico. The New Mexico chile crop tripled between 1950 and 1980. In both 2002 and 2003 the state's total chile harvest was around 95,000 tons, a cash crop that brings more than $200 million to the state annually. A bumper crop in 2000 yielded 99,000 tons. Texas and Arizona are in the top five producers of this Southwest staple and export.

A field guide, dozens of recipes, and a bibliography on chiles can be found in *The Whole Chile Pepper Book* by Dave DeWitt and Nancy Gerlach. Mark Miller's *The Great Chile Book* is a handsome full-color field guide.

FOOD FESTIVALS IN THE SOUTHWEST

Harvest festivals have been around as long as people and crops have. To celebrate a season of hard work and a bumper crop, one can finally gather friends and family together and let go a little. Even in times of famine, any kind of harvest at all was cause for thanks and celebration before careful planning for surviving the coming months.

In the Southwest, festivals have been celebrated for harvests and prosperity as well as for holy days and saints' days.

Thai chicken satay is a well-known festival food that shows the strong Asian influence in the Southwest. Courtesy of Jay Cox Hayward.

Chiles are harvested once or twice a year, depending on the growing season for the microregion. The ancient preparation method is simply to dry them in the sun in long, attractive strings called ristras. These strings can be found in roadside stands as well as gourmet markets. Ristras have become such a popular decorative motif that artificial chiles are available. Courtesy of Jay Cox Hayward.

Therefore, one can find present-day festivals year-round that either celebrate an event in the church calendar, a historical event, or a particular crop.

Festival food has a special set of conditions to meet: it must be somehow typical of a culture, it must meet local health regulations, and it must be something that people will buy, so that vendors will find participation worthwhile.

Adaptations must be made, then, to make the food palatable to a large number of festival goers and to keep them healthy and happy. Perhaps a dish that calls for tripe will be bypassed for one that has more widely accepted ingredients. Another adaptation might be the method of preparation or presentation. Sausages that might more typically be served on a bed of sauerkraut with a side of potato pancakes and applesauce, might better be sold and served on a stick or in a bun for ease of eating in a festival setting. An item that requires deep frying might be prepared more easily in a wok filled with oil rather than in a deep fat fryer.

Festival food tends more toward the more fatty and sweet dishes. It's a party, so everything must be keyed toward fun rather than being a strict representation of cultural heritage. Thus, festival food at any particular event on any given day might deviate a little—or a lot—from the "authentic" item. But no one usually cares, and judging from the amount of trash generated by food festivals, everyone goes home happy and well fed.

Texas Festivals

Texas is a big place and has many regions. Some scholars say that the Southwest really starts at Interstate 35, which neatly dissects the state between Deep South and Old West. The food festivals across Texas show its variety and ethnic diversity, as well as Texans' passion for eating and for celebrating food.

The Texas Folklife Festival, held in June in San Antonio, embraces the entire breadth of ethnic groups in the state. Over 275 organizations participate in folk demonstrations, food booths, music and dance performances, and crafts demonstrations. Everyone shows up—the Texas Cajuns, the Alsatian Texans, the German Texans, the Nigerian Texans, and the Chinese Texans—and they all party for four days. The prime focus is to show the heritage and diversity of Texas, but with over thirty booths, it's easy to just show up and eat. Everything from barbeque and barbacoa to spanakopita and sourdough biscuits can be found on the menu.

An older celebration in San Antonio is known simply as Fiesta. Held in late

April, well past the solemn days of Lent and Easter, Fiesta San Antonio lasts for more than a week and includes parades, performances, and large quantities of the city's best food. This fiesta kicks off several weeks of celebration, because it's close to Cinco de Mayo, the Return of the Chili Queens event over Memorial Day weekend, and then the Texas Folklife Festival in June.

In Athens, Texas, the Black-Eyed Pea Jamboree is held the third weekend in July and has been since the 1970s. In parts of Texas and across the Deep South, eating black-eyed peas is a symbol of good luck. Athens' economy depended largely on the legumes for many years, so this community celebrates this heritage with a fun-run, a carnival, and craft booths, as well as plenty of black-eyed pea dishes.

The Chilympiad is held the third Friday and Saturday in September in San Marcos, Texas, a lovely town just south of Austin. Begun in the 1970s, the activities include a beauty pageant, a fun-run, dancing, music, and some serious chili-cooking competitions. The Chilympiad is said to be the largest cook-off in existence and is for men only.

Almost on the Louisiana border, Mauriceville hosts the Crawfish Festival every year on the third weekend in April. Beginning with a parade to honor "mudbugs," the festivities include a cook-off and picnic, crafts booths, a carnival, and an auction.

The Stonewall Peach JAMboree and Rodeo is held at the height of peach harvest in late June, in this tiny community tucked between Austin and Fredericksburg. Stonewall peaches are highly prized, and people flock here to gobble cobbler, pie, ice cream, and cake—and barbeque—all while watching the crowning of the rodeo and Peach Queen.

As do other predominantly German

Will the "Real" Gordita Please Stand?

Recipe variations often fuel controversies among food writers, scholars, and historians. But variations and substitutions can show the dynamic nature of food and the passion we feel for traditions: the recipes we use, or that were handed down to us, are the best, the most authentic, and that's that. But in fact, because of the fluid nature of food, variations are to be expected. An example of this is the humble *gordita*, a thick, hand-patted corn tortilla.

Among the Tejanos (Mexican Texans) at the Texas Folklife Festival who make and sell thousands of gorditas, there was considerable debate about what a "real" gordita is. Many feel that one must use the old techniques for mixing the masa and patting out the dough—no machines, no shortcuts. There have been stories told along the border about how women in Mexico of the 1930s and 1940s were observed shaping corn tortillas on their bare knees, the skin of which gained a certain softness from the dough. Many dispute this preparation method, perhaps taking exception to this sensual and unsanitary method, claiming that their mothers and aunts draped their knees with towels instead.

While the women at the festival booths pat out the dough by hand (but not on their knees), it is the men of the group who prepare the dough in large quantities, by hand, because, as one of the ladies said, "Our hands aren't strong enough to knead five pounds of dough at once."

Another element in this controversy is how a "real" gordita is fixed. Is a gordita the tortilla itself, or is that just a shell, requiring toppings to make it a gordita? The food booth at the festival prepares the gordita with meat, cheese, lettuce, and salsa. Yet old-time San Antonio residents claim that a "real" gordita is thick enough to be sliced and stuffed with its ingredients—again, meat, cheese, and salsa. When ordered in a restaurant in San Antonio, however, a gordita is topped, not stuffed. Restaurants from Texas to Arizona also often call these items *chalupas* or *tostadas*.

On the other hand, Taco Bell's gordita is a piece of wheat flatbread folded like a taco and stuffed, which bears little resemblance to the "real" thing, which would warrant its classification as appropriation, not a variation.

It is evident that within a certain range of variables, there are some key elements that are required—corn masa, a thick pancake, and some toppings—to make the real thing, and everything else is up for debate. And this law of variations is true of almost any recipe: within certain limits, it is the deviation from the rule that gives each cook and each regional cuisine its own unique style.

towns in central Texas, New Braunfels hosts an annual festival in October, to coincide with the festivities back in Germany during the same month. Wurstfest is held usually toward the end of the month and features strudel, pretzels, funnel cakes, polka music, and, of course, the best "wurst" on a stick around.

In the still very German town of Fredericksburg, Oktoberfest is an annual event held on the first weekend of October. In addition to music and the beer, the food is a major focus: sausages, kraut, potato pancakes, and all things strudel made with the area's plentiful peach and pecan harvests.

Salsa Strategies

There are three general types of salsa: *salsa fresca*, *salsa picante*, and hot sauce. The first is an uncooked, chunky relish, usually with tomatoes, onions, garlic, and chiles, and sometimes with cilantro. Salsa picante, picante sauce, or commonly known just as salsa, is a thick, cooked liquid made from tomatoes (or *tomatillos* for green salsa), onions, garlic, chile peppers, and sometimes other vegetables.

The rise in salsa consumption across the country now has almost everyone familiar with salsa, but then, in order to sell the spicy food "north of the border," interesting marketing strategies were employed, contrasting sharply with those used south of the border.[14]

Dallas–Fort Worth Metroplex (the Dallas–Fort Worth metropolitan area) is a collection of cities and towns and is one of the country's largest population centers. Food festivals occur almost weekly in the Metroplex, but one highlight is the Corndog Festival, which coincides with the opening of the State Fair of Texas in October. The corndog is said to have been invented here. One can see corn dogs in costumes and oddball dioramas as well as all-you-can-eat corndogs.

The Greek Food Festival, sponsored by the Holy Trinity Greek Orthodox Church, is one of Dallas' oldest food fests, having marked fifty years of Greek dishes such as domas, spanakopita, and gyros.

A huge chili cook-off in north Texas is the Prairie Dog Chili Cook-Off, which is doubled-billed with the World Championship of Pickled Quail Egg Eating. A two-day chili competition, this event is held in Grand Prairie and satisfies vegetarians and animal lover alike, since there is also a pinto-bean cook-off, and no prairie dogs are harmed to present this festival.

Not all Dallas festivals recall the cowboy heritage. The Asian Festival features Asian food as a backdrop for dance, music, martial arts, and other entertainment.

Also worth noting in the Texas food festival calendar are the Poteet Strawberry Festival, the Luling Watermelon Thump, Yamboree in Gilmer, Sweetwater's Rattlesnake Round-up (yes, they serve rattlesnake there), the Jalapeño Festival in Laredo, and the Onion Festival in Weslaco. The weirdest and most wonderful food festival in Texas, though, has to be Spamarama, held close to April Fools' Day every year in Austin. Events includes sculpting with Spam, a cook-off, a Spam toss and plenty of roasted corn, funnel cakes, music, and oddball entertainment. The festival benefits local charities and has its own cookbook as well.

New Mexico Festivals

With the hundreds of feast days in the pueblos and communities across the state, New Mexico has a long tradition of festivals dating back to the first human occupation in the region, specifically the fertile Rio Grande Valley.

The Santa Fe Indian Market is held in June on the famous old plaza in the center of town. At this premier art market, food vendors offer delicious contempo-

"We Call It Tucson Eat Yourself"

Southern Arizona is home to a diverse blend of people, from the Native American and Hispanic communities to members of widely different cultural groups who now find themselves living in the area. In 1974 "Big Jim" and Loma Griffith noticed this unique blend and decided to hold a festival as a way to showcase folk arts of different cultures for the whole community. Thus was born a festival called Tucson Meet Yourself.

For the past thirty years this three-day festival has featured food, music, dance, and traditional arts. This festival is remarkable for its longevity and focus but also because of two key elements: it is run completely by volunteer staff and accepts no donations from large food or beverage manufacturers. These factors have kept the festival successful and community-based and make it one of the most popular events in southern Arizona's cultural calendar.

Held each year at the site of the original walled presidio, many participants and guests feel that the heart of Tucson Meet Yourself is the nearly thirty food booths, which offer traditional foods for sale to the more than 30,000 attendees. In fact, "the entire event can be said to hinge on the preparation and sale of the traditional ethnic foods that provide the central public image of "Tucson Meet Yourself"[15] resulting frequently in the pun Tucson Eat Yourself.

Tucson Meet Yourself provides a general atmosphere of festival fun, but in the food plaza in particular, visitors can see a microcosm of the Southwest itself. The side-by-side food booths become a living testament to the spirit of tolerance and acceptance. One can see a Native American church youth group booth, at which fry bread is sold, next to the Chinese school's booth, where they're selling egg rolls and beef hunan. Brazilian, Colombian, and Panamanian booths selling pork and rice, banana-leaf-wrapped potato tamales, or flan, may be interspersed with booths selling freshly roasted corn on the cob, Thai chicken satay served with *Pad Thai*, and German knackwurst and kraut. In recent years, the festival has expanded to host food booths from Afghan, Armenian, Croatian, Norwegian, and Italian groups, to name a few. The oldest food booth to participate is the Swedish group VASA, who began their food booth at the first festival in 1974.

Each food-booth participant at Tucson Meet Yourself finds it necessary to adapt traditional recipes to suit practical factors such as health and convenience and for fear of turning off customers with food that is too spicy or exotic. But the end result is still a "gringo" version of that culture's food.

What happens when a critical mass of Tucsonans assemble at El Presidio Park to eat each other's food? Something quite magical. Because of food sharing and the temporary relaxation of ethnic and racial boundaries, a new community is created complete with its own structure, rules, and geography. Organizers discuss the festival in terms of its geography, even though the booths and stages are stored for the entire year and the park is returned to its ordinary state following the event. Some long-time visitors to the festival see themselves as citizens of a little city that rises up from nowhere every year, like Brigadoon. And indeed, even the first-time visitor to Tucson Meet Yourself is drawn into this world quickly when he or she shares the communion of *paella* (Spanish Stew), trifle, and *aguas frescas* (sweet drinks). For some, the approach to Tucson Meet Yourself is one of cafeteria-style tourism—eating as many different items as possible throughout the weekend to absorb the diversity viscerally.

The event is held in Tucson's downtown El Presidio Park, usually the second weekend in October. It is free, open to the public, and welcomes volunteers and visitors alike.

rary versions of native American foods: mutton stew, roasted corn, blue-corn pancakes, and fry bread, which is made sweet with powdered sugar and/or honey, made savory with beans, cheese, and chili. Only food vendors who are members of a federally recognized tribe and serve a menu that reflects their tribal background are eligible to apply.

Buñuelos are fried batter dusted with cinnamon sugar or powdered sugar. These fancy buñuelos, made by the thousands for the Texas Folklife Festival by a Mexican food booth, use a cross-cultural cooking technique. Scandinavian irons are used for dipping in the batter and frying. Homemade buñuelos are typically flat pancakes or tortillas, made sweet with cinnamon sugar. Courtesy of Jay Cox Hayward.

The Hatch Chile Festival, held over Labor Day weekend, is the state's largest harvest festival, attracting nearly 30,000 to this small town of 2,000 in central New Mexico.

Also of interest to culinary enthusiasts are two Ruidoso festivals, the New Mexico Chile Cook-off in early October and the Lincoln County Barbeque War in late October.

The tiny community of Cuchillo holds the Pecan Festival at the end of February. Spiced pecans, pecan candy, barbeque, and hundreds of pies mark this harvest festival. From there, it's a short trip down I-25 to Mesilla to visit Stahmann's orchards for taffy, toffee, whole nuts, and their famous chile pecans.

High Rolls, New Mexico, celebrates two fruits of the area, the cherry in June and the apple harvest in October. Pies and bake-offs are the order of the day, rounded out by arts and crafts and entertainment.

In late September, Las Cruces hosts the Whole Enchilada Fiesta with continuous entertainment of street dancing, a parade, and children's activities, and it ends with the cooking of the world's largest enchilada, ten ft. in diameter.

Arizona Festivals

It's not only its Tucson Meet Yourself event (see sidebar) that shows Tucson really knows how to eat and celebrate food. The Norteño Festival in August is a blazing hot night of great regional music set against booth after booth of tacos, *birria* (lamb and chile dish), chimichangas, and Navajo fry bread. La Fiesta De Los Chiles, held in October, is one big party celebrating chiles and all things made from chiles (including artificial ones). Local salsa makers, restaurants, artists, specialty-food manufacturers, and non-profit groups such as Desert Survivors and Native Seed/SEARCH have booths at this two-day event at the Tucson Botanical Gardens.

Held in April for the past twenty-six years, the unique Scottsdale Culinary Festival rounds up the upscale chefs from the state to celebrate food and eating. Highlights of this event are the Great Arizona Picnic, where visitors can sample from nearly a hundred caterers, and the Southwest Festival of Beers.

Also notable in Arizona is the Tucson Greek Festival, which serves up gyros, spanakopita, and baklava, along with Greek dancing, music, and culture every September.

Nevada Festivals

The National Cowboy Poetry Gathering, Elko Nevada, sponsored by Western Folklife Center, is usually held in late January. Cowboy lore, bonafide poetry from working cowhands, and immense steaks have a very loyal following. The festival has grown in its twenty years to be a premier event.

Started in 1919, the Genoa Candy Dance in Genoa, Nevada, has grown into a long-awaited annual downtown event in this northern Nevada town. Originally begun as a way to make a little money by selling candy, this late-September festival is more a crafts fair than food festival, but the fudge is still a big draw.

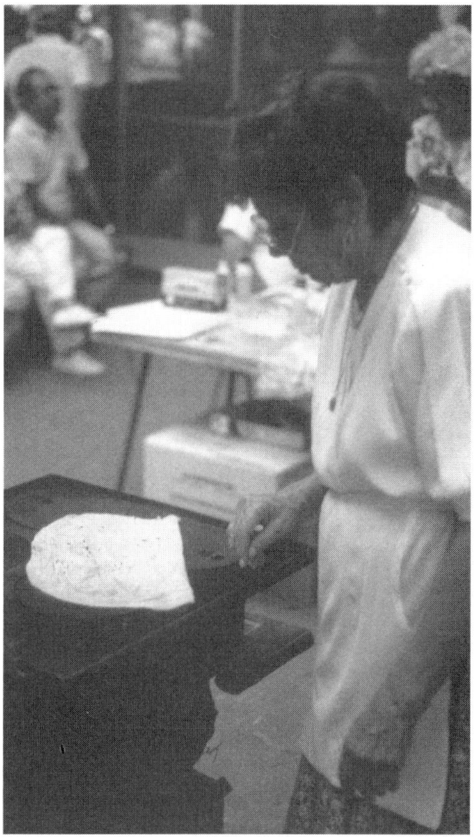

At Tucson Meet Yourself, a member of the COMWOLEI group demonstrates how to transform a ball of dough into a large, translucent, delicious flour tortilla, which is a familiar item in the Sonoran cooking of southern Arizona. Flour tortillas are then placed on a hot surface, such as a comal or the top of this cast iron wood-burning stove and cooked on both sides. Infrequently, the patterns burned into the surface resemble a face or a shape that is interpreted to be a miraculous appearance of, for example, Jesus or the patron saint of Mexico, La Virgen de Guadalupe. Worthy of tabloid headlines, these special tortillas sometimes become the focal point of temporary shrines in homes, attracting devout pilgrims who come to view the miracle. Courtesy of Jay Cox Hayward.

RESOURCE GUIDE

Printed Sources

Amador, Adela. *Southwest Flavor: Adela Amador's Tales from the Kitchen*. New Mexico Magazine, 2000.

Arnold, Samuel P. *Eating Up the Santa Fe Trail: Recipes and Lore from the Old West*. Golden, CO: Fulcrum Publishing, 1990, 2001.

Arrington, Leonard J., and Davis Bitton. *The Mormon Experience: A History of the Latter-Day Saints*. Urbana: University of Illinois Press, 1992.

Barbas, Samantha. "'I'll Take Chop Suey': Restaurants as Agents of Culinary and Cultural Change." *Journal of Popular Culture* 36 (Spring 2003): 669–686.

Bentley, Amy. "From Culinary Other to Mainstream America: Meanings and Uses of Southwestern Cuisine." *Southern Folklore* 55, no. 3 (1998): 238–252.

Bishop, Marion. "Speaking Sisters: Relief Society Cookbooks and Mormon Culture." In *Recipes for Reading: Community Cookbooks, Stories, Histories*, edited by Anne Bower. Amherst: University of Massachusetts Press, 1997.

Brown, Linda Keller, and Kay Mussell, ed. *Ethnic and Regional Foodways in the United States: The Performance of Group Identity*. Knoxville: University of Tennessee Press, 1984.

Brown, M.H. de la Peña. "Una Tamalada: The Special Event." *Western Folklore* 40 (1991): 64–71.

Busca Isusi, José María. *Traditional Basque Cookery*. Reno: University of Nevada Press, 1987.

Camou-Healy, Ernesto and Alicia Hinajosa. *Cocina Sonorense*. Hermosillo (Sonora, Mexico): Instituto Sonorense de Cultura, 1990.

Camp, Charles. *American Foodways: What, When, Why and How We Eat in America*. Little Rock, AR: August House, 1989.

Coe, Sophie. *America's First Cuisines*. Austin: University of Texas Press, 1994.

Cushing, Frank. *Zuni Bredstuff*. New York: Museum of the American Indian, Heye Foundation, 1920.

Davis, Mary Ancho. *Chorizos in an Iron Skillet: Memories and Recipes from an American Basque Daughter*. Reno: University of Nevada Press, 2001.

Dent, Huntley. *The Feast of Santa Fe: Cooking of the American Southwest*. New York: Simon and Schuster, 1985.

De Witt, Dave, and Nancy Gerlach. *The Whole Chile Pepper Book*. Boston: Little, Brown, 1990.

De Witt, Dave, and Mary Jane Wilan. *The Food Lover's Handbook to The Southwest*. Rocklin, CA: Prima Publishing, 1992.

Dirlik, Arif, ed. *Chinese on the American Frontier*. Lanham, MD: Rowman & Littlefield, 2001.

Fennelly, Michael, Charles Greer, and James Bibo. *East Meets Southwest*. San Francisco: Chronicle Books, 1991.

Foster, Nelson and Linda S. Cordell. *Chilies to Chocolate: Food the Americas Gave the World*. Tucson: University of Arizona Press, 1992.

Gabaccia, Donna. *We Are What We Eat: Ethnic Food and the Making of Americans*. Cambridge, MA: Harvard University Press, 1998.

Gilbert, Fabiola Cabeza de Baca. *The Good Life: New Mexico Traditions and Food*. 2nd ed. Santa Fe: Museum of New Mexico Press, 1982.

Goody, Jack. *Cooking, Cuisine and Class: A Study in Comparative Sociology*. Cambridge: Cambridge University Press, 1982.

Griffith, James S. *Southern Arizona Folk Arts*. Tucson: University of Arizona Press, 1988.

Humphrey, Theodore C., and Lin T. Humphrey, eds. *"We Gather Together": Food and Festival in American Life*. Ann Arbor, MI: UMI Research Press, 1988.

Inness, Sherri. *Dinner Roles: American Women and Culinary Culture*. Iowa City: University of Iowa Press, 2000.

Jaramillo, Cleofas M. *The Genuine New Mexico Tasty Recipes: With Additional Materials on Traditional Hispano Food*. 1939. Reprint, Santa Fe, NM: Ancient City Press, 1981.

Jorgan, Randolph. *Flavor of the Hill Country: Texas-German Recipes from the Sauer-Beckmann Living History Farm*. Tucson, AZ: Southwest Parks and Monuments Association, 1992.

Kavena, Juanita Tiger. *Hopi Cookery*. Tucson: University of Arizona Press, 1998.

Lèvi-Strauss, Claude. "The Culinary Triangle." *Partisan Review* 33 (1966): 595 ff.

Linck, Ernestine Sewell, and Joyce Gibson Roach. *EATS: A Folk History of Texas Foods*. Fort Worth: Texas Christian University Press, 1989.

Long, Lucy M. "Culinary Tourism: A Folkloristic Perspective on Eating and Otherness." *Southern Folklore* 55, no. 3 (1998): 198–204.

———. "Nourishing the Academic Imagination: The Use of Food in Teaching Concepts of Culture." *Food and Foodways* 9, no. 3–4 (2001): 235–262.

McNutt, James C. "Folk Festivals and the Semiotics of Tourism in Texas." *Kentucky Folklore Record* 32, no. 3–4 (1986): 118–129.

Miller, Mark. *The Great Chile Book*. Berkeley, CA: Ten Speed Press, 1991.

———. *East Meets Southwest*.

Montano, Mario. "Appropriation and Counterhegemony in South Texas: Food Slurs, Offal Meats and Blood." In *Usable Pasts: Traditions and Group Expressions in North America*, edited by Tad Tuleja. Logan: Utah State University Press, 1997: 50–67.

Mormon Cooking: Authentic Recipes. Salt Lake City: Great Mountain West Supply, 1996.

Nabhan, Gary Paul. *Coming Home to Eat: The Pleasure and Politics of Local Foods*. New York: Norton, 2002.

Niethammer, Carolyn J. *American Indian Cooking: Recipes from the Southwest.* Lincoln: University of Nebraska Press, 1974, 1999.

———. *The Tumbleweed Gourmet: Cooking with Wild Southwestern Plants.* Tucson: University of Arizona Press, 1987.

Padilla, Carmella. *The Chile Chronicles: Tales of a New Mexico Harvest.* Santa Fe: Museum of New Mexico Press, 1997.

Parades, Américo. *Folklore and Culture on the Texas-Mexican Border.* Austin: University of Texas Press, 1993.

Pilcher, Jeffrey M. *¡Que Vivan los Tamales! Food and the Making of Mexican Identity.* Albuquerque: University of New Mexico Press, 1998.

———. "Tex-Mex, Cal-Mex, New Mex, or Whose Mex?: Notes on the Historical Geography of Southwestern Cuisine." *Journal of the Southwest* 43, no. 4 (Winter 2001): 659–679.

Polzer, Charles. *A Kino Guide: A Life of Eusebio Franscico Kino and a Guide to His Missions and Monuments.* Tucson: Southwestern Mission Research Center, 1974.

Ruffner, Melissa with Budge Ruffner. *Arizona Territorial Cookbook.* Prescott, AZ: Primrose Press, 1982.

Smith, Jeff. *The Frugal Gourmet on Our Immigrant Ancestors.* New York: William Morrow, 1990. (Contains sections on Basque, Mexican, Thai, and Vietnamese immigrants.)

Thorpe, Madeline Gallego, and Mary Tate Engels. *Corazón Contento: Sonoran Recipes and Stories from the Heart.* Lubbock: Texas Tech University Press, 1999.

West, John O. *Mexican-American Folklore.* American Folklore Series, edited by W. K. McNeil. Little Rock, AR: August House, 1988.

Web Sites

Chili Appreciation Society International
http://www.chili.org/chili.html

Chili has its own international organization that produces and hosts chili competitions around the country. The society's Web site contains guidelines for entry, scholarships, and tips for getting into the competition as well as entertaining photos, recepies, and bulletin boards. The premier competition in all of chilidom is the Terlingua Championship Cookoff, held the first Saturday of November in Terlingua in the Big Bend area of Texas.

Mexican Food and History
http://www.gourmetsleuth.com/mexicanfoodhistory.htm

Extensive resources and bibliographies on Mexican food and its influences and adaptations in the Southwest U.S. and Americas.

Nativetech: Native American Technology and Art: Food & Recipes.
http://www.nativetech.org/food/

An index of hundreds of submitted recipes and incorporation native foods.

Santa Cruz Chile and Spice Co.
http://www.santacruzchili.com/

Founded in 1943, this company is known for the special and distinctive chilies that grow in the Santa Cruz valley, one of the best chili growing areas in the world.

Southwest Food Service News
http://www.sfsn.com/SW/

This Web site features a bimonthly newsletter that covers all segments of the food-service industry in Texas and the Southwest. Each issue features news and information about food service people, companies, events, products, and services. The Web site has a search engine subscription form, advertising information and a special section for feedback and news tips.

Texas Cooking/Texana
http://www.texascooking.com

An informative site with current articles, book reviews, recipes, and restaurant listings for all things Texan.

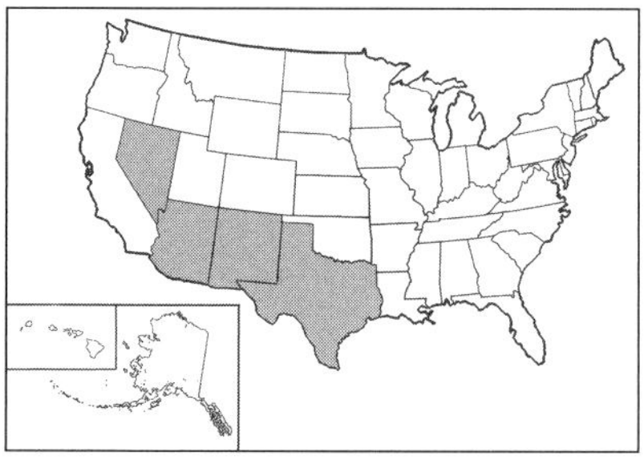

LANGUAGE

Carol Lea Clark

Beginning some 500,000 years ago, small bands of migratory big-game hunters crossed from Siberia to North America on a land bridge and began to populate southward. These immigrants possessed ancient knowledge, developed in the Orient, of social organization. By the time of first contact with Spanish explorers in the Southwest in the sixteenth century, social customs and languages were complex and adequate for the indigenous peoples' needs. Their languages allowed them to express to each other ways to live in harmony with their surroundings. First the Spanish, then the English and mixed Europeans arrived, and their interaction with Native Americans was cataclysmic in the Southwest as elsewhere. Battles and disease led to the most obvious effect, population loss, but continuing contact also influenced the Native Americans' social structure and languages.

The Southwest is one of the most linguistically heterogeneous regions of the United States. While English is certainly predominate today, with Spanish less so, within this region an array of American Indian languages are all represented by sizable numbers of speakers. Other languages can also be found, including German, Vietnamese, and Basque. A substantial number of the region's inhabitants are bilingual or multilingual, and there are dialects formed by the intersections of languages.

According to the *Dictionary of American Regional English*, American settlers migrating inward from the Atlantic Seaboard looked for climates and living conditions like those they left behind.[1] Following this reasoning, it is easy to understand that Southern culture moved into eastern Texas. But the arid nature of the Southwest was unlike any climate English speakers had previously encountered in America. The endless wide spaces and lack of navigable rivers forced settlers to travel overland, an arduous task. The scarcity of rain prevented the planting of traditional crops. Once the movement of settlers westward reached the 98th parallel of longitude, many either sped to the Pacific Coast or turned back. But some did not. Something about the arid Southwest attracted them. Eventually, English Eastern

Often Mispronounced Place Names of the Southwest

Bexar County, TX (BAY-er)	Moab, UT (MOE-wab)
Bourne, TX (BUR-nee)	Mogollon, AZ (mug-gy-OWN)
Casa Grande, AZ (kas-sa-GRAND)	Montague County, TX (MON-tayg)
Deseret, UT (de-zer-RET)	Oquirrh, UT (OH-kurr)
Duchesne, UT (due-SHANE)	Peoa, UT (pee-OH-ah)
Fort Huachuca, AZ (Wah-CHEW-ka)	Pioche, NV (Pee-OACH)
Genoa, NV (Juh-NO-ah)	Quincy, TX (QUIN-zee)
Hazen, NV (HAY-zen)	Refugio, TX (re-FUR-ee-o)
Hurricane, UT (HURR-a-cun)	Toiyabe, NV (Toy-AH-bee)
Kanab, UT (kuh-NAB)	Tooele, UT (tah-WILL-lah)
Lamoille, NV (La-MOYLE)	Toquima, NV (Toe-KEE-mah)
Mantua, UT (MAN-too-way)	Vya, NV (VIE-ya)
Mexia, TX (muh-HAY-a)	

regional pronunciations migrated into the interior of the Southwest, where it was influenced by contact with other varieties of regional English as well as by European immigrant groups and American Indian speech. Place names in the Southwest today often are mispronounced words from European languages (including Spanish and English) and Native American languages.

Today, English is the official language, and it is also reinforced endlessly through television, film, books, radio, and other media. However, other languages maintain vitality, and the numbers of their speakers may, in some cases, be increasing.

NATIVE AMERICAN LANGUAGES

The concept of "Indians" as one ethnic group that speaks one language is inaccurate. *Indian* is a label Europeans gave to the indigenous people of the Americans. Similarly, the names we have for various Indian tribes are generally labels that the white man gave, not what the Indians called themselves. Historically, some individuals have believed that Native American languages are somehow primitive because the groups speaking them lived in small-scale foraging and horticultures and possessed less sophisticated technology than did the Europeans encountering them. Rather, according to *American Indian Languages*, "Every natural language has a highly perfected sound system, an equally well-developed grammar, all the vocabulary required by the culture of its speakers, and the capacity for expressing intellectual and aesthetic ideas and feeling."[2]

Sound Systems (Phonology)

There is no consistent number of sounds in the Native American languages of the Southwest. Acoma, for example, has thirty-nine consonants, while some of the Athabascan languages have almost fifty. Many speech sounds found in the majority of the world's languages, such as stops, nasals, or vowels, are also found in Native American languages, although glottalized consonants are more typically found in Native American languages than in European languages. Some Southwest Native American languages use differences in relative pitch to distinguish meanings;

for example, "Navajo *nílí* 'you are' and *nílí* 'he is' have the same sequence of consonants and vowels, and are differentiated only by a difference in tone."[3]

In the Acoma language, possession is a crucial part of grammar. Nouns, similarly to English (e.g., "my apple"), may have a possessive pronoun. A noun may also be possessed by another noun (like the English "my father's car"). Possession is not, in Acoma, as in many Native American languages, however, indicated by a separate word, as it is in English, but as a prefix to the word. As in English, Acoma has possessive pronouns for the three persons (*my*, *yours*, *theirs*), plus an additional person for an indefinite. Acoma is also gender neutral, so possessive pronouns can be translated as either his or hers. To complicate matters, Acoma has two patterns of possession: alienable (or temporary possession) and inalienable (permanent possession). For example, "girl's notebook" is alienable, while "body parts" are inalienable.

In Apachean languages (including Navajo, Chiricahua Apache, and Mescalero Apache, as well as languages spoken in Alaska and Canada), verbs consist of a stem. One or more prefixes indicate person and tense, as well as adverbs that show direction of the verb's action (*up*, *down*, *toward outside*, etc.). Verb stems also indicate classification of the object. For example, the verb stem *tooz* means to handle a "flat, flexible object, such as a sheet, shirt, handkerchief, as well as a small sackful of objects, such as a small stack of coffee or groceries." The verb stem *jool* means "to handle noncompact or wool-like material, such as loose hay, gaseous material such as fog, smoke, dust."[4]

Pueblo Indians

The nineteen pueblos of New Mexico, sometimes called the Rio Grande Pueblos, are clustered in eight counties of New Mexico. The Pueblo Indians have a common traditional religion, although ceremonies and rituals may vary, as well as a common economy based on the arid high-desert region where they have lived for millennia. But they are not one people, and each Pueblo functions independently, similarly to city-states.

There are three distinct and different Pueblo language families with diverse origins. These language families are grouped as Keresan, Tanoan, and Zunian. The Tanoan language is further divided into three dialects: Tewa, Tiwa, and Towa. In prehistoric times, Pueblo peoples were often multilingual. The Keresan-speaking Pueblos could communicate with the Tanoan-speaking Pueblos and with the Hopis and Zunis. In addition, the Pueblo peoples, in order to trade, often acquired a working knowledge of Apache, Navajo, Kiowas, and Comanche languages.

The Keresan language is quite distinct from other Native American languages. Seven varieties or dialects of Keresan are spoken at seven different pueblos. Eastern Keresan is spoken in the Rio Grande Valley area pueblos of Cochiti, Santo Domingo, San Felipe, Santa Ana, and Zia. Western Keresan is spoken at Acoma and Laguna. The Keres Pueblos immigrated to the Southwest by incursion around 4,500 years ago. Àcoma Pueblo was established at its present location as early as 900 C.E.

Linguists call the Zuni language an isolate, although some have attempted to place it in other language families such as Aztec-Tanoan or Penutian. Zuni has been in its present locale, and the Zuni people have been speaking their language, since at least 1200 C.E.

Of the Tanoan language dialects, Northern Tewa is spoken at Taos and Picurís; Southern Tiwa is spoken at Isleta and Sandia. Tewa is spoken at San Juan, Santa Clara, San Ildefonso, Nambe, Pojoaque, and Tesuque, as well as at Hano on the Hopi reservation. Towa is spoken at Jemez Pueblo. Evidence shows the extinct Pecos Pueblo to have had a Tanoan language, perhaps Towa.

The Pueblo Indians have lived much the same way of life in settled farming villages for 1,500 years, and they have been able to maintain distinct languages and cultures after centuries of contact, first for four hundred years with the Spanish and then a century and a half with the English-speaking Americans, though there have been changes. When the Spanish arrived their language and culture mingled to some degree with that of the Pueblos, especially the eastern Pueblos. Spanish was the language of trade and official documents, but the Pueblo Indians were able to survive the Spanish period with their languages and ceremonies mostly intact.

When the American territorial government moved into New Mexico after 1846, English began to be the universal means of communication between the Pueblos and the U.S. immigrants. Some borrowings of Spanish and English words occur in the everyday Pueblo language. However, in the religious or cultural ceremonies, the native language vocabulary and terminology remain unchanged.

Now, most Pueblo Indians speak their own native language and English as a second language. Older Pueblo people may also speak Spanish and have some knowledge of other Pueblo languages. The trend, though, is toward bilingual native- and English-language knowledge.

The Athabascans: Navajo and Apache

Many archaeologists believe that Athabascans arrived in the Southwest as late as the beginning of the sixteenth century, although others think that they arrived as early as 1000 C.E. The ancestral Athabascans gradually spread to occupy a broad expanse of territory surrounding the Pueblos, including much of what is now Texas, New Mexico, Arizona, Colorado, and northern Mexico. Their arrival and possible warfare that followed might partially explain the abandonment of some Pueblo sites in the twelfth and thirteenth centuries.

At the time of the Spaniards' arrival in the Southwest, Athabascan groups spoke closely related languages; they were essentially the same. Linguists have calculated that the Navajo and Chiricahua Apache languages diverged from each other during a period of only 149 years. The Navajo are separated by 279 years from the San Carlos and Jicarilla Apaches, and by 335 years from the Lipan Apache.[5]

The Navajo adopted many practices of the Pueblo Indians around them, such as the cultivation of corn. By 1730 the Navajo had become a large and powerful people. They dwelled in earth-covered houses and grew corn, beans, and squash. They gathered wild foods and hunted widely, and they engaged in extensive trade with other Indians and the Spanish settlers.

Unlike the Pueblo peoples who preferred to live in proximity to others, the Navajo groups and families scattered over the landscape, though they retained a close association for ceremonies and rituals. The Navajo language was the exclusive method of communication for most of the tribe well into the twentieth century. Not until the 1950s did a majority of the Navajo population have an opportunity to attend school, though a fraction of children went to boarding schools. Since 1950, however, the use of the Navajo language steadily declined as the Navajo people became more acculturated. The main Navajo reservation of some 16 million acres is located in the Four-Corners area and encompasses portions of Arizona, New Mexico, and Utah. Several off-reservation Navajo groups live in New Mexico: the Ramah, in the town of Ramah; the Puertocito, or Alamo, living some thirty-five miles north of Magdalena; the Cañonito, located approximately thirty-five miles from Albuquerque.

The label *Apache* was first recorded in 1598; it was the Spaniards' identification for Indians of the Texas and New Mexico plains. Those who gathered mescal, an agave cactus, for food became named the Mescalero Apache. The ones who dominated the Chiricahua mountain strongholds became known as the Chiricahua Apache. Other branches were named after regional terms, such as the Gila, San Carlos, White Mountain, Tonto, and Cibecue Apache.

At first, the Apache dwellings were mud-covered huts resembling the Navajo hogan, and their lifestyle was also similar. Over time, however, they became more migratory and took over many attributes of the horse-based Plains Indian culture, such as tipis, bison-hunting, and even language elements.[6] They traded with Spaniards and sometimes cultivated corn and other vegetables like the Pueblo Indians.

Several bands of Apaches, in the nineteenth century, learned the Plains Sign Language and used it to communicate with other tribes they encountered. The language was primarily iconic, which means a direct association between the sign

Navajo Athabascans won fame for being used in WWII for radio code. © Corbis.

and its referent. For example, the word *eat* was created by a hand gesture that mimicked eating.

After the Treaty of Guadalupe Hidalgo of 1848 ceded the area to the United States, tensions increased between the Apache and whites. The U.S. government's and settlers intentions of obtaining land and mining natural resources were at odds with the Apache's nomadic bison-based lifestyle. The Apache became known as warriors. Beginning in the 1860s, however, Apache, as well as Navajo, were forced onto reservations. Today, the Mescalero Apache have a 460,000-acre reservation east of Tularosa, New Mexico, on U.S. Highway 70. The Jicarilla Apache's reservation consists of 750,000 acres between Cuba, New Mexico, and the Colorado–New Mexico border.

The Uto-Aztecan: Shoshone, Paiute, and Papago-Pima

Today's Shoshone, Paiute, and Papago-Pima tribes speak Uto-Aztecan languages: the Shoshone's language is also called Shoshone; the Paiute speak Northern Paiute; and the Papago-Pima speak O'odham. Their ancestors, ancient Uto-Aztecans, likely dwelled in the area of today's Arizona and northern Mexico, perhaps extending into California. From there, speakers spread as far north as Oregon, east to the Great Plains, and south to Panama. Even widely separated Uto-Aztecan languages have a similar basic vocabulary for body parts, simple activities, and natural phenomena such as weather. Also, basic grammatical structures are similar, generally placing the verb after the direct object, for example. The ancient Paiutes and Shoshone may have learned pottery and other semisedentary living skills from the Pueblo Indians, although they also gathered wild plants and hunted for game.

In the early nineteenth century, the Shoshone occupied parts of southeast California, northwest Utah, southwest Montana, western Wyoming, southern Idaho, and northeast Nevada. The Paiutes were, at that time, composed of two distinct groups, both speaking Shoshonean languages. The Northern Paiute ranged over central and eastern California, western Nevada, and eastern Oregon. The Southern Paiute occupied northwest Arizona, southeast California, southern Nevada, and southern Utah. The Upper Pimas (now called Akimel O'odham) lived in area of the Gila and Salt rivers; and the Papago (now called Tohono O'odham) dwelled in the foothills and valley floors of northern Sonora (Mexico) and southern Arizona.

The Uto-Aztecan tribes of the Southwest were little disturbed by the early Spaniards, with whom they came in slight contact during the sixteenth and seventeenth centuries. It was not until the 1820s that the Paiute and Shoshone had persistent interaction, first with mountain men hunting beaver and other furs and then with travelers crossing the Rocky Mountains and Great Basin as they headed for gold and silver discoveries in California and Nevada. After the United States annexed New Mexico and California, the tribes' domains were encroached on steadily, and some Indians groups were forced onto on reservations. The majority, however, remained scattered through their native land. Friction was minor until the 1840s, when it increased greatly as the number of settlers, and American military to protect them, increased.

The Western Shoshone reservations are in central to northeastern Nevada, the Shoshone-Bannock at the Fort Hall Reservation in Idaho, the Northern Shoshone in Wyoming, and Goshute on the Goshute Reservation in western Utah. Paiute is spoken on about twenty reservations spread out over 1,000 miles in northern Nevada and contiguous areas of Oregon, California, and Idaho. The Papago-Pima live on seven reservations in south-central Arizona.

Native American (Navajo) girls and white men pose outdoors at Theodore Roosevelt School in Fort Apache, Arizona, 1924. The girls wear tags on their dresses. Courtesy of the Denver Public Library.

BILINGUAL AND ENGLISH-ONLY EDUCATION

Anglo-American policies about Indian languages varied over time. Many Indian children in missionary-founded schools in the seventeenth and eighteenth centuries were instructed in both their native tongue and in English. This approach supported the viability of the native languages while enabling native speakers to communicate in English, the dominant language. When the Bureau of Indian Affairs was created in the late nineteenth century, the federal government's goal was to provide an environment that would acculturate Indian children into an English-speaking way of life. Many children were placed in boarding schools, such in the Albuquerque Indian School, which removed them from the influence of their parents and their native cultures.

The federal English-only policy began to relax in the 1930s. Bilingual materials were provided to some tribes, including the Sioux, the Navajo, and several of the Pueblos. Teachers began to be taught techniques of bilingual instruction. This approach was suspended during World War II, however, and was not resumed after the war.

The 1968 Bilingual Education Act brought back a focus on the native languages. In tribes such as the Zuni, whose native language was still spoken widely, the programs taught English as a second language, but in other tribes such as the Tewa Pueblos, the native language had to be taught as the second language. The Native American Language Act in 1990 gave further impetus to the movement of fostering vitality in native languages, and it acknowledged that language is an "integral part" of a Native American group's culture and identity.[7]

A number of Native American language programs involve disseminating a written alphabet and grammar for previously oral-only languages. For example, The American Indian Language Development Institute (AILDI) was founded in 1978 with the mission of helping Southwestern tribes develop language and curriculum materials. The assumption is that language forms the basic medium for the transmission of a group's heritage and thus is necessary for the survival of the group's culture, history, and values.

PRESERVING NATIVE AMERICAN LANGUAGES

For more than a century and until as late as the 1960s, many tribal children were required to attend federal boarding schools that banned children from speaking their native languages. More recently, tribal parents focused on teaching their children English, so that they could function in the English-speaking culture of the United States. Adults would speak the native language to each other but not to their children. Inée Slaughter, director of the Indigenous Language Institute in Santa Fe, confirms, "We're seeing the age of speakers increase, and the youth not using the languages. And it only takes a generation or two to lose a language."[8]

Actions at Cochití Pueblo are typical of attempts to reverse the trend toward speaking only English among the tribe's younger members. A 1992 survey of Cochití Pueblo showed that the tribe's under-thirty-five population tended not to be fluent in Keres. The tribal council responded to this survey and other evidence by creating programs such as elementary-school classes to invigorate native language use. Another is a "language nest," a day-care program for children under school age where only Keres is spoken.

At Cochití Elementary School, approximately 110 students, from kindergarten through sixth-grade, study their native language, Keres, for 45 minutes a day. The school enrolls students from a variety of ethnic groups; the only ones taking the Keres classes are the Cochití Pueblo children. The language classes are offered though a special arrangement with the school district that allows fluent tribal members to teach the classes. The programs at Cochití seem to be working. "We have 6-year-olds going home and teaching their parents the language. And the older ones are asking their parents who speak Cochití to do so at home so they can practice. The children are teaching the adults," reported teacher Anna Ka-Hee.

The Indigenous Language Institute in Santa Fe provides assistance to the Cochití and other tribal-language programs, training teachers and suggesting curriculums, as well as encouraging tribes to network with each other about program problems and successes.[9]

SOUTHWEST SPANISH

Spanish flourished in the Southwest partially for historic reasons, beginning with Coronado's initial exploration in 1540. New Mexico's upper Rio Grande Valley (Rio Arriba), including Santa Fe, Sandoval, and Taos counties, is one of the earliest identifiable European-settled regions in the United States. Spaniard Juan de Oñate established a Spanish colony there in 1598 as part of his exploration venture in the Southwest. During the Spanish period, and later the Mexican, the core of the Spanish presence in the Southwest was in this geographic region, particularly the area from present-day Albuquerque on the south and Taos on the north, the Sangre de Cristo Mountains on the east, and the Jemez Mountains on the west.

As the Spanish presence grew over the years, Hispanic culture slowly became dominant over the Indian cultures. English is a relative newcomer, becoming dominant only in the nineteenth century. Furthermore, the proximity of Mexico occasioned close and continual contact with Mexico's Spanish-speaking culture and reinforced the use of Spanish in border areas; also, the continued influx of immigrants from Mexico adds more and more Spanish speakers to the area. Indeed, the Spanish language has continued to flourish in the Southwest despite sometimes hostile reactions from monolingual English speakers.

For example, El Paso, Texas, currently the most thoroughly Hispanic of the cities in the Southwest, has Indian, Spanish, Mexican, and American roots. Language has changed in the city as the prevailing groups have changed. When significant numbers of Spaniards first crossed the Rio Grande in 1598, they found Indians they named Sumas and Mansos. Priests followed conquering expeditions, and as the priests began to convert the Indians to Catholicism, they taught them Spanish, and Spanish became the primary language in the area.

Juan de Oñate, Spanish colonizer who founded the first European settlements in the Southwestern United States © Bettmann/Corbis.

When Americans began to enter El Paso in the early 1800s, primarily as traders, they found they had to learn to speak Spanish to be successful in this growing community. Because of the scarcity of American women, the traders often intermarried with Spanish or Indian women. Americans began to come in family groups, on wagon trains and stagecoaches, in the 1840s. After the Civil War, more and more Americans came to the area and, slowly, English took the lead away from Spanish. El Paso was an English-speaking American town, and the Mexicans then learned that they needed to know English to succeed in business. The railroad's arrival in the 1880s only reinforced the English-speaking culture of the town. People began to note that they lived on an international border and to think of Juarez not as a next-door neighbor but as part of Mexico, a foreign country.

The language balance changed again at the time of the Mexican Revolution in 1910, as thousands of Mexican citizens fled north of the border. In succeeding years, migration to El Paso from other parts of the United States was strong, but not as strong as Mexican immigration. Over time, the Mexicans became American citizens and learned English, which enabled them to lead and prosper. In more recent years, with many residents being bilingual and with continued immigration of Mexican immigrants who speak only Spanish, Spanish has again become a major force in the region and is regaining dominance.

In the twentieth century the road to bilingualism in the Southwest has not been smooth, however. As the Hispanic population increased, so did the prejudice of Anglo-Americans. In 1970 a landmark court case, *Cisneros v. Corpus Christi Independent School District*, held that Mexican Americans, as an "identifiable ethnic minority group," were being discriminated against in Corpus Christi schools.[10] As such, they were entitled to the same legal protection against school discrimination extended to African Americans by the decision of *Brown v. Board of Education of Topeka, Kansas*.

Hispanic groups began to organize themselves to combat discrimination in schools, housing, the workplace, and other parts of society. The League of United States Latin Citizens (LULAC) was formed in 1927 to promote the interests of Hispanics and fight segregation. In more recent decades, moreover, groups of young people, calling themselves Chicanos, have pressed for immediate social change. The

Mexican American Youth Organization (MAYO) was founded in 1967 and the Mexican American Legal Defense and Educational Fund (MALDEF) in 1968.

Hispanics have slipped past blacks as the nation's largest minority group, based on the 2000 Census. More than 50 percent of the American Hispanic population reside in two states, California (11.0 million) and Texas (6.7 million). The highest percentage of Hispanics (42 percent) live in New Mexico, followed by California (32 percent) and Texas (32 percent) (8).[11] The continued population growth of Hispanics in the first two years of the twenty-first century, was called "dizzying" by the *New York Times* in June 2003.[12] According to U.S. Census Bureau statistics, the Hispanic population in 2003 had increased by 9.8 percent over the April 2000 census figures. The Census Bureau concluded that immigration, both legal and illegal, accounts for roughly 53 percent of the increase. The remainder, presumably, is because of a higher birth rate among Hispanics than among other segments of the population. "It suggests a demographic momentum so powerful," said Roberto Suro, director of the Pew Hispanic Institute, "that the immigration flow is somewhat impervious to the economic downturn or fears over national security."[13]

Considering the demographic trend of increased numbers of Hispanics in the United States, it will be interesting to see if places of high concentrations like El Paso, will experience increasing acceptance of the Spanish language in the future.

Spanish/English Language Mixing

A common practice among bilingual English-Spanish speakers is code switching, which means that speakers alternate between Spanish and English, often within a single sentence. Some speakers label code switching as bad Spanish. Sociolinguists point out, however, that code switching enables bilingual speakers to use all available linguistic constructions to talk with a variety of audiences. Hispanics who are bilingual also use code switching to establish a unique identity for themselves as a group. A code switcher generally switches from one language to the other at only one point in a sentence. He or she might say, "*A veces* (sometimes) we take too many things for granted" or, "*Yo sé, porque* (I know, because) I went to the hospital to find where he was at." The beginning of each sentence is in Spanish, and the latter part is in English.

Alternatively, an English word or phrase occurs within the grammatical frame of a Spanish sentence. A code switcher might say, "*Hizo* improve *mucho* (She improved much)" or, "*Los estan* busing *pa otra escuela* (They are busing them to another school)."

A third option is for an English word, or a word derived from English, to be adapted grammatically to the norms of the Spanish language. The code switcher might say, "*Taipeo las cartas* (I type the letters)," with *taipeo* derived from the English "type," or, "Va a mistir el tren (He is going to miss the train), with *tren* derived from *train*."[14]

REGIONAL ENGLISH

English in the Southwest is less than 150 years old. As Craig M. Carver observed, "If American English as a whole is a youth compared to the European national languages, western American speech is a mere infant. And like an infant, its personality and features are not yet well formed."[15] Presumably, the same could be said of American English in the Southwest. In addition to the linguistic changes wrought by the confluence of English speakers from different regions of the United States, European immigrant groups, and Native Americans, English was also influenced by the landscape of the Southwest. And it is here that intersections with Spanish or Indian words are especially prevalent. For example, the word canyon (from the Spanish *cañon*), is rarely used in the eastern United States, where mountains such as the Appalachians have gentle ravines and hollows. A word borrowed from Spaniards already acclimated to the region became the appropriate word for the sharp-sided mountains of the Southwest and West.

People of African descent in the Southwest date back to the arrival of Estevanico in 1528, with Cabeza de Vaca's expedition. Black and mixed-blood people were among the first Spanish who settled the Southwest beginning in 1598. By 1680 there were almost 3,000 of these individuals in New Mexico alone. By 1792, 34 blacks and 414 mulattoes were among the residents of Texas. Over the centuries, blacks have lived and worked alongside Americans of Mexican, European, and Native American descent. Many slaves helped settle Texas; by 1860 slaves numbered 182,000, approximately 30 percent of the population. After the Civil War, free African Americans comprised a substantial number of the pioneers who traveled hundreds of miles to settle the Southwest.[16] African words have entered the language; for example, the word *"doggies"* as in the cowboy lyric "get along little doggies, for Wyoming shall be your new home," may be derived from the African word *kidogo*, meaning "a little something," or "something small."

English Borrowings from Spanish

English spoken in the Southwest has been influenced by Spanish. Some English speakers of Hispanic descent speak a variety of English with a Spanish accent and phonology. This variety of English, which is often called Chicano English by researchers, is comparable to the speech of some Texans that sounds either "black" or "white" to listeners. Moreover, most English speakers in the Southwest, and speakers elsewhere who are describing aspects of the Southwest, use words borrowed from Spanish. *Chili*, *bronco*, and *adobe* fall into this category.

EDUCATION

Language in the Southwest was influenced by the educational process in the nineteenth century. People were interested in speaking so-called better English, or having their children learn it from teachers. Nineteenth-century teacher education in the eastern United States affected portions of the Southwest, although perhaps not to the degree it did in other regions. In the twentieth century, college-educated teachers influenced speech patterns and reduced regional and ethnic differences in pronunciation.

Television, radio, and film, as in other parts of the country, "educate" the listener with their generally standard English pronunciation. However, films and television programming depicting parts of the Southwest contribute to a clichéd image of area residents that may or may not be true in actuality.

English dialects continue to flourish in the Southwest and, perhaps particularly, in Texas. Many Texans consider their dialect part of their identity. Some utter-

Spanish Words in English

adios: friendly expression of leave-taking, equivalent to *goodbye*
adobe: mud-based building material
amigo: friend, companion
arroyo: ravine
bandido: outlaw, bandit
bonanza: good fortune, profitable enterprise
bravo: expression of approval
bronco: wild horse
burro: donkey
camino real: main highway
cantina: a bar or saloon
chile or chili: Mexican pepper
compadre: friend
corral: pen or enclosure
diablo: the devil
frijol, frijole: bean, particularly Mexican pink or pinto
hacienda: ranch, especially a large one
hombre: man
junta: a political group or gathering
lobo: wolf
machete: a large, sharp knife
mañana: tomorrow
mesquite: a type of tree that thrives in the high desert Southwest
padre: priest
patio: courtyard
plaza: public square
poncho: blanket-like outer covering
pronto: quickly
ramada: a shelter made of tree branches
rancho: a ranch or stock-raising business
rodeo: large show involving bronco riding, calf-roping
señor: a man, a husband
siesta: afternoon nap
sombrero: a broad-brimmed hat
tequila: an alcoholic beverage made from the agave plant
tornado: wild wind storm
tortilla: a flat cake made of corn or wheat
vaquero: cowboy

ances of these Texas dialects such as *ain't* are criticized by outsiders as incorrect English. But Texans will continue these "mistakes" because they consider themselves different from other Americans. Outsiders, for example, often adopt such Texas Southernisms as *y'all*, *fixin' to*, and *might could*. In this way, language enables Texans, native or naturalized, to maintain their separate identity.

Cowboy English is a particular dialect that has spread into mainstream English, at least in the Southwest. The history of the cowboy identity can be traced to the *vaquero*, the Spanish cowboy, who managed cattle in the semidesert area of the Southwest before the arrival of Anglo-American settlers. Thus, many cowboy terms are derived from the Spanish language, though others are English words with the meaning redefined.

EUROPEAN LANGUAGES

Migrations into the Southwest continued in large numbers into the present; indeed, it might be said that, in terms of language dialects, the Southwest is still being settled. Immigrants from Germany and elsewhere brought their languages and cultures with them. The vitality of the languages have generally depended on groups clustering enough to develop cultural centers, the rate of marriage within an ethnic group, the amount of discrimination by other resident ethnic groups, the desire of an ethnic group to maintain its own language and culture as part of group and individual identity, and the function of language in a group.

Cowboy Words and Expressions in the Southwest

aim to: intend, as in "I aim to attend church"
antelope range: open country of the type inhabited by antelopes
barrel: midsection of a horse
bedding down: bringing cattle herd to rest; also refers to a human fixing a place to sleep
cutting out: selecting cattle for market
bit: metal part of bridle put in horse's mouth
bite the dust: be thrown off a horse
blaze: to mark a path or trail
boot hill: cemetery, as in for cowboys who died with their boots on
brand: to use a hot iron to make a permanent mark of ownership on cattle
break: to ride a will horse until it is tame; also, for a man, "to make a break" was to escape
camp: a ranch house or cabin occupied temporarily or seasonally
cattle baron: owner of large cattle-raising ranch
cattle trail: route used to take cattle to market; rutted or beaten path marked by cattle
chaps: leather leggings used to protect against brush or cactus
chuck wagon: wagon that carried all tools and supplies for cooking during a trail drive or roundup
corral: from Spanish, an enclosure for cattle or horses
dutch oven: heavy iron pot, constructed so hot coals could brown both top and bottom of food
greenhorn: a man unfamiliar with cowboy life
grub: food
hayseed: farmer
jerky: dried strips of meat
lasso: from Spanish, a rope used to catch horses or cattle
loco weed: a poisonous plant cattle sometimes consume
mustang: wild horse
nester: farmer
norther: a cold wind
open range: range land that had no fences or impediments
round-up: gathering of cattle to brand them
rustler: a horse or cattle thief
saddle blanket: a blanket placed between the horse and saddle
sourdough: fermented dough used to make bread on cattle drives
stampede: uncontrolled running of alarmed cattle
steer: castrated male cow
stray: a cow or horse not in its appointed herd or range
string: horses allocated to one cowboy or group of cowboys
wrangle: to herd horses
yearling: a year-old horse or cow

Texas Czech and Texas German, for example, are dialects and different in substantial ways from Czech or German spoken in Europe. This is due to the isolation of the language groups, contact with American English, and its usage mostly in ceremonial or cultural contacts rather than for everyday communication.

The largest Western European ethnic group in Texas were and are Germans; after Hispanics, German-origin peoples are the second largest ethnic group in the state. Germans first arrived in Texas in the 1830s, and they immediately settled in ethnic enclaves with other Germans, particularly in the south-central part of the state. In 1850 Germans comprised more than 5 percent of the state's population. In 1990 the U.S. Census found that 2,951,726, or 17.5 percent of the total population claimed pure or partial German ancestry. In the late nineteenth century and the twentieth century the German groups increasingly assimilated into the Anglo-Texas culture. Anti-German feeling during the two world wars accelerated the process.[17]

Czechs, a Slavic people from Bohemia, Moravia, and Silesia, though a smaller group than the Germans, numbered about 700 in Texas by the time of the Civil War. By 1900 the number had climbed to 9,204 and by 1910 to 15,074, but then the Czech immigration slowed. Approximately 250 Czech communities had been settled in Texas by the turn of the twentieth century. They were generally rural communities in agricultural areas. Czech language education began as early as 1855, although it declined in the late nineteenth century. Czech organizations encouraged study of the Czech language, and this advocacy has continued. Language is considered an integral part of Czech ethnic identity. Some thirty-three Czech-language newspapers and periodicals have been published in Texas, which reinforced use of the language.[18]

A number of Basques settled in Nevada, beginning at the time of the gold rush in the 1800s, although most found more success in herding livestock, especially sheep, than in prospecting for gold. Basques have essentially assimilated into typical occupations of the state, though many of them work in construction, gardening, and baking. According to the 1990 census Nevada had a total of 4,840 residents who identified themselves as Basque, with 1,156 in Reno and 254 in Sparks. The homeland of the Basques is a small region (about the size of Rhode Island) that straddles the border of Spain and France. Euskara, the Basque language, is in a language family by itself and is unrelated to the Indo-European languages of the peoples who inhabit countries surrounding the Basque homeland. Though use of the Basque language in Nevada is not widespread, the University of Nevada at Reno has a Basque Studies program and offers Basque-language courses.[19]

VIETNAMESE

Vietnamese began to arrive in Texas in 1975, after the collapse of the American-supported Saigon regime. The first to arrive were well-educated members of the former privileged elite. Later in the 1970s, refugees, referred to as boat people, joined them. Indeed, Vietnamese who originally settled in other parts of the United States relocated to Texas because of economic opportunity and the similarity in climate of some of its coastal areas to Vietnam. In 1985 the state Vietnamese population was projected at 52,500. The 2000 Census recorded 135,000 individuals of Vietnamese descent.[20]

The Vietnamese, like other ethnic groups, found that they had to learn English to be successful in the professions. By centering in large population areas such as Houston, Dallas, and Austin, though, the Vietnamese have been able to support radio, theater, publications, and holiday celebrations that reinforce Vietnamese heritage and language.

CONCLUSION

One of the most linguistically diverse regions of the United States, the American Southwest includes English and Spanish as dominant languages; an array of American Indian languages with sizable numbers of speakers; and other languages such as German, Vietnamese, and Basque. A substantial number of the region's inhabitants are bilingual or multilingual. This variety began some 500,000 years ago when small bands of migratory big-game hunters crossed from Siberia to North America on a land bridge and moved southward. The next wave came with first contact with Spanish explorers in the Southwest in the sixteenth century. First the Spanish, then the English and mixed Europeans arrived, and their interaction with Native Americans was calamitous—battle and diseases, population loss, altered social structures and, of course, changed languages. The kind of continuing change, particularly a mixture of languages, marks the course of language in the Southwest and will, no doubt, characterize language development in the region throughout this millennium and beyond.

RESOURCE GUIDE

Printed Sources

Campbell, L., and M. Mithun, eds. *The Languages of Native America: Historical and Comparative Assessment*. Austin: University of Texas Press, 1979.

Cassidy, F., ed. *Dictionary of American Regional English*. Vol. 1. Cambridge: Belknap Press of Harvard University Press, 1985.

Dutton, B. *American Indians of the Southwest*. Albuquerque. University of New Mexico Pr.; 1983.

Sando, J. *Pueblo Nations: Eight Centuries of Pueblo Indian History*. Santa Fe: Clear Light, 1998.

Sedillo Lopez, A, ed. *Latinos in the United States*. New York: Garland, 1995.

Silver, S., and Wick R. Miller. *American Indian Languages: Cultural and Social Contexts*. Tucson: University of Arizona Press, 1997.

Sturtevant, W., gen. ed. *Handbook of the Indians of North America*. Vols. 8–10. Washington, DC: Smithsonian Institution.

Web Sites

American Indian Language Development Institute
http://w3.arizona.edu/~aisp

Cassidy, Frederic. *Dictionary of American Regional English*.
Dictionary of American Regional English. March 23, 2004.
http://polyglot.lss.wisc.edu/dare/dare.html

The main page of one of the *DARE* projects, which was compiled under the direction of the late Frederic Cassidy, from field work carried out in 1965–1970.

Center for Basque Studies
http://basque.unr.edu

Ethnologue
http://www.ethnologue.com

The Handbook of Texas Online
http://www.tsha.utexas.edu/handbook/online/index.html

Institute for the Preservation of the Original Languages of the Americas (IPOLA)
http://www.collectorsguide.com/fa/fa059.shtml

Labov, William. *TELSUR*.
The Atlas of North American English. March 23, 2004.
http://www.ling.upenn.edu/phonoatlas/

The Web site through which one can access the TELSUR project, a survey of linguistic changes now under way in North America, as well as maps.

Varieties of English (with sound samples)
http://www.ic.arizona.edu/

This dialect site has a good overview of general linguistics (phonology, IPA, etc.). Features information on African American, American Indian, British, Canadian, Chicano, Northeastern, and Southern English.

Organizations and Institutes

American Indian Language Development Institute
Department of Language, Reading and Culture
College of Education, Room 517
University of Arizona
P.O. Box 210069
Tucson, AZ 85721-0069

Center for Basque Studies
University of Nevada, Reno / 322
Reno, NV 89557-0012

Ethnologue
7500 W. Camp Wisdom Road
Dallas, TX 75236

Institute for the Preservation of the Original Languages of the Americas (IPOLA)
560 Montezuma Avenue, Suite 201-A
Santa Fe, NM 87501-2590

Linguistic Institute for Native Americans (LINA)
2201 San Pedro N.E., Bldg. 4
Albuquerque, NM 87110

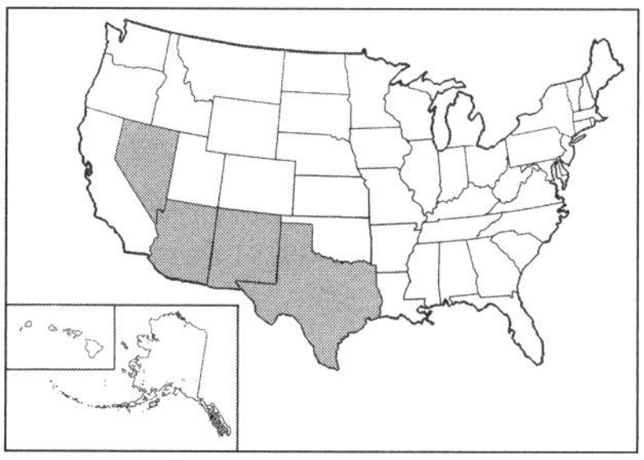

LITERATURE

Cory Lock

Far, far; the eye strains; it is a kind of warm pursuit to look on farther, it is as if one hunted the distance; one grows eager, then sated, then tired, with one's acquisitions of spaces. The earth seems larger than the heavens: one feels that yonder horizon cannot circumscribe this vastness.

—Sidney Lanier, "Letters from Texas"

I am reminded of a small example used in every Spanish class about a central cultural difference between English speakers and Spanish speakers. In English, one says, *I dropped the glass*, should such a thing happen. It is an "I"-centered instance, rugged individualism in its smallest moment. In Spanish, one says, "*Se me calló el vaso,*" which means, "The glass, it fell from me." This is a different world view, a way of accommodating the world, of living with it instead of changing it. Which is the better view is not the point, but I do think that our notions of the West as representing rugged individualism may, in fact, be faulty. There's a messy middle, something in between. I think that's the language of this place. It's a rugged pluralism.

—Alberto Ríos, "Introduction: West Real," *Ploughshares*

If you look with the mind of the swirling earth near Shiprock you become the land, beautiful. And understand how three crows at the edge of the highway, laughing, become three crows at the edge of the world, laughing.

—Joy Harjo, "Secrets from the Center of the World"

The nature of the Southwest and its people is a hotly contentious topic. Perhaps the most dominant mainstream perspective on the Southwest, and on the West as a whole, has been that of writers like Sidney Lanier (1842–1881), a man who visited Texas in the 1870s in hopes of improving his health and beginning a new life. He associated the Southwest's landscape with an overwhelming vastness—of territory, of sky, of possibilities. That he uses the term *acquisition* in describing his survey of the land is not surprising. For Lanier and those like him the Southwest offered the opportunity to make a piece of land one's own, to profit, or to better oneself. Many of the writers have shared this view, seeing the Southwest as a frontier, a place where civilization meets wilderness. Less stratified and confined than Eastern society, the Southwest from this perspective may seem dangerous, yet it also offers expansive possibilities for personal advancement. Carving out a niche for oneself in a harsh terrain and less-than-refined society may pose difficulties, but through hard work a miner, cowboy, schoolteacher, land speculator, or homesteading family may claim their piece of the American dream. The Southwest from this perspective is truly a place of rugged individualism.

Yet, as Alberto Ríos (1952–), a contemporary Chicano writer, suggests, the story of manifest destiny, of the myth of the frontier, of rugged individualism is only one world view. The hero of this cultural mythology has been predominantly Anglo and male. In recent decades scholars have critiqued this model, revealing that though the frontier meant promise for some, it meant fruitless struggle, injustice, and oppression for countless others. Further, as Ríos stresses, the very philosophy behind the concept of the frontier—the emphasis on individuality and the assumption of an "empty" land of plenty awaiting Anglo settlers—is culturally and racially biased.

Ríos reminds us of the diversity of the Southwest. It is a place with multiple landscapes, races, cultural traditions, and economic classes. It is rural *and* urban, rich in history *and* extremely modern, a place of wilderness *and* civilization. Many Southwestern writers express an ambivalence at such binaries and multiplicities. Approaches to region within Southwestern literature thus vary from work to work, and even within the same work. Yet many, like Ríos, find a richness within this uncertainty and inscrutability. Consequently, the "rugged pluralism" he describes brings with it the promise of fertility.

Both Lanier and Joy Harjo (1951–) use the Southwest's land to inspire and express the region's more intangible qualities. This too is a major trend among the writers of the Southwest. Writers frequently relate the land's qualities to the people who inhabit it. Though their interpretations may differ—land may signify individuality, inhospitality, openness, danger, promise, or doom—an overwhelming number of authors associate themselves and their communities with distinct local flora, fauna, and terrain. They describe the natural world as a source of beauty, nourishment, shelter, tradition, and cultural identity. Reflections on man's complex relationships with the land are central to Southwestern writing, and travel narratives—stories of journeys through the region's rich variety of terrains—take on potent significance.

Harjo also quite elegantly reveals the importance of region and of regional writing. Region helps determine how people work, how they play, and, in essence, who they are. From this perspective, the macro (the region) shapes the micro (the individual). The writers who remain close to home in their work should not be dismissed as provincial or isolated. Instead, we must pay attention to the local because its particularities are ours. What we learn on the local scale, say, from three crows laughing at the edge of a Shiprock highway, can become a powerful means of understanding and expressing global concerns.

SOUTHWESTERN WRITERS AND LITERARY MOVEMENTS

The first great stories of the Southwest, like those of almost all other regions and cultures, were oral. Native American tribes of the region, such as the Apache, Hopi, Navajo, Pueblo, and Zuni peoples, told stories of the world's creation, the origin of animals and man, the struggles of heroes, and the cunning of tricksters. Spanish explorers passed along legends of the fountain of youth, the golden cities of Cíbola, and hidden gold and silver mines. Mexicans and Mexican Americans tell folktales, such as those of La Llorona, the crying woman searching for her drowned children, and Malinche, the Indian woman said to have betrayed her people by acting as Cortez's interpreter and concubine. African Americans in the Southwest, particularly in Texas where black communities developed under the institution of slavery and remained even after emancipation, have rich oral traditions that include inspirational stories of resistance and terrifying tales of strange apparitions. Folk accounts by Anglo settlers of both historical and purely mythical heroes, such as Davy Crockett, Pecos Bill, and Billy the Kid, inspired much of the Southwest's early written literature, and the vital role these oral traditions and folk tales play in nourishing Southwestern literature as a whole should not be forgotten (see chapter on **Folklore**). There is a continuity between the stories and concepts that appear and reappear within oral tradition and the tales and thoughts that individuals have chosen to record in writing, making up the literature of the region.

EARLY SOUTHWESTERN LITERATURE

In their journals, letters, and reports on the people and places they encountered, Spanish missionaries and explorers provided the first written accounts of what today is known as the American Southwest. In his renowned *Relación* (1542), Álvar Núñez Cabeza de Vaca (1490–1557) described his experiences as part of the Narváez expedition to Mexico after his group's 1528 shipwreck off the Texas coast. Cabeza de Vaca and his companions, already famished and debilitated from a long, difficult voyage, are thought to have washed up on what is now Galveston Island, which they named Malhado (Misfortune) Island. After a brief period of recuperation the crew attempted to launch their barge, removing their clothes to keep them dry. But the boat was almost immediately capsized by an enormous wave, and as a result several crew members drowned. The naked and possessionless men who remained were enslaved by Texas Indians and soon became separated from each other. As years went by, Cabeza de Vaca gained some freedom and status among the native peoples while he served as a mediator and trader between various tribes. In 1533 he encountered three other survivors of the Narváez expedition: Castillo, Dorantes, and Estevanico the Moor. A year later they managed to escape their captors and journey westward. The group interacted with numerous Native Americans as they traveled through Texas and New Mexico; eventually they turned south to Mexico, where they reached a Spanish settlement in 1536.

Cabeza de Vaca has proved invaluable to historians and anthropologists because his is the first written account by a European of the Southwest and its peoples. Yet he has been equally important to literary scholars, who value *La Relación* as a prototype of several early forms of American literature, including the captivity narrative, the westward journey of discovery, and the tale of spiritual revelation. *La Relación* has gained particular attention for its detailed descriptions—and open admiration—of many aspects of Native American culture. Despite his early enslavement, Cabeza de Vaca gained increasing respect and compassion for Native Americans as he ventured across the Southwest and lived among various native peoples. Though he began his expedition as a conquistador, he ended it eight years later as an advocate of racial tolerance and human compassion.

Though the most well known of Spanish Southwestern writers, Cabeza de Vaca should by no means be understood as representative of all his contemporaries. From the sixteenth through the nineteenth centuries, numerous Spanish explorers, missionaries, and settlers recorded their impressions of what is today the American Southwest. English translations of many Spanish journals remain in print today, and they provide a valuable array of perspectives to anyone interested in early Southwestern literature, history, or culture. The authors of these reports include Fray Marcos de Niza (1539), Pedro de Castañeda (1540), Gaspar de Villagrá (1610), Fray Alonso de Benavides (1630), and Diego Vargas (1692). Of particular interest is Gaspar Pérez de Villagrá's *Historia de la Nueva México* (1610), a verse history of the Juan de Oñate expedition to New Mexico, and America's first epic poem, and a Portuguese account of the De Soto/Moscoso Expedition from Florida to Texas written by an expedition member known only as the Gentleman of Elvas (1557). During the late seventeenth and eighteenth centuries, Spaniards produced more formal histories of the present day Southwest; they include Juan Bautista Chapa's *Historia del Nuevo Reino de León de 1650–1690* and Fray Juan Augustín de Morfi's *History of Texas, 1673–1779*. Missionaries and others also continued to produce diaries during this period, many of which were not published until over a century later. Surviving diaries include those of Pedro de Rivera y Villalón (covering 1727), Fray Francisco Céliz (covering 1718–1719), Fray Juan Antonio de la Peña (covering 1721–1722), Marqués de Rubí (covering the year 1767), and Fray Jose de Solis (covering the year 1767).

NINETEENTH-CENTURY SOUTHWESTERN LITERATURE

Ongoing battles over territory, race, and culture dramatically affected the Southwest's literary development during the nineteenth century. In previous centuries Spain had only sparsely settled the area, choosing to focus primarily on searching for gold and other riches, subduing the Indian tribes it encountered in doing so, and, in some locations, attempting to convert these native peoples to Catholicism. When Mexico won its independence from Spain in 1821, the new government began to institute its own new policies in this region. Mexico wanted to firmly control its northernmost territory, but this required a much higher population density than the relatively small and distant Spanish missions provided. The Mexican government therefore implemented colonization laws that welcomed settlers of any nationality willing to swear allegiance to Mexico and to practice Catholicism. Anglo-Americans made up a large majority of these new settlers. This dramatic increase in Anglo-American settlement, legal and illegal, quickly led to conflict between the Mexican government and the portion of newcomers who abandoned the original settlement conditions. It also introduced a new dimension to the already existing racial conflict in the Southwest between Hispanics and Native Americans.

Anglo-Americans and the enslaved blacks many of these settlers brought with them created an entirely new set of race and culture-based perspectives. In the decades that followed the Mexican Revolution, the Southwest was the scene of intense conflict, including the Texas Revolution, U.S.-Mexican War, Civil War, Indian Wars, and countless smaller-scale but equally violent disputes over land and lifestyle.

Southwesterners documented much of this conflict in letters and journals that in many ways resembled those of their Spanish predecessors. For example, the Texas Revolution and its mythic battles, such as those at the Alamo and San Jacinto, fostered dynamic accounts from both the revolutionary and the Mexican perspectives. *Col. Crockett's Exploits and Adventures in Texas* (1836), by an unknown author, dealt with myth as much as historical fact, but it served to catapult Davy Crockett into American legend. Anthony Ganilh provided a less inflated account of the same war in *Mexico versus Texas* (1838), a history based on his own experience. Mexican accounts of the conflict were also numerous. One famous example is Juan N. Almonte's *Noticia Estadistica Sobre Tejas* (*Statistical Report of Texas*) (1835), which details the events leading up to the revolution. José Enrique de la Peña's *La Rebelión de Texas: Manuscrito Unédito de 1836, Por un Oficial de Santa Anna* (published in English as *With Santa Anna in Texas*) has received particular attention in recent years due to the Mexican officers' claim that David Crockett and six other Alamo defenders survived the battle and were later executed under Santa Anna's orders. Though most accept the document as authentic, a vocal minority have claimed it is a forgery.

While other conflicts, such as the Civil War and the U.S.-Mexican American War also captured the attention of Southwesterners, it was the Indian Wars that produced the military literature most directly associated with this region. Some of the most famous of these narratives are General Nelson A. Miles' *Personal Recollections and Observations* (1896), which he later revised and published as *Serving the Republic* (1911). Miles' account describes the military campaigns in Arizona, Texas, and other Western locales. Lieutenant John Bigelow Jr.'s *On the Bloody Trail of Geronimo* discusses the Apache Wars in Arizona, New Mexico, and Mexico. It was first published serially in *Outing Magazine* in 1886 and was eventually released in book form by historian Arthur Woodward in 1958. Journalist George W. Kendall provides a fascinating sequel to these accounts in *Narrative of the Texan Santa Fe Expedition* (1844), which chronicles the failed attempt to persuade the New Mexico territory to join Texas' newly formed republic.

Equally engaging nonfiction narratives describe the experiences of Anglo settlers seeking to find fortune or to start a new life in the Southwest. These autobiographies were generally written by homesteading men and women working to create a home and family on the frontier or by young men struggling to build their fortunes through ranch work, mining, or land acquisition. They testify to the authors' individual fortitude, traits that have been celebrated by later writers as distinctly American characteristics. Josiah Gregg's *Commerce of the Prairies* (1844) is one such account considered to be a classic of frontier literature. Gregg (1806–1850) first journeyed from Missouri to Santa Fe in 1831 in order to restore his health. He thrived on the expedition, became a trader, learned Spanish, and began regular business-related journeys through New Mexico, Texas, and Mexico. *Commerce of the Prairies* records his experiences as a traveling merchant, as well as observations on politics, customs, topography, and vegetation. The diversity of cultures which Gregg encountered in his travels is suggested by the members of just one of his expeditions: one Frenchman, two Germans, two Polish exiles, two American Indians (a Creek and a Chickasaw), several Mexicans, and a number of "backwoodsmen" Americans. Other notable accounts of frontier life include James O. Pattie's *Personal Narrative* (1831), Lewis H. Garrard's *Wah-To-Yah and the Taos Trail* (1850), and Noah Smithwick's *The Evolution of a State; or, Recollections of Old Texas Days* (1900). Frederick Law Olmsted's *A Journey through Texas* (1857) differs from many of these exuberant descriptions of Southwestern life in its critique of much of frontier civilization, particularly the institution of slavery in East Texas. John Crittenden Duval offers another unique account in his *Early Times in Texas* (serial form, 1868–1871; book, 1892) and *The Adventures of Big-Foot Wallace* (1870). Like other early nonfiction writers, Duval addresses regional history, but he is also highly conscientious of the mythic figures of Texas, whom he captures with the art of a true storyteller.

Most of the above accounts deal to some extent with life on the trail, but some of the most popular nineteenth-century nonfiction from the Southwest concentrates specifically on the experiences of cowboys. Perhaps the classic of all such nonfiction is Charlie Siringo's *A Texas Cowboy: or Fifteen Years on the Hurricane Deck of a Spanish Pony* (1885), which he revised and published later as *Riata and Spurs* (1927). Born to an Italian father and an Irish mother in Matagorda County, Texas, Siringo (1855–1928) began working as a cowboy at age fifteen. During the years that followed he acted as a trail driver for a number of ranchmen, helped establish the LX ranch, and met Billy the Kid. He wrote *A Texas Cowboy* soon after marrying in 1884 and moving to Kansas to become a merchant. In 1886 Siringo arrived in Chicago, where he became a cowboy detective and began hunting down outlaws throughout the West. He was appointed a New Mexico ranger in 1916, and during the 1920s he worked occasionally as a film advisor and extra on silent Westerns in California. Siringo's later books drew from many of these experiences. They include *A Cowboy Detective* (1912), *A Lone Star Cowboy* (1919), *History of "Billy the Kid"* (1920), and his last book, *Riata and Spurs* (1927), in which he compiled and revised his first two autobiographies.

Though much early literature depicts the Southwest as a uniformly masculine domain, women in fact produced a great quantity of nonfiction that describes a diverse range of settings and cultures, including life on the trail, in frontier settlements, in military camps, and in the natural world. One of the earliest of these accounts is Mary Austin Holley's *Texas* (1833), the first book in English that dealt entirely with Texas. Cousin to land developer and founder of Anglo-American Texas, Stephen F. Austin, Holley was able to witness and describe Austin's colony in its early stages. She revised and expanded her work into *History of Texas* (1836) and included accounts of the Texas Revolution. Another engaging nonfiction work is *Down the Santa Fe Trail and into Mexico, 1846–1847* (first published in 1926), the diary of eighteen-year-old Susan Shelby Magoffin, the first Anglo woman known to travel the Santa Fe Trail. Susan Wallace, the wife of New Mexico governor Lew Wallace, provides a unique perspective on nineteenth-century New Mexico in *The Land of the Pueblos* (1889). Though Wallace creates romanticized portraits of New Mexico, she also advocates for the preservation of Hispanic and Native American culture. Military wives also offered a unique view of Southwestern life as both insiders and outsiders of the American armed forces.

Elizabeth B. Custer wrote three books describing the military campaigns of her husband, George Armstrong Custer. These glorify her husband's career, yet they also voice the difficulties and frustrations of life as an army wife on the frontier. Of these three, *Tenting on the Plains, or Gen'l Custer in Kansas and Texas* (1887) most directly describes the Southwest. Another military wife's account, which was published just at the beginning of the twentieth century but is still in keeping with the subject and style of other nineteenth-century nonfiction, is Martha Summerhayes' description of the Apache wars, *Vanished Arizona: Recollections of the Army Life of a New England Woman* (1908).

As Southwestern nonfiction grew in quantity and quality throughout the nineteenth century, so, too, did the burgeoning school of fiction. Southwestern fiction often drew from the topics and style of the biographies and the histories of the Southwestern experience. A number of writers dramatized major historical events. For example, the Alamo inspired numerous dramatic fictions, including Augusta J. Evans Wilson's *Inez, a Tale of the Alamo* (1855) and Amelia Barr's *Remembering the Alamo* (1888). In the early twentieth century, Sara Driscoll, the woman responsible for the preservation of the physical structure of the Alamo, published a collection of short stories, *In the Shadow of the Alamo* (1906).

During the second half of the nineteenth century the Western also began to develop as a genre. The dime novel began to flourish throughout America and England as well. Consumed by a youthful, working-class audience, these works generally relied on highly romanticized formula plots. They included detective stories, society romances, rags-to-riches tales, and stories of cowboys and outlaws in the American West. Many of these Western precursors were also published in magazines, such as the *Saturday Evening Post*, *Collier's*, *McClure's*, *Cosmopolitan*, *American*, and *Everybody's*. *Wolfville* (1897), by Alfred Henry Lewis (1857–1914), is another such Western predecessor. The stories in this collection describe the fictional town of Wolfville, which Lewis based loosely on Tombstone, Arizona. Lewis' works, and others like them, describe larger-than-life male heroes and rely heavily on scenes of physical action, such as fights and chases. Mayne Reid (1818–1883), an Irish immigrant who came to the Southwest to fight in the U.S.-Mexican war, also wrote early Western-theme novels, such as the war romance, *The Rifle Rangers* (1850), and adventure tales such as *The Scalp Hunters* (1851). His works were successful in England and popularized an image of the Southwest as a land of adventure and romance.

Nevada was the home base for a particularly interesting group of writers, many of whom produced exceptional work as both journalists and fiction writers. The most famous member of this "Sagebrush School" was Samuel Clements, or Mark Twain (1835–1910), who as a young man lived in Nevada for three years while he worked for the newspaper, the *Virginia City Territorial Enterprise*. During this time period Twain produced a number of short, humorous, but also sharp and socially critical, sketches, including "Petrified Man" and "Washoe—'Information Wanted.'" Dan De Quille, the pen name of William Wright (1829–1898) was another major figure of the Sagebrush School, and he remains one of Nevada's most notable authors. Although De Quille's journalistic endeavors for the *Territorial Enterprise* are discussed later in this essay, his fiction deserves a mention in its own right. De Quille, like Twain, became famous for a number of literary hoaxes in which he would describe fantastic "news" stories and test readers' gullibility, and his short stories, such as "An Indian Story of the Sierra Madres," "The Goblin Frog," and "The Fighting Horse of the Stanislaus," reflect that same robust sense of humor. De Quille also produced several novellas that reveal the sensibilities of a remarkable storyteller. They are *The Gnomes of the Dead Rivers* (1880), *The Sorceress of Attu* (1894), *Dives and Lazarus* (mid-1890s), and *Prince of the Land of Lakes* (mid-1890s). Other major fiction writers of the Sagebrush School include Rollin Mallory Daggett, Samuel Post Davis, Charles Carroll "Judge" Goodwin, and James W. Galley.

The frontier-focused fiction and nonfiction that dominated Southwestern literature of the nineteenth century was not just important as regional literature. Frontier themes and Southwestern settings dominated American literature as a whole, and many began to see the frontier experience as the central defining factor of American identity, the crucible that formed unique national characteristics, such as independence, openness, self-sufficiency, and determination. Wisconsin native Frederick Jackson Turner was the theorist most closely associated with this perspective; he first presented his "frontier thesis" at the 1893 World's Colombian Exposition. In it, Turner described the frontier as the foundation of American individualism and democracy and pondered the results its "close" (due to decreasing availability of land for Anglo settlement) would have on society as a whole. Yet while the social, political, and economic aspects of the lives of people in the West were undergoing dramatic transformations by the end of the nineteenth century, as the nation urbanized and industrialized, literature's focus on the frontier and the traits Americans had come to associate with its inhabitants only increased. Though the era of the American pioneer may have been coming to a close, the mythology of the frontier was just beginning.

SOUTHWESTERN LITERATURE FROM 1900 TO THE PRESENT: WRITING THE MYTH OF THE WEST

Biographies, autobiographies, and histories continued to make up much of Southwestern literature throughout the twentieth century, particularly during its first half, when writers sought to document the ways of life that were quickly being erased by modernization. As in the previous century, the unique and mythic elements of ranching culture and frontier life inspired everyday people to document their own personal stories and those of the people around them. Such nonfiction works are numerous, but some examples from this time are J. Marvin Hunter and George W. Saunders' *The Trail Drivers of Texas* (1924), J. Evetts Haley's *The XIT Ranch of Texas* (1929) and *Charles Goodnight* (1936), Hilda Faunce's *Desert Wife* (1934), Sally Reynolds Matthews' *Interwoven: A Pioneering Chronicle* (1936), Edward C. Abbott and Helena Huntington Smith's *We Pointed Them North* (1939), and Agnes Morley Cleaveland's *No Life for a Lady* (1941).

It was during this nostalgic period that the Western genre became a mainstay of American literature. Western short stories and novels are most often set in the last decades of the nineteenth century, perhaps the most romanticized period of American history. They typically revolve around the cowboy protagonist but feature a cast of characters that includes lawmen, outlaws, railroadmen, Indians, and Mexicans. They often center around binary conflicts, such as white settlers versus Indians, ranchers versus farmers, and Western freedom versus civilization in the

East. Although the lifestyle of the open range most Westerns depict lasted only a few decades, from the end of the Civil War to the 1890s, its legacy continues in literature, film, clothing, music, and elsewhere in American popular culture.

Today, most scholars credit *The Virginian* (1902), by the Pennsylvania writer Owen Wister, as the first true Western novel. Its plot follows the love relationship of a handsome young cowboy and an Eastern school mistress. The conflict between Western values of freedom and independence and the civilization and culture represented by the East looms large throughout the work. Yet, in recent decades, some critics have suggested that a Texas writer, Mollie E. Moore Davis (1844–1909), should actually hold the title of first Western novelist. *The Wire-Cutters* (1899) describes the fence-cutting wars of the late nineteenth century; in doing so, it moves away from the romantic conventions that dominated earlier Western-theme works toward more realistic content and "serious" form. Davis is also known for her other literary works, including poetry, short stories, a history, plays, and novels, including *Under the Man-Fig* (1895) and *In War-Times at La Rose Blanche* (1888).

Many early Western fiction writers strove for the same historical authenticity we find in the nonfiction memoirs of this period. Though born in Indiana, Andy Adams (1859–1935) used his own experiences as a cowboy in Texas as a base for his fiction. The most famous of his works is *The Log of a Cowboy* (1903), which describes a trail drive from Texas to Montana. In it, Adams depicts the cowboy as a hardworking, everyday man and purposely avoids the romance many of his contemporaries were already attributing to cattle culture. New Mexico's Eugene Manlove Rhodes (1869–1934) likewise provides true-to-life tales of cowboy life in many of his novels, such as *Good Men and True* (1910), *Bransford in Arcadia* (1912), *The Desire of the Moth* (1916), *Copper Streak Trail* (1917), and *Stepsons of Light* (1920). Rhodes also produced two well-known stories of noble outlaws, *Pasó por Aquí* (1927) and *The Trusty Knaves* (1931), that possess the realistic qualities of his cowboy stories.

Other writers chose to romanticize Western themes by exaggerating a hero's attributes, developing extravagant plot lines, and weaving love stories into the works' overall plots. Though often associated with New York City, where he lived and wrote for the last ten years of his life, William Sydney Porter (O. Henry; 1862–1910) also wrote a number of Southwestern stories in this romantic vein, many of which were collected in *Heart of the West* (1907). These short stories are informed by his experiences in Texas, where he lived from 1882 until 1898. Most focus on South Texas, where O. Henry worked as a cowboy for two years. His stories draw heavily from sentimental and melodramatic formulas, often relying on standard romantic plots or surprise endings to engage a wide popular audience. Yet, enriched by his personal experience, stories such as "An Afternoon Miracle," "The Princess and the Puma," "The Hiding of Black Bill," and "The Last of the Troubadours" are engaging to read and offer useful insight into Southwestern culture at the beginning of the twentieth century. Other romanticized tales of the Southwest that continue to enthrall readers today are Emerson Hough's *Heart's Desire* (1903) and *North of 36* (1923), Steward Edward White's *Arizona Nights* (1904), and Conrad Richter's *Sea of Grass* (1937).

Though the cowboy dominates frontier fiction, outlaw stories have been a popular subgenre of Westerns since their inception. This literature generally depicts the outlaw character as a good man gone bad due to social or political persecution. Though the outlaws are law breakers, they often are depicted as Robin Hood figures, dark heroes who uphold a personal sense of justice in fighting legally sanctioned wrongs. At times these characters are completely fictional, but the most enduring of these stories have been based on historical characters, such as Jesse and Frank James, the Dalton gang, and Sam Bass. The most prominent Southwestern outlaw is, without a doubt, Billy the Kid, who has become a central figure in American literature, drama, song, and other popular culture. Nineteenth-century depictions of "the Kid" treated him as a ruthless killer; it was not until the twentieth century that his reputation was revised to that of a good badman. Perhaps the most prominent contributor to this revision was Walter Noble Burns, whose *Saga of Billy the Kid* (1926), part history and part mythology, revitalized and reworked the Billy the Kid legend. Burns' work inspired the first major film on the outlaw, MGM's *Billy the Kid* (1930), which was directed by King Vidor. Two notable works that predate *Saga of Billy the Kid* are those of Pat Garrett, the man who shot Billy the Kid, and Charles Siringo. Both Garrett's *The Authentic Life of Billy, the Kid* (coauthored with Ash Upson, 1882) and Siringo's *History of "Billy the Kid"* provide dynamic accounts of Billy the Kid's life that draw from the authors' own personal experiences. Numerous other versions of "the Kid's" story followed; some of the most prominent include John William Poe's *The Death of Billy the Kid* (1933), Miguel Antonio Otero's *The Real Billy the Kid* (1936), and J. W. Hendron's *The Story of Billy the Kid* (1948).

Another major author of outlaw fiction—and that of lawmen as well—is the popular Western writer Zane Grey. Though he grew up in Ohio, Grey's turn to Westerns was inspired by a visit to an Arizona ranch, and he continued to be drawn to the Southwest ever since. In his novels Grey creates superhuman characters inhabiting true to life Western backgrounds. Consequently, his historical romances are often valued by Grey fans for their realistic depictions of the geography, natural world, and sense of place unique to the Southwest. Yet Grey has also been criticized for stereotypical and even racist representations of American Indians and Mexicans. Grey's Southwestern novels are too numerous to list comprehensively here, but they include *The Heritage of the Desert* (1910), *The Light of the Western Stars* (1914), *The Lone Star Ranger* (1914), *To the Last Man* (1921), *The Thundering Herd* (1925), and *Arizona Ames* (1932).

In examining the Western genre, we most often find male authors penning the exploits of highly masculinized protagonists. From this perspective the genre seems to buy in wholeheartedly to that (in)famous saw about the Texas frontier originated by memoirist Noah Smithwick: "it's an adventure for men and dogs, but hell on women and horses." However, a number of women writers have successfully adapted the Western to recognize women's place within the history and mythology of the West while also retaining the popular elements that appeal to mainstream women audiences. A good example of such writers is New Mexico's Elsa Barker. Barker, who was married to writer and poet S. Omar Barker (1894–1985), was a regular contributor to the Western pulp magazine, *Ranch Romances*. Her female characters appealed to women readers because they were more complicated than their counterparts in male-authored novels. Barker's novels, all published under the name E. M. Barker to mask their author's female identity, include *Riders of the Ramhorn* (1956), *Clouds over the Chupaderos* (1957), *Cowboys Can't Quit* (1957),

Showdown at Penasco Pass (1958), *War on the Big Hat* (1959), and *Secrets of the Badlands* (1960). More recent female Western writers include Judy Alter, a prolific author of such works as *Mattie* (1987), *A Ballad for Sallie* (1992), *Libbie* (1994), and *Cherokee Rose* (1996), and Cindy Bonner, author of *Lily* (1992), *Looking after Lily* (1994), *Right from Wrong* (1997), and *The Passion of Debbie O'Barr* (1996).

The "Texas Triumvirate": Dobie, Webb, and Bedichek

As the frontier-focused Western genre developed during the first half of the twentieth century, a related interest in the peoples and traditions of the Western frontier influenced a significant number of folklorists. The unique school of Texas folklore, which blurred the line between folklore and fiction, is worth noting here. The leading figure of this group was Texas literary giant J. Frank Dobie (1888–1964). Dobie's greatest legacy was bringing Southwestern literature and culture into the light as material worthy of both serious scholarship and popular consumption. Some of Dobie's most famous tales are of Mexico and the Spanish Southwest, such as *Coronado's Children* (1931), *Apache Gold and Yaqui Silver* (1939), and *Tongues of the Monte* (1935, reprinted as *The Mexico I Like* in 1942). Yet his greatest concern was, without a doubt, ranching culture. Dobie published a host of works on the subject, including *A Vaquero of the Brush Country* (1929), *The Longhorns* (1941), *The Mustangs* (1952), and *Cow People* (1964). In his folklore Dobie sought to capture the feel of Southwestern folk tales. Consequently, he deemphasized accuracy and instead strove to create narratives that captured the rhythms, themes, and drama of Southwestern lore.

Dobie undeniably left a legacy throughout Texas and the Southwest. He constantly strove to reach the Southwest's general public in a variety of ways, and in addition to writing books, he wrote a syndicated newspaper column, had a radio program, published a Southwestern literature curriculum, and was very active in the Texas Folklore Society and the Texas Institute of Letters, all of which established him as one of the "big three" of Texas literature and culture. He inspired a generation of writers that followed him, although many of them sought to reveal aspects of Texas culture they felt Dobie had either distorted or ignored, such as African American Texas (J. Mason Brewer), Mexican American Texas (Américo Paredes), and Texas' Southern culture (William A. Owens). Yet, Dobie is also remembered for the liberal political leaning he developed in his later years, as he began vocal support of such causes as civil rights and freedom of speech.

J. Frank Dobie. Courtesy of the Library of Congress.

The other members of this Texas Triumvirate were historian Walter Prescott Webb (1888–1963) and naturalist Roy Bedichek (1878–1959). Although in recent years Webb has come under criticism for his stereotypes of Mexicans and Native Americans and his glorification of Anglo settlers, his works, particularly *The*

Great Plains (1931) and *The Texas Rangers* (1935), were instrumental in shaping the history and mythology of the West. His works are still indispensable to historiographers of the American West. Bedichek's distinctive talent lay in capturing the rich details of central Texas: the "poetry" of a mockingbird's song, the "gentle droop" of the black-eyed Susan, or the unique flora and fauna of a particular creek.[1] *Adventures of a Texas Naturalist* (1948) is considered the classic Bedichek work, but *Karánkaway Country* (1950) and *The Sense of Smell* (1960) also provide thoughtful, eye-opening reflections on the natural world that inspire in his readers an appreciation for the local environment. In the decades spanning the 1930s through the 1960s, the works and personalities of Dobie, Webb, and Bedichek solidified a school of Texas letters, and their emphasis on the state's Western, as opposed to Southern, characteristics remains today.

New Mexico Writers

At the same time that Dobie, Webb, and Bedichek were establishing their names in Texas, writers in other areas of the Southwest were focusing on similar themes: self-reliance, Anglo colonization, and regional myth. Many of these writers brought an precedented level of artistry to Southwestern fiction. New Mexico, in particular, inspired a number of skillful writers to capture the drama of the frontier. Born in Buffalo, New York, in 1903, Paul Horgan (1903–1995) moved to Albuquerque with his family in 1915. He also lived in Roswell for many years, first as a cadet at the New Mexico Military Institute and then later as its librarian. Many of Horgan's short stories and novels are set in the East, yet he has produced a masterful body of frontier-themed fiction sensitive to the Southwestern landscape and its effect on the human psyche. Horgan's works include poetry, short stories, essays, reviews, and descriptive sketches he called word-pictures. His major Southwestern novels include *The Fault of Angels* (1933), *No Quarter Given* (1935), *Main Line West* (1936), *The Common Heart* (1942), *Whitewater* (1970), *The Thin Mountain Air* (1977), and *Mexico Bay* (1982). Though an accomplished fiction writer, Horgan gained some of his greatest national acclaim for his nonfiction; his history of the Rio Grande, *Great River* (1955), and his biography of Juan Bautista Lamy, *Lamy of Santa Fe* (1975), both won the Pulitzer Prize for literature.

Three other major New Mexico writers of the 1930s through 1950s and beyond who likewise established themselves through frontier fiction are Harvey Fergusson, William Eastlake, and Conrad Richter. Fergusson (1890–1971) was one of Horgan's favorite writers, as well as a personal friend. Born in Albuquerque, Fergusson spent almost all his adult life outside the Southwest. Although he was physically distant, the history and culture of the Southwest captivated him throughout his life, a fact evident in his fascinating nonfiction, such as *Rio Grande* (1933) and *Home in the West* (1944), and his historical fiction, including *Wolf Song* (1927), *In Those Days* (1929), *Grant of Kingdom* (1950), and *The Conquest of Don Pedro* (1954). Though a less popular writer than Horgan or Fergusson, William Eastlake (1917–1997) has received significant critical acclaim, particularly for his first novels, *Go in Beauty* (1956), *The Bronc People* (1958), and *Portrait of an Artist with Twenty-Six Horses* (1963). This lyric trilogy, set in the mountainous New Mexican terrain he calls "Indian Country," describes the Bowman family adventures, rivalries, passions, and betrayals. Eastlake emphasizes the power of myth—both

American Indian and Anglo—to shape mankind and its perception of the natural world. Born in Pennsylvania, Conrad Richter (1890–1968) lived in New Mexico from 1928–1950. The landscape, history, and culture of this region inspired a number of his works, including a collection of short stories, *Early Americana* (1936), and several novels, *The Sea of Grass*, *Tacey Cromwell* (1942), and *The Lady* (1957).

The Taos Art Colony

Beginning in the 1910s, a unique group of intellectuals, writers, and artists settled in New Mexico, particularly in the Taos area. New Mexico drew these immigrants and visitors from other American regions less for its frontier legends than for its reputation as a mystical, spiritual, or inspirational environment. The scene also included visual artists, such as Georgia O'Keeffe, Paul Berlin, Alfred Steiglitz, and Raymond Johnson, who mingled with visiting writers. A foundational member of this artist society was Mabel Dodge Luhan (1879–1962), who settled near Taos in 1917 and over the following decades invited dozens of photographers, poets, writers, painters, and composers for long stays at her spacious, twenty-two room home. Luhan herself was the author of a number of admirable autobiographical reflections; two of the strongest are *Winter in Taos* (1935), *Edge of the Taos Desert* (1937), both of which highlight the power and richness of New Mexico's history and landscape. When English novelist D.H. Lawrence (1885–1930) and his wife, Frieda, first visited Taos in 1922, they stayed with Luhan. She later gave them a nearby ranch, where the couple lived from 1924 to 1925. It was there that he penned parts of *The Plumed Serpent* and drew inspiration for much of his essay collection, *Mornings in Mexico* (1927). Willa Cather (1873–1947) also lived and worked at Luhan's Taos home. Though best known for her depictions of the American Midwest, one of Cather's best works, *Death Comes to the Archbishop* (1927), provides a moving and historically accurate account of two French priests, Bishop Jean Baptiste L'Amy and Father Joseph Vaillant, living in the Spanish colonies of the New World.

Nevada Writers

The mid-twentieth century also produced one of Nevada's most renowned writers, Walter Van Tilburg Clark (1909–1971). Clark moved to Reno with his family at the age of nine, when his father became president of the University of Nevada. Clark himself entered academia, attending graduate school at the University of Nevada and, later in life, teaching creative writing at a number of universities. Throughout the 1930s Clark devoted himself to poetry, but it was his first novel that drew national recognition. Set in 1885, *The Oxbow Incident* (1940) is a dramatic portrait of a declining frontier and an indictment of mob violence. Clark's later novels, *The City of Trembling Leaves* (1945) and *The Track of the Cat* (1949), likewise use the mythic West to comment on contemporary, national concerns.

In the second half of the twentieth century, Southwestern writers continued to describe cattle ranching and frontier life, and many did so with a sensitivity to history, character, and landscape that distinguished them from formula Westerns. Robert Laxalt (1923–2001) provided unique portraits of Basque immigrants' lives on Nevada's high desert plains. Laxalt's first book, *Sweet Promised Land*, tells the experiences of his Basque sheepherder father in a classic story of American immigration. His novels include *A Man in the Wheatfield* (1964); his trilogy, *The Basque Hotel* (1989), *Child of the Holy Ghost* (1992), and *The Governor's Mansion* (1994); and *Time of the Rabies* (2000). Laxalt, the brother of former Nevada governor and U.S. senator Paul Laxalt, has also published extensively on Nevada and Basque immigrant history. Other eloquent contemporary descriptions of frontier life include the historical novels *Filaree* (1979), by Arizona's Marguerite Noble, and *A Beautiful, Cruel Country* (1987), by Arizona's Eva Antonia Wilbur-Cruce.

Mabel Dodge Luhan, 1934. Courtesy of the Library of Congress.

Texas Writers

In Texas a number of fiction writers have also created complex, compelling stories of frontier life. Benjamin Capps (1922–2001) distinguished himself through his authentic representations of historical circumstances in both fiction and nonfiction. All his novels describe inhabitants of the Great Plains during the last half of the nineteenth century. Three of these, *A Woman of the People* (1966), *The White Man's Road* (1969), and *Woman Chief* (1979), focus on Native American cultures, while the others, such as the award-winning *Trail to Ogallala* (1964), *Sam Chance* (1965), and *The White Man's Road* (1969), describe the experiences of Anglo setters. Robert Flynn (1932–) creates humorous depictions of trail life and traditional Texas in his many short stories and novels; best known among his works are *North to Yesterday* (1967) and *Wanderer Springs* (1987). Russell G. Vliet (1929–1984) established himself as a poet, playwright, and fiction writer. His lyric novels, *Rock Spring* (1974), *Solitudes* (1977; republished posthumously in revised version as *Soledad* in 1986), and *Scorpio Rising* (1985), bring to life the landscape and people of Texas' cedar country. One of the most beloved Texas writers of Western fiction is San Angelo's Elmer Kelton (1926–). Like Capps, Kelton published several admirable nonfiction works, but he is famous for his cowboy novels, which address the power of the frontier myth and its implications for contemporary life. Best known among these are *The Day the Cowboys Quit* (1971), which describes the 1883 cowboy strike of the Canadian River area, and *The Time It Never Rained* (1973), whose protagonist, Charlie Flagg, struggles to protect his land, his workers, and his own reputation through the devastating Texas drought of the 1950s. Kelton's other novels have also been well received; they include *The Good Old Boys* (1978), *The Wolf and the Buffalo* (1980), and *Stand Proud* (1984).

Larry McMurtry

In a 1981 lecture, "Ever a Bridegroom: Reflections on the Failure of Texas Literature," Larry McMurtry (1936–) somewhat infamously denounced Texas fiction as, on the whole, a failure. He particularly targeted nostalgia and sentimentality as the primary cause of a mediocre body of fiction that constantly rehashes the past rather than drawing from the compelling experiences of contemporary urban Texans. At this point McMurtry was a well-established author known for his own portraits of small-town Texas, including *Horseman, Pass By* (1961), *Leaving Cheyenne* (1963), and *The Last Picture Show* (1966). Yet, beginning in 1970 McMurtry had turned to urban life in a Houston trilogy: *Moving On* (1970), *All My Friends Are Going to Be Strangers* (1972), and *Terms of Endearment* (1975); then, to the Hollywood-set *Somebody's Darling* (1978). He continued to focus on urban life outside the state of Texas in *Cadillac Jack* (1982), set in Washington, D.C., and *Desert Rose* (1983), set in Las Vegas; however, neither of these works won much critical acclaim.

In 1985 McMurtry made a complete turnabout, looking away from the urban and back in time, as he penned the first of a series of mythic stories about the Western frontier. *Lonesome Dove* (1985), the story of Woodrow Call's and Augustus McCrae's frontier trail drive from Texas to Montana, was the best seller of McMurtry's career. McMurty later produced a sequel to this novel, *Streets of Laredo* (1993), and two prequels, *Dead Man's Walk* (1995) and *Comanche Moon* (1997). And he continued to create other stories of a mythic Western past, such as his version of the Billy the Kid legend, *Anything for Billy* (1988) and of Calamity Jane in *Buffalo Girls* (1990). McMurtry also wrote sequels to some of his earlier novels; *Texasville* (1987) and *Duane's Depressed* (1999) follow the characters of *The Last Picture Show* and *The Evening Star* (1992), which continued the story of *Terms of Endearment's* Aurora Greenway. Recently, he completed a new frontier series: *Sin Killer* (2002), *The Wandering Hill* (2003), *By Sorrow's River* (2003), and *Folly and Glory* (2004) that follows the British Berrybender family in the 1830s as they journey through the Great Plains. McMurtry has created many more novels and essay collections than those listed here; he is, perhaps, the premier writer of Southwestern literature today. A concrete testament to his popular reception has been the regular conversion of McMurtry's books to other media; these miniseries and films include *Hud* (1963), *Texasville* (1990), *Lonesome Dove* (1990), *Streets of Laredo* (1995), and *Dead Man's Walk* (1997).

Cormac McCarthy

Though McMurtry is, perhaps, today's best-known Southwestern writer, another Texas writer has received both glowing critical reception and a significant popular reception. Cormac McCarthy (1933–   ) wrote a number of powerful novels about the American South before moving from Tennessee to Texas in the early 1980s. Critic Harold Bloom called his first Southwestern work, *Blood Meridian* (1985), one of the greatest twentieth-century novels. Set in the Texas-Mexico borderlands of the 1940s, it reworks the classic Western plot in a dark and ruthless coming-of-age tale on a frontier consumed by horrifying violence, dehumanization, and epic power struggles. McCarthy followed *Blood Meridian* with his border trilogy, *All the Pretty Horses* (1992), *The Crossing* (1994), and *Cities of the Plain* (1998), which likewise focus on coming of age amid complex, often inscrutable struggles between innocence and evil on Southwestern borders.

Despite the power of the frontier myth, it has always been an ambivalent symbol. Like McCarthy, many Southwestern writers play on this ambivalence, using the frontier as an ideal site to narratively enact struggles between a host of polarized values: individual versus community, nature versus civilization, good versus evil. In considering Southwestern literature, it is essential to note the conflicts surrounding the Southwest's "true" identity and to understand it as a site that authors have connected not only with mainstream American tales of progress and hegemonic dominance but also with artistic retreat, revision, and resistance.

SOUTHWESTERN LITERATURE 1900–PRESENT: REVISING THE MYTH OF THE WEST

The concept of the frontier as a site fostering individualism, adventure, and self-improvement is central to the literature of the Southwest. Yet, it is equally important to recognize that the Southwest is not a monolithic space. As both physical place and ideology, it has meant many things to many different people. Some writers have reworked the myth of the West and Southwest in significant ways by emphasizing the presence of women and people of color within its boundaries, forwarding new conceptions of people's relationship with the land, revealing economic injustice, complicating the popular emphasis on stereotypical Western characteristics, and insisting on the urban and modern qualities of the contemporary Southwest.

Women have been significantly involved in rewriting the Southwest's frontier myth. The traditional story forwarded not only by Westerns, but also by personal narratives and historical fiction, has often overlooked the presence of women in the region. Consequently women have responded with direct critiques of frontier culture and social structure. Many of these writers emphasize the importance of women's lives and culture in the making of the contemporary Southwest. For example, *The Wind* (1925) by Dorothy Scarborough (1878–1935) features a woman protagonist and suggests how both the physical and cultural climate of the Southwest can destroy a sensitive and cultured woman. Scarborough wore several hats, including those of author, folklorist, and scholar; she held a PhD from Columbia University and taught literature and creative writing at both Baylor and Columbia Universities. Scarborough's folklore collections are *On the Trail of Negro Folksongs* (1925) and *A Song Catcher in the Southern Mountains* (1937, posthumous).

Other women have put forward virulent critiques of other forms of discrimination within the region, particularly racism. A powerful work written at the beginning of the twentieth century is Marah Ellis Ryan's *The Flute of the Gods* (1909). In this historical romance, Ryan portrays the sixteenth-century conflict between Hopi Indians and Spaniards from the Hopi perspective. *Giant* (1952) by Edna Ferber (1887–1968) is an epic novel of a twentieth-century Texas cattle empire, which also openly criticizes the sexism and racism prevalent in the state. Ferber's work was the basis of the classic film by the same name, which was released in 1955 and starred Rock Hudson, Elizabeth Taylor, and James Dean. Ferber's other works were also critically acclaimed; they include the Pulitzer Prize–winning *So Big* (1924), *Showboat* (1926), *Cimarron* (1929), and *Ice Palace* (1958).

Another classic critique of Texas racism is *Divine Average* (1952), by Lena Elithe Hamilton Kirkland (1907–1992). In it, Kirkland depicts Anglo Mexican American conflict in south Texas in the period between Texas statehood and the Civil War. All of Kirkland's works, including *Love Is a Wild Assault* (1959), *On the Trellis of Memory: A Psychic Journey into Pre-history* (1971, with Jinny Lind Porter), and *The Edge of Disrepute* (1984), feature women as central protagonists. Yet the works of Kirkland, Ferber, Ryan, and Scarborough are only a few of the many reworkings of the frontier myth that have been written by women. They are intended to emphasize, rather than survey, the role of women in such critiques. Many more women writers are included in the sections that follow.

Environmental Literature

Southwestern naturalists and environmentalists challenge traditional conceptions of the frontier as an inexhaustible supply of natural resources, such as water, timber, minerals and precious metals, and land for grazing, farming, or settlement. Many of these nature writers have turned to the essay or other forms of nonfiction both to document the powerful beauty of the Southwestern landscape and to call for preservation of its flora and fauna. A foundational work of Southwestern nature writing is John C. Van Dyke's *The Desert* (1901), one of the first works to celebrate the beauty and biological diversity of American deserts. Just a few years later, New Mexico's Mary Austin (1868–1934) published the seminal *Land of Little Rain* (1903), a moving collection of personal reflections on the cultures and natural environment of the Southwestern desert land she calls "the Country of Lost Borders."[2] Austin authored twenty-seven books and hundreds of articles; her publications include her autobiography, *Earth Horizon* (1932), other works of nonfiction, such as *The Land of Journey's Ending* (1924), and fictional works, such as *A Woman of Genius* (1912).

Nature writers have continued to have a strong presence within Southwestern literature since 1950. Joseph Wood Krutch (1893–1970) was already a well-established naturalist and literary scholar before he and his wife retired to Arizona in the 1950s. While there, he published a number of excellent works focused on the physical and philosophical connections of humans with the natural world; they include *The Desert Year* (1952), *The Voice of the Desert* (1954), and *The Great Chain of Life* (1956). Another Arizona writer, Charles Bowden, indicts man's voracious appetites and demonstrates their consequences, the ubiquitous destruction of the environment, in works like *Blue Desert* (1986), *Desierto: Memories of the Future* (1991), *Blood Orchid: An Unnatural History of America* (2002), and *Blues for Cannibals: The Notes from the Underground* (2002).

Roy Bedicheck, previously mentioned in the section on the "Texas Triumvirate," was the father of Texas naturalists. Following directly in his footsteps, John Graves (1920–) reveals the interconnection and rich diversity of Southwestern history, folklore, philosophy, and literature. Reminiscent of Henry David Thoreau's writing, Graves' essay collections, such as *Goodbye to a River* (1960), *Hard Scrabble* (1974), and *From a Limestone Ledge* (1980), are poetic ruminations inspired by the peoples and the places of north-central Texas. In a similar manner, Sessions S. "Buck" Wheeler (1911–1998) celebrates that which is unique and irreplaceable in the Nevada landscape. His works include *The Nevada Desert* (1971) and *The Black Rock Desert* (1978). Susan J. Tweit lives in Colorado, but in works such as *Barren, Wild, and Worthless: Living in the Chihuahuan Desert* (1995) and *Seasons in the Desert: A Naturalist's Notebook* (1998) she shares thoughtful, detailed reflections on the Mojave, Sonoran, Great Basin, and Chihuahuan desert landscapes.

Beginning in the 1970s, writers began to use fiction as another arena for communicating their fascination with the Southwestern environment. Prominent among such writers is New Mexico's John Nichols (1940–). Like other nature writers, Nichols often employs fiction to demonstrate the beauty of his adopted state. His novels use humor and engaging plot lines to draw in audiences while still strongly maintaining his sociopolitical message. *The Milagro Beanfield War*

Novelist Edward Abbey sits above the water playing his flute, Lake Powell, Utah. © Jonathan Blair/Corbis.

(1974), the best of these works, follows New Mexico water politics through the eyes of its protagonist, Joe Mondragon. Nichols' other fictional works also often address the hardships of working-class people struggling to make a living in the Southwest's harsh land. Among these are his New Mexico trilogy, *The Magic Journey* (1978), *A Ghost in the Music* (1979), and *The Nirvana Blues* (1981). His most recent work, *The Voice of the Butterfly* (2003), is a dark comedy describing the conflict that results when a new highway threatens an endangered butterfly.

Though he writes of Western landscapes both inside and outside the Southwest, Edward Abbey (1927–1989) is still the best-known environmental fiction writer of this region. Born in Indiana, Pennsylvania, Abbey first hitchhiked through the Southwest as a teenager. Abbey received both undergraduate and graduate degrees from the University of New Mexico. He is best known for *The Monkey Wrench Gang* (1975); in this cult classic, a group of ecological anarchists sabotage development projects throughout Utah and Arizona. *Fire on the Mountain* (1962), *Black Sun* (1971), *Good News* (1980), and *Hayduke Lives!* (1990) likewise describe memorable protagonists who struggle against the annihilating forces of civilization and modernity. Abbey is equally well known for his nonfiction works. Based on his own experiences as a ranger at Arches National Monument, Utah, *Desert Solitaire* (1968) contains both moving reflections on and poignant lamentations about civilization in the form of tourists, dams, and bureaucracy infiltrating the desert he sees as one of the last bastions of American wilderness. Other excellent nonfiction works by Abbey include *The Journey Home* (1977), *Abbey's Road* (1979), *Down the River* (1982), and *One Life at a Time, Please* (1988).

The Southern Southwest

A number of Texas writers offer descriptions of their state's Southern culture that, like much nature writing, stands in sharp contrast to the Westerns and frontier-focused writing that is most readily associated with the Southwest. Rather than examining ranching culture, these writers generally concentrate on farm life, particularly the cotton-farming culture. In addition to her book *The Wind* (1925), Dorothy Scarborough created many other excellent works on Texas farming culture. Many of them, including *In the Land of Cotton* (1923), *Can't Get a Redbird* (1929), and *The Stretch-Berry Smile* (1932), expose the injustices of the tenant-farm system. Mattie Ruth Cross (1887–1981) was another Texas woman who established herself through her fictional accounts of Texas cotton culture. *The Golden Cocoon* (1924) and *The Big Road* (1931) depict the struggles of tenant farmers, emphasizing the monotony and ignorance resulting from their rural isolation.

During the 1940s Texas writers produced some of the classics of Texas literature, which, like Scarborough's and Cross' works strove to expose the injustices of sharecropping and tenant farming. Known best among these is George Sessions Perry's *Hold Autumn in Your Hand* (1941), which describes one year in the life of a Texas tenant farmer. *Hold Autumn in Your Hand* received both the National Book Award and a Texas Institute of Letters award, and John Renoir, a well established French filmmaker, subsequently transformed Perry's novel into the film *The Southerner* (1945). Perry (1910–1956) created several other works about Texas' Southern cotton culture; they include his two memoirs, *My Granny Van* (1949) and *Tale of a Foolish Farmer* (1951). Two other famous indictments of the sharecropping system are Edward Everett Davis' *The White Scourge* (1940) and John W. Wilson's *High John the Conqueror* (1949). Wilson's account is unique because of its focus on the struggles of African American sharecroppers.

Whereas these works concentrate specifically on the institution of cotton farming, other Texas writers have focused more broadly on the Southern culture of East and Central Texas. One of the best of these writers is Katherine Anne Porter (1890–1980). Porter's close attention to everyday events and relationships, combined with her eloquent writing style, eventually established her as one of the best American short fiction writers of the twentieth century. Porter's personal experiences in her native state inspired many of her short stories, yet her relationship with Texas was a complicated one. Although national critics celebrated Porter's writing, awarding her both the Pulitzer Prize and the National Book Award, Texan critics were slow to appreciate her talent, quite likely because of her reputation for focusing on Texas' Southern, rather than Western, characteristics. Porter did describe Mexican culture and revolution (in stories such as "María Concepcíon," "Virgin Violeta," "The Martyr," "Flowering Judas," and "Hacienda") and violence on a South Texas farm (in her novella, *Noon Wine*). Yet she is best known for her accounts of such Southern topics as the legacy of slavery ("The Old Order"), family relationships ("The Jilting of Granny Weatherall," "The Old Order," "Old Mortality," and "Pale Horse, Pale Rider"), and farm life ("Rope," "He," and "Holiday"). Further, Porter's elegant, lyric style distances her from many of the linguistically minimalist Western writers. Porter's short-story collections include *Flowering Judas and Other Stories* (1935), *Pale Horse, Pale Rider* (1939), and *The Leaning Tower and Other Stories* (1944). She is the author of one full-length novel, *Ship of Fools* (1962).

Katherine Anne Porter, 1940. Courtesy of Photofest.

After World War II, three writers rose to prominence within this Southern tradition; these were "the three Williams": William Goyen (1915–1983), William Humphrey (1924–1997), and William Owens (1905–1990). Goyen established his name as a Southern writer in *The House of Breath* (1950), a modernist novel. Experimental in form, *The House of Breath* describes the dead members of a family, as narrated through the consciousness of Boy Ganchion as he revisits the East Texas family home. Goyen produced a number of other creative works, including short stories, plays, and poetry. His work has been widely translated and particularly well received by German and French audiences, intrigued by both his insight into American Southern culture and his modernist sensibility. William Humphrey's fiction describes the culture of northeast Texas, where he spent his early life. *The Ordways* (1965) follows the successes and tragedies of the Ordway family; mock-epic in form, it parodies Southern nostalgia and sentimentality. Humphrey's memoir, *Farther Off from Heaven* (1977), tells the story of his father's early death and its effect on Humphrey's life; but it also chronicles East Texas life in general from the 1930s to the 1960s, a change also documented in another of Humphrey's novels, *Proud Flesh* (1973). Folklorist William Owens is best known for his account of the struggles of poor Lamar County farmers in a trilogy memoir that consists of *This Stubborn Soil* (1966), *A Season of Weathering* (1973), and *Tell Me a Story, Sing Me a Song* (1983). These works are remarkable for the way they weave folklore, particularly songs and music traditions, throughout the story of his own life. There have been many other accomplished Texans writing in the Southern tradition in recent years; among them are Leon Hale, author of *Half a Look of Cain: A Fantastical Narrative* (1994); Mary Karr, author of *The Liar's Club* (1995) and *Cherry* (2000); and Jane Roberts Wood, author of the trilogy *The Train to Estelline* (1987), *A Place Called Sweet Shrub* (1990), and *Dance a Little Longer* (1993), as well as *Grace* (2002) and *Roseborough* (2003).

African American Literature

Many African American authors of the Southwest have come from and written about this same farm-based culture of East and Central Texas. This is in part a legacy of the institution of slavery in nineteenth-century Texas. During that period many African Americans were brought to the state, particularly to the cotton-farming areas of East Texas. By 1860, 30 percent of Texas' population consisted of enslaved African Americans. Many blacks remained in Texas following the Civil War, a fact that continues to affect demographics today. The 2000 U.S. Census shows that Texas is 12 percent African American, and in many East Texas counties this percentage reaches 20 percent. In comparison, African Americans make up of 3 percent of Arizona, 7 percent of Nevada, and 2 percent of New Mexico. Thus, the literature and culture of East Texas is fundamental to any examination of blacks in the nineteenth-, twentieth-, or twenty-first-century Southwest.

Writing at the beginning of the twentieth century, Sutton E. Griggs (1872–1933) created extremely political novels that suggested the ongoing social and cultural oppression of African Americans in the United States, and in them he called for radical change. Griggs is best known for his first novel, *Imperium in Imperio* (1899), which describes a Waco-based revolt in which African Americans attempt to seize Texas for an all-black nation. Griggs' other novels, *Overshadowed* (1901), *Unfettered* (1902), *The Hindered Hand* (1905), and *Pointing the Way* (1906), likewise virulently denounce the status quo of race relations in the United States and call African Americans to political action. Another black Texan, J. Mason Brewer (1896–1975), achieved national recognition as a folklorist for his ability to capture the unique culture of black Texas—and later of black America—particularly through his attention to dialect. His major works are *The Word on the Brazos* (1953), *Aunt Dicey Tales* (1956), *Dog Ghosts and Other Texas Negro Folktales* (1958), *Worser Days and Better Times* (1965), and *American Negro Folklore* (1968). Two other captivating works are C.C. White's memoir, *No Quittin' Sense* (1969), which details the struggles of black Texans in the segregated society of East Texas, and Annie Mae Hunt's *I Am Annie Mae* (1983, collected and edited by Ruth Winegarten), which documents Hunt's struggle for personal and economic independence. All these works are important to Southwestern literature as a whole for the way they challenge and rework dominant myths of regional identity.

Although many black Southwestern writers draw from the Southern tradition, this is by no means exclusively the case. Contemporary author Terry McMillan (1951–) is a case in point. Though born in Port Huron, Michigan, McMillan lived in Tucson, Arizona, for a number of years while she held a faculty position at the University of Arizona. Her best seller, *Waiting to Exhale* (1992), details the lives of four black Phoenix women. McMillan's other works include *Mama* (1987), *Disappearing Acts* (1989), *How Stella Got Her Groove Back* (1996), and *A Day Late and a Dollar Short* (2001). Jewell Parker Rhodes, a professor of creative writing at Arizona State University, excels at bringing to life overlooked moments of African American history. *Douglass' Women* (2002) is a historical novel that describes the lives of two women, the black wife and the white mistress who loved the famous self-taught former slave Frederick Douglass. Rhodes' earlier works include the critically acclaimed *Voodoo Dreams* (1993), the story of Marie Laveau, a voodooist in nineteenth-century New Orleans, and *Magic City* (1997), an imaginative rendering of the 1921 Tulsa Riot. Houston's Anita R. Bunkley writes romances that center around African American women and weave together history, family, and ongoing struggles for self-improvement. Her works include *Emily, the Yellow Rose* (1989), *Black Gold* (1994), *Wild Embers* (1995), and *Starlight Passage* (1996).

American Indian Literature

For many centuries American Indian folklore has been a major cultural force in the Southwest, but the late twentieth century witnessed a flowering of written works related to American Indian culture and experiences. These fiction writers drew from oral traditions and from earlier American Indian histories and memoirs. Among these earliest authors of personal and tribal history was Sarah Winnemucca Hopkins (1844–1891). Born among the Paiutes of Nevada, Winnemucca dedicated her life to the public defense of her tribe's cause. Her *Life among the Piutes* (1883) tells the story of her own life, but it also dramatically illustrates the Paiute struggle to protect their lands and culture. Another notable early work is James Paytiamo's *Flaming Arrow's People* (1932), an illustrated account of his childhood and of the Acoma way of life.

The 1960s witnessed a notable increase in fiction by Native American authors. One of the best known of such writers is Pulitzer Prize winner N. Scott Momaday (1934–). Although Kiowan, Momaday spent much of his life among Navajo, Pueblo, and Apache Indians on reservations where his parents were teachers. He received his BA from the University of New Mexico and his doctorate from Stanford University. It was his first novel, *House Made of Dawn* (1968), that won the Pulitzer and thrust Momaday—and American Indian writing—into the national spotlight. *House Made of Dawn* describes the return of Abel, a Tano Indian, to his New Mexican home after World War II. There he struggles with a conflict of cultures, the traditional and harmonious world of his grandfathers and the modern, materialistic culture of Anglo Americans. Abel seeks to find a way to survive in the modern world while still upholding the Tano world view. In addition to a number of poetry volumes, Momaday has also written a second novel, *The Ancient Child* (1989), a memoir called *The Names* (1987), and a collection of short stories, *In the Presence of the Sun* (1992). Momaday has lived in Tucson since 1982, where he is a professor at the University of Arizona.

Like Momaday, New Mexico's Leslie Silko (1948–) is both poet and fiction writer. Silko was raised on the Laguna Pueblo Indian reservation and later attended school in Albuquerque. Her first novel, *Ceremony* (1977), also parallels Momaday's first fiction in that it describes the struggles of a World War II veteran as he returns to his home town and native culture. *Almanac of the Dead* (1991) is Silko's darkest work. Silko spent ten years writing the 700-page novel, which is set in Tuscon and traces that city's long history of corrupt trade and exploitation of both the land and native peoples. A harsh critique of Anglo injustice, *Almanac of the Dead* suggests that the only hope for Native Americans is the day when they reclaim their land. Silko's other novels have also been well received by both critical and popular audiences; they include *Storyteller* (1981), *Yellow Woman* (1993), *Yellow Woman and a Beauty of the Spirit* (1996), and *Garden in the Dunes* (1999).

A number of Anglo authors have also established themselves through their fictional descriptions of American Indian cultures. Though his father was part Cheyenne, Frank Waters (1902–1995) himself grew up in Colorado in a predominantly Anglo culture. Waters' early works dealt with a range of topics related to the West, yet over time Waters grew increasingly fascinated by the spirituality of the Hopi, Navajo, Pueblo, and pre-Columbian peoples. *The Man Who Killed the Deer* (1941), a classic of Southwestern literature, tells the story of Martiniano, an Indian boy who returns home from a government school to find himself in conflict with both Native American and Anglo cultures. A prolific writer of both fiction and nonfiction, Waters' other works include his novels *People of the Valley* (1940) and *Flight from Fiesta* (1986) and two memoirs, *Pumpkin Seed Point* (1969) and *Mountain Dialogues* (1981).

Oliver La Farge (1901–1963) is another Anglo who wrote about a range of topics related to the Southwest but who is best known today for his fictional accounts of American Indian life. La Farge won the Pulitzer Prize for his first novel, *Laughing Boy* (1929), which depicts the encroaching influences of Anglo culture on Navajo society during the early twentieth century. His other fictional works that depict Native American life include *Sparks Fly Upward* (1931) and *The Enemy Gods* (1937), as well as a number of short stories from his collection, *All the Young Men* (1935).

Richard Bradford's *Red Sky at Morning* is a classic coming-of-age story. In it, Josh, an Anglo boy from Mobile, Alabama, moves to Santa Fe in the 1940s. As Josh adapts to the Indian and Hispanic cultures that surround him, Bradford conveys a sensitive portrait of Indian culture and of race relations in general in the New Mexico of the 1940s. Finally, Tony Hillerman is a contemporary Anglo author who, like Waters and La Farge, has established himself through his representations of American Indian life; his mystery novels are discussed later in this essay.

Mexican American Literature

During the twentieth and twenty-first centuries, Mexican American writers in particular have been influential in revising the myth of the West. Previously, much Southwestern literature depicted Anglo heroes as valiantly defending what were deemed civilized values against the supposedly barbaric Native Americans and corrupt Mexicans. Chicano writers have worked hard to revise this version of history, revealing both the violence of Anglo intruders and the richness of American Indian and Mexican cultures. Folklorist and author Américo Paredes (1915–1999), was one of the major early figures driving this revision. His scholarly cultural analysis, *With His Pistol in His Hand* (1958), which examined the *corridos* (folk ballads) and legends surrounding the folk hero Gregorio Cortez, established Paredes as a major ethnographer. His novel, *George Washington Gomez*, was written between 1935 and 1940 but published in 1990. It is a compelling story of a young man's search for both Mexican and American identity during the Great Depression. Paredes' short-story collection, *The Hammon and the Beans and Other Stories* (1994) is also a skillful portrait of cultural conflict in the Texas-Mexico borderlands at a range of historical moments.

Another major force in revising mainstream perceptions of Mexican-American literature and culture has been the project called Recovering the U.S. Hispanic Literary Heritage. Founded in 1990, this program has worked to reintroduce into print literature by Hispanic Americans written before 1960. Though its scope was nationwide, the Recovery Project helped reshaped the face of Southwestern Literature. The program has published or republished a number of Southwestern works, including a new translation of Cabeza de Vaca's *Relación* (1993; written in 1542), Leonor Villegas de Magnón's memoir, *The Rebel* (1924; written in the 1920s), Miguel Antonio Otero's *The Real Billy the Kid* (1998; originally published 1936), Jovita González's *Dew on the Thorn* (1997; written between 1926 and the late 1940s), and Cecilo García-Camarillo *Selected Poetry* (2000; written in the 1960s).

Many Mexican American writers choose to publish in Spanish. One such writer was Tomás Rivera (1935–1984), the son of Mexican immigrants who worked as migrant farm laborers. He wrote his seminal *. . . y no se lo trago la tierra* (*. . . And the Earth Did Not Devour Him*) (1970) in Spanish, and by doing so he could directly reach other Latinos with immigrant backgrounds who spoke Spanish as their first language. His tale of migrant farm workers of the 1940s and 1950s has subsequently been translated into English and today is considered a classic of Southwestern literature. Rolando Hinojosa-Smith is best known for his serial work, the *Klail City Death Trip Series*. Hinojosa has chosen to write part of this work, which depicts the changing cultural climate of the fictional Belken County, South Texas, in English and part in Spanish. *Estampas del Valle y otras obras* (1971) is one such Spanish-language work, *Mi querido Rafa* (1981) is more or less bilingual, and works such as his *Korean Love Songs* (1978) were conceived of and written in English. Hinojosa's more recent works move in and out of the Belken County world as its residents fight in the Korean War and investigate crime on the Mexican side of the border; they include *The Useless Servants* (1993) and *Ask a Policeman* (1998).

Chicanas have been major figures in recent Southwestern literature. Kleya Forté-Escamilla (1941–) often publishes under the name Edna Escamill. She is of Peruvian, Mexican, and Anglo descent and has spent much of her life in southwestern Arizona. Not surprisingly, Forté-Escamilla emphasized multiculturalism in her works, such as *Daughter of the Mountain* (1991), *Mada: An Erotic Novel* (1994), and *The Storyteller with Nike Airs and other Barrio Stories* (1994). Denise Chavez (1948–) was born and still lives in Las Cruces, New Mexico, where she teaches creative writing at New Mexico State University. As an actress, she draws on storytelling and dramatic traditions in all her literary works. She is the author of numerous plays including *The Wait* (1970), *Plaza* (1984), and *Women in the State of Grace* (1989), as well as the novels *The Last of the Menu Girls* (1986), *The Woman Who Knew the Language of Animals* (1992), *Face of an Angel* (1994), and *Loving Pedro Infante* (2000).

One of the biggest celebrities in Southwestern literature today is San Antonio's Sandra Cisneros (1954–). Her award-winning first novel, *House on Mango Street* (1984), speaks to both young readers and adult audiences in describing a Mexican American girl growing up in a working-class Chicago neighborhood. Cisneros' short-story collection, *Woman Hollering Creek* (1991), likewise addresses the coming-of-age of young Mexican Americans, but its broad scope also reveals many different faces and personalities of the Latino community: widows, grandfathers, mothers, children, artists, lovers, vendors, teachers, dishwashers, and exterminators. In attempting to capture the multiple facets of the Mexican American community, *Woman Hollering Creek* also pays close attention to a range of folk and popular culture traditions. *Caramelo* (2002), Cisneros' most recent work, is a multigenerational saga of the Reyes family that spans from the late nineteenth century to the mid-twentieth, and extends its reach to Chicago, San Antonio, and Mexico City. Cisneros' coming-of-age themes appeal to diverse audiences, and this, combined with her progressive feminist messages, has led her to be one of the most often anthologized Mexican American writers.

Like Cisneros, many Chicano and Chicana writers have tried to capture the folk traditions of Mexican Americans. The works of many of these writers have a lyric, mythical quality that remind the reader of how the Southwest's diverse cultural history continues to enrich present-day life. Arturo Islas (1938–1991) is one such writer. His novels, *The Rain God* (1984), *Migrant Souls* (1990), and *La Mollie and the King of Tears* (published posthumously in 1996) portray everyday people living extraordinary lives. In his subtle, poetic novels, Islas weaves the supernatural into the fabric of modern day life and such issues as divorce and homosexuality.

A mythical quality also permeates the works of New Mexico's Rudolfo Anaya (1927–). His trilogy composed of *Bless Me, Ultima* (1972), *Heart of Aztlán* (1976), and *Tortuga* (1979) deals loosely with the search for self-identity and the healing power of belief. Some of Anaya's more recent works, such as *Jalamanta* (1997), have moved from the magical realism of the earlier novels to New Age philosophy that some reviewers find "preachy" and overly simplistic in its reliance on binaries.[3] Yet *Alburquerque* (1992) won the PEN Center West award for fiction, and Anaya's recent mysteries, *Zia Summer* (1995), *Rio Grande Fall* (1996), and *Shaman Winter* (1999), have also been very well received.

Other writers have chosen to focus on urban life and the struggles of modern Mexican Americans. Dagoberto Gilb's (1950–) short-story collections, *The*

Magic of Blood (1993) and *Woodcuts of Women* (2001), and his novel, *The Last Known Residence of Mickey Acuña* (1995), provide compelling portraits of working-class Chicano life that are rooted in the cities of the Southwest. Highways, building sites, airports, and department stores define the landscape of these stories; among them, very real characters struggle with the tragedies and indignities of life. The gay themes and Los Angeles setting of many of John Rechy's works have at times distanced him from others in the Southwestern Chicano tradition, but the El Paso native has also set many of his novels in his home state, including *City of Night* (1964), *This Day's Death* (1969), *The Fourth Angel* (1972), *Marilyn's Daughter* (1988), and *The Life and Adventures of Lyle Clemens* (2003). All these works give a vivid sense of the rhythms of the urban Southwest, while also taking a more complicated and complex view of Mexican American identity.

Urban Writers

A final way contemporary writers have revised the myth of the West has been through an emphasis on modern, urban life. As previously noted, in 1981 Larry McMurtry, after denouncing nostalgic, pastoral literature, made a famous call for urban-based Texas fiction and during the 1970s and 1980s made this switch himself. Yet there were writers in Texas and throughout the Southwest who preceded McMurtry. One of the most famous of these writers is Billy Lee Brammer (1929–1978). His *The Gay Place* (1961) is a canonical American political novel often compared with Robert Penn Warren's *All the King's Men*. It consists of three interrelated novellas, each of which eloquently describe the idiosyncrasies of Austin's political and cultural climate of the 1950s. Arthur Fenstemaker, a character who looms large throughout the three works, is based on Lyndon Johnson, a man Brammer himself knew through work on LBJ's staff. Through such characters Brammer is able to convey a new Texas, Southern in political tradition, Western in individualism, yet modern through and through. Other excellent urban-based works by Texas writers followed Brammer's, and many of them, including Edwin Shrake's *But Not for Love* (1964) and *Strange Peaches* (1972), Peter Gent's *North Dallas Forty* (1973), and Larry McMurtry's *Moving On*, *All My Friends Are Going to Be Strangers*, and *Terms of Endearment*, focused on the big money, conservative politics, and wild lifestyles of Dallas and Houston.

Texas women have also made names for themselves through their accounts of urban and suburban life. Beverly Lowry, Laura Furman, Shelby Hearon, and Sarah Bird are four of the most prominent writers whose works often focus on Texas middle- and upper-class society. For example, Beverly Lowry's *Daddy's Girl* (1979), Shelby Hearon's *Now and Another Time* (1976), and Sara Bird's *Alamo House* (1986) and *Virgin of the Rodeo* (1999) emphasize Texas' cultural idiosyncrasies. Other works, like Hearon's *The Second Dune* (1973) and *Hannah's House* (1975) and Bird's *Mommy Club* explore women's roles within contemporary marriage, while Hearon's *Group Therapy* (1984) and *Ella in Bloom* (2001) and Bird's *The Yokota Officer's Club* (2001) focus on mother-daughter relationships. A surprising number of these writers' works also deal with death and dying, including Lowry's *The Perfect Sonya* (1987), *Breaking Gentle* (1988), and *Crossed Over: A Murder, a Memoir* (1992); Furman's *The Shadow Line* (1982) and *Ordinary Paradise* (1998); and Hearon's *Life Estates* (1994) and *Footprints* (1996). Overall, Lowry, Furman, Hearon, and Bird, bring to Southwestern literature a refreshing emphasis on the modern, city-dwelling woman's life. They explore the heartaches and tragedies that everyone must face but do so with remarkable insight and humor.

Arizona has been another major site of urban Southwestern literature. Though Barbara Kingsolver (1955–) writes on a variety of locations and topics, many of her works deal explicitly with the urban Southwest. She is an extremely popular writer who won numerous book awards despite some critics' claims that her works are too simplistic or politically correct.[4] Yet most readers consistently praise Kingsolver's engaging heroines and unfailing humor. Her works include *The Bean Trees* (1988), *Animal Dreams* (1990), and *Pigs in Heaven* (1993). Arizona State University's Ron Carlson is the author of the short-story collections *The News of the World* (1987), *Plan B for the Middle Class* (1992), *The Hotel Eden* (1997), and *At the Jim Bridger* (2002), as well as of the novels *Betrayed by F. Scott Fitzgerald* (1977) and *Truants* (1981). Terry McMillan's work, mentioned earlier, centers on contemporary urban African Americans.

An extremely popular subgenre of urban Southwestern fiction is that of detective novels and mysteries. Though it was the 1980s when Southwestern writers began to turn to the mystery genre in large numbers, Nevada's Virginia Coffman (1914–) has been creating nationally recognized gothic mysteries since the 1960s. Beginning with her first novel, *Moura* (1959), Coffman has produced a steady stream of such works under her own name, as well as under the pen names Kay Cameron, Victor Cross, Jeanne Duval, Virginia C. Du Vaul, Diana Saunders, and Ann(e) Stanfield. Among her best known works are *The High Terrace* (1966), *Black Heather* (1966), *Night at Sea Abbey* (1972), and *Passion's Rebel* (1983). Coffman was inducted into the Nevada Writers Hall of Fame in 1990.

New Mexican Tony Hillerman has produced successful detective fiction that follows Native American characters in Southwestern settings. Hillerman (1925–) is a past president of Mystery Writers of America and has received their Edgar and Grand Master Awards. His numerous other honors include the Silver Spur Award for the best novel set in the West, the Navajo Tribe's Special Friend Award, the National Media Award from the American Anthropological Association, and the Public Service Award from the U.S. Department of the Interior. Hillerman's Navajo Mysteries series of books feature Native American tribal police detectives Jim Chee and Joe Leaphorn. They number over a dozen and include *The Blessing Way* (1970), *Dance Hall of the Dead* (1973), *Skinwalkers* (1986), and *The Thief of Time* (1988). Recently, *Skinwalkers* has received national attention because it was released to television audiences as part of PBS's *Mystery!* series.

Today Southwestern detective and mystery fiction is popular throughout the United States. In addition to Hillerman, New Mexico boasts a number of major mystery authors, including Lauren Haney, Michael McGarrity, Connie Shelon, and Rudolfo Anaya. In Arizona, Sinclair Browning has received highly enthusiastic critical acclaim for her Trade Ellis series of cowboy mysteries, and former Arizona State technology professor Renee Horowitz, has established herself through an unusual series of Rx mysteries that follow pharmacist/crime sleuth Andrea Felder. Bernard Schopen of Nevada was inducted into the Nevada Hall of Fame in 2000 for his mysteries featuring Reno detective Jack Ross. Texan crime writer James Crumley has been producing critically acclaimed fiction for three decades. A number of his works, including *The Mexican Tree Duck* (1993), *Bordersnakes*

(1996), and *The Final Country* (2001), are set in the West Texas landscape. A sense of place is also inseparable from one of Texas' best-known mystery writers, David Lindsey, although Lindsey concerns himself, for the most part, with the gritty underside of Houston's high society. Lindsey's two most recent works, however, are set in central Texas. *Animosity* (2001) describes a murder in an artist colony, while *The Rules of Silence* (2003) alternates between Austin and San Miguel de Allende, Mexico. Musician Kinky Friedman has also tried his hand at mysteries in such works as *A Case of Lone Star* (1987), *Armadillos and Old Lace* (1994), *Road Kill* (1997), and *Meanwhile Back at the Ranch* (2002). Other well-known Texas mystery writers include Rolando Hinojosa, Susan Wittig Albert, Bill Crider, and Jeff Abbott.

JOURNALISM

The importance of journalism in the Southwest cannot be underestimated. It was one of the first ways the written word took root in this region, and it remains central to the area's culture and politics. Small towns established local newspapers and magazines long before communities could support more literary presses. Thus, many famous fiction writers made their start—and their living—in the world of journalism, whereas others have grown to be household names through their reporting alone. In addition to the critical work of reporting local occurrences and politics, journalists shaped—and continue to shape—the way the readers both inside and outside of the Southwest understand the region's landscape and its inhabitants.

Early newspapers, here loosely defined as newspapers printed before or in the decades just following a region's statehood, differed from the twenty-first-century newspaper in both form and focus. Often they were four pages long, and they appeared in a variety of sizes. Though there were a few dailies, more often newspapers were printed weekly, semiweekly, or triweekly. They published reprints from other newspapers, foreign news, official notices, literary features, and varying amounts of local news. In addition to informing residents about current events and culture, newspapers often served to promote their area to settlers. Thus, they were vocal proponents for the social improvement of their region and territory or state. Newspapers often took quite partisan positions on politics, vilifying some candidates and office holders and praising others. Some of the earliest papers that remain in publication today include Arizona's *Tucson Citizen*, *Daily Sun* (Yuma), and *Arizona Republic* (Phoenix); New Mexico's *Albuquerque Journal* and *Alamogordo Daily News*; Texas' *San Antonio Express News*, *Herald-Zeitung* (New Braunfels), and *News* (Galveston); and Nevada's *Virginia City Territorial Enterprise*.

Beginning in 1860 and continuing well into the twentieth century, the *Virginia City Territorial Enterprise* produced some of the Southwest's most remarkable journalists. Notable among the "Sagebrush School" of writers was their crossover between journalism and fiction. Not only did many writers produce both, but many individual works reflected this hybridity: fictional short stories and novels were spun out of real events and news reports by writers who prided themselves on being masters of the practical joke.

Unforgettable among such writers is Samuel Clemens, better known as Mark Twain. From 1862 to 1864 Twain worked for the *Enterprise*, reporting on topics as varied as the Nevada Constitutional Convention, Saturday night dances, the

Pony Express, trials, and other local current events. Twain's ironic sensibility was whetted during his tenure at the *Enterprise*; his colleagues, such as Dan De Quille, Joseph T. Goodman, Rollin M. Daggett, and James W. E. Townsend, were masters of the use of humor to reveal scandal. Dan De Quille, the pen name of William Wright, in particular established himself as humorist because of his frequent and extravagant hoaxes. He also became Nevada's most popular writer of the nineteenth century through his newspaper columns, as well as through his short fiction and travelogues. Most famous of these is *The Big Bonanza* (1876), an entertaining history of Virginia City's Comstock Lode, a silver vein that fueled the city's boom economy and local lore.

For many decades, state-owned magazines have helped create a sense of regional identity for resident Southwesterners and visitors alike. Founded in 1923, *New Mexico Magazine* is the oldest state-produced magazine in the nation, and it is closely followed by *Arizona Highways*, which was first published in 1925. In the 1940s, *Nevada Magazine* was created, and in 1974 *Texas Highways* was first produced. *Arizona Highways* and *Texas Highways* are each produced by their state highway departments, whereas *New Mexico Magazine* and *Nevada Magazine* are sponsored by state tourism departments. Each of these periodicals is intended, at least in part, to promote tourism. Yet, their glossy photographs of scenic vistas and informational articles on local history, culture, arts, and environments have helped define in each of these states a sense of place that goes beyond mythology to reveal the region's cultural and geographical diversity, as well as the singularity of local communities.

One recent group of journalists especially worthy of attention is Texas' "Mad Dog" writers. Though their peak of influence lasted from the late 1960s through the 1970s, many of these writers are still very productive today. They were loosely associated through a shared counterculture attitude, though the ways these artists chose to rebel against mainstream society took many forms, such as wild parties, ironic or outspoken published critiques of Texas politics and culture, and blatant attempts to distinguish themselves from the urban American intellectuals who congregated in the Northeast. The Mad Dogs were a hyper-masculine, hyper-Texan boys' club, gathered predominantly in the Austin and Dallas areas. However, they were also earnestly interested in reworking the stereotypical Texan image. Their members included writers Billy Lee Brammer and Larry McMurtry, musicians Willie Nelson and Jerry Jeff Walker, painters such as Fletcher Boone, and actors Dennis Hopper, Peter Boyle, and Warren Oates, all in Austin for the filming of Bud Shrake's *Kid Blue*. Yet, the heart of the Mad Dogs was journalism. Many of its most prominent members, such as Gary Cartwright, Larry L. King, Bud Shrake, Jan Reid, Dan Jenkins, and Jay Milner made names for themselves in publications such as the *Dallas Times-Herald*, *Texas Monthly* magazine, and the *Texas Observer*, a liberal weekly devoted primarily to Texas politics. And though each of these writers also published fiction and memoirs, they must also be remembered for their steady contribution to Texas letters through articles that both informed readers about Texas politics and culture and challenged them to look at their society in new ways.

The Texas Mad Dog writers are not, of course, the only names in contemporary journalism. In Texas their masculine voices have been answered by the witty, but equally pointed, writing of women such as Molly Ivins and Prudence Mackintosh. Nevada's Lucius Morris Beebe is famous for his literary journalism and his reinvigoration of Virginia City's historic *Territorial Enterprise*. The Southwest also has its share of environmental reporters, such as Arizona's Ben Avery, and excellent columnists, including Nevada's Rollan Melton of the *Reno Evening Gazette* and *Nevada State Journal*.

POETRY

In the stereotypical conception of Southwestern literature, poetry does not always immediately come to mind. Yet there are several thriving contemporary strains of poetry, many of which have deep roots in the past. American Indian poets often combine elements of oral tradition with contemporary concerns. The work of two previously discussed authors, N. Scott Momaday and Leslie Silko crosses literary forms and includes poetry. Momaday's poetry collections include *The Gourd Dancer* (1976), *In the Presence of the Sun* (1992), and portions of *In the Bear's House* (1999); Silko is best known for her collection *Laguna Woman* (1974).

The Southwestern landscape features prominently in the work of Pueblo poet Simon Ortiz (1941–). Through his poetry he criticizes the modernization of New Mexico, particularly its effect on American Indian peoples. Ortiz's major works are *Going for the Rain* (1976), *A Good Journey* (1977), *Fight Back: For the Sake of the People, for the Sake of the Land* (1980), *Woven Stone* (1992), *After and Before Lightning* (1994), *From Sand Creek: Rising in This Heart Which Is Our America* (2000), and *Out There Somewhere* (2001).

One of the most prominent American Indian writers today is Joy Harjo. Like Ortiz, Harjo focuses on the natural world in her poems and on the survival of American Indians in contemporary society. Her works include *The Last Song* (1975), *She Had Some Horses* (1983), *In Mad Love and War* (1990), *The Woman Who Fell from the Sky* (1994), *A Map to the Next World* (2001), and *How We Became Human: New and Selected Poems, 1975–2001* (2002).

Joy Harjo with her saxaphone. © Christopher Felver/Corbis.

Paula Gunn Allen (1939–) is of Laguna, Sioux, Scotch, and Lebanese descent, but she grew up amid the female-centered Pueblo culture in New Mexico. In collections such as *The Blind Lion* (1974), *Coyote's Daylight Trip* (1978), *Shadow Country* (1982), and *Skin and Bones* (1988), she explores racial and sexual boundaries, while also emphasizing the importance of women in American Indian—and in all—societies.

Language is central to the works of both Luci Tapahonso (1953–) and Ofelia Zepeda (1954–). Tapahonso grew up speaking Diné (Navajo) in Shiprock, New Mexico, on the largest Indian reservation in the United States. She publishes in English, but because Tapahonso conceptualizes her poems in Diné, that language infuses her work both structurally and in the many Diné words she retains even after English translation. Tapahonso's works include *One More Shiprock Night* (1981), *Seasonal Woman* (1981), *Saanii Dahataal:*

The Women Are Singing (1993), and *Blue Horses Rush In* (1997). Like Tapahonso, Zepeda learned English as a second language. She grew up speaking O'odham in the rural community of Stanfield, Arizona. Today Zepeda is a linguistics professor at the University of Arizona, where she studies and teaches the O'odham language. In addition to her translation work, she has collected her own poetry in *Ocean Power: Poems from the Desert* (1995) and *Jewed 'I-Hoi/Earth Movements* (1997).

Born and raised in northern Nevada, Adrian C. Louis is of Lovelock Paiute and Anglo descent. He has taught English at the university level in South Dakota and Minnesota, where he currently resides. Louis' most recent poetry collections include *Vortex of Indian Fevers* (1995), *Skull Dance* (1998), and *Bone and Juice* (2001). His novel, *Skins* (1995), which depicts life on the Ogala Sioux reservation at the site of the Wounded Knee Massacre, was released in 2002 as a movie of the same name.

Like American Indian poetry, much contemporary Mexican American poetry in the Southwest references traditional culture. It often draws from the *corrido* (ballad) tradition prevalent in northern Mexico and much of the American Southwest. A majority of Mexican American writers also blend English and Spanish, although the degree of this mixing varies considerably among individual writers.

Though much Chicano poetry has been produced since the 1960s, there have been earlier writers of considerable talent. One such poet is Fray Angelico Chavez (1910–1996). Born Don Fabian Chavez and raised in Mora, New Mexico, he entered the Franciscan seminary at age fourteen. Chavez received the name Fray Angelico when he received his Franciscan habit in 1929. Although he ministered to the people of New Mexico most of his life, he served as an army chaplain during both World War II (1943–1946) and the Korean War (1950–1952) and was discharged honorably with the rank of major. An accomplished writer, Chavez published short stories, essays, a novel, drama, and histories and biographies pertinent to New Mexico. But he is also well known for his lyric poetry, which is collected in *Clothed with the Sun* (1939), *Eleven Lady Lyrics and Other Poems* (1945), *The Single Rose* (1948), *The Virgin of Port Lligat* (1959), and *Selected Poems with an Apologia* (1969).

Like Chavez, some of the best Mexican American poets are also well known for their work in multiple forms. So it is with Sandra Cisneros, previously discussed in this article, whose fiction has published the following poetry collections, *Bad Boys* (1980), *The Rodrigo Poems* (1985), *My Wicked, Wicked Ways* (1987), and *Loose Woman* (1994). Gloria Anzaldúa (1942–2004) developed a strong critical following for *Borderlands/La Frontera: The New Mestiza* (1987), her collection of essays and poetry in which she sought to define and redefine female, Chicana, and queer identities.

Jimmy Santiago Baca's (1952–) memoir, *A Place to Stand* (2001), describes his five years in prison, during which he developed a love of literature and eventually became a highly accomplished poet. His collections include *Black Mesa Poems* (1989), *Immigrants in Our Own Land* (1991), *In the Way of the Sun* (1997), *Set This Book on Fire* (1999), *Healing Earthquakes* (2001), and *C-Train and 13 Mexicans* (2002). He has also written a play, a screenplay, and a number of essays and short stories.

Arizona writer Alberto Ríos has authored much humorous yet poignant short fiction, such as *The Iguana Killer: Twelve Stories of the Heart* (1984), *Pig Cookies and*

Other Stories (1995), and *The Curtain of Trees: Stories* (1999), but is equally well known for his poetry collections, *Whispering to Fool the Wind: Poems* (1982), *Five Indiscretions: A Book of Poems* (1985), *The Lime Orchard Woman: Poems* (1988), and *Teodora Luna's Two Kisses: Poems* (1990).

Born in San Marcos, Texas, to a family of migrant workers, Tino Villanuevo (1941–) writes in both English and Spanish, often alternating between the two. He has published many volumes of poetry; they include *Hay Otra Vez: Poems* (1973), *Chronicle of My Worst Years* (1987), *Scene from the Movie "Giant"* (1993), *La Llaman America* (1997), and *Primera Causa* (1999).

Pat Mora (1942–) was born and raised in El Paso and currently divides her time between Santa Fe and Cincinnati. Her works reflect her attraction to Southwestern places and history. *Aunt Carmen's Book of Practical Saints* (1997) explores a tradition native to northern New Mexico of carving saints in wood, while poems in collections such as *Agua Santa* (1995) and *Chants* (1984) reveal intimate details of the Texas landscape.

Like American Indian and Mexican American poetry, cowboy poetry also has its roots in oral tradition, specifically the late nineteenth-century ballads of working cowmen. While many of these cowboy songs were anonymous, others, such as Frank Desprez's (1853–1916) "Lasca" (1882) have retained distinct authorship. Early collections of such songs include Jack Thorpe's *Songs of the Cowboys* (1908) and John Lomax's (1867–1948) *Cowboy Songs* (1911). It is from this oral heritage that cowboy poetry draws its generally simple rhyme scheme and regular meter, which facilitate easy memorization. Early examples of such poetry include William Lawrence Chittenden's (1862–1934) famous poem "The Cowboys' Christmas Ball" (1885) and his collection *Ranch Verses* (1897), as well as S. Omar Barker's twentieth-century collections, *Buckaroo Ballads* (1928), *Songs of the Saddlemen* (1954), and *Rawhide Rhymes* (1968).

In recent decades, cowboy poets have expanded their use of poetic forms, such as in their increasingly frequent use of free verse. Most cowboy poets today live in the American West and are in some way associated with the cattle industry either through their own work or through their family's work traditions. Though white males make up a large portion of Southwestern cowboy poets, there is also an established tradition of women and Mexican American writers among their ranks. This is clear at the most famous cowboy poetry event, the Cowboy Poetry Gathering in Elko, Nevada, where a diverse mix of cowboy poets gather annually to share their work. Nevada is also home to one of the most famous contemporary cowboy poets, Waddie Mitchell, who gained national fame in part due to his regular television appearances on Johnny Carson's *Tonight Show*. Mitchell publishes his works as recordings so as to retain an emphasis on their spoken qualities. These collections include *Lone Driftin' Rider* (1992), *Buckaroo Poet* (1993), *Live* (1998), and *That No Quit Attitude* (2002). Another famous cowboy poet who also frequented the *Tonight Show* and who continues to make regular appearances on National Public Radio is Baxter Black. Black has lived and worked as a large-animal veterinarian in both New Mexico and Arizona; his works include *Coyote Cowboy Poetry* (1987), *Croutons on a Cow Pie* (1992), *A Cowful of Cowboy Poetry* (2000), and *Horseshoes, Cowsocks & Duckfeet* (2002).

In addition to the various oral traditions that have helped shape contemporary American Indian, Mexican American, and cowboy poetry, there was also a nineteenth-century written tradition crafted in the vein of such mainstream American poets as William Cullen Bryant, Henry Wadsworth Longfellow, and Frances Sargent Locke Osgood. These works were generally formal in tone, often focusing on public subject matter, such as praises of the American nation or odes to war dead. Most were not exceptional, but one such poet worthy of note is Mollie E. Moore Davis (1844–1909). Her work is representative of the period in tone and subject matter and it is above-average in quality. Davis' poems, collected in *Minding the Gap and Other Poems* (1867) and *Selected Poems* (collected and published posthumously in 1927), frequently addressed patriotic themes and support of the Confederacy. Other early Southwestern poets writing before the 1960s and worthy of mention are Glen Ward Dresbach, Lexie Dean Robertson, Arthur M. Sampley, and William Barney.

Some of the best early Southwestern poetry was produced by New Mexico's immigrant artist communities from the 1920s through 1940s. Witter Bynner (1881–1968) was a central figure in both the Santa Fe and Taos artist communities and today he is celebrated by many for his openness about his own homosexuality, both in his everyday life and in a number of his poems. His poetry also reflects a deep influence by Eastern philosophy. Bynner produced an excellent translation of the Chinese philosophy the *Tao Te Ching*, which he titled *The Way of Life According to Laotzu* (1944), as well as several collections of poetry, including *Indian Earth* (1929), *Selected Poems* (1943), *Take Away the Darkness* (1947), and *New Poems* (1960). Alice Corbin Henderson (1881–1949) moved to Santa Fe with her husband in the late 1910s for medical reasons. There the couple soon devoted themselves to fighting for the civil rights of American Indians and preserving local New Mexico traditions. Henderson's poetry, collected in *Red Earth, Poems of New Mexico* (1920), reflects these concerns; she also edited anthologies of poetry by New Mexico artists. Henderson cofounded Writers' Editions, a cooperative press dedicated to publishing local authors, with another writer and poet, Haniel Long (1888–1956).

It is in recent decades, however, that Southwestern poetry has truly flourished. Today, the region hosts a dynamic contemporary scene. In Nevada, A. Wilburs Stevens (1921–1996) was the founding editor of the poetry and fiction journal *Interim* and a professor of English at the University of Nevada, Las Vegas. His verse collections are *The World Is Going to End Up in Burma* (1988) and *From the Still Empty Grave* (1995). Other major Nevada poets include Joanne de Longchamps, Gary Short, Gailmarie Pahmeier, and William Wilborn. New Mexico's Greg Glazner teaches at College of Santa Fe; his works include *From the Iron Chair* (1992) and *Singularity* (1996). In Arizona Norman Dubie (1945–) is a professor of English at Arizona State University. He has published numerous volumes of poetry, including *In the Dead of the Night* (1975); a trilogy consisting of *The Springhouse* (1986), *Groom Falconer* (1990), and *Radio Sky* (1991); and *Mercy Seat* (2001). Lubbock's Walter McDonald (1934–) uses verse to reveal the power and the harsh beauty of the West Texas landscape. A few of his many poetry collections are *Witching on Hardscrabble* (1985), *Rafting the Brazos* (1988), *Where Skies Are Not Cloudy* (1993), *Blessings the Body Gave* (1998), *All Occasions* (2000), and *Climbing the Divide* (2003). Other major contemporary Texas poets include Cynthia Macdonald, William Barney, and Dave Oliphant.

One of the most apparent features of today's Southwest is the growing ethnic diversity of its writers and the corresponding range of poetic perspectives this nourishes. As previously discussed, American Indian and Mexican American poets are some of the most prominent figures in the Southwest's contemporary scene. Yet there are many modern writers who do not fit into the most common Southwestern racial categories of Indian, Mexican, or Anglo. These writers suggest the diversity of histories contained in the Southwest and often encourage readers to reexamine their initial conceptions of the identity of the Southwesterner.

Two of the best known Asian American poets in the Southwest today are Stephen Shu-Ning Liu (1930–) and Arthur Sze (1950–). Nevada's Liu grew up in China and after college immigrated to the United States in 1952. Since 1973 he has resided in Las Vegas, where he taught English at the Community College of Southern Nevada until his retirement in 2001. Liu writes in English but is informed both by modern American and ancient Chinese traditions. His works include *Dream Journeys to China* (1982) and *My Father's Martial Art* (1999). Sze, a second-generation Chinese American, has been teaching creative writing at Santa Fe's Institute for American Indian Art for well over a decade. He is known both for his skillful translations of classic Chinese poetry, as well as for his own award-winning, avant-garde work. Sze's most recent volumes include *The Archipelago* (1995), *The Red-Shifting Web* (1998), and *Silk Dragon* (2001).

Jay Wright (1935–) likewise sees his poetry as a mixture of cultural influences. Wright was born and raised in Albuquerque and played professional baseball in Oklahoma as a young man. He now lives in Vermont where he devotes himself full time to poetry and playwriting. Though he often references Mexico and the Spanish language, jazz music, the African American experience, and African cultural roots are all central to his work. Wright's work includes *The Double Invention of Komo* (1980), *Explications/Interpretations* (1984), *Boleros* (1991), and *Transformations* (1997). Other prominent African American poets in the Southwest today include Lorenzo Thomas and Harryette Mullen.

Other poets are even more difficult to locate within a distinct ethnic poetic tradition. For example, Reno's Emma Sepulveda-Pulvirenti (1950–) shares a bilingual background with many Latinas, yet the Argentinian poet also reveals her own unique cultural inheritance. Her poetry collections include *Tiempo Complice del Tiempo* (1989) and *Death to Silence—Muerte al Silencio* (1997). Tom Meschery (1938–) was born in Manchurian China to Russian immigrant parents. During World War II he was held with his family in a Japanese internment camp near Tokyo. Later, after Meschery's family immigrated to the United States, he played professional basketball for ten years for the Golden State Warriors and the Seattle Supersonics. Today, Meschery sees his poetic work as directly influenced by both the Russian poetic tradition, in which poetry is a mainstream part of culture and family life, and by the American Beat poets he encountered during his youth in San Francisco. Meschery currently resides in Reno, Nevada, and his collections include *Over the Rim* (1971) and *Nothing We Lose Can Be Replaced* (1999).

Ai (1947–) stresses cultural diversity throughout her work. Born Florence Anthony in Albany, Texas, she changed her name to the Japanese word for *love*. Ai is of African American, Japanese, Choctaw-Chickasaw, Southern Cheyenne, Comanche, and Irish heritage, and she consciously infuses her tumultuous works, including *Killing Floor* (1979), *Sin* (1986), and *Greed* (1993), with a similar sense of multiplicity.

Another Texan, Naomi Shihab Nye (1952–), has served as a cultural ambassador to Asia and the Middle East. Born in St. Louis, Missouri, of an American mother and Palestinian father, Nye is today a longtime San Antonio resident. Her work has appeared in journals throughout the United States, Europe, and the Middle and Far East; among her collections are *Red Suitcase* (1994), *Fuel* (1998), *Come with Me* (2000), and *19 Varieties of Gazelle* (2002).

These poets have, for the most part, reached their readers through traditional poetry readings and through published works. But a recent trend in performance poetry has helped revitalize oral tradition within contemporary society. Poetry slams are competitive performance poetry in which original works are delivered to an audience and scored on the poem's content and aural qualities, as well as on the author's performance. Competing poets do not use props during their performances, so that the focus remains on the spoken word. They can participate as individuals or teams, and each spoken poem must last three minutes and ten seconds or less. Southwestern cities that host regular poetry-slam tournaments include Flagstaff, Mesa, and Tempe in Arizona; Las Vegas in Nevada; Albuquerque and Taos in New Mexico; and Austin, Conroe, Corpus Christi, Dallas, Fort Worth, Houston, and San Antonio in Texas.

CONCLUSION

From twenty-first-century poetry slams to Western novels or centuries-old correspondence, Southwestern literature is many things to many people. Writers struggle to introduce new voices into the Southwestern canon, whereas others demand the preservation of classic genres and traditional Southwestern values. In his *Guide to Life and Literature of the Southwest*, J. Frank Dobie argued that regional literature's importance lies in that it helps the "people of the Southwest see significances in the features of the land to which they belong, to make their environments more interesting to them, their past more alive, to bring them to a realization of the values of their own cultural inheritance, and to stimulate them to observe."[5] Through it, we gain intimate acquaintance with a place and its peoples, a sense of solidarity with like-minded individuals, and an awareness of perspectives different from our own. As the writers, genres, and mediums of Southwestern literature continue to evolve, this essential role of education and inspiration continues to hold true.

RESOURCE GUIDE

Printed Sources

Busby, Mark. "Texas and the Great Southwest." In *A Companion to the Regional Literatures of the United States*, edited by Charles Crow, 432–457. New York: Blackwell, 2003.

Byrkit, James W. "Land, Sky, and People: The Southwest Defined." *Journal of the Southwest* 34 (1992): 257–387.

Chavez, John R. *The Lost Land: The Chicano Image of the Southwest*. Albuquerque: University of New Mexico Press, 1984.

Dasenbrock, Reed Way. "Southwest of What?: Southwestern Literature as a Form of Frontier Literature." In *Desert, Garden, Margin, Range: Literature of the American Frontier*, edited by Eric Heyne, 123–132. New York: Twayne, 1992.

Dobie, J. Frank. *Guide to Life and Literature of the Southwest*. Rev. ed. Dallas: Southern Methodist University Press, 1952.

Dunaway, David King. *Writing the Southwest*. New York: Penguin, 1995.
Francaviglia, Richard, and David Narrett, eds. *Essays on the Changing Images of the Southwest*. Arlington: University of Texas Press, 1994.
Lensink (Temple), Judy Nolte, ed. *Old Southwest, New Southwest: Essays on a Region and Its Literature*. Tucson: Tucson Public Library, 1987.
———. *Open Spaces, City Places: Contemporary Writers on the Changing Southwest*. Tucson: University of Arizona Press, 1994.
Riley, Michael J. "Constituting the Southwest, Contesting the Southwest, Re-Inventing the Southwest." *Journal of the Southwest* 36 (1994): 221–241.
Teague, David W. *The Southwest in American Literature and Art: The Rise of a Desert Aesthetic*. Tucson: University of Arizona Press, 1997.
Western Literature Association. *A Literary History of the American West*. Fort Worth: Texas Christian University Press, 1987.
———. *Updating the Literary West*. Fort Worth: Texas Christian University Press, 1997.

Web Sites

General

Center for Environmental Arts and Humanities (NV)
http://www.unr.edu/artsci/ceah/

Center for the Study of the Southwest (TX)
http://swrhc.txstate.edu/cssw

The Handbook of Texas Online
http://www.tsha.utexas.edu/handbook/online/

The Southwest Center (AZ)
http://info-center.ccit.arizona.edu/~swctr/

Southwest Regional Humanities Center (TX)
http://swrhc.txstate.edu/

Texas Institute of Letters
http://www.stedwards.edu/newc/marks/til/

Collections

Center for American History (Strong Collections for Texas and the SW)
http://www.cah.utexas.edu/

Harry Ransom Humanities Research Center (The University of Texas at Austin)
http://www.hrc.utexas.edu/home.html

Hispanic Writers Collection
http://www.library.txstate.edu/swwc/misc/hispanic.html

Nettie Lee Benson Latin Collection
http://www.lib.utexas.edu/benson/

Southwest Collection/Special Collections Library
http://swco.ttu.edu/

Southwestern Children's Literature Collection (University of Texas, El Paso)
http://libraryweb.utep.edu/swchildlit.html

Southwestern Writers Collection (Southwest Texas, San Marcos)
http://www.library.swt.edu/swwc/

Journals

American Indian Quarterly: Journal of the Southwest
http://info-center.ccit.arizona.edu/~swctr/journal.html

Borderlands Texas Poetry Review
http://www.borderlands.org/

ISLE: Interdisciplinary Studies in Literature and Environment
http://www.unr.edu/artsci/engl/isle/

Southwest Review
http://southwestreview.org/

Southwestern American Literature
http://swrhc.txstate.edu/publications/journals/shq

Texas Books in Review
http://swrhc.txstate.edu/cssu/publications/sal.php

Western American Literature
http://www.usu.edu/westlit/

Literary Festivals

Arizona Book Festival (Phoenix), since 2002
http://www.azbookfestival.org/

The Border Book Festival (Mesilla, NM), since 1995
http://www.zianet.com/bbf/

Judy and A. C. Greene Literary Festival (Salado, TX), since 1998
http://www.1rtsalado.com/Festival.html

National Cowboy Poetry Gathering (Elko, NV), since 1984
http://www.westfolk.org/gathering.html

Northern Arizona Book Festival (Flagstaff), since 1998
http://www.flagstaffcentral.com/bookfest/Subjects/about.html

Santa Fe Festival of the Book, since 1998
http://sfweb.ci.santa-fe.nm.us/sfpl/festival.html

Santa Fe Writers' Conference, since 1985
http://www.santafewritersconference.com/

Taos Summer Writers' Conference, since 1999
http://www.unm.edu/%7etaosconf/

Texas Book Festival (Austin), since 1995
http://www.texasbookfestival.org/

Tucson Poetry Festival, since 1981
http://www.tucsonpoetryfestival.org/

Vegas Valley Book Festival (Las Vegas), since 2003
http://www.vegasvalleybookfest.org/

Organizations

Arizona Authors Association
http://www.azauthors.com/

Arizona Center for the Book
Arizona State Library, Archives, & Public Records
1700 W. Washington, Suite 200
Phoenix, AZ 85007

Arizona State University Creative Writing Program (Tempe)
http://www.asu.edu/clas/english/creativewriting/

Gemini Inc (San Antonio)
http://www.geminiink.org/

Inprint, Inc. (Houston)
http://www.inprint-inc.org/

James A. Michener Center for Writers, The University of Texas at Austin
http://www.utexas.edu/academic/mcw/

Lannan Literary Foundation (NM)
http://www.lannan.org/

Nevada Center for the Book
Nevada State Library and Archives
100 N. Stewart St.
Carson City, NV 89701

New Mexico Center for the Book
P.O. Box 31188
Santa Fe, NM 87594–1188
http://www.nmcb.org/

Nuestra Palabra: Latino Writers Having Their Say (Houston)
http://www.nuestrapalabra.org/

Southwest Literary Center (a branch of Recursos de Santa Fe)
http://www.recursos.org/swlc.html

Texas Center for the Book
Dallas Public Library
1515 Young St.
Dallas, TX 75201
http://www.dallaslibrary.org/tcbintro.htm

Texas Institute of Letters
http://www.stedwards.edu/newc/marks/til/index.htm

The Writer's Garrett (Dallas)
http://www.writersgarret.org/

The Writers' League of Texas (Austin)
http://www.writersleague.org/

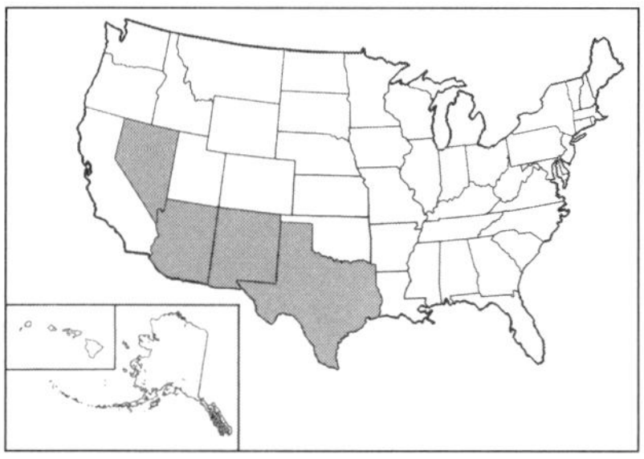

MUSIC

Richard Holland

The defined region for this reference work is problematical when it comes to music because of the very different demographics, settlement patterns, and cultural landscapes that have created modern Texas, New Mexico, Arizona, and Nevada. In brief, these four states share little in the way of musical history, except that every American place after the mid-twentieth century to some extent has shared much of the same popular music that played on the radio, in motion pictures, and on television. The history of twentieth century popular music in America is largely that of expanding audiences from the local to the regional to the national. Some of the elements in this gradual transformation were technological: the spread of the radio in most American homes beginning in the 1920s, the popularity of motion picture musicals beginning the 1930s, and the television era that coincided with the beginnings of rock and roll in the early 1950s all played a part in this growth toward a mass audience.

Likewise, the transformation of the middle class American home from a setting where family and friends participated in music making through singing and performing to a more passive environment based on listening to recordings was a paradigm shift. Between 1890 and the 1930s, hundreds of American piano manufacturers went out of business as home record players became almost as common as the living room radio. The basis of the spread of American popular music was the publication and sale of sheet music through the 1930s—this was supplanted in the decades to come by the rise of the record industry, particularly after "long-playing records" (LPs) were introduced and "45" rpm singles were manufactured for the new rock and roll consumers. The spread of recordings and the rise of nationally popular radio variety shows helped create musical stars who for the first time were popular from coast to coast. A good example of this is Bing Crosby, who started singing jazz with Paul Whiteman and Bix Beiderbecke in the 1920s to relatively small audiences but by 1940 had his own nationally broadcast radio program that was regularly listened to by millions of Americans on their home radio sets. After Crosby's "White Christmas" became a huge national hit in 1942, it was no longer unusual for Americans in every town to be whistling the same song. Yet the regional musics, particularly in the South and Southwest remained intact. Their roots in the region and their influence throughout the United States and internationally are what we will examine.

Each of these four Southwestern states contributed something of its own, although Texas because of its proximity to Mexico and its placement as the easternmost part of the South and the bottom of the Midwest has perhaps the richest and most diverse musical culture of any individual state in the United States.

BLUES AND JAZZ

Early Blues

Early Southwestern blues music refers to music made by self-taught African American singer / guitar players from the eastern half of Texas. Musicologists have surmised that itinerant black singers, usually alone and playing a guitar, entertained in both rural and urban black working communities as early as 1900. Although not as well documented as the same phenomenon in the Mississippi Delta, the Texas music and audiences were similar. In the country, families of sharecroppers would gather on weekend nights to drink and dance, often breaking church vows to do so. In the cities, particularly Houston and Dallas, even the most famous of the early singers usually played on the street, passing a hat. The content and style of the early Texas blues performers prior to the recording era is thought to have been dance music, with the lyrical content being a snippet of the singer's autobiography. Some reports of this early music say that popular blues or ragtime songs from as far away as New Orleans were performed. In the prerecording era, Jelly Roll Morton's double-entendre anthem "C. C. Rider" was a favorite with Texas audiences.

By the mid-1920s Dallas had become a center for the recording of "race" records. Texas blues scholar Alan Govenar has pointed out that during that period the major record labels Okeh, Vocalion, Brunswick, Columbia, RCA, and Paramount all set up studios and talent scouts in Dallas. This was largely due to the celebrity of Clarence (?) Blind Lemon Jefferson, whose Paramount and Okeh records had tremendous sales outside of Texas. Jefferson, who was born in the small East Texas town of Wortham to a family of sharecroppers, was known to have played on the streets of Dallas by 1912, the year that Huddie Ledbetter (Leadbelly) later mentioned as their having met. Jefferson is thought to have first heard the forms of blues music in his hometown in performances by black entertainers who sometimes traveled in shows that resembled an African American version of vaudeville.

One of these very early bluesman who Jefferson heard was Henry "Ragtime Texas" Thomas, born around Big Sandy, Texas, in 1874, the child of former slaves. Thomas disliked the cotton sharecropping life of his parents and became an itinerant bluesman, traveling by foot and by rail as far away as Chicago. Ragtime Texas Thomas' signature sound was created by his combination of guitar and panpipes that he attached around his neck and played with his mouth. The handmade pipes were made of quills and are thought to have been an adaptation of an African instrument. Thomas was over fifty when he first recorded in Chicago on the Vo-

Blind Lemon Jefferson. Courtesy of Getty Images.

calion label in 1927 and 1929. His influential songs included "Fishing Blues," covered by Taj Majal, and "Honey Won't You Allow Me One More Chance," sung by Bob Dylan on his 1962 album *The Freewheelin' Bob Dylan.*

Another blues pioneer was Alger "Texas" Alexander, born in 1900. Alexander performed with Blind Lemon Jefferson on the streets of Dallas and at gatherings in rural Texas. He began recording in 1927 and made several notable blues and jazz records with King Oliver, Clarence Williams and the Mississippi Sheiks, and others. These recordings, mainly on the Okeh label, were done primarily in San Antonio, Fort Worth, and New York City. His early recording career was interrupted by a five-year prison sentence for murdering his wife. Later in his career he was closely associated with his cousin, Houston bluesman Sam "Lightnin'" Hopkins, with whom he recorded in 1947.

But it was Blind Lemon Jefferson who became the mythic early blues figure. His profound influence on subsequent Texas singers including Lightnin' Hopkins, Mance Lipscomb, and Aaron "T. Bone" Walker is clear, but his significance also influenced the work of artists as diverse as Bessie Smith, Bix Beiderbecke, Louis Armstrong, Carl Perkins, and the Beatles. His most frequently covered songs are "Matchbox Blues," "See That My Grave Is Kept Clean," "Black Snake Blues," and "Tin Cup Blues." Massachusetts folk singer Geoff Muldaur created a touching tribute to Jefferson in his songs "Got to Find Blind Lemon, Part One" and "Got to Find Blind Lemon, Part Two."

Blind Willie Johnson, born in Marlin, Texas, in 1902, brought his blues sensibility into church. A master of the bottleneck guitar, Johnson had a powerful bass voice that dramatically contrasted with his keening guitar lines. Johnson traveled throughout the South in the 1920s, mostly performing for church audiences, including his legendary performance of "If I Had My Way I'd Tear This Building Down," which he sang while standing in front of the New Orleans Custom House. Following the powerful call and response number, the police arrested him for inciting a riot. The rest of Johnson's songwriting legacy includes "Nobody's Fault But Mine," "Dark Was the Night—Cold Was the Ground," "Jesus Make Up My Dying Bed," and "God Moves on the Water."

One of America's finest female blues singers was Sippie Wallace, born in Houston in 1898. Something of a prodigy, she grew up playing the organ in her father's church. By 1916 she was a dancer and vaudeville comedian in traveling tent shows. In 1923 she met Okeh Records talent scout Ralph Peer (the man who discovered the Carter Family and Jimmie Rodgers), who recorded her. Soon she became a nationally popular artist, known for her blunt songs about men and women, such as "Mighty Tight Woman" and "Women Be Wise (Keep Your Mouth Shut, Don't Advertise Your Man)." Wallace enjoyed a revival in the 1960s when Bonnie Raitt covered those two songs. In her seventies Wallace made frequent appearances with Raitt and rerecorded "Women Be Wise" with her. Wallace died on her eighty-eighth birthday.

In 1937, San Antonio's place in blues history was sealed when the most powerful of the early Mississippi singers, Robert Johnson, made a recording there. Always secretive, Johnson played and sang in a secluded room in the Gunter Hotel, his back to the recording engineers. The mysterious Johnson's only other recordings were made in a subsequent session in Dallas.

Early Jazz

The history of jazz is the story of talented band leaders, sidemen, and singers who left home to be where the music was played and recorded. The American Southwest, particularly Texas, has produced perhaps more than its share of important jazz personages, but what part a home place plays in the development and importance of a jazz player who leaves to be in Kansas City or New York or Los Angeles is a question worth exploring. What follows is a brief listing of some of the more important early jazz figures with Southwestern roots.

Jack Teagarden (born in Vernon, Texas, in 1905; died in New Orleans, in 1964) is widely considered the finest jazz trombone player and a subtle singer with a distinctive style. His blues interpretations of standards such as "St. James Infirmary" betrayed his Texas roots.

Saxophonist Buster Smith was born in Alsdorf, Texas, in 1904. He developed a loud playing style on the alto saxophone that made him heard above the brass. This technique plus his high-quality musicianship made him a star in Hot Lips Page's Orchestra and teamed him with Count Basie in Kansas City before Basie had a full big band. He died in Dallas in 1991.

Oran "Hot Lips" Page was born in Dallas in 1908. He began playing jazz trumpet in Ma Rainey's band in the 1920s. In 1928 he played with the most important of what have come to be known as the territory bands, Walter Page's Blue Devils. Page went on to play with Bennie Moten, Count Basie, Artie Shaw, and Eddie Condon. He died in New York City in 1954.

Jump Music and Rhythm and Blues

In many ways black music and country music followed the same paths in the Southwest during the 1930s and 1940s. Blues became more commercial, and primarily black nightclubs began to pop up in cities that had black music consumers, such as Houston and Dallas. Particularly just after World War II, there was a dramatic increase in black music venues (although in the segregated parts of the Southwest, whites frequented black venues but blacks could not reciprocate), and by the late 1940s, an increased mobility meant that many African American entertainers left the Southwest (especially Texas) and moved to California.

The father of the amplified blues guitar is Aaron "T-Bone" Walker, born in Linden, Texas, in 1910. Both his mother and father played instruments and sang. When he was a boy, Walker's family moved their home to Dallas. Blind Lemon Jefferson was a frequent guest, and he picked the eight-year-old Walker to be his "lead boy" who directed him from club to club in Dallas' Deep Ellum neighborhood. Walker won a talent contest when he was nineteen, played the banjo briefly with Cab Calloway's big band, and signed a record deal with Columbia in 1929. Walker was a natural entertainer, and in the early 1930s he stopped playing music professionally and traveled through the South with different black medicine shows, for which he worked as an acrobatic dancer (to draw crowds). He died in Los Angeles in 1975.

Aaron "T-Bone" Walker, c. 1930. Courtesy of Getty Images.

The development of the amplified guitar in jazz and blues is thought to be the work of three Texas musicians: Eddie Durham (b. San Marcos, Texas, 1906; d. New York City, 1987) who was the architect of the early Count Basie band's sound, Charlie Christian (b. Dallas, 1916; d. Staten Island, 1942), whose brilliant, brief jazz career linked him with Benny Goodman and T. Bone Walker. As the oldest of the group, Durham tutored the other two. The challenge, particularly in large groups with horns, was for the guitar to be heard. Durham developed amplification for the straight 4/4 rhythm-guitar style that later became associated with longtime Basie sideman Freddie Green. In 1935 Durham became the first musician to record an amplified guitar on Jimmie Lunceford Orchestra's piece "Hittin' the Bottle." Charlie Christian, who died at age twenty-five, invented the guitar as a jazz solo instrument in his important recordings with Goodman's sextet. His innovation was the single line solo, similar to that played by horn players. Another important black musician from Texas, Teddy Wilson (b. Austin, 1912; d. New Britain, Connecticut, 1986) played piano in Goodman's small group, and both he and Christian helped Goodman pioneer racially integrated bands.

But it was T-Bone Walker who influenced the future of music for decades to come. Playing a large hollow-body guitar, Walker became a master of dynamics and tone. He invented the conversational style of playing, then singing, then playing. Later blues artists who played in the same style, including B. B. King and Eric Clapton, always acknowledge Walker's legacy to their music. By the time his medicine-show days were over, he moved to southern California, where he began working as an emcee, dancer, singer, and guitar player for Big Jim Wynn's band. Soon he struck out on his own and became wildly popular. When T-Bone played in package shows with the likes of Lowell Fulsom and Ray Charles, he always played last because no one wanted to follow him.

In 1946 and 1947, he recorded fifty classic songs on Black and White Records in Los Angeles. This seminal body of work included his often-covered numbers "T-Bone Shuffle" and "Stormy Monday." Walker loved to drink and to gamble (there is a funny story about him playing poker with the blind Ray Charles), and the drinking resulted in bleeding ulcers so severe that most of his stomach was removed. Like many other bluesmen, Walker was hurt by the rise of rock and roll, but he recorded on Atlantic for a time and in 1960 actually sang with the Count Basie Orchestra. When the blues revival came along in the early 1960s, Walker was the toast of many European blues festivals, settling down for some time in Paris. When he returned to California from France in 1972, he discovered that he had won a Grammy Award for a record he had made in Paris on the Black and Blue label. In the early 1970s Walker and Texas singer Eddie "Cleanhead" Vinson (b. Houston, 1917) were both seriously injured in a car accident. Before Walker died in 1975 he saw the Allman Brothers' rendition of "Stormy Monday" become a national hit. Without his example there would have been no B. B. King, no Eric Clapton or Jimi Hendrix, and later, no Texas inheritors of his style such as Johnny Winter and Stevie Ray Vaughan.

Other important blues/jazz guitarists who migrated from Texas to California were the brothers Johnny Moore (b. Austin, 1906; d. Los Angeles, 1969) and Oscar Moore (b. Austin, 1912; d. Las Vegas, 1981). In the 1930s the Moore family moved to California, and Johnny Moore had established his jazz/blues trio the Blazers by 1942. Texas City–born Charles Brown (b. 1922; d. 1999) joined the Blazers the next year as their piano player and singer. During the next fifteen years Brown became one of the most distinctive and influential vocal stylists in popular music, his direct influence can be heard in the early vocal styles of both Nat King Cole and Ray Charles. While singing with the Blazers, Brown's big hit was "Drifting Blues," in 1946. His other signature tune, also recorded with the Blazers, was the perennial Christmas favorite "Merry Christmas Baby." Two years later Brown and Johnny Moore had a falling out, and Brown began recording for Alladin Records. It was at this juncture that Oscar Moore joined his brother's band. Although Brown had several successful recordings on Alladin, including "Black Night," his recording career effectively ended when he and the record label had a disagreement over royalties. After a long retirement in northern California, Brown reemerged in the 1980s and 1990s, recording several albums and touring with Bonnie Raitt. In 1997 he received a National Endowment for the Arts Heritage Award. He died in January 1999.

Stevie Ray Vaughan. Courtesy of Photofest.

Other influential Texas blues and R&B artists from this era include the pianists Amos Milburn (b. Houston, 1927; d. Memphis, 1974) and Ivory Joe Hunter (b. Kirbeyville, Texas, 1914; d. Houston, 1980), the brilliant and irascible guitar player and violinist Clarence "Gatemouth" Brown (b. Vinton, Louisiana, 1924–) and the alto saxophonist and bandleader Eddie "Cleanhead" Vinson (b. Houston, 1917; d. Los Angeles, 1988). Milburn's piano style was based on boogie woogie, which can be heard on his hit "Chicken Shack Boogie," which he recorded twice, the second time with a rock and roll drummer and fast tempo. Another style he used was influenced by stroll piano and is exemplified by "One Scotch, One Bourbon, One Beer." Hunter's lasting contribution to American music was his hit "Since I Met You Baby," recorded on Atlantic Records. Gatemouth Brown was a fiery instrumentalist who had many guitar showdowns with T. Bone Walker. His Louisiana and deep East Texas roots are most evident in his Cajun-style fiddle music. Vinson had a long career as a singer and bandleader that began when he was a bandmate of T-Bone Walker and Arnett Cobb in Milt Larkin's band. His Texas jump music was popular with dance audiences and included several bawdy songs that were not permitted play on the radio. His career took him to New York and to California, where he performed with the Johnny Otis Revue and with Cannonball Adderly's band.

Blues in the 1960s and 1970s

Blues music in the 1960s and 1970s saw the cross-fertilization of the music crossing racial lines. One of the most influential guitarists and singers of this period was Freddie King (b. Gilmer, Texas, 1934; d. 1976). Growing up in East Texas, King played the guitar under the tutelage of his mother. After he moved to Chicago at age sixteen, he learned from some of the best bluesmen who performed there, including B. B. King and T-Bone Walker. In the 1950s he worked with the Sonny Cooper Band and Earlee Payton's Blues Cats. Like many other blues stars of the 1960s, Freddie King played a big role in teaching white musicians to play. Eric Clapton, when he played with the Yardbirds, the John Mayall Blues Band, and Cream, always cited Freddie King as his favorite for his slashing guitar style.

Among King's most popular songs were "Hide Away," "Have You Ever Loved a Woman," and "Tore Down." In 1970 he signed with Leon Russell's Shelter Records and was backed by Russell's crack band that later played behind Joe Cocker and Eric Clapton. During the 1970s, Freddie King played frequently at the Armadillo World Headquarters—a huge Jim Franklin painting on the wall depicted an armadillo running through King's chest as he played his guitar. He died at the age of 42 from bleeding ulcers and heart problems.

A key figure in the history of regional blues was Don Robey (b. Houston, 1903; d. Houston, 1975), who ran Duke/Peacock Records in Houston from 1949 to 1973. Robey began promoting black dances in Houston in the early 1930s. After running a club in Los Angeles, Robey returned to Houston and opened the Bronze Peacock Dinner Club in 1945, a tremendously successful venue that featured the best blues and jazz acts in the country. This led to his beginning a talent agency in 1947, and he quickly signed Clarence Gatemouth Brown and terminated Brown's recording contract with Alladin Records. In 1949 Robey founded Peacock Records, named after the club. Over the years he recorded a number of important artists on Peacock, including Memphis Slim, Floyd Dixon, and Willie Mae "Big Mama" Thornton (b. Montgomery, Alabama, 1926; d. Los Angeles, 1984), who recorded "Hound Dog" in 1953, a version far superior to the Elvis Presley rendition that later eclipsed it.

In 1953 Robey gained control over Duke Records, another Houston label. This acquisition brought him artists of the stature of Johnny Ace, Little Junior Parker, and Bobby "Blue" Bland (b. Roseville, Tennessee, 1930), who between 1957 and 1970 recorded sixteen R&B hits that made the national charts. Some questioned

Robey's role in the shooting death of Johnny Ace, who officials reported shot himself playing Russian Roulette backstage during a concert on Christmas day, 1954. Robey sold Duke/Peacock to ABC-Dunhill in 1973 and died in 1975.

Other influential African American bluesmen of this era were Johnny Clyde Copeland (b. Haynesville, Louisiana, 1937; d. New York City, 1997), who lived in Houston, and Albert Collins, born in Leona, Texas, in 1932. Both of these artists were acclaimed for their guitar styles. Copeland had played extensively in Texas, Louisiana, and Arkansas before he moved to New York in 1974, where he was a very popular attraction in both black and white clubs. After he signed with Rounder Records in 1981, Copeland released *Copeland Special* and *Make My Home Where I Hang My Hat. Texas Twister*, released in 1983, was a best-selling album that featured Copeland playing with Albert Collins and the young Robert Cray. Albert Collins, nicknamed "the Iceman," was a virtuoso guitarist, known for his extremely long guitar cord that allowed him to walk out into the audience, and occasionally, all the way to the parking lot. He died in Las Vegas in 1993.

Two East Texas bluesmen, Sam "Lightnin'" Hopkins (b. Centerville, Texas, 1911; d. Houston, 1982) and Mance Lipscomb (b. near Navasota, Texas, 1895; d. Navasota, 1976) were nationally prominent during the acoustic blues revival of the early 1960s. Hopkins was one of the most recorded of the mid-century blues artists—over thirty-five years he recorded for twenty different labels, sometimes cutting songs for one when under contract with another. In 1959 Hopkins began working with the legendary blues producer Sam Charters, who helped market his records to white audiences. In the early 1960s Hopkins played Carnegie Hall with Pete Seeger and Joan Baez, and by the end of the decade he was opening shows for the Grateful Dead and Jefferson Airplane, but he kept his Texas roots well nourished. In 1972 he worked on the soundtrack for the film *Sounder*, and in 1970 he was the subject of a documentary, *The Blues According to Lightnin' Hopkins*. Hopkins died in Houston in 1982.

Mance Lipscomb lived in the Brazos River valley close to his hometown of Navasota for most of his life, working as a tenant farmer. He did not play music regularly until he moved to Houston at the age of 61. It was there that he fell under the influence of Lightnin' Hopkins and other blues figures. He was discovered by the Houston blues archivist Mack McCormick and by Chris Strachwitz of Arhoolie Records, who recorded Lipscomb in 1960 on the album *Texas Blues, Volume 2*. For the next ten years this humble farmer became legendary for his story songs that he performed at blues festivals, including the Berkeley Folk Festival, where in 1961 he played for an audience of 40,000. In 1970 he was the subject of Les Blank's documentary film *A Well-Spent Life*. Lipscomb died in Navasota in 1976.

Texas' White "Blues Brothers"

Among the strongest of the 1960s generation of white bluesmen was Johnny Winter, born in Beaumont, Texas, in 1944. When he was fourteen, Winter formed a band with his keyboard-playing younger brother, Edgar Winter (b. Beaumont, 1946), called Johnny and the Jammers. A single on Dart Records was released when Johnny was fifteen years old. In 1968 Johnny formed a blues/rock trio, with Tommy Shannon on bass and Uncle John Turner on drums. They played to big audiences at Austin's Vulcan Gas Company (a precursor to the Armadillo World headquarters) and cut an album on Imperial Records as the Progressive Blues Experiment. Winter moved the group to England, looking for a better reception for his work. After a rave article on him in *Rolling Stone*, every major record company called him. Winter signed a million-dollar deal with Columbia Records, thought to be the biggest signing for a new artist to that date. Columbia promoted him as America's white blues guitar hope who would compete with Eric Clapton, Jeff Beck, and Jimmy Page in England. Winter cut four powerful albums with Columbia, the best selling being *Johnny Winter and Live*. In the 1970s Winter began a fruitful collaboration with Muddy Waters, playing behind the Chicago Bluesman and producing the records *Hard Again and I'm Ready*. After a four-year break, Winter signed with Chicago's Alligator records in 1984 and recorded some of his best work.

The other leading pair of Texas white blues brothers are Jimmy Vaughan (b. Dallas, 1951) and his little brother Stevie Ray Vaughan (b. Dallas, 1954; d. 1990). The Vaughan brothers grew up in the working-class neighborhood of South Oak Cliff in Dallas. After a junior-high-school football injury, Jimmy Vaughan was given a guitar to play during his recuperation. By the time he was fifteen, Jimmy had his own band, the Swinging Pendulums. The next year, he joined a leading Dallas band, the Chessmen, a rock band that opened for Jimi Hendrix in Dallas. After seeing Muddy Waters and Freddie King play in Dallas, Jimmy Vaughan became devoted to the blues. In 1969 Jimmy Vaughan helped form Texas Storm, a blues soul band that became very popular when they moved to Austin. In the early 1970s Jimmy's kid brother Stevie Ray moved to Austin and started playing bass in Texas Storm. In 1974 Jimmy Vaughan cofounded the Fabulous Thunderbirds with singer/harmonica player Kim Wilson (b. Detroit, 1951), who had moved to Austin from California. Vaughan and Wilson were joined by the ultra-funky Keith Ferguson (b. Houston, 1946; d. 1997) on bass and a succession of drummers that included Mike Buck (b. Fort Worth, 1952). The Thunderbirds became the house band at Antone's, the new blues club located in downtown Austin. Vaughan and the others backed the leading blues artists of the period, including Muddy Waters, Albert King, and Buddy Guy. Jimmy Vaughan's understated guitar riffs caught everyone's attention. He recorded eight albums with the T-Birds, including *Girls Go Wild*, *Tuff Enough* (a platinum album), and *Wrap It Up*. Between tours with his band, Jimmy often played shows with Stevie Ray. This led to their recording an album together, *Family Style*, which was finished just weeks before Stevie Ray's fatal helicopter crash in August 1990. After recovering from Stevie Ray's death, Jimmy opened for Eric Clapton for sixteen nights at London's Royal Albert Hall in 1993 and later the same year recorded his first solo album, *Strange Pleasures*. This was followed by another successful recording, 1998's *Out There*.

After Jimmy Vaughan abruptly left home to play music, his parents tried to keep Stevie Ray away from the guitar, but he would stay up late to play the guitars Jimmy had left behind. As soon as he could manage it, Stevie Ray followed Jimmy down to Austin. After playing bass in Jimmy's band, he began sitting in on guitar wherever he could. In the late 1970s he formed Triple Threat with the powerful blues singer Lou Ann Barton (b. Fort Worth, 1954). This group eventually evolved into Double Trouble, with Tommy Shannon and Reese Wymans. In 1982 the trio played the Montreaux Jazz Festival in Switzerland and were seen by David Bowie and Jackson Browne, who both used Vaughan in their next recordings. Stevie Ray was signed to Columbia Records by the legendary John Hammond, who had been the first to sign the Count Basie Band, Billie Holiday, Bob Dylan, and Bruce Springsteen. Double Trouble's first Columbia album, *Texas Flood*, was an immediate success. A steady stream of Columbia records enhanced Stevie Ray's reputation, and in 1984 he was the first white artist to win the Entertainer of the Year award from the National Blues Foundation. He collapsed during a 1986 European tour and went through drug and alcohol rehabilitation. By 1989 he was playing at his best, and the records and concerts reflected it. His final concert in East Troy, Wisconsin, featured him on stage with Buddy Guy and Eric Clapton, who both considered Vaughan a master. There have been a number of excellent posthumous releases, including *The Sky Is Crying* in 1991. The city of Austin erected a memorial statue of Stevie Ray on the shores of Town Lake in 1993.

Other leading white female blues artists in Texas would include Angela Strehli (b. Lubbock, 1945) and Marcia Ball (b. Orange, Texas, 1949) both of whom have had solid recording careers. Ball was in Austin by the late 1970s, when she was lead singer for the country folk group Freda and the Firedogs. She went on to have great success as a solo artist, playing the piano in Professor Longhair–inspired New Orleans style. Strehli played many stirring dates at Antone's, backed by their house band. Ball and Strehli joined Lou Ann Barton for a "girl group" album recorded for Antone's Record company. Titled *Dreams Come True*, it was released to acclaim in 1990.

Fort Worth's Delbert McClinton (b. Lubbock, 1940) is frequently described as a musician's musician. McClinton is noted for his harmonica playing, a craft he learned while playing in a Fort Worth group in the 1950s called the Straitjackets, who played in blues bands on the Jacksboro Highway behind Jimmy Reed, Big Joe Turner, and Howlin' Wolf. In 1962 McClinton toured Europe with Bruce Channel, playing harmonica on his hit "Hey! Baby." It was on this tour that Delbert famously tutored Beatle John Lennon in harmonica. The results can be heard on the Fab Four's "Love Me Do."

After having regional hits in the 1960s with the Ron-Dels and with Delbert and Glen, McClinton began a solo career in the early 1970s. At first he was marketed as a country artist, but his blues and honkytonk roots always burned through. His essential albums from this period are *Victim of Life's Circumstances* (1975), *Genuine Cowhide* (1976), *Second Wind* (1978), and *Keeper of the Flame* (1979). In 1980 his song "Giving It Up for Your Love" was a top ten hit, and in 1989 his *Live From Austin* won a Grammy Award for best contemporary blues album. In 1992 he won again, this time for a duet with Bonnie Raitt. Still active, his 2001 album *Nothing Personal* demonstrated his very fine songwriting skills and singing. McClinton's entry in *The Penguin Encyclopedia of Popular Music* ends by saying: "the musicians all know who he is, an unclassifiable talent with a solid following."[1]

COUNTRY AND WESTERN

Early Country Music

As Anglo settlers moved east to Texas from Mississippi and Tennessee, they brought with them their musical traditions, most of them based on Protestant church music and English and Scottish ballads. Typically, country people would play and sing music together, sometimes in a church setting and sometimes at home. The instrumentation was usually fiddles, banjos, and guitars, whose virtue is their portability, and in churches and more prosperous homes there might be a piano. The content of the religious songs varied according to denomination, but most of them were present in the early twentieth-century Protestant hymnals. The lyrical content of the secular music often dwelt on morbid details surrounding the death of loved ones.

According to music historian Gary Hartman, the first commercial recordings of country music were the fiddle tunes "Arkansas Traveler" and "Sallie Gooden," issued by Victor Records in 1922. Appalachian-style string music had traveled a long distance from North Carolina and Tennessee, because the fiddler on the recordings, Eck Robertson (b. Delany, Arkansas, 1887; d. Berger, Texas, 1975), had grown up in Amarillo, Texas. In 1924 Vernon Dalhart, a native of the old East Texas town of Jefferson, recorded the first country song to sell over a million copies, "The Wreck of the Old 97." Soon, record companies began signing promising artists and the field of "country and western" music was recognized in New York as a niche market with an eager audience. Other artists with Texas connections included the singing cowboys Gene Autry (b. Tioga, Texas, 1907; d. Los Angeles, 1998) and Tex Ritter (b. Carthage, Texas, 1905; d. Nashville, 1974) and the singing cowgirl Dale Evans (b. Uvalde, Texas, 1912; d. Apple Valley, California, 2001). Nothing demonstrates the power of the movies over popular music taste more than the enormous popularity of the cowboy singers. Gene Autry and the others quickly became national celebrities.

Known as the father of country music, Jimmie Rodgers was born in Meridian, Mississippi in 1897, and was discovered by Ralph Peer in Bristol, Tennessee, where his first recordings were made. Yet Rodgers always seemed to have an attraction to Texas, oftentimes working the Lone Star state into his song lyrics and eventually moving to Kerrville, Texas, a Hill Country town thought to have a dry climate that would help Rodgers' tuberculosis. Part of Rodgers' tremendous influence on American music stemmed from his blending of traditional Anglo styles with that of the blues and jazz styles that he had heard while growing up in the South. He died in 1933.

Western Swing

Western Swing can be seen as perhaps the first American hybrid popular music, combining the basic elements of country string bands with jazz rhythms and instrumentation. The result was a tremendously exciting dance music that has entertained audiences for seventy-five years. In the often muddled history of music, the origins of Western swing are refreshingly straightforward.

In 1929 Bob Wills (born in Kosse, Texas, in 1905) moved to Fort Worth and formed a small band that he called the Wills Fiddle band. The next year, Milton Brown joined the small aggregation as vocalist. In 1931 Wills changed the name of the band to the Lightcrust Doughboys, a reference to the "lightcrust flour" manufactured by Fort Worth's Burrus Mill and Elevator Company, who agreed to sponsor the band on a daily radio broadcast on Fort Worth's KFJZ and Dallas' powerful WBAP. The president of the Burrus Mill, W. Lee O'Daniel, soon canceled the band's contract, however, citing his dislike of "hillbilly music." After strong protests on the part of the radio audience, O'Daniel rehired the band and became the daily show's master of ceremonies. By the time "Pappy" O'Daniel ran for governor of Texas, backed on the campaign trail by the Lightcrust Doughboys, both Bob Wills and Milton Brown had left the group.

Milton Brown and Bob Wills are recognized as the cocreators of Western swing, but Brown's brilliant career was cut short when he was killed in April 1936 in a car wreck. He was 33. Having left the Lightcrust Doughboys, Milton Brown had formed Milton Brown and the Musical Brownies in 1932. The hot band's frequent appearances at Fort Worth's Crystal Springs Dance Hall were legendary—Milton Brown was one of the most electrifying singers in the history of country music. The Brownies were the first Western swing band to record; in 1934 and 1936 they cut over one hundred songs for Decca and RCA's Bluebird label. This sizable legacy of recordings seamlessly combines country sentiments, jazz technique, and outrageous humor. Their best recorded work includes standards—"Shine On, Harvest Moon" and "The Sheik of Araby"—bawdy songs—"Somebody's Been Using That Thing"—regional favorites—"The Eyes of Texas" and "Cielito Lindo"—and humorous ditties—"I'll Be Glad When You're Dead You Rascal You" and "You're Bound to Look Like a Monkey When You Grow Old."

One brilliant instrumental innovator was Bob Dunn (b. Ft. Gibson, Oklahoma, 1908; d. 1971), whom Milton Brown hired in 1934. Dunn had been influenced by the Hawaiian-style guitars and developed a design for an amplified steel guitar. But Dunn loved jazz and especially the Texas trombonist Jack Teagarden, so he developed a single-note, horn-like approach to the instrument. His innovations can be heard on most of the recordings of Milton Brown and the Brownies.

When Bob Wills left the employ of W. Lee O'Daniel (who went on to become governor of Texas), he formed one of the legendary American music ensembles: Bob Wills and the Texas Playboys. Unlike Milton Brown, Wills left Fort Worth and moved to Tulsa, Oklahoma, where he lived from 1934 to 1943, the most formative period of his band. In 1940 Wills and the Playboys recorded what became a nationwide hit, "New San Antonio Rose," the same year he made the first of nineteen movie appearances. The Playboys were a large ensemble in the 1930s and early 1940s, with instrumentation similar to that of a big jazz band, though fiddles stood in for some of the horns. Wills is also attributed with adding drums to country music.

After "San Antonio Rose" became a hit, the Playboys were invited to play at the Grand Ole Opry, a very rare invitation for a group located west of the Mississippi River. Wills was told that the Opry did not allow drums because they would violate the purity of the music. Wills got them to allow the drummer to play behind the curtain. During a lively number, Wills took his fiddle bow and pushed the curtain back, and the crowd responded with enthusiasm. Bob Wills was not invited back, but the conservative tastemakers in Nashville soon changed their policy.

The Texas Playboys became a training ground for generations of musicians during Wills' long and productive career (Wills played until his death in 1973). Among the notable Playboys were the singer Tommy Duncan and instrumentalists Smokey Dacus, Jesse Ashlock, Sleepy Johnson, Leon McAuliffe, Eldon Shamblin, Herb Remington, Tiny Moore, Millard Kelso, Curly Lewis, Johnny Gimble, and Bob Wills' brother, Johnnie Lee Wills. Like Milton Brown's Brownies, the Playboys recorded a number of standards, but it was their original tunes that are still played. These tunes include "New San Antonio Rose," "Roly-Poly," "Ida Red," "Steel Guitar Rag," "Time Changes Everything," "I'm a Ding-Dong Daddy from Dumas," "Milk Cow Blues," "Cherokee Maiden," "Right or Wrong," "Bring It on Down to My House," "Faded Love," and "Take Me Back to Tulsa."

After World War II, the economics of music changed, and the Texas Playboys changed into a smaller, more portable band. This coincided with their greatest popularity when they played all up and California in the big ballrooms of the day.

Other notable Texas-based Western Swing bands were Bill Boyd and His Cowboy Ramblers, The Tune Wranglers, Cliff Bruner's Texas Wanderers, the Crystal Spring Ramblers, and Ted Daffan's Texans. Later, Adolph Hofner's band, and two Austin-based groups, Alvin Crow's Pleasant Valley Boys and Asleep At the Wheel, which is led by Ray Benson have kept the "country jazz" tradition vital.

Lomax Legacies

John Avery Lomax and his son Alan Lomax pioneered the collecting of folk, country, and blues archives and the techniques of field recording. John Lomax worked on the staff of the University of Texas during the 1910s and for the three decades that followed, raising his family in Austin. When he was a child in Bosque County, Texas, the senior Lomax heard cowboys on trail drives singing songs to the cattle, and he became fascinated with the music. He began transcribing the songs at a young age. Similarly, he became fascinated with the work songs and gospel tunes of blacks in East Texas. It was Lomax who discovered Huddie Ledbetter (Leadbelly) in a Louisiana penitentiary, helped him obtain freedom, and took him to New York City to perform in Carnegie Hall.

Alan Lomax followed his father's musical path but strongly differed with him politically. Alan was an intrinsic part of the left-leaning intelligentsia in New York in the 1940s and 1950s, making the music of the people that he and his father recorded an intrinsic part of American culture. Their archival work on American music at the Library of Congress is continued to this day in its Archive of Folksong.

John Lomax's books include *Cowboy Songs and Other Frontier Ballads*, *Folk Songs: U.S.A.*, *Negro Songs as Sung by Leadbelly*, and his autobiographical *Adventures of a Ballad Hunter*. Alan Lomax's important book is *The Land Where the Blues Began*. His worldwide field recordings have been reissued on compact disc and have been sampled by several contemporary hip-hop and pop artists, including Moby.

Honky-Tonk Music

Country music historians customarily point to Al Dexter (born in Jacksonville, Texas, 1902) as the first honky-tonk singer. In the early 1930s he and his band played in clubs on the outskirts of the wild East Texas oil boomtown of Longview. In 1936 he recorded "Honky Tonk Blues," the first song that used the term. Dexter admired pop music as much as country and had considerable success crossing over to popular audiences. He and his band, the Troopers, recorded "Pistol Packin' Mama" and "Rosalita" in 1943, augmented by Gene Autry's popular group. The record sold a million copies in six months and topped *Billboard Magazine*'s pop chart for eight weeks—and this was before Bing Crosby recorded the song and sold millions more copies.

After World War II, country music and its audience changed. Soldiers were home from the war, and the birth rate went up for obvious reasons, but so did the divorce rate. Postwar music audiences were ready for more reality and less of the sentimentality of the music that helped them make it through the war. After families had cars again, their mobility took music lovers to little clubs on the edge of towns. They started being called honky-tonks and featured either small live bands or new jukeboxes, which were at first stocked with 78s. Although similar in many ways to the earlier country music instrumentally, the mid- and late 1940s country songs often directly addressed heartbreak and infidelity for the first time. Among the greatest exponents of this new music were five Texans: Ernest Tubb, Floyd Tillman, Lefty Frizzell, Hank Thompson, and Ray Price.

Country great Ernest Tubb was born in Crisp, Texas, in 1914 and raised by relatives in Ellis County, Texas. As a teenager he worked at KONO in San Antonio and was befriended by Jimmie Rodgers' widow. Carrie Rodgers helped Tubb land a recording contract and in 1936 he signed with RCA Records. Four years later he was with Decca and began recording hits. The first one was his signature song "Walkin' the Floor Over You," a million seller that led to his becoming a regular on the Grand Old Opry show in Nashville. In 1948 he had three songs on Billboard's top-ten chart. He went on to record over 250 songs and to sell 30 million records. Among his other early hits were "Have You Ever Been Lonely (Have You Ever Been Blue)," "Filipino Baby," "Don't Rob Another Man's Castle," and "Waltz across Texas." Tubb's outgoing personality and unmistakable baritone voice made him a favorite with country fans for over forty years. He was constantly on the road, even when he was ill late in his life. Toward the end of each show he would sing his hit "Thanks (Thanks a Lot)" and turn over his guitar to reveal the word *thanks* taped to the back. His stripped down, simple sound was summarized in his instructions to his band: "Keep it low to the ground." In the 1980 biopic of Loretta Lynn, *Coal Miner's Daughter*, he played himself.

In the early 1950s the one country artist who gave Hank Williams a run for his money was Lefty Frizzell, born William Orville Frizzell in 1928 in Corsicana, Texas. Lefty's father was a roustabout in the Corsicana oilfields, and the family was itinerant. By age sixteen, Lefty was playing guitar and singing in country fairs, dances, bars, and clubs in North Texas. Before he was twenty he had moved to El Dorado, Arkansas, with his family, where he continued his performing career. By age twenty-two Frizzell had a recording contract with Columbia Records. His first single, recorded in July 1950, made his reputation: it was "I Love You a Thousand Ways," backed with "If You've Got the Money (I've Got the Time)." By 1951 he was a recording star, with four songs on Billboard's top-ten chart.

Many later singers, including Merle Haggard and Willie Nelson, thought that Lefty Frizzell was the greatest country vocalist and certainly a great influence on their generation of country artists. The Scottish country-music writer Duncan McLean called Lefty "the thinking man's Hank." Despite a chaotic personal life that resulted in jail time in Roswell, New Mexico, for statutory rape, Frizzell's career prospered through the 1960s. A 1964 number-one hit, "Saginaw, Michigan," revived his career. His other hit songs included "Always Late (With Your Kisses)" and the old American tune "Long Black Veil."

Floyd Tillman moved to the West Texas town of Post three months after he was born in Oklahoma in 1914. When he was growing up he played the mandolin and banjo, but by the time he joined Adolph Hofner's German-Czech swing band at age eighteen, Tillman played the guitar too. Houston was a hotbed for innovative country music in the early 1930s, and Tillman landed there in 1933, eventually playing in the Blue Ridge Playboys, led by Leon "Pappy" Selph (b. Houston, 1914; d. 1999). At a young age Tillman wrote the classic "It Makes No Difference Now," thought to be "too hillbilly" until it became a hit for Gene Autry and for Bing Crosby. Tillman's talented cohorts in the Blue Ridge Playboys included Moon Mullican (b. Polk County, Texas, 1909; d. 1967), later billed as "king of the hillbilly piano players," and the steel-guitar player Ted Daffan (b. Beauregard Parish, Louisiana, 1912; d. 1996), whose lasting songs were "Worried Mind," and "Born to Lose," immortalized in the 1960s by Ray Charles. After World War II, Tillman continued writing hits, including the slow waltz "I Love You So Much It Hurts." His shocking 1949 hit, "Slipping Around" is considered the first popular "cheatin' song," dealing as it does with an adulterous couple that has to resort to slipping around in order to spend time together. Floyd Tillman was still a beloved and vital performer right through the 1990s. He died in August 2003.

Hank Thompson, born in Waco, Texas, in 1925, was voted the number-one country singer in 1952, during the heyday of Hank Williams. Thompson joined the Navy at age eighteen and often made up songs to entertain his shipmates. By 1946 he had formed the Brazos Valley Boys and began playing clubs in central Texas. In 1947 Thompson had formed a friendship with the cowboy singer and movie star Tex Ritter, who helped Thompson sign a contract with Capitol Records, a business relationship that lasted eighteen years. His first popular record on Capitol was "Humpty-Dumpty Heart," released in 1947. His infidelity anthem "The Wild Side of Life" was the number-one country song for three months in 1952. Kitty Wells (b. Nashville, 1919) immediately recorded a sort of answer song, "It Wasn't God Who Made Honkytonk Angels," which became the first million-selling country record by a female artist. Thompson's later hits included a honky-tonk drinking song, "Six Pack to Go." Thompson and his band were still performing in the late 1990s.

The multitalented singer Ray Price was born near Perryville, Texas, in 1926. He had planned to become a veterinarian after serving in World War II but began singing in a local café and was signed to Bullet Records in 1949. In 1951 Price signed with Columbia Records and was befriended by Hank Williams, who gave Price his song "Weary Blues." In 1956 Price put his own stamp on honky-tonk music with his number-one song "Crazy Arms." The aggressive 4/4 shuffle beat of this tune was developed further with his next hit, "Heartaches by the Number," written by Harlan Howard. Price's band, the Cherokee Cowboys, was a training ground for future country stars including Roger Miller (b. Fort Worth, 1936; d. 1992), Johnny Paycheck, and Willie Nelson, who played bass in Price's band. By the mid-1960s Price began recording ballads that sold very well. The hit records in this style were "Make the World Go Away," "For the Good Times," and "Night Life" (written by Willie Nelson). Decades later, Price and Nelson recorded two compelling duet albums. As recently as 2001 Ray Price was a headliner at Austin's South by Southwest Music Festival.

Country Music: The Golden Years

Country music featuring artists and imagery from the Southwest really came into its own beginning in the late 1950s. This dynamic period lasted about twenty years.

Marty Robbins was born in 1925 in Glendale, Arizona. By the late 1940s he hosted "Chuck Wagon Time," an early-morning radio program on Phoenix's

KPHO. Grand Ole Opry star Little Jimmy Dickens came through Phoenix in 1951 and was so impressed with Robbins' voice that he helped him get a contract with Columbia Records, with whom he would record for more than twenty years. Robbins' first hits were "Singing the Blues" in 1956 and the anthemic prom song, "A White Sport Coat and a Pink Carnation," released in 1957.

In 1959 Robbins released his important concept album *Gunfighter Ballads and Trail Songs*. The single "El Paso," one of the most compelling American narrative songs, was a number-one hit in January 1960 and won Robbins his first Grammy Award. Later in his career Robbins appeared in several films and had a notable career as driver on the early NASCAR race car circuit. He died in 1982 at age fifty-seven.

Country music has no greater connoisseur of misery than perhaps its finest singer, George Jones (b. near Sarasota, Texas, 1931). Jones was born in a log cabin in the Big Thicket, now a national forest, and his father was a hard-drinking working man named George Washington Jones. In the late 1940s, when still a teenager, Jones had his own radio show in Beaumont. He began recording in 1954 for the Houston record executive H. W. "Pappy" Dailey. The first hit on Dailey's Starday Records was "Why Baby Why" in 1955. This rocking number began a brief rockabilly career for Jones, a departure that he later regretted. Jones left Starday for Mercury Records in 1959, for whom he had an immediate hit, "White Lightnin'" written by his Beaumont disc jockey friend J. P. Richardson (the Big Bopper) (b. Sabine Pass, Texas, 1930; d. 1959). Jones recorded many hits for United Artists and Musicor in the 1960s, during which time he was still produced by Pappy Dailey. Among these classic recordings were "The Window Up Above," "She Thinks I Still Care," "We Must Have Been Out of Our Minds," "Love Bug," "The Race Is On," and "When the Grass Grows Over Me."

Jones married his third wife, Tammy Wynette, in 1968. The story goes that she was a Mississippi beautician who did George's hair when they met. The 1970s were a decade of chaos for Jones, filled with heavy drinking, gunfire, and wife-beating allegations. Nonetheless, Jones and Wynette were a dynamic singing duo, recording the hits "We Can Make It," and "Once You've Had the Best" in 1972 and 1973. By then recording for Epic and produced by Billy Sherrill, Jones' other fine recordings in that decade were "The Grand Tour," and "A Picture of Me Without You." Jones' biggest hit, "He Stopped Loving Her Today," won him a Grammy Award and many country kudos in 1980. George's fourth wife partially reformed him, and from the mid-eighties on he has been productive. Jones' 1999 album, *The Cold Hard Truth*, contained his finest work in years.

Willie Nelson (b. Fort Worth, Texas, 1933), no longer belongs just to Texas or the Southwest, but his national and international acclaim has its roots in the region. After his father died, Willie Nelson and his sister Bobbie were raised by their grandparents in Abbott, Texas, a small community south of Dallas. Young Willie showed musical talent by the time he was seven. By the time he was eleven he had produced a handwritten book of songs that touched on the themes of drinking (accompanied by hangovers) and infidelity. After high school, Nelson got a job as a disc jockey at a Fort Worth Station. He recorded his first song, "Lumberjack," in 1956.

In 1961 Nelson was living in Nashville, where he landed a music publishing contract, and that year he saw three of his songs that had been recorded by other artists hit the charts. These were Faron Young's "Hello Walls," Billy Walker's "Funny How Time Slips Away," and one of the great American records, Patsy Cline's recording of Willie's "Crazy." During this decade Nelson made his own records, and in 1965 he became a member of the Grand Ole Opry after he signed with RCA.

Disgusted by the formulaic Nashville music of the time, Nelson moved back to Texas in the early 1970s, settling in Austin. By that time he had formed the band that he still performs with. They started modestly, playing free concerts, some of them in the parking lot of automobile dealers. In 1973 Nelson signed a contract with Atlantic Records after Atlantic's Jerry Wexler made a talent-scouting trip to Austin. The result was two of the decade's innovative country albums, *Shotgun Willie* and *Phases and Stages*, a concept album whose first side was written from the woman's point of view in a breakup ("Sister's Coming Home"); side two was from the standpoint of the man ("Bloody Mary Morning"). Nothing like this was coming out of Nashville, and Willie soon grew a beard and shaggy hair and began playing at the Austin's Armadillo World Headquarters, a converted military Quonset hut that featured notables in the music business ranging from Van Morrison to the young Bruce Springsteen to the old Count Basie and his Band.

In 1975 Nelson jumped to Columbia Records and recorded another concept album, *Red-Headed Stranger* (technically a soundtrack record) that contained his first smash hit as a singer, the remake of Roy Acuff's "Blue Eyes Crying in the Rain." Nelson's biggest crossover was his 1978 album *Stardust*, which featured him singing standards like "Blue Skies," "Stardust," and "Georgia On My Mind." Two fine albums in 1980 solidified his popularity—one was the soundtrack to his film *Honeysuckle Rose*, which featured a song that became his anthem, "On the Road Again." The other notable release the same year was *San Antonio Rose*, a fine example of honky-tonk and Western swing that featured Willie singing with his old bandleader/boss Ray Price.

During the last two decades Nelson has released over fifty albums, many of them duets where he sings with artists as varied as George Jones, Merle Haggard, Latin crooner Julio Iglesias, Sinead O'Connor. In 2003 his very earliest work was recognized in a fascinating release titled *Crazy, the Demo Sessions*, that literally were cuts from his earliest years in Nashville as a songwriter making demos for the likes of Patsy Cline.

Willie Nelson's nonmainstream success in Austin helped create the "outlaw" movement in country music in the middle and late 1970s. The "outlaws" were renegades from the country-music establishment in Nashville that at the time was more interested in string arrangements and cookie-cutter artists who looked and sounded alike. Several of these artists were Texas natives or transplants there, and the principal talent in this group, after Nelson, was Waylon Jennings (b. Plainview, Texas, 1937). Jennings grew up in West Texas listening to Jimmie Rodgers, Ernest Tubb, and the blues artists B. B. King and Bobby Blue Bland. By age fourteen he was a disc jockey on KDAV, and it was at that station in 1955 that Jennings met Buddy Holly. He soon became Holly's bass player in the Crickets, and it was Jennings who gave up his airplane seat to the Big Bopper on the flight that, tragically, crashed in February 1959, killing all aboard, including the Big Bopper, Buddy Holly, and Richie Valens.

In the mid-1960s Jennings was a headliner at a Phoenix club called JD's. It was there that his rough and ready rockabilly style was discovered by Herb Alpert's A&M Records. Jennings later switched to RCA, where he was signed by Chet Atkins. His early 1970s albums *Lonesome, On'ry and Mean* and *This Time* were critical successes and caught the attention of people who weren't usually fans of country music. Particularly fine was Jennings' album of songs written by Billie Joe Shaver (b. Corsicana, Texas, 1939), *Honkytonk Heroes*. Two signature Jennings songs—"Low Down Freedom" and "Ain't No God in Mexico"—were on the Shaver-penned album. In 1976 Jennings, along with Tompall Glaser and Willie Nelson, released *Wanted: The Outlaws*, and it became country music's first platinum record. Jennings' and Nelson's duet version of "Good Hearted Woman" played on the jukebox of every beer joint in America. Jennings' other hit songs in this fertile period were "Are You Sure Hank Did It This Way," "Amanda," and two more duets with Nelson, "Luckenbach, Texas," and "Mamas, Don't Let Your Babies Grow Up to Be Cowboys," the latter of which won the two Texans a Grammy for best vocal by a duo or group. Jennings' career continued through the 1980s, and in the 1990s he toured as part of "The Highwaymen," a country supergroup made up of Jennings, Willie Nelson, Johnny Cash, and Kris Kristofferson (b. Brownsville, Texas, 1936). Waylon was slowed down a bit by poor health at the end of that decade. He died in Phoenix in February 2002 and is buried in Mesa, Arizona.

The Cosmic Cowboys and Country/Folk

Partly a marketing ploy and partly a genuine subgenre was the phenomenon in the 1970s known as the cosmic cowboys. A triangulation of the movement would include a radio station in Austin (KOKE-FM), a cavernous concert hall where hippies and rednecks listened to music together (Armadillo World Headquarters), and a cozy little beer joint (the Split Rail) where the music was nurtured. The music itself ranged from some of Willie Nelson's best concept albums to good-times music that celebrated an unbridled lifestyle to hippie-band appropriations of country and folk. Joe Gracy was the station manager at KOKE-FM, an FM station that promoted and played new albums and singles by Nelson, Waylon Jennings, Jerry Jeff Walker (Ronald Clyde Crosby) (b. Oneota, New York, 1941), Michael Murphey (b. Dallas, 1945), B. W. Stevenson (b. Dallas, 1949), and Willis Alan Ramsey (b. Birmingham, Alabama, 1949), among others. The image of this music and the individuals who played it was decidedly more "cosmic" (i.e., bohemian) than it was cowboy. Jerry Jeff Walker and Michael Murphey shared the personnel in what became known as the Lost Gonzo band, a talented aggregation that featured singers Gary P. Nunn and Bob Livingston, ace guitar player John Inmon and drummer Freddie Krc. Two important albums by these artists were released in 1972: Walker's, *Jerry Jeff Walker*, which featured "L.A. Freeway" and "Hill Country Rain," and Murphey's *Geronimo's Cadillac*, which elicited a rave review from Chet Flippo in *Rolling Stone*. The next year, Walker recorded his most popular album, *Viva Terlingua*. B. W. Stevenson's career was notoriously mishandled by RCA, who presented him as a pop singer. Yet his haunting ballads "My Maria" and "Shambala" are still played on oldies stations. Willis Alan Ramsey's 1972 Shelter Records album *Willis Alan Ramsey* is an American perennial and to date his only recorded work in album form. Popular songs from the album include "Muskrat Love" and

"Goodbye Old Missoula." Lyle Lovett included a couple of new Ramsey songs on his 1998 tribute to Texas songwriters, *Step Inside This House*. B. W. Stevenson died in 1988 at the age of 39.

Jerry Jeff Walker's career has been revived by his manager/wife, Susan; their son, Django, is an emerging singer/songwriter. Michael Murphey is now Michael Martin Murphey and for several years has been a performer of cowboy songs. Willis Alan Ramsey lives in Wimberley, Texas, and is still performing in small clubs, and about every third year there is a rumor about his recording a second album.

The imaginative bookings at the Armadillo would juxtapose the emerging Austin singers with touring bands that might include Little Feat, Van Morrison, or Bruce Springsteen, who in the 1970s would play a packed hall for a two-dollar cover charge. The Split Rail on Sunday night was a beloved gig that usually featured Freda and the Firedogs, a soulful hippie-country band that included Marcia Ball on piano and on vocals singing Loretta Lynn covers, Bobby Earl Smith on bass, and John Reed, from Lubbock, on guitar. The entire scene was institutionalized by Willie Nelson's Fourth of July picnic, which in its first year, 1972, was held in a broiling hot limestone pasture a little west of Dripping Springs, Texas.

Country Music of the 1980s and 1990s

The mainstream male country star with the greatest longevity during the last two decades of the twentieth century was George Strait, born in Poteet, Texas in 1952. After attending Southwest Texas State University, he formed and began playing with a band named Ace in the Hole. From playing small halls and wedding parties in the late 1970s, Strait went on to almost instant success after his first album *Strait Country* was released in 1981. Since that initial effort he has recorded twenty-five albums that went platinum, with 1995's *Strait Out of the Box* selling over seven million copies. Strait still works with his original band and adheres to a pure version of country music, he usually includes two or more covers of classic songs and is especially adept at Western swing. His renditions of Bob Wills tunes like "Take Me Back to Tulsa" are always popular in his sold out concerts. His own best-selling singles have been "Amarillo By Morning," "Write This Down," and "I Can Still Make Cheyenne."

The popular and controversial female trio the Dixie Chicks keep producing excellent records. They began in Dallas in 1989, when the group consisted of the sisters Martie (b. 1969) and Emily (b. 1972) Erwin (now Martie Maguire and Emily Robison), who respectively play fiddle and guitar. The other two original members were Laura Lynch and Robin Lynn Macy. Robin Lynn Macy left the group in 1992, looking for a purer bluegrass style. In 1995 Laura Lynch was replaced by the singer Natalie Maines (b. Lubbock, Texas, 1974), daughter of the Lubbock pedal-steel-guitar player and record producer Lloyd Maines. The new trio immediately had a hit album, *Wide Open Spaces*, on Monument Records. This was followed by another best seller, *Fly*. After a two-year-long dispute with Sony Records, the trio recorded their most mature album, *Home*, an independent production done by Lloyd Maines. *Home* won the Grammy Award for best country album in 2002. In March 2003 Natalie Maines became the most controversial artist in country music when she said during a concert in London that the band was "ashamed the

President of the United States is from Texas." She later apologized, but many conservative fans were upset. The upset did not appear to hurt the group's record sales or concert attendance.

FOLK

The American folk poet Woody Guthrie (b. Okemah, Oklahoma, 1912; d. 1967) began writing songs and playing music in Pampa, Texas, in the early 1930s. He had moved to the Texas Panhandle town at age nineteen, after a string of tragedies in his hometown of Okemah, Oklahoma, including the tragic death of his sister and the institutionalization of his mother. By 1937 the inhabitants of western Oklahoma and the northern-most counties of Texas began abandoning the drought-ridden countryside that had become the bottom tier of the Dust Bowl. Woody, like many others, headed west to California, traveling by car, by rail, and by foot through New Mexico and Arizona to the fields of Southern California, where he worked as a tenant farmer and began entertaining the other workers. He quickly became popular and soon played live on big radio stations in Los Angeles and Tijuana, Mexico. His constant crisscrossing of the American Southwest and the misery he saw and experienced there resulted in his classic ballads "I Ain't Got No Home," "Goin' Down the Road Feelin' Bad," and "Hobo's Lullaby." His sharp-edged political pieces included songs of tribute to the Southwestern outlaws Jesse James and Pretty Boy Floyd.

Always restless, Guthrie moved to New York City in 1939, where he was adopted by intellectuals and folk audiences whose knowledge of the rural side of the Great Depression was learned to a large degree through Farm Security Administration photographs and from Woody's music. "This Land Is Your Land," became his anthem, as well as that of audiences who had experienced, and overcome, hard times during the Great Depression.

Huddie Ledbetter, better known as Leadbelly was born in Mooringsport, Louisiana, in 1888. His family moved to an East Texas farm when he was ten. Migrating to Dallas, Ledbetter fell under the spell of Blind Lemon Jefferson, with whom he sang on the street corners of the black neighborhoods. In 1918 Ledbetter was convicted of murder and sent to the Texas penitentiary, where he acquired his nickname after surviving a gunshot to the abdomen. After writing a song for Texas governor Pat Neff, he was released in 1925. Back in prison in Louisiana in 1930, Leadbelly was discovered by the Texas musicologist John Avery Lomax, who had heard of the singing killer. The relationship between the two of them was complex, with Leadbelly calling Lomax "bossman" and driving the white man's car for him, while Lomax arranged for the singer to make his debut at Carnegie Hall in New York wearing a striped convict's suit. The result was that Leadbelly became a sainted figure in the early years of the East Coast folk revival. He eventually became much closer to Alan Lomax, the folk music archivist son of John Lomax. It was under Alan's guiding hand that Leadbelly wrote and recorded populist songs such as "The Bourgeois Blues." The publishing rights to Leadbelly's most famous song, "Goodnight Irene," were retained by John Lomax. Leadbelly died in New York in 1949.

The vitality of the country music and early rock and roll scenes dominated music in the Southwest, but an important contribution to American folk music began in

1972: the Kerrville Folk Festival. Kerrville, Texas, is a picturesque town in the Texas Hill Country, where Jimmie Rodgers had moved for his health. Jazz and folk-music promoter Rod Kennedy (b. 1930) staged his first folk festival in Kerrville's Municipal Auditorium in June 1972. There were thirteen performers, including Carolyn Hester, Allen Dameron, Townes Van Zandt, Kenneth Threadgill, Rusty Weir, Steve Fromholz, Bill and Bonnie Hearne, Mance Lipscomb, Jerry Jeff Walker, and Michael Murphey. The following year, the festival was again in the auditorium but had expanded to five concerts in three days—the paid attendance was 5,600, and among the new performers was Willie Nelson.

In 1974 the festival relocated to a sixty-acre location outside Kerrville that Kennedy named Quiet Valley Ranch to assuage the concerns of the suspicious neighbors. At the ranch, folk fans could now camp for several days and hear music both formally and informally. One of the "new folk" competition's finalists in 1974 was a young Arkansas singer, Lucinda Williams. By 1981 the festival had expanded to eleven days that stretched over several weekends. Among the "unknown" singers that the festival helped highlight (and get recording contracts) were Lyle Lovett, Nanci Griffith, Hal Ketchum, John Gorka, James McMurtry, Tish Hinojosa, Robert Earl Keen, and Steve Earle. By the late 1990s attendance was regularly close to 30,000. In 1999 Rod Kennedy sold his interest in the festival to a Dallas investment group.

One of the strongest ingredients in contemporary acoustic music is the singer/songwriter, a phrase that seems to have supplanted "folk singer" sometime in the 1970s. Of the many excellent Texas musicians who might be described by the term, the most respected without question is Townes Van Zandt (b. Fort Worth, 1944). Townes was born to a wealthy, well-connected Texas family. As a young man he was diagnosed as being manic-depressive, and the remainder of his life was a struggle with this disease and with alcoholism. He had begun to record by 1969 and soon had produced a string of fine acoustic albums for Tomato Records that included some of his best-known songs: "For the Sake of the Song," "If I Needed You," "Flyin' Shoes," "Tecumseh Valley," and "Pancho and Lefty." By 1970 Van Zandt was living in Nashville. He began to get national attention when Emmy Lou Harris recorded "Pancho and Lefty," in 1977 (there was a later hit version of the song done by Merle Haggard and Willie Nelson). In 1981 Don Williams' cover of "If I Needed You" was number one on the country charts.

But Van Zandt was his own worst enemy. He had little discipline when it came to the business of recording and no discipline at all when it came to performing. At venues like Austin's Cactus Café, the question was always, will Townes show up, and if so, will he be able to play? Yet his live performances, when they happened, were legendary—an example is captured on *Live at the Old Quarter*, recorded in Houston. Up until his death on January 1, 1997, of heart failure, there were always new projects talked about. Since his death there have been countless tributes and covers of his songs. His oldest child, J.T. Van Zandt, is now performing as a singer in Austin.

Guy Clark (b. Rockport, Texas, 1941) was Townes Van Zandt's closest songwriting friend. Clark was living in Houston in the late 1960s, when Van Zandt was married and sporadically attending law school. Clark was also friends with Jerry Jeff Walker, and two of Clark's songs, "L.A. Freeway" and "Desperadoes Waiting for a Train," were first recorded by Walker. Clark's first album of his own songs was *Old Number One*, released in 1975. This was followed the next year by *Texas Cookin'*. Neither of these made the charts, yet Clark was liked so well by other artists that many of them appeared on these records—his guests included Emmylou Harris, Rodney Crowell, Hoyt Axton, and Steve Earle. This pattern of underground and critical success has followed Clark, who has continued to perform and write good material. One of his best recent albums is *The Dark*, released in 2002.

Lyle Lovett was born in 1957 in Klein, Texas, north of Houston. Klein was founded by his mother's great-grandfather. He graduated early from high school and entered Texas A&M University in College Station, Texas, where he majored in German and in journalism. He immediately was attracted to the coffee house scene there and in Austin and was very influenced by several singers, but especially by Willis Alan Ramsey, whom he first saw perform in Austin's old downtown movie theater, the Paramount. One of Lovett's classmates at A&M was Robert Earl Keen (b. Houston, 1956), another aspiring songwriter. Together they wrote a song they both still perform, "This Old Porch." In 1984 Lovett spent time in Nashville singing backup on Nanci Griffith's album *Once in a Very Blue Moon*.

Nanci Griffith (b. 1954, Seguin, Texas) passed along a Lovett tape to Guy Clark, who contacted MCA Records. Two years later *Lyle Lovett* was released, followed in 1988 by *Pontiac*. The first two albums were an unusual combination of plaintive ballad ("This Old Porch," "Closing Time,") and jaunty jazz arrangements, with Lovett backed by a jazz band ("An Acceptable Level of Ecstasy," "Black and Blue"). By 1989, upon the release of *Lyle Lovett and His Large Band*, everyone knew that he was not a conventional Nashville songwriter. That year he won the Grammy Award for best male vocalist. In 1992 Lovett appeared in his first Robert Altman film, *The Player*, which is where he met actress Julia Roberts, whom he soon married, from whom he was divorced less than two years later. In 1993 Lovett won another Grammy, this one for a duet with Al Green singing Willie Nelson's standard "Funny How Time Slips Away." Notable albums since then have been *Joshua Judges Ruth*; his tribute album to Texas songwriters, *Step Inside This House*, and in 2003, *My Baby Don't Tolerate*.

In 1981 Robert Earl Keen moved to Austin with his band, the Incredible Robert Keen and Some Other Guys band. In 1984 he financed his first album, *No Kinda Dancer*. By 1988 he was making his living writing in Nashville and spending time with Nanci Griffith and Lyle Lovett. His 1994 album, *Gringo Honeymoon*, is probably his best. His popular concerts, at least in Texas, are marked by enthusiastic (and drunk) Texas A&M students singing along with Keen.

ROCK AND ROLL

Many music historians date the beginnings of rock and roll to the day in July, 1954 when Elvis Presley recorded "That's All Right Mama" in Memphis' Sun Studio. Presley's innovation on that day was to combine two strains of American music: African-American blues and hillbilly country. Presley was nineteen. The same summer, an eighteen-year-old from West Texas was making experimental recordings of his own, in a little studio located in Wichita Falls, Texas. His name was Buddy Holly.

The Far Southwest

Buddy Holly was born on September 7, 1936, in Lubbock, the youngest of four children. While still in high school, Holly formed a trio with Bob Montgomery and Larry Wellborn, who played a regular show on Lubbock's KDAV. In 1954 when Holly was eighteen, the trio began making experimental recordings at a studio in Wichita Falls. In 1956 Holly had a short-lived solo contract with Decca records. He was dropped after a year when he didn't fit into their country mode. Holly formed a new group in 1957 that included drummer Jerry Allison and Niki Sullivan. Calling themselves the Crickets, they drove over to Clovis, New Mexico, to the recording studio run by Norman Petty. Brunswick Records signed the Crickets, and Coral, a subsidiary of Brunswick, signed Holly to do solo work. The first song released, "That'll Be the Day," was an instant hit, rising to number three on the pop chart and number two on the rhythm-and-blues chart. Indeed, many listeners thought that the Crickets were a black group, and when they first flew East in July 1957, they were packaged with black R&B acts at Harlem's Apollo Theater. The next Holly single was "Peggy Sue," backed with "Every Day," and after that came "Oh Boy" backed with "Not Fade Away." By the end of the year the group had appeared on the Ed Sullivan Show, on American Bandstand, and in numerous package shows. Before they toured Australia, Niki Sullivan quit the band and was replaced by Tommy Allsup.

In 1958 Holly moved from Lubbock to New York, leaving behind Petty's Clovis studio, where all of the hits were recorded, and the original Crickets. One of the newly formed Crickets was the bass player, Waylon Jennings, who later became a country superstar. After a show in Clear Lake, Iowa, on February 3, 1959, Holly chartered a plane to get him quickly to Fargo, North Dakota, close to his next show. Two other stars, Richie Valens and J. P. Richardson (the Big Bopper), bumped two of the Crickets. The plane crashed soon after takeoff, killing all passengers. The event was memorialized in Don McLean's 1971 song "American Pie" as "the day the music died." Indeed, Buddy Holly was the prototype of much that was to come—the small, hardriving, self-taught band, full of confidence and tight songs. His influence was acknowledged by the Beatles, the Rolling Stones, Bob Dylan, and Elvis Costello, among others. After the release of the film *The Buddy Holly Story* in 1978, the city of Lubbock began to celebrate its native son.

Norman Petty was the first successful independent producer in popular music. After Holly's death he released unfinished Crickets songs using overdubs. Petty had retained the rights to all of Holly's songs, and in 1973 he sold them to Paul McCartney, who purchased the entire Buddy Holly song catalog.

A West Texas contemporary of Holly's was the great singer Roy Orbison (b. Vernon, Texas, 1936) who grew up in the oilfield town of Wink. As a high school student he formed a country-and-western band called the Wink Westerners, which featured Orbison as lead singer. This group was transformed into a rock and roll band, the Teen Kings, when Orbison was attending North Texas State College (where he was acquainted with fellow student Pat Boone). The Teen Kings recorded his composition "Ooby Dooby." Orbison was quickly signed to Sun Records in Memphis in 1956, and he rerecorded his first hit. Although Sun was the little studio that made stars out of Carl Perkins, Johnny Cash, Jerry Lee Lewis, and Elvis Presley, Orbison had no further success and left Sun. In 1959 he joined Monument Records in Nashville and began recording a string of the most eerily beautiful songs in pop music. These included "Only the Lonely" (1960), "Running Scared" (1961), "Blue Bayou" (1963), and in 1964, "It's Over" and "Oh, Pretty Woman." In the late 1960s and 1970s Orbison experienced a series of personal tragedies, and his recording dwindled. In 1980 he won a Grammy Award with a duet he made with Emmy Lou Harris. In 1986 his song "In Dreams" was featured in the film *Blue Velvet*. The same year he was inducted into the Rock and Roll Hall of Fame in a touching ceremony that featured Bruce Springsteen making the presentation. In the year of his death, 1988, he filmed a very successful television special and recorded *The Traveling Wilburys* along with Bob Dylan, George Harrison, and Tom Petty. Decades before, Elvis Presley had called Orbison "the greatest singer in the world."

Two other important early West Texas rockers were Buddy Knox, born near Happy, Texas, in 1935, and Bobby Fuller, born in Goose Creek in 1943. In 1956 Knox and his group recorded "Party Doll," a song he had written when he was sixteen. The hit was recorded on Triple D, a small label out of Dumas, Texas, and the record was subsequently bought by Maurice Levy, who released it as the first song from his new company, Roulette Records. Knox had other popular songs but was not fairly treated by the record company. By 1970 he was living in Canada and touring Europe as part of an "oldies" show. He died in Bremerton, Washington, in 1999. Bobby Fuller's family moved to El Paso in the 1950s, and by the end of that decade he played drums in a group called the Counts. In 1962 he formed the Bobby Fuller Four and, with his parents' help, built a recording studio in their house, where he recorded his signature song "I Fought the Law (And the Law Won)." Fuller then opened a popular teen club in El Paso called the Teen Rendezvous Club. After it burned in 1964, Fuller moved to Los Angeles and began recording with Bob Keene. He rerecorded "I Fought the Law" and released another hit, "Let Her Dance." The Bobby Fuller Four decided to break up, and in 1965 and 1966 a number of albums were released. On July 18, 1966, Fuller was found shot dead behind the wheel of his automobile. His death was ruled a suicide, but many of his friends thought that Fuller had met with foul play.

After Buddy Holly's death, Lubbock continued as a musical town. Holly's father encouraged a new generation, including an up and coming band called the Flatlanders, who played a combination of folk, country, and rock and roll. The group included three talented songwriters who went on to contribute a number of memorable numbers to the Texas songbook. Butch Hancock was born in Lubbock in 1945 and was the most prolific of the group's songwriters. His best songs have intricate wordplay akin to that in Bob Dylan's songs—among these are "The West Texas Waltz" and "If I Were a Bluebird," both recorded by Emmy Lou Harris and the Joe Ely Band recorded those as well as "She Never Spoke Spanish to Me" and "Boxcars," Hancock's bandmate and childhood friend Jimmie Dale Gilmore (b. Tulia, Texas, 1945) was one of the lead singers for the Flatlanders and a songwriter as well. Gilmore is known for his keening tenor voice and for such songs as "Treat Me Like a Saturday Night" and "Dallas." The third songwriter and singer in the Flatlanders was Joe Ely (b. Amarillo, 1947). The original Flatlanders, which was largely acoustic and featured a musical saw, mainly played in Lubbock and West

Texas. By 1978 Hancock, Gilmore, and Ely had each individually made their ways to Austin. The Flatlanders had produced one record that was available on an eight-track tape (it was reissued by Rounder Records in 1990 as *More a Legend Than a Band*). The Joe Ely Band was signed by MCA, and their second album, *Honky-Tonk Masquerade*, was full of fine songs by Gilmore and Hancock and by Ely himself ("Cornbread Moon"). A tremendous band in person, the Ely group featured Lloyd Maines on pedal steel guitar, Jesse Taylor on lead guitar, and Ponty Bone on accordian. Ely's great voice and electric stage presence won fans all over the world—this was especially true in England, when the band opened for the Clash in a major tour in 1982. The resulting live album, *Live Shots*, was one of their best. MCA dropped the Ely Band in 1983.

Jimmie Gilmore had success in his solo albums released in 1988 and 1989 and had quite a bit of national exposure on television. In 1993 his album *Spinning Around the Sun* was released, and in 1996 he recorded *Braver Newer World*, produced by Fort Worth native T-Bone Burnett. Butch Hancock remained ubiquitous, releasing his songs on his own label, Rainlight. In 2000 the Flatlanders began to tour again, and in 2002 the three friends recorded a new Flatlanders album titled *Now Again*.

The biggest maverick in the Lubbock scene is the painter/singer/gadfly Terry Allen (b. Wichita, Kansas, 1943). Although not as heralded as Ely, Gilmore, or Hancock, Terry Allen's far out persona and far-flung connections and interests have brought the world to Lubbock. Allen is not primarily a musician, although he keeps his hand in. As a Guggenheim Fellowship winner, he has been a multimedia artist in Los Angeles and New York, accomplished in the media of painting, sculpture, film, video, and multimedia installations. In music, Allen is often bunched with the Flatlanders' members, and this is true as far as his generation and playing mates are concerned. Allen, however, has his own offbeat take on reality on West Texas subjects, including football ("The Great Joe Bob"), late night radio ("The Wolfman of Del Rio"), and the dangers of picking up hitchhikers who turn out to be Jesus ("Give Me a Ride to Heaven Boy"). Allen's most diverse album is *Lubbock, On Everything*, released in 1979.

The South Texas Sound

San Antonio has been a cultural crossroads for four hundred years, and this is clearly reflected in the music it has produced. As the major population center of South Texas, it has been a natural home for the Mexican and Tejano music styles. San Antonio Tex-Mex cafés regularly feature mariachi orchestras, and for decades the west-side clubs have featured the best conjunto ensembles. San Antonio has produced many virtuosos in this music, including the three legendary push-button accordian players Santiago Jiminez Sr. (b. San Antonio, 1913; d. 1984) and his sons Flaco Jiminez (b. Leonardo, San Antonio, 1939) and Santiago Jiminez Jr. (b. San Antonio, 1944).

But when it comes to rock and roll, the Alamo City's hometown favorite was the Texas legend Doug Sahm, born Douglas Wayne Sahm in 1941. Sahm was a prodigy who at a young age played steel guitar, mandolin, and fiddle; he made his San Antonio radio debut at age five on KMAC. Soon he was performing on the Louisiana Hayride in Shreveport as Little Doug Sahm. He would sit in with the big country stars of the time, including Webb Pierce, Hank Thompson, and Faron Young. In December 1952 Sahm was called to the stage by Hank Williams in what proved to be Williams' final show at Austin's Skyline Club. As a teenager, Sahm was offered a regular spot on Nashville's Grand Ole Opry, but his mother made him turn it down.

But it was the blues that formed Sahm's musical direction. In a reminiscence, Sahm recalled, "Across a plowed field from my house was a place called the Eastwood Country Club. On any given night you had T-Bone Walker, Junior Parker, the Bobby 'Blue' Bland Review, Hank Ballard, and James Brown. At about twelve or thirteen, my neighbor would bring over these great 45s with colorful labels like Excello, Atlantic, and Specialty, and dudes like Lonesome Sundown, Jimmy Reed, and Fats Domino." By 1964 Sahm's band, the Markays, was playing opposite Augie Meyers' band, the Goldens, both opening for the Dave Clark Five. The British Invasion had prevailed in America, and finally Texas record producer Huey Meaux agreed to record Sahm, but only if he and his new band, the Sir Douglas Quintet (now with Augie Meyers [b. San Antonio, 1941] on keyboards) would pretend to be English and dress in matching suits like the Beatles. This charade only lasted until the audience heard Sahm's drawl or the Tex-Mex patois spoken by the rhythm section. But Meaux's recording of the quintet's "She's About a Mover" proved to be a big hit in January 1965. After a 1966 marijuana bust in Corpus Christi, the Sir Douglas Quintet moved to California, settling in Marin County, north of San Francisco. The quintet performed in Bay Area ballrooms and cut several stellar albums on Smash Records, including *Mendocino*, whose single of the same name became a minor hippie anthem.

By this time Sahm's band, made up almost entirely of old pals from San Antonio who could and did play a bewildering mixture of country, blues, Mexican music, soul music, and rock and roll, moved back to Austin. This coincided with Sahm's being signed to Atlantic Records by Jerry Wexler, the man who had recorded Ray Charles and Aretha Franklin. Sahm's tenure there was relatively short-lived but included *Doug Sahm and Band*, a Sahm supergroup album that included Bob Dylan, Dr. John, and Flaco Jiminez. In Austin, Sahm was a fixture at the original Soap Creek Saloon, where he wore long hair, a cowboy hat, and granny glasses, mixing his sets with songs written by himself and by his influences, including T-Bone Walker, Bob Wills, Bob Dylan, and Creedence Clearwater Revival. There was nothing like dancing to Sahm playing Walker's "T-Bone Shuffle" followed by Will's "Faded Love" followed by Guitar Slim's "The Things That I Used to Do" followed by his own "Groover's Paradise," his tribute to the Austin of the period. Later in his Austin days, Sahm revived his San Antonio blues band that included the West Side Horns, which featured Rocky Morales on tenor sax, Al Gomez on trumpet, and Arturo "Sauce" Gonzalez on Hammond B-3 organ. In the 1990s, Sahm helped form another super group—the Texas Tornados—made up of Sahm, Tejano singer Freddy Fender, accordianist Flaco Jiminez, and keyboardist Augie Meyers. These old friends recorded a number of country hits, including Meyers' "Hey Baby, Que Paso?" and Sahm's "Who Were You Thinking Of." Doug Sahm died at age fifty-nine in 1999, in Taos, New Mexico, of a heart attack. The week he died, the *Austin Chronicle* devoted its entire issue to Sahm, calling him the "state musician of Texas."

The Texas/San Francisco Connection

Janis Joplin was born in Port Arthur, Texas, in January 1943, and by junior high school was showing signs of a bohemian rebellion directed against her conservative parents and her conventional classmates. Before she finished high school, she was part of an adventuresome group that traveled to Louisiana to hear music and drink. She began to sing and to listen to old blues records by Bessie Smith and Big Mama Thornton. By the time she reached the University of Texas in 1962, she was a regulation folk singer, wielding an acoustic guitar. She played at a student housing co-op called the Ghetto and at the old service station run by the country singer Kenneth Threadgill (b. Peniel, Texas, 1909). Two years in San Francisco, 1963–1965, led to nothing but drug problems and exhaustion. After resting up back in Port Arthur, she returned to the Bay Area, this time hooking up with the rock band Big Brother and the Holding Company. She and the band hit it big, growing in popularity through 1966 and making a particular impact at the Monterey Pop Festival in the early summer of 1967. Captured in the documentary film *Monterey Pop*, Joplin's performance is mesmerizing. The psychedelic blues style of Big Brother perfectly set off Joplin's wispy, gravelly, shrieking singing that was perfect for some of the older material, including Big Mama Thornton's anthem "Ball and Chain" and George Gershwin's "Summertime."

With her new fame Joplin came under the management of Albert Grossman, who felt that Big Brother and the Holding Company held her back. He was wrong, as her subsequent group, The Kosmic Blues Band, quickly demonstrated. A third group, the Full Tilt Boogie band, worked better, but her original San Francisco fans felt betrayed. By the time of her death of an overdose in 1970, she was widely regarded as the finest white female blues singer America produced. Her final studio album, *Pearl*, includes some notable work, including her version of Kris Kristofferson's "Me and Bobby McGee." Fans of the Big Brother band should listen to *Janis Joplin and Big Brother and the Holding Company: Live at Winterland, 1968*.

Janis Joplin. Courtesy of Photofest.

During the time Joplin lived in Austin, one of the experimental bands was the Thirteenth Floor Elevators, an ensemble most commentators credit with the invention of psychedelic music. Led by the powerful singer and poet Roky Erickson (b. 1947), the band played original songs and covers at Austin clubs of the mid-1960s, like the New Orleans, on Red River Street. The band featured Tommy Hall, who played the electric jug, literally a ceramic jug that was amplified. After their first hit record, "You're Gonna Miss Me," in 1966, the band moved to San Francisco, where they usually played at the Avalon Ballroom, a dance hall operated by a group of Texas expatriates that included Chet Helms (a close friend of Janis Joplin). Much of the later San Francisco sound came from this Texas group. Back in Austin, Roky was arrested with six marijuana joints, and after pleading an insanity defense was sent to Rusk State Prison for the Criminally Insane, where he underwent electroshock and liquid-Thorazine treatments. In prison Roky formed a band and wrote over one hundred songs. He was released in 1972. He never quite regained his mental health but is cared for by a charitable bank fund. In 1991 Reprise record executive Bill Bentley, the former drummer in the Austin group LeeAnn and the Bizarros, produced a fine tribute album titled *Where the Pyramid Meets the Eye*.

Steve Miller (b. Milwaukee, Wisconsin, 1943) and Boz Scaggs (b. William Royce Scaggs, Ohio, 1944) played music together in Dallas in a high school group called the Marksmen. Miller's father was a physician and a good friend of guitar pioneer Les Paul, as well as a guitar player himself. When he was growing up, Miller met various guitar greats as they came through town and visited his home, including T-Bone Walker. The Marksmen played blues clubs in Dallas and once backed Jimmy Reed. Miller asked Scaggs to join the group as a vocalist. Miller left for college at the University of Wisconsin when he was sixteen, and Scaggs soon followed him there. In Madison both played in a blues band called the Ardells and then the Knightranes. Returning to the United States from Europe, Miller spent a summer in Chicago working with the blues harpist Paul Butterfield. This band played with Muddy Waters, Howlin' Wolf, and Buddy Guy, all of whom encouraged Miller in his blues guitar playing.

In 1966 Miller moved down to Austin in hopes of taking music classes at the University of Texas. He was not admitted to the music school, so he bought a VW minibus and drove to San Francisco. He soon moved in with Paul Butterfield, and Miller quickly formed the Steve Miller Blues Band, which debuted at the Avalon Ballroom in January, 1967. After playing at the Monterey Pop Festival, they did a live recording backing Chuck Berry at the Fillmore Auditorium. Miller soon hammered out a lucrative contract with Capitol Records, who gave him total artistic control. Now called the Steve Miller Band, Scaggs joined Miller again as vocalist. Soon the band produced hits like "Living in the U.S.A." and "Gangster of Love." Personnel changed, but Miller's success continued, rising to a peak with the 1976 album *Fly Like an Eagle*.

Boz Scaggs left Miller's band in 1968 to begin a solo career. With the help of *Rolling Stone*'s Jann Wenner, Scaggs signed with Atlantic Records. Duane Allman of the Allman Brothers played on his Atlantic album *Loan Me a Dime*. Three records in the 1970s established Scaggs' smooth style. These were *My Time* (1972), *Slow Dancer* (1974), and *Silk Degrees* (1976). Scaggs was in retirement for much of the 1980s, buying and operating a San Francisco club, Slims. In 2003 Scaggs released an album of standards titled *But Beautiful*.

Duane Eddy (b. Corning, New York, 1938) moved to Arizona in the mid-1950s with his family, eventually settling in Phoenix. A local disc jockey, Lee Hazlewood, liked the young Eddy's guitar style and helped him develop what became known as his "twangy" guitar. The style involved powerful single-note melodies reinforced by the bass line playing in unison. Eddy signed with Dick Clark's Jamie label and had a hit record in 1958, "Rebel-'Rouser," an instrumental that featured rebel yells and handclaps. His backing group on the single was the Rivingtons. Duane Eddy was twenty years old. During the next five years he had fourteen more top-forty hits, most of them instrumentals. In the 1960s Eddy began working on songs for television and the movies, including the television show *Peter Gunn*. In 1962 Eddy married the teenaged Phoenix singer Jessi Colter (b. Mirriam Johnson, Phoenix, 1947), who became a successful singer in her own right. They were divorced by 1968, and she later married country star Waylon Jennings. In the 1970s Eddy was still popular in England and recorded with the British group the Art of Noise. In 1987 he recorded his album *Duane Eddy* on Capitol. Among the stars who contributed to the album were Paul McCartney, Jeff Lynne, Ry Cooder, George Harrison, Steve Cropper, and James Burton. Eddy was elected to the Rock and Roll Hall of Fame in 1994. He is considered by many the finest rock and roll instrumentalist of all time.

Linda Ronstadt was born in 1946 on an Arizona ranch outside of Tucson. Her father, who owned the ranch and a hardware store, encouraged her to investigate the musical heritages in her multiethnic background—German, English, Dutch, and Mexican. Her father especially schooled her in the Mexican mariachi songs, many of which she later recorded on her album *Canciones de me Padre*. When she was eighteen Ronstadt moved to Los Angeles with the guitarist Bob Kimmel, and they joined Kenny Edwards to form the Stone Poneys. The group became an integral part of the L.A. folk-rock scene, but soon Ronstadt signed as a solo artist with Arista Records. Her first solo albums, 1969's *Hand Sown Home Grown* and 1970's *Silk Purse* were solid country-influenced albums, but it was the 1974 *Heart Like A Wheel* album that made her one of the decade's leading recording stars. She proved her rock and roll merit in 1977 with two cover songs, the Rolling Stones' "Tumbling Dice," and Warren Zevon's "Poor Pitiful Me." In the early 1980s she took a recording break and performed in the Broadway production of Gilbert and Sullivan's *Pirates of Penzanze*, and later she was featured in the film. A very fine country album, *Trio*, with Emmy Lou Harris and Dolly Parton, was released in 1987. In that decade she also recorded three bilingual albums, *Canciones de mi Padre* (1987), *Mas Canciones* (1991), and *Frenesi* (1992).

After the midpoint of her illustrious career, she virtually stopped performing live—there were rumors of a devasting stage fright. But through almost every type of American music—including an album of standards conducted by Nelson Riddle, Ronstadt had demonstrated her depth as a singer.

The Live Music Capital of the World

Austin's calling itself the "live music capitol of the world" may be largely hyperbolic, yet the slogan does contain more than a kernal of truth. There is no doubt that in certain periods of the last forty years Austin has been an innovative center for individual musicians and bands. Part of this has been institutionalized by the South by Southwest Music festival, held annually in March, by the popular television program *Austin City Limits*, and by an active club scene that has endured despite waves of club closures, some at the hands of the city of Austin. The striking thing is the variety of the music that has been available to musicians and fans over the years.

In the 1940s and 1950s the preeminent country spot was the Skyline Club, up on the old Dallas Highway. Not remarkable except for the fact that Hank Williams played his last show there, it did feature the best touring country artists of the day. The same building was transformed in the late 1970s and became the second location of Soap Creek Saloon, a barny building that featured many Texas and Louisiana artists at their peaks, including the Joe Ely Band, Delbert McClinton, Doug Sahm, and the Neville Brothers. One of the country's finest blues clubs, Antone's, started downtown on Sixth Street in 1975. In its early days the club was a second home for the great Chicago artists, including Muddy Waters. Many young blues aspirants got their first glimpse of masters there, and some began to play there themselves.

Austin City Limits

The popular public television program *Austin City Limits* began in 1974 in the studios of Austin's KLRU, which is still its home. The early seasons focused on progressive country acts, with Willie Nelson being a special favorite. As the popularity of the show expanded, it became easier for the show to book a wider variety of acts. By the end of its fifth season the show had presented both Ray Charles and Chet Atkins. By the early 1980s the show began winning awards for the show's founder Bill Arhos, and its primary producer, Terry Likona. The musical selection expanded to folk in the late 1980s with a series of songwriting shows. Two tribute shows were tremendously popular: a tribute to Stevie Ray Vaughan that featured B. B. King and Eric Clapton, and a Townes Van Zandt show that presented Willie Nelson, Guy Clark, Nanci Griffith, and Lyle Lovett. The shows are shot live in a small studio on the campus of the University of Texas.

College students in the 1950s and 1960s spent a fair amount of time in the clubs on Red River Street and in East Austin at black clubs like Charley's Playhouse and the I. L. Club. Back then there was a hint of danger in traveling into a segregated neighborhood, but the club owners were always hospitable. In the late 1960s a downtown space calling itself the Vulcan Gas Company opened. It was a version of a San Francisco–style ballroom, with psychedelic posters, lightshows, and mainly local groups like Greezy Wheels, Balcones Fault, and Ramon Ramon & the Four Daddios. The Armadillo World Headquarters became world famous for its innovative booking and live albums. Just before it closed in 1980, after ten years in business, there were a number of farewell concerts, including a Lubbock Night. The last concert there was the Berkeley California honkytonk band Commander Cody and His Lost Planet Airmen playing with Asleep at the Wheel.

One of the finest venues for adventurous music in the 1970s and 1980s was Liberty Lunch, on Second Street close to the river. Partially open-air, the club booked everyone from the Meters to Sun Ra to Dwight Yoakum. The last week it was open there was a twenty-four-hour performance of the Van Morrison song "Gloria." The building was razed to make room for the new City of Austin offices. Late in the 1970s, punk music hit Austin hard (shortly after the Sex Pistols concert in San Antonio), and the club to hear it at was Raul's, close to the university campus. Groups such as the Skunks, the Bad Boys, and the Dicks were very popular there and could also be heard at the Continental Club on South Congress. A fine venue for folk rock was the original location of the Waterloo Icehouse on Congress Avenue. Operated by Steve Clark, the club featured the accomplished folk trio Uncle Walt's Band.

Most of Austin's clubs participate in the South by Southwest festival, booking four bands a night for three or four nights. The result is a very rich aural environment with choices of music all over town. Usually up and coming (and unrecorded) bands play the festival, but mixed in the schedule over the years have been artists of the stature of Tony Bennett, Randy Newman, and Tom Waits.

Venerable clubs that still book good music include the Continental Club (roots music) on South Congress, The Broken Spoke (country and western, swing) on South Lamar, and Antones, now at its fourth location. Perhaps the best and most consistent Austin club for quiet music is the Cactus Café on the campus of the University of Texas. A fall music festival, the Austin City Limits Festival, began in 2002 and has made a promising beginning.

Las Vegas, Nevada

Las Vegas as a musical destination is somewhat overshadowed by its primary purpose, which is to entertain people while lightening their bank accounts. Yet music has been important there, particularly in the 1960s when Frank Sinatra and the other members of the Rat Pack entertained, primarily at the Sands Hotel, located on "the strip," which is the old highway that comes into Las Vegas from Los Angeles. The Sands is now gone, but from the late 1950s and through the 1960s, the club in the hotel featured the top entertainment of the day, including Frank Sinatra backed by the Count Basie Band, and variety shows that might include Sinatra's pals Dean Martin or Sammy Davis Jr. It is said that Sinatra, by insisting that the Sands feature Davis, integrated the city.

In 1969 Elvis Presley, then age thirty-four, began his first shows at Las Vegas' International Hotel. Elvis, 637 performances later, also performed his last show in the International, on December 12, 1976. The mature Elvis has been parodied, yet he had much musical and entertainment merit. Overlapping with the King were Liberace and Wayne Newton, perhaps more in the mold of the schlock we associate with the city. As of this writing show biz acts of the caliber of Elton John, Celine Dion, and Cher still play Las Vegas several times a year.

NATIVE AMERICAN MUSIC

Native American music in the Southwest was documented in the earliest written accounts, in Álvar Núñez Cabeza de Vaca's *Relacion* (1542), by the Rodriguez expedition (1582), and by that of Alonso De Leon in 1645. Cabeza de Vaca encountered tribes who chanted, clapped their bodies in rhythm, and shook rattles made of gourds and pebbles. The Rodriguez party reported a festival gathering, close to what is now the Presidio on the Texas-Mexico border, that featured both unison and harmony singing. Likewise, Alonso De Leon wrote about group singing at ceremonial gatherings close to what is now Monterrey, in northern Mexico.

Archeological evidence in the Southwest discloses remnants of shaken rattles made from gourds and dried beans, rasps used to scrape hollow gourds, bone whistles, drums, and rattles made from the tails of rattlesnakes. Other percussion instruments were made from the large scapula, or shoulder bones, of deer and elk, and on the Texas coast, ankle- and wrist-bracelet rattles were made by stringing together mussel shells. Most early drums have not survived because the wood and hide deteriorated, but some cave paintings record the presence of drums in dancing. The Alarcón expedition of 1718 described a large kettledrum made of a waterjug, with a stretched head made from dampened deer skin. In many sites the most numerous music-making objects are whistles, made from the perforated long bone of birds.

Traditional dances still performed include the following:

The Buffalo Dance is a celebration of thanksgiving. The dance depicts the hunter stalking the buffalo, and to participate is considered an honor. The dances are major events in December and are held at the Acoma, Cochiti, Pojoaque, San Idelfonso, Santa Clara, Taos, and Tesuque pueblos.

The Corn Dance is fertility dance that may be held on varying dates. One spectacular event is the Santa Domingo Pueblo corn dance held in midsummer and featuring virtually every man, woman, and child in the community playing different formal roles, and the pueblo elders adorned with their finest silver jewelry. The drumming at this event is especially powerful.

The Deer Dance is associated with Christmas and like most of the modern dances combines elements of the Christian religion (introduced by Spanish missionaries in the seventeenth and eighteenth centuries) with ancient tribal spiritual rituals. The dancers wear antlers and dance with long sticks that represent the deer's front legs. The deer dance is customarily performed on Christmas day or King's day (January 6) at Acoma, Cochiti, San Idelfonso, San Juan, Santa Clara, and Taos.

The Turtle Dance is a fertility and rain dance that celebrates the harvest. The singing and dancing celebrates the gods of rain and thunder and honors mother earth. This is another December dance, usually held before Christmas at Acoma, Cochiti, San Idelfonso, San Juan, Santa Clara, and Taos.

An important gathering day occurs on September 30, San Geronimo Day, at the Taos Pueblo. The day begins at seven in the morning with intrapueblo footraces and in the afternoon culminates with a corn dance and the climbing of tall wooden poles. The day is open to all visitors and brings together many native artists and craftsmen, who sell their works at a fair on the grounds of the ancient Taos pueblo.

West of these pueblos are the home places of the Hopi and the huge Navajo nation, centered in the area outlined by Flagstaff, Arizona, and the small tribal towns of Window Rock and Tuba City. Hopi dances occur in several of the eleven villages, all scattered throughout the Black Mesa. Hopi dances are based on the four hundred different *kachina* figures that symbolize all aspects of native life. Navajo dances are accompanied by modernized ancient flute music and often last several days. Some are private ceremonies, but several are open to visitors. All the major Native American groups that

The Santa Fe Opera

The founder of the Santa Fe Opera, John O'Hea Crosby, was a Yale-educated New Yorker who first visited New Mexico to attend the Los Alamos Boys School. One of his Yale professors was the composer Paul Hindemith. Crosby fell in love with opera and decided to start a company that would afford young American singers the opportunity to learn classic and new roles. His father bought an old ranch seven miles north of Santa Fe, a place that impressed Crosby with its flourishing art community. The first Santa Fe Opera performance in 1957 was Pucccini's *Madame Butterfly*, with Crosby conducting. An early friendship between Crosby and Igor Stravinsky resulted in performances of most of Stravinsky's operas in Santa Fe during the first six years of its existence. In 1961 Hindemith conducted his new opera, *News of the Day*. In 1963 Alban Berg's *Lulu* had its American premiere. John Crosby championed the operas of Richard Strauss, usually conducting one each season.

The opera's apprentice program for singers was an important aspect of its success. American singers of the stature of Sherill Milnes, James Morris, and William Burden began as apprentices in Santa Fe, and Kiri Te Kanawa and Bryn Terfel made their American debuts there.

In 1967 a fire destroyed the theater. The following year the new theater opened, and the first production in the new building was another production of *Madame Butterfly*. The new opera house featured an open roof—opera-goers frequently wore rain gear—and off in the clear desert distance the lights of Los Alamos were usually visible. Highlights of the 1970s and 1980s included bass Samuel Ramey debuting in *Carmen* in 1975, the pop artist Robert Indiana designing Virgil Thompson's *The Mother of Us All* in 1976, James Morris debuting in *The Rake's Progress* in 1981, and in 1984 Elisabeth Söderström debuting in Richard Strauss' *Intermezzo*. In 1991 John Crosby received the National Medal of the Arts from President George H.W. Bush. Crosby died in December 2002. A new space, the John Crosby Theater, was dedicated on his birthday in July 2003. The Santa Fe Opera is still the highlight of the summer tourist season in Santa Fe.

perform music and dance maintain Web sites that contain dates and locations.

Native American adaptations of country music, folk, and rock and roll often feature native instruments such as the flute. Native American artists who crossed over into pop culture include the folk singer Buffy Saint Marie and the rock guitar player Jesse Ed Davis.

Singers Natalie Dessay, left, who plays Amina, and Shalva Mukeria, right, who plays Elvino, sing during a dress rehearsal of *La Sonnambula* at the Santa Fe Opera in Santa Fe, New Mexico on Tuesday, July 27, 2004. © AP/Wide World Photos.

MEXICAN MUSIC

Mexican music is a large subject, but we will briefly examine three genres: *conjunto*, *mariachi*, and *corrido*. In the nineteenth century, Mexican music along the United States–Mexico border was little different from the popular music of interior Mexico. Dance orchestras with strings played conventional romantic songs to the beat of waltzes, polkas, and schottisches. What became known as *música norteño* (music of the north) or *conjunto* (literally, a group or band) began after the introduction of the European-style push-button accordion into the Mexican bands. A city like San Antonio was a crossroads of musical styles, and the German settlers there played accordions at their dances that featured dance forms such as the polka, similar to those in Mexico. The advantage of the accordion was its portability, and soon every ranch and small border town had bands that played them. The other primary instrument in the small conjunto band was the *bajo sexto*, a big-bellied guitar that had extra bass strings. By the 1930s two accordion players, Narcisco Martinez and Santiago Jiminez, began to make records in this style. The songs were usually sung in close harmony by two lead singers and were romantic songs, often about heartbreak. Instrumentally, the music was so close to its European dance models that records without vocalists were often marketed as Czech or Polish bands.

Mariachi bands are more widely spread throughout the Southwest and are much more complex in instrumentation. It is thought that mariachi, really a modified big-band form, has its origins in the Mexican state of Jalisco. There can be as many as fifteen, or even more, instruments, with the basic elements consisting of trumpets, violins, guitars, the *guitarrón* (small guitar), the *vihuela* (rounded-back small guitar), and the bajo sexto. The large mariachi band is a very exciting affair that features both male and female singing, soaring (and loud) trumpet lines, and maybe as many as four violins playing in unison. The mariachi costumes are very formal—usually black wool trousers with silver decorations down the pant legs, and a short, bolero-style jacket. Often the women singers or violin players wear sombreros or have elaborately decorated hair. Many high schools, universities, and colleges in south Texas, New Mexico, and Arizona have mariachi programs. Among the most notable is the Arizona-Mariachi program at the University of Arizona. Mariachi bands in a somewhat debased form can be heard in Mexican restaurants all through the Southwest, playing loudly and working for tips. But the genuine mariachi is a long-held tradition that has produced many fine musicians and singers.

The corrido is a folk form traditionally performed by singers who traveled throughout the Mexican border on horseback. The structure of the corrido is that of a traditional ballad, with a four-line stanza sung to a simple melody. It is the content that sets this form apart. It is often the news of the day: the songs began to catch on during the Mexican Revolution as a means of spreading the news of Pancho Villa up and down the Texas-Mexico border. Historians have pointed out that the corrido is a direct descendant of the romance, a form that exclaims the details of a battle or the virtues or a hero or the exploits of a bandit. The leading Texas scholar of this form was Americo Paredes (b. Brownsville, Texas, 1915), a University of Texas folklorist who published a distinguished history of this music in his landmark book *With a Pistol in His Hand: A Border Ballad and Its Hero*, published in 1958. Paredes himself knew hundreds of these songs and passed them on to a younger generation, including the singer Tish Hinojosa (b. San Antonio, 1955).

The subject matter has always kept up with the times—from the Kennedy assassination to the Challenger explosion, the border ballads have provided commentary. In the 1990s a new topic became all the rage—the drug trafficking between Mexico and the United States. These "narco-corridos" often named names and the routes that the smugglers used. Another major event that elicited many songs was the murder of the popular Tejana singer Selena (b. Lake Jackson, Texas, 1971; d. 1995) in 1995.

CONCLUSION

The American Southwest is a crossroads and its music reflects the patterns of hundreds of years of coming and going. The indigenous music of the pueblos of New Mexico and Arizona have served a spiritual and a social purpose in those deeply individualistic cultures.

Beginning in the late nineteenth century, the music of the rest of the region began contributing to and reflecting the rest of American music. The rich variety of musical traditions in Texas are reminiscent of what bird fanciers say about the Lone Star state: there is a an enormous number of native species and a significant number of "flyovers," that is, imports from the state's richly musical neighbors, Mexico and Louisiana. At the same time, Texas has exported some of the most influential American musicians in the fields of jazz, blues, R&B, and country. Icons such as Buddy Holly, Janis Joplin, and Willie Nelson are just the top of a huge pyramid of music.

Like the indigenous music of the Native Americans, twentieth century music has continued to play a strong social role in the region. The traditions of families gathering at dance halls is strong throughout Texas, and runs parallel to the live music and recordings that the state and the region continue to produce.

RESOURCE GUIDE

Barkley, Roy, Douglas E. Barnett, Cathy Brigham, Gary Hartman, Casey Monahan, Dave Oliphant, and George B. Ward, eds. *The Handbook of Texas Music*. Austin, TX: State Historical Association, 2003.

Clarke, Donald, ed. *Penguin Encyclopedia of Popular Music*. 2nd ed. London: Viking Penguin, 1998.
Malone, Bill. *Country Music USA*. 2nd Rev. ed. Austin: University of Texas Press, 2002.
Reid, Jan. *Improbable Rise of Redneck Rock*. Rev. ed. Austin: University of Texas Press, 2004.
Townsend, Charles. *San Antonio Rose: The Life and Music of Bob Wills.* Urbana: University of Illinois Press, 1976.

Web Sites

All Music Guide
www.allmusic.com

The Handbook of Texas
www.tsha.utexas.edu/handbook

Joseph Levy, "Doug Sahm and the Sir Douglas Quintet: A Brief History."
http://www.laventure.net/tourist/sdq_hist.htm

The Red Hot Jazz Archive
http://redhotjazz.com

Rolling Stone
www.rollingstone.com

Texas Montly
www.texasmonthly.com

Events

Kerrville Folk Festival
Kerrville, TX
May/June annually.

Santa Fe Opera
Santa Fe, NM
July/August annually.

South By Southwest Music Festival
Austin, TX
Third week of March annually.

Willie's Picnic
Location varies.
July 4, annually.

Collections

Center for American History
University of Texas at Austin

Recordings, archives, business records, posters, sheet music.

Cowgirl Hall of Fame Museum
Fort Worth

Materials on singing cowgirls.

Fine Arts Library
University of Texas at Austin

Harry Ransom Humanities Research Center
The University of Texas at Austin

Jazz collections including recordings, archives, sheet music, and manuscripts.

Music Library
University of North Texas
Denton, TX

Southwestern Writers Collection
Alkek Library
Texas State University

Archives, manuscripts, costumes, recordings, photographs.

Discography

Terry Allen, *Lubbock on Everything*
Blues Masters, Volume 3: *Texas Blues*
Joe Ely, *Honkytonk Masquerade*
The Fabulous Thunderbirds, *Tuff Enuff*
The Flatlanders, *More a Legend Than A Band*
Buddy Holly, *The "Chirping" Crickets*
Lightnin' Hopkins, *The Very Best of Lightnin' Hopkins*
Janis Joplin, *Janis Joplin and Big Brother and the Holding Company Live at Winterland*
George Jones, *She Thinks I Still Care: The George Jones Collection*
Robert Earl Keen, *Gringo Honeymoon*
Lyle Lovett, *Lyle Lovett*
Delbert McClinton, *Victim of Life's Circumstances*
Willie Nelson, *The Essential Willie Nelson*
Roy Orbison, *For the Lonely: 18 Greatest Hits*
Marty Robbins, *Gunfighter Ballads and Trail Songs*
Linda Ronstadt, *Canciones de mi Padre*
Doug Sahm, *The Best of Doug Sahm and the Sir Douglas Quintet*
Frank Sinatra, *Sinatra at the Sands*
Ernest Tubb, *Live 1965*
Townes Van Zandt, *Anthology 1968–1979*
Stevie Ray Vaughan, *The Sky Is Crying*
T-Bone Walker, *The Complete Recordings 1940–1955*

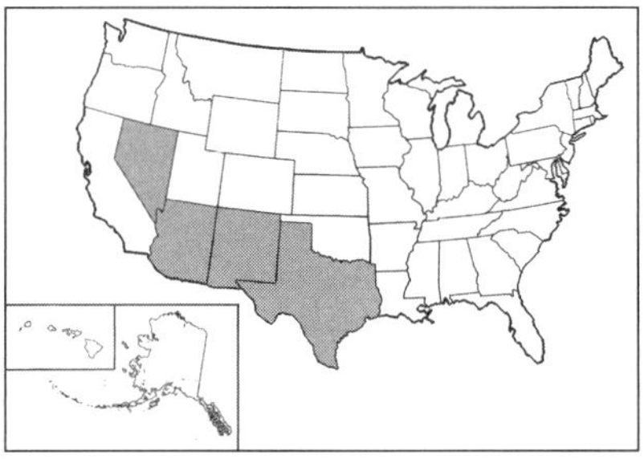

RELIGION

Jeremy Bonner

The dominant religious culture in the Southwest reflects the intersection of two cultures: Anglo-American and Hispanic. No other part of the United States has had such a long association with Spanish culture or Roman Catholicism, one that dates back to 1598. Yet the Southwest was a marginal region to Spain, Mexico, and finally the United States, at least until the 1950s. Local Catholic culture was forced to develop a fortress mentality in the face of neglect by the Spanish Catholic Church. After Mexican independence, the northern provinces considered themselves inadequately represented in the constitutional debate and resisted efforts to impose a centralized state system on them. The emergence of the independent nation of Texas and the subsequent American conquest of the rest of the Southwest brought the region's laicized Catholics into confrontation both with the American Catholic hierarchy, who sought to eliminate the folk religion of the region, and with Protestant missionaries intent on their conversion. In largely Protestant eastern Texas, the initially dominant Methodists were overtaken by the Southern Baptists in the decades following the Civil War. Texas Baptists took upon themselves the mantle of evangelical witness, seeking to bear the Gospel to every community in the region.

The Southwest thus exchanged a tradition of religious neglect during the eighteenth century for one of religious conflict during the nineteenth. Indigenous Hispanic Catholics were challenged both by their new church leadership and by a host of Protestant advocates to abandon the folk religion of their fathers. In eastern Texas, religious revivals cemented a strong sense of Protestant identity that united Texas Baptists and Methodists with their respective denominations east of the Mississippi. In sparsely populated western Arizona and Nevada, early settlement was driven by mining booms that brought a fairly irreligious group of citizens into the region. The Southwest thus proved to be less open to transdenominational experiments and ecumenism than some other parts of the West. Religious culture defined communities more distinctly and offered greater possibilities for conflict than for cooperation.

The Southwest can be viewed in terms of three distinct sections: eastern Texas, which is the westward extension of the Bible Belt; western Texas, New Mexico, and southeastern Arizona, which form the Catholic core; and northern and western Arizona and Nevada, historically Catholic but with a growing Mormon population and many residents completely uninterested in religion. This chapter begins by tracing the nature of indigenous religious expression by various Native American groups in the Southwest, explores the cultural clash that followed the arrival of missionaries and settlers in the sixteenth century and particularly during the 1850s, and then examines the Southwest from around 1890 until 1920. The chronological approach then shifts to a thematic one, and the examination turns to the internal operation of the leading religious groups in the Southwest, the role of religious organizations in sustaining and upholding the social needs of the local community, and the part played by the various denominations in the public-policy process. The chapter concludes with selective consideration of the role of the churches in the urban life of the region.

PRE-1848 NATIVE AMERICAN RELIGION

Before 1865, Native American religious systems were the dominant cultural force in much of the Southwest. Although most were broadly communal, they ranged from the tightly controlled Pueblo Indian communities to the Papago, Athabascan, and Yuma tribes, who adopted a markedly individualistic style. The Pueblo were divided into western tribes, whose sophisticated rituals focused on weather control and crop growth, and eastern ones that emphasized medicine. Both segments were broadly agricultural communities organized into villages and governed by a collective leadership drawn from the heads of the religious societies. The western Pueblo held most of their rites in a *kiva* (ceremonial chamber), and their liturgical calendar was shaped by seasonal festivals, beginning with observance of the winter solstice in December, continuing in February with a bean dance to aid germination, followed by ceremonies in August and September to bring rain and assure a successful harvest, and concluding with the initiation of young men into adulthood in November. Singing, praying, smoking of tobacco, and consumption of medicine water might accompany all such activities. The Pueblo laid great stress on the cult known as *Kachinas*, the only tribe-wide body open to boys and girls, which celebrated the visitation of ancestral spirits to the tribe between the winter and summer solstices. Kachinas also played a central role in the winter solstice celebrations. The Pueblo tribes had puberty rites for girls, which involved their seclusion for four days to grind corn, prepare bread, and have their hair arranged in a ritual fashion to prepare them for marriage, and initiation of boys into one of four tribal societies. Certain subgroups had rituals peculiar to their community; one example is the Hopi's Snake Dance, which involved dancers performing while holding snakes and, at the end of the dance, grabbing as many as they could carry and depositing them at tribal shrines.

Amongst the eastern Pueblo, where rainfall was more assured, the focus fell on the medicine societies, some general and some devoted to specific illnesses. Membership generally stemmed from being cured by a member of that society and was for life. Cures were the responsibility of shamans, who might either use songs and the "brushing away" of evil with an eagle feather or, in more severe cases, "draw out” disease objects (a worm or a stone) and ritually wash the patient. Tribal societies included a Kachina cult, whose dancing stimulated rain, fertility, and general well-being, and warriors’ and hunters’ associations, served respectively by warrior priests and shamans. The *cacique* (village chief) was an important figure who watched over the pueblo, prayed for its welfare, and was the possessor of an important fetish.

West of the Pueblo villages were the Papago (now called Tohono O’odham) Indian communities. Similar in many ways to the Pueblo, particularly in that their rituals, too, were geared to the production of rain, the main sites of Papago worship were the dance area and ceremonial house. The principal rainmaking rite was held in July and was preceded by two days of dancing and the conduct of rainmaking magic by the shamans. Village representatives and invited guests then consumed a portion of fermented cactus juice, sang rain charm songs, and dropped some of the juice on the ground, after which all the villagers returned to their homes to drink the juice privately. Seasonal observances concluded with the *Viikita* (Prayerstick Festival), held every four years in winter by the northern Papago and every summer by the southern Papago, as a festival of thanksgiving and to assure the maintenance of world order. The Papago had a number of power ceremonies, intended mainly for young men. These included the salt pilgrimage to the Gulf of California, first undertaken at age sixteen and on at least three subsequent occasions. Participants collected salt from the salt beds, threw cornmeal into the waves, and ran along the beach, in the course of which they received visions. Spiritual power might also be derived from shooting or trapping an eagle and plucking it in a ritual fashion, with the spirit of the dead bird becoming the slayer’s guardian. The Papago had a girl’s puberty dance similar to that of the Pueblo; it involved a four-day seclusion that concluded with purification by a shaman. No marriage ritual existed, and the observance of death, apart from some stylized wailing, was similar to that of the Pueblo.

The religious culture of the Athabascan tribes of Arizona—the Apache and Navaho—were less village centered but highly ritualistic nevertheless. Like the Papago and unlike the Pueblo, the Apaches recognized the importance of an individual’s search for power, whether unsought and revealed in a vision, or learned from someone who already controlled that power. Supernatural powers, once acquired, gave the owner protection, the power to cure, and general success in life. The Apache laid great stress on life-cycle rituals, beginning with cradle ceremonies and hair-cutting rites in early childhood. An elaborate girl’s puberty rite lasted four days and included seclusion, anointing with pollen, and social dancing, while a shaman smoked, prayed, and sang with the girl to assure her a long and successful life. Death rituals were also elaborate, including wailing, the removal of unnecessary clothing, and the cropping of hair. For fear of ghosts, which were believed to cause sickness, the body was buried quickly, the relatives purified, and the camp moved. Given their warring tendencies, the Apaches had a variety of war rituals, the most colorful being the four-day scalp dance that followed a successful war party. A generally more peaceful society than the Apaches, the Navajo people placed more emphasis on liturgical forms. Every Navajo ritual or chant was a framework into which many elements could be inserted according to context. Navajo prayers, often extremely long, had to be intoned without error. The mechanistic nature of Navajo worship was reflected in the variety of equipment used, including pollen, prayersticks, drums, rattles, and fumigants. Medical practitioners fell into two classes: diviners, who were concerned with the causes of disease and whose powers were acquired unsought, and singers, who were concerned with curing and who had learned the appropriate rituals.

The Yuma Indians represented the region's closest links with the tribal culture of the Great Basin. The search for power among the Yuma was confined to the dream experience, sometimes enhanced by the use of hallucinogens, in which animal, natural, or supernatural spirits might visit the dreamer. The role of the shaman was principally to achieve cures through methods already detailed, while other Indians with special powers were deputed to lead war parties. Puberty rites for girls were comparatively simple, usually involving the girl lying in a depression filled with hot sand for four nights in a row. Death rituals did not reflect the Athabascan fear of ghosts; the deceased were cremated, ritual wailing and funeral orations were performed, and close relatives cropped their hair. The Yuma demonstrated the least religious complexity of any Southwestern Indian tribe and subordinated learning to the experiences of visions and dreams.

NATIVE AMERICAN RELIGION TODAY

In the aftermath of the Civil War, federal seizure of Indian lands intensified, particularly after the federal government ceased to acknowledge the tribes as bodies with whom it was obliged to negotiate. By the 1880s a majority of Indians had been confined to reservations of varying size, though some groups, such as the Apaches, continued to wage war. The federal government delegated management of these reservations to the mainstream Protestant churches, particularly the Methodists and Presbyterians, and many missionaries traveled west to serve in the process of conversion. German-born Charles Cook, a Presbyterian missionary to Arizona's Pima (now called Akimel O'odham) Indians, urged tribal members to cut their hair and adopt Western clothing and surnames; he also founded several reservation schools to teach carpentry and irrigation techniques. By introducing the Presbyterian ecclesiastical system and making several tribal leaders into Presbyterian elders, Cook revitalized the tribe and restored the moral authority of its leadership. Arizona was also the site of many Presbyterian Indian schools and hospitals at the towns of Ganado, Indian Wells, and Fort Defiance, the latter an Episcopal institution. Many Indians joined the Protestant denominations, and missionaries also helped preserve Indian languages, artifacts, and folklore.

The exposure of the tribes to the work of Protestant missionaries and the suppression of outward manifestations of indigenous religious expression did not destroy Native American religion so much as change its form. In the 1890s there arose a movement that ultimately gave rise to a pan-Indian religious body—the Native American Church—and the Tipi and Cross Fire peyote ceremonies, the latter the more overtly Christian of the two. Peyote use began among the tribes of Oklahoma and became widespread among the Taos Indians during the 1890s. During the 1920s it spread to the Navajos, where it acquired a considerable hold. Today, about half of the Navajo nation are members of the Native American Church. Tribal opposition to peyote use in the Southwest was considerable, however, and both Pueblo governors and the Navajo Tribal Council waged a campaign against it during the 1920s and 1930s.

Peyote ceremonies require both a sacred fire, the embers of which are arranged in a particular pattern, and a sand altar and are generally conducted on a Saturday night. Peyotists sit on the floor in a circle, peyote buttons are distributed and consumed by the participants, and the organizer sings four songs before surrendering the floor to the next participant. Singing occupies much of the meeting, with the rest devoted to individual public prayer. At dawn, a breakfast of corn, meat, and fruit is consumed, and participants have an opportunity to socialize. Significantly, the Cross Fire ceremony is a syncretic observance that is viewed as an extension of the Christian faith and may include a Bible reading. Peyote is viewed as something from God that cures and heals and provides the user with a more acute sense of the transcendent. Despite this outlook, the non-Indian establishment generally looked with disfavor on peyote use, because of its association with narcotics and hallucinogenics. Arizona, Nevada, and New Mexico all banned peyote use off the reservation between 1917 and 1925, to which Native Americans responded by incorporating state Native American churches and organizing the Native American Church in North America in 1955. While some tribes today continue attempts to revive the old religious traditions of their particular tribes, the future of Native American spirituality is much more evident in syncretic pan-Indian religion than in the plethora of tribal practices that existed in the Southwest before 1848.

MISSION AND SETTLEMENT

Alone among the American regions the Southwest witnessed an aggressive program of Christianization that worked in tandem with the assertion of imperial power. As Spain sought both to exploit the mineral wealth of New Mexico and build colonial outposts during the sixteenth and seventeenth centuries, both the Franciscan and Jesuit orders developed a subsistence economy and a mission system to reach the region's Indians that supplemented the state's establishment of military installations, and the first church in New Mexico—San Juan Batista—was erected on August 23, 1598. Resistance to the occupiers, particularly in the more isolated settlements of Texas and Arizona, slowed the pace of conversion, especially after the Pueblo Revolt of 1680 and the Pima Rebellion of 1751. In Arizona Padre Eusebio Kino helped revive the mission ethos at the end of the seventeenth century, most notably through the San Xavier del Bac mission, founded in 1700. Texas boasted the parishes of Our Lady of Mount Carmel (1682), La Purisima (1683) in El Paso, and, later, Sacred Heart in Nacogdoches (1716), and San Jose de Bexar (1720) and San Francis Espada (1731) in San Antonio, but the Texas missions were even more of a fringe enterprise than those in the rest of the Southwest.

The mission structure emphasized the direct link between proselytism and economic development, which took the form of an extensive program of agricultural investment, with a particular focus on stock raising. Despite these efforts, the religious hierarchy proved quite as unconcerned as the secular authorities about making the region's Catholics feel connected to the empire's destiny. With little aid from the Spanish Crown and denied the right to trade with foreign countries, New Mexico languished economically throughout the eighteenth century. Although a church was erected at Santa Fe as early as 1606 for the province's Hispanic settlers, followed by churches at Albuquerque in 1706 and Santa Cruz in 1733, these

San Xavier del Bac Mission in Tucson. © Art Directors/TRIP Archive.

were all erected at the expense of the local Catholic population. Furthermore, despite the regular levying of tithes by the Spanish government, no bishop was appointed for New Mexico under Spanish rule. As a result, the region's Catholics (both the descendants of colonists and converted Indians) developed a sense of insularity and regional separatism that would outlast both independence from Spain in 1821 and conquest by the United States in the 1840s.

Mexican independence served only to accentuate lay authority. Although Padre Miguel Hidalgo was the first to voice the call for rebellion that gave rise to the Texas revolt of 1811–1813 led by Juan Batiste de las Casas against the Spanish, the new Mexican state tended to regard the clerical establishment as opposed to it. Most of the missions of the Southwest were dissolved, and Spanish-born priests were expelled from Mexico. Into the vacuum created by this absence of clerical leadership stepped the *Penitentes*, a lay brotherhood that helped preserve the communities of faith in the absence of a regular priest, most notably in the matter of funerals and festivals surrounding the celebration of Holy Week. For almost thirty years, many borderland Catholics rarely saw a priest, helping to develop a faith more centered on personal and family devotions than on reception of the sacraments. After Texas independence in 1836, the Bishop of New Orleans sent Father John Timon to reorganize the church in the region. Missionary bishops, including Jean Marie Odin of Galveston, played a critical role in sending out priests to organize the scattered rural communities into vast parishes and to erect temporary chapels.

The U.S.-Mexican War marked the transfer of the Southwest's Catholics from a largely autonomous existence to direct rule in 1850 by an American hierarchy in the person of Bishop Jean-Baptiste Lamy of Santa Fe. Lamy regarded the folk religion of the region as contrary to proper Catholic practice and preferred to rely on French priests from his own circle rather than on the local Catholic clergy. He reintroduced diocesan tithing during the 1850s to cover the costs of new construction and encouraged educational orders like the Sisters of Loretto to open academies that would provide a Catholic education for Hispanics. Nevertheless, his strongly Americanizing stance and deprecation of local customs brought him into conflict with the Hispanic clergy, most notably with Father José Martinez of Taos. Within the Hispanic churches, moreover, there was a continued emphasis on lay spirituality, in the form of prayers, penances, and works of corporate mercy. In Texas the Catholic Church grew rapidly, aided by the enthusiasm of Catholic circuit riders like Father Peter Keralum (who was lost in the Rio Grande Valley in 1872) and the support of European missionary societies (the Diocese of Galveston received $250,000 from abroad between 1846 and 1901).

Unlike the rest of the Southwest, eastern Texas was a Protestant stronghold that adhered mainly to Methodism before the Civil War and then gradually gave way to the Southern Baptists. The 1870s and 1880s were a time when Protestant missionary zeal was at its zenith, and many congregations were established in West Texas and New Mexico. Local communities took pride in their new churches and would sometimes subscribe to their erection, even if they were not members, as when the Jewish Seligman family contributed to the building of the Catholic cathedral in Santa Fe. Some frontier ministers also held prominent public offices; Episcopal priest Joseph Tays, for instance, served on the El Paso city council, was director of the First National Bank of El Paso, and was part owner of the *El Paso Times*. Protestant ministers also challenged the region's cultural mores, as when Methodist minister Alexander Groves condemned Sunday mine operations in Prescott, Arizona, during the 1870s.

Protestant missionaries also vigorously attempted to convert the Hispanic population of the Southwest to Biblical Christianity. The earliest attempts were made by Baptist minister Hiram Read, who arrived in the Southwest in the 1850s and resided in El Paso from 1883 to 1895. Read generally visited individual households and read aloud to the inhabitants selections from his Spanish Bible, but he also corresponded with sympathetic Mexican American priests, including Father Martinez. The real push for evangelization, however, came with the arrival in New Mexico of Methodists Thomas and Emily Harwood and Presbyterians David McFarland and John Annin in the 1860s. The Harwoods started a school and the newspaper *El Abogado Christiano*. With the coming of the railroad, many of their coreligionists settled in the region, and El Paso, Texas, also became a focus of missionary activity. Not only were many missions, schools, and settlement houses located there, but the Baptists also built the largest Spanish Baptist publication house in the world. The later missionaries generally followed Hiram Read's strategy toward the region's Hispanics, distributing Spanish Bibles to all who would accept them. Even this restrained approach provoked clashes with the Catholic establishment, especially in the pages of the Jesuit *Revista Catolica* and editor Sheldon Jackson's *Rocky Mountain Presbyterian*. Ultimately, the Presbyterians began to ordain Hispanics as elders, beginning with José-Yves Perea in 1880.

One of the most contentious areas of conflict was New Mexico's education system, for which the Sisters of Loretto continued to serve as teachers after 1890. All

The Santa Fe Cathedral. © Art Directors/TRIP Archive.

the Protestant denominations established schools and academies in the region, which helped to Americanize many Hispanics, but most had been phased out by the end of the century. By 1900, despite a great investment of resources, only about 5 percent of the residents of Arizona and New Mexico were Protestant.

RELIGION DURING THE GROWTH OF THE SOUTHWEST

Although the Southwest was largely settled by 1892, only Texas (1846) and Nevada (1864) had been admitted as states; the territories of Arizona and New Mexico did not become states until 1912. By the beginning of the twentieth century, the rapid Texas population boom and the mass migration of Mexican clergy following the Mexican Revolution of 1910 had begun to change the shape of Texas religion and make it the center of Catholic activity in the Southwest. New urban dioceses were created in 1890 (Dallas), 1912 (Corpus Christi), and 1914 (El Paso), and the Catholic Church Extension Society helped build 315 chapels in Texas between 1905 and 1921, including four-fifths of the churches and schools in Amarillo. A new Catholic urban landscape also began to emerge, and some separate parishes for racial minorities were founded, including St. Peter Claver in San Antonio (1888) and Holy Rosary in Galveston (1889) for African Americans, as well as many Mexican parishes in the dioceses of Corpus Christi and San Antonio.

The role of the Protestant clergy in the Southwest from 1880 to 1930 was multifaceted. The level of education of mainline Protestant clerics was generally higher than much of the local population (although this was less true for the Southern Baptists), and they therefore performed not merely common pastoral functions like counseling but also served as the principal distributor of charity at times of natural disaster and as community librarians, as well as offering lectures on issues of religious and public interest. By the 1890s, as the value of the land they owned increased, many churches were able to erect new, elaborate structures for worship. Tucson's First Methodist Church, erected in 1906, cost $23,000, whereas St. Clement's Episcopal Church, El Paso, erected in 1908, cost $60,000.[1] Many of the new Western churches drew upon the Romanesque style and dominated the urban landscape in a fashion that had not previously been experienced in the Southwest.

The churches of the Southwest also played a key role in the advancement of social welfare. "Unlike their northern or southern counterparts," notes Ferenc Szasz, "from the 1890s to the WW I era the forces of organized religion in the West essentially created the institutional infrastructure for their subregion."[3] Foremost in the field of education was the Episcopal Church, which had established an academy in every diocese in the region by 1900. These academies focused on character formation, which the Church feared would be neglected in the public schools, but they also provided a rigorous academic grounding that enabled many non-Episcopal Westerners to attend college in the East. Although the Baptists came late to Texas education, by 1900 they had established fifteen colleges. Religious universities from this era that have subsequently achieved a high academic standing while retaining their religious identity include Southern Methodist University, Fort Worth, Texas, and Baylor University, Waco, Texas. One alternative solution to what they perceived to be the problem of secular education was the idea of the denominational hall of residence at the state university pioneered by Episcopal Bishop Herbert Kinsolving of Texas, who helped establish Grace Hall at the University of Texas, Austin.

Despite the rise of the urban churches, many congregations were heavily rural and provided much, if not all, of the social recreation for their community. Such institutions as the Ladies Aid Societies and women's guilds were critical to the organization of dramatic productions, readings of Shakespeare's works, public addresses, church suppers and, in some denominations, church dances, found in so many towns in the Southwest. These events almost always had a fund-raising component and sought to attract as many nonmembers from the immediate community as possible, particularly as support from the Home Mission Boards declined after 1890.

Evangelization was fostered by itinerant preachers, who distributed large num-

Lutherans in Texas

Migration to Texas included a sizable influx of Lutherans from Germany and Scandinavia, who settled mostly in the center and southwest of the state. The First Evangelical Lutheran Synod of Texas was founded in 1851. Norwegian Lutherans settled near Waco and Dallas, Swedish Lutherans around Austin, and German Lutherans in the central Hill Country. The majority of the latter aligned with the Midwestern Iowa Synod in 1896 and experienced great growth in the mid-twentieth century. With 50,000 members in 1945, the Texas Synod swelled to 100,000 after the establishment of the American Lutheran Church in 1960 and provided financial support for Texas Lutheran College and Lutheran General Hospital. In 1987 it was absorbed into the Evangelical Lutheran Church in America. Some German Lutherans also belonged to the more conservative Lutheran Church–Missouri Synod, which arrived in Texas in 1855. In 1990 the Evangelical Lutheran Church in America claimed 155,276 members in 401 congregations, and the Lutheran Church-Missouri Synod claimed 134,280 members in 345 congregations.[2]

bers of religious periodicals and other literature, but also by means of more modern technology such as the chapel car—and later the auto chapel—as when the Baptists sent their "Emmanuel" car to Arizona. Inevitably, some transdenominational forms of religious education emerged, the most influential being the Sunday School program, whose printed lesson plans enabled the unordained (and even women) to lead religious discussions. In the Southwest, particularly in Texas, with its conservative evangelical traditions, there was much greater scope for revivalism. Leander Millican of El Paso became the leading itinerant evangelist in New Mexico and West Texas in the 1890s, denouncing prize fights, dancing, and card playing. West Texas was also the venue for the Bloys Camp Meeting, established in the Fort Davis Mountains by a Presbyterian in 1890. A popular interdenominational body that held up the life of Christ as an ideal to live by and encouraged boys to declare their faith and live by it, Bloys served as a contrast to the denominational schisms evident in much of East Texas.

The Southwest also witnessed the rise of the Social Gospel, a nationwide phenomenon in mainstream Protestantism that called for greater ecclesiastical attention to the material needs of the underprivileged. Certain features of the Social Gospel peculiar to the Southwest included language classes and special missions to immigrant Chinese communities in Tucson, Albuquerque, and El Paso and the development of medical care for the treatment of tuberculosis in Arizona, New Mexico, and West Texas. In Albuquerque the Sisters of St. Joseph established a hospital in 1902, the Baptists sent a trained nurse in 1904, and the Methodists established a sanatorium in 1912. The Episcopal Church built St. Luke's Hospital in Phoenix for TB sufferers, and the Baptists erected similar establishments in El Paso and Tucson. By 1920, 10 percent of New Mexico residents were persons recovering from tuberculosis.

BELIEF SYSTEMS AND CHURCH ORDER

Two different measures of church membership in 2000 illustrate the extent of the Southwest's religious diversity: the degree to which people are involved in any religious organization and the relative share of the church-going population that the various denominations enjoy.[4] In Texas, where Catholics and Baptists divide the population, participation stands at 55.5 percent, whereas in neighboring New Mexico the figure is 58.2 percent. In historically Catholic but increasingly secular Arizona and Nevada, by contrast, the figures are only 39.9 percent and 34.3 percent, respectively.[5] Accounting as it does for roughly three-quarters of the region's population, Texas is a religious powerhouse. The state is narrowly tied between Roman Catholics, who represent 37.7 percent of believers, and the Southern Baptist Convention, who have 30.4 percent. Other significant groups are the United Methodist Church with 8.8 percent, Churches of Christ with 3.3 percent, and the Assemblies of God with 2.0 percent. Geographically, the centers of Southern Baptist strength are a swathe of counties stretching from the northern Panhandle to the edge of the Dallas–Fort Worth Metroplex, a cluster of counties northeast of Dallas, and another on the Louisiana border. The Catholic presence is concentrated in the El Paso corridor in the far west and throughout south Texas, including San Antonio, while Catholics also enjoy a plurality in Houston.

Table 1. Religious denominations in the Southwest, 2000

Denomination	Number	Percentage of Total Adherents
Roman Catholic	6,346,207	41.3%
Southern Baptist Convention	3,830,883	24.9%
United Methodist	1,127,623	7.3%
Church of Jesus Christ of Latter-Day Saints	566,611	3.7%
Churches of Christ	413,046	2.7%
Assemblies of God	355,661	2.3%
Jewish congregations	297,275	1.9%
Evangelical Lutheran Church in America	246,044	1.6%
Presbyterian Church in the United States of America	234,295	1.5%
Episcopal Church in the United States of America	226,702	1.5%
Lutheran Church-Missouri Synod	178,321	1.2%
Other	1,541,851	10.1%
TOTAL	15,364,519	100.0%

Source: Dale E. Jones, Sherri Doty, Clifford Grammich, James E. Horsch, Richard Houseal, Mac Lynn, John P. Marcum, Kenneth M. Sanchagrin and Richard H. Taylor, *Religious Congregations and Membership in the United States 2000: An Enumeration by Region, State and County Based on Data Reported for 149 Religious Bodies* (Nashville, TN: Glenmary Research Center, 2002).

Prevalent Religions in the Southwest

At 63.4 percent New Mexico is the most Catholic state in the region. The Southern Baptist Convention accounts for 12.5 percent of believers in New Mexico, the United Methodists claim 3.9 percent, and the Church of Jesus Christ of Latter-Day Saints claim 4.0 percent. The Catholic heartland is in Albuquerque and counties to the northwest of it, whereas the Southern Baptists are stronger on the Texas border. In Arizona, Catholic adhesion is noticeably weaker than in New Mexico (47.6 percent), and the Southern Baptist Convention manages only 6.8 percent. Northern Arizona is part of the Mormon cultural zone, and the Latter-Day Saints enjoy 12.3 percent support throughout the state. Additionly, cosmopolitan Arizona has attracted minority denominations, including Jewish congregations (4.0 percent), the Assemblies of God (4.0 percent), the Evangelical Lutheran Church in America (3.4 percent), and the United Methodists (2.6 percent). Mormons are strongest in the northwest portion of the state; the Catholics' heartland is found in the southeast, around Tucson. Of the three intermountain states, Nevada's commitment to religion is the most uncertain. Like Arizona, the state is split between Catholics in the northwest around Reno and in southern Clark County (48.4 percent) and Mormons in the rest of the state (17.1 percent). The Southern Baptist Convention attains 5.9 percent and the Assemblies of God have 3.3 percent. Also striking is the 11.3 percent share recorded by Nevada's Jewish community.

Catholicism

The strength of Catholicism in the Southwest is clearly evident, with one believer in three adhering to the denomination. That ascendancy antedates the establishment of the United States and is buttressed by the moral authority that the Roman Catholic Church enjoys throughout the American continent. Although its outlook underwent a dramatic change at the time of the Second Vatican Council (1962–1965), it continues to stress the sacramental life: Baptism; frequent reception of the Eucharist; Confession and Unction; veneration of the saints, especially the Virgin Mary; and an all-male celibate priesthood. There are currently twenty-two dioceses in the region, fifteen of them in Texas, and the number of urban parishes in the Sunbelt has swelled in recent years. However, many parishes now provide special services as opposed to being solely a worshipping community, and the old emphasis on parish jurisdiction is declining.

The Second Vatican Council refocused the church toward a more lay-centered ministry, something that has led to significant changes at the parish level. Parish staffs are now more likely to include permanent deacons and members of the laity, and there has been a rise in the number of parish councils intended to help set priorities and act as a clearinghouse for parish organizations. Such bodies, however, can only be as effective as the priest is willing to allow them to be, since they do not have ultimate authority over the conduct of church policy. One area in which organizational resources have increased is in outreach to minority groups, both Native American and Hispanic. During the 1970s an increasingly large number of Catholic-run institutions were turned over to the Indian tribes they served, and the Tekakwitha Conference (founded in 1939 by missionary priests from the northern Great Plains) opened itself to Native American participation and created a basis for dialogue. Among Hispanics, the rise of Chicano militancy during the 1960s led to the establishment of a national Secretariat for Hispanic Affairs and comparable agencies on the diocesan level. Eight

Religious Diversity in Texas

It should not be assumed that Texas lacks religious diversity. It is a measure of the changing state population profile that the state capital of Austin plays host to Madelyn Murray O'Hair's American Atheists Inc., founded in 1963. Headed by Ellen Johnson since 1996 after O'Hair's disappearance in 1995, American Atheists Inc. maintains a 40,000-volume library and produces a cable-television show, *The Atheist's Viewpoint*. In addition to forthright unbelievers, Texas contains increasing numbers of non-Christians. Just outside Austin, the Barsana Dham Hindu Temple is now home to one of the biggest Janmashtami celebrations in North America. Buddhist groups are found in Dallas, Houston, and El Paso, the largest being followers of Nichiren Shoshu, a sect that emphasizes the pursuit of world peace, prosperity, and happiness in this life; there is also a Korean Buddhist community in Houston. Texas also has the eighth-largest Muslim community in the United States, with 57,000 Muslims and twenty-two Islamic centers in Houston, and 30,000 Muslims and fifteen Islamic centers in Dallas.[6]

Perhaps the most newsworthy Texas religious story of recent years was the FBI siege of the Branch Davidian compound in 1993. Founded in 1930 by Victor Mouteff, the Branch Seventh-Day Adventists moved to Waco in 1935 where they established a communal and agricultural Adventist society called the Mount Carmel Center. After Houteff's death in 1955, the movement fell prey to internal feuding and was ultimately taken over by Vernon Howell, who took the name David Koresh and saw himself as the Lamb mentioned in the fifth chapter of the Book of Revelation. Koresh adopted a positive attitude toward polygamy and accusations of child abuse and the stockpiling of weapons led to a confrontation with federal officials on February 28, 1993, and a siege that ended on April 19 with the incineration of the compound and many deaths.

regional offices and four pastoral institutes now exist—the oldest of the latter being the Mexican American Cultural Center in San Antonio. Perhaps the greatest weakness has been in the area of recruiting Hispanic priests to the ministry. It was not until 1970 that the first Hispanic bishop, Patricio Florez of San Antonio, was appointed, and Hispanics still represent a small percentage of priests, sisters, and brothers.

Southern Baptists

If the Southwest has tended to be viewed as a historically Catholic region, it has also witnessed considerable growth on the part of the Church's most determined competitor, the Southern Baptist Convention (SBC), both in Texas and elsewhere. That growth has come at a price, however, namely the disruption of a body that has prided itself on its ability to embrace a wide spectrum of belief. Since 1920 the SBC has seen a considerable shift away from its original focus on congregational autonomy toward denominational centralization, albeit under fundamentalist leadership since 1980. Prior to 1980 the SBC existed under the framework of a "Grand Compromise" that allowed for considerable theological diversity within its member congregations. This was particularly true for Texas Baptists, who generally took a conservative but pragmatic approach in their mission to evangelize the Southwest, although they opposed efforts at ecumenical activity outside the denomination. Prominent Texas Baptists included Benejah H. Carroll (1843–1914), the founder of Southwestern Baptist Seminary in Fort Worth, and George Truett (1867–1944), pastor of First Baptist Church in Dallas.

According to Bill Leonard, "theology [in the SBC] was defined narrowly enough to establish common Baptist identity but broadly enough to include a variety of historical interpretations relating to faith and practice. Efforts to narrow doctrine and practice—efforts that might exclude segments of the community from the great missionary endeavor—were avoided whenever possible."[7] Baptists have constantly contested the cardinal tenets of their faith. Despite a reputation for Calvinism, there has always been a strong Arminian slant to their views on election, atonement, and free will (Arminian teaching argued that man was free to choose God, in contrast with the Calvinist emphasis on predestination), and there is a considerable element of "balance" in Baptist belief. Thus, although the authority (and in recent years the inerrancy) of the Bible is of great importance, so is the right of personal interpretation and the notion that the laity should not receive the truth unquestioningly from those in authority. The principal confession, the Baptist Faith and Message—drafted in 1925 and revised in 1963—emphasized the local community of believers, Baptist definitions of Baptism and the Lord's Supper, evangelism, freedom of conscience, and church-state separation. The ordinances of Baptism and the Lord's Supper are themselves not uniform, with everything from immersion to sprinkling being practiced, and Holy Communion (though accepted as a memorial by all) is in some churches open to all evangelicals, in some to all Baptists, in some only to Southern Baptists. At the heart of Baptist belief is a determination to convert the world, but the understanding of the conversion process has changed from a nineteenth-century belief in an extended process of conversion to the more immediate transformation effected by revivalist techniques.

Structurally, the SBC has traditionally left individual congregations free to determine their own budgets, ministries, and theological emphasis. Above the congregation comes the regional association (also autonomous) and the state convention, the latter receiving funding from individual congregations for the purpose of establishing new churches and supporting local colleges and universities. A portion of the state convention's dues is provided to the national convention for maintenance of the denomination's six seminaries, the home and foreign mission boards and various other agencies, including the Christian Life Commission. The national convention meets annually, and every congregation is entitled to send "messengers." In 1917 the SBC created its Executive Committee to coordinate programs and serve as the voice of the denomination between conventions. In 1925 it established the Cooperative Program to regularize the collection of funds for the national agencies and determine the allocation of resources. In recent years the national bureaucracy has grown apace, and there has also been a decline in the idea that a pastor derives his authority from his congregation. As the ministry has become professionalized, the congregation's role in fiscal affairs has diminished and fundamentalists have sought to elevate the status of the pastor relative to his congregation. The previous division of authority between pastor and the deacon (an ordained lay minister from within the community) has to some extent given way to a clerical elite.

Separatist Baptists

Although the Southern Baptist Convention is the dominant influence in Texas, there are at least two important separatist Baptist groups. The World Baptist Fellowship in Arlington is the legatee of J. Frank Norris (1877–1952), the controversial fundamentalist pastor of First Baptist Church, Fort Worth. Conservative fundamentalist in theology and congregational in polity, the fellowship is strong in Texas and Ohio and operates Arlington Baptist College. The American Baptist Association in Texarkana is an older body that represented nineteenth-century Landmark Baptists (those who refused to recognize baptisms performed by other denominations, rejected shared pulpits, practiced closed communion and opposed interdenominational mission work). Landmarkism was never endorsed by the SBC, although it was supported by a sizable minority in the movement. The association is congregationally organized and operates a publishing house in Texarkana.

Mainline Protestants and Methodists

Mainline Protestants have not done well in the Southwest, despite the missionary endeavors of the nineteenth century. The Episcopal Church accounts for only 1.6 percent of the region's believers, and the Presbyterians account for only 1.9 percent. Only the United Methodist Church enjoys significant representation at 8.2 percent. That denomination is a product of the 1939 reunion of the northern and southern branches of American Methodism and owes its origins to John Wesley and his American disciple, Francis Asbury (b. 1745; d. 1816). Methodism was historically distinguished by its espousal of Arminianism—the belief that Christ died for all, not just for the elect, and that man is a free moral agent with the ability to choose or reject God—and pietism—a movement that began among seventeenth-century Lutherans and emphasized a devotional life for the laity and private study of the Bible. It affirms the sufficiency of the Bible for salvation and recognizes the sacraments of Baptism and the Lord's Supper. The largest American Protestant denomination, the Methodists had a distinguished record of social service during the twentieth century but have, in recent years, voiced an increasingly liberal theological perspective. The Methodist Church is organized around district and annual conferences that form a hierarchy of authority, with the quadrennial general conference being the church's highest legislative and policy-making body.

The heart of Methodism in the Southwest is in Texas, yet even here it is very much a junior partner to the SBC, despite having been the leading Protestant denomination before the Civil War. It retains a certain intellectual standing, having under its auspices such institutions as Southern Methodist University, Dallas College, McMurry University, and Texas Wesleyan University. At the heart of the system is Southern Methodist University's Perkins School of Theology, which was established in 1951 to provide theological training. Today, Perkins is the regional seminary for the southern and western sections of the United Methodist Church, providing education in pastoral care, the sociology of religion, and Christian ethics, and women represent an ever-increasing proportion of candidates (Doris Neal [n.d.] was the first woman to be ordained Elder after completing a course of seminary education in 1961).

The church has established a wide range of family and urban ministries since the 1970s. Its national paper, the *United Methodist Reporter*, had its origins in the Texas-based *Southwestern Christian Advocate*, and Texas Methodists carry their message to the airwaves by means of the United Methodist Communications Council of Texas and the Wesleyan Satellite Network. Texas Methodists have tended to be more open to theological innovation and to the social implications of the Gospel than their counterparts in the Southeast, though less so than those in the North, and are generally more optimistic in their view of human progress. They maintain hospitals in Dallas, Fort Worth, and Houston, each of which has a program to pay for care for indigents and draw on church auxiliaries for nonmedical support. They also operate the Southwestern Center for the Hearing Impaired and the Southwestern Maternity Center in San Antonio and the Methodist Home in Waco.

African American Baptists in the Southwest

African Americans constitute a significant minority population in the Southwest, of which the largest religious component are the Black Baptist churches of East Texas, particularly the urban communities of Dallas, Galveston, and Houston, to which many African Americans moved at the beginning of the twentieth century. In 1990 they accounted for 872,122 residents of the Southwest and 6.3 percent of the church-going population. The African American Baptists are divided into various associations, predominantly the American Baptist Church of Texas, the Missionary Baptist General Convention of Texas, and the Central Missionary Baptist General Convention of Texas. Although professing a theology very similar to that of their white counterparts, the Black Baptists remain a separate religious culture in which certain theological features of African American culture are evident. While they accept the need for individuals to have a personal relationship with Christ, they view sin as having both personal and communal aspects. There is much greater stress, too, on the notion of God as immanent as well as transcendent, directly connected with the trials of suffering humanity. Overall, however, Black Baptist theology is much more conservative than other African American denominations, and women play a much less prominent role in church life, even though most congregations are around 60 percent female.

Mormonism

The corporate religious life of the Black Baptist churches would be quite comprehensible to members of the Church of Jesus Christ of Latter-Day Saints who primarily reside in Arizona and Nevada. Mormonism asserts a theology considerably removed from mainstream Christianity, relying on the Book of Mormon as a historical and theological text equal in weight to the Bible. The organizational nature of the church reflects a strongly hierarchical structure and a great dependence on lay activism. Divine revelation is understood to be something that comes directly from God and goes to the president of the church. At the local level are the ward (or parish) presided over by a bishop and the stake (roughly equivalent to a diocese). The Mormon priesthood is universal, and all males in good standing can expect to be called to it. Auxiliary organizations include educational groups like primary school (children's religious education), Sunday school (adult religious education), and the Relief Society (the women's auxiliary concerned with a variety of family and social service activities within the church).

Church of Christ

A final group that has some limited impact on regional culture (particularly in Texas) are Churches of Christ, heirs to the efforts of Alexander Campbell and Barton Stone to "restore" the primitive church during the 1830s. Although the heartland of Churches of Christ is central Tennessee, the Texas wing helped push the movement away from its pacifist and nonpolitical roots and toward a more denominational alignment, under the leadership of fiery author of *Soldier of the Cross*, Foy E. Wallace Jr. (1896–1979). Churches of Christ form a heavily congregational organization that reject most forms of clerical authority, and none of their regional or national gatherings have the power to dictate policy. During the 1950s, after Highland Church of Christ in Abilene pioneered radio broadcasts of sermons, the Texas congregations were subject to vigorous debate over the appropriateness of operating homes for orphans and the elderly or even of cooperating in missionary work. Heavily conservative on most secular issues, they can be viewed as somewhat to the right of the Southern Baptist Convention. In Texas they maintain Abilene Christian College, Southwestern Christian College, and Lubbock Christian College.

RELIGION-CENTERED SOCIAL LIFE AND ACTIVITIES

There is a divide in Catholic community life in the Southwest between the Hispanic and non-Hispanic communities. The latter have been strongly affected by Vatican II's emphasis on the ministry of the laity, and there has been a marked rise in the number of permanent deacons, especially in Arizona and New Mexico, and a greater involvement of women in a variety of church functions. As the Catholic population has become increasingly well-educated, the focus on Christian education at the parish level has grown and lay ministry has expanded to include services to church youth, the sick, and the dying, a marked shift from a hundred years ago, when most lay ministries focused chiefly on the maintenance of the church building and interior. Many lay Catholics now serve on parish councils, giving them a sense of involvement in decision making. The parish church, however, is less the integrated and self-contained community that it was at the beginning of the twentieth century, a change epitomized by the erection, adjacent to churches, of family centers that are viewed more as community resources (and sometimes rented to non-Catholic groups) than as part of a wider Catholic social fabric.

The Vatican II changes have had a lesser impact on the Hispanic parishes of the region, which remain closer in style to the ethnic parishes of the nineteenth century. During the 1930s, the Bishop of Tucson tried to strengthen their attachment to mainstream Catholicism in rural Arizona by dispatching the Catholic Church on Wheels to them, as his Protestant counterparts had done forty years before. The existence of a Hispanic culture and the enduring strength of family life puts Hispanic religious life in a different category from that of more Americanized groups. Throughout the Southwest, folk customs and old religious artifacts, such as murals and altar screens, are being restored to many older churches. Although the civil authority of the Penitentes is a shadow of its former self, the brotherhood retains a core of members. New novices are drawn principally from existing Penitente families and are obliged to practice fraternity, community, and piety. They are nevertheless orthodox Roman Catholics who refrain from usurping priestly functions. Most of their penitential rites are performed on holy days—Corpus Christi, the Annunciation, All Saints' Day, and All Souls' Day. The high point is *La Cuaresma* (the rites of Lent) which includes recitation of the Stations of the Cross on Fridays and the famous flagellant processions that sometimes include the dragging of a wooden cross or a simulated crucifixion. A carved figurine of Death sometimes accompanies these processions. On Good Friday, the brothers reproduce the events of the Passion, with vigils and public processions (a Penitente-sponsored Passion play is performed at Talpa, New Mexico, each year).

The cult of the saints is also strong among Hispanic Catholics, who venerate local saints in the form of wooden *santos*, shaped by local craftsmen, which are viewed not merely as images for contemplation but also as instruments of power. *Fiestas* for a village's guardian saint (known as *la funcion*) are also common in the region and are an important expression of popular piety, involving a high mass, games, eating, and a closing dance. Among the Papago Indians, there is an annual celebration of the Fiesta Magdalena de Kino at the Church of Magdalena de Sonora in Mexico, a transborder celebration emphasizing ethnic and cultural bonds, which jointly celebrates Francis Xavier, Francis of Assisi, and Padre Kino. Marian devotions are also an important part of Hispanic culture, as revealed in the annual observance of repossession by Our Lady of Conquest (brought to New Mexico in 1625) in Santa Fe Cathedral. Finally,

Penitentes in a self-flagellation ceremony in front of a wooden cross near Taos, New Mexico. Courtesy of the Library of Congress.

such ceremonies as weddings and funerals give evidence of accretions of popular piety, such as family blessings before the marriage ceremony and processions from the family home to the church. But the church has faced a growing problem of keeping younger Hispanic men in the faith, losing many either to Pentecostalism or to the secular world.

Protestant Hispanics

Protestant Hispanics represent one of the more unusual religious phenomena of recent years. It is estimated that between one-quarter and one-third of Hispanics nationally may now be Protestant, though in the Southwest that figure is probably lower. They cover a wide range of denominations and theological positions but share a common sense of marginality in the historically Euro-American denominations. For them, the folk religion of their Catholic peers continues to have appeal, as does the use of Pentecostal language, personal "testimonies," and Hispanic music, but they are also decidedly Bible-centered. They retain a strong emphasis on group rights, the importance of the extended family, and the need to act *with* rather than *for* the poor and oppressed. Their Protestant credentials are nevertheless evident in their stress on the need for self-discipline and lay participation in the governance and life of the church. Recruitment of Hispanics by the Latter-Day Saints and conservative evangelicals has risen dramatically in the Southwest in recent years, particularly in Arizona.

Religious Outreach in the Southwest

While the region's Catholic culture has a distinctly Western hue, the orientation of the SBC, to a great extent, remains Southern. From 1865 to 1965 it was the principal guardian of the heritage of the "Lost Cause," and many of the Southern Baptist enclaves created in the West at this time were formed solely by migrant Southerners. Since the 1960s that regional uniformity has broken down. The broad spectrum of opinion has been replaced by contending church parties and the use of designated giving as a means of upholding a particular theological position. Southern Baptists do have a structure of religious behavior, at the core of which is the belief in the need for every Christian to have a personal evangelical encounter with Christ. Baptist piety stresses the need for individuals to strengthen their relationship with God through private devotion, personal morality, and evangelism.

All this is achieved by regular church attendance, participation in Bible study, and midweek prayer meetings, which meet to share personal and collective needs and to offer intercessory prayer. The SBC has a church calendar that congregations are encouraged to observe, based on the periodic need to raise funds for missions. In more recent years other special Sundays have been added to that calendar, including Race Relations Sunday, Cooperative Program Day, World Peace Sunday, and Sanctity of Life Day. Sunday worship is supplemented by morning Sunday school and evening Training Union, which provides instruction in Baptist doctrine, history, ethics, and Christian citizenship. Many Baptists also use study courses, all of them written by Southern Baptist theologians. Training is provided in evangelistic technique, particularly in how to witness for Christ and "give testimony" about one's own experience. While most religious-education courses seek to show how Bible stories can be applied to contemporary daily life, the focus is more on a personal rather than a corporate ethic, with little time devoted to issues of social justice. Moreover, the round of church-sponsored events, including church socials, revival meetings, the Women's Missionary Union and the Men's Brotherhood, tend to be very focused on the internal life of the church, offering few opportunities for interaction in the outside world, aside from missionary work.

Southwestern Methodist church life has many similarities with that of the

Southern Baptists but has, since 1945, laid a much greater stress on social outreach through groups such as the Women's Society of Church Service and the Methodist Youth Fellowship. Beginning in 1949 the Lakeview Methodist Assembly began to host a youth camp at Palestine, Texas, and other camps followed at Bridgeport, Kerrville, Glenlake, Ceta Canyon, and Butman. The 1950s witnessed a steady decline in the denomination's hostility to social dancing, though not its advocacy in favor of temperance. During the 1960s the Methodists began to develop different forms of evangelism for resorts, recreational centers, and apartment buildings. Retreat and study centers for Methodist youth were steadily expanded, as were small prayer-study-witness groups. In 1962 First United Methodist Church in San Augustine, Texas, instituted what became known as the "faith promise," a twelve-month commitment to give for mission work, and the parish developed ties with a number of missionary groups, including several that were nondenominational.

Black Baptist church life reflects the importance of corporate worship to spiritual growth. Corporate worship is meant to elevate the community at prayer over the individual's personal connection with God. Music—both spirituals and gospel music—affirms the principle that all human beings are made in the image of God, while the identification of African Americans with the Children of Israel or even the sufferings of Jesus binds the community to the working out of the divine plan. The pastoral sermon is, if anything, more important than in many Protestant churches, since it is the instrument for developing the message of scripture into a guide for life and addressing the needs and issues of the particular congregation. The giving of personal testimonies—from persons of any age—and vocal prayers and altar calls also serve to unite the congregation. Admonitions to the young to stay in school and avoid drugs and alcohol are commonplace. Ebenezer Baptist Church in Austin is known for its missionary work, choirs, scholarships, programs for the elderly, and volunteer council for the Texas State Hospital.

For the Southwest's Mormons, church work represents a considerable portion of the Latter-Day Saint's working hours, and perhaps the two most overt symbols of commitment are the tithe and missionary service. The church requires the commitment of one-tenth of a member's income to the support for church work and calls on all unmarried young men and women to undertake missions, mostly abroad, a process that they or their families must finance themselves. Mormonism tends to stress the active over the contemplative life, demanding high levels of participation and commitment. Holders of the priesthood are charged with making monthly visits to families in their community and becoming personally acquainted with their needs and concerns. Ward councils form a supportive apparatus for organizing ward functions and identifying individuals who may need special help. Family life is an essential component of the Mormon experience, and to support it, in 1965 the church launched the family home-evening program, a weekday night devoted to a family meal and recreational activities.

There is less to be said about church life among Churches of Christ, because the denomination has had a tradition of simple worship, despite the erection of more elaborate churches since World War II. Rural Texas churches have nevertheless rejected any further institutionalization of the church and insist on maintaining a focus on the congregation. During the 1980s there was some softening regarding outreach at time of natural disasters, especially to Eastern Europe. Prestoncrest Church of Christ, in Dallas, helped to raise $3.5 million for relief, and the World Church Broadcasting Company has been established, but Churches of Christ have paid less attention to social service than the SBC has.

SOUTHWESTERN CHURCHES AND THE WIDER WORLD

Politics and religion have been an uneasy combination in the Southwest. During the 1920s there was a strong fundamentalist reaction in Texas and Arizona that helped fuel the temporary ascendancy of the Ku Klux Klan. Until the 1950s, however, the churches took little interest in politics, and it was only the pressures of secularization and a new pattern of domestic migration that transformed the West into a political battleground. Fights over creationism and gay rights have inevitably involved the interests of churchmen on both sides of the issue, and in Arizona and Nevada, at least, there is no assurance of a majority for either social conservatism or social liberalism. In most of these debates the Catholic Church been obviously political, even though church leadership has come down on the side of social conservatives. Nevertheless, it did join liberal Protestant groups in supporting the Sanctuary movement for refugees fleeing the civil wars in Central America and in opposing military research. One of the more vocal pacifist bishops was Leroy Matthiesen (1921–) of Amarillo.

By contrast, the Southern Baptist Convention has taken very public policy stances. In 1959 T. B. Maston of Southwestern Baptist Theological Seminary in Fort Worth published *The Bible and Race*, a challenge to segregation on religious grounds. Maston's students included future Christian Life Commission president Foy Valentine and future director of the Baptist Joint Committee on Public Affairs James Dunn. The SBC's Christian Life Commission quickly took a prominent role in backing the civil-rights agenda, but such activism evoked a largely negative response from many SBC members. Moreover, the 1960s witnessed a growing interest in biblical criticism in SBC seminaries that proved very threatening to many conservatives. In 1979 Houston lawyer Paul Pressler reacted to what he perceived as the theological failings of Baylor University by orchestrating the election of Adrian Rogers as the first fundamentalist president of the SBC. Since that date, fundamentalists have controlled the presidency, including Texas pastors James Draper (1982–1984), Morris Chapman (1990–1992), Edwin Young (1992–1994) and Paige Patterson (1998–2000). Winfred Moore of First Baptist Church, Amarillo, carried the standard of the moderates in 1985, but his challenge fell short.

The triumph of the fundamentalists had, in part, to do with simple theology. Fundamentalists demanded adherence to the principle of biblical inerrancy as a test of orthodoxy and sought to enforce this through selective appointments to SBC boards and seminary positions. In 1985 controversy arose after moderate president Russell Dilday of the Southwestern Baptist Seminary tried to dismiss a professor for political intrigue but failed to get the approval of the trustees, which was seen as a victory for the fundamentalist viewpoint. The intradenominational debate, nevertheless had implications for the SBC activities in the world. In 1984 fundamentalists sought to reduce the role of women in the ministry by denying aid to congregations with female pastors. In 1988 they passed a resolution affirming the role of the pastor as the shepherd of his flock, reflecting the increasing dominance of the pastors of urban megachurches in the decision-making process.

Perhaps most significant was the SBC's strong endorsement of the social policies of the Reagan administration on abortion, family life, and school prayer. In 1988 Richard Land, a former academic vice president of Criswell College in Texas, replaced a moderate as head of the Christian Life Commission. During his tenure he repudiated abortion, endorsed school prayer, and rejected the notion of ordaining women and giving them ruling authority. In response to the leftward drift of the Baptist Joint Committee on Public Affairs, whose head, James Dunn, opposed school prayer and aid to parochial schools and had ties to People for the American Way, a progressive public advocacy group, the SBC created the Public Affairs Committee to be a voice for conservative Baptists; this committee endorsed the nomination of Robert Bork for Supreme Court justice. In recent years the SBC endorsed the conservative agenda in support of Israel and school prayer and opposition to the Equal Rights Amendment.

Southern Methodism since the 1950s, or even earlier, has shown itself to be quite ready to engage in social reconstruction and political activity. Confronting segregation earlier than its Protestant neighbor, the Perkins School of Theology admitted African American students in 1950, followed by McMurry University in 1954 and Lon Morris College in 1961, and the Methodist Youth Fellowship set up a racially integrated work camp in San Antonio in 1954. Calls to abolish the (black) Central Jurisdiction were initially resisted, however, and this was not finally achieved until 1968. The church was also a leading participant in ecumenical dialogue, with Dr. Albert Outler of the Perkins School serving as the Methodist observer at Vatican II, and played a leading role in the Texas Council of Churches. It remained a vocal opponent of pari-mutuel betting and liquor by the drink, and it was sharply divided over the Vietnam War. In 1968 a quota system for representation of women and minorities was introduced, and more democratic procedures for church governance were adopted. Some projects for minority communities in Dallas, Fort Worth, and Waco were also financed, but black participation declined, and many churches remained effectively segregated. Conservative Methodists viewed these changes with disquiet and helped organize the Good News Fellowship in Texas, but the general trajectory of the church was more liberal than that of the SBC.

Black churches of all denominations have always preached involvement in worldly affairs, and the pulpit has often been a stepping-stone to political office. During the 1960s as Texas grappled with ending racial segregation, the black churches were prominent in advancing voting and civil rights. During the 1970s the churches underwent a period of decline as black nationalists argued that they were too much concerned with individual pietism and too little concerned with the problems of the race, but most Black Baptist leaders rejected the "black" theology of intellectuals like James Cone (1939–). In the 1990s the churches rebounded as African Americans came once again to appreciate the need for a guiding moral ethic in family life. The Black Baptists have also begun to develop institutional outreach in business, housing, and education, to a degree that puts them ahead of the Pentecostal denominations but behind the black Methodist churches. Some concerns about what has been referred to as environmental racism have been voiced, most notably with regard to the siting of landfills in black neighborhoods of Houston. The social conservatism of Black Baptist clergy has been to some extent vindicated by the scourge of drugs that affects even rural Texas communities. The tradition of black political involvement remains a vibrant force, even in the socially conservative Southwest.

Although the Latter-Day Saints may not be a dominant political force throughout the Southwest, they are extremely influential in the Arizona state legislature. During the Great Depression, the church launched its own faith-based initiative, the Welfare Plan, to care for unemployed Latter-Day Saints, providing supplies to the needy from a network of bishops' storehouses in exchange for work by all the able-bodied unemployed. The Welfare Plan caught national attention and won approval for the church from many non-Mormons, including U.S. president Franklin Roosevelt. Beginning in the 1950s, observers reported a shift by the church to the political right as cultural issues began to supersede economic ones in the political dialogue. It supported Sunday closing and right-to-work laws and in recent years has spearheaded or supported campaigns against abortion, gambling, homosexual rights, and pornography.

Although the Church of Christ has left behind the pacifist traditions of its founders, it does not have much to do with world matters. The issues of the Civil Rights era were discussed even less within Churches of Christ than among the Southern Baptists, despite the presence of institutional racism within their membership. Several female members of Churches of Christ, including Lottie Beth Hobbs of Fort Worth, campaigned against the Equal Rights Amendment, but Texas Churches of Christ, while taking a conservative stand on issues of law and order and national security, generally avoided discussing political involvement. Although their pattern of voting has shifted from Democratic to Republican, they continue to be issue-driven populists who are not reliably Republican.

RELIGION AND THE URBAN SOUTHWEST

The rise of the city on the late-nineteenth-century frontier produced one of the most profound revolutions in the history of the American churches. The "urban problem," which exercised the minds of secular reformers, also suggested to religious leaders that they must adapt their mission to deal with ethnic and religious minorities who were flooding into the urban environment and implement new types of outreach ministry to assist the downtrodden. In the West, the idea of the Social Gospel was not new, but the metropolitan centers that nurtured it in the East were not a factor west of the Mississippi until the 1950s. In more recent times, the dramatic transformation of the Sunbelt cities of the Southwest has presented many problems for the urban churches. Secularism is rife, many of the newcomers to the region have tenuous ties to church life, and rapid growth outstrips the resources of many established organizations.

There are eleven major cities in the Southwest, and seven of these are in Texas.[8] In general, the secularization of the urban landscape seems to have had little effect in the Catholic culture zone of western Texas. In El Paso County, which is 81.2 percent Catholic, 63.4 percent of the population participates in any church life, while in Bexar County (San Antonio), which is 63.3 percent Catholic, the participation rate is 65.1 percent, and in Nueces County (Corpus Christi), which is 49.5 percent Catholic, it is 55.7 percent. Denominational challenges are practically nonexistent in El Paso, whereas the Southern Baptist Convention has 13.2

percent support in San Antonio and 24.8 percent in Corpus Christi. The United Methodists command 7.0 percent support in Corpus Christi and 4.5 percent support in San Antonio, and the latter also boasts a significant group of independent charismatic congregations (4.9 percent).

St. Mary's Cathedral in Austin. © Art Directors/TRIP Archive.

Where Catholicism only manages a plurality, as in Travis County (Austin), Harris County (Houston), and Dallas County, or the Southern Baptist Convention has the advantage, as in Tarrant County (Fort Worth), overall church participation is noticeably lower. The state capital, Austin, trails in participation, with only a 46.2 percent rate. Austin's Catholic population (44.2 percent) has a clear advantage over the Southern Baptists (20.6 percent), while the United Methodists have 5.9 percent, the Episcopal Church has 3.5 percent, and the Evangelical Lutheran Church in America has 3.1 percent. There are also a significant number of Jewish congregations (3.6 percent). Among the three eastern cities, Dallas leads with 55.1 percent participation, Fort Worth follows with 52.4 percent, and Houston trails with 50.4 percent. In Fort Worth, the Southern Baptists enjoy a plurality of 35.7 percent, the Catholics follow with 22.0 percent, and the United Methodists have 13.0 percent. Independent noncharismatic congregations account for 4.5 percent and Churches of Christ for 4.1 percent. Noncharismatic congregations are non-denominational faith communities that do not emphasize manifestations of the Holy Spirit—such as speaking in tongues—among believers. Dallas and Houston have Catholic pluralities of 39.3 percent and 36.1 percent, respectively. The corresponding figures for the Southern Baptists are 23.1 percent and 28.3 percent, while those for the United Methodists are 8.7 percent and 10.0 percent. Dallas also enjoys a significant presence from the Community of Christ (3.7 percent) and Jewish congregations (3.1 percent).

High participation rates in Catholic cities start to fade once one crosses the Texas border. Participation in Bernalillo County, New Mexico (Albuquerque), stands at 54.7 percent, below the statewide average; Pima County (Tucson), Arizona, reports 44.9 percent participation, above the statewide average; Maricopa County (Phoenix), Arizona, is only 39.7 percent; and Las Vegas, Nevada, is only 36.2 percent, although that is actually above the statewide figure of 34.3 percent. The basic pattern is one of a clear Catholic advantage over the Southern Baptists in Albuquerque and Tucson and a narrower Catholic advantage over the Latter-Day Saints in Phoenix and Las Vegas. In Albuquerque, Catholics claim 62.9 percent to the Southern Baptists' 7.3 percent and the United Methodists' 3.7 percent, while in Tucson, Catholics claim 59.5 percent to 6.0 percent for the Southern Baptists, 5.3 percent for Jewish congregations, and 4.5 percent for the Latter-Day Saints. In Phoenix, the Catholic share is 43.4 percent, compared to 12.6 percent for Latter-Day Saints, 6.3 percent for the Southern Baptist Convention, 4.9 percent for Jewish congregations, 4.7 percent for the Assemblies of God, and 4.2 percent for the Evangelical Lutheran Church in America. Finally, in Las Vegas, Catholics represent only 47.5 percent of the church-going population compared to 16.4 percent for Latter-Day Saints, 15.0 percent for Jewish congregations, 5.3 percent for the Southern Baptist Convention, and 3.5 percent for the Assemblies of God.

Jews in the Southwest

The urban Southwest has proved fertile ground for Jewish migration. Jews have long resided in Texas, with the first chartered congregation, Beth Israel, being organized in Houston in 1859 and other sizable communities emerging around the same time in Galveston and San Antonio. Texas Jews remained extremely heterogeneous, widely scattered, and prominent in public life—Simon Mussina founded Brownsville, Henri Castro founded Castroville and Vandenburg, and Rabbi Henry Cohen helped organize the Galveston Movement (1907–1914) to resettle 10,000 Russian Jews trying to escape the pogroms of that period. Since 1945 Texas Jews have organized youth camps and campus ministries and have been active in city and state politics, perhaps the most prominent figure being Congressman Martin Frost. More recent, but growing more rapidly, are the Jewish communities of Phoenix, which expanded from 45,000 to more than 100,000 between 1984 and 2002, and of Las Vegas, which grew from 25,000 to 75,000 between 1990 and 2002. These communities are well educated, include many retired members, and are heavily skewed toward Reform Judaism. Attachment to synagogues is much smaller than in the Northeast, and rates of intermarriage with non-Jews are high (40 percent in Phoenix and 26 percent in Las Vegas), with a corresponding lack of attachment to Jewish customs in such families. Many Jews who move to these communities are seeking to avoid an intensive Jewish lifestyle, and the lack of specifically Jewish schools is particularly marked.[9]

Religion in Las Vegas

Las Vegas presents a peculiar problem that was already acknowledged in the 1960s. "Being in Las Vegas is like being on a battlefield," declared the pastor of Las Vegas Community Church. "I wish that every minister could spend an internship here instead of in some eight-hour town. If you want to find out about human beings, this is the place to do it, in this 24-hour town."[10] In a community where, in 1961, 15 percent of the churches' annual budgets came from the gambling industry and almost everyone worked in it, attacks on gambling were generally ineffective, although Bishop Robert Dwyer of Reno won applause for his denunciations of nude shows and instructions to the state's Catholics to boycott them. The Catholic Church also made some effort to reach the unchurched by holding masses in downtown hotels for gambling-industry workers.

Tourists from California were generally regarded as a lost cause, however, and often represented a burden to church welfare agencies obliged to pay their travel expenses home after they had lost all their money. A new focus came to the Las Vegas Strip in the mid-1960s, when several Protestant denominations sought to create a ministry specific to the entertainment community. Foremost among these was Richard Mawson (1935–), a United Church of Christ minister from Union Theological Seminary who had initially been sponsored by the National Council of Churches as a summer volunteer. Working on a golf course and as a check clerk, he came into contact with the ordinary workers and the racial and economic problems they faced. Although initially distrusted by local churches who suspected him of being a wedding counselor looking for business, Mawson gradually established a profile as a diligent chaplain offering personal counseling, leading Bible studies, and working with the city's human-relations commission. In 1963 he was joined by a Methodist student who worked as a security guard and got to know the cocktail waitresses, bartenders, and dealers. Mawson himself stressed the need for any clergyman to make use of such "Salty Christians" scattered through the community who could alert him to unexpected pregnancies, suicides, divorces, and abuse of intoxicants, but Mawson insisted that he was not an evangelist.

Las Vegas is clearly an extreme example of secular urban culture. In Texas, by contrast, urban growth brought challenges of a different type. Urban Catholic churches certainly grew in importance during the 1950s and 1960s, one example being St. Pius X, in Dallas, founded in 1954. Within two years it had grown from 192 families to 700, and by 1961 it was sustained by 1,100 families. As well as traditional parish ministries, it hosted Operation Understanding in 1957 to explain the Catholic faith to outsiders, and a branch of the Catholic Family Movement was established. The parish also operated a school-lunch program and sent two papal volunteers to Bolivia during the 1960s.

Churches and Urban and Suburban Growth

Many Protestant churches were unprepared for rapid change in membership. By 1956 Second Presbyterian, in 1904 a suburban church, had become Houston's only downtown church. With a membership of around 1,600, the church lost 1,200 members between 1946 and 1956, but it regained a similar number. While moving to the suburbs was an option, church leaders decided that it would be better to stay in inner-city Houston and serve as a center for Protestant activity and a location for meetings of the city's Council of Churches. Indeed, Second Presbyterian saw itself as an excellent location for training the next generation of church leaders for suburban churches. The work of the church was expanded through the School of Christian Living program, which met every Sunday evening for supper, a hymn sing, and programs of study for all ages. Eight Sunday school classes also served to keep the adult members in touch with one another, and the church invited members of other denominations to observe the latest methods in Christian education. In addition to Young Adult and Retired prayer groups, Second Presbyterian began a program of men's lunches on Fridays at noon, followed by a short service in which local firms were invited to participate. It also launched a neighborhood recreation program with the local grade school, YMCA, and various firms, offering a program on Fridays for eighty children aged 8–12, staffed by church personnel. In this way they cultivated additional ties with the local community.

The mid-1960s forced local congregations to move toward a direct confrontation with the social issues of the day, especially segregation and racism. One such ministry was that performed by former football coach Jim Self's "people workers" at First Presbyterian Church in Houston: a mission to the slums that called on local congregations to pool their resources of money and talent. Self's volunteers were sent out to get to know children in the ghetto, breaking up fights and organizing baseball teams as a first step toward making local residents aware of welfare resources. In building relationships the volunteers were expected to follow a three-step process of exploration, training, and, ultimately, commitment. In the long term, Self hoped to train up to 15,000 laymen to form a service corps to help weak congregations and take on inner-city assignments. A more direct attempt to resolve racial tensions came in 1970, when the Presbyterian Church's metropolitan ministry in San Antonio recommended that its member congregations adopt

Project Equality, a merit employment program. The member congregations were divided, with several wealthy churches, including First Presbyterian Church, strongly opposed and expressing concern about Roman Catholic involvement, the impact on negotiations for reunion with the United Presbyterian Church, and competition between Mexican American and Anglo-American employees. A 1971 Presbytery meeting on the issue produced a record attendance, but Project Equality was ultimately rejected by a vote of 35 to 71. However, the debate had served to make equal opportunity a legitimate subject for debate amongst San Antonio Presbyterians. Shortly after the meeting, First Presbyterian hired a Mexican American bookkeeper, and the San Antonio Presbytery pledged to make the next employee it hired a Mexican American. Supporters of Project Equality concluded that they would have to undertake more grassroots education before they tried to have the measure debated publicly.

By the early 1980s inner-city parishes faced further problems of population contraction. In 1982 six United Methodist congregations with a largely white and aging population came together to form the East Dallas Cooperative Parish (EDCP), which covered an ethnically and religiously diverse neighborhood with high crime rates. By 1989 there had been a net membership gain, baptisms had increased, and community-based ministries served 55,000 people in eastern Dallas. The aim of EDCP was to develop geographic parish "grids" for missions, while attracting volunteers from any church to impart a sense of mission identity. Thus, the church best known for distributing food was transformed into a food and clothing pantry that by 1989 was serving approximately fifty families per day.

Another church located near a Cambodian refugee community hired a former Buddhist, who became the first Cambodian-born United Methodist minister in 1988. His church was around one-quarter Cambodian by 1989, when it published *The Voice of Cambodian Americans.* Two parishes provided Spanish-language services, a family medical clinic, tutorial programs for schoolchildren, and an immigration-assistance center for the local Hispanic population. One parish provided meals, recreation activities, and Bible study five days a week for retirees and also organized a home-companion service. In 1989 EDCP purchased a twenty-four-unit apartment complex for low-income families and for housing a number of non-church groups—a refugee advocacy group, state literacy and training programs, and a pro bono legal clinic. That same year the EDCP had fifty employees and 2,000 volunteers in 1989. That year, a hundred-member Southern Baptist congregation joined the EDCP network, marking a new phase in interdenominational cooperation among Dallas churches.

Increasingly after 1970, however, the trend was toward parachurch organizations like Bill Bright's Campus Crusade for Christ, which in 1972 organized an 87,000 person meeting in Dallas. Explo 72 provided a foretaste of the evangelistic training conferences that would be a feature of the 1980s. Here, the postwar generation gathered to hear addresses by Bill Bright and Billy Graham and to learn the business of door-to-door evangelism, which they then practiced in the Dallas suburbs. While accepting that Explo 72 focused on making a "willed" rather than an emotional commitment to Christ, critics nevertheless felt that it often presented too rigid a formula, with excessive emphasis on "selling" one's personal testimony. They also argued that Campus Crusade for Christ was less ecumenical than it claimed to be, that it recommended delegates to attend fundamentalist churches in Dallas such as the Believer's Chapel and Scofield Presbyterian Church, and that it was insufficiently critical of existing social and economic power structures.

A more subtle parachurch body born in the Southwest was Christian Conciliation Service (CCS), founded by lawyer Laury Eck in Albuquerque in 1986. Moving west after a conversion experience, Eck was struck by the fact that lawsuits in Albuquerque had risen from 16,000 in 1978 to 30,000 in 1980, which was a large increase for a city of 400,000. Few local pastors had had much success in resolving their parishioners' disputes, so Eck sought to organize a ministry involving volunteer layers, pastors, and laypeople. By 1986 CCS was handling about fifty cases per month, two-thirds of them business-related and one-third marital disputes. Maintaining that the civil legal system lacked any concept of forgiveness, Eck and his associates focused on finding out the real reasons behind disagreements and discovering what was truly important to the contending parties. The option of arbitration was always available, whereby both parties agreed to accept the final decision of the three-person panel—a lawyer, a pastor, and a layman. Despite the concerns of some lawyers about going outside the legal framework and relying on too literal an interpretation of biblical injunctions, CCS has continued to grow and has spread well beyond Albuquerque.

CONCLUSION

Religious culture in the Southwest reflects the dramatic socioeconomic changes that have transformed the West in the last fifty years. Where once the majority of the region's residents lived in small mining and farming towns, today they reside in ever-expanding metropolitan corridors where high-tech jobs and large areas of unspoiled environment serve to bring in many people who grew up outside the region. Many of these migrants do not bring with them a faith community or even a coherent religious identity. Priests and pastors who, in times past, could at least count on an acquaintance with holy scripture and religious iconography, now face an often spiritually illiterate populace. The secularization that is already considerably advanced in the West Coast states has begun to make its way eastward.

Urban church life in recent years has demonstrated considerable adaptability. Protestant churches in Texas, including the Baptists, who had previously chosen to focus solely on individual pietism, began to develop programs of social service and outreach that were often remarkably wide-ranging. The Methodist experience with Houston's East Dallas Cooperative Parish reveals how combining resources allowed faith communities to play to their strengths and not overextend themselves with overambitious programs. The rise of parachurch structures that engaged the young has also been of importance in an age of increasing alienation from organized religion. The notion of the Christian Conciliation Service is an excellent example of a nondenominational yet Christian ministry established in the West but now adopted as a model throughout the nation. The Southwest thus continues to contribute to national religious innovation.

There are two world views struggling for ascendancy in the Southwest, Roman Catholic and Southern Baptist. Both have endured internal cultural and political struggles during the last fifty years, which have minimized the conflict between them. The Southern Baptists have both held the line in Texas and carried their mission westward, moves which have been accompanied by the rise of Texas Baptists to the leadership of the Southern Baptist Convention. Just as Texans today play leading roles in national secular politics, so do they determine the course of the most identifiably "Southern" Protestant denomination. Baptist identity is now heavily fundamentalist and politically engaged, changes which are of comparatively recent origin, and is dominant in northern and eastern Texas.

Roman Catholicism in the Southwest is almost inseparable from Hispanic culture, something accentuated by the growing numbers of Mexican immigrants to the region. Hispanic Catholic culture had a separatist identity, which often rejected the authority of the episcopate in favor of a communally based faith, something exploited by Protestant missionaries during the nineteenth century. Folk religion, though less condemned than in the past, has kept priests and laity at arm's length for much of the twentieth century. It remains unclear whether that distance can now be reversed, even though the church is now much more focused on serving Hispanic Catholics. With over one-third of the region's church-goers belonging to the Catholic Church, this is not a region church leadership can afford to abandon.

Other denominations with significant presence include three Texas-based Protestant groups—the United Methodist Church, the Black Baptist associations, and Churches of Christ—and the Mormons of Arizona and Nevada. The Black Baptists are divided from the SBC not by theology so much as by a legacy of racial prejudice among Southern Baptists and cannot really be considered competitors. The Methodists and Churches of Christ, by contrast, can be viewed as representing the left and right flanks of the SBC, at least with regard to social activism. Both are Protestant traditions that are not as distinctly Texan in outlook, although both have achieved a significant constituency. The Mormon communities of the Southwest represent the fringes of the Mormon heartland and compete more with the Catholic Church than with evangelical Protestantism.

For more than a century the churches were a fundamental part of daily life in the Southwest. They converted and educated a sizable portion of the Native American population, provided teachers and scholars for frontier communities, and contributed to the erection of a social welfare system in many states. Contrary to popular belief that the frontier lacked a religious sensibility, the regional evidence suggests that priests and pastors, as well as believing Christians, were key players in the transformation of the West from frontier to settled society. Today, secularism has gained ground in the states adjoining California, while Catholicism wrestles with the problem of its Hispanic communicants and the Southern Baptist Convention seeks to complete its conversion from regional denomination to national denomination. What occurs in the Southwest may reveal a great deal about the shape of American Christianity in the twenty-first century.

RESOURCE GUIDE

Printed Sources

Bradley, Martin B., Norman M. Green Jr., Dale E. Jones, Mac Lynn, and Lou McNeil. *Churches and Church Membership in the United States 1990: An Enumeration by Region, State and County Based on Data Reported for 133 Church Groupings*. Atlanta, GA: Glenmary Research Center, 1992.

Bullock, James R. "The Challenge of the City Church." *Presbyterian Survey* 46, no. 10 (October 1956): 10–11, 37, 44.

Byars, Larry L. "Peace on Earth, Good Will in Albuquerque." *Christian Herald*, December 1986, 20–24.

Collins, John J. *Native American Religions: A Geographical Survey*. Lewiston, NY: Edwin Mellen Press, 1991.

Cutting, Tom. "A Presbytery Considers Project Equality." *Chicago Seminary Theological Register* 62, no. 4 (September 1972): 31–39.

Evans, J. Claude. "The Jesus Explosion in Dallas." *Christian Century* 89, no. 27 (July 19, 1972): 767–769.

Hooper, Robert E. *A Distinct People: A History of the Churches of Christ in the 20th Century*. West Monroe, LA: Howard, 1993.

Jensen, Carol L. "Deserts, Diversity and Self-Determination: A History of the Catholic Parish in the Intermountain West." In *The American Catholic Parish: A History from 1850 to the Present*, edited by Jay. P. Dolan, 2:137–276. Mahwah, NJ: Paulist Press, 1987.

Jones, Dale E. Sherri Doty, Clifford Grammich, James E. Horsch, Richard Houseal, Mac Lynn, John P. Marcum, Kenneth M. Sanchagrin, and Richard H. Taylor. *Religious Congregations and Membership in the United States 2000: An Enumeration by Region, State and County Based on Data Reported for 149 Religious Bodies*. Nashville, TN: Glenmary Research Center, 2002.

Kostyu, Frank A. "Win or Lose: Rick Mawson Ministers on the Las Vegas Strip." *United Church Herald* 8, no. 18 (October 1965): 7–11.

Leonard, Bill J. *God's Last and Only Hope: The Fragmentation of the Southern Baptist Convention*. Grand Rapids, MI: William B. Eerdmans, 1990.

Maldonado, David, Jr., *Protestantes/Protestants: Hispanic Christianity Within Mainline Traditions*. Nashville, TN: Abingdon Press, 1999.

McQueen, Clyde. *Black Churches in Texas*. College Station: Texas A&M University Press, 2000.

Melton, J. Gordon. *Encyclopedia of American Religions*. 6th ed. Detroit, MI: Gale Research, 1999.

Montgomery, William E. "African-American Churches." In *The New Handbook of Texas*, edited by Ron Tyler, Douglas E. Barnett, Roy R. Barkley, Penelope C. Anderson and Mark F. Odintz, 1:43–46. Austin: Texas State Historical Association, 1996.

Nolan, Charles E. "Modest and Humble Crosses: A History of Catholic Parishes in the South Central Region (1850–1984)." In *The American Catholic Parish: A History from 1850 to the Present*, edited by Jay P. Dolan, 1:235–346. Mahwah, NJ: Paulist Press, 1987.

Orsi, Robert A. "Introduction: Crossing the City Lines." In *Gods of the City: Religion and the American Urban Landscape*, edited by Robert A. Orsi, 1–78. Bloomington: Indiana University Press, 1999.

Pinn, Anthony B. *The Black Church in the Post-Civil Rights Era*. Maryknoll, NY: Orbis Books, 2002.

Quinn, D. Michael. "Religion in the American West." In *Under an Open Sky: Rethinking America's Western Past*, edited by William Cronon, George Miles and Jay Gitlin, 145–166. New York: Norton, 1992.

Reid, Ed. "Religion in Gambling Town, U.S.A." *Christian Herald* (November 1961): 13–14, 54–55.

Stewart, Omer C. *Peyote Religion: A History*. Norman: University of Oklahoma Press, 1987.

Swierenga, Robert P. "The Little White Church: Religion in Rural America." *Agricultural History* 71, no. 4 (Fall 1997): 415–441.

Szasz, Ferenc M. *The Protestant Clergy in the Great Plains and Mountain West, 1865–1915*. Albuquerque: University of New Mexico Press, 1988.

———. *Religion in the Modern American West.* Tucson: University of Arizona Press, 2000.

Szasz, Ferenc M., and Margaret C. Szasz. "Religion and Spirituality." In *The Oxford History of the American West*, edited by Clyde A. Milner II, Carol A. O'Connor and Martha A. Sandweiss, 359–391. New York: Oxford University Press, 1994.

Taylor, Betty Jo. "You Walk the Streets." *Presbyterian Survey* 57, no. 3 (March 1967): 14–18.

Thornburg, John, and Elizabeth Thornburg, "East Dallas Cooperative Parish: Born to Serve, Grown to Redeem!" *Circuit Rider* 14, no. 10 (December 1990–January 1991): 6–7.

Vernon, Walter N. *The Methodist Excitement in Texas: A History.* Dallas: Texas United Methodist Historical Society, 1984.

Weigle, Marta. *Brothers of Light, Brothers of Blood: The Penitentes of the Southwest.* Albuquerque: University of New Mexico Press, 1976.

Web Sites

Baptist General Convention of Texas
http://www.bgct.org

Baylor University
http://www.baylor.edu

Catholic Archdiocese of Santa Fe
http://www.archdiocesesantafe.org

Catholic Diocese of Corpus Christi
http://www.goccn.org/diocese/

Southern Methodist University
http://www.smu.edu

Festivals

Calendar of Indian Dances and Events at the New Mexico Pueblo and Other New Mexico Tribes

http://www.indianpueblo.org/index.cfm?module=ipcc&pn=17

Santa Fe Fiesta
P.O. Box 4516
Santa Fe, NM 87502
http://www.santafefiesta.org
First week of September.

St. Louis Day Church Festival
St. Louis IX of France Church
1306 Angelo Street
Castroville, TX 78009
Sunday closest to August 25.

Organizations

Mission Nuestra Señora de la Purisima
807 Mission Road
San Antonio, TX 78210

Mission San Xavier del Bac
1950 West San Xavier Road
Tucson, AZ 85746
http://www.sanxaviermission.org
Daily, 8:00 a.m. to 5:00 p.m.

San Francisco de Asis Church
101 Valerio Road
Taos, NM 87557

St. Francis Cathedral
131 Cathedral Place
P.O. Box 2127
Santa Fe, NM 87504

Texas Baptist Historical Center Museum
10405 FM 50
Brenham, TX 77833
Wednesday–Saturday, 10:00 a.m. to 4:00 p.m.

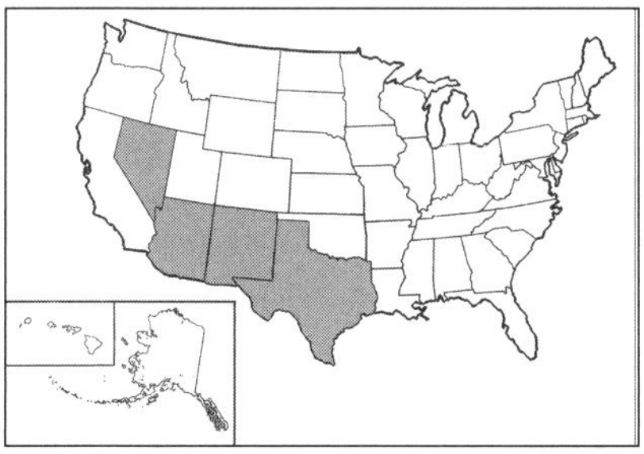

SPORTS AND RECREATION

Margaret Dwyer

As recreational destinations go, the American Southwest is second to none. Arizona, Nevada, New Mexico, and Texas not only have thriving tourist industries and major-league team play, they are accommodating ever-growing numbers of retirees who move to the region in search of mild winters and a wide range of recreational options. These states all offer the ubiquitous American sports and recreational options of theme parks, golf courses, country clubs, sports teams, and stadiums, but they also have individual reputations regarding their sports preferences—many Americans believe that Texans are crazy about football, that Arizonans adore golf, that New Mexicans love basketball, and that Nevadans can see beyond the bright lights of the casinos to spend their time engaging in skiing and other mountain sports. Although these generalizations are broad, they are lent credence by the culture and geography of these states.

This region's uniqueness comes from its wild areas and the Indian cultures, which are some of the earliest documented in North America. These factors also influence the urban cultures of the region. As Aldo Leopold observed many years ago in *A Sand Country Almanac*, the rugged landscape of desert, mountain, prairie, pine forest, bayou, and coastal lands have shaped the human cultures that grew up there:

> Wilderness is the raw material out of which man has hammered the artifact called civilization. Wilderness was never a homogeneous raw material. It was very diverse, and the resulting artifacts are very diverse. These differences in the end-product are known as cultures. The rich diversity of the world's cultures reflects a corresponding diversity in the wilds that gave them birth.[1]

SPORTS IN EARLY NATIVE AMERICAN CULTURE

Gritty sun-baked earth, a hot wind, a landscape of red-hued mesas and arroyos and Indian ruins are what visitors have come to expect when visiting any of the many archaeological parks throughout the Southwestern desert. One is likely to learn about cultural markers such as the types of buildings and their placement, ceramics, agriculture in a dry climate, the distances native people traveled to hunt and find plant and mineral resources, and in the case of Arizona's Anasazi and Hohokam cultures, conjecture on why they apparently "disappeared" around 1300 C.E. Because the Native American languages were oral rather than written, understanding of their lives generally comes from the remnant physical evidence. Indeed, archaeologists date the clear beginnings of Hohokam culture to when they began to make their distinctive, red-on-buff pots, or, as Patricia Crown writes in her essay "Hohokam: Current Views of Prehistory and the Regional System," when they are clearly identified "as sedentary, pottery-producing horticulturists."[2]

Sport was distinctly important in Hohokam society. Found among their middens and ruins are clues to this: their rubber balls and evidence of the hundreds of ball courts they built, which are some of America's first public architecture dedicated to sport. However, this may be too simple an explanation, because Native American origin stories and general world view placed these games in an entirely different realm or context than today's modern games played with rubber balls.

Little is known about the origins of the Hohokam, who are considered to be the ancestral peoples of the Tohono O'odham (Papago), but they are presumed to have evolved or arrived in the Salt and Gila river valleys between 500 and 300 B.C.E. However, their ball game and elaborate equipment are directly linked to the courts found throughout the Mexico and Central American region, called Mesoamerica. Although the Hohokam culture was no longer in existence by the time Coronado began his grand tour of the Southwest in 1540, there were many ball courts and players in Mexico for the Spanish to write about. More important, the Maya themselves, in what is present-day Mexico, wrote about their ball games in their books, or codices, such as the *Popol Vuh* and represented players in statues, stone carvings on structures, and pottery. The Hohokam of Arizona are the northern-most culture that incorporated ball courts into their public architecture and were a culture for which ball games had ontological, or spiritual, significance. In order to understand the Hohokam game in contrast to the modern world's view of sports as business and entertainment, it is important to examine why these ball courts were far more than the means to a friendly little game of handball at lunchtime. And much can be construed about the Hohokam worldview by examining other regional cultures that shared in these games.

Throughout Mesoamerica there is a great body of evidence for enthusiasm for team sports in the form of games played in ball courts, according to Jane Day, chief curator of the Denver Museum of Natural History. She believes that there is a marked difference between games in these ancient cultures when compared to others around the world, because these earliest of American games focused on teams rather than individual prowess. This team focus has been adapted through the centuries and is still highly prized in modern American sport. Day writes:

> It is in the use of rubber balls that modern games are most clearly linked to the Pre-Columbian past. Rubber itself was a product of the Americas and unknown in Europe and Asia before the arrival of Columbus in 1492. The bouncing rubber ball was at first viewed by the amazed Spanish invaders as magical, an instrument of the devil. Cortes took teams of players and num-

> bers of rubber balls back to Spain soon after the Aztec conquest in 1521. There the Indian teams played for spectators at the royal court of Charles V. Soon the superior elastic qualities of the New World ball became appreciated and rubber began to replace wood and leather in European games.[3]

When Day published her research in 1992, more than six hundred I-shaped, stone ball courts had been documented in Mesoamerica. The ball games were played by all the major cultures of the region, including the Aztecs, Maya, Olmecs, Toltecs, and Zapotecs. In the Nahuatl language of the Aztecs one of these games was known to have been called Ullamalitzli, and ball courts were found to have been constructed in all communities of any size. This "sport of kings," according to Day, was played by nobility and was "both a competitive contest and a ritual ceremony." She adds that "the game held religious as well as secular significance for players and spectators."[4]

In Arizona the Hohokam built at least 206 oval-shaped ball courts at 166 locations, in a region that begins near the Mexican border and extends to north of Flagstaff. Archaeologists trace the territorial boundaries and the evolution of the Hohokam culture itself by its development of these ball courts between 700 C.E. and 1250 C.E., a period that apparently concluded with a social upheaval that resulted in the cessation of the construction of ball courts and the appearance instead of large ceremonial platform mounds in villages. Another hundred years would see the end of the Hohokam culture. Excavations have brought to light rubber balls and figurines of ballplayers wearing protective gear, found among fragments of trade goods from Mexico such as turquoise, copper, shell, and macaw feathers. "The distribution of ball courts provides a second means of bounding the [Hohokam region] . . . , particularly when viewed in comparison to the distribution of red-on-buff ceramics" according to Crown.[5]

The National Park Service is one of many agencies and organizations entrusted with the job of preserving these ancient sites. At Wupatki National Monument in northern Arizona, the park policy is to state that while these ball courts were important social sites in each village, "the evidence suggests that the northern most game court that was [actually] used was 150 miles south in Phoenix at the end of the runway at what is the present-day Phoenix airport," where a rubber ball fragment was found next to a court. Archaeologist Allen Dart of the Old Pueblo Archeology Center in Tucson explains that "there is no hard evidence of playing ballgames on those northern courts," noting that "unless both teams were struck by lightning and left lying there on the court to be found in the act of playing the game, evidence is scarce."[6] The balls wouldn't be left on the court when not in use, so they must be found elsewhere, and the connections will be made that way.

LAND USE: EARLY SURVIVAL, MODERN RECREATION

Archeologists know that Ullamalitzli, or Ulama, was and is clearly a socially significant ritualized game, unlike popular sports such as today's football and basketball, but these modern sports, too, are played with rubberized balls. In addition to these games American Indians practiced many other activities such as hunting and fishing, that have spanned centuries and cultures but are today practiced more as sport than for survival. When people hunt for food the necessity is clear, and the

The ballcourt at Wupatki National Monument. Courtesy of the National Park Service.

ritual aspect is apparent in the stories and ceremonies of tribes and in the literature and poetry of modern Indian writers. Modern Indian novels, such as Leslie Marmon Silko's *Ceremony* and N. Scott Momaday's *House Made of Dawn*, clearly portray the skill and pride in hunting to be equal to that of modern hunters.

The major differences today are the access to the land, and the "sportsmanship" handed down through privileged classes in Europe and America, restricting what is hunted and when it may be taken. In 1895 an important legal challenge was waged by the state of Wyoming against the Bannock tribe of the Fort Hall Reservation in Idaho, enforcing new state hunting laws and effectively eliminating Indian access to treaty hunting grounds around Jackson Hole. Despite the murder and disappearance of Indian hunting-party members after their arrest and the confiscation of all their material goods, this event, according to historian Louis Warren in his book *The Hunter's Game*, represents a major change from traditional hunting schedules and methods to a codified system that favored white sportsmen.[7] Modern tribal managers in the Southwest now host fine hunting for Indians and non-Indians alike on reservation wildland.

The most recent hunting, fishing, and wildlife survey taken by the U.S. Census bureau, indicates that in 2001 hunters in Arizona, New Mexico, Nevada, and Texas spent $1.5 million on their pastimes.

A New Tribal Development: Native American–Operated Golf Courses

Residing in the Southwest means learning to live with heat or little rain or both heat and little rain, and the Southwest comes with a larger-than-life reputation of hosting tenacious ancient cultures such as the Pueblo, Apache, Navajo, Hohokam, Paiute, and Comanche, to name a few of the indigenous American Indian cultures. It should come as no surprise that enterprising tribal leaders have found a way to use some of their large tracts of land to attract local residents and tourists to their remote locations: build golf courses, and they will come. According to golf journalist Shane Sharp, "They are devoid of ubiquitous Sun Belt housing, ungainly condominiums and all the undesirable trappings of modern golf course developments. They have become so popular with golfers that their tee sheets are typically filled weeks and even months in advance."[8] These courses, particularly in Arizona and New Mexico, have attracted a great deal of attention due to the quality of the layout combined with the beauty of the remote landscapes. In Arizona these clubs include We-Ko-Pa Golf Club in Fountain Hills, northeast of Phoenix, run by the Fort McDowell Yavapai Nation. The name, designated by the tribe, translates to "Four Peak Mountain," one of the four scared mountains (the others being the McDowell Mountains, Red Mountain, and the Superstitions). On the Gila River (Akimel O'Odham/Pee Posh) Indian Reservation, south of Phoenix, is the Whirlwind Golf Club and its two courses, Devil's Claw and Cattail. In New Mexico several of the pueblos have built courses, including the Pueblo de Cochiti Golf Course, between Albuquerque and Santa Fe, the Twin Warriors Golf Club located on the Santa Ana Reservation just north of Albuquerque, the Isleta Eagle Golf Course, south of Albuquerque on the Isleta Pueblo Reservation, and the Towa Golf Resort on the Pojoaque Pueblo north of Santa Fe.

Golf courses run by Indian tribes are not only a valuable addition to the number of courses local golfers have access to in this golfer's paradise, they are an excellent form of economic diversification for the area Indian tribes. According to Sharp,

> So far so good from a design perspective, but the business side of the equation is just as, if not more important for the Native American tribes that get involved in owning and operating golf courses. That said, why have a handful of Arizona tribes opted to make a go at this tempestuous business when the casino industry has yielded substantial profits? We-Ko-Pa general manager Jeff Lessing says that tribal business objectives are not that different from those of private developers entering the golf course fray. "Golf courses have a way of attracting other business and serve as a good centerpiece," says Lessing. 'In the case of tribal lands, it's not residential development but rather casinos and hotels they are looking to promote and stimulate through golf. And while the courses aren't the main money makers, they still make a profit."[9]

Golf is only one of many ways to fill leisure time with play in the Southwest.

MODERN RECREATION

Recreation today encompasses much more than the obvious sports and game pursuits. By the most liberal definition recreation is anything that we choose to do during our leisure time, that part of the day, week, month, or year when we aren't working or doing chores. What constitutes "recreation" is limited only by the imagination—whether it is fulfilled via a hobby, a physical activity, a cultural event, or a social gathering. Wild land has, as already demonstrated, been for decades considered a primary destination for recreational activity, but today we see much more polarized views on land use and value judgments regarding some recreational choices. Non-motorized-vehicle pursuits are placed in opposition to mechanized recreation, and hunting and fishing are opposed by animal rights groups. What some individuals consider recreational, others consider criminal. Thus, how we "play" is a transaction that not only involves choosing activities to suit ourselves within the limitations of available time, financial resources, physical ability, and access to the places, spaces, and materials necessary to any given activity, it is conducted on a playing field where access is not equal and special interest politics can give it a complex, occasionally bitter flavor. Hunters pass protestors on their way to hunting grounds, hikers are more than disgruntled when motorized vehicles speed past them on public trails. Tourists travel over contested ground when their destinations include sacred lands, ruins, or currently occupied Indian communities. Ski areas have on occasion been proposed for placement on public lands that hold spiritual importance for local tribes.

Without belaboring the issue, it is important to acknowledge that there are some serious conflicts within the field of recreation, but for most activities and most Americans, these issues rarely arise, and the family vacation is still a major American institution that attracts millions of visitors to the Southwest annually. In 1997 Americans living in and visiting Arizona, Nevada, New Mexico, and Texas spent $3.25 billion on fitness and personal sports activities (skiing, golf, fitness clubs, and so forth), $4 billion on sporting goods, $3.1 billion on recreational and off-road vehicles, $1.1 billion on commercial team sports (such as football, basketball, baseball, and hockey), and $19.3 billion on tourism in the region. The following table reflecting the 2000 U.S. Census survey figures regarding recreational expenditures demonstrates the importance of recreation and sports to the economy of the region:

Early Twentieth Century Land Management in the Southwest

Much land management in the Southwest today results from the work of a forester and game manager who got his start in New Mexico and Arizona after the turn of the last century. In 1909 Arizona and New Mexico were still territories when Aldo Leopold (1887–1948) arrived by stagecoach in Springerville, Arizona, to begin working on the Apache National Forest. An avid hunter and fisherman, Leopold recognized that promoting healthy populations of game and fish in national forests would benefit recreational uses. Wilderness became a central focus of his attention as a land manager, and in 1921 his essay "The Wilderness and Its Place in Forest Recreation Policy" appeared in the *Journal of Forestry*. Noting that Gifford Pinchot (1865–1946) had made good on his promise that the newly established national forests would open the land to forestry instead of "bottling up" the resources, Leopold argued that some land be designated wilderness and be managed in such a way to exclude logging and roads. "Recreation plans are leaning toward the segregation of certain areas from certain developments, so that having been led into the wilderness, the people may have some wilderness left to

Table 1. U.S. dollars spent on recreation and sports (categories include services, equipment, vehicles, lodging)

These numbers have been parsed from several U.S. Census Bureau categories and are not intended to be added to or subtracted from one another. Some categories had dual figures for profit and nonprofit status, and at times one or the other was undisclosed to maintain anonymity within the state's business category.

Category	Arizona	Nevada	New Mexico	Texas
Sports Teams and Clubs				
Spectator Sports (teams, racing, trainers, etc.)	309,480,000	47,181,000	31,343,000	724,015,000
Teams and Clubs	224,656,000	undisclosed	4,346,000	514,971,000
Other spectator sports (golf, tennis, rodeo, etc.)	8,875,000	21,296,000	10,445,000	34,277,000
Racetracks (auto, horse, dog)	75,949,000	undisclosed	16,552,000	174,767,000
Recreation for Individual Participants				
Master totals for fitness, skiing, golf, amusement parks, bowling, etc.	769,391,000	301,443,000	152,368,000	2,030,000,000
Fitness—gyms and pools	214,336,000	68,657,000	41,703,000	546,396,000
Sports and rec. clubs, miniature golf, amusement parks	11,283,000 (plus undisclosed)	62,749,000 (plus undisclosed)	19,593,000	352,260,000 (plus undisclosed)
Skiing	undisclosed	8,454,000	27,134,000	none
Golf courses and Country Clubs	356,644,000	136,286,000	48,065,000	899,824,000
Bowling	44,258,000	4,245,000	12,454,000	124,846,000
Marinas	59,743,000	16,437,000	3,419,000	106,674,000
Recreational Vehicles, Campers, Trailers, ATVs, Mopeds, Motorcycles, Boats, Personal Watercraft				
All vehicles in this category	755,666,000	297,258,000	174,869,000	1,931,433,000
Recreational vehicles (self-contained campers, modified vans, etc.)	436,221,000	154,565,000	95,681,000	752,017,000
Motorcycles, mopeds, ATVs, personal watercraft	170,750,000	80,245,000	59,738,000	421,028,000
Boats	104,374,000	37,529,000	11,040,000	545,326,000
Retail Sporting Goods, Games, Toys, and Musical Instruments				
Retail Sporting Goods, Games, Toys, and Musical Instruments	713,600,000	307,038,000	212,703,000	2,787,904,000

Table 1. U.S. dollars spent on recreation and sports (*continued*)

Category	Arizona	Nevada	New Mexico	Texas
Sporting Goods Stores alone	336,055,000	163,774,000	111,194,000	1,291,107,000
Musical groups & artists	5,734,000	47,019,000	11,815,000	163,380,000
Musical Instrument & supply stores	79,636,000	undisclosed	15,985,000	272,924,000
Hobby, Toy & Game stores	238,729,000	96,620,000	70,669,000	1,007,059,000
Tourism: Hotels, Food, Parks, Zoos				
Traveler Accommodations (hotels, motels, B&Bs, NO casino hotels)	2,084,135,000	12,339,474,000	548,904,000	4,339,458,000
Recreational Vehicle parks, campgrounds	110,441,000	20,602,000	11,158,000	48,908,000
Resorts & vacation camps, NO campgrounds	21,767,000	1,615,000	17,133,000	75,760,000
Gambling				
Casino Hotels	undisclosed	12,993,478,000	none	none
Casinos	600,905,000	579,779,000	251,066,000	undisclosed
Entire Gambling Industry without Casino hotels	836,631,000	948,688,000	294,914,000	252,277,000
Other (slot machines, lottery, bingo, betting)	235,726,000	368,909,000	43,848,000	undisclosed

enjoy."[10] "By wilderness," he states later in the paper, "I mean a continuous stretch of country preserved in its natural state, open to lawful hunting and fishing, big enough to absorb a two weeks' pack trip, and kept devoid of roads, artificial trails, cottages, or other works of man."[11]

Today's land managers are still struggling with the issue of appropriate access to wild areas and face steady and mounting pressure for more access with motorized conveyances ranging from four-wheel-drive vehicles and two- and three-wheeled all-terrain vehicles to floatplanes and helicopters flying passengers into remote wilderness areas. At the 1999 Congress on Recreation and Resource Capacity held in Snowmass, Colorado, federal and state land managers and "stakeholders" (private organizations and businesses that organize trips and sell equipment) met to discuss outdoor recreation capacity issues. Within a given park or forest, how many people are enough, and how many are too many before the quality of the experience is diminished? Congressional proceedings published after the meeting reveal that all in attendance, land managers and stakeholders alike, recognize the need to limit access through quotas, fees, and permits and to educate visitors about the carrying capacity of any given parcel of land. This is a plan that has its origins in Leopold's ideas about the health of the land.

Environmentalists have articulated opposition to the encroachment of roads and vehicular traffic of all kinds into wild areas. Activist and author Edward Abbey noted in *Desert Solitaire* that today's "industrial tourism" forces the hand of the Park Service, an agency set in place in 1916 to "provide for the enjoyment of [park lands] in such manner and by such means as will leave them unimpaired for the enjoyment of future generations."[12] Abbey further notes:

> This appropriately ambiguous language, employed long before the onslaught of the automobile, has been understood in various and often opposing ways ever since. The Park Service, like any other big organization, includes factions and factions. The Developers, the dominant faction, place their emphasis on the words "provide for the enjoyment." The Preservers, a minority but also strong, emphasize the words "leave them unimpaired." It is apparent, then, that we cannot decide the question of development versus preservation by a simple referral to holy writ or an attempt to guess the intention of the founding fathers; we must make up our own minds and decide for ourselves what the national parks should be and what purpose they should serve.[13]

Aldo Leopold and His Land Ethic

Leopold's evolving ethos of recreation grew in later years into his concisely stated "Land Ethic," the final essay in his book *A Sand County Almanac*. This essay in particular and that book as a whole are recognized today as a major building block of American environmental philosophy. When Leopold's collected essays were published posthumously in 1949, what debuted was not only a sublime work of literature but the cornerstone of the debate regarding what constitutes the health of the land and how people should use it in order to retain that health. Admittedly, Leopold's attitudes about hunting and fishing as sport arose from his privileged Midwestern roots and were learned from his German-immigrant father. The rules of "sportsmanship," as subjective as they are, came into play early in his career as a naive Leopold attempted to intercept Apache hunters who had a different view on the appropriate use of their traditional hunting lands, but the Indians eluded him. What Leopold, his forestry crews, and the Apaches had in common was that they all approached the land on foot or horseback, and it was this type of access to wild lands that Leopold promoted the rest of his life.

That dialogue continues today and is apparent when tourists make choices about how to reach many popular parks. For example, visitors can drive to Grand Canyon National Park, Arizona, but park managers recognize that the intense traffic and crowded parking lot conditions diminish the park experience. While studying the possibility of a light rail system, the park's management plan currently calls for eventually excluding private cars from the places like the popular Grand Canyon Village in favor of parking outside the boundaries and providing bus service into the village. Both Leopold and Abbey predicted the problems that would result from the successful marketing of parks and services surrounding them, but the agencies and the tourist industry are learning to accommodate the demands of visitors, ranging from quiet isolation to the excitement of off-road motorized-vehicle activities, and everything in between.

THE AMERICAN SOUTHWEST AS A RECREATIONAL DESTINATION

Each succeeding wave of settlers in the Southwest has learned to live here by adapting to the rugged and dramatic geography and the climate, and their games and sport reflect the place. This territory consists of bioregions as varied as beautiful deserts, forested mountains, high basin and range terrain, staked plains and prairies, vast pine forests, and the green and lush bayous, and a stunning 367-mile stretch of shoreline. Each of these zones offers unique opportunities for play within the landscape, whether golfing, riding, hiking, climbing, skiing, spelunking, fishing, hunting, or boating, to name just a few.

Public Lands and Recreation

Public- and private-sector entities in the American Southwest have for many years promoted the region for both living year-round and vacationing. The intense beauty of the landscape that stretches from the Sierra Nevada to the Gulf of Mexico is well-suited to travel brochures, and part of the package is experiencing some aspects of the territory referred to as the Old West. Local chambers of commerce encourage tourists to visit dude ranches, movie studios, museums, ghost towns, and historic sites or to dine in a local steak house where Western wear is optional but neckties are rejected with the simple motion of a pair of shears. State tourist boards encourage other pursuits such as visiting local parks, Indian reservations, pueblos, or modern villages or traveling through Spanish and Mexican land grants and historic city squares with their centuries-old hacienda or nineteenth-century Victorian architecture. Ecotourism businesses are in place to help visitors go one-on-one with the landscape, backpacking, climbing mountains (or just some of their rock faces), biking, kayaking, whitewater rafting, skiing, ballooning, or choosing some of the extreme versions of these sports. This frontier landscape, complete with an exciting history, is the stuff of Westerns.

Today's tourists may wish to rough it on foot or horseback, but they have additional choices such as air travel, personal vehicles, motor homes and other camping vehicles, and several types of personal off-road transportation, as well as boats and personal watercraft. Their most frequent destinations? National and state parks, water recreation areas and beaches, and wild lands managed by the National Forests, the U.S. Fish and Wildlife Areas, the Bureau of Land Management, and the U.S. Army Corps of Engineers, to name just a few.

The federal government is the largest landowner in Arizona, New Mexico, and Nevada, followed closely by American Indian tribal lands, most of which are managed by the federal Bureau of Indian Affairs. Federal (non-Indian) agencies manage 43 percent of Arizona's territory, 85 percent of Nevada, and 31 percent of New Mexico. Texas, with its unique history of separate nationhood boasts only 2 percent federal lands and Indian lands. According to the *Texas Handbook Online*, "after the annexation of Texas [in 1845], the federal government assumed control of Indian affairs but had no authority to settle the Indians on reservations in the state since Texas retained ownership of the public lands."[14] In most regions American Indians allow some access onto their tribal lands, that portion of their tribal holdings that excludes individual allotments and government-held land for schools and Bureau of Indian Affairs agency operations. In Arizona that amounts to nearly 10 percent of the total land, or 19.8 million acres, followed by 7.2 million acres in New Mexico and 1.1 million acres in Nevada. Texas has less than 5,000 acres of tribal lands. In addition to the federal land holdings, each of these states has invested heavily in state recreational facilities. Arizona has 30 state parks, historic, and natural areas, Nevada has 24 state parks, New Mexico has 31 state parks, and Texas has 120 state parks and historic sites. Visitors to the American Southwest have access to the kind of acreage Leopold envisioned when he began planning and campaigning for wilderness recreational lands, though the struggle to maintain these lands continues to be an active political issue in every presidential administration. With the exceptions of the National Park Service, the U.S. Army Corps of Engineers, and the Fish and Wildlife Service, which have always had strong recreation ties, and the Bureau of Land Management and the U.S. Forest Service, which have always had large recreation components in addition to their logging, grazing, and mining activities, the transition of federal agencies from managing resource extraction to more general resource management that includes recreation has been gradual, but landmark legislation and important studies helped pave the way.

A significant shift occurred in the federal land management focus following the passage of the federal Wilderness Act of 1964 and the 1972 Roadless Area Review and Evaluation (RARE) and 1979 RARE II studies. This law and these public evaluations heralded a rise in the public interest in recreational access to wild areas. Numerous small towns that had previously been supported by resource extraction saw years of decline as public pressure restricted or closed some or all of these operations. The financial turn-around for many of these communities came with the realization that developing a public/private tourism industry could allow local entrepreneurs to take advantage of the wild public lands in their regions. These operations have become some of the stuff that vacations are made of.

A man goes white water rafting in the Grand Canyon. Courtesy of Getty Images/PhotoDisc.

Table 2. Dollars spent on hunting, fishing, and wildlife watching

	Arizona	Nevada	New Mexico	Texas
All activities, total participants	1.7 million	657,000	884,000	4.9 million
Fishing	419,000	172,000	314,000	2.4 million
Hunting	148,000	47,000	130,000	1.2 million
Wildlife watching	1.5 million	543,000	671,000	3.2 million
Total spent in state on wildlife recreation	1.6 billion	681 million	1 billion	5.4 billion
Trip related expenses	512 million	168 million	302 million	1.7 billion
Equipment expenses	1 billion	472 million	583 million	2.9 billion
Fees, licenses, donations, leases, property	67 million	40 million	138 million	844 million

Source: U.S. Census Bureau, National Survey of Fishing, Hunting, and Wildlife-Associated Recreation.

Hunting, fishing, and wildlife watching are such big business and recreational draws that major state and federal government surveys are conducted regularly. The U.S. Census Bureau's National Survey of Fishing, Hunting, and Wildlife-Associated Recreation (FHWAR) is conducted every five years, most recently in 2001, to reveal the interests of U.S. residents both in the Southwest and throughout the United States Survey results must be read with the understanding that participants are usually involved in more than one activity on the list. Residents aged sixteen and older hunt and fish, or they may be birdwatchers that also fish. By far the most popular activity is wildlife watching, and it must be noted that the categories allow for travels out to wild areas as well as animal and bird watching close to home (as the following table indicates).

Of the many federal agencies that manage millions of acres in the Southwest, one can make some generalizations regarding allowable public access. Typically, the public is permitted access for recreational activities of many sorts, but each agency is subject to different sets of enabling legislation, so all federal lands are not equally open or accessible. Camping, hiking, off-road driving, fishing, hunting are activities that may occur on some federal land but not necessarily on all federal land.

National Parks and Recreation Areas

The Southwest is home to many parks and recreation areas. Arizona has twenty-three national parks, monuments, and recreation areas. Nevada has four, counting two historic trails. Fifteen parks, monuments, and historic trails are found in New Mexico, and Texas has fourteen federal parks, monuments, and recreation areas. Each state has a well-developed state park system, and in Texas there are far more state lands than federal lands available for recreational use.

The National Park Service and the U.S. Forest Service alone account for the management of more famous tourist destinations than all other agencies combined, everything from the Big Thicket in Texas, Lake Mead in Nevada, the Gila Wilderness in New Mexico, to Arizona's Grand Canyon. Other federal agencies in the Southwest and some high profile recreational sites include the U.S. Army Corps of Engineers, the Bureau of Land Management, the U.S. Fish and Wildlife Service, and the Bureau of Reclamation. The U.S. Forest Service and the National Park Service manage the lion's share of the well known (and not so well known) parks and forest locations throughout the United States.

National Forests

Established in 1905 with the mission to "sustain the health, diversity, and productivity of the Nation's forests and grasslands to meet the needs of present and future generations," the U.S. Forest Service now administers 191 million acres of land, roughly equivalent to the size of the state of Texas. "The mission of the USDA Forest Service is to sustain the health, diversity, and productivity of the Nation's forests and grasslands to meet the needs of present and future generations."[16] Set up as a conservation agency (in contrast to a preservation agency, such as the National Park Service), the resources on the ground are intended to be used in some form or fashion by present and future generations. Logging, mining, grazing, and watersheds protection were early agency tasks, and through the work of individuals like Aldo Leopold, wildlife management and recreation were added. Wilderness areas exist in Forest Service and other agency land holdings. The original owners of mining claims generally retain historic mineral rights, and activities such as hunting and fishing are permitted.

Arizona has six national forests. They are the Apache-Sitgreaves, Coconino, Coronado, Kaibab, Prescott, and Tonto. Federal lands in Nevada are managed primarily by the Bureau of Land Management. In the northern half of the state, however, is the Humboldt-Toiyabe National Forest, its many segments forming in sum

Multi-Agency Land Management

Restrictions (fish and game laws, primarily) are layered onto federal lands by each state and sometimes by other agencies, making too many variables to try to include in a single chapter. Internet searches on state and federal agencies will provide up-to-date information. An example of a unique land-use situation exists in Arizona, where the Barry M. Goldwater Air Force Range abuts the Cabeza Prieta Wildlife Refuge on its northern and western boundaries. To the south lies Organ Pipe Cactus National Monument, a National Park Service site where the public is free to roam. But upon entering the National Wildlife Refuge, the protected nature of the Air Force bombing ranges forces closure of access across the refuge except for scheduled openings. According to the agency,

> before entering the refuge, you must obtain a valid Refuge Entry Permit and sign a Military Hold Harmless Agreement. Free permits are available from the refuge office or they can be sent through the mail. Most of the refuge falls within the air space of the Barry M. Goldwater Air Force Range. Numerous low-flying aircraft cross the refuge on their way to air-to-air bombing and gunnery ranges located to the north. Some military training exercises over the refuge may require limitations on travel and even short periods of closure of the refuge to the public. Military schedules are known in advance, so refuge staff can help with your schedule.[15]

Cooperative relationships between federal agencies are not uncommon when it comes to land and resource management. The National Park Service and the U.S. Forest Service have joint visitor centers in many remote regions of the United States. A unique experimental partnership is getting underway with the establishment of the Valles Caldera National Preserve, established in 2000 on "89,000 acres of the Baca Ranch in northern New Mexico. The Valles Caldera Preservation Act designated these spectacular lands as the Valles Caldera National Preserve, a unit of the National Forest System. The Act also created the Valles Caldera Trust to manage the Preserve."[17]

the largest national forest found outside Alaska. New Mexico, like Arizona, has a wide variety of landscapes and a healthy distribution of national forests throughout. It also boasts the first official wilderness, the Gila Wilderness Area, a major accomplishment by a then little-known forester named Aldo Leopold.

Texas has relatively little federal land for recreational opportunities when compared to the other states discussed in this region. The state's timber industry, and national forests, are all found in the eastern Piney Woods region of the state, and this is where the Angelina National Forest, the Davy Crockett National Forest, the Sabine National Forest, and the Sam Houston National Forest are located. The only Texas Forest Service site not in the Piney Woods are the Caddo National Grasslands and Lyndon B. Johnson (LBJ) National Grasslands, two sites managed as a single entity, which are located north of the Dallas–Forth Worth area.

In each state all these forests and grasslands permit recreational access, and the most popular activities are hiking, camping, fishing, hunting, horseback riding, mountain biking, skiing, wildlife viewing, and photography. A newer, and at times controversial activity is that of off-road travel, and access to public land is managed differently in each forest. Where off-road vehicles (ORVs) are permitted, there may be day-use permits required. In Texas, "each Forest has different restrictions on off-road riding. It's your responsibility to know the rules. Visit our Web site for maps and additional information, or call the District Office of the forest where you would like to ride. Volunteering to help maintain trails is a great way to show your support."[18]

National Parks, Monuments, and State Parks

Besides the national forests, the Southwest is a major destination for people in search of outdoor recreation because of the numerous appealing national and state parks and monuments throughout the region.

Arizona has many beautiful and appealing places with physical beauty and historical significance. The Grand Canyon National Park is the most famous park in the United States, visited by millions for its spectacular views. Saguaro National Park, near Tucson, has large forests of Saguaro cactus including the large-armed cactus that has dominated western film sets everywhere. Canyon De Chelly National Monument is a deep canyon on Navajo land with many cliff dwellings. The Chiricahua National Monument features eroded rocky pinnacles and unusual wildlife in a remote corner of Arizona. The Lake Mead National Recreation Area is between Nevada and Arizona, where three of America's four desert ecosystems meet: the Mojave, the Great Basin, and the Sonoran Deserts. It was formed by the Hoover Dam (originally Boulder Dam) on the Colorado river. The Organ Pipe Cactus National Monument celebrates the Sonoran Desert landscape, including the organ pipe cactus, a large cactus rarely found in the U.S. The Petrified Forest National Park features brightly colored fossilized trees, and the Sunset Crater Volcano National Monument includes cinder cone volcanoes. Other Arizona recreational sites are the Casa Grande Ruins National Monument—large four story Indian ruins south of Phoenix; Montezuma Castle National Monument—an Indian cliff dwelling; the Pipe Spring National Monument—a nineteenth-century Mormon fort; Tonto National Monument—well-preserved cliff dwellings high above Roosevelt Lake; Tuzigoot National Monument—a large ruin looking down on the Verde River valley; the Walnut Canyon National Monument—sandstone cliff dwellings in a canyon near Flagstaff; Wupatki National Monument—the tallest, largest, and probably the most influential pueblo 800 years ago; Alamo Lake State Park—a distant, desert lake in central Arizona; and Tonto Natural Bridge State Park—the largest travertine bridge in the world.

New Mexico also features numerous historical sites that demonstrate the ancient Southwest, such as the Aztec Ruins National Monument—a large twelfth-century walled settlement; the Bandelier National Monument—ancient dwellings carved into volcanic cliffs; and the Chaco Culture National Historical Park—a collection of Anasazi village ruins. Others focus on physical features of the state, including the Carlsbad Caverns National Park—probably the most famous cave system in the world; El Malpais National Monument—miles of black, twisted lava and other volcanic formations; El Morro National Monument—Ancestral Puebloan ruins and signatures, dates, and messages from Spanish travelers such as Juan Oñate, whose signature is prefaced by the Spanish phrase, "Pasó por aquí" ("Passed by here"); and the White Sands National Monument—spectacular dunes of pure white gypsum. Other scenic places are the Angel Peak National Recreation Area—badlands in the high desert, and the Bisti Badlands—a remote desert landscape.

Texas has fewer public lands than the other Southwestern states, despite its size. Most have been added to the national registry in recent years, such as the Amistad National Recreation Area—an artificial lake on the Rio Grande; Big Bend National Park—a large desert, canyon, and mountain wilderness in the bend of the Rio Grande; the Fort Davis National Historic Site—in the Davis Mountains of west Texas, and one of America's best surviving examples of the Indian War's frontier military post in the Southwest, where black Buffalo Soldiers were stationed; the Guadalupe Mountains National Park—a mountain range growing out of the Chihuahuan Desert; the Big Thicket National Preserve—in east Texas with eastern hardwood forests, Gulf coastal plains, and midwest prairies in one geographical location; the Lyndon B. Johnson National Historical Park—celebrating the life of Lyndon Johnson, the 36th President; Padre Island National Seashore—an eighty mile undeveloped beach along the Gulf of Mexico; and the San Antonio Missions National Historical Park—five Spanish missions (not including the Alamo) dating from 1718. Other important Texas sites include, the Big Bend Ranch State Park—a wilderness area west of Big Bend, Black Gap Wildlife Management Area—a large part of the Chihuahua desert east of Big Bend, Dinosaur Valley State Park—fossilized dinosaur tracks; the Enchanted Rock State Natural Area—a large granite batholith near Fredericksburg in the Texas Hill Country; the Lost Maples State Natural Area—featuring an isolated strand of Uvalde Bigtooth Maple and steep limestone canyons; Palmetto State Park—with exotic plants and a semitropical environment at the edge of the desert; and Pedernales Falls State Park—a scenic waterfall on the Pedernales River between Johnson City and Austin.

Besides Lake Mead, Nevada also shares major sites with other states including, the Death Valley National Park—shared with California, with the lowest point in the western hemisphere at 282 feet below sea level and with an average rainfall of only 1.96 inches a year, the driest place in North America; and Lake Tahoe—also shared with California, a major recreation lake surrounded by high mountains, no-

Backpackers in Big Bend National Park, Texas. Courtesy of the National Park Service.

table for its connection with the 1960 Winter Olympics at nearby Squaw Valley. Within the Nevada state borders are, the Great Basin National Park—created in 1986 and probably the least known National Park in the Southwest, with varied climate zones, caverns, a glacier, and the high desert Great Basin with its distinctive sage and the 13,063-foot Wheeler Peak; the Red Rock Canyon National Conservation Area—with its distinctive red cliffs and canyons just west of Las Vegas; the Ash Meadows National Wildlife Refuge—large springs at the edge of the Mojave Desert, and the Lunar Crater National Natural Landmark—featuring volcanic formations in a remote region. Important state parks in Nevada are the Cathedral Gorge State Park with eroded rock structures, caves, and ravines, and the Valley of Fire State Park with weathered red rock formations close to Lake Mead.

SKIING AND OTHER WINTER SPORTS

Despite the relative aridity of much of the Southwest, there are substantial mountain and forest areas for winter sports. Bordered on the west by the Sierra Nevada, Nevada tops the list of Southwestern states with good downhill ski areas and many other opportunities for winter sports. Around Lake Tahoe are many ski areas and resorts, and other ski areas include Incline Village, Diamond Peak, Las Vegas Ski, Mt. Rose, Heavenly, and for cross country, places like Spooner Lake. And, although Minnesota comes to mind when ice fishing is mentioned, Nevada is unique in the Southwest in being able to offer ice fishing in a few of its frozen mountain lakes.

The northern and mountainous portions of Arizona and New Mexico have ski areas that are open most, though not all, years. Cross-country skiing is not bound by the restrictions of downhill skiing, and depends largely on access to a good snow-covered landscape or roads. These Southwestern locations for downhill skiing compensate for their typically warmer southern latitudes with high elevations and cold-weather patterns that favor them with snow. Many of these ski areas also provide space to snowboard or snowslide. In New Mexico there are several, including one owned by the Apache Indian nation and aptly named Ski Apache. Others include Sandia Peak, Angel Fire, Sipapu, Ski Santa Fe, Taos, Red River, and Enchanted Forest. Downhill skiing in Arizona is found in several areas of the state. The Arizona Snowbowl, in the San Francisco Peaks northwest of Flagstaff has operated since 1938 and is one of the oldest ski areas in the Southwest. Thirty miles west of Flagstaff is the Williams Ski Area. Sunrise Park Resort in the northeastern side of the state is owned and run by the White Mountain Apache tribe, and Mt. Lemmon, the southernmost ski area in the United States, is in the Santa Catalina Mountains near Tucson. Commercial cross-country ski areas can be found around the state as well, in several locations in the region surrounding Flagstaff.

Texas has no commercial ski areas.

FISHING AND HUNTING

Fly-fishing, fishing from boats and piers, fishing along lake and stream banks, and even ice fishing in Nevada's high lakes are all practiced in the Southwest. The fish themselves are both fresh and saltwater varieties, with trout and bass fishing popular in streams and lakes and deep-sea fishing common in the Gulf of Mexico. States heavily regulate fishing activities and manage populations with fisheries and research. Many fishing clubs, organizations, and journals have online resources such as articles, databases, and discussion lists for sharing the vital statistics of the best spots and lures and the usual fish stories. Of particular interest in the Southwest are the operations on American Indian reservations. Several of them provide excellent sport fishing.

The White Mountain Apache Reservation in Arizona and the Pyramid Lake Paiute tribe Reservation in Nevada have special fisheries established to both protect their lakes and to encourage regulated tourism, but they are not regulated in the same way as on non-Indian lands. As independent nations they establish their own rules and policies. It is possible in Arizona, for example, to rent an entire lake for your exclusive use on the White Mountain Apache Reservation. Also, "the tribe has set aside certain Reservation waters for the management of high quality, trophy fisheries. Access is limited in these areas to provide visitors a trophy fishing experience," according to their official Web site.[19]

In Nevada, Pyramid Lake is a salty remnant of the prehistoric Lahontan Lake and was for many years a resort destination for trophy fishermen wanting to catch the famed Lahontan cutthroat trout. As the fish perched on the edge of extinction due to overfishing and decreasing lake water levels, the tribe took control of the fishery and have restored the population of both Lahontan cutthroat and the cui-ui lakesucker. In his article "Pyramid Lake Lahontans," Stephen Trafton wrote "In 1844, the explorer John Fremont's Paiute Indian hosts fed him trout 'as large as the Columbia salmon.' Pyramid's Lahontan cutthroat . . . grew to reported weights in excess of 60 pounds."[20] The ecosystem is not as easily regenerated as the lake's fish population, so until the Truckee River waters all flow into Pyramid Lake, the largest trout fly fishermen and fisherwomen will catch are going to be approximately eight pounds.

Most people concerned with the environment agree that a healthy environment is one in which predators remain. For example, this came on the heels of the infamous "Kaibab Affair" in which the Kaibab Plateau in Arizona was denuded of its predators, with a view toward leaving the deer and elk for human hunters. The rapid growth of the deer population soon lead to severe browse damage of the forest and starving deer. Although Leopold was not a part of that experiment, he took the lesson to heart and in 1933 published *Game Management*, a seminal work in the growing field of game and wildlife management.

Census figures show a general decline in the popularity of hunting, but it is still one of the more popular activities on public lands, as demonstrated in Table 2 and in the Resource Guide at the end of this chapter. Hunting and fishing are two of a number of sports that take land users deep into the land, far from roads. Mountain climbing, rock climbing, hiking and backpacking, kayaking, and travel by horse are also popular in park and forest areas. But most of the visitors to these wild areas rarely get more than a few yards from their cars. A small percentage of public land gets the lion's share of the travel as campgrounds, lodges, hotels, short nature trails, driving trails, scenic overlooks, and various concessions absorb most of the traffic. Traffic management, animal control, waste management, and law enforcement are major jobs for front-country foresters and rangers in popular recreational areas.

GROUP SPORTING EVENTS AND TEAM SPORTS

Many of the personal and occasionally solitary recreational activities already listed are holdover activities of the Southwest's pioneer past. Traveling on foot or by horseback, fishing and hunting for subsistence, camping, and skills with animals were once necessary for survival. In modern times, increasing leisure time has allowed these activities to evolve into the present-day events that are frequently the basis of competitions, such as rodeo, cutting horse competitions, and livestock shows.

Rodeos and Stock Shows

What would the Southwest be without the old-fashioned cowboy events? Ranching has been an operation in the west ever since Europeans set foot there and Indians started catching their escaped horses. The Southwest is a region known the world round for its cowboys and cowgirls who work in the cattle and livestock industries, many of whom also rodeo. But these events are so popular that they are no longer exclusively associated with ranching. Horses are ridden for pleasure in urban areas as well as rural, and they are bred and trained for pleasure riding, ranch work (such as cutting horses), and rodeo competitions. They are also used in a growing number of therapeutic programs for children with disabilities. These four states host various competitions for dressage and cutting horses and hold many Professional Rodeo and Cowboy Association (PRCA)–sanctioned rodeos in a year-round operation, thanks to indoor arenas. American Indian and African American

Cowboys at the rodeo in Arizona. Courtesy of Getty Images/PhotoDisc.

rodeos, as well as occasional *charreada* (Mexican rodeo) are found in all four states. Other competitions like these can be found at each state's state fair and at livestock shows such as the Southwestern Exposition and Livestock Show in Fort Worth, Texas, and the Arizona National Livestock Show in Phoenix. Nevada hosts a Junior Livestock Show for 4-H and Future Farmers of America (FFA) participants, and at the New Mexico State Fair the horse and livestock shows are rolled all into the one event. Some livestock events have come under increasing criticism for injury to animals. This is particularly true of rodeo and charreada, in which horses can be tripped in a number of events. Sports and ethical behavior have come a long way in preventing injuries in athletics, whether the players have four legs or two.

Company Teams and Municipal Sponsorship of Sports

Sports in the Southwest in the years following the European movement onto the continent are notable for both the variety of games and activities introduced and the transformation of those games and activities in the years that followed as different cultures gained dominance in any given region. Sometimes a sport simply vanished, in other instances it matured under pressure. Games such as baseball were introduced in company towns throughout the West for a variety of reasons. First and foremost, they kept men busy in their spare time. Leagues encouraged disparate groups to work as a cohesive unit on the field of play. One must make note of some important intermediate sports developments when approaching the main competitive sports as they exist today. In particular, there is a major but often overlooked period in the development of company teams and leagues of the early twentieth century. Some company and community teams were established not just for the purpose of recreation but also as a tool toward socialization into mainstream culture in the United States. As is typical with a plan with a single goal (develop more Americanized workers) there were unintended consequences—ardent national pride among immigrant workers and the beginnings of what amounted to a minor league pool of players to be drafted into the major league sports. This is historical territory occupied by migrant workers, agribusiness and mining companies, and the birth of labor unions. For the owners of mines, agricultural industries, and other big businesses who wanted to instill a solid work ethic in their labor force, sport was a powerful tool. When labor problems in the early twentieth century conflicted with employer goals of maintaining a stable workforce, employers began to institute "social welfare programs to win over worker's loyalty."[21] One program that was widely promoted was industrial recreation, bringing baseball and other sports to the workers in many communities. In his article "Mexican American Baseball," a study of racial struggle and labor politics in Southern California, José Alamillo, outlines the pattern of sports sponsorship as it occurred across the Southwestern states in general:

> Before arriving in the United States, Mexicans had already been introduced to America's "national pastime" by U.S. railroad, agricultural, and mining companies during the Porfiriato, the thirty-four year period (1876–1910) of Porfiro Díaz's presidencies characterized by modernization such as the construction of railroads. During leisure hours, the Mexican National and the Mexican Central Railroad Companies organized baseball matches between Anglo supervisors and Mexican track laborers. By the late 1880s, baseball had gained popularity and spread to the border towns and Mexico City, where some of the first matches drew large crowds, convincing Porfirian liberals of the sport's potential to teach modern industrial values to the masses.[22]

Alamillo also states that "American employers hoped that skills and 'good sportsmanlike' habits learned on the playing field among Mexican employees would be channeled into higher productivity in the workplace and increased company loyalty."[23]

All the Southwestern states had their variations on this theme. In Nevada where the economy was heavily dependent on mining from 1849 forward, with the Comstock discovery in 1859 setting off a big rush in mining development. Much of what constituted sport in the early years of mining towns was harsh, such as dogfights and cockfights, which have long been outlawed. Most company towns by the late nineteenth or early twentieth centuries had settled into stable routines with baseball, wrestling, and boxing teams that were sponsored by the copper companies or the railroad. Following this trend, schools in the early twentieth century had both curricular and extracurricular sports activities, for boys and girls, including the new game of basketball. The value of these programs goes beyond forming good workers; they also contribute to good physical health, more cohesive communities, and lower crime rates.

To this day there is a general expectation that sports will be promoted in both physical education classes and as extracurricular activities in public schools and in city and county parks and recreation departments. Often, when high schools limit sports participation to those students who qualify to be on varsity-level teams, youths turn to municipalities for sports and recreation opportunities. Cities throughout the Southwest are developing recreation programs that can make serious inroads into preventing youth crime and gang activity. For example, a youth-at-risk program in Phoenix targets adolescent and preteen girls "with gender-specific programming designed to help them find positive personal and social fulfillment."[24] According to City of Phoenix park and library departments budget documents, the "Plan It" program brings in professional women basketball players from the Phoenix Mercury to "teach basketball skills to high school girls, who then operate a league for elementary school girls."[25] Fort Worth, Texas, invested millions of dollars and with the assistance of four city departments ran the "Comin' Up" program with the area Boys' Club. The Fort Worth late-night basketball program evolved because the park department and city council recognized the need for organized team sports for high-school-age teens and young adults. These late-night games are generally held in areas of town with concentrated minority populations and high numbers of at-risk youth and gang membership. As one Fort Worth police chief said of the program, "we can't arrest our way out of social problems."[26] Sports are not just a venue for play, they are a means for social change. Such is also the case for the early-to-mid-twentieth-century Negro League baseball teams.

MAJOR SPORTS

While cities and schools make athletic activities available to the general public, the scope of these programs and number of people they serve are not usually common knowledge in their communities. Far fewer athletes participate in collegiate and professional sports than the spectators who see them—in other words, professional sports are entertainment for the masses and only provide exercise for a few players. Professional sports teams today are multimillion-dollar businesses with complex funding, facilities, and sponsorship arrangements that are far removed from the simple Victorian-era beginnings

Negro League Baseball

Since as far back as 1884 African American athletes have played on professional baseball teams. Andrew "Rube" Foster (1897–1930), born in Calvert, Texas, was the founder of the Negro League and became a member of the Baseball Hall of Fame posthumously in 1981. He played on several teams in the north, pitching for the Chicago Union Giants and the Philadelphia Giants, and in 1903, as a pitcher, he won four games of what was called the Colored World Series.[27]

Willie Wells (1905–1989), another Texas Negro League player, was also elected to the Baseball Hall of Fame posthumously, in 1997. He played shortstop in sandlot baseball in Texas, where he was discovered and recruited to several northern teams. He also played in an integrated league in Cuba against both Cuban players and white players and in a similarly integrated league in Mexico.

During the years there were many attempts to form teams and leagues, and many of them failed, and the league had to be reformed season after season. An 1890 International League ban on African-American players was upheld six years later, along with many other segregationist policies, when the U.S. Supreme Court ruled in favor of the "separate by equal" doctrine that upheld a Louisiana segregation law in the infamous *Plessy vs. Ferguson* case. A few African-American teams did play against major league clubs.

Sometime after 1910 the Austin (Texas) Black Senators team was formed, and they played, in various leagues and team organizations, into the 1930s. They played for the Independent League, the Texas Negro League, and the Texas-Oklahoma Negro League, and often they played in exhibition games against black colleges in Texas (primarily the Texas A&M branch at Prairie View, Texas). In 1948 the Negro National League disbanded, and in 1952 the Negro American League also disbanded, after many of its former players were drafted onto the now-integrated teams of organized baseball.

of professional teams, when sponsorship meant that a company provided matching uniforms and perhaps a field on which to play.

Golf

As demonstrated above, sports vary from state to state according to both economic and population demographics, and golf, important in the Southwest, is dominant in Arizona, a state that is established as a major retirement destination. Although Arizona has an even larger percentage of federal and government-held lands than New Mexico, which limits the tax base, the retirees moving there bring retirement income and are largely focused on golf, a sport that benefits from private-sector investment. This relatively small state has more than 275 golf courses, according to the Arizona Chamber of Commerce. The chamber further boasts that "the depth of Arizona's love affair with golf is seen on worldwide television every January on Super Bowl Sunday. That is the final round of The Phoenix Open, which attracts more than 400,000 avid annual fans—the largest PGA gallery in the world—including those fun-seekers doing the "wave" on the infamous 16th hole."[28] Neighboring Nevada, with over one hundred golf courses, promotes heavily to attract out-of-town players but is well-suited to grooming local talent like Patty Sheehan (1956–), an LPGA Hall of Famer. New Mexico has a growing reputation for fine golf courses and fine young golfers, notable among them is Notah Begay III, of the Dine (Navajo) and San Felipe and Isleta (Pueblo) nations. In 1995, his first year as a professional, Begay earned more than $1 million in tournament winnings.

Babe Didrickson Zaharias. Courtesy of Photofest.

While golf may not be as flamboyantly popular as football in Texas, there are more than eight hundred golf courses to be found around the state. Many famous players hail from Texas, including Ben Hogan (1912–1997), Lee Trevino (1939–), Don January (1929–), and Byron Nelson (1912–). One of Texas' most enduring sports legends of all time is golfer Babe Didrikson Zaharias.

Mildred "Babe" Didrikson, (1911–1956), who could swing a baseball bat like the Sultan of Swat she was nicknamed for, was not only the best woman athlete of her day, she was the best American athlete of her day. This Port Arthur, Texas, native excelled in several sports at the state level and was a 1932 Olympic track and field gold medallist in javelin and hurdles. She would have won gold for the high jump if she hadn't been disqualified for going head first over the bar, which wasn't allowed in her day. Deciding on professional golf as a lucrative sport that would help support her large family, she won many tournaments around the world and helped found the Ladies Professional Golf Association (LPGA).

Football

The Arizona Cardinals football team was originally established as the Morgan Athletic Club in Chicago in 1898. After several name changes and moves, the team moved to Phoenix in 1988. Since then they have played their games in Arizona State University's Sun Devil Stadium, although a 2000 bond vote approved funds for a new stadium, the Tostitos Fiesta Bowl, which is expected to open in 2005. In 1997, the Cardinals drafted Arizona State star quarterback Jake Plummer, and in 1998, Plummer led Arizona to its first playoff berth.

Texas is the home of the Dallas Cowboys, a team that began as an expansion franchise in the National Football League (NFL) in 1960, with Tom Landry as their first coach. Their history includes playing in eight Super Bowls and winning four of them. Hall of Fame members from the Cowboys include Tony Dorsett, Tom Landry, Bob Lilly, Mel Renfro, Roger Staubach, Tex Schramm, and Randy White. The Houston Texans is Houston's expansion team, inaugurated in 2002, after the Houston Oilers moved to Tennessee and became the Titans. The Houston Oilers began in 1960 as one of the original six franchises in the newly formed American Football League (AFL) under longtime owner K. S. "Bud" Adams, who selected the name Oilers for his Houston franchise. In the first AFL draft the Oilers made Billy Cannon, who won the Heisman Trophy his senior year at Louisiana State University, their first pick. Cannon gave instant credibility to the Oilers and the entire league. The Oilers won the first game they played at the Astrodome in 1968.

In 1975 Adams hired O. A. "Bum" Phillips as the team's tenth head coach. Among the best-known Oilers during the period were Billy "White Shoes" Johnson and Heisman Trophy winner Earl Campbell from the University of Texas. Warren Moon, who played for the Houston Oilers from 1984–1993, and Steve McNair, who has been with the franchise since 1995, have proven that black quarterbacks could be successful and reach All-Pro status in the NFL. The franchise moved to Tennessee in 1997. The Houston Texans began playing in 2002 in the Reliant Energy Stadium, with Dom Capers as the coach and former Fresno State star David Carr at quarterback, and they became the first expansion team in forty-one years to win their opener, stunning state rival the Dallas Cowboys.

Baseball

Major League Baseball was introduced to the region in 1962 when the Houston Colt .45s began play. In 1965, the team changed its name to the Astros and began to play in the Astrodome, the world's first multipurpose, domed stadium, which came to symbolize the future of professional sports venues in America. The Astros moved out of the Astrodome into Enron Field in 1999, renamed Minute Maid Park after Enron's collapse. Among the notable players include Rusty Staub, Joe Morgan, Nolan Ryan, Jose Cruz, and its most durable players of the 1990s, Jeff Bagwell and Craig Biggio. In 2004 the Astros lured famed pitcher Roger Clemens out of a short retirement to pitch in his home state.

Texas gained another Major League franchise when the Washington Senators moved to Arlington, Texas, in 1971 and became the Texas Rangers. The Rangers' most famous player has been Nolan Ryan. In 1989, Ryan became the first pitcher to record five thousand strikeouts; in 1991, at the age of 44, he became the oldest pitcher to throw a no-hitter. Ryan was elected to the Baseball Hall of Fame in 1999.

The Arizona Diamondbacks are new in Arizona as of 1998 after their expansion draft in 1997. This new team shot to the top quickly, winning the 2001 World Series against the New York Yankees and setting a record for taking the shortest time of any expansion team to win the Series. Team players of note include pitcher Randy Johnson, who won his fourth Cy Young award in 2001, and pitcher Curt

Arizona Diamondbacks celebrate defeating the New York Yankees 3-2 in Game 7 of the World Series, Sunday November 4, 2001, at Bank One Ball Park in Phoenix. At center foreground is Diamondbacks' Steve Finley © AP/Wide World Photos.

ABC sportscaster Bob Uecker and Nolan Ryan, 1979. Courtesy of Photofest.

Schilling. Johnson and Schilling were co-winners of the 2001 World Series Most Valuable Player Award.

Basketball

The Houston Rockets, originally a San Diego team, moved to Houston in 1967 after four disappointing years in California. They moved to Houston at a time of great expansion within the National Basketball Association and floundered for a few years as they established themselves in Texas. By the 1980–1981 season they made it to the playoffs but were defeated in the championship series against the Boston Celtics. They returned to the playoffs again in 1985 and 1986, then after several down years won the championship in 1994 against the New York Knicks, repeating the win in 1995 against the Orlando Magic.

In 2004 a new Southwestern Division went into effect in the Western Conference, and the Houston Rockets moved into that division, as did the Dallas Mavericks.

The Southwest is able to support several professional basketball franchises. Arizona's professional basketball passion is centered around the Phoenix Suns and the Phoenix Mercury basketball teams. The Suns began playing in the 1968–1969 season. The first player selected in the 1968 expansion draft was Dick Van Arsdale, who also happened to score the first point in the team's first game and who still works for the team. The Mercury, established in 1997, is one of fourteen teams in the Women's National Basketball Association.

The San Antonio Spurs arrived in San Antonio in 1973 with their tails between

Hakeem Olajuwon. Courtesy of Photofest.

their legs after five lackluster years as the Dallas Chaparrals (and briefly as the Texas Chaparrals) of the American Basketball Association. Their draw was so poor that at their last Dallas game they had just 134 paid seats occupied in the audience. The turnaround in the team was immediate, and in their first year they finished the season in second place in the Western Division. In 1999 and 2003 the Spurs finally came out on top, winning the championship by beating the New York Knicks and the New Jersey Nets, respectively. The Dallas Mavericks were formed in 1980 when the National Basketball Association owners voted in this new Texas franchise. This team was not the first to play in Dallas; from 1967 until 1972 the Chaparrals were the resident American Basketball Association team there. The Women's National Basketball Association is represented in the Southwest by the Phoenix Mercury, the Houston Comets, and the San Antonio Stars. All three were established in 1997.

Hockey

Rounding out the big four of sports are the National Hockey League teams. Arizona is home to the Phoenix Coyotes, a team that moved to Phoenix in 1996 after many years as the Winnipeg Jets. New Mexico has one minor league hockey team, the New Mexico Scorpions. Texas is the home state to winners of the 1999 Stanley Cup, the Dallas Stars. Dallas saw professional hockey action beginning in 1941: the Texans played on the rink at Dallas Fair Park, first under the American Hockey Association, then the United States Hockey League. In 1947 the Texans became the farm team for the powerful Montreal Canadiens. Professional hockey left Dallas in 1950 when a new hockey league under development failed to materialize. The present professional hockey team, the Stars, arrived in Dallas in 1993. Texas also has several minor league hockey clubs, including the Austin Ice Bats, the Amarillo Rattlers, the Fort Worth Brahmas, the Lubbock Cotton Kings, the Odessa Jackalopes, and the San Angelo Outlaws.

This rough outline of the professional teams in the Southwest will serve for some as a mere footnote to the sport that really counts in the region: high school football.

AMATEUR SPORTS

If one asks the question "why are Texans crazy about football, while in New Mexico high school and college basketball are all the rage, Arizonians are most interested in golf, and Nevadans are particularly fond of motor sports?" the answer might be as simple as "political boundaries." State lines and something within the character and population size of each state keeps Southwesterners and their visitors from becoming a homogenous group of fans and sports participants. In *Pigskin Pulpit*, Ty Cashion's 1998 examination of high school football coaches in Texas, he suggests that, for example, Texans' love of high school football has to do with the culture in coaching and the resulting roles coaches played in popular culture. "High school football in Texas emerged during the twentieth century as one of the state's identifying institutions, a pastime shaped in the image of its coaches."[30] Friday night football is akin to a religion in small towns across this state that has a large and diverse population and a tax base to support extracurricular high school sports. In Arizona and New Mexico, smaller states with much smaller populations, the recreational balance tips in favor of different sports. Football gear is expensive and managing league play is a major operation undertaken in Texas by the University Interscholastic League (UIL). Youthful athletes in a poorer state, like New Mexico, where the high percentage of government land skews state tax revenues, may choose a sport based on economics—every kid can have a hoop and a basketball and most schools have gymnasiums. Hence, the indigenous population grew up with the more egalitarian and easily sustainable sport of basketball. Arizona has an even larger percentage of federal and government-held lands to limit the tax base, but as a major retirement destination, the interest in recreational sports by those moving into the state with retirement income veered toward golf, a sport that benefits from a great deal of private sector investment. Nevada is a law unto itself, with the powerful influence of odds-makers in the gambling community, and the continual interest within both the state and the gambling busi-

Sun Devil Stadium in Tempe, Arizona, 2003. © Dave G. Houser/Corbis.

nesses to attract visitors with new and innovative sports and recreational opportunities—everything from the big shows of Las Vegas to indoor skydiving.

Football fans can love or hate their favorite teams' coaches, but when a really exceptional coach like Gordon Wood (1914–2003) comes along, fans take notice and pour their hearts into supporting him. At the time of his death Wood was "the second-winningest high school football coach in Texas football history and one of the top five nationally . . . Gordon was a truly a legend and one of a kind in a state that prides itself on its caliber of football," according to Dave Campbell, publisher since 1960 of the annual *Dave Campbell's Texas Football*, a longtime sports editor of the *Waco Tribune-Herald*, and a member of the Texas Sports Hall of Fame. "Football is the unofficial religion of Texas."[31]

In Wood's forty-five-year coaching career, his teams at Brownwood and Stamford won a total of nine state championships between 1955 and 1981, and he retired with a record 396 wins. Among the honors Wood received were memberships in the Texas Sports Hall of Fame, the National High School Hall of Fame, and the Big Country Hall of Fame. In 1999 the *Dallas Morning News* named him the Coach of the Century.[32] For many of those players, that success they made of themselves was through winning scholarships to play football in college.

"The possibilities of player recruitment and scholarships to college teams are excellent for young men from this state," according to Dave Campbell. He has written of Texans' passion for football that, while popular throughout the Southwest, is number one in Texas. The Texas high school program develops such powerful athletes that coaches and recruiters travel to Texas from around the country in search of players. In an interview with Campbell, coach Randy Rogers, recruiting coordinator at the University of Texas from 1992 to 1997, said that in the most recent season prominent recruiters from universities in Wisconsin, Michigan, Illinois, Oklahoma, Louisiana, Mississippi, and Florida made extended trips to Texas communities to offer players scholarships. According to Rogers, high school coaches help their players strategize by encouraging them to apply to several universities of their choice, so that if the highly coveted Division 1 scholarship is not offered, access to another program, and eventually a scholarship, is possible.

However, Texas is not alone in having larger-than-life popular high school coaches. Jack Rushing (1915–2003), a member of the Creek Nation, was a much-honored "old school" teacher and coach in Albuquerque, New Mexico. Rushing was an Oklahoma native who was that state's amateur heavyweight boxing champion in 1938 before he moved to New Mexico. As a tackle on the University of New Mexico football team he was the first American Indian to earn All-Border Conference honors in 1938 and 1939. After graduating with a degree in history and physical education, Rushing taught and coached baseball, football, wrestling, tennis, and track at Albuquerque High School, beginning in the 1940s. Later he coached and was athletic director at Highland High School. Rushing's teams won eight state titles, and in recognition of all his sports contributions, Rushing was inducted into five halls of fame. "Jack Rushing was from the old school era of the do-it-all, no-nonsense kind of coach" remembered *Albuquerque Journal* staff writer Paul Logan.[33] Today, if high school coaches don't have the background to "do it all," then the interscholastic associations most schools belong to, do.

Each state in the Southwest has at least one governing body that oversees interscholastic sports competitions. Membership is voluntary, but all these interscholastic associations have wide participation from schools. In Arizona the body is the Arizona Interscholastic Association, and in New Mexico schools may participate through the New Mexico Activities Association. Schools in Texas compete on the terms established by the University Interscholastic League, while the Nevada Interscholastic Activities Association governs many students in that state. The ubiquitous 1a (1–200 students) through 5a (1900 or more students) rankings apply.

Each state has many sporting and athletic competitions in addition to football. Among other options are badminton, baseball, basketball, cross-country, dance, golf, gymnastics, soccer, softball, swimming and diving, tennis, track and field, wrestling, and volleyball. Additionally, scholastic competitions such as academic decathlon, chess, band, debate, and speech have statewide competitions. The Texas UIL "offers the most comprehensive literary and academic competitive program in the nation, with 22 high school and 18 elementary and junior high contests. More than a half million students participate in UIL academic contests."[34]

A word on college athletics: Like its high school and professional counterparts, college sport is a large and important field, with oversight by the National Collegiate Athletic Association (NCAA). A list of regional university athletics programs can be found in the Resource Guide at the end of this chapter.

URBAN RECREATION

Despite the popular early twentieth-century imagery of poets, such as T. S. Eliot in his remarkable poem "The Waste Land," and popular novels like F. Scott Fitzgerald's *The Great Gatsby*, most American cities are not fetid landscapes; they are simply busy places with lots of concrete and crowding. Moreover, cities in the Southwest rarely fit the stereotypical mold cast in novels and cinema; of small-parched spots of pioneer activity surrounded by a cactus-studded wilderness. Instead, many large Southwestern cities provide green spaces for vigorous outdoor activities in modified forms (such as fishing in urban lakes and rivers, hiking in parks, bird watching in neighborhoods, biking along abandoned railroad tracks, skateboard parks, rock climbing, swimming pools, and water sports.). These cities have enough open space to be able to provide a natural experience for these activities, and more people will participate in these city activities than will ever do them in federal or state wilderness areas far from home.

Beyond the presence of sporting facilities in Southwestern cities and their suburbs, in schools and city recreation facilities, there is a lot of nature and wildlife recreation with in these heavily populated regions. Urban nature recreation might seem an oxymoronic idea to some, but nature doesn't stop at the city limits, and more city park and recreation departments are making the most of their urban landscapes with parks, long connected interurban trails, botanical gardens, zoos, and nature centers. Often these enterprises cross many boundaries and agencies, such as the Pony Express Trail in Nevada, the Continental Divide Trail from Canada to Mexico that runs through New Mexico, or the Trinity Trails project in North Texas, which involves the cities of Fort Worth and Dallas and many smaller cities in between, as they link their trial systems along the Trinity River. Branches of the trail stretch to the north to reach the Okalahoma border, and the Trinity River Greenway is possible due to participation by the U.S. Army Corps of Engineers, the Trinity River Authority, numerous Texas counties and small municipalities, and more than a few private landowners. The result is hundreds of miles of trails (http://www.dfwinfo.com/envir/trin/outdoor/ttfact.html) to travel by foot, bicycle, or on horseback. Many major cities in the Southwest have similar urban trail systems.

Large tracts of open land and landscaped and cultivated city parks are magnets for nature, and city dwellers are drawn to these oases of wilderness in growing numbers. One category in the Fishing, Hunting, and Wildlife Survey cited in the table on page 389 showed that millions of Southwest residents actively view or feed "home" wildlife, those animals and birds within a mile of their homes. Just as there are specialized sporting goods stores, there are specialized wildlife businesses, selling feeders, food, identification materials, and landscaping materials, bringing the nature to the cityscape.

CONCLUSION

Sports and recreation are multibillion dollar-a-year industries just in these four states alone. This chapter has covered a history of sports and recreation in the American Southwest, from ancient ritual games through the development of important philosophical developments regarding the health of the land and its recreational use. The discussion has touched on many types of games and types of land on which sports and recreation take place, as well as the many commercial sporting teams in the region. Whether in pursuit of outdoor recreation or indoor sporting events, residents of and visitors to the American Southwest place great value on this nebulous thing called recreation. To reprise Aldo Leopold, "few enterprises are undertaken with such abandon or by such diverse individuals, as that group of avocations known as . . . recreation."[35] The growth of the sunbelt demonstrates that the region draws people both because of its appeal as a place for personal recreation, and because of the diversity and reach of the organized sports. The words "Play ball," and "Let the game begin," will continue to ring across the Southwest.

RESOURCE GUIDE

Printed Sources

Abbey, Edward. *Desert Solitaire: A Season in the Wilderness.* New York: Ballantine Books, 1971.

Abstracts, Congress on Recreation and Resource Capacity. 1999, Colorado State University Published online at http://www.cnr.colostate.edu/nrrt/capacity/boa.pdf.

Alamillo, José M. "Mexican American Baseball: Masculinity, Racial Struggle, and Labor Politics in Southern California, 1930–1950." In *Sports Matters: Race, Recreation, and Culture,* edited by John Bloom and Michael Nevin Willard, 86–115. New York: New York University Press, 2002.

Bissinger, H. G. *Friday Night Lights: A Town, a Team, and a Dream.* New York: HarperCollins, 1990.

Cashion, Ty. *Pigskin Pulpit: A Social History of Texas High School Football Coaches.* Austin: Texas State Historical Association, 1998.

Cayleff, Susan. *Babe: The Life and Legend of Babe Didrikson Zaharias.* Urbana: University of Illinois Press, 1995.

Coleman, Annie Gilbert. "The Unbearable Whiteness of Skiing." *In Sports Matters: Race, Recreation, and Culture*, edited by John Bloom and Michael Nevin Willard, 141–168. New York: New York University Press, 2002.

Crown, Patricia L., and W. James Judge. *Chaco and Hohokam: Prehistoric Regional Systems in the American Southwest*. Santa Fe: School of American Research Press, 1991.

Day, Jane S. "The Mesoamerican Ballgame." Denver: Denver Museum of Natural History, 1992. http://linux.tlc.north.denver.k12.co.us/~gmoreno/gmoreno/Mesoamerican_Ballgame.html.

Duran, Diego. *Book of the Gods and Rites and the Ancient Calendar*. Reprint, Norman: University of Oklahoma Press, 1977. The writings of Fray Diego Duran (1537–1588).

Gent, Pete. *North Dallas Forty*. New York: Morrow, 1973.

Jenkins, Dan. *Semi-Tough*. New York: Signet, 1977.

Leopold, Aldo. *Game Management*. New York: Charles Scribner's Sons, 1933.

———. *A Sand County Almanac*. New York: Ballentine, 1949.

———. "The Wilderness and Its Place in Forest Recreational Policy." In *The River of the Mother of God and Other Essays*, edited by J. Baird and Susan Flader Callicott, 78–81. Madison: University of Wisconsin Press, 1921.

McMurtry, Larry. *The Last Picture Show*. New York: Simon and Schuster, 1966.

Meine, Curt. *Aldo Leopold: His Life and Work*. Madison: University of Wisconsin Press, 1988.

National Park Foundation. *Complete Guide to America's National Parks: Official Visitors Guide of the National Park Foundation*. 11th ed. New York: Fodor's, 2001.

Noble, David. *The Hohokam: Ancient People of the Desert*. Santa Fe: School of American Research Press, 1990.

Scarborough, Vernon L. and David Wilcox. *The Mesoamerican Ballgame*. Tucson: University of Arizona Press, 1991.

Shipnuck, Alan. *Bud, Sweat and Tees: A Walk on the Wild Side of the PGA Tour*. Simon and Schuster, 2001.

Sherrington, Kevin. "Always in the Game: Football, Gordon Wood Style, Still Absorbs Coach of Century." *Dallas Morning News*, November 17, 1999, Sports Day, 1B.

"Sports." In *Texas Handbook Online*. Austin: Texas Historical Association, 2002.

Sharp, Shane. "Reservation Courses Scoring Big with Valley Golfers." *GolfArizona.com*. Tucson: Travel Golf Media, 2004. http://www.golfarizona.com/

Trafton, Stephen. "Pyramid Lake Lahontans." *Fly Fisherman* 33, no. 2 (2004): 32.

U.S. Census Bureau, http://factfinder.census.gov.

Warren, Louis. *The Hunter's Game*. New Haven, CT: Yale University Press, 1997.

Witt, Peter A., and John L. Crompton, eds. *Recreation Programs That Work for At-Risk Youth: The Challenge of Shaping the Future*. Venture Publishing, 1996. (Book out of print, but complete text online at http://www.rpts.tamu.edu/Faculty/Witt/CasestudyBook.htm.)

Web Sites

History

Arizona Historical Society

The AHS has links to several major libraries in collections that include excellent images of sports teams. The collections are in Tucson, Tempe, and at the Cline Library Special Collections at Northern Arizona University in Flagstaff.

http://www.arizonahistoricalsociety.org/

(Only the Flagstaff portion of the collection is online as this book goes to press.)

Center for the History of Ancient American Art and Culture, University of Texas at Austin

This site includes links to museums, exhibits, archives, and publications about the ancient ball games.

http://www.utexas.edu/research/chaaac/index.html

Handbook of Texas Online

Texas has pulled many of its historical resources into one huge online guide. "The *Handbook of Texas Online* is a multidisciplinary encyclopedia of Texas history, geography, and culture sponsored by the Texas State Historical Association and the General Libraries at UT Austin."

http://www.tsha.utexas.edu/handbook/online/

Historical Society of New Mexico

This organization is involved with many aspects of state history and provides links and access to museum resources. Sports information and photos may be obtained here.

http://www.hsnm.org/

Nevada Department of Cultural Affairs

This organization maintains a Web site with links to the Division of Museums History and the State Library and Archives and other sites with historic information. The Nevada Historical Society has many early images of company towns and company sports teams.

http://dmla.clan.lib.nv.us/

Online Archive of New Mexico

This "is a single, integrated source for searching and navigating finding aids to archival collections. These finding aids contain descriptive information about archives and manuscript collections housed at research institutions in New Mexico." Sports information may be found here.

http://elibrary.unm.edu/oanm/

Trinity Trails

This is "a continuous public-access recreation corridor with a multi-use trail along the Trinity River Corridor in North Central Texas and northward to the Red River," the border between Texas and Oklahoma.

http://www.dfwinfo.com/envir/outdoor/ttfact.html

Wupakti National Monument, National Park Service

For information and images of ball courts at the monument.

http://www.nps.gov/wupa/

High School Sports Resources

Arizona Interscholastic Association
http://www.aiaonline.org/

Dave Campbell's Texas Football
High school pages may be found at

http://www.texasfootball.com/highschool.asp

Nevada Interscholastic Activities Association
http://nevada.ihigh.com/

New Mexico Activities Association
http://www.nmact.org/

Texas—University Interscholastic League
http://www.uil.utexas.edu/

Barry Sollengerger's Phoenix Metro Football Magazine

This publication and Web site are "a popular recruiting tool for colleges in the western United States, with Arizona's population boom and storied sports past. Since 1990, close to 100 former Arizona high school students have moved on to play in the National Football League."

http://www.phoenixmetrofootball.com/

Public Outdoor Sports and Recreation

Arizona Game and Fish Department
http://www.gf.state.az.us/h_f/hf_resources.html

Arizona State Parks
Thirty state parks, historic areas, and natural areas.
http://www.pr.state.az.us/

Arizona White Mountain Apache
Wildlife and Outdoor Recreation Division
http://162.237.6/wmatod/index.htm

Cabeza Prieta Wildlife Refuge
http://Southwest.fws.gov/refuges/arizona/cabeza.html

Nevada Department of Wildlife
http://www.ndow.org/

Nevada Pyramid Lake Paiute Tribe
Fisheries information
http://www.pyramidlakefisheries.org/

Nevada State Parks
Twenty-four parks in the system.
http://parks.nv.gov/

New Mexico Department of Game and Fish
http://www.gmfsh.state.nm.us/

New Mexico State Parks
Thirty-one parks in the system.
http://www.emnrd.state.nm.us/nmparks/

Texas Parks and Wildlife Department
A total of one hundred and twenty parks and historic sites in the system.
http://www.tpwd.state.tx.us/

U.S. Census Bureau
This site contains the Fishing Hunting and Wildlife Associated Recreation (FHWAR) survey.
http://www.census.gov/prod/www/abs/fishing.html

Wilderness Act
Full text of the 1964 act.
http://www.fs.fed.us/htnf/wildact.htm

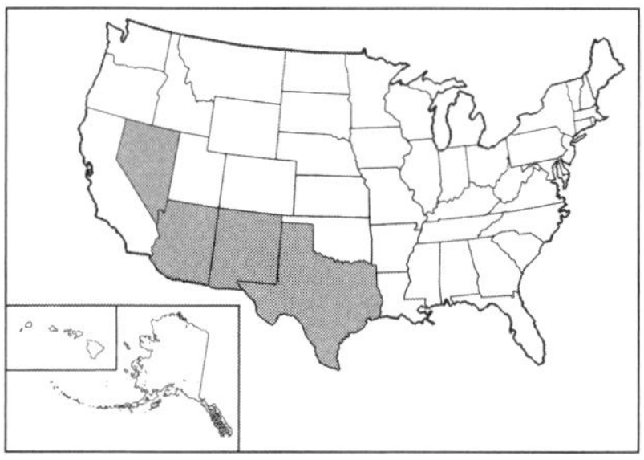

TIMELINE

c. 25000 B.C.E.	Sandia people demonstrate evidence of human existence in area that is now New Mexico.
c. 10000–9000 B.C.E.	Clovis hunters search for mammoth, bison, and other game.
c. 9000–8000 B.C.E.	Folsom people flourish throughout Southwest toward end of the last ice age.
2000 B.C.E.	Indians introduce agriculture to Arizona.
c. 1000–500 B.C.E.	Cochise people cultivate corn, squash, and beans.
1–700 C.E.	Anasazi basketmakers create baskets, clothing, sandals, and utensils.
300–1400 C.E.	Mogollon culture produces highly artistic pottery and early architecture in the form of pit houses.
700–1300 C.E.	Chaco Canyon civilization (Anasazis) develops.
1200–1500s C.E.	Along the Rio Grande and its tributaries, Pueblo Indians establish villages.
1200 C.E.	Hopi village of Oraibi is founded. May be oldest continuously inhabited American town.
1492	Columbus lands in the Bahamas.
1519	Explorer Alonso Alvarez de Piñeda explores and maps the Texas coastline.
1521	Cortés plunders Aztec empire.
1534	In captivity since their shipwreck on Texas coast near Galveston in 1528, Cabeza de Vaca, Estevan the Moor, and two others escape and begin journey across Texas.

1536	Cabeza de Vaca reaches Culiacan, Mexico, after possibly crossing Texas and what is now southern New Mexico, and begins rumors of the Seven Cities of Cíbola.
1539	Fray Marcos de Niza and Estevan lead expedition to find Cíbola and reach the Zuni village of Hawikuh, where Estevan is killed, then de Niza claims Arizona for Spain.
1540s	Francisco Vasquez de Coronado explores SW. De Cardenas discovers Grand Canyon.
1598	Juan de Oñate establishes the first Spanish capital of San Juan de los Caballeros at the Tewa village of Ohke north of present-day Española.
1600	San Gabriel, second capital of New Mexico, is founded at the confluence of the Rio Grande and the Chama River.
1605	Oñate expedition to the Colorado River; visits El Morro, leaves message on Inscription Rock.
1608	Oñate removed as governor of New Mexico and sent to Mexico City to be tried for mistreatment of the Indians.
1609–10	New governor Pedro de Peralta establishes a new capital at Santa Fe. Construction begins on the Palace of the Governors. Gaspar de Villagrá publishes epic history on the founding of New Mexico.
1620s	The Woman in Blue, María de Agreda, supposedly visits the Jumanos in West Texas to instruct them in Christianity.
1626	Spanish Inquisition begins in New Mexico.
1680	Pueblo Indian revolt. Spanish survivors flee to El Paso del Norte.
Late 1600s	Navajos, Apaches, and Comanches begin raids against Pueblo Indians.
1685	La Salle erects Fort Saint-Louis and begins exploration of Texas interior.
1692	Father Kino starts work and founds Guevavi mission.
1700	San Xavier del Bac mission (White Dove of the Desert) is founded.
1706	Villa de Albuquerque founded.
1749	La Bahía is moved to Goliad, Texas.
1776	A *presidio* (fort) is built at Tucson.
1807	Zebulon Pike leads first Anglo-American expedition into New Mexico. Publishes account of way of life in New Mexico upon return to the United States.
1821	Mexican independence achieved. Mexican President Agustín Iturbidé grants Moses Austin land on the Brazos River in Texas. Mexico declares independence from Spain. Santa Fe Trail is opened to international trade.

1825 As part of his Snake River expedition, Peter Skene Ogden becomes first white man in Nevada.

1828 First major gold discovery in Southwest is made in Ortiz Mountains south of Santa Fe.

1834 Captain John C. Frémont names Pyramid Lake, thirty miles northeast of the present-day city Reno, also becoming first white man to see Lake Tahoe.

1836 Texas declares independence from Mexico at convention at Washington-on-the-Brazos, Fall of the Alamo (March 6), and Battle of San Jacinto (April 21).

1841 Santa Fe Expedition, Texas soldiers invade New Mexico and claim all land east of the Rio Grande.

1842 Mier Expedition to Mexico, black bean episode—captured Texans are forced to draw bean; those who select black bean are killed.

1845 Texas is annexed by United States.

1846 U.S.-Mexican War begins. Stephen Watts Kearny annexes New Mexico to the United States. The Donner Party delays their journey too long in the Truckee Meadows near the present-day city of Reno, Nevada, later trapped in the heavy snows of the Sierra Nevada, engage in cannibalism to survive the winter, forty-seven out of eighty-seven die.

1848 Treaty of Guadalupe Hidalgo ends U.S.-Mexican War. Discovery of gold in California begins the gold rush. Nevada Truckee River and Meadows becomes a rest stop for settlers to California.

1849 Over 22,500 settlers pass through the Truckee Meadows, then 45,000 in 1850, and up to 52,000 in 1852.

1850 New Mexico (which included present-day Arizona, southern Colorado, southern Utah, and southern Nevada) is designated a territory but denied statehood.

1854 The Gadsden Purchase from Mexico adds 45,000 square miles to the territory.

1854 Copper is discovered in Arizona.

1857 First stagecoach runs in Arizona.

1858 Gold is discovered on Gila River.

1861 Texas secedes from the Union and enters the Confederacy. Confederates invade New Mexico from Texas. The Confederate Territory of Arizona is declared with the capital at La Mesilla. Territory of Colorado is created.

1862 Battles of Velarde de and Glorieta Pass end Confederate occupation of New Mexico. Chief Cochise and Apaches attack soldiers at Apache Pass in Arizona, beginning decade-long war with settlers.

1863–68	In what is known as the Long Walk, Navajos and Apaches are relocated to Bosque Redondo in New Mexico; finally allowed to return to their homelands after thousands die of disease and starvation.
1863	New Mexico is partitioned in half. Territory of Arizona is created with Prescott as capital.
1864	During the Civil War Nevada becomes thirty-sixth state; adopts state motto "Battle Born." Kit Carson captures approximately seven thousand Navajo in Canyon de Chelly and forces them to leave Arizona.
1865	Black Texans learn of their emancipation on "Juneteenth."
1869	John Wesley Powell explores the Grand Canyon by boat.
1878	Railroad arrives in New Mexico, opening full-scale trade and migration. Lincoln County War erupts in southeast New Mexico.
1880	Phoenix becomes capital of Arizona Territory.
1881	Sheriff Pat Garrett shoots Billy the Kid in Fort Sumner, New Mexico.
1881	Railroad crosses Arizona.
1881	The gunfight at the O.K. Corral occurs.
1884	Sarah Winnemucca, daughter of Chief Winnemucca and the granddaughter of Chief Truckee, establishes Nevada's first school for Native Americans.
1886	Geronimo surrenders; Indian hostilities cease in the Southwest.
1898	First movie filmed in New Mexico, *Indian Day School* by Thomas A. Edison. Young American artists Ernest L. Blumenschein and Bert G. Phillips are forced to stop near Taos, New Mexico, when the wheel of their surrey breaks. The delay gives them time to become captivated by spectacular landscape and cultures of Taos valley.
1900	Galveston is devastated by hurricane.
1901	Oil is discovered on Spindletop.
1902	Owen Wister publishes *The Virginian.*
1903	Vitagraph Theater, the first movie house in Nevada, in Reno, opens.
1906	People of New Mexico and Arizona vote on issue of joint statehood, New Mexico in favor and Arizona against.
1911	Roosevelt Dam is completed.
1912	New Mexico is admitted to the Union as forty-seventh state. Arizona becomes the forty-eighth State with Phoenix as capital. Taos Society of Artists is founded; artists have been there and in Santa Fe since turn of the century.
1915	Plan de San Diego proclaimed.

1916 Pancho Villa raids Columbus, New Mexico. Georgia O'Keeffe first arrives in Southwest, teaching at West Texas State Normal College in Canyon, Texas.

1919 Grand Canyon National Park is founded.

1920 Adoption of the nineteenth Amendment gives women the right to vote.

1923–24 Oil is discovered on the Navajo Reservation.

1924 Vernon Dalhart records "The Wreck of the Old 97" considered the first country recording.

1925 Houston ship channel opens.

1930–43 During the Great Depression, federal New Deal funds provide employment for many and cause construction of numerous public buildings.

1931 Nevada governor Fred Balzar approves gambling bill. Bob Wills forms Light Crust Doughboys, with Milton Brown as singer.

1932 Texas unemployment rises to 350,000 to 400,000 people.

1936 Hoover Dam is completed. Alexandre Hogue, Lone Star regionalist painter with Jerry Bywaters and others, paints *Mother Earth Laid Bare*.

1939 John Ford's *Stagecoach* starring John Wayne is released.

1940 Jerry Bywaters completes *Oil-Field Girls*.

1942–45 Japanese capture New Mexico soldiers serving during World War II and force them to endure Bataan Death March. Navajo Codetalkers help end the war. Secret atomic laboratories established at Los Alamos, New Mexico.

1945 World's first atomic bomb is detonated at Trinity Site in southern New Mexico after its development at Los Alamos.

1946 T-Bone Walker records "Stormy Monday." Las Vegas' Flamingo Hotel is opened by Benjamin "Bugsy" Siegel.

1947 UFO allegedly crashes near Roswell, New Mexico; believers claim U.S. governew mexicoent engages in massive coverup of the incident.

1948 Native Americans win the right to vote in New Mexico elections.

1949 Herman Sweatt becomes first African American admitted to University of Texas Law School. Georgia O'Keeffe moves to Abiquiqui, New Mexico.

1950 Uranium is discovered near Grants, New Mexico.

1951 Atomic testing begins at the Nevada Proving Grounds.

1957 Buddy Holly records "Peggy Sue" at Norman Petty Studio in Clovis, New Mexico.

1959 On February 3, small plane crash kills Buddy Holly, Big Bopper, and Richie Valens.

1960 Marty Robbins releases "El Paso."

1964 Barry M. Goldwater, Senator from Arizona, runs for president but loses to Texas's Lyndon Johnson.

1966 Farm workers strike in Rio Grande valley in Texas and march on state capitol. New New Mexico state capitol, the "Roundhouse," is dedicated. *Bonnie and Clyde* released.

1968 London Bridge is moved to Lake Havasu City, Arizona. Congress authorizes Central Arizona Project to bring Colorado River water to Phoenix and Tucson.

1970 Armadillo World Headquarters in Austin opens October 4; Janis Joplin dies of drug overdose.

1971 Rudolfo Anaya publishes *Bless Me, Ultima.*

1975 Raul H. Castro becomes the first Mexican American governor of Arizona. Willie Nelson releases the album *Red-Headed Stranger.*

1976 Preston Jones' three plays of *A Texas Trilogy* open on Broadway.

1979 Sam Shepard wins Pulitzer Prize for drama for *Buried Child.*

1981 Oil prices peak; Texas state economy booms.

1981 Arizona Justice Sandra Day O'Connor becomes the first woman on the U.S. Supreme Court.

1982 Space shuttle Columbia lands at White Sands Space Harbor near Alamogordo, New Mexico.

1985 Oil prices plunge; Texas state recession ensues. Larry McMurtry publishes *Lonesome Dove.*

1986 Congress establishes the Great Basin National Park, Nevada's only national park. Lyle Lovett releases his first album.

1988 George H. W. Bush of Texas is elected U.S. president. Arizona governor Evan Mecham becomes the first U.S. governor in fifty-nine years to be impeached.

1992 New Mexico observes Columbus Quincentenary, welcomes Cristobal Colon XX, direct descendent of Christopher Columbus.

1995 District court in Texas Hopwood case rules against affirmative action admission system.

1996 John Sayles' *Lone Star* is released.

1997 Townes Van Zandt dies January 1.

1998 New Mexico celebrates its *cuartocentenario*, commemorating its 1598 founding by Juan de Oñate.

2000 Texas governor George W. Bush is elected U.S. president

2003 Space shuttle Columbia crashes over East Texas.

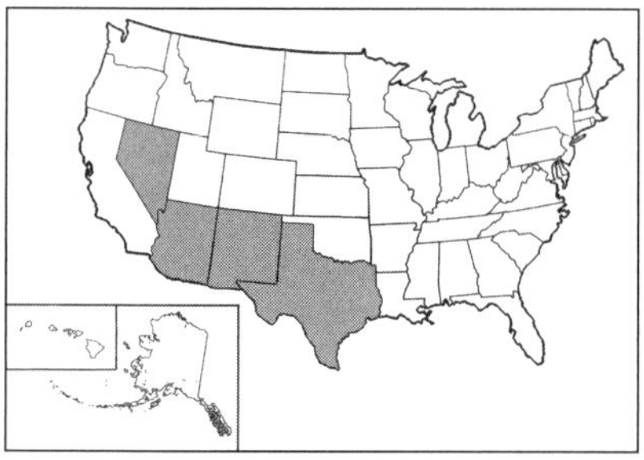

NOTES

Introduction

1. A version of this paper was presented at the "Regionalism and the Humanities Conference" in Lincoln, Nebraska, in November 20, 2003.

2. Pat Conroy, *Book-of-the-Month Club News* December 1986, quoted in *Simpson's Contemporary Quotations*, compiled by James B. Simpson (New York: Houghton Mifflin Company, 1988).

3. W. Eugene Hollon, *The Southwest: Old and New* (New York: Knopf, 1961), 6.

4. Kenneth Kurtz, *Literature of the American Southwest, A Selective Bibliography* (Los Angeles: Occidental College, Ward Ritchie Press, 1956), 7.

5. Erna Fergusson, *Our Southwest* (New York; London: A.A. Knopf, 1940), 20.

6. Lawrence Clark Powell, *Southwest Classics: The Creative Literature of the Arid Lands: Essays on the Books and Their Writers* (Los Angeles: W. Ritchie Press, 1974).

7. Charles C. DiPeso, *Casas Grandes and the Gran Chichimeca* (Santa Fe: Museum of New Mexico Press, 1968).

8. Bertha P. Dutton, *American Indians of the Southwest*, rev. English ed. (Albuquerque: University of New Mexico Press, 1983), 4.

9. Ross Calvin, *Sky Determines: An Interpretation of the Southwest* (New York: Macmillan, 1934), ix.

10. Rupert Norval Richardson and Carl Coke Rister, *The Greater Southwest: The Economic, Social, and Cultural Development of Kansas, Oklahoma, Texas, Utah, Colorado, Nevada, New Mexico, Arizona, and California from the Spanish Conquest to the Twentieth Century* (Glendale, CA: The Arthur H. Clark Company, 1934).

11. Herbert Eugene Bolton, *The Spanish Borderlands* (New Haven: Yale University Press, 1921).

12. Howard Roberts Lamar, *The Far Southwest, 1846–1912: A Territorial History*, rev. ed. (Albuquerque: University of New Mexico Press, 2000).

13. Dan Flores, *Horizontal Yellow: Nature and History in the Near Southwest* (Albuquerque: University of New Mexico Press, 1999), ix.

14. Stanley Vestal, *The Book Lover's Southwest: A Guide to Good Reading* (Norman: University of Oklahoma Press, 1955), 8.

15. William T[om] Pilkington, *My Blood's Country: Studies in Southwestern Literature* (Fort Worth: Texas Christian University Press, 1973), 8.

16. Keith L. Bryant, *Culture in the American Southwest: The Earth, the Sky, the People* (College Station: Texas A&M University Press, 2001), 5–6.

17. J. Frank Dobie, *Guide to Life and Literature of the Southwest* (Dallas: Southern Methodist University Press, 1942), 14.

18. William T. Pilkington, "Epilogue," in *Cabeza De Vaca's Adventures in the Unknown Interior of America*, translated by Cyclone Covey (Albuquerque: University of New Mexico Press, 1983, 1961), 145–46.

19. Frederick Turner, *Beyond Geography: The Western Spirit against the Wilderness* (New York: Viking Press, 1980).

20. Roy Bedichek, *Adventures with a Texas Naturalist* (Garden City, NY: Doubleday, 1947), 115.

21. http://www.cpluhna.nau.edu/Biota/merriam.htm.

22. I have also discussed these ideas in "The Significance of the Frontier in American Literature," in *The Frontier Experience and the American Dream*, edited by David Mogen, Mark Busby, and Paul Bryant (College Station: Texas A&M University Press, 1989), 95–103.

23. Pilkington, *My Blood's Country* (Fort Worth: Texas Christian University Press, 1973), 3.

24. Larry McMurtry, *In a Narrow Grave* (Austin: Encino, 1968).

25. Larry McMurtry, *Lonesome Dove* (New York: Simon and Schuster, 1985).

26. Larry Goodwyn, "The Frontier Myth and Southwestern Literature," *American Libraries* (Feb. 1971, 161–67; Apr. 1971, 359–66), reprinted in *Regional Perspectives: An Examination of America's Literary Heritage*, edited by John Gordon Burke (Chicago: ALA, 1973), 175–206.

27. Larry McMurtry, "The Texas Moon and Elsewhere," *Atlantic* 235, no. 3 (March 1975): 29–36.

28. Richard Slotkin, *The Fatal Environment: The Myth of the Frontier in the Age of Industrialization, 1800–1890* (New York: Atheneum, 1985); *Regeneration Through Violence: The Mythology of the American Frontier, 1600–1860*, (Middletown, CT: Wesleyan University Press, 1983); and *Gunfighter Nation: The Myth of the Frontier in Twentieth-Century America* (New York: HarperPerennial, 1993).

Architecture

1. Antoine Predock, http://www.predock.com/nelson.html.

Ecology and Environment

1. Lawrence, 142–143.
2. Mares, 26, 31.
3. Ibid., 29.
4. Gehlbach, 12.
5. Ibid., 7, 18.
6. Woodhouse, 100.
7. Gehlbach, 5.
8. Woodhouse, 105.
9. Gehlbach, 41.
10. Krech, 48–55.
11. Jennings, 54.
12. Ibid., 105–106.

13. Flannery, 227.
14. Krech, 77.
15. Ibid., 59.
16. Jennings, 51.
17. Krech, 58; Woodhouse, 102.
18. Weber, 308–309.
19. Ibid., 58.
20. Diamond, passim.
21. Weber, 58.
22. Gehlbach, 51.
23. Weber, 311.
24. Gutiérrez, 136; Weber, 136–137; 303.
25. Krech, 54.
26. DeBuys, 92–98.
27. Strom, 52.
28. DeBuys, 111.
29. Gehlbach, 110.
30. Ibid., 11.
31. DeBuys, 222.
32. Ibid., 225.
33. Maxwell and Baker, 159.
34. DeBuys, 231.
35. DeBuys, 224.
36. Strom, 49–74.
37. Gehlbach, 179.
38. Montejano 65–68.
39. Morris, 52.
40. Flores, passim.
41. Ibid.
42. West, 20.
43. Worster, 77.
44. Worster, 156–157.
45. Maxwell and Baker, passim.
46. DeBuys, 241, 268.
47. Jacoby, 175.
48. Wilkinson, 13.
49. White, 254–262.
50. Flores 2003, 224.
51. Gehlbach, 183.
52. Davis 1998, 54–59.
53. Davis, 45.
54. Gallagher, xxxii.
55. Wilkinson, 13, 65.
56. Abbey, 6.
57. Baker, passim.

Ethnicity

1. *Merriam-Webster's Collegiate Dictionary*, 11th ed., s.v. "Ethnic."
2. Ibid., "Ethnicity."
3. Ibid., "Ethnic."
4. Menchaca, 83–85.

5. Officer 1987.
6. Spicer 1962.
7. Chavez 1984.
8. Gonzalez-Berry and Maciel 2000.
9. Meier and Gutiérrez, 92–93.
10. Garcia 2002, 136–153.
11. Meier and Ribera 1993, 233–248.
12. Dulaney, 1.
13. Menchaca, 230.
14. Dulaney, 1.
15. Menchaca, 230.
16. Ibid., 238.
17. Crouch, 10.
18. Rusco 1975, 192–200, cf. Rusco 1994, 326.
19. Chan et al. 1994; Leubke 1998.
20. Castile 1981.
21. Martinelli 1989.
22. Jordan 2002, 1.
23. Tobias 1990.
24. Ibid.
25. Fong 1980, 8.
26. *Arizona Daily Star*, November 9, 1884.
27. Fong, 9.

Fashion

1. Martha Summerhayes, *Vanished Arizona: Recollections of the Army Life of a New England Woman* (Lincoln: University of Nebraska Press, 1979), 146.
2. Lon Tinkle and Allen Maxwell, eds. *The Cowboy Reader* (New York: Longmans, Green and Co., 1959), 81.

Film and Theater

1. For a shorter version of this discussion of film, see Mark Busby, "Texas and the Southwest," in The *Columbia Companion to American History on Film*, ed. Peter Rollins. (New York: Columbia University Press, 2003), 488–496.
2. Will Wright, *Sixguns and Society: A Structural Study of the Western* (Berkeley: University of California Press, 1975), 40–52.
3. Don Graham "Moo-vie Cows: The Trail to Hollywood," *Southwestern American Literature* XVIII:1 (Fall 1992), 1–12.
4. Jane Tompkins, *West of Everything: The Inner Life of Westerns* (New York: Oxford University Press, 1992), 118.
5. Don Graham, *Cowboys and Cadillacs: How Hollywood Looks at Texas* (Austin: Texas Monthly Press, 1983), 59–62.
6. Richard Warren Lewis, "*Playboy* Interview: John Wayne," *Playboy* 209 (May 1971), 154+.
7. Stephen Harrigan, "The Making of *Lonesome Dove*," *Texas Monthly* 16:6 (June 1988), 82–86, 156–159.

Folklore

1. Americo Paredes, trans., *"With His Pistol in His Hand": A Border Ballad and Its Hero* (Austin: University of Texas Press, 1958).

Food

1. From Lèvi-Strauss.
2. See Cushing.
3. Gary Paul Nabhan, "The Desert Can Heal: Desert Walk for Health, Heritage, and Biodiversity." *Herbal Gram* 49:29 (2000), publication of the American Botanical Council.
4. Mark Twain, in Chap 13 of *Roughing It* (reprinted in Dirlik), remarks that the house cooks and servants in California and Nevada "were chiefly Chinamen." Twain also writes of their resourcefulness in making jewelry from cast-off tins, fortunes from mining claims, and gardens from sand piles. "All Chinamen can read, write and cipher with easy facility—pity but all our petted *voters* could" (emphasis retained).
5. Dirlik 138, quoting newspaper accounts from Virginia City, Nevada.
6. Dirlik 67 and 92, quoting newspapers account from territorial Prescott, Arizona.
7. Dirlik 80.
8. The term *gastronomic tourism* has received critical attention in the years since my doctoral dissertation ("Eating the Other: Ethnicity and the Market for Authentic Mexican Food in Tucson, Arizona," University of Arizona, 1993). See esp. Bentley, Long 1998, Long 2001, Pilcher 1998, and Pilcher 2001.
9. In my doctoral research, I explored the relationship between ethnic producer–tourist consumers and the invention of authenticity. I argued that gastronomic tourists who flock to a region for a certain type of food are being served a hybrid cuisine as part of the law of supply and demand. Producers in restaurants and food companies will provide what the market will buy. Visitors may not be interested in eating the foods that locals eat at home—they want more marked dishes, such as festival foods, or blander versions of traditional fare.
10. See Bentley.
11. Dave and Nancy Gerlach, *The Whole Chile Pepper Book* (Boston: Little, Brown Co., 1990).
12. Amador, 57.
13. *Merriam-Webster's Collegiate Dictionary*, 11th ed., s.v. "Chili."
14. An exhibit of salsa labels was displayed at the Main Library of the University of Arizona in March 1992, and was co-curated by James S. Griffith and Jay Ann Cox.
15. Griffith 1988, 222.

Language

1. *Dictionary of American Regional English* ed. F. Cassidy, vol. 1 (Cambridge: Belknap Press of Harvard University Press, 1985), xvi–xvii.
2. Shirley Silver and Wick R. Miller, *American Indian Languages: Cultural and Social Contexts* (Tucson: University of Arizona Press, 1997), 5.
3. Ibid., 18.
4. Ibid., 20–21, 32–33.
5. Bertha P. Dutton, *American Indians of the Southwest* (Albuquerque: University of New Mexico Press, 1983), 70.
6. Ibid., 105.
7. Shirley Silver and Wick R. Miller, *American Indian Languages* (Tucson: University of Arizona Press, 1997), 12–13.
8. Steve Larese, "Preserving the Language," *New Mexico Magazine* (August 2002): 50–56.

9. Ibid.

10. Sedillo Lopez, Antoinette, ed., *Latinos in the United States* (New York: Garland Publishing, 1995), 930–931.

11. "Executive Summary: A Demographic Profile of Hispanics in the U.S.," Population Resource Center, available from http://www.prcdc.org/summaries/hispanics/hispanics.html.

12. Lynette Clemetson, "Hispanic Population Is Rising Swiftly, Census Bureau Says," *New York Times*, June 19, 2003. Late edition, final, Sec. A, 22, col. 3.

13. Ibid.

14. Reyes, Rogelio, "Language Mixing in Chicago Bilingual Speech," in *Studies in Southwest Spanish*, ed. J. Donald Bowen and Jacob Orstein.

15. Craig M. Carver, *American Regional Dialects* (Ann Arbor: University of Michigan Press, 1987), 1.

16. "African-Americans," *Handbook of Texas*, available from http://www.tsha.utexas.edu/handbook, accessed December 15, 2003.

17. "German," *Handbook of Texas*, available from http://www.tsha.utexas.edu/handbook, accessed August 12, 2003.

18. "Czech," *Handbook of Texas*, available from http://www.tsha.utexas.edu/handbook, accessed August 12, 2003.

19. Center for Basque Studies, University of Nevada at Reno, available from http://basque.unr.edu, accessed December 15, 2003.

20. "Vietnamese," *Handbook of Texas*, available from http://www.tsha.utexas.edu/handbook/online/articles/view/VV/pjv1.html, accessed August 12, 2003; U.S. Census Bureau, available from http://factfinder.census.gov, accessed December 15, 2003.

Literature

1. Roy Bedichek, *Adventures with a Texas Naturalist* (Austin: University of Texas Press, 1988), 214, 186.

2. Mary Austin, *The Land of Little Rain* (Albuquerque: University of New Mexico Press, 1974), 3.

3. Rudolfo Anaya, review of "*Jalamanta*: A Message from the Desert," *Publisher's Weekly*, January 1, 1996: 58.

4. Harriet Malinowitz, "Down-home Dissident," rev. of *Small Wonder: Essays* by Barbara Kingsolver, *Women's Review of Books* 19, no. 10 (2002): 36; Laura C. Moser, "Serial Adultery, Seriously: The Perils of Pretentious Pulp," rev. of *Peyton Amberg* by Tama Janowitz, *New York Observer* 8 (December 2003), 23.

5. J. Frank Dobie, *Guide to Life and Literature of the Southwest*, rev. ed. (Dallas: Southern Methodist University Press, 1952), 9.

Music

1. *Penguin Encyclopedia of Popular Music*, 2nd ed., p. 790.

Religion

1. Church costs in Szasz, 1988, 53.

2. Lutheran numbers in Texas in "Lutheran Church," *The Handbook of Texas Online* http://www.tsha.utexas.edu/handbook/online/articles/view/LL/ill1.html.

3. Szasz, 2000, 21.

4. Unless otherwise stated, all percentages are derived from Jones et al.

5. The Nevada figure is lower than all the other states except Oregon (31.3 percent) and Washington (33.0 percent).

6. Figures for Texas Muslims and Buddhists in "Muslims," *The Handbook of Texas Online*, available at http://www.tsha.utexas.edu/handbook/online/articles/view/MM/irmxh.html and "Buddhism," *The Handbook of Texas Online*, available at http://www.tsha.utexas.edu/handbook/online/articles/view/BB/irb1.html.
7. Leonard, 8.
8. Urban percentages derived from Jones et al.
9. Figures for the newer Jewish communities in Phoenix and Las Vegas derived from *The 2002 Greater Phoenix Jewish Community Study*, http://www.jewishphoenix.com/jewishCommunity/2002study/highlightssummary.pdf and Andrew Muchin, "Vegas has high-rolling hopes for its unaffiliated Jews," http://www.jewishsf.com/bk021101/us43.shtml.
10. Reid, 14.

Sports and Recreation

1. Leopold, *A Sand County Almanac*, 188.
2. Crown, 144.
3. Day, Internet essay.
4. Ibid.
5. Crown, 156.
6. Allen Dart, telephone interview with author, December 12, 2003.
7. Warren, 3–4.
8. Sharp.
9. Ibid.
10. Leopold, "The Wilderness and Its Place in Forest Recreational Policy," 79.
11. Ibid., 79.
12. Abbey, *Desert Solitaire*, 55.
13. Ibid., 55.
14. "Indian Reservations," *Texas Handbook Online*, http://www.tsha.utexas.edu/handbook/online/articles/view/II/bpi1.html, accessed August 2 16:31:23 US/Central, 2004.
15. http:/southwest.fws.gov/refuges/arizona/cabeza.html.
16. http://www.fs.fed.us/aboutus/mission.shtml.
17. http:/www.vallescaldera.gov/about.php.
18. http://www.southernregion.fs.fed.us/texas/recreation/orv_info_ang_de_sab.shtml.
19. http://162.42.237.6/wmatod/index.htm.
20. Trafton.
21. Alamillo, 89.
22. Ibid., 88–89.
23. Ibid., 89.
24. http://ojjdp.nejrs.org/pubs/principles/pro8.html.
25. Witt.
26. Ibid.
27. *Texas Handbook Online*.
28. http://www.azchamber.com/fun/golf.shtml.
29. http://www.house.gov/judiciary/san0613.htm.
30. Cashion, 1.
31. "On Gordon Wood," *Dave Campbell's Texas Football*, http://texasfootball.com/03front_1218.html.
32. Sherrington, Sports Day, 1B.
33. "Rushing Was Outstanding Coach," *ABQJournal.com*, http://www.abqjournal.com/obits/profiles/116766profiles12-02-03.htm.
34. http://www.uil.utexas.edu/aca/index.htm.
35. Leopold, *A Sand Country Almanac*, 189.

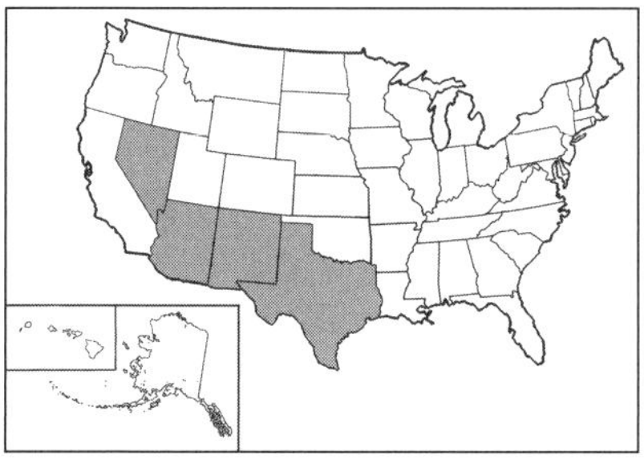

BIBLIOGRAPHY

Abbey, Edward. *Beyond the Wall.* New York: Holt, Rinehart and Winston, 1984.
———. *The Brave Cowboy.* New York: Dodd, Mead, 1956.
———. *Desert Solitaire: A Season in the Wilderness.* New York: McGraw, 1968.
———. *The Journey Home: Some Words in Defense of the American West.* New York: Dutton, 1977.
Adams, Andy. *The Log of a Cowboy.* Boston: Houghton Mifflin, 1903.
———. *Reed Anthony, Cowman: An Autobiography.* Boston: Houghton Mifflin, 1907.
———. *A Texas Matchmaker.* Boston: Houghton Mifflin, 1904.
Allen, Paula Gunn. *Grandmothers of the Light: A Medicine Woman's Sourcebook.* Boston: Beacon Press, 1991.
———. *Shadow Country.* Los Angeles: Native American Series, UCLA, 1982.
———. *The Woman Who Owned the Shadows.* Albion, CA: Spinsters Ink, 1983.
Anaya, Rudolfo. *Aztlan: Essays on the Chicano Homeland.* Albuquerque: El Norte Press, 1989.
———. *Bless Me, Ultima.* Berkeley: Quinto Sol, 1972.
Anderson, John Q., Edwin W. Gaston Jr., and James W. Lee. *Southwestern American Literature, A Bibliography.* Chicago: Swallow, 1980.
Austin, Mary. *Earth Horizon.* 1932. Reprint, Albuquerque: University of New Mexico Press, 1991.
———. *The Land of Little Rain.* 1903. Reprint, New York: Penguin, 1988.
Barthelme, Donald. *Sixty Stories.* New York: Putnam, 1981.
Basso, Keith. *Wisdom Sits in Places: Landscape and Language among the Western Apache.* Albuquerque: University of New Mexico Press, 1996.
Bedichek, Roy. *Adventures with a Texas Naturalist.* Garden City, NY: Doubleday, 1947.
———. *Karánkaway Country.* Garden City, NY: Doubleday, 1950.
Berger, Bruce. *The Telling Distance: Conversations with the American Desert.* 1990. Reprint, Tucson: University of Arizona Press, 1997.
———. *There Was a River: Essays on the Southwest.* Tucson: University of Arizona Press, 1994.
Bowden, Charles. *Blue Desert.* Tucson: University of Arizona Press, 1986.
Brammer, William. *The Gay Place.* Boston: Houghton Mifflin, 1961.

Bibliography

Brewer, J. Mason. *Dog Ghosts and the Word on the Brazos*. Austin: University of Texas Press, 1976.

———. *Killing the Hidden Waters*. Austin: University of Texas Press, 1977.

Busby, Mark, *Larry McMurtry and the West: An Ambivalent Relationship*. Denton: University of North Texas Press, 1995.

———. *Preston Jones*. Western Writers Series #58. Boise: Boise State University, 1983.

———. *Ralph Ellison*. New York: Twayne/Macmillan, 1991.

———. "Texas and the Great Southwest." In *A Companion to the Regional Literatures of the United States*, edited by Charles Crow, 432–457. New York: Blackwell, 2003.

———, ed. *New Growth/2: Contemporary Short Stories by Texas Writers*. San Antonio: Corona, 1993.

Busby, Mark, and Dick Heaberlin, eds. *From Texas to the World and Back: Essays on the Journeys of Katherine Anne Porter*. Fort Worth: Texas Christian University Press, 2001.

Byrkit, James W. "Land, Sky, and People: The Southwest Defined." *Journal of the Southwest* 34, no. 3 (Autumn 1992).

Cabeza de Vaca, Álvar Núñez. *The Account: Álvar Núñez Cabeza de Vaca's "Relación."* Translated by Martin A. Favata and José B. Fernández. Houston: Arte Publico Press, 1993.

Capps, Benjamin. *The Brothers of Uterica*. New York: Meredith, 1967.

Cather, Willa. *Death Comes for the Archbishop*. New York: Knopf, 1927. Reprint, New York: Vintage, 1971.

———. *A Lost Lady*. New York: Knopf, 1923. Reprint, New York: Vintage, 1972.

———. *The Professor's House*. New York: Knopf, 1925. Reprint, New York: Vintage, 1973.

———. *The Song of the Lark*. Boston: Houghton Mifflin, 1915. Reprint, Sentry revised (1932 edition), 1963. Reprint, Lincoln: University of Nebraska Press (1915 edition), 1978.

Cervantes, Lorna Dee. *Emplumada*. Pittsburgh: University of Pittsburgh Press, 1981.

Chin, Frank. *The Chickencoop Chinaman, The Year of the Dragon: Two Plays*. Seattle: University of Washington Press, 1981.

Church, Peggy Pond. *The House at Otowi Bridge: The Story of Edith Warner and Los Alamos*. Albuquerque: University of New Mexico Press, 1959.

Cisneros, Sandra. *The House on Mango Street*. Houston: Arte Publico Press, 1983.

Clark, H. Jackson. *"The Owl in Monument Canyon," and Other Stories from Indian Country*. Salt Lake City: University of Utah Press, 1993.

Coburn, D.L. *The Gin Game*. New York: Samuel French, 1978.

Crawford, Stanley. *A Garlic Testament: Seasons on a Small New Mexico Farm*. New York: HarperCollins, 1992.

———. *Mayordomo: Chronicle of an Acequia in Northern New Mexico*. 1988. Reprint, New York: Doubleday, 1989.

Dobie, J. Frank. *The Mustangs*. Boston: Little, Brown, 1952.

———. *Some Part of Myself*. Boston: Little, Brown, 1967.

———. *Tongues of the Monte*. Austin: University of Texas Press, 1935.

———. *A Vaquero of the Brush Country*. Austin: University of Texas Press, 1929.

Ellison, Ralph. *Invisible Man*. New York: Random House, 1952.

Fletcher, Colin. *The Man Who Walked through Time*. New York: Knopf, 1967.

Flores, Dan. *Caprock Canyonlands: Journeys into the Heart of the Southern Plains*. Austin: University of Texas Press, 1990.

———. *The Natural West: Environmental History in the Great Plains and Rocky Mountains*. Norman: The University of Oklahoma Press, 2001.

Flynn, Robert. *North to Yesterday*. New York: Knopf, 1967.

Garreau, Joel. *The Nine Nations of North America*. Boston: Houghton Mifflin, 1931.

Geiogamah, Hanay. *New Native American Drama*. Norman: University of Oklahoma Press, 1980.

Gilb, Dagoberto. *The Last Known Residence of Mickey Acuña*. New York: Grove Press, 1994.

———. *The Magic of Blood*. New York: Grove Press, 1994.

———. *Woodcuts of Women*. New York: Grove Press, 1994.

Goyen, William. *The House of Breath*. New York: Random House, 1950.

Graham, Don. *Cowboys and Cadillacs: How Hollywood Looks at Texas*. Austin: Texas Monthly Press, 1983.

———. *Texas: A Literary Portrait*. San Antonio, Corona, 1985.

Graham, Don, James W. Lee, and William T. Pilkington, eds. *The Texas Literary Tradition: Fiction/Folklore/History*. Austin: College of Liberal Arts, University of Texas, 1983.

Graves, John. *From a Limestone Ledge: Some Essays and Other Ruminations about Country Life in Texas*. New York: Knopf, 1980.

———. *Goodbye to a River: A Narrative*. New York: Knopf, 1960.

———. *Hard Scrabble: Observation on a Patch of Land*. New York: Knopf, 1974.

Greene, A. C. *The Fifty Best Books on Texas*. Dallas: Pressworks, 1981.

———. *A Personal Country*. New York: Knopf, 1969.

Grey, Zane. *The Trail Driver*. New York: Harper, 1936.

Griggs, Sutton E. *Imperium in Imperio*. New York: Arno Press, 1969.

Harjo, Joy. *She Had Some Horses*. New York: Thunder's Mouth Press, 1983.

———. *What Moon Drove Me to This*. New York: I Reed Books, 1979.

Harjo, Joy, and Stephen Strom. *Secrets from the Center of the World*. Tucson: University of Arizona Press, 1990.

Harrigan, Stephen. *Aransas*. New York: Knopf, 1980.

———. *Gates of the Alamo*. New York: Knopf, 2000.

———. *Jacob's Well*. New York: Knopf, 1984.

Heifner, Jack. *Patio/Porch*. New York: Dramatists Play Service, 1978.

———. *Vanities*. New York: Samuel French, 1977.

Hinojosa, Rolando. *Rites and Witnesses*. Houston: University of Houston, Arte Publico Press, 1983.

———. *The Useless Servants*. Houston: University of Houston, Arte Publico Press, 1993.

———. *The Valley*. Ypsilanti, MI: Bilingual Editions, 1983.

Hogan, Linda. *Calling Myself Home*. Greenfield Center, NY: Greenfield Review Press, 1979.

———. *Daughters, I Love You*. Denver: Loretto Heights College Publications, 1981.

Horgan, Paul. *Great River: The Rio Grande in North American History*. New York: Rinehart, 1954.

Hough, Emerson. *North of 36*. New York: Appleton, 1924.

Humphrey, William. *Farther Off from Heaven*. New York: Knopf, 1977.

Jones, Preston. *Santa Fe Sunshine*. New York: Dramatists Play Service, 1977.

———. *A Texas Trilogy*. New York: Hill & Wang, 1976.

Kappel-Smith, Diana. *Desert Time: A Journey through the American Southwest*. Boston: Little, Brown, 1992.

Kelton, Elmer. *The Time It Never Rained*. Garden City, NY: Doubleday. 1957.

———. *The Wolf and the Buffalo*. Garden City, NY: Doubleday, 1980.

King, Larry L. *Of Outlaws, Con Men, Whores, Politicians, and Other Artists*. New York: Viking, 1980.

King, Larry L., and Peter Masterson. *The Best Little Whorehouse in Texas*. New York: Samuel French, 1981.

Krutch, Joseph Wood. *Grand Canyon: Today and All Its Yesterdays*. 1957. Reprint, Tucson: University of Arizona Press, 1989.

———. *The Voice of the Desert*. New York: William Sloane, 1954.

Lea, Tom. *The King Ranch*. Boston: Little, Brown, 1957.

———. *The Wonderful Country*. Boston: Little, Brown, 1952.

Leopold, Aldo. "Arizona and New Mexico." *A Sand County Almanac*. New York: Oxford University Press, 1949.

Lewis, Alfred Henry. *Wolfville*. Chicago: A. L. Burt, 1897.

———. *Wolfville Days*. New York: F. A. Stokes, 1902.

———. *Wolfville Nights*. New York: F. A. Stokes, 1902.

Luhan, Mabel Dodge. *Edge of Taos Desert: An Escape to Reality*. New York: Harcourt Brace, 1937.

———. *Winter in Taos*. New York: Harcourt Brace, 1935.

McCarthy, Cormac. *All the Pretty Horses*. New York: Knopf, 1992.

———. *Cities of the Plain*. New York: Knopf, 1998.

———. *The Crossing*. New York: Knopf, 1994.

McLure, James. *Lone Star*. New York: Dramatists Play Service, 1980.

———. *Pvt. Wars*. New York: Dramatists Play Service, 1980.

McMurtry, Larry. *All My Friends Are Going to Be Strangers*. New York: Simon and Schuster, 1972.

———. *Boone's Lick*. New York: Simon and Schuster, 2000.

———. *Buffalo Girls*. New York: Simon and Schuster, 1990. Reprint, Pocket Books, 1991.

———. *Comanche Moon*. New York: Simon and Schuster, 1997.

———. *Dead Man's Walk*. New York: Simon and Schuster, 1995.

———. *The Evening Star*. New York: Simon and Schuster, 1992. Reprint, Pocket Books, 1993.

———. *Horseman, Pass By*. New York: Harper, 1961.

———. *In a Narrow Grave*. Austin: Encino, 1968.

———. *The Last Picture Show*. New York: Dial, 1966.

———. *The Late Child*. New York: Simon and Schuster, 1994.

———. *Leaving Cheyenne*. New York: Harper, 1963.

———. *Lonesome Dove*. New York: Simon and Schuster, 1985.

———. *Moving On*. New York: Simon and Schuster, 1970. Reprint, Touchstone, 1989.

———. *Paradise*. New York: Simon and Schuster, 2001.

———. *Sin Killer*. New York: Simon and Schuster, 2002.

———. *Some Can Whistle*. New York: Simon and Schuster, 1989.

———. *Terms of Endearment*. New York: Simon and Schuster, 1975.

———. *Streets of Laredo*. New York: Simon and Schuster, 1993. Reprint, Pocket Books, 1994.

———. *Walter Benjamin at the Dairy Queen*. New York: Simon and Schuster, 1999.

McMurtry, Larry, and Diana Ossana. *Pretty Boy Floyd*. New York: Simon and Schuster, 1994.

———. *Zeke and Ned*. New York: Simon and Schuster, 1997.

Medoff, Mark. *Children of a Lesser God*. New York: Dramatists Play Service, 1981.

———. *The Wager: Two Short Plays*. Clifton, NJ: James T. White, 1976.

———. *When You Comin' Back, Red Ryder?* Clifton, NJ: James T. White, 1974.

Meinig, D. W. *Imperial Texas: An Interpretive Essay in Cultural Geography*. Austin: University of Texas Press, 1969.

Momaday, N. Scott. *The Gourd Dancer*. New York: Harper & Row, 1975.

———. *House Made of Dawn*. New York: Harper & Row, 1968.

Nabhan, Gary Paul. *The Desert Smells Like Rain: A Naturalist in Papago Indian Country*. San Francisco: North Point, 1982.

———. *Gathering the Desert*. Tucson: University of Arizona Press, 1985.

Nichols, John. *A Fragile Beauty: John Nichols' Milagro Country*. Layton, UT: Gibbs M. Smith, 1987.

———. *If Mountains Die: A New Mexico Memoir*. New York: Knopf, 1986.

———. *Keep It Simple*. New York: Norton, 1992.

———. *The Last Beautiful Days of Autumn*. New York: Henry Holt, 1982.

———. *On the Mesa*. Layton, UT: Gibbs M. Smith, 1986.

———. *The Sky's the Limit: A Defense of the Earth.* New York: Norton, 1991.

Olmsted, Frederick Law. *A Journey through Texas; a Saddle-trip on the Southwestern Frontier.* New York: Dix, Edwards, 1857.

Ortiz, Simon. *Going for the Rain.* New York: Harper & Row, 1976.

———. *A Good Journey.* Berkeley: Turtle Island, 1977.

Owens, Louis. *Bone Game.* Norman: University of Oklahoma Press, 1994.

———. *Dark River.* Norman: University of Oklahoma Press, 1999.

———. *Nightland.* New York: Dutton Signet Publishers, 1996.

———. *The Sharpest Sight.* Norman: University of Oklahoma Press, 1992.

———. *Wolfsong.* West End Press, 1991; Oklahoma, 1995.

Owens, William A. *Fever in the Earth.* New York: Putnam, 1958.

Paredes, Américo. *"With His Pistol in His Hand": A Border Ballad and Its Hero.* Austin: University of Texas Press, 1958.

Pilkington, William T. *Imagining Texas: The Literature of the Lone Star State.* Boston: American, 1981.

———. *My Blood's Country.* Fort Worth: Texas Christian University Press, 1973.

Porter, Katherine Anne. *The Collected Essays and Occasional Writings of Katherine Anne Porter.* New York: Harper, 1955.

Powell, John Wesley. *The Exploration of the Colorado River and Its Canyons.* 1895. Reprint, New York: Penguin, 1987.

Quanamen, David. "The Face of a Spider." *The Flight of the Iguana.* New York: Dell, 1988.

Rhodes, Eugene Manlove. *Bransford of Arcadia, or The Little Eohippus.* New York: Henry Holt, 1914.

———. *Good Men and True.* New York: Henry Holt, 1910.

———. *Once in the Saddle.* Boston: Houghton Mifflin, 1927.

———. *Pasó par Aquí.* Boston: Houghton Mifflin, 1927.

Richter, Conrad. *The Sea of Grass.* New York: Knopf, 1937.

Rivera, Tomás. *. . . y no se lo tragó la tierra/And the Earth Did Not Part.* Berkeley: Quinto Sol, 1971.

Rose, Wendy. *Academic Squaw—Report to the World from the Ivory Tower.* Marvin, SD: Blue Cloud Quarterly, 1977.

———. *Hopi Roadrunner Dancing.* Greenfield Center, NY: The Greenfield Review Press, 1973.

Russell, Sharman Apt. *Songs of the Fluteplayer: Seasons of Life in the Southwest.* Reading, MA: Addison-Wesley, 1991.

———. *When the Land Was Young: Reflections on American Archeology.* Reading, MA: Addison-Wesley, 1996.

Scarborough, Dorothy. *In the Land of Cotton.* New York: Macmillan, 1923.

———. *The Wind.* New York: Harper & Brothers, 1925.

Shelton, Richard. *Going Back to Bisbee.* Tucson: University of Arizona Press, 1992.

Shepard, Sam. *Buried Child.* New York: Urizen Books, 1979.

———. *Five Plays.* Indianapolis: Bobbs-Merrill, 1967.

———. *Four Two-Act Plays.* New York: Urizen Books, 1980.

———. *Seven Plays.* New York: Bantam Books, 1981.

Silko, Leslie. *Ceremony.* New York: Viking Press, 1977.

———. *Laguna Woman.* Greenfield Center, NY: Greenfield Review Press, 1974.

Soto Gary. *Black Hair.* Pittsburgh: University of Pittsburgh Press, 1984.

———. *The Elements of San Joaquin.* Pittsburgh: University of Pittsburgh Press, 1977.

———. *The Tale of Sunlight.* Pittsburgh: University of Pittsburgh Press, 1978.

———. *Where Swallows Work Hard.* Pittsburgh: University of Pittsburgh Press, 1981.

Stegner, Wallace. *Beyond the Hundreth Meridian: John Wesley Powell and the Second Opening of the West.* New York: Penguin, 1953.

Tapahonso, Luci. *Seasonal Woman*. Santa Fe: Tooth of Time Books, 1982.
Valdez, Luis. *Actos*. San Juan Bautista, CA: Centro Campesino Cultural, 1971.
Van Dyke, John C. *The Desert*. 1901. Salt Lake City: Peregrine Smith, 1980.
Watt, Donley. *The Journey of Hector Rabinal*. Forth Worth: Texas Christian University Press, 1994.
Webb, Walter Prescott. *The Great Plains*. New York: Grosset & Dunlap, 1931.
Williams, Terry Tempest. *Desert Quartet*. New York: Pantheon, 1995.
————. *Pieces of White Shell: A Journey to Navajoland*. 1984. Albuquerque: University of New Mexico Press, 1992.
————. *Refuge: An Unnatural History of Family and Place*. New York: Pantheon, 1991.
Wister, Owen. *The Virginian*. New York: Macmillan, 1902.
Woodin, Ann. *Home Is the Desert*. 1964. Reprint, Tucson: University of Arizona Press, 1984.
Zwinger, Ann. *Downcanyon: A Naturalist Explores the Colorado River through the Grand Canyon*. Tucson: University of Arizona Press, 1995.

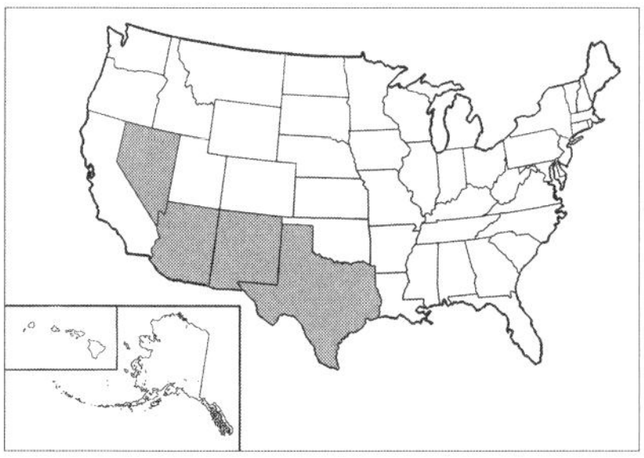

INDEX

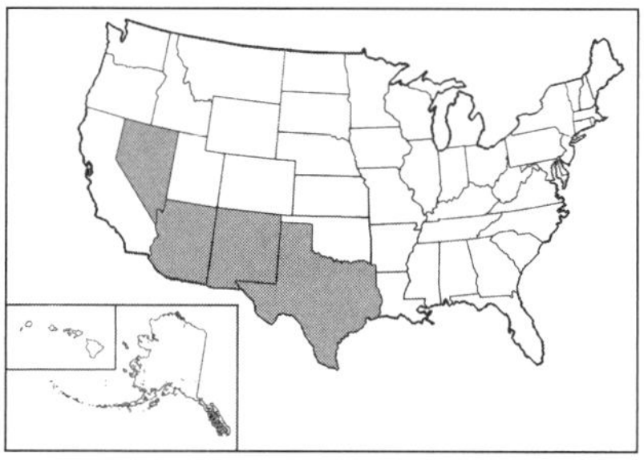

ABOUT THE EDITOR AND CONTRIBUTORS

MARK BUSBY is director of the Southwest Regional Humanities Center and Professor of English at Texas State University–San Marcos. A native of Ennis, Texas, he is author of *Larry McMurtry and the West: An Ambivalent Relationship* and *Ralph Ellison*; and editor of *New Growth/2: Contemporary Short Stories by Texas Writers*. He is coeditor (with Dick Heaberlin) of *From Texas to the World and Back: Essays on the Journeys of Katherine Anne Porter* and the journals *Southwestern American Literature* and *Texas Books in Review*. He has also published *Preston Jones* and *Lanford Wilson*, coedited *The Frontier Experience and the American Dream*, and was a contributing editor of *Taking Stock: A Larry McMurtry Casebook*. He has published in *Western American Literature*, *MELUS*, *New Mexico Humanities Review*, *A Literary History of the American West*, and elsewhere. His first novel, *Fort Benning Blues*, was published in 2001.

JEREMY BONNER holds a PhD in American history from the Catholic University of America in Washington, D.C., and is currently an independent scholar in Baltimore, Maryland. He has published on political and religious history in such journals as the *Journal of Mormon History* and *Anglican and Episcopal History*. He is currently working on a biography of Victor J. Reed, the Catholic Bishop of Oklahoma City and Tulsa from 1958 to 1971.

BRENDA BRANDT, PhD, is the education and community outreach manager at the Arizona Capitol Museum in Phoenix, Arizona. Previously, she held the position of exhibits curator and historian at the Phoenix Museum of History; she has also served as a faculty member in design programs at the University of Arizona and Colorado State University. Her research focuses on the relationships people have with material culture. She has published several articles on army wives and on men's and women's clothing practices in the American West.

CAROL LEA CLARK is an associate professor and director of first-year composition at the University of Texas–El Paso. She holds a PhD in rhetoric and composition from Texas Christian University, an MA in composition studies from California State University at San Bernardino, a M.Ed in Counseling Psychology from the University of Houston, and a BA in English and psychology from Rice University. Her books include *The Genre Reader* (forthcoming), *eSearchers: An Electronic Research Guide*, *Imagining Texas: Early Texas Newspapers 1824–1836*, *The Wired Society*, *Working the Web*, *Hits on the Web*, and *Interconnections: Writer, Culture and Environment*. Her research and teaching interests include applied rhetoric, history of rhetoric, the Internet, and composition studies.

MARGARET DWYER is a writer for the University of Texas–Arlington libraries. She received her MA in English from UT–Arlington in 1999, has nearly completed an MA in environmental philosophy from the University of North Texas, and earned a BA in recreation and park management from Western Washington University in 1980. She spent fifteen years working as a park naturalist and forester and served six years on the City of Fort Worth, Texas, Park and Community Services Advisory Board.

JAY COX HAYWARD, PhD, earned her doctorate in 1993 from the University of Arizona and currently is an independent scholar in the areas of food, festival, material culture, and ethnic literature of the Southwest. Based in Tucson, Arizona, she has published biographical works on notable Southwest literary figures and Native Americans for reference works. Hayward works full-time as an editor for a newspaper and magazine group and also writes freelance features on food, living, and popular culture for various regional publications. She guest-edited a recent issue of *Southwestern American Literature*, devoted to her late friend Louis Owens.

RICHARD HOLLAND is a senior lecturer in the Liberal Arts Honors Program at the University of Texas at Austin, where he teaches courses in the history of popular music and in Texas culture. In 1999 he edited *Larry L. King: A Writer's Life in Letters, or Reflections in a Bloodshot Eye*. He was the founding curator of the Southwestern Writers Collection at Texas State University, San Marcus.

HOLLE HUMPHRIES earned a BFA in art from Carnegie Mellon of Pittsburgh, Pennsylvania, an MA in art education, and a PhD in fine arts from Texas Tech University in Lubbock. She has published in state and national journals, presented at conferences throughout the United States, and authored and edited work about art for nationally adopted textbooks. Based on her background in philosophical aesthetics, art history, and art education, her contribution for this volume emphasizes how physical and cultural geography influenced the evolution of regional art in the Southwest.

BENJAMIN JOHNSON teaches history at Southern Methodist University, in Dallas, Texas. He is author of *Revolution in Texas: How a Forgotten Rebellion and Its Bloody Suppression Turned Mexicans into Americans* and coeditor of *Steal This University: The Labor Movement and the Corporatization of Higher Education*. His essay

"Subsistence, Class, and Conservation at the Birth of Superior National Forest" in the January 1999 issue of *Environmental History* won the 2000 Ralph Hidy Award and has been republished in *American Environmental History* edited by Louis Warren. He is currently at work on a study of urban development and conservation politics in the early-twentieth-century United States.

CORY LOCK teaches at St. Edwards University in Austin. She received a PhD in literature from the University of Texas–Austin, an MA from the University of Chicago, and BA from the University of Virginia.

RUBEN G. MENDOZA is the founding director and professor of the Institute for Archaeological Science, Technology, and Visualization at California State University, Monterey Bay. He was awarded a PhD in anthropology from the University of Arizona. A specialist in the archaeology and ethnohistory of Mesoamerica and the Southwest, his current area of research is with the historical archaeology of Hispanicized Mission Indian communities of early California and the Southwest. Professor Mendoza's previous reference works include contributions to the *Handbook of Hispanic Cultures in the United States*, *Encyclopedia of the History of Science, Technology, and Medicine in Non-Western Cultures*, *Oxford Encyclopedia of Mesoamerican Cultures*, and the *Encyclopedia of Food and Culture*.

J. RHETT RUSHING is a native Texan who has spent his life studying and exploring the American Southwest. A graduate of Texas A&M University and Western Kentucky University, and currently a PhD candidate in the Folklore and Ethnomusicology Department of Indiana University, Rhett has taught classes on folklore, Mexican American folklore, Hispanic popular Catholicism, and writing at Indiana University, Texas State University, and Texas Lutheran University. He is currently the staff folklorist in the Research Department of the University of Texas Institute of Texan Cultures at San Antonio, and he is an officer of the Texas Folklore Society.

DAVID L. SHAUL is librarian and archivist for the Tohono O'odham Nation, a federally recognized tribe. He studied at the University of Arizona, where he earned degrees in Chinese, music, and anthropology. His PhD in anthropological linguistics is from the University of California–Berkeley. He is a specialist in Uto-Aztecan languages, as well as Native American cultures of the American Southwest. Professor Shaul's recent publications include, with Louanna Furbee, *Language and Culture* and *Hopi Traditional Literature*.

MAGGIE VALENTINE holds a PhD in Architecture and Urban Planning from UCLA. She is Professor of Architecture and Interior Design at the University of Texas at San Antonio and the author of *The Show Starts on the Sidewalk: A History of the Movie Theatre* (1994).

The Greenwood Encyclopedia of American Regional Cultures

The Great Plains Region, *edited by Amanda Rees*

The Mid-Atlantic Region, *edited by Robert P. Marzec*

The Midwest, *edited by Joseph W. Slade and Judith Yaross Lee*

New England, *edited by Michael Sletcher*

The Pacific Region, *edited by Jan Goggans with Aaron DiFranco*

The Rocky Mountain Region, *edited by Rick Newby*

The South, *edited by Rebecca Mark and Rob Vaughan*

The Southwest, *edited by Mark Busby*

DATE DUE
